The International Series in

ELEMENTARY EDUCATION

Consulting Editor

JOHN M. KEAN

University of Wisconsin

Readings on Reading

Readings on Reading

ALFRED R. BINTER

JOHN J. DLABAL, Jr.

LEONARD K. KISE

Department of Elementary Education
Northern Illinois University

INTERNATIONAL TEXTBOOK COMPANY
Scranton, Pennsylvania

Second Printing, November 1970

Standard Book Number 7002   2208   1

Preface

AUTHORS of textbooks in reading instruction have as their primary concern the transmission of specialized knowledge, skills, and understandings peculiar to this area of pedagogy. In order to help the teacher or teacher candidate extend and expand his view of what is of concern in reading today, the reading instructor will require his students to familiarize themselves with specific materials in professional journals. However, the problems that students encounter in acquiring these materials are well known to those who have made such assignments. Therefore, books of readings are utilized by reading instructors to aid the student in understanding the complexity and scope of reading today. Unfortunately, the selection from which to choose is limited in respect to number.

The authors of this book of readings have selected topics as representative of what reading instruction should encompass, excluding the technical aspects which can be acquired in any good text of reading instruction. These areas include articles relating to such traditional but unresolved problems as "What is reading?" "What are the most desirable ways of organizing the classroom for reading instruction?" In addition, such contemporary themes as technical and material innovations, contributions to reading instruction from the science of linguistics, and reading instructional problems related to the culturally deprived child are included as being important to gaining an insight and an intelligent understanding of reading today.

This book of readings can serve several functional roles in a course in the instruction of reading. First, the editors have carefully surveyed the literature in the selected topics of this book to bring to the reader that which is current and pertinent to the topic. Second, the editors have selected readings, not on the basis of a prescribed philosophy for the teaching of reading, but for the purpose of exposing the reader to several points of view about the teaching of reading. Third, the editors believe that the readings selected should stimulate intellectual inquiry and curiosity on the part of the reader to question any one particular orientation to the teaching of reading. It is hoped that the reader will seek further readings to answer their personal questions about the reading process. Fourth, the editors believe that this text can be fruitfully used in the classroom to encourage questions about reading processes that will enhance the reader's understanding about reading. The editors also believe that this book of readings is a useful and productive source of information for teachers in the classroom setting. This book can be used as a supplementary text or for individual reading assignments to extend or enhance the common core of learnings expected of people engaged in the teaching of reading.

Alfred R. Binter
John J. Dlabal, Jr.
Leonard K. Kise

DeKalb, Illinois
February, 1969

Acknowledgments

THE editors of this book wish to gratefully acknowledge the many people and organizations that cooperated in making this book possible.

First, to the authors of the articles in this book for their time and energy in the thoughtful presentation of their topics. Also, we wish to thank the authors for their permission to use their materials in this book.

Second, we wish to thank the editors and staff of the several organizations who have granted us permission to reprint their materials. Particular thanks should go to Miss Elaine Fraze of the International Reading Association and Mrs. June Schuster of the University of Chicago Press for their extensive cooperation and efforts in assisting the editors.

Third we wish to gratefully acknowledge the administrative, professional, and clerical staff at Northern Illinois University who have facilitated us in our professional efforts in this book of readings.

Fourth, a special note of thanks should go to contributors who wrote original materials for this book at the editors' request. We wish also to thank our families who made a personal sacrifice by graciously forgiving us our lapses in assuming home responsibilities. Thank you Thyliss, Martie, and Lucia.

A.R.B.
J.J.D.
L.K.K.

Contents

xi

I

Overview

1. What Is Reading?*

FRANK G. JENNINGS

Editor-at-large, *Saturday Review*
and education consultant, New World
Foundation

WHAT is reading? Where does it start? How can it be done well? With these questions you can make a fortune, wreck a school system or get elected to the board of education. Most people who try to think about reading at all conjure up these little black wriggles on a page and then mutter something about "meaning." If this is all it is, very few of us would ever learn anything. For reading is older than printing or writing or even language itself. Reading begins with wonder at the world about us. It starts with the recognition of repeated events like thunder, lightning, and rain. It starts with the seasons and the growth of things. It starts with an ache that vanished with food or water. It occurs when time is discovered. Reading begins with the management of signs of things. It begins when the mother, holding the child's hand, says that a day is "beautiful" or "cold" or that the wind is "soft." Reading is "signs and portents," the flight of birds, the changing moon, the "changeless" sun, and the "fixed" stars that move through the night. Reading is the practical management of the world about us. It was this for the man at the cave's mouth. It is this for us at the desk, the bench, or control panel.

The special kind of reading that you are doing now is the culmination of all the other kinds of reading. You are dealing with the signs of the things represented. You are dealing with ideas and concepts that have no material matter or substance and yet are "real." But you can not do this kind of reading if you have not become skilled in all the other kinds. Unless you know down from up, hot from cold, now from then, you could never learn to understand things that merely represent other things. You would have no language, as you now understand it, and you could not live in the open society of human beings. It is quite conceivable that a true non-reader can only survive in a mental hospital.

For most of the world's people the act of reading what is written down is still surrounded with an aura of mystery and the black arts. Throughout most of our history reading has been the prerogative of elite classes. Its earliest

*From *This Is Reading* (New York: Teachers College Press, 1965), 1-22. Copyright © 1965 by Teachers College, Columbia University. Reprinted by permission of the publisher.

3

practitioners were priests and their special agents. The terrible power of the "remembering line" of writing held kings in bondage and made wisdom a commodity for sale at the temple. The owner of the book was the possessor of strong magic and so was respected, or feared, which amounted to the same thing. But the man who could wrest from a book its core of meaning and make it completely his own, was still stronger. The Egyptian god Horus, as a child, was able to possess the "wisdom" of a scroll merely by touching it. Everyone who hopes or wishes for some magical way of committing the printed word to understanding memory, without a struggle, is repeating the essence of this myth.

Until the beginning of the twentieth century, reading was thought of as a simple unitary act. Books were to be "mulled over," "studied," and struggled with. The teaching of reading was begun as a sort of matching game in which the child was trained to fit appropriate symbols together, beginning with the letters and building up to words and sentences. The child's formal introduction to the joys of reading began with the line, "A is for Adam. In Adam's fall, sinned we all." Here was a somber and sobering thought for the tyke. It was guaranteed to get rid of any notion that there ought or might be pleasure in reading.

The reading habits of any age are the direct products of the pressures of society and the world in which we live. You can easily see this in the ways in which we have used reading in this country. During colonial days and immediately thereafter in education, religion dominated the drama of life. The literature of the Bible and other kinds of religious writing provided almost all of the reading material available for most of the people. Some writers of the history of reading say that this kind of reading fulfilled a "felt need" (a favorite and not inaccurate phrase of many educators). They say that because of the hostile environment of the day-to-day struggle for some kind of security, man became sensitive to his spiritual resources. This is probably a superficial reading of our social history, but it is true that when all of the people, except for the usual cranks and subversives, keep their thoughts on God and their eyes on the acts of their neighbors, most people wouldn't be caught with anything other than an approved text. When the approvers happened to be New England divines who were quick with torch, rope, and dunking stool, the intelligent and the wise would repair to the good book. And since pleasure whelped sin, they wisely suffered as they read.

This, of course was not true of all of the people, or even of some of the people all of the time. You have to read secular instructions if you are to survive in a world of waves and wilderness. You have to get the clear meaning out of what is written down if you are anxious to avoid financial or physical disaster. Road signs say their piece only once. The governor's edict in declarative prose had to be understood and acted upon. People in the colonies were busy trying to break even with life, so they had little time for reading that was not utilitarian.

The Industrial Revolution turned a lot of things upside-down, including our reading habits, and our notion of the proper place and function of religion.

The New England theocracy was bound to shatter on the rock-bound coast of opportunity in the new world. If religion were to continue to suppress rather than to support the interests and capacities of man it would be ditched for a kinder contact with God, so religion, always willing, however reluctantly, to meet the "felt needs" of the people, turned a little toward the light and said that it was good. More and more, there was evidence that faith in the value of secular knowledge paid handsome dividends and more and more writers and speakers of influence announced that the printed word was in fact a safeguard against the corrosive influences of ignorance. Under the pressure of this kind of publicity many people read many books that their grandfathers would have burned, along with the reader, writer, and publisher. The announcement of moral standards was no longer the central service sought from the book. Men wanted to know things and facts and if the book could instruct them, they would read.

Long before the middle of the nineteenth century, publishing in the United States had become a flourishing industry. Without the let or hindrance of copyright and with the aid of translators of widely varying talent, a flood of books carrying the world's knowledge was washed across the country. The hindsight of history always makes us out to be splendid solvers of jigsaw puzzles. With an expanding agrarian economy as a background and the bright light of an apparently limitless frontier to illumine the board, the pieces fell into their appointed places. In the last half of the nineteenth century, daily newspapers flourished. Public and private libraries were set up in the smallest cities. Jefferson's notion of appropriate educational opportunities was considerably expanded and public instruction in literacy was accepted as a social responsibility. Science was getting its hands dirty in mine and mill, filling the purses of the enterprising. The kind of power that was respected and sought was the kind that moved and made things and the knowledge of this power was eminently democratic. It required no school tie, no proper family connection, only an eagerness to know, a willingness to seek out the little truths that turned wheels and lighted the dark houses. With this explosive expansion of the desire for and the use of knowledge there came too, a recognition of the obligation of anyone who would be anybody, to read widely and skillfully. So, although the teaching of the alphabet might still be a key to the library's treasure, it was a shining, inviting instrument, promised joys to children, pride for the parents, and the world's riches for the whole community.

But change and development have always been most characteristic of the American community. And there have been enormous changes in our world during the last half-century. As Dr. La Brant said, "It would be absurd to think that the methods and purposes in the teaching and the learning of reading have not also changed with our world."[1] Until this century, reading, talking and

---

[1] Lou La Brant, "Personal Factors in Reading," in *Reading in an Age of Mass Communication.* William S. Gray, Editor, New York: Appleton Century Crofts, 1949, 56.

actual demonstration were the only ways in which information could be transmitted. Now we get our information and our entertainment from many sources. The world of words in which we are immersed is so radically different from that of our grandfathers' and even our fathers' that some of them have been overwhelmed and have been forced to retreat from it. In many ways our children are living on a planet that differs from the one we knew.

It all began innocently enough, in the "good old American way" of competition. The news had to be gotten to the public more quickly, the public had to be wooed with flashy, easy-to-read pages, excited and stimulated by any means to read and later to look at one paper, one magazine above all others. The end product is the picture magazine that puts almost no strain upon the literacy of its purchaser and the tabloid newspaper that reduces current events to slogans, nicknames, and exclamations.

Mergenthaler made it easy with his linotype machine, but the tramp printer had already started things with his lightning fingers, and a hundred gadgeteers and inventors brought mass production to printing long before anyone else suspected it could be applied to factory work.

A word-avalanche was started in the late days of the nineteenth century that built up the pressures that created the needs for more and more information, faster and faster. The telegraph and the telephone wiped out distance between towns, and made and shrank time into the tight little ball of the present. The moving picture, spawned out of electricity, silver nitrates, and celluloid, followed an ancient Chinese injunction about words and pictures, and compressed an experience of a lifetime into a matter of minutes. There was a new kind of reading that had to be learned here, but it was learned quickly since the skills required were not far removed from those of watching the old shadow plays or the more recent jack-o-lantern.

There was a pause of brooding power as the new century dawned. Scientists and tinkerers were toying with strange new invisible waves, and the way the earth's atmosphere reacted to them. Edison's electric lamp made electrons behave oddly and the galvanic secret of the compass needle became common knowledge. Count Rutherford made electric sparks jump little gaps, as had Franklin long before him, but then the Italian, Telsa, made a veritable Jovian bolt, and his compatriot. Marconi, used it to hurl words across the Atlantic.

Man, it seems is always trying to make his words go farther, loom larger, and stay longer. This last skill he learned early and so invented history. For the others, he had used everything from pigeons and kites, to cupped hands, billboards, megaphones, and pulpits. But it wasn't until 1920, when radio station KDKA went on the air with the results of the presidential elections that the world of words began to envelop the earth.

For a generation the phonograph had sung songs to the nation but it was a readily domesticated instrument. It didn't stop the family from living its life as usual. Now with the dancing electrons pounding into private earphones, the family, as individuals, was tied to and transfixed by a little black box. They sat through the night and listened for sense through squawks and squeals and whistles. They stopped talking. They stopped reading. A newborn radio trade magazine noted in the early 1920's, "The rate of increase of the number of people who spend at least a part of their evening in listening is almost incomprehensible. . . .It seems quite likely that before the movement has reached its height. . .there will be at least five million receiving sets in this country." This sounds like warnings about post-war television. The youngsters were shooed off to bed and the parents braved the chill quiet of the night to be able to brag the next morning of having "pulled in" a station three hundred miles away.

During this whole period public education was becoming more public. Although sanctioned by law as available to all, less than 700,000 boys and girls were enrolled in high schools in 1900. But when KDKA went on the air, that number had climbed to almost two and one half million, and by 1930 it had reached six and one half million. Of course it is true that our total population has also doubled in this period, but the point for all pundits to consider is that up to 1900 the high school was a highly selective institution in which only those possessing high verbal skills could hope to survive. It was in fact a preparatory school for our intellectual elite. Today, although we still tend to judge intelligence in terms of verbal proficiency, we are committed to the proposition that all America's youth have opportunities to develop and learn a wide variety of skills that will enable them to be full-functioning citizens in our communities.

Now this is a grand commitment, fully worthy of such a nation as ours. It is the substance from which we draw much moral strength as well as our seemingly limitless production and creative powers; but the specter of the New England schoolman haunts us. When we look in upon ourselves and consider what we are, we see an image that is not cast by a student's lamp but by an acetylene torch. We are as brawling and as sprawling as Whitman and Frost and Sandburg have seen us. We are at once rough and subtle, but the brawn bulks larger and we are self-conscious, ashamed.

What is the first thing that we do to a newborn child? We talk to it. We wrap it round with a welter of sound before its brain can sort out any of the reports of its senses. We interpret any wriggle or squawk as a sign that we are understood. This gives us immense satisfaction, and at the beginning it costs the child nothing since it hasn't yet learned to be confused. Not until it becomes aware of confusion and seeks to get rid of it, does it begin to function in ways we like to call human, but from the very beginning the rest of us are in frantic haste that it should be aware of us and the world. We want this awareness so that we may act as human beings toward the child and the difficulties that we and it are confronted with in reaching such a point can only be resolved when some level of understanding is reached.

Put very simply, this means we are trying to talk to the infant. We have trouble from the very beginning—first because he doesn't know and later because he won't pay attention. Notice too that "it" has become a male child on whom it is easier to heap the sins of omission and commission than on a girl. We have trouble getting through to him and later on that trouble increases in direct proportion as we try to help him understand. And then the school steps in and the critics howl: they say that the trouble multiplies because teachers are not anywhere nearly as professional at teaching as parents are at "parenting." Schools have been following a descending scale of performance at least since Socrates. Most parents know from experience that the schools are not as good as they used to be. "Why, when I was in high school, everybody was a good reader!" "We never wasted time on trips and games the way they do today." "Imagine, promoting a child because it is old enough for the next grade!" It is probably because of the nature of education in a democratic society that everyone feels called upon to say something about it. There have been more committees and commissions on the problems of education in the last twenty years than on most of the other institutions in our society. Everyone wants to get into the act.

Our language heritage, misread in the nineteenth century parlors appears still to hold us to the adventures of the written word, to the battle of books. Despite all we know and it is a very great deal, we as a people can be thrown into a panic by a garrulous and argumentative scholar, new to our language and ignorant of our usage, who looks through the wrong end of his research telescope and discovers a little boy who doesn't "read" his mother tongue with the polished skill that he, an adult foreigner has acquired.

As a nation of educators, and we are that as surely as the antique Greeks ever were, we know a vast amount about what learning is and what it entails. We make and have made mistakes, but that's the asking price of adventure and experiment. When we realized that the three R's were necessary but not sufficient for the full development of our children, we went overboard in our practice sometimes, although our more competent philosophers and guides were more cautious than us in their theories. We have liberated our children even as the very shape of the family was being changed by packaged foods and the automobile. We have produced generations which, for all their mistakes, have done things that no legend dared imagine. And we have done this by teaching our children to read.

But reading, remember, is not restricted to the printed page. Actually it never was. In one sense reading *is* the art of transmitting the ideas, facts and feelings from the mind and soul of an author to the mind and soul of a reader, with accuracy and understanding, and much more. But throughout his history man has "read" many things: the flight of birds, the guts of sheep, sun spots, liver spots, and the life lines on a hand. He has read the lore of the jungle, the spoor of the beast, and the portents in a dish of tea. But whatever he has read and however he has read, it has always been for "reason." It was only when man invented symbols for the words in his mouth and the ideas in his teeming brain that other kinds of reading became useful, possible or even desirable. Yet even then, as it still in a large measure is today, this kind of reading was essentially magical. It was and is converted to practical use when man realized that words written down could pin down his purposes, hold his plans still, the better to study and understand them. Word magic is one of man's most wonderful and most dangerous tools. It builds air castles, raises an army of dragon men, fixes a star on a name, and sends human blood running through dirty gutters.

Reading begins at the womb when the body first senses the universe, and the message center of the brain scans the scrambled reports of the senses. Reading gains precision as the sign of an ache or an emptiness is correctly translated into appropriate and soothing action. Reading gains in scope when faces and features become organized into personalities. Reading begins to encompass that universe when the mother, standing with the child at the window, "reads" the beauty of the day.

Now this is using "reading" in a very odd way; what I'm discussing here might well be called "life-orientation." We can play such useful games with the written and the spoken word. The point is that without this orientation, we cannot have a healthy human being, capable of the mind-taxing disciplines required by the special kind of reading you now are doing.

There are many skills that go to make an efficient reader of printed words. Some are psychological, some are physical, others are social. None can be slighted. The teaching of reading should begin as early as possible, never sooner. It is fully within the range of human capacities to produce an intellectual monster of three or four years who can make the sounds represented by printed words. It is a mark of the toughness of the human personality that some such man-made monsters can survive as relatively whole persons able to live in the society of their fellows. But even as the Biblical sages knew, there is a time for everything and things are best accomplished in their season. So it is with this reading. The schools call it "readiness." The child who has been prepared shows it by a willingness, an eagerness to learn.

But the secret is in the preparation. For too long in this country, probably because of the general excellence of the schools, parents have more and more relinquished their own peculiar responsibilities towards preparing their children for what they want and expect.

The Harvard Committee in their report, *General Education in a Free Society*, observed that

A child brought up where books are read, interests are in the air, and promptings everywhere solicit his own small explorations will evidently stand a better chance of exhibiting intelligence, as our society judges it, than one who has felt no such promptings.[2]

[2]*General Education in a Free Society*, Cambridge, Mass.: Harvard University Press, 1946, p.10.

The learned committee is dealing with the special case but after all this is the one kind of reading we usually have to talk about, so far as the parents are concerned. Because of our traditional interest in the academic aspects of education and because of the relative ease with which achievement in this area can be seemingly gauged by the nonprofessional, it has been the proverbial touchstone for anxiety and hysteria and in recent years a source of wealth for the unscrupulous, the gadget-minded, and the educational confidencemen.

We are a paper and ink civilization. Before and after we are anything else, we are *that*. We scribble notes from the day we learn how to mar wallpaper to the terrible moment when we affix our signatures to the last amended codicil to the final version of our ultimate will and testament. We consume a mountain of print before we die, for amusement, for escape, for enlightenment and for living. And we do all of this usually without ever pausing to wonder at many things. In this nation especially, this wonderment often degenerates into an obsession. If the obsession is diet, we'll eat anything from hay to marbles. If it's "peace of mind" we'll mumble Coué's formula or Peale's positive apostrophe——but today our abiding obsession is with reading. Look at the explosive growth of reading clinics, the do-it-yourself books that offer the same services more cheaply and even less legitimately, the damn-their-eyes books that accuse the teacher, on *misread evidence,* of preventing the child from reading at all. Consider the doleful report of the American Book Publishers Council, " . . . reading is still unattractive to the majority." Yes, something must be done about this . . .

I suspect that it might be a sociological axiom that every such obsession creates a kind of commodity vacuum into which the gadget makers rush with their wonder tools, or tricks, or drugs. Scrabble begets a Scrabble Lazy Susan and even a Scrabble Dictionary. The capable householder becomes a do-it-yourself man with more power tools than his housebuilder ever needed. And so it is with reading. There are kits that are marketed in bookstores. There are correspondence courses too. We have a gadget that pushes the child's nose down the page at the prescribed rate and another that whips his eyes back and forth with the speed of a sidewinder's tail. We have films that make him scan, skip and skim and cameras to picture his eyes' fixations. All we lack is a pill to make him want to read . . . Oh, but we will make him read all right! We have only to organize our know-how, tool up for production and then get the ad men to compose the appropriate incantations.

Reading difficulties are much easier to see than social or psychological problems. A fifth-grade boy who cannot manage a third-grader reader appears to be in much more difficulty than a well-behaved classmate who masters intellectual skills easily, is complaisant and apparently content to be left alone. The very good boy can be in very bad shape. Saying this, however is to throw a sop to some educationists, a goad to some psychological cranks and in general to commit the same pathetic fallacy that the destructive critics of the schools are usually guilty of.

No single facet of human behavior can ever explain the whole personality. It is tempting to seek one, but if one were to exist, the personality in which it was found would be less human because of its existence. The uniqueness of man is the variety of his interests, his goals, his behavior. The wonder of the universe is its multiplicity. Man seeks single answers. This is his passion for neatness. This is how he reaches nearer the angels, how he sees God. But for every-day affairs of life he must blind himself to other possibilities, to see the world in terms of black and white, right and wrong. This too he must do in order to act, or else he must spend his life in paralyzed indecision. The "crazy, mixed-up kid" asks too many questions. The mature adult has made an armed truce with life in order to find the small and partial answers that mean food, shelter and sanity.

"My child can't read," says the troubled parent. "They are not teaching him properly." A visit to the school confirms the fear. Half a dozen groups of children, reading books of varying difficulty may be scattered about the room. Some children may "only" be looking at pictures. The teacher may be working with one group on the recognition and association of words with things and actions. Depending on the age and experience of the group, she may be helping them take words apart and put them together. She may be urging some to read aloud. She may be trying to persuade others not to pronounce the words as they read silently. She may move to another group and talk with them about the story and she may even allow the talk to drift off on tangents of personal remembrances.

The puzzled and worried parent who does not or cannot understand the teacher's explanations of what is going on, will have fears confirmed and may turn for solace and advice to someone who chants the song of the "good old days."

There are basic skills that must be acquired, of course. There are fundamentals to be absorbed, but so it is in every area of human endeavor. A particular kind of knowledge is good for dealing with a particular kind of information. There was once a notion which fortunately continues to have currency, more in the colleges than in the schools, that the learning of Latin or Greek or mathematics somehow "trained" the mind to deal with life problems. The survivors of this "classical" education often achieved considerable success in society. And so that kind of education gained and maintained a reputation for social inefficiency that in fact it never contained.

There has always been a kind of hidden or secret education that goes on whenever people deliberately try to teach skills or knowledge to others. It has become open and purposeful in the last generations. It has always been the actual source of human excellence. It has nothing to do with subject matter, although it uses all knowledge. It is dependent on no specific teaching method, although it experiments with methodology. It has no completely articulated "philosophy of education," although philosophers who are concerned with education tend to agree about general goals and values. This kind of education exists just because some people want to help others to learn to think, to live. They are the wonderful few who have themselves learned how to excite in others the desires to "find out for themselves." They are the ones who can make the dissection of frogs "come alive," who can make the mixed-up mutterings of ancient poets "make sense"; who can make it important that the stars be counted; who can make man's interminable difficulties with himself and others a source of adventure and a cause for hope. They teach people to ask questions, to accept every answer as provisional, to rely for practical affairs only on the kind of information that anyone can get to and check. The students of these teachers learn to think purposefully and solve real problems. They may, incidentally, learn to speak Greek.

In one sense we are all Texans. We go "whole hog" whether it's busting the atom or denying the existence of hard liquor. And we are always nursing a hangover from one or another of our binges. We even invented mass advertising so that we could keep up the noise level on our tricks. We made something called elementary education a free gift of all to each, then we made it compulsory; then we added more education and some of us aren't fazed by the notion of life-long education free for all to the extreme limits of individual needs, urges, and desires.

We have a nationwide concern that all be educated. We will not abide a nationwide operation of that institution. We are anxious to give or get help, as the case may be, but no strings attached! We have a naive and abiding faith that education will solve all social personal ills, but then we join groups to keep the schools absolutely free from every influence except ours. We expect our children to be turned into citizens who are as good as or better than we are. Yet when the schools, which we develop, make timid but professional suggestions about how this might be done, we imagine that the foundations of society are tottering. "Keep sex out of the schools." "Keep God in the classroom." "Don't hunt for the skeletons in our historical closets." "Make the children civic-minded but don't make them nosey." "Teach them to be objective about other ways of living." "Teach them to accept the American Way."

Most people are intimidated by professionals. The dentist might be a political moron but we'll accept his judgment on dental affairs until it is contradicted by a physician, or the corner druggist. We assume, usually rightly, a high level of technical competence in our professional people; all but the teachers.

Teachers are not professional, they're—well, they're teachers. In a way, we're in the same business. You had the kids, we handle them. But you were there first, so—so you can talk, and you do, as you should. But whereas a physician can diagnose a non-existent ulcer and you will properly behave as an ulcer-owner, you greet a teacher's suggestion about child care or family relations with suspicion or even contempt.

In a way your attitude is not unwarranted. Many teachers and many of their organizations are status-hungry. They want to be respected. They whimper about their need in staff room, conference room and church socials. They cry poor-mouth in the presence of bank clerks and do the weak-sister act before a trade unionist. They are seedy-looking and faceless, the very spit-and-image of the thing no honest teacher ever was or could be. They can be panicked by an equally under-paid professor of education or a child psychologist on a dry run. So they are fair game for you, but hunting them only hurts your child.

Where human learning is concerned there is no one best way of doing anything, but for the professional person, there are always certain ways that are more appropriate than others. No two children can be made to want to read in the same way. Most children come to school eager to learn everything. But what you have done with and for them in the years before will determine what things they are most anxious to learn. As the Harvard committee pointed out, a child surrounded by an atmosphere rich with the joys of reading, will want to read. One who has come from a home that is barren of books, in which reading by the parents rarely goes beyond the comics and the sport sections of the papers, is hardly going to think very much of the idea of "reading" a story he can see on television. His parents won't be reading this book. Yet our society has decided that he be given reading skills so that he can take full advantage of his "unalienable rights." Where the teacher is faced with one or a few such children in the classroom, her task isn't insurmountable. But where, in addition she has children who for many other reasons, are not either ready or willing to learn to read, then the whole class may be in for difficult times.

Our literary heritage—the wit, wisdom, and knowledge of the world's civilizations—is the rightful possession of every child, but some will never claim that inheritance. Yet even they will share in the riches of others. How they will share will depend to a large measure on where they are born, how they grow, who loves them, what they become.

See the conflict here. This is the province of all. The domain of human enterprise. All are called but some do not choose to heed. They are not the less for the choice, nor necessarily the poorer. This world machine of ours is a wonderful servant, far more dependable than the dreamed of genie. Not only has it made books talk. It makes them be. It teaches without tears.

Let us face this fact: There are, there have been and there will be in increasing numbers, boys and girls who will grow up in this country with little in the way of reading skills. They learn how to make out directions. They can read road signs, price tags, and the myriad labels that name our world. They will be word-minded only in the simple social sense. Not that they could not have been otherwise, but we fortunately still refuse to make a person become even what would benefit him most. These children will grow, as they have in the past, into full-functioning citizens, fully able to share, and willingly sharing, the burdens of that citizenship. They in turn will rear children, pay taxes, engage in our common defense, contribute to some of our arts. They will neither read nor write books.

In the recent past and today, we have not been serving these people as well as they serve us. They keep wheels going. They make power flow. They make the machines behave. They sing for us. They paint. They even make us laugh. The only thing they cannot do is make the printed and written word behave. What have we given them, we who prefer and know the use of the printed word? Consider television, the film, display advertising, the theatre. These are their major avenues of enlightenment, instruction, entertainment, and escape. The words are there, in the air or behind the scenes.

Words are expendable; that is the nature of language. Their meanings wear out and shift. They lose their bite and punch and precision. But words are devalued before their time by the truncated thinking that produces sentences such as, "What type shoes do you want?" "This cigarette is milder." "Let's finalize this contract." When words are cut off from the things and acts which they are used to refer to, the thinking that they are meant to express becomes confused and crippled. The words are debased!

The attitude that fosters this, however, doesn't start on Madison Avenue, although it ends there. It begins, for example, with an off-hand publicity release from an important university about some research on ways, other than reading, of getting basic information. This release is picked up by a responsible newspaper whose careful headline writer understands the sense of the story to mean "PICTURES HELD TO RIVAL WORDS." The newspaper reporter in his story indirectly quotes someone to the effect that "One minute of motion picture (is) the equivalent of thirty minutes of talk." This story also includes a direct quote from John E. Burchard that "the idea which a reader derives from Ernest Hemingway's *The Old Man and the Sea* comes after the reader has absorbed some sixty thousand words. This takes at least an hour." The newspaper report concludes with the statement that, "Mr. Burchard ventures the opinion that a similar understanding could come after a few minutes study of a painting by a skillfull artist."

It is quite possible that you could get just as superficial an understanding of Hemingway's book, "reading" at a thousand words per minute as you would from looking at a painting for a few minutes. However, these points of view are not to be argued with here. What is important is that a conscientious copywriter, an earnest headline writer, a responsible newspaper, a group of thoughtful and dedicated people all conspire, in spite of their own most cherished aims, in giving life to a monstrous notion which is the very opposite of their intentions. Pictures are not better than words except where the words are not understood or the "meaning" of the picture is clearer to the viewer than the words. Pictures are very effective for telling the *what* of things but rarely the *why* or *worth*. Where pictures begin to approach words in this function they lose their visual values in the same proportion as they gain in communicating ideas. But ideas sometimes shrink and harden from use and we make marks to stand for them. This is how alphabets are born and changed.

What has to be clearly understood is that there is no one sovereign way of getting information. Pictures are good. So are smells, yells, and bellyaches. But information is the raw material of communication. Information isn't even that unless it is used or a use is contemplated for it. Communication is a social act. It is always concerned with other people. It can be done with a grunt, a bump, or a glance. It can be rich with "meanings" or with feeling or with a mixture of both. The *what* of things can be reduced to the simple symbols of mathematics but the *why* and its *worth* needs the poets' magic and the shared remembrance of dreams and hopes. The crudest television commercial pays homage to this when the dancing bottles or marching cigarettes picket the screen with little signs, pleading for closer attention.

Words are slippery things. They won't stay put. They pick up meanings and colors not "intended" for them. They suffer or profit by the company they keep. In the mouth of one man the word "love" can be a plea. Other lips can make it a curse. Its meaning can be reduced to the equivalent of "like" or expanded to mean "worship." The word *red* may mean truth, beauty, or falsehood. *Liberty* can become a dirty name; *chain* a term of endearment.

What happens to words can and does happen to any symbol. A flag, a statue or a city can "stand for" opposite things for different peoples. But we trust the words we share with others until we or they are misunderstood and even then we distrust them more than their words. We often have a very firm belief that the words that we use are the same as and as real as the things they stand for the acts they represent. Languages are filled with reverent remarks like "I give you my word!" The tyranny of the two-letter word *is* forces us to act, sometimes as if the word we use for a thing is as real as the thing in itself. This causes us to misjudge the nature of the actual world. It worries us and even makes us sick. Some people in this world, not of course as civilized as we are, even think that it is dangerous to let anyone know their real names for fear that the name-knower would have power over them. But let any man call another a fool or a liar or question the social regularity of his parents' marital relations and he will act as violently as any other primitive.

We are a nation of loudmouths. We got that way on the tinker's trail and at the boasting parties around frontier campfires. We have more tall tales in our folklore than you can find in all of Europe. But our tallest tales have become merely conservative estimates of our actual performances. Pecos Bill rode a tornado. His great-grandchild rides a Thunderjet at ten times the speed. Paul Bunyan's Blue Ox would be worn out by a medium sized bulldozer and Johnny Inkslinger couldn't even feed the cards to an obsolete IBM bookkeeping machine.

We wallow in this flood of words, but it's of our own making. We've painted the clouds with ads for soap, curtained the country-side with billboards for baby foods, and crammed the general air with electronic declarations about the benefits of laxatives and deodorants. But the anxiety we should suffer in the face of this flood is only apparent in the warnings of the permanently disenchanted.

Of course it is true that the shell game is played on us everyday in the year by peddlars, purveyors, and producers of everything that we need and use and a lot we don't need, never wanted, but cannot do without.

It is certainly true that our intelligences, however great or meager are insulted and conned by the anti-logic of the huckster but it is about time that someone blew the whistle on the anxious applicants for our intellectual guardianship. This is not to say that there should be no concern about the connivance of the wool-pullers and pharmaceutical wolf-criers but, rather, that those individuals with off-center sensitivity over the sodden plasticity of the masses ought to learn to read their dials and counters with more accuracy and objectivity. The mass mind is a myth.

The mass media for communcation, and we have invented and perfected all of them here, are effective upon the masses only so far as distribution of "information" is concerned. The only apparent mass movement that television has so far has been able to effect is the concerted and collective use of plumbing during the commercials. Mass action can still only be effected where there are masses. The motion picture could do this, but we lack the indecency of Hitler's Leni Reifensthal; besides, our whole population is never anxious about the same thing at the same time. We rarely suffer more than a few mob scenes during any year, and these are engineered by methods that were invented by the old Greeks and still require a man with leather lungs and a ruptured psyche.

No, we live splendidly and dangerously in this word ocean of ours. Its currents are strong. Its shoals are treacherous but it is not the whole of our environment. We inhale and exhale words for our social living, but we do this for purposes, to make or change things or keep them as they are. To do this we must take thought and to think we must be able to hold ideas still long enough to compare them. To make comparisons we must be able to choose and choice requires that we have preferences. None of these acts are possible if we cannot manage and master the words that we use. The mastery that we have gained is the measure of the cultural distance we have traveled from the cave. It is a long long way. We have negotiated it through our ability to make, read, and act upon signs. Early man was a good sailor on the sea of life. We are navigators.

In the following sections of this book the sources of our skills will be examined. To do this we will have to see how words are born and how they die. We will need to know what changes man has made in his living since he learned how to freeze ideas onto a page and yet make them more alive. Then perhaps we can understand what is involved in the act we loosely call reading and what it means to initiate a child into its open mysteries.

2. Reading As Experience In Inquiry*

RUSSELL G. STAUFFER

INQUIRY is fundamental to reading. When a person reads he is gathering and processing information; and this is inquiry. A reader who raises questions, builds hypotheses, reads and processes data, and tests findings to determine validity is actively involved in inquiry. To be able to inquire is a necessary condition for independent research-type reading that results in learning.

A reader who cannot perform as an inquiring reader needs to have all of his reading programmed for him. Material has to be fed to such a reader. Questions have to be raised for him; inferences have to be drawn for him; and he must be told what conclusions should be reached. Such a reader is obviously a totally dependent reader and learner.

Since inquiry is fundamental to reading, the method of teaching reading must be such that inquiry is fostered. When a person tries to promote conceptual changes in another by giving him something to read and showing him how to read it, he is engaged in teaching reading. When a person tries to promote these changes on his own by gathering and processing information through reading, he is engaged in inquiry.

SCHEMATA

Inquiry is native to the mind. As an infant a child is busy gathering data from his environment in order to conceptualize it.[3][1] When an infant learns that rubber rings may be sucked as well as thrown, pulled at, pegged, and so on, he is internalizing properties in his environment. Such interactions with environment occur long before formal education begins and help a child to form intuitive schemata or some sort of structure system.

Schemata are plastic organizations that adapt and change as man's ability

---

*From *Education Leadership,* 24, 5 (February, 1967) 407-412. Copyright ©1967 by the Association for Supervision and Curriculum Development. Reprinted by permission.

[1] Numbers in brackets refer to references at the end of the article.

to understand and control his environment increases. As a child grows older he learns to become more systematic in making his conceptual systems correspond to reality. His searching and collecting and processing of data become broader and more complex. His schema becomes more sophisticated and reflects more closely the complexities of the real world. The developmental changes that occur as schemas are not only generalized but also differentiated and may best be described as a process of assimilation and accomodation [3].

The first of these two basic processes consists of taking in and incorporating what is perceived in terms of what is known and understood at the time. When a child begins to discriminate objects that are to be sucked when he is very hungry, an element of recognition occurs. He has assimilated his perception of the objects in terms of his established schemas related to sucking. As long as events encountered do not differ too sharply from concepts which are known, assimilation occurs without difficulty.

When, though, a child faces an experience that he cannot readily assimilate—a discrepant event—he needs to examine more carefully and perhaps create new schemas. Thus he may have to reshape and reorganize conceptual structures until they fit and account for the new circumstances. This is known as accommodation. It paves the way for conceptual reorganization and the subsequent assimilation of a formerly discrepant event.

Inquiry involves both assimilation and accommodation in complementary roles. The inquirer, faced with a discrepant event, may first attempt to break it down into component parts, to analyze it in terms of variables which he has already conceptualized . . . and use them in finding greater meaning and unity in experience [6, p. 60-61].

INQUIRY AND DIRECTED READING

Inquiry being native to the mind and fundamental to reading, particularly critical and creative reading [4], it follows that the processes of assimilation and accommodation operate in both circumstances. Therefore, a person reading needs to know how to deal with concepts that are readily assimilated and with discrepant events that require accommodation as well as assimilation.

Directed reading-thinking activities can be accomplished on a group basis or an individual basis. In both, the process of inquiry can and should be incorporated [5].

In a group-type directed reading-thinking activity, four requirements need to be met. First, the number of children in the group should not exceed a range of eight to twelve. This size will permit each pupil to be an active participant in the activity. Second, the children in the group should have about the same reading ability. Third, all should be required to deal with the same selection at the same time. Fourth, the teacher must direct the activity in such a way that the major responsibility for purposes for reading rests with the children, and the tyranny of a right answer resides in the text. This demands devotion to the belief that inquiry is native to the mind and that children are curious, will inquire, and will be interested if they are permitted to inquire.

In an individual-type directed reading activity, certain requirements have to be met, too. First, even though there may be thirty children in a class, each is required to be on his own. Each pupil operates as an individual. Second, each pupil decides what topic of interest he wants to pursue or read about, and why. Third, he selects his own material and is limited in his choice primarily by the library available. Fourth, the teacher is a resource person and is available to give help and encouragement as needed and as requested. Fifth, what a pupil does with what he reads and learns is paced largely by the process of assimilation and accommodation required to incorporate the ideas within his conceptual system and by the experience of sharing these attainments with his peers.

Inquiry can be accomplished with or without teacher direction. Primarily, though, when the mode of learning is inquiry, the person proceeds on his own. "When the mode of learning is inquiry . . . the process of data gathering, analysis and experimentation is under the control of the learner himself." [6, p. 60]. The person is free to reach out in whatever direction he chooses. He decides on the topic of interest he wishes to pursue and how thoroughly he needs to investigate it. He decides what conceptual changes he wishes to accomplish and how discrepant they are. He gathers and selects data and processes the information in whatever sequence is meaningful to him. He programs and paces his own learning and does so in terms of his own cognitive needs as dictated by his style of learning.

It is possible, of course, for one person to shape the concepts of another by programming a series of experiences and engineering a child's conceptual reorganization. This is called teaching. In order to be effective, though, the teacher must be thoroughly acquainted with a learner's existing conceptual structures so that he may start at the level of the learner with an event that is not too discrepant. In addition, he must keep a constant check on the conceptual modifications that are occurring and must do so at every step along the way.

In the preschool years the schemata formed largely represent by-products of a child's attempts to manipulate and control his environment. Later the data gathering and processing take on a more organized form as he shifts his concern from producing effects to seeing relationships. When he sees his operations as experiments that can be done or undone or replicated, and as tentative and reversible, his inquiry takes on more the character of research. Now he can experiment in a more or less controlled fashion. At the stage where he reaches mental maturity, he is capable of going beyond concrete operations to the point where he can declare and test hypotheses by means of formal logical operations. The older child constructs or invents conceptual models of causality by obtaining the data needed to try out his concepts. He does so by testing and revising and learning how "... his manipulations as causes correlate with outcomes as effects" [6, p. 63]. The mature mind can bypass even the empirical or concrete operations and can test the validity of an hypothesis logically.

If a child is going to reorganize his conceptual systems by reading, he must be given the opportunity to try out his store of conceptual models by using them to make predictions and design objectives. Then he must be free to gather the data he needs to resolve his predictions or cognitive conflicts. This he must do until he can assimilate what he reads or evolve a conceptual system by restructuring his models and accommodate to the new data.

It should be apparent that the process of inquiry as well as the process of inquiry-type reading has a large creative component. Even so the reader cannot depart from the realm of logic or reason. In turn the problem of how to develop inquiry-type reading in the elementary school becomes basic to all learning. This is why the process of directed reading-thinking activities—both group-type and individual type—assumes paramount importance. Children need to be taught to read in such a way that their conceptual growth is engineered by them and not by their teachers, and so that they know how to achieve this autonomy by asking questions to gather information. Since inquiry is fundamental to human behavior from its earliest stages of development, reading instruction must be done in a manner which exercises rather than denies this talent.

MEANS OF PROMOTING INQUIRY-TYPE READING

A group-type directed reading-thinking activity serves many useful purposes and, in a way, provides training that is fundamental to individual activities. Performing in a group permits an individual to compare his questions, the efficiency of his data processing, and the effectiveness of his validity yardstick with those of others. He can observe at firsthand some of the effects of various strategies of data gathering and processing as used by different children. Henderson [2] noted that comprehension is influenced by the capability of children to set individual purposes for reading, that pupils who set better purposes for reading on their own are likely also to be more successful in attaining purposes supplied by someone else, and that good and poor purpose setters differ in the comprehension of story material even when the material is at their independent reading level.

Whatever story or selection is used, it should be real and meaningful to the children. At the primary level such materials may be largely of the story type—filled with human interest factors, and with an evolving plot that leads to a plausible and, preferably, unique climax.

Story type material can be used in such a way that problems are posed that puzzle the children. To obtain a discrepant event, the children should be asked to speculate about the story plot and its likely outcome. Speculation can be based on different amounts of information, thus requiring inquiry strategies that are flexible and can be adjusted to the demands posed when little is known or when much is known. For example, pupils may be asked to speculate after seeing only a story title ("A Newspaper Helps," "Stopping an Airplane"); after reading a third of a selection; or a half of a selection; or all except the last page. Greater divergent (creative) responding is invited when the amount of data available is limited. When, however, almost all of the data has been processed, convergent-type thinking is required [1].

The children must be given the freedom to use the data or story facts to speculate as they desire, and as *they* see fit. Teachers must not impose their predictions and must avoid giving their speculations or summations. These conditions allow each child to pursue his own summations as he follows the consequence of ideas, and in the end satisfies his own cognitive needs.

Beginning readers who can read comfortably at a first reader level can be taught to react to story content by using it to speculate about plot direction and plot outcome. They can do this if the plot, its characters and setting, are within their range of experience. The human factor of people doing things and interacting makes the drama of everyday happenings a ready source of conceptual systems which children can use to speculate and conclude. Their interactions with their environment provide schema whereby children internalize the properties and events of their environment.

As they grow older and become more mature readers, the children learn to deal with more complex plots and do so in a more sophisticated way. Reading provides an early opportunity for the young minds to learn how to go beyond concrete operations and manipulate ideas and hypotheses through increasingly more logical operations. As a result, through reading they are able to build increasingly more elaborate and accurate schemata which reflect more and more closely the realities and complexities of their real world.

From plots to accounts of events in the social sciences and the humanities is a ready transition. Human interest factors predominate and permit the reshaping and reorganization of conceptual structures until they are understood anew. Truth becomes stranger and as fascinating as fiction as the course of human events provides the opportunity to relate new meaning to old conceptual structures.

Mathematics and the sciences are dealt with in much the same way. The reader deals with the data provided, abstracts relationships, tries out hypotheses, and adjusts his conceptual models by the causality observed and by the operations used.

All this is done in a group situation where one reader-thinker can compare his inquiry performance with that of others. He sees how others deal inductively with a story or an account. He sees new understandings come to light through the forum of discovery-type reading.

Such group-type directed reading-thinking activities can provide the reading-inquiry training needed for the learner to perform through self-directed actions. Then the autonomy of the learner, his interests and tastes and ambitions, can be translated into plans and actions—as problems are posed, materials are identified, answers are sought, and new concepts are developed. The individual reader goes to the library and selects the materials he needs, or produces the data he needs for his conceptual reorganizations. He does not have a group to rely on. Neither does a teacher program his conceptual reorganization by selecting material, explaining data, and demonstrating relationships. He does research type reading by experimenting and gathering his own data, by trying out various combinations of schemata, and by testing each until he has found a proper solution. Of course, the teacher is engaged in teaching reading—research and discovery-type reading-with the universe as the boundary for pupil interests and the library as the source of materials.

In this type of individualized reading instruction, the teacher keeps a constant check, even though the gathering and processing of data are under the control of the learner. In turn, the learner not only programs his own reading in terms of his own cognitive and informational needs of the moment, but also is influenced by whatever sharing he does with the group. A principal feature of individualized reading *instruction,* where the learner is autonomous, is the sharing he does with and for his classmates. The activity of gathering and processing information is exciting and pleasurable in its own right; but it becomes even more so when pupils are given the opportunity to share their findings with their classmates.

How to organize material and present it to a class in such a way as to be both clear and attention-holding poses a real challenge. But it is just this type of demand for planning and constructing that creates in the learner a sense of power. The group serves as auditor, asking questions, censoring presentations, and seeking clarity. The presentations are either oral or written or both, are illustrated or dramatized—as the occasion demands. The satisfaction derived has immediate consequences. It serves to motivate further reading because it occurs in this kind of inquiry-research type context. Individualized-type directed reading-thinking activities, just like inquiry training, are, borrowing Suchman's words: "a joyous experience of discovery" and "a highly satisfying and stimulating activity."

In conclusion, when inquiry-type reading instruction is the dominant mode of learning, school libraries become the heart of the school's reading program, and basic readers are used as auxiliary training aids. Individualized reading-inquiry training is paralleled and supported by group-type training. Both teaching procedures are essential.

By providing both the climate and the training for reading-inquiry and reading-thinking, the teaching becomes a motivational force that promotes curiosity and builds up irresistible learning pressures. Pupils are constantly seeking answers. School and classroom libraries are filled with inquiring minds gathering data and satisfying interests. They will find ways to assimilate and accommodate discrepant events because each is being taught how to adapt the reading-learning process to his own cognitive needs.

If a child is going to learn how to read in accord with his own cognitive needs, he must have the opportunity to ask questions, make predictions, and gather and process data. In short, he must be taught to be an inquiring reader.

References

1. J.P. Guilford, "Three Faces of Intellect," *American Psychologist,* 14 (1959,) 469-79.
2. E.H. Henderson, "A Study of Individually Formulated Purposes for Reading in Relation to Reading Achievement Comprehension and Purpose Attainment." Unpublished doctoral dissertation. College of Graduate Studies, University of Delaware, 1963.
3. J.Piaget, *The Origins of Intelligence in Children.* New York: International Universities Press, Inc., 1952.
4. R.G. Stauffer, "Critical Reading: A Preface to Maturity of Choice," *The Journal of Reading* (in press).
5. R.G. Stauffer, "Individualized and Group Reading Instruction," *Elementary English,* **27** (October, 1960).
6. J.R. Suchman, "The Child and the Inquiry Process," *Intellectual Development: Another Look.* Papers and Reports from the ASCD Eighth Curriculum Research Institute. Washington, D.C.: Association for Supervision and Curriculum Development, 1964, 59-77.

3. Personal Values In Reading*

DAVID RUSSELL

READING is responding. The response may be at the surface level of "calling" the word. It may be at the somewhat deeper level of understanding the explicit meaning of sentence, paragraph or passage. Sometimes reading may be at a third level. It may involve going beyond the facts to the discovery of new and personal meanings. It may be a stimulus to images, memories, identification or fresh and creative thoughts.

Teachers are concerned with each of the three levels of response. First, we want children to be accurate in what they read—to see the difference between *broad* and *board*. Second, we want them to get accurate meaning from a story or article, especially if the passage is a factual one such as is found in a science or a health textbook. But sometimes we aim to have children go beyond accuracy and literal meaning to some personal interpretation of what they read. We want them to say. "I think Ginger is a funny dog" or "It was very brave of Manuel to scare away the bull."

In other words we want children to find in a story humor or beauty or new meanings. We want them to see for themselves such qualities as courage or friendliness or loyalty.

Put another way, we as teachers need to help children discover that printed materials can be treated in these three ways. Teachers and pupils can decide whether to read for the surface meaning or whether it is worth while to dip below the surface. This habit of diving below the surface may start to develop in the primary grades. After the primary child has been helped over some of the first hurdles of learning to read he may read widely in the many attractive and easy readers and short storybooks available today. As he begins to branch out into current materials—the newspaper, the advertisements, the magazines and a wider range of books—he must learn how to discriminate among these materials, to differentiate between the superficial and the thoughtful, the evanescent interest and the permanent value. He can learn that the comics are on

The Reading Teacher, **15,** 3,(December, 1961), 172-178 Reprinted by permission of the International Reading Association.

25

the surface—to be read quickly and forgotten. He can be helped to decide that many newspaper and news magazine stories are in this same, temporary category. He can be guided in seeing that some factual materials are very useful for understanding the solar system or for building a model plane. But he can also be helped in seeing that some poems, stories and books have hidden meanings that must be explored and, if possible, understood. Although a child will not name them directly, these meanings and symbols may represent some of the important, unifying ideas in our culture such as the importance of the individual or the value of co-operative effort. Now these concepts will not be stated explicitly in the story—they must be "read into" it by the reader. And usually the young reader needs help in finding such symbols and deeper meanings.

Two stories in a well-known reading series and from a well-loved poem illustrate my point. The stories have been picked from readers with deliberate intent to show that in this available source are materials which should not be skimmed over in a quick attempt to get the story read and the book closed. Instead, here are typical examples of how the teacher, with broader background and deeper understanding, may help children see symbols and find deeper meanings.

The first story is from the third reader called *Friends Far and Near*. This story is called "A Little Black Bear Goes to School." Notice the opportunities for developing personal values in this one short third-grade story. It begins:

" 'Take it back!' puffed Henry, striking a blow at Sam.

" 'Won't!' came the answer as the two boys rolled over and over. Legs and fists flew. The fight was on again.

"The boys did not see the stranger who stepped into the clearing just in time to watch the fight. His blue eyes were bright with fun. But when he saw the blows were coming down hard, he leaped toward the boys.

" 'Hold on, you young wildcats!' he called, pulling the boys apart. 'Now, then. Speak up. What's the matter?"

" 'Sam says Johnny Appleseed is just an old tramp,' cried Henry, pushing the hair out of his eyes. 'And I'm making him take it back.'

"The stranger's eyes danced. 'Well, maybe Johnny Appleseed *is* just an old tramp.'

" 'Sure he is,' said Sam gruffly.

" 'No, sir,' cried Henry. 'You don't know him if you think that. He is kind to everybody. My father says he walks a long, long way every year planting apple trees so that people can have fruit.'

" 'What started you boys talking about Johnny Appleseed?' asked the stranger.

" 'He's going to teach school next week. The master is sick,' said Sam. 'And who wants to go to school to an old tramp!' cried Henry.

The story continues the next week at a pioneer schoolhouse. Sam and Henry get to this little log building and there is the old man who had stopped their fight. He is Johnny Appleseed. While he is telling the children about his apple trees and the wild animals he has met, into the classroom walks a hungry little bear. Johnny says, " 'As I was saying, it's well to respect the rights of bears. I think this little fellow's hungry.' " The children feed the bear most of their fourteen lunches and after he is well filled Johnny Appleseed says, " 'Henry, can you and Sam look after this bear without getting into a fight?' " The boys do so happily and decide to call the bear Johnny.

This is a typical third-grade story. Similar examples from second-grade or even first-grade books could be given. If a teacher follows the manual for this story, here are some of the questions the children must think about as they read, reread and discuss the story:

> At the beginning, one boy calls Johnny a tramp.
> At the end, the boys are saying "Sir," Why did they change? What about our attitudes to older people?
> What about Johnny Appleseed's work?
> Was he a person to respect?
> Is fighting a good way of settling difficulties?
> What did Johnny mean by showing respect for the rights of bears?
> How did Johnny settle difficulties between two boys?
> Is getting people to work together a good way of settling difficulties?

The second story is from "The Big Word" in the fifth reader, *The New Days and Deeds*. The big word is "responsibility." Robert learns to spell it for a spelling match at school which he dearly wants to win. But when his father is hurt, and the whole corn crop is in danger, he learns that responsibility is more than a word. He gives up the match for the sake of the family and he and his older brother begin to harvest the corn as partners in a job to be done.

In the reading and rereading of the story questions such as the following may be discussed:

> What were the two sides of the argument about Robert's going to the spelling match?
> Did Robert exaggerate his real feelings when he talked to his brother?
> While Mr. Beachum was deciding to pick the corn, what do you think was going through Robert's mind?
> Do you think it was more important for Robert to do the farm chores or his homework?
> Do Robert's and his brother's arguments over responsibility for feeding the animals remind you of similar arguments in your family?
> Why is *responsibility* more than a word?

Not all stories have important meanings as found in the two illustrations and not all the questions can be answered simply. Indeed, one mark of a good discussion will be the suggesting of different kinds of answers to these questions and to others raised in the discussions.

The poem selected to illustrate the possibility of finding deeper meaning is Rachel Field's "If once you have slept on an island" found in different anthologies and readers.

> If once you have slept on an island
> You'll never be quite the same;

In introducing the poem, the teacher has probably been able to use testimony from children who have actually been on islands—what they are like and how they felt when they were surrounded by water. Perhaps she has been able to show a copy of Golden MacDonald's and Leonard Weisgard's charming picture book *The Little Island.* Then the children have been ready to hear the whole poem and perhaps parts of it two or three times. Now comes the time, when the poem has been savored, to look for possible deeper meanings.

> Can we sometimes make our own islands?
> Can we have an "island" in a tree-house or our own room?
> Have you ever had a feeling you wanted to get away from brothers or sisters and just be alone?
> Is it a good thing to go off by ourselves and just think things over quietly?

The teacher, with a greater breadth of experience, may know that escape to a private world is not always possible. She may have in mind John Donne's "No man is an Island, intire of it selfe; every man is a peece of the Continent." Most fifth or sixth graders are not ready for subtleties but they can often see that this poem and other good poems suggest ideas beyond the literal words. Again, the wise teacher expects different responses from different children. Some may be bored by the poem, others may be transported to private worlds.

Since, in the words of Walter de La Mare, "A poem may have as many different meanings as there are different minds" another teacher or child may prefer to discuss certain lines of the poem.

> But you'll see blue water and wheeling gulls
> Wherever your feet may go.

How many of you can see pictures of the sea? What other pictures do you see clearly? And so perhaps to the deeper truth that we all have memories and images which we may carry with us for the rest of our lives.

Perhaps some children will be attracted by the lines

> Oh, you won't know why and you can't say why
> Such a change upon you came

and the whole question of events that have changed one's life will emerge. But with all these possibilities, the teacher must be aware that to some children this is just a poem about some other child and an idea that has nothing whatever to do with themselves. In a sense, this poem is not for them. But perhaps some other poem is!

The three examples illustrate the idea that deeper meanings can be found in different kinds of writing and books. Most children will read at the surface level habitually unless the teacher encourages occasional penetration into new territory. Such encouragement is most rewarding in imaginative literature. Even the second-grader can find some plus-values in the simple folk and fairy tales he is able to read. For the average child, by the time he can read fourth-grade materials a whole world of books and ideas is beckoning. The classroom and school libraries should contain works of literature, with ingredients of imagination and fantasy, as well as the factual books needed in a world where concrete knowledge accumulates so quickly. Imaginative literature is more intrepid in its approach to problems than a single child or adolescent can be. A judicious mixture of fact and fiction is the aim of most teachers. Perhaps even the comics should not be written off as part of the imaginative literature which may stimulate thinking. For example, in a recent television program on humor, cartoonist Al Capp, originator of "Li'l Abner," called the comic strip "the world's most popular literary form." He went on to say,

I think comics should create a cheerful, healthy disrespect for everything everyone tells us is perfect. It's true Daisy Mae is sweet and virtuous, but she is also one of the most irritating girls in the world-like practically every nice girl that practically every one of us marries.

Most comic strips do not contain "universal truths" but Capp suggests that, even here, the meanings one gets from reading depend upon the attitude one brings to reading and the habit of occasionally looking below the surface.

If the teacher is to help the third-grader or tenth-grader dive below the surface, the question may be asked, "But what do we look for?" The response to the question is as varied as pieces of literature or as individuals themselves, but the general answer lies in two words, *symbols* and *values*. Most children recognize the flag as a symbol; they know that the lion is a symbol of courage or that Mercury was a swift messenger. In addition, they can be helped to see symbols in the incident involving Johnny Appleseed, the story of the farm boy who learned about responsibility, the poem about the islands, and most of the other imaginative literature they read and share. Johnny Appleseed himself is a symbol of the opening of the West to agriculture. Islands may be symbols of security or of withdrawal. So in every book, story or poem children with some help can discover meanings and symbols.

So with values. In literature children and adolescents can find many of man's most important social-ethical ideas. Our values are the things we live by. One man's values may be in Cadillacs or a full stomach, another in building beautiful bridges or in service to mankind. Values are usually described in the lovely words of our language such as truth, justice, loyalty and faith. These are puzzling and difficult ideas for adults and even more for children, and yet they are the foundations of our society. A child's or adolescent's grasp of such concepts is slow agrowing. Only a wide variety of experience can give some understanding of tolerance or perseverance or sacrifice, but sometimes the process of getting to understand such ideas can be quickened through literature.

Such talk of values may make reading and the teaching of reading seem, to some, a difficult and grim affair. It is difficult, but it need not be grim. The teacher has neither the time, the energy, nor the background to ferret out all values in a piece of literature. Some stories *are* to be read quickly and forgotten. Teacher and children alike must relax over their reading and have fun with much of it. From the adult point of view, the point is made nicely in a recent issue of the *Columbia University Forum* in an article by Norman Podhoretz, entitled, "Why I Can't Get Through *The Charterhouse of Parma.*" His point is that even a great novel is not for all of us. It has to be *relevant,* to talk somehow about life as one is living it from day to day. Just being a classic is not enough of a true cause for reading by an adult or a child.

Similarly, we must always remember that children read a great deal of "trash." What is worthless to the serious adult may still have some function in the child's life. Not all reading is a search for ultimate values. Cornelia Otis Skinner makes the point nicely in her book *Family Circle.* She says:

> I wish I could state that my reading matter was the sort which gave marked indications of instinctively esoteric choice, for I cherish a grudge filled with envy against those biographers who claim that their nursery shelves groaned (the verb is apposite) with lovingly thumbed-up volumes of Henty, Scott, Fenimore Cooper, and Maria Edgeworth. My taste in literature was a good deal like my taste in art, which ran riotously true to Harrison Fisher.
>
> The furthest I could go in the classics was Howard Pyle's *Knights of the Round Table,* and then only because I could ruin the pages by hand-coloring the black-and-white illustrations. *Sara Crewe, or What Happened at Miss Minchin's* had its moments, but my real delight was that 'honeychile' of the Old South, *The Little Colonel.* Less genteel, but more absorbing than the *Little Colonel* books was a series known as *The Automobile Girls,* thrilling tales of four stalwart young things who, complete with goggles and linen dusters, toured the country in an open Chalmers, encountering every possible sort of adventure. These I read and re-read, and I regarded *The Automobile Girls in the Berkshires* with the same reverence I now hold for *War and Peace.* Then a schoolmate started lending me books from her aunt's library and, as Chapman's *Homer* burst upon Keats, Elsie Dinsmore swam into my ken. The *Elsie* books, to be sure, belonged to an earlier and more heavenly minded

generation, and I don't know what their charm could have been, dealing as they did with a religious fanatic of a child, who spent her days praying, hymn-singing, and reproving her less spiritual contemporaries with lengthy quotations of Scripture. The author of this morbid series must have known how to cast a spell, for Elsie had a way of carrying piety to extremes as absorbing as those to which Dick Tracy today carries adventures. Her life of sanctimony I found most beautiful. Other children wanted to be like Joan of Arc or Queen Guinevere, or even like Captain Kidd. I wanted to be just like Elsie Dinsmore. For a brief but intense period, I got religion.

But despite these examples of the fact that people will always want to read some trash, the teacher of reading and literature must accept responsibility for inculcating essential values, not in the sense of imposition, but in terms of discovery and thoughtful appraisal. The teacher in this case may be supplementing the efforts of home and church but cannot assume that the values are being developed elsewhere. The truth is that life offers the ten-year-old or the fifteen-year-old a bewildering variety of values. One neighbor may be relieving the suffering in the community but another may be chiefly interested in the "fast buck." And yet both are "neighbors." It is hard for children to develop what the psychologist calls a "scale of values." In the analogy of William Temple, the world is like a shop window in which someone, during the night, has mixed up all the price labels. In the morning, what shall we do? The high school senior may be looking forward to becoming what White calls "the organization man" but he is also to be a husband, a father, a citizen—in other words, a person. In such complexity the child or youth needs guides. Television, the pulps and the movies are not ordinarily concerned with the higher values. In good books, stories and poems the child may read of courage or kindness or co-operation and perhaps grasp something of the importance of these ideas. Reading about such things at one's leisure, or in a small group where unhurried discussion follows, is our best hope that such values will become part of the lives of boys and girls.

In one of the apocryphal books associated with the Old Testament the prophet Esdras is given the splendid assurance:

I shall light a candle of understanding in thine heart, which shall not be put out."

Perhaps the same promise can be made to children when teachers seek to help them find values in what they read.

4. Developing Life Values Through Reading*

MAY HILL ARBUTHNOT

WHEN Longfellow uttered his portentous warning, "Life is real! Life is earnest!" he neglected to add that life can also be a lot of fun and more full of intriguing people and interesting things to do and see than one lifetime can possibly encompass. The problem is to make the most of life and, as adults, we do have to admit that growing up is also a chancey process. What forces, for instance, made you what you are? And when and where did you begin to grow into the You that is sitting here today? As a group of teachers we may not be in the higher echelon of world shakers, but on the whole we are a fairly competent lot of people. What image of ourselves grown to maturity made us so and prevented us from going in the direction of the unhappy law-breakers of one kind or another?

As teachers we would be the first to admit that the child's home and the people he is associated with are of paramount importance in forming his ideals of what he himself wants to be. But for the most part these influences are beyond our control. Today we are also concerned about the influence of mass media on the child's developing image of himself. And again his use of these media, outside of school, we can do little about except to know their scope and character. Certainly all forms of mass media—newspapers, pictorial magazines, moving pictures, radio and television-are very much with today's child. Along with their fine documentaries and other substantial offerings, today's child is bombarded daily with closeups of brutality, banality, scandal, and violence. Over the din of the Beatles with their screaming hordes, Western heroes forever fighting and movie Queens forever misbehaving, what chance to make a deep impression, for instance, has the image of Herbert Hoover's quiet dedicated life? The hopeful element in this mass presentation of savage and silly examples of maturity is their evanescence. Pictures and words come and go with great rapidity and are immediately replaced by something equally brief and easily forgotten. But are they forgotten? We know so little about the image of himself

*From *Elementary English*, **43**,1 (January, 1966), 10-16, Reprinted by permission of the National Council of Teachers of English and May Hill Arbuthnot.

32

that is gradually forming in that secret, inner world of the child's mind and spirit. But one thing we do know. If we can induct children into a genuine enjoyment of books, we can guide them to stories in which they will discover pictures of noble maturity and of children growing and changing into more competent and more lovable human beings at every stage of development.

Reading an absorbing story is a continual process of identification. The child sees himself as the smart, third Little Pig or as Tom Sawyer or Caddie Woodlawn or whoever his current hero may be. Then, because even fluent, rapid reading is a slower, steadier process than the interrupted piecemeal presentation of television with its station identifications and endless commercials, the hero image in a book has a chance to make a deeper, more lasting impression. Books are a bright hope if we can find the right book for a child at the right time.

FOR THE YOUNGEST—REASSURANCE AND ACHIEVEMENT

The youngest children in our schools, the prereaders and beginners in reading, just because they are small and inexperienced, are uncertain, insecure and generally find themselves in the wrong. Someone is always saying, "Don't do that," or "No, you aren't old enough for that." So, of course, these young pilgrims need lots of reassurance about their place in the world, that they are loved, needed and capable of doing things on their own. Notice how their first picture stories stress both loving reassurance, and also achievement. For example, these qualities account, in part, for the popularity of *The Happy Lion* series by Louise Fatio with pictures by Roger Duvoism. The Lion, like small children, is cribbed, confined, and misunderstood. But he has ideas of his own, whether it is going for a walk in the town or getting himself a beautiful lioness, he carries out his plans gently but firmly. And children, after feeling sorry for him, chuckle over his achievements and say, "read it again." Then they pore over those inimitable pictures which are completely one with the text and they triumph again with the Happy Lion.

This autumn has brought one of the most beautiful and satisfying picture stories for the prereaders that we have had. It is called, *Whistle for Willie*, written and illustrated by Ezra Jack Keats who did the Caldecott Medal book *Snowy Day*. This new one is even more beautiful, in luscious pinks against the whole spectrum of colors, and with the same little colored boy in a pink and white shirt trying desperately to whistle for his dog, Willie. Failing, he crawls into a big carton to practice. Then, feeling more grown-up by the addition of his father's hat, he plays father, and all sorts of other things, but always working for a whistle. Suddenly, there is Willie his dog, and suddenly Peter whistles! Willie stops dead in his tracks and then comes flying. Here is a climax and from that point on, sheer triumph! But there is more to this slight story than this briefing indicates. There is the enviable pattern of big boys whose dogs come when they whistle and a little boy struggling to be equally competent. There is an understanding mother, a proud father, love and achievement happily combined to make a small masterpiece.

If you look back over the picture stories that have enjoyed lasting popularity with children, you discover how these two notes—reassuring love and independent achievement—recur over and over again from *Peter Rabbit, Little Black Sambo,* and *Millions of Cats,* through the *Little Tim* and *Madeline* series to last year's splendid and more mature story of *Hans and Peter* by Heidrum Petrides. All of Robert McCloskey's beautiful picture stories stress reassurance. When children identify their own helplessness with the Ducklings or with Sal picking blueberries or losing a tooth or with the family in *Time of Wonder,* they come away from these books feeling that they too, when their time of trial comes, can weather the storm. They are stronger, more confident children for such books. And at an older level, the importance of Alice Dalgliesh's *The Bears of Hemlock Mountain* lies in the fact that Jonathan was genuinely afraid. Nevertheless, he went ahead with his scary undertaking and discovered in himself unexpected resources. A fine achievement tale for the primary.

Certainly, the carefully selected folk tales we use with young children—the fours and fives, sevens and eights— present a lively gallery of up-and-doing heroes and heroines, as, for example, the dauntless Bremen Town Musicians, the Three Pigs, Three Billy Goats, Boots, Beauty, Snow White and their like. These and the more complex tales for the older children are saying to the child, "If you show kindness as well as courage, if you beware of silly credulity and use your head as well as your heart, you too can accomplish wonders." These old stories are worthwhile if only to build in children the firm conviction that evil need not be endured; that giants, ogres and all the other big bullies in the world can be laid low, and meanness, greed and cruelty exterminated. Our generation may not have finished the job but some progress has been made and maybe the next generation will do better. Anyway, these old tales are good medicine for children to grow on, so don't miss the beautiful new editions of single tales illustrated by such artists as Marcia Brown, Adrienne Adams, Eric Blegvad, and many others. These entrancing editions are bound to revive the popularity of these old tales, and it is about time.

MIDDLE YEARS—7-10, CURIOSITY AND ZEST FOR LIVING

Love and achievement continue to motivate stories for all ages, but by the middle school years children seven, eight, and nine should be developing a lively curiosity about an ever expanding world and should have such a gay, coltish zest for living that they seek fun, adventure, and sometimes pure nonsense. Apathy and boredom in these transition years are unthinkable, and yet teachers say there are plenty of both, especially among deprived children in our big cities.

Perhaps the bite of frustration and failure has set in. In these years, 7 to 10, the child has taken a giant step. He has learned to read for himself, but alas, not fluently! There's the rub. Learning to read is all very exciting to begin with, but when difficulties pile up, discouragement mounts. These are the years when teachers must try consciously to fill the gap between what the slow learning child can read for himself and what he would like to read. There is often a lag of from one to three years between reading skill and the ability to understand and enjoy. Teachers must fill that gap with plenty of practice in easy-to-read books and by reading aloud to their children books that delight them but are well beyond their reading ability.

There are many lists of easy-to-read books but frequently the content is too immature for the children who need them. Take Else Minarek's *Little Bear* books. They are charming for the fives and sixes, but babyish at seven and eight. Here the books of Clyde Bulla help mightily. He has an easy but never commonplace style and a stepped-up content which the sevens and even the elevens respect and enjoy. He always tells a lively adventure story and his books fit into many subject matter areas as the titles indicate—*Squanto, Friend of the White Men, Down the Mississippi, The Sword in the Tree,* and others. Alice Dalgliesh's *The Courage of Sarah Noble* will balance these boys' stories and give even the mildest little girls a sense of achievement. While we are on historical fiction, these may be good years to read aloud one of William Steele's stories of pioneer boys to introduce children to these books—*Tomahawks and Trouble, Winter Danger,* or any of them. Their importance lies in the fact that besides being exciting adventure stories, these ignorant, wrong-headed boy heroes grow and change in the course of a story, forged into something stronger and better by trials of endurance that call out all their stamina. Such books build up children's self-respect. They are antidotes for discouragement, apathy, and giving up the struggle. It is far too easy for children to accept failure and to downgrade themselves accordingly. Strong stories are energizing. The hero image gives them a clear idea of a competent maturity and the satisfaction of putting up a good fight.

Children also need a sense of fun along the way. The more school or home or personality difficulties increase, the more a child needs the release of laughter or even pure nonsense. Laughter can break tensions and restore balance. Nonsense verse or what children call "funny stories" help. If they can read for themselves those two indestructibles—*Mr. Popper's Penguins* or *Mary Poppins*—they'll chuckle and recover from the doldrums. If they can't, then take time to read one of them aloud. Of if you prefer, choose Oliver Butterworth's *Enormous Egg,* about the hen that hatched out not an Ugly Duckling, but no less than a mammoth dinosaur, amiable but outsize for domesticity. For a group of children to laugh together is to break down hostilities, tensions, and unhappiness. It is well worth the time. And E. B. White's matchless *Charlotte's Web,* which *is* beyond their reading skill but not their enjoyment level, will give them not only the therapy of laughter but the therapy of tears. Children need both. How else can they learn compassion?

These examples of the child's "funny stories" have all been in the field of fantasy, but there is also humorous realism to reassure routine-weary youngster. If they cannot read Beverly Cleary's *Henry Huggins,* read them the first book and they'll tackle the next one as soon as possible. The hilarious Huggins' adventures with Ribsey, the dog, and the neighborhood children lead naturally to Keith Robertson's *Henry Reed, Inc.,* one of the funniest books available. Henry, with his complete lack of humor, decides to go in for research. He puts up a sign, "Henry Reed, Inc. Research," to which his pushy girl neighbor adds, "Pure and Applied." He explains that only girls keep diaries "about their dates and different boy friends. But pirates and explorers keep journals." So, in his journal he records their summer adventures in research and these should leave any child a little better able to laugh at himself when he gets into absurd messes of his own making. The second book, *Henry Reed's Journey,* is as amusing as the first. Both are enhanced by some of Robert McCloskey's funniest drawings.

In these years the child's curiosity is boundless, or should be, and so are the informational books written to answer his questions and promote new ones. In any field of science, from dinosaurs to insects, and from stones to stars, there are excellent books at almost any reading level you desire. The same is true in the field of the social studies. But factual books are not the province of this paper which is concerned with literature for children. Fiction may also meet his curiosities about people, places, and ways of living. So his fiction goes back in time to include historical events of long ago and out in space to embrace the diverse regions and peoples of our United States and of other lands. Stories about Amish, Indians, Negroes, Jewish families, ranchers, farmers, fishermen, migrant workers, city folk, all give a colorful and sympathetic introduction to diverse peoples and customs in this vast country of ours. Young readers get delightful glimpses of life in other countries in such old favorites as Chinese *Little Pear* by Eleanor Lattimore, or Hungarian *The Good Master* by Kate Seredy, or Natalie Carlson's tender and humorous story of Paris *The Family Under the Bridge,* or Harry Behn's Mexican *The Two Uncles of Pablo.* From all these areas of reading—historical, regional, foreign lands—children get the reiterated truth that peoples of every age or place or country have similar difficulties, suffer deprivations and failures, and are more alike than different in their struggles to achieve a place in the sun.

For these middle years you may have noticed a dearth of recent titles, but there is nevertheless rich treasure in the books available if you are not too dedicated to recency. And why should you be? Just remember, it is the children who are forever recent, the books don't have to be, and a strong book twenty years old is worth a dozen bits of mediocrity just off the press.

PREADOLESCENTS—10 TO 12 OR 14, COMPASSION AND COURAGE

In the last years of elementary school reading there is such a wide variation in reading abilities and social maturity that placing books by age levels is complete nonsense. A thirteen-year-old who thoroughly enjoyed *The Agony and the Ecstasy* and could discuss it eagerly, play by play, is not going to be satisfied with *Caddie Woodlawn,* Nor will a twelve-year-old who has a struggle to get through *Henry Huggins.* give more than a passing glance at *Rifles for Watie.* Adults who guide children's reading in the years from ten to twelve or fourteen are pretty much on their own and can let those brashly graded reading lists fall where they may.

Oddly enough there is one area of reading where children and adults frequently meet on common ground and that is the well-written story about animals. By well written we mean authentic, true to the animal species, and neither humanized nor sentimentalized. For instance, *The Incredible Journey* by Sheila Burnford, which meets all these standards, was intended for adults, but the children took it over. The same thing happened to Marjorie Rawlings' *The Yearling* and to that poignant little masterpiece by the late James Street, *Good-Bye, My Lady.* And, of course, the values of such books and those by Marguerite Henry, Jim Kjelgaard, Joseph Lippincott, the Georges and others, are manifold. Of first importance, however, is the fact that they stir the readers' compassion for animals. Albert Schweitzer calls this "reverence for life, all life worthy of development." Such reverence is made up of sensitivity to the needs and sufferings of others, compassion and a strong identification that we call empathy. These are all aspects of the same emotion, love. Going out to others selflessly is the most civilizing force in life. Never have we needed it more.

Teachers who have worked in the deprived areas of big cities where children have never been responsible for farm animals or pets, know all too well the horrible acts of sadism practiced by unthinking children against small animals, especially defenseless cats. Only this autumn there have been two such terrible examples of 'cat-torture that they have made the front pages of the papers. These could not have happened had those children ever cherished a pet cat or a rabbit or a dog of their own. And next to owning or growing up with animals are the vicarious experiences of reading about them. The process of identification that goes on when a child reads about *Smoky* or *Lassie* or *King of the Wind* means that he suffers with and for the animal hero. He also senses nobility and sacrifice of the great gorilla in Lucy Boston's *Stranger at Green Knowe* or the patient endurance of mistreated Smoky or the curious loyalty and first aid the cat gave her two dog companions in *The Incredible Journey.* Perhaps compassion and reverence for life are ambitious terms for the child's emotional response to these books, but certainly they evoke tenderness and the desire to cherish and protect. These are the qualities that make the well-written animal story of great importance to young readers of every age and the reason why a story about animal torture in the bull ring, ballet style, seems regrettable.

The last years between childhood and the budding maturity of youth are hard on children. These preadolescents need almost as much encouragement as the youngest. They try their wings and fall flat on their faces. Failure is bitter and it takes courage to get up and try again. They are acutely aware of their own imperfections—too fat or too skinny or not sufficiently sought after. They are even more critical of the frightful imperfections of their parents. In no book has this ever been more accurately reflected than in those opening paragraphs of Emily Neville's *It's Like This, Cat.* Here they are:

> My father is always talking about how a dog can be very educational for a boy. This is one reason I got a cat.
>
> My father talks a lot anyway. Maybe being a lawyer he gets in the habit. Also, he's a small guy with very little gray curly hair, so maybe he thinks he's got to roar a lot to make up for not being a big hairy tough guy. Mom is thin and quiet, and when anything upsets her, she gets asthma. In the apartment—we live right in the middle of New York City—we don't have any heavy drapes or rugs, and mom never fries any food because the doctors figure dust and smoke make her asthma worse. I don't think it's dust; I think it's Pop's roaring.
>
> The big hassle that led me to getting Cat came when I earned some extra money baby-sitting for a little boy around the corner on Gramercy Park. I spent the money on a Belafonte record about a father telling his son about the birds and the bees. I think it's funny. Pop blows his stack.

By the way, whoever said this book lacked style? It may not have the lyric style of *Wind in the Willows,* but a family conflict is not a lyric. Styles do and should differ, and this is valid for the subject it describes. Incidentally, notice how in these brief paragraphs, the reader gets the theme, problem, and conflict of the entire book, as well as the brash, caustic judgments of youth. The fact that in the course of the story Dave comes to reevaluate his parents and even to see a new image of his own maturity through his father's eyes, makes this a choice book and one of our best big-city stories of a boy growing up.

There are different kinds of courage and it takes a special kind to accept physical handicaps or humiliating failures. That was the special value of the Newbery Medal book by Marguerite De Angeli, *The Door in the Wall.* Young, active, ambitious Robin has to accept the cruel fact of his semi-paralyzed limbs. But thanks to Brother Luke's ministrations and his philosophy—"Always remember . . . thou hast only to follow a wall far enough and there will be a door in it. . . ." Robin learned to use his hands again and to get around agilely on crutches. The conclusion is not a cure, but a heart-warming triumph for Robin that should give courage to all permanently handicapped children. The thing is to find a door in every wall.

To come to grips with failure is part and parcel of growing up. Most children's stories grant the hero success in the end. That happened to David in that remarkable book of 1963—*The Loner* by Ester Weir. This is a great book. But there is a recent book that is memorable because in *Skinny* by Robert Burch, the boy's failure to achieve his heart's desire is unalterable. Skinny is an illiterate, eleven-year-old orphan. Miss Bessie has taken him in temporarily to help her in her small town hotel. The work and Miss Bessie suit Skinny fine, and he dreams of adoption. Everyone likes Skinny but at the end of a happy summer the dreaded orphanage is inevitable. The board has refused Miss Bessie's request to adopt Skinny because she is unmarried. Everyone keeps saying, "The orphanage is only forty miles away." To which Skinny replies sadly, "Forty miles is a far piece." And so it is, a far piece from love and a home. But at least he can return to Miss Bessie for vacations and at long last he is going to learn to read and write. It is a sad ending but somehow the right one, for the reader knows that Skinny will make out wherever he lands. He'll put his grief behind him and do with a flourish whatever there is to do.

In Joseph Ullman's older book *Banner in the Sky,* Rudi also saw his bright hope destroyed. This is a new step for children in their reading and in facing life. Things do not always come out happily in the end. Hopes are blasted, struggles are defeated, but the young reader must catch from his reading the image of the hero who picks himself up after defeat to make a new start. That is what reading in these last years of childhood must reiterate, and that is what all of Rosemary Sutcliff's magnificent historical novels are saying over and over. They were discussed last year in detail, but get your good readers into these books as soon as they can handle them.

Still another kind of courage, often thankless, is the patient's plodding courage to endure. The recent *Across Five Aprils* by Irene Hunt tells such a story. It is another Civil War book, usual in subject but unusual in treatment. Five years of war are seen through the eyes of Jethro, a farm boy, nine years old when war begins and fourteen when it ends. With his brothers gone off to fight, his father paralyzed, even his beloved school master gone too, all the back breaking toil of maintaining the farm falls on young Jethro. The unusual quality of this book lies in the vivid portrayal of every person in the story, even minor characters. It is a beautifully written chronicle of the enduring courage of one unsung hero, a boy, who did what had to be done.

Another 1964 story of courage at a more mature level is Ann Petry's relentless account of the Salem witch-hunting hysteria, *Tituba of Salem Village.* Tituba was a slave, and from her arrival in Salem, her dark skin and unusual skills made her suspect. There is a grim foreboding and suspense about this story of mounting evil that grips the reader from the first page to the last. Yet with others hanged or burned, Tituba, honest, brave, and patient, miraculously survived. Only mature readers can take this bitter record of white civilization gone wrong. But it has a message for today, not underlined in the book, but there nevertheless. This is probably the most powerful book of the season in the juvenile field, not to be missed by good readers.

CONCLUSION

In suggesting some of the needs of children at different ages that books can help to satisfy, the list began with reassuring love and independent achievement. It ends with much the same—compassionate love and the kind of courage that is another phase of achievement. These qualities, by the way, motivate fiction for all ages and help to tie children's books into the whole stream of literature. But in children's books, the quality of love must grow and change as the child matures, until he can begin to see himself vicariously through his book heroes as loved and bestowing love, as dealing compassionately with others and, above all, as picking himself up after failures or shattered hopes or grievous mistakes to try again. These are some of the things strong books can do for children besides giving them keen enjoyment. Books can show them patterns of compassionate love and courageous achievement of many kinds.

5. What Have We Accomplished In Reading?*

NILA BANTON SMITH

THIS last half-century stands out as a truly golden period in the progress of reading instruction. More innovations have been effected in reading during the last fifty years than during the entire three hundred years antedating this period of American history. I am sure that progress has been equally notable in the other phases of the language arts constellation. It is most appropriate that accomplishments in all of the language arts areas be reviewed upon this momentous occasion —the Golden Anniversary of The National Council of Teachers of English!

Progress in reading instruction has been marked by a succession of turning points. For a period of years reading methods and materials all over the country are quite similar—so similar, in fact, that an unbiased examiner might arrive at the conclusion that all had been turned out of the same mold, with just a slightly different crimp here and there in the contour of the pan. Then, rather suddenly, a new plan becomes popular, and we teach reading in this manner until another turning point arrives. Thus, epoch after epoch of reading instruction passes [26].[1]

Fortunately printed records are available to which we can turn in delineating these epochs and ascertaining their characteristics. In attempting to obtain information to bring to you about reading epochs during our recent half century the following source materials, published between 1910 and 1960, were explored: prominent educational magazines that usually contain reading articles, yearbooks of learned societies, summaries of published investigations in reading, lists of unpublished master's and doctoral researches completed or under way. More than 300 pieces of materials were surveyed for the purpose of picking up the sequence of events and trends which marked the pilgrimage of reading in its upward march from 1910 to the present time. This information will be presented to you by decades.

*From *Elementary English*, **28**,3 (March, 1961), 141-150. Reprinted by permission of the National Council of Teachers of English and Nila Banton Smith.

[1] Numbers in brackets refer to references at the end of the articles.

ACCOMPLISHMENTS FROM 1910 TO 1920

The dramatic decade beginning with 1910 ushered in the first truly great break-through in reading progress. This was the birth of the scientific movement in education. In 1909 Thorndike made the initial presentation of his handwriting scale before a meeting of the American Association for the Advancement of Science, and in 1910 it was published [29]. Generally speaking, the publication of the Thorndike scale has been recognized as the beginning of the contemporary movement for measuring educational products scientifically. In the immediately ensuing years scales and tests appeared rapidly: Courtis arithmetic tests, Hilligas' Composition Scale, Buckingham Spelling Scale—and then a reading test—The Gray Standardized Oral Reading Paragraphs[13]. This test was published in 1915. Other reading tests followed shortly.

As a result of the strong new surge of interest in placing education on a scientific basis together with its correlative motives for developing instruments of measurement, we would naturally expect that the scientific study of reading problems would take a vigorous spurt. And this it did.

Through all the years up to 1910 only 34 studies had been reported in reading. During the 1910-20 decade, 200 accounts appeared, about six times as many as had been reported during the entire history of reading preceding this time. These studies had to do mostly with tests and school surveys as would be expected.

As for method: the most revolutionary thing happened that had happened since clergy began to teach reading in churches, and dames began to teach reading in kitchens. "For hundreds of years oral reading had maintained a supreme and undisputed claim on teaching methods" [25]. During this decade, however, the concept of teaching *silent* reading burst into our slumbering complacency like a bombshell. It came suddenly and in the midst of a period in which school people were serenely content in the use of sentence-story methods applied to the oral reading of selections in literary readers. For the most part they continued to use these practices to the end of the decade but the startling new idea was at least launched. Discussions of the advantages of silent reading appeared for the first time in the Sixteenth [16] and in the Eighteenth [17] Yearbooks of the National Society for the Study of Education. Speakers at educational conventions began to talk about it, magazine articles began to discuss it. The idea had been born.

To sum up: developing the concept of applying scientific techniques to the study of reading, devising standardized instruments to measure reading achievement, increasing the number of studies tremendously, initiating the silent reading idea. These seem to have been the major accomplishments from 1910 to 1920.

ACCOMPLISHMENTS FROM 1920 TO 1930

The period extending from 1920 to 1930 is perhaps the most golden decade in this golden era of progress in so far as fundamental changes in reading practices are concerned. These changes were largely due to the scientific movement which had shaped up during the preceding period and which now was opening up fresh wells of information with improved and extended applications.

The new studies conducted during this decade carried with them three distinct earmarks of progress: the number increased tremendously; they covered a wider scope of problems; many of them were conducted in classrooms by teachers and other school personnel, rather than being confined to the laboratory.

As to the number of investigations: Gray's summaries reveal that 763 were reported as compared with 200 during the preceding decade. This unprecedented increase reflected the zeal and enthusiasm with which school people were searching for more information about the important subject of reading.

The studies of this period probed a variety of problems, but there were three problem areas which were most highly significant. They were significant because they resulted in sweeping changes in practice. These three areas were: (1) silent reading, (2) individual differences, and (3) remedial reading.

The first half of this decade might well be called "The Age of Silent Reading." "These years were marked with an exaggerated, often exclusive emphasis on silent reading as opposed to the traditional oral reading techniques" [25]. As previously mentioned, the concept of teaching silent reading was initiated during the latter part of the preceding period, but it didn't really take hold as a nation-wide classroom practice until during the years of 1920 to 1925. This sudden and widespread reversal in practice was largely due to two influences: the development of tests which revealed that silent reading was superior to oral reading in speed and comprehension; and the publication of The Yearbooks of the National Society for the Study of Education. As already indicated, one article each appeared in the Sixteenth [16] and the Eighteenth [17] Yearbooks. The climax, however, came with the publication of the Twentieth Yearbook, Part II [19] of which was devoted entirely to the report of the "Society's Committee on Silent Reading." Following the appearance of this Yearbook, "textbook writers began to produce readers based on silent reading procedures; other authors prepared professional books on silent reading; teachers busied themselves in preparing exercises that would check comprehension of silent reading by means of drawings, true-false statements or completion sentences and so forth. The whole country for a time seemed to be obsessed with the idea of teaching silent reading" [25].

This extreme emphasis, however, was soon balanced with other factors. By

1925 the novelty of the new idea had worn off, somewhat; investigations revealed some unique uses of oral reading, school people discovered that there still were some special needs for oral reading in the school program. Perhaps, the culminating influence came with the publication of the Twenty-Fourth Yearbook, Part I [20] which appeared in 1925. This Yearbook advocated a broader program of reading instruction which among other things recognized both oral and silent reading. New courses of study, professional books and readers immediately reflected the broadened objectives of this Yearbook and methods during the years 1925-1930 were shaped largely by its contents. So during the first two decades of the last fifty years we progressed from extreme oral reading to extreme silent reading to a broader program which recognized both. In my opinion, this was an indication of real accomplishment.

As for individual differences: with the administration of the newly developed tests, a very great fundamental truth became apparent with a violent impact—the realization that there were wide individual differences in the reading achievement of children, in the same grade and in the same classroom. This discovery spurred school people to experiment with a variety of adjustments in classroom organization and instruction, designed to cope with this newly revealed variation in the learning rate of children.

There were reports of adjustments made in classrooms which maintained the regular organization such as ability grouping, flexible promotions, and differentiated assignments. But the pulsating new idea was that of breaking up class organization entirely to permit of individual progression. This plan of organization received as much attention at this time as it is receiving at the present moment. Speeches, articles, and Yearbooks dealt with the subject. San Francisco; Los Angeles; Detroit; Winnetka; Madison, Wisconsin; and other school systems reported [21] results they had obtained by individual instruction. The states of Connecticut and Illinois reported [21] experiments in individualizing instruction in rural schools.

The various plans, on the whole, were patterned after the Winnetka or the Dalton ideas, in both of which individual progression in reading and other subjects was made possible by means of assignments in which the child worked through subject material that increased in small increments of difficulty. The important point to note is that attention to individual differences in reading received its first great impetus during this decade of remarkable progress.

The concept of *remedial* reading was launched from its small island of study during this period and sent out over unexplored seas in quest of answers to disability problems. The movement was spurred on by the use of standardized tests. These tests revealed that thousands of boys and girls were failing each year to make normal progress in reading. Published reports of work in the reading disability field indicate that the chief interest at this time was in diagnosing individual cases. As for method, it was during this period that Fernald evolved her kinesthetic method, and that Orton expounded his theory on mixed dominance and the treatment that accompanied it. Remedial reading did get under way during this period.

In beginning reading there also were innovations. Experience charts first came into use. The Nineteenth Yearbook [18], published in 1920, dealt with reading materials. In it examples were given of charts based on children's experiences, and the practice of introducing children to beginning reading through the use of such material was advocated. This practice was not widely accepted until much later, but progress had been made in evolving the idea.

And last but not least, mention must be made of another mark of progress which clearly stamped itself into the later annals of this decade. The reading readiness concept began to take shape at this time.

In 1926 the International Kindergarten Union in cooperation with the United States Bureau of Education conducted an investigation on "Pupils' Readiness for Reading Instruction upon Entrance to First Grade." The first articles on this subject were published in Childhood Education in January, 1927. Two of these articles used the term "reading readiness." In so far as I am aware, this was the first time that this phrase crept into our reading vocabulary [27]. In Gray's summaries published in 1928, he reported for the first time three studies on reading readiness. A few master's theses and a trickling of articles on this subject also appeared before the close of the decade. The new concept, however, was still in the formative stage, and little was done about it in a practical way until the following period, but the movement was on its way.

Much more could be said about the accomplishments made during this unprecedented period. I should like to dwell longer on the accumulation of information gathered about reading and the auspicious innovations in classroom practice that were inaugurated at this time, but I must pass on to other conquests and other days.

ACCOMPLISHMENTS FROM 1930 TO 1940

This period may be characterized largely as one of extension and application rather than one of revelation and initiation.

Investigations continued at an accelerated pace. In round figures about 1200 studies were reported between 1930 and 1940. Not only were these studies greater in number, but they were superior in isolation of problems, in designs, and in controls.

Some of the embryo ideas that had sprouted in the preceding decade came into full bloom and fruited profusely at this time. For example: the reading readiness interest reached its zenith in this period [27]. Published investigations on this topic increased steadily during each successive year of this decade [9], reaching their climax of frequency in 1940 when Gray reported 22 studies relating to this topic in one year. Since that time the number has decreased steadily.

Turning to unpublished research, this was the hey-day of aspiring masters and doctors in finding problems for research in the readiness area. The first doctoral dissertation on readiness was reported in 1927. From that time on, the number of master and doctoral studies increased, reaching its peak in the years 1937 to 1940. Fourteen such studies were completed in 1937, 15 in 1938, 14 in 1939, and 12 in 1940. Since that time only 2 or 3 academic studies on readiness have been reported each year.

A similar trend is seen in published articles on reading readiness. Periodicals abounded with discussions on readiness topics from 1930 to 1940. Articles on this subject rarely appear in present-day literature.

In the light of this evidence, it may be concluded that this was the period of most vigorous emphasis, both on investigations of reading readiness and applications of the readiness theory. The concept has been accepted now and we hear little about it at the present time.

Remedial reading, which had experienced a touch-and-go recognition during the preceding period, now became established and gained stature. Many significant studies were conducted in the remedial reading areas: causes of difficulties, diagnosis, and corrective procedures. Professional books devoted exclusively to remedial reading were first published. Some laboratory studies were still made but the majority of studies now were conducted in schools. Remedial reading, which had started in laboratories, now became a topic for practical experimentation in the public schools themselves.

A new trend that began to emerge was that of giving beginning attention to high school, college, and adult reading. Studies made at these levels, however, were mostly concerned with interest in, and uses of reading, rather than with reading achievement and teaching procedure.

Every decade reviewed so far has been characterized by one or two events of great distinction. In the 1910-1920 decade, it was the application of scientific measurement and investigation to reading, in the 1920–'30 era, it was the startling innovations of silent reading and of individual progression. What was the spectacular event in the nineteen-thirties?

The Activity Movement swept the country during these years, and the startling new idea in reading was to teach this skill as a part of the Activity Program. In such a program children worked freely and spontaneously and actively in following their own interests; and teachers were intrigued with the new "game" of trying to get all of their subject matter across through "Units of Work."

In so far as reading was concerned, pupils had access to a considerable number of books bearing largely on the topic of their "Unit of Work." This was the first big impetus for bringing a quantity of books into the classroom for reading. There was a profusion of charts and school-made booklets growing out of children's interests. Pupils read functionally from their co-operatively prepared materials and out of many books in doing research in connection with their Units. In a word, this was how reading proceeded in the Activity Program in the thirties.

We no longer hear of the Activity Program at this time nor of the teaching of reading in connection with this program. The Activity Movement, however, made a vigorous impact on the teaching of reading and other subjects at this time—an impact so strong that its influence still continues. The Activity Movement distracted the school public from its age-old concept of schools centered almost exclusively on subject-matter goals to schools in which consideration is given to the child, himself, his stage of development, his interests, his activities, his choices and his decisions.

In summary, we may say that progress in this decade was characterized by continuing investigations, greater in number, higher in quality than in the preceding decade; intensive application of the readiness concept; transfer of remedial activities from laboratory to classroom; beginning attention to reading at higher levels; and wide-spread interest in teaching reading as an integral part of the Activity Program.

ACCOMPLISHMENTS FROM 1940 TO 1950

An event resulting from progress in science overshadowed all other indications of progress during this period. The "birthday of the atomic age" is officially set as December 2, 1942, when Dr. Enrico Fermi turned on the first successful nuclear energy machine in Chicago. The first atomic bomb destroyed Hiroshima on August 6, 1945. On the face of things this terrifying discovery with its possibilities for good or for evil reduced to comparative insignificance our little scientific achievements in reading. Yet, could this achievement have been possible without reading? Can we cope adequately with its future destructive or beneficent effects, as the case may be, without more efficient reading skill and a wider reading citizenry? The atomic age and reading immediately become interactive.

But we didn't realize this at the time. We were too close to this earth-shaking event to sense its import for reading instruction. The war probably only had two *immediate* effects on reading. One of these was a diminution in the number of reading investigations. This was probably due to the fact that many of the psychologists and educators who conducted research in reading, or stimulated others to do so, were in the armed services.

The other major effect of the war was the shocking discovery that at this day and age thousands of young men in the military service could not read well enough to follow the simple printed instructions for camp life. Coupled with this discovery was the revelation that reading could be taught to these young men in army camps in an amazingly short time. Concurrently, several new investigations disclosed reading deficiencies in large numbers of high school and college students. These several influences combined to produce a spurt in attention to reading at these higher levels. Immediately following the war, a great deal of professional literature on reading emerged and among these publications several bulletins and one Yearbook appeared dealing with high school and college reading. Chief among these publications was a bulletin of the National Education Association titled *Reading Instruction in Secondary Schools* [15], and the Forty-Eighth Yearbook, Part II of the National Society for the Study of Reading, titled *Reading in High School and College* [24]. The actual teaching of reading at these levels had not progressed far at this time but the idea was vigorously expanding.

During this period, reading in the content subjects also became a matter of wide discussion and the subject of a few investigations. The studies at this time pointed to the general conclusion that while good readers can read well in all subject fields, special practice in reading in particular subject areas is helpful to average and poor readers.

In the forties, wide recognition was given to the interrelationships amongst the language arts. Studies, articles, speeches were concerned with the relationship of reading to spelling, handwriting, vocabulary, and composition. As a result we came to recognize that reading was not an isolated skill independent of other skills used in the interchange of ideas, but that it was just one aspect of the total language arts constellation mutually dependent upon and interactive with all other skills in the communication dimension.

A strong new concern also sprang up in regard to the effects of three of the newer media for mass communication: comics, movies and radio. Television did not come in for much attention until the next decade but during this period wide dissemination of entertainment through the first named agencies stirred up worry on the part of school people and parents. They feared that interest in listening to radio, looking at comics, viewing movies would reduce interest in reading and thus decrease the amount of reading done. Numerous popular articles bemoaned the situation and pointed out its dangers. Several studies were conducted directed toward the exploration of students' interests in this area and finding out how much time they devoted to the offerings of these types. Thus initial steps were taken in obtaining information to combat what was thought to be the first threat to reading.

Remedial diagnosis and treatment continued to claim a large segment of the spotlight. Mechanical instruments and devices which had been introduced during the preceding period increased in numbers and use. There were fewer studies reported on psychological factors such as dominance, handedness, eyedness, and reversals. An increasing number were devoted to personal factors as related to reading: personal interests and attitudes, personal status in social, emotional, and experiential maturity. This attention to other growth and development factors as related to reading was certainly one of the most notable advances made during this period.

To sum up: the chief points of progress during this decade were: increased attention to teaching reading at the higher levels; growing attention to reading in the content subjects; concerns about mass communications; attempts to find relationships between reading and handwriting, spelling, vocabulary and composition; and perhaps, most important of all, a growing consciousness of the profound truth that reading doesn't develop in a vacuum by itself, but that it is part and parcel of general child development and is affected by all other aspects of child growth.

ACCOMPLISHMENTS FROM 1950 TO 1960

A most exciting decade! For one thing, interest in reading instruction became almost universal during this period. There was a time when primary teachers were the only people interested in the teaching of reading. Now teachers of all subjects and at all levels want to know more about reading. Parents are asking questions, pursuing books and articles on reading. Students at high-school and college levels and adults beyond college are flocking to reading centers. Slick magazines and laymen are discussing reading freely. A great conflagration of interest has been ignited amongst teachers and students, and more especially amongst the lay public. And this is good.

During this period, however, for the first time in history, reading instruction in American schools underwent harsh and severe criticism by laymen. School people maintained that the criticisms were unfair and rose to the defense of their methods through articles, speeches, discussions, and investigations. Several comparative studies of "Then and Now" were made. These studies, on the whole, showed that we were teaching reading as well as or better than in preceding years.

Insofar as progress is concerned the criticism by laymen probably had three good effects; its caused school people to examine their present methods more carefully; it stimulated the interest of parents and other laymen in reading instruction; it offered motives and opportunities to school people to explain the research, psychology, and philosophy on which present methods are based. So in this situation, as is often the case in other situations, even criticism caused reading to move forward.

Perhaps as an off-shoot of interest and criticism, coupled with a growing awareness of the complexity of the reading process, there has been a spurt of activity in the re-instatement and increase of reading courses in the curriculums of teacher-training institutions. Concurrently with this interest in adding more courses, standards are being raised in regard to the qualifications of teachers of reading and of reading specialists. This movement toward better-trained teachers in reading is a big step forward.

As for the number of investigations: studies during this period reached incredible proportions. Gray reported over 1,000 studies in his 1960 summary, but in his introduction he said for the first time in his thirty-five years of annual summarizing, "The number of studies are increasing so rapidly that it is no longer possible to report all of them in this annual summary. Those referred to this year represent either a new or distinctive approach to a problem or suggest significant issues in need of further study." Not only was this increase apparent in the published reports of reading investigations, but it also was reflected in the reports of dissertations completed or in progress which soared to new numerical heights, the number reported averaging about 90 per year as compared with about 50 in the preceding decade.

Advance is shown in the subjects of investigation. Reading in the content fields, adult reading deficiencies, and television as related to reading came in for strong additional attention. The most gratifying trend revealed, however, is that we are at present delving more deeply into the reading process and more broadly intc the factors that affect it. The former popular topic of phonics now seems to have been replaced with studies of perception. Comprehension is no longer treated as a lump sum; the emphasis at present is upon the higher thinking processes of interpretation and critical reading. The old readiness studies are replaced with investigations of prediction and expectancy. Remedial reading is not so much concerned now with studies of gadgets and specific teaching remedies as it is with organismic and personality factors. Parental personality, attitudes, and interactions with the child as related to reading entered the research scene for the first time during this period, and many reading investigations concerned with parents and their children are now being reported. Studies are made in regard to the climate of the classroom and its effect on reading. This mere glimpse at some of the subjects of the most recent studies is indicative of a trend toward probing to greater depths and in wider breadths than was evident in most of the studies preceding this period.

Special mention should be made of a clearly discernible advance in regard to reading and the other language arts. In the preceding decade we became strongly concerned about the relationships of reading to the subjects of spelling, handwriting, vocabulary, and composition. During this decade we have moved on to a concern about aspects of the language arts which perhaps are less tangible than the subject matter areas but more inclusive in their application to the entire block of communication skills. Listening studies have increased by leaps and bounds. Some of the most recent dissertation topics have to do with semantic studies of reading content, multiple meanings, figures of speech in reading, and the linguistic approach to reading. Is it not an accomplishment to have moved on from subject interrelationships to relationships dealing with listening and the various aspects of linguistics?

The innovation in reading method which has loomed large on the horizon of late is the plan known as *individualized instruction.* The amount of attention given to this plan in this decade is comparable to that given to individual instruction in the nineteen-twenties. It probably is the most popular topic of discussion at present in educational magazines and often at teacher gatherings.

This individualized plan of the present is different from individual instruction which was popular in the twenties. The earlier plan was subject-matter oriented. Each child was given subject matter assignments divided into small increments of difficulty and he was permitted to progress as fast as he, personally, could complete each successive increment. The present plan is child-psychology oriented utilizing particularly Dr. Willard Olsen's theory of *seeking, self-selection,* and *pacing* in that the child seeks that which stimulates him, selects the book he desires to read, and proceeds at his own rate.

This plan has been used too recently for research reports to have crept into published summaries of investigations. Most of the research on this topic at present falls into the unpublished category of theses, dissertations, or mimeographed reports of experiments carried on in certain school systems. An examination of the most recent sources listing dissertations completed or under way indicates that a quantity of research is now taking place in regard to this topic. Much of it will undoubtedly find its way into print in the near future.

Much more could be said about this period, but because of lack of time we now shall let the curtain fall over the last scene in fifty years of reading accomplishment. As we review the stirring events of the past, we have a right to feel cheered, grateful, proud. In looking back in retrospect we might wonder whether another fifty years could possibly bring about so many changes. This was the first period in which experimentation could be conducted scientifically. In consideration of the newly developed tools, our eagerness to learn, and studies conducted, we might reason that practically all facets of reading instruction have been explored and thus another era could never be so great as this.

If we do reason to this conclusion, we probably are wrong. We pioneered during this period in unexplored territory. We chopped down and cleared away the large virgin trees, but perhaps some of the humble shrubs or creeping vines or fragile mosses may hold even more significance for us than the strikingly obvious, first-sight timbers. But these more obscure growths won't yield their significance with the use of heavy saws and axes. We shall need fresh, piercing insights in choosing which of these to select for dislodgment, and then we shall need unique, delicate tools to pry them loose from their tangled environment and to test the potency of their effect.

What I am trying to say is that while our accomplishments have been very great, indeed, it may be that we have only penetrated the first layer, the troposphere, so to speak. Undoubtedly, brilliant new insights will be revealed, ingenious new techniques of experimentation will be evolved. Possibilities of such developments portend opportunities for unlimited achievement in the future.

Most assuredly, we shall not rest complacently in the glory of achievement during this past golden age. Rather shall we look forward to still greater accomplishments in reading. Let us push on and on with more and more vigor in the next decade, and the next decade, and in all of the other decades ahead!

References

This bibliography would be too voluminous if each separate piece of material examined were listed. In case of educational journals, yearbooks, and summaries of investigations, each successive issue or publication was examined during the period of years indicated by dates accompanying the general reference. In cases in which a specific reference was made, or a quotation was stated from one particular publication, that publication is listed. Professional books on reading were examined but the titles are too numerous to include in this list.

1. Emmett Albert Betts, and Thelma Marshall Betts. *An Index of Professional Literature on Reading and Topics.* American Book Company, New York: 1945.
2. *Childhood Education,* 1-37, 1924-1960.
3. *College English,* 1-22, 1939-1960.
4. *Doctoral Dissertations Accepted by American Universities* H. W. Wilson Co., New York: 1934, 1955.
5. *Educational Index,* 1-31, H. W. Wilson Co., New York: 1930-1960.
6. *Elementary School Journal,* 10-60, 1910-1960.
7. *Elementary English,* 1-37, 1924-1960.
8. *English Journal,* 1-49, 1911-1960.
9. Carter V. Good, "Doctoral Studies Completed or Under Way," *Phi Delta Kappan,* 1923-1953; (Separate publications) Lyda, Mary Louise; Jenson, Glenn; Brown, Stanley; Anderson, Harold, Phi Delta Kappa, Bloomington, Ind. 1954-1959.
10. William S. Gray, *Summary of Investigations Relating to Reading,* University of Chicago Supplementary Monograph, No. 28, Chicago: 1925.
11. William S. Gray, "Summary of Investigations Relating to Reading," *Elementary School Journal,* 26-32, 1925-1932.
12. William S. Gray, "Summary of Investigations Relating to Reading," *Journal of Educational Research,* 5-54, 1932-1960.
13. William S. Gray, *Oral Reading Paragraphs Test,* Public School Publishing Co., Bloomington, Indiana: 1915.
14. National Education Association, "Newer Practices in Reading in the Elementary School," *The National Elementary Principal,* Seventeenth Yearbook, 1938.
15. National Education Association, *Reading Instruction in Secondary Schools,* Research Bulletin, Vol. 22, No. 1, 1942.
16. National Society for the Study of Education: *Sixteenth Yearbook, Part I,* 1917.
17. *Eighteenth Yearbook, Part II,* 1919.
18. *Nineteenth Yearbook, Part I,* 1920.
19. *Twentieth Yearbook, Part II,* 1921.
20. *Twenty-Fourth Yearbook, Part I,* 1925.
21. *Twenty-Fourth Yearbook, Part I,* 1925.
22. *Thirty-Sixth Yearbook, Part I,* 1937.
23. *Forty-Eighth Yearbook, Part I,* 1949.
24. *Forty-Eighth Yearbook, Part II,* 1949.
25. Nila Banton Smith, *American Reading Instruction,* Silver Burdett, New York: 1937.
26. Nila Banton Smith, "Historical Turning Points in Reading," *National Education Association Journal,* (May, 1952), 280-282.
27. Nila Banton Smith, *Readiness for Reading and Related Language Arts,* National Council of Teachers of English, 1950.
28. *The Reading Teacher,* International Reading Association, 1-14, 1947-1960.
29. E. L. Thorndike, *The Thorndike Scale for Handwriting of Children,* Bureau of Publications, Teachers College, Columbia University, New York: 1910.
30. Arthur E. Traxler, Educational Records Bureau, New York: *Ten Years of Research in Reading* (with Seder, Margaret), 1941. *Another Five Years of Research in Reading* (with Townsend), 1946. *Eight More Years of Research in Reading* (with Townsend), 1955, *Research in Reading During Another Four Years* (with Jungeblut).
31. U. S. Library of Congress Catalog Division, *American Doctoral Dissertations* Lists Government Printing Office, Washington: 1913-1940.

II

Psychology of Reading

6. Reading as a Cognitive Process*

RUSSELL G. STAUFFER

University of Delaware

COMPREHENSION is the function of a large number of variables. When the value of a variable changes, the value of comprehension changes also. Mathematically it can be said that $c = (f)\ x$; or that c (comprehension) is a function of x (a variable). When the function of x changes, the efficiency of c may also. Even though the exact relationships among variables cannot be stated precisely, it is possible to identify the principal variables that influence the teaching-learning process in purposeful learning.

Undoubtedly certain independent variables in a reading instruction situation influence learning: the teacher—her actions and interactions with the children; the student—his abilities and motivation; the instructional materials—their nature and difficulty; and the group and its cohesiveness. The dependent variable-reading efficiency—is also dependent upon processes essential to purposeful learning. The processes include setting a goal, gathering and processing information, accepting or rejecting information through critical thinking, reaching or not reaching a goal, and experiencing feelings of success or failure. It is with reading-thinking processes that this presentation is primarily concerned.

THE INDEPENDENT VARIABLES

The history of research in teaching and learning shows that the single most significant independent variable in a purposeful instructional situation is the teacher. The findings reported by the twenty-seven USOE studies of first-grade reading instruction reconfirm this [10]. Encouraging and guiding pupil discovery [6:247] is not only the trend in recent years but is also the salvation of the learner caught up in the midst of a series of knowledge explosions [3]. Rote learning and lock-step practices are giving way before teaching and learning

*From *Elementary English,* 44, 4 (April, 1967), 342-348. Reprinted with the permission of the National Council of Teachers of English and Russell G. Stauffer.
Numbers in brackets refer to references at the end of the articles.

which encourage the student to raise questions and find answers and *use* the answers in different situations. Adler says [1:43] "The art of reading, in short, includes all the same skills that are involved in the art of discovery: keenness of observation, readily available memory, range of imagination, and, of course, a reason trained in analysis and reflection . . . To whatever extent it is true that reading is learning, it is also true that reading is thinking."

The role of the teacher takes on new dimensions when the art of discovery is taught. A delicate balance is required between giving too much direction to students and giving too much freedom and responsibility. The immediate teaching situation determines largely how much help a teacher should give as well as when and why to give help. "Where students are assisted in discovery, usually three features are incorporated into motivation: bringing to the students a problem that is real and meaningful, [2] encouraging and guiding students in gathering information, and [3] providing a responsive environment in which students get accurate feedback promptly so they can ascertain the adequacy of their responses" [4:247].

Efficiency of learning is influenced by several factors in the cognitive domain; particularly intellectual ability both general and specific, and previous experience. In the affective domain such variables as interests, attitudes, values, and so on are determiners of readiness for learning and efficiency of learning.

While it is true that the knowledge and experience that students bring with them materially influences their learning, it is considered equally true that motivation or set or intention to learn strongly influence meaningful learning. The highest form of motivation in inquiry learning seems to be intrinsic to the process itself [14]. The excitement inherent in gathering and processing information is tremendously satisfying. Focusing on the cognitive aspects of learning, by involving the learner intellectually—his questions, his hypotheses, his processing of information, his evaluation—mobilizes pupil effort and concentration of attention. As a result the information processed is more clearly differentiated, more functional in new situations, and more resistant to forgetting.

The material to be read must be potentially meaningful to the student. In other words, the material may not be too discrepant. It must be discriminable from what is already known, because students process data in terms of their established conceptual systems. As long as the information encountered consists of reasonably familiar events and situations, the process of assimilation occurs without too much difficulty [9]. When faced with conceptual categories that can be readily assimilated, conceptual reorganization needs to occur. This process of reshaping and reorganizing conceptual structures is known as accommodation. The learner experiments and may attempt to break down data into component parts and analyze it in terms of variables he already knows. Material that can be organized so as to be assimilated is retained for a longer period of time. This is especially so if the conceptual models have stability and clarity.

When the experience and knowledge of the reader are not sufficiently broad or relevant so that ready assimilation can be accomplished, a promising technique is to help the reader gain a better grasp of the material by presenting to him advance-organizer type passages [2]. Advance organizers are short expository passages that provide a general overview of the material, its organizational elements, and show how concepts already learned are similar to or different from the new concepts being presented.

Group cohesiveness can be guided to achieve useful goals. The nature of the task at hand and the group temperament or interaction can foster desired interactions among the pupils. Children performing at about the same level and capable of maintaining group prestige tend to develop group cohesiveness. To accomplish this, teachers may divide a whole class so that each member experiences success and secures prestige for a job well done.

Each of the independent variables described significantly influence reading instruction and learning. Efficient reading skills to be accomplished, must be taught. This means that if efficient pupil learning is to be accomplished expert teaching is required. Needed are teachers who are not only well-educated but also thoroughly acquainted with the reading-thinking process.

THE DEPENDENT VARIABLE

Comprehension as the dependent variable takes on a different significance when viewed from a teaching-learning point of view. Now comprehension efficiency becomes the major objective of reading instruction. Some of the criteria used to determine efficiency of comprehension are accuracy, thoroughness, speed, and style. The abilities that need to be developed are to be versatile and to think critically.

The versatile reader is one who has the ability to adapt his rate of reading to his purpose for reading and to the nature and difficulty of the material. The thinking reader attains his goal through productive thinking and sound judgments.

Comprehension efficiency is inferred from performance during and immediately after reading instruction, at a later time, and in different situations. Instructional effectiveness is a composite of many characteristics and varies from one directed reading activity to another. Much depends upon teacher behavior; pupils' cognitive abilities, and intellectual characteristics; and the materials used. Much depends also on how a reader performs in the library, at home, in the curriculum areas of the school program, and so on.

Efficient reading blends process, content, and product in such a way that the purposes for reading are accomplished in the most economical time and way. This happens only when the reader knows why he is reading what he is reading, and tries to do it well.

THE NATURE OF THE
READING-THINKING PROCESS

A moment's reflection calls to mind many illustrations to support the fact that language and reading embody concepts used to communicate about objects, events, and principles. It is readily apparent, too, that much of the knowledge one gains throughout life and many of the conclusions one reaches are based upon concepts of a second-hand variety. Historical concepts are particularly illustrative. No one can go back in time and meet or see Caesar or experience living at the time of Caesar. The concepts any scholar has of that period in time are based on perceptual experiences that have had to be transformed and used abstractly. The same may be said when projecting plans into the future. The net result is that the cognitive structures a student forms perceptually by seeing, manipulating, and experimenting need to be established with the greatest of care, since it is on these structures or schemas that concepts learned by reading and study are based. If the inclusiveness and generality of these experienced happenings, events, and actual state of affairs are not thoroughly and thought-fully established, the subsequent concepts based on these mental structures will be all the more arbitrary and faulty. In other words, if the things we see and manipulate in our everyday affairs are examined only casually, they will provide schema of limited usefulness.

Dewey [4] considers reflective thinking an essential learning aim because it emancipates the student from merely impulsive and merely routine activities. Reflective thinking requires a turning over of ideas in the mind and giving them serious and consecutive thought so as to find something new or to see what is already known in a different light. In turn, he does not give the name *thinking* to the automatic, unregulated, and autistic ideas that course through the mind.

In school it is assumed that students read and study textbooks and similar expository materials in a reflective way and without rotely memorizing the content. By so doing they acquire new concepts and extend and refine old concepts. Of course, they may also read just to be entertained and may do so in such a way that a minimum of intellectual effort is required. Even so, books written primarily for entertainment can be examined as they are in literature appreciation courses.

When *meaningful reception learning* is compared with *discovery learning*, noteworthy distinctions can be identified [7:Chaps. 7 and 8]. The virtues of discovery learning seem readily apparent, but the utility value of the method takes on a different perspective when it is realized that a student does not have to discover all concepts independently and that he does not have time to do so. In discovery learning a student attains concepts by observing their common attributes through active searching and productive thinking, by using them in new situations, and by evaluating their usefulness. In meaningful reception learning "... the entire content of what is to be learned is presented to the learner in final form" [4:85]. He is asked to internalize it so that it will be available and reproducible at some other time. The process of meaningful reception learning, like that of discovery learning, requires the student to have a meaningful purpose and to use material that is potentially meaningful.

Undoubtedly, the reading-thinking process as a way to operate takes on major significance as the prime independent variable in the learning activity of a student. It does so because it focuses on the cognitive aspects of learning and is an indispensable condition of *meaningful learning* as well as a principal way of attaining concepts *by discovery learning.*

Setting a goal influences retention of meaningful material more than intention to remember after a goal has been reached. Retention is better, too, when practice is done with intent to learn, rather than incidentally. When learning is done with intent it is called purposeful learning.

Discovery type reading, motivated by pupil purposes, can be taught in a *group* situation where all the material is presented at one time to be internalized, as well as in *individualized* reading instruction where the reader is on his own and materials are made available, and he has to select what he needs to meet his purposes.

In the former procedure all the pupils are presented at the same time the same selection or the same textbook to be read. Now the teacher must direct the activity in such a way that the major responsibility for purposes for reading rests with the student [12]. This is necessary because the learner has to know how to bridge the gap between what he already knows and what he is about to learn.

The use of advance organizers is one way of doing this. Subconcepts are provided which increase the familiarity and meaningfulness of the new material [2]. Purposeful mental activity is developed by focusing on the cognitive aspects of the material to be learned and relying on a motivation that is developed retroactively from successful learning.

A survey of the material can be made so that a set can be obtained. Such a survey is made with the intent to raise questions and speculate about answers. A question well asked is half the answer and this, along with the speculation, helps the student marshall his knowledge and experience and compare it with what the context leads him to anticipate [11]. Or one may ask students to note similarities and differences between the material to be studied and what they already know [15].

Questions can be raised for the learner. Then the students must be instructed to speculate about the answers [13]. This speculation causes them to mobilize their knowledge, compare and contrast it with the nature of the question, and in turn help them make the question more or less their own. Such a procedure focuses on the motivational aspect of the students' intellectual commitment and concentration of attention.

Purposeful intellectual involvement of a student asked to reorganize his conceptual systems by reading is an indispensable condition of the reading process. The learner must be given an opportunity to try out his conceptual models by using them to make predictions, design objectives, or to set goals. Lorge [8:173] defines the teacher's task in a practical way and supports the need for learner involvement.

> The teacher's task in the development of thinking is important and significant. The steps must, by suggesting, hinting, or questioning, lead the learner through the phases of understanding the problem, suggesting hypotheses or reasons for the existence of the problem, and formulating hypotheses for the solution of the problem. Here the teacher can help the learner by asking him to formulate questions. Good questioning is good hypothesis formulation.

This procedure implies a disposition to incorporate new ideas into the existent level of the student's cognitive structure by starting at and with the learner's level of ignorance.

In an individualized situation, inquiry reading is dictated by pupil interest, and material is selected by the pupil. The pupil decides on what conceptual changes he wishes to accomplish and how discrepant they are. He gathers and selects data, and processes the information in whatever sequence is meaningful to him. He programs and paces his own learning. Of course, teaching is involved. The teacher keeps a constant check on the purposes for reading—their nature and complexity. Skillful questioning by the teacher may help clarify the learner's purposes or bring them into better focus. Furthermore, to avoid having the pupil proceed randomly and inefficiently, the teacher arranges the learning situation so that productive inquiry-type individualized reading can be accomplished.

The gathering and processing of information varies from one arranged reading instruction situation to another. In a meaningful reception type situation in which the material or textbook to be learned is given to the students to read, all of the information has been programmed for him. Now the great importance of cognitive structure is readily apparent because the data have been gathered and assembled for the reader. How he processes the information depends largely on the degree to which the reader focuses upon a problem. If a situation or problem has been intellectualized by the reader and stated, or restated, in such a way as to be clear to him, then the reading and thinking may be productive.

On the other hand, when the mode of learning is inquiry and the gathering of data takes as its limits all sources available, efficient learning proceeds differently. Now the learner must know when to select material, how to select it, and how to determine its reliability. In order for instruction to be effective, the teacher must be thoroughly acquainted with a learner's existing conceptual structures so that the gathering and processing may start at the level of the learner and not be too discrepant. In addition, the teacher must keep a check on the conceptual modifications that are occurring and must do so at every step along the way. In some situations the solutions may be readily found and processed; in others the search may require continuous effort for a week or a month or longer.

When the production aspect of reading or learning has been accomplished and a solution has been tentatively accepted, it must be tested out or evaluated. This is done through *critical thinking;* and the teaching of critical thinking is thought to be a most important teaching job.

Ennis [5:84] viewed critical thinking as the correct assessing of statements. He declared twelve aspects of critical thinking that would help a student perform at the various stages in the process of assessment:

1. Grasping the meaning of a statement
2. Judging whether there is ambiguity in a line of reasoning
3. Judging whether certain statements contradict each other
4. Judging whether a conclusion follows necessarily
5. Judging whether a statement is specific enough
6. Judging whether a statement is actually the application of a certain principle
7. Judging whether an observation statement is reliable
8. Judging whether an inductive conclusion is warranted
9. Judging whether the problem has been identified
10. Judging whether something is an assumption
11. Judging whether a definition is adequate
12. Judging whether a statement made by an alleged authority is acceptable.

It is to be noted that the judging of value statements is not included in this list. Neither does the list allow for those aspects of thinking that would be grouped under creative or divergent thinking.

In addition, Ennis proposed a three-dimensional model of critical thinking: a logical dimension, a criterial dimension, and a pragmatic dimension. A person competent in the logical dimension knows what follows from a statement or group of statements because he has examined their meaning. He is particularly alert to such logical qualifiers as "all", "some". "if . . . then", and so on. A person competent in the criterial dimension is capable of using a set of rules or criteria for judging the adequacy or reliability of statements about the world of things, men, and events. These criteria must be applied with discretion.

The pragmatic dimension covers the impression of the background purpose on the judgment. It also includes the decision as to whether the statement is good enough for the purpose. This dimension recognizes the necessity for the balancing of factors preceding the judgment, because it is the purpose that helps the reader judge how important it is to be right and when there is enough evidence. Since complete criteria can most likely never be established, an element of judgment is needed over and above the ability of applying criteria and knowing logical meaning.

Confirming or rejecting, testing, verifying, require application of: logical dimensions by the recognition of instances and the application of principles; criterial dimensions through the knowledge of criteria or judgmental yardsticks; and pragmatic dimension in deciding that there is or is not enough evidence and how strict one must be about the evidence, to satisfy the purposes of the inquiry. Teachers can arrange learning situations to facilitate this kind of critical reading and thinking. Even in the lowest grades children can be given the challenge of dealing with fiction by recognizing problems and organizing information so as to suggest solutions or hypotheses.

Cognitive processes can be directed toward finding a logical conclusion or an already accepted conclusion, as in convergent thinking or critical thinking. Or, the cognitive processes can be directed toward finding the new or the novel conclusion, as in divergent thinking.

The experiencing of feelings of success or failure comes to be regarded by students as an intrinsic aspect of the reading-thinking process and the making of judgments. In finding the path from what is known to what is unknown and is to be discovered, the learner obtains satisfaction from verifying his thinking or solving a problem. It is an active process of seeking and searching, collecting and organizing, generalizing and solving. The activity is exciting and pleasurable in its own right. Overcoming obstacles within a student's range of assimilation and accommodation has as its concomitant the feelings of genuine learning of the sage.

The cognitive abilities that have been emphasized do not develop unrelated to the personality of the students. Children must be taught to test their own attitudes, habits, and interests to try to find out why they act as they do, or why they treat certain people as they do. Teachers must examine their attitudes toward children to determine which are associated with firm, stimulating, warm, and productive learning situations.

CONCLUSION

Reading, thinking, problem solving, and creating always occur in a context. Reading is about something. Purposeful reading is directed toward a solution or goal, as is problem solving. Creativity is involved in expressing something in a new form or another form.

The cognitive processes involved are those of assimilation and accommodation. The first of these two processes consists of taking in and incorporating what is perceived in terms of what is known and understood at the time. The second paves the way for conceptual reorganization. It may require the reshaping and reorganizing of conceptual structures until they fit and/or account for the new circumstances.

Inquiry is native to the mind. Children are by nature curious and inquiring, and they will be so in school if they are so directed and if they are permitted to inquire. It is possible to direct the reading-thinking process in such a way that children *will* be encouraged to think when reading—to speculate, to search, to evaluate, and to use.

The dependent variable—reading efficiency—can be accomplished if teachers and students are thoroughly acquainted with the reading-thinking process. The process can be taught in a small group situation where it can be honed and sharpened as the various members bring a variety of purposes to bear upon the outcome. However, the object is to prepare scholars who can work alone, who can initiate searches, locate and process data, and arrive at solutions.

References

1. Mortimer J. Adler, *How to Read a Book.* New York: Simon and Schuster, 1940.
2. D. P. Ausubel, *The Psychology of Meaningful Verbal Learning.* New York: Grune and Stratton, 1962.
3. J. S. Bruner, "The Act of Discovery," *Harvard Educational Review,* 31 (1961) 21-32.
4. John Dewey, *How We Think.* Boston: D. C. Heath and Co., 1933.
5. Robert H. Ennis, "A Concept of Critical Thinking," *Harvard Educational Review,* 32 (Winter 1962) 81-111.
6. R. W. Heath, (Editor), *New Curricula.* New York: Harper and Row, 1964.
7. Herbert J. Klausmeier, and William Goodwin, *Learning and Human Abilities.* New York: Harper and Row, 1966.
8. Irving Lorge, "The Teacher's Task in the Development of Thinking," *The Reading Teacher,* 13 (February 1960) 170-175.
9. J. Piaget, *The Origins of Intelligence in Children.* New York: International Universities Press, Inc., 1952.
10. *Reading Teacher, The,* R. G. Stauffer, Editor. May 1966 and October 1966.
11. Frank Robinson, *Effective Study.* New York: Harper and Brothers, 1941.
12. R. G. Stauffer, "Reading as Reflective Thinking,"(Proceedings of Schoolmen's Week Conference, University of Pennsylvania, Philadelphia, Pa.) 1961.
13. R. G. Stauffer, Alvina T. Burrows and Dilys M. Jones, *Skillbook for Skyways to Tomorrow.* New York: Holt, Rinehart and Winston, Inc., 1962.
14. J. R. Suchman, "The Child and the Inquiry Process," *Intellectual Development: Another Look.* Papers and Reports from the ASCD Eighth Curriculum Research Institute. (Washington, D.C.: ASCD, NEA, 1964), pp. 59-77.
15. M. C. Withrock, "Effects of Certain Sets upon Complex Verbal Learning," *Journal of Educational Psychology,* 54 (1963), 85-88.

7. Critical Appraisal of Research on Children's Reading Interests, Preferences, and Habits*

ETHEL M. KING

University of Calgary

MUCH effort is expended today in developing new and more efficient methods of teaching reading, and in evaluating the reading achievement of pupils. Evaluation of the total reading program, however, should be concerned with assessing more than the acquisition of reading skills. This evaluation should also include an assessment of the development of children's reading interests and habits. Curriculum guides in reading usually include some objectives related to the development of interests and the establishment of habits of reading, voluntarily, a wide variety of good literature. This kind of broad objective is perhaps one of the most important today because of the number of people who *can* read but *don't*. The process and the results of reading become equally important goals since they are interdependent.

What are the factors which influence what children are reading? A great many investigators have attempted to answer this question. Some begin by studying the attitudes of children, reasoning that a child's attitude towards reading is of prime importance in learning to read and in establishing habits of reading. Attitudes are general predispositions toward reading which are developed or modified with experience.

More specifically, the stimulus or generator of activity is the individual's interest in reading. Interest has been defined as "a characteristic disposition, organized through experience, which impels an individual to seek out particular objects, activities, understandings; skills or goals, for attention or acquisition" [9]. Interest in reading develops with the skills and abilities of learning to read and is generally proportionate to the meaning a child receives from reading. According to Kopel, "What makes an activity interesting is not that it is 'easy' but rather, that it is challenging—which means that it presents obstacles that can be overcome—necessarily through effort" [16]. The responsibility of the teacher, then, is to nurture an interest in reading by his own enthusiasm for reading and by skillfully guiding the pupils in a stimulating reading program.

While competency in reading affects interests in reading, particular

*From *Canadian Education and Research Digest,* 7, 4 (December, 1967), 312-326. Reprinted with the permission of the publisher and Ethel M. King.

interests, or special competencies in other areas of learning, are often important determinants of reading interests. For this reason, studies of reading interests frequently become much broader in order to include a general study of children's interests.

Reading *interests* are not necessarily the same as reading *preferences.*

The difference between a preference and an interest is that the preference is relatively passive, while the interest is inevitably dynamic. A preference is a readiness to receive one object as against another; it does not induce us to seek out the object. In contrast, the basic nature of an interest is that it does induce us to seek out particular objects and activities. [9]

For example, a child might express a preference for *Wind in the Willows* over the *Bobbsey Twins* but not be interested in reading either one.

After pursuing reading interests, the reader will develop reading tastes. Harris points out that "Children do not develop discrimination by being allowed contact only with superior reading matter....Taste develops through comparison and contrast, not from ignorance". [11]

As taste in reading improves, it is probable that interest in reading will increase. Such an increase may well lead to more reading and this repetition of an act which satisfies a motivating condition may determine reading habits.

If we accept as one of the objectives of elementary education the development of children who want to read, then knowledge of significant research findings can contribute to improved selection and use of books. The history of research in children's reading interests dates back to the beginning of this century. Over 300 studies in this area have since been completed. With the findings that have been accumulating, certain trends and characteristics can be identified.

Kinds of Studies

Many studies have been conducted on the general interests of children and their relationships to reading interest. Other studies have been concerned with changes in reading interests according to chronological age, sex differences, and intelligence. A third group of studies are those determining children's preferences in form, style, and format. Finally, there are studies which have tried to determine the reading habits of children.

READING INTERESTS

Reading Interests and General Interests

A number of the studies of reading interests are concerned with the general interests of children and the way these are reflected in reading interests. A commonly accepted assumption is that an individual's reading interests at any given time will be largely influenced by the kind of person he is, the kinds of activities he engages in, and the ideas about which he likes to think and talk. The topics favored by one reader may be rejected by another. Readers' preferences will change as new interests, reflecting increased maturation, are developed.

Reading interests do not necessarily reflect children's informational needs. Over 1,000 children were asked by Baker [1] to write questions they would like to ask. The responses indicated an emphasis on animal life, communication, and the earth. In analyzing the science interests of intermediate grade children, Young [40] found that the universe, animals, earth, human growth, and weather ranked high. Shores [30] found that boys asked questions more in the field of science, particularly about geology, geography, and rockets. Girls, on the other hand, wanted information on foreign countries, history, authors, and artists. Intermediate grade pupils are more interested in reading to find the specific information needed rather than to read an entire book on the general topic. Shores concluded that children are not necessarily interested in reading the same things about which they ask questions. To find the answers to their questions, children often use sources of information other than reading.

Librarians report that the basic reading interests of children have changed very little over the years. However, topics of current interest, such as outer space, are reflected in the reading choices of children. Current movies may influence the popularity of certain books.

Until recently, studies of children's interests did not reflect the effect of watching television programs. Larrick [18] believes that urban and rural children may be developing interests which are more alike as a result of having the opportunity to watch the same television programs. After a study on general interests of children, Howes [12] concluded that television viewing ranks first among preferred activities. If such is the case, preferences in television programs could be expected to have a significant effect on the reading interests, preferences, and tastes of young children. Mauch and Swenson [25] reported that among recreational interests, reading ranked fourth.

Reading Interests and Chronological Age

The typical reading interests of children at different stages of development have been the concern of many investigators.

Studying interests of kindergarten children, Cappa [3] reported a preference for fanciful stories over realistic ones, providing they were not completely unrealistic. In spontaneous group discussions, children of seven revealed to Gunderson [10] that they enjoyed humor, excitement, suspense, adventure, magic, and a satisfying ending.

The content of stories selected by primary grade children will be largely realistic stories about everyday activities. They tend to favor fairy tales, animal stories, nature stories, humorous tales, comics, and how-to-do-it books. In the intermediate grades, pupils prefer adventure, animal stories, tall tales, family-life stories, famous people, sports, humor, science, and social studies.

Rudman's study, [29] using questionnaires to children, parents, teachers, and librarians, indicated that children generally enjoy stories of action, mystery, adventure, horses, and dogs. Interest in mysteries, recreation and sports continues to increase, and interest in cowboy stories and fairy tales decreases.

A very comprehensive study of children's interests was conducted by Norvell [26] with 24,000 children in New York State from grades three to eight. Some Mother Goose rhymes were enjoyed throughout the elementary grades, and others were rejected by grade three. Fables and fairy tales were popular in grades three to five and after that myths, legends, and folk tales were favored. Animal stories ranked first and biography second with children from grade three to six.

Recent studies reveal a trend among children of younger ages toward maturing faster in their reading interests. McAulay [20] identified more mature interests in social studies materials among younger children as being probably due to the influences of television, radio, movies, and travel.

Reading Interests of Boys and Girls

Studies of children's interest in reading reveal few differences between the sexes up to age nine. Young boys, however, generally show an unusual interest in stories about trains.

One of the classic studies in the field of reading interests was published in 1925 by Terman and Lima. [33] These two investigators described the typical interests of boys and girls at each age level, from pre-school through adolescent years. Girls preferred fairy tales, poetry, and sentimental fiction, while boys favored adventure and vigorous action.

In studying responses of 3,000 children, ages 10 to 15, Thorndike [34] reported that boys of all ages were more interested than girls in science, invention, sports, and violent adventure. In contrast, girls favored stories of home life, romance, school adventures, fairy-tales, and animals.

Later Lazar, [19] investigating sex differences in reading interests, outlined the rank-order of preferences of boys as mystery stories, adventure, detective, history, invention, science, nature and animal, fairy stories, biography, novels, stories about home and school, and poetry. Girls listed, in descending order, mystery stories and stories of home and school activities.

Norvell [26] corroborated the findings of earlier studies which indicated that sex differences in children's reading interests appear at about age nine. Girls were found to enjoy many boys' books, but boys did not enjoy almost all girls' books. Boys were interested in the following: detective stories, humor, physical struggle, history, courage and heroism, invention, and science. Favorites among the girls were stories of: home and school life, domestic animals and pets, sentimental fiction, mystery, the supernatural, and fairy tales. During the middle grades, boys responded unfavorably to description, didacticism, fairy tales, romantic love, sentiments, physical weakness in males, and females as the leading characters in the stories. Girls disliked violent action, description, didacticism, slightly younger children, and fierce animals.

McKenzie studied the reading interests of pupils in Medicine Hat, Alberta. He found "Sex differences in reading interests appeared in Grade 4, and increased appreciably in Grades 5 and 6. In the latter grade the girls outnumbered the boys two to one in their choice of mystery books and children's stories, whereas the boys nearly reversed the score in preferences for non-fiction." [23]

Several other studies have been in general agreement with these findings on sex differences in reading interests.

Reading Interests and Intelligence

Intelligence is an important factor in determining what children read. Thorndike [34] studied the reading interests of thousands of children grouped according to superior (median I.Q. about 123), average, and weak pupils (median I.Q. about 92). The superior group indicated interests more like pupils in the slow group who were two or three years older. Lazer, [19] too, found that the choice of books did not vary much with bright, average, and dull pupils. The patterns of reported reading interests were much the same for all groups. Within a class, however, the areas of interest of more intelligent children will be more mature than the less intelligent children.

The types of reading preferred by less able pupils, according to Stone, [32] varies only slightly from those preferred by average and bright pupils. The most notable exception is humor which is chosen less by dull pupils. While the slow-learning child has interests which are slightly immature for his chronological age, nevertheless, they are usually more mature than those of younger children of the same mental age. As a result, this group tends to select books which are at a reading level that is too difficult for them.

Summary of Factors Influencing Reading Interests

1. Reading interests tend to change as new interests are developed.
2. Reading interests do not necessarily reflect informational needs.
3. Audio-visual aids may play an important role in changing reading interests.
4. Primary grade children prefer fairy tales and realistic stories based on everyday activities and animal stories.
5. In the intermediate grades, pupils prefer mystery, adventure, animal stories, family life stories, biographies, sports, science, and social studies.

6. Children appear to be maturing faster in their reading interests.
7. There are few sex differences in reading interests up to age nine.
8. Definite differences in reading interests among girls and boys become apparent after age eight.
    a. Boys read more non-fiction than girls.
    b. Girls read more poetry than boys.
    c. Both boys and girls rank adventure, action, mystery, animal stories, patriotism, and humor high in their preferences.
    d. Boys prefer stories of science, invention, and vigorous action.
    e. Girls prefer stories of home and school life, sentimentalized fiction, and fairy tales.
    f. Boys have a wider range of interests than girls.
    g. Girls will read a book considered to be of interest to boys but the reverse is seldom true.
9. The reading interests of children who are above average in intelligence mature faster than those of slow learners.

READING PREFERENCES

Factors influencing reading preferences have been studied in many different ways: pupil's reasons for choosing books, kinds of reading materials, literary form, style of writing, type of print, and illustrations.

Reasons for Selection

From studies which included 600 intermediate grade pupils, Humphreys [13] listed the reasons why children selected books. A recommendation from a personal friend was the reason stated most frequently.

A number of studies, such as those by Wightman, [36] Coast, [4] and Cappa, [2] indicated that the teacher's enthusiasm for literature is an important factor in the development of reading preferences.

Kinds of Reading Material

The reading interests, preferences, and habits of children are influenced by the amount and kind of materials they read. In addition to reading books, children often devote much time to reading comics and magazines.

Interest in reading comic books begins in the primary grades and continues beyond the elementary school. Witty and Sizemore [39] found 90 percent of the pupils ages 8 to 13 read comics regularly.

In another study, Witty [37] concluded that boys tend to read more magazines than girls. A number of adult magazines enjoy popularity with children. [17]

Literary Form

Children throughout the elementary grades show a preference for narrative material. Fiction is preferred and read more frequently than non-fiction.

Girls show a greater interest in poetry than boys. Mackintosh [22] reported that the qualities children liked most in poetry were: rhyme, emotional tone, vocabulary, story, and descriptions. According to Norvell's study, [26] children preferred humorous poems and poems about animals.

Style of Writing

Factors which appeal to children in the style of writing have changed very little. In 1921, Dunn [8] described the preferred qualities as: surprise, action plot, repetition, and liveliness.

Primary grade children favor a story with a good plot and lots of action. Humor and nonsense rank high in their preferences.

Summarizing several studies, Jordan [14] concluded that the following characteristics were favored: action, adventure, mystery, excitement, and humor.

For factual and informational books to be popular with young readers, they must be simply written.

Type of Print

Young children prefer larger type and a page which is uncluttered. With growth in reading skills, their preferences change. Type size should decrease from 18 to 14 points in grade one to 12 points in grade six. [7] Sometimes books with smaller print may be judged to be more "grown-up." If a child is seeking approval, he may select a book more on the basis of what he thinks is expected of him rather than what he actually prefers.

Illustrations

Again, many studies have been conducted on the effect of various characteristics of illustrations on reading preferences. Whipple's study [35] indicated that preference for a book increases with the following factors: the proportion of the illustrations that depict action, along with the color, size of illustration, and number of illustrations. Other studies support the finding that the children prefer colored pictures to black and white ones. Whether a picture is colored or not is less important than the success of the picture in making the content appear real or life-like. [28,24] Interpreting research findings in terms of the more recently published children's books is difficult because of the marked changes that have taken place in the last five years in the kinds of illustrations.

Summary of Factors Influencing Reading Preferences

1. Personal recommendations rank high in determining the selection of reading materials.
2. Pupils read a variety of reading materials including books, comics, and magazines.
3. Prose form, particularly narrative, is preferred to poetry.
4. Children prefer stories with a good plot, much action, and humor.
5. Colored pictures are preferred to black and white ones.
6. Realism tends to be a more important factor in illustrations than color.

READING HABITS

The Committee on Children's Recreational Reading in Ontario concluded that "reading problems are largely solved by making good books available in abundance and by directing children in their approach to them, and that where there is no great interest in books on the part of the central authorities, reading standards decline." [5] This point of view emphasizes the importance of making books available if we are to establish desirable reading habits.

In interviewing children about their reading habits, McCracken [21] found children could seldom give specific reasons when asked why they liked to read. All the avid readers, however, said they had liked reading and had had books around ever since they could remember. Once a good supply of books is available, children develop their own preferences, tastes, and methods of selection. The books preferred are not necessarily the same books as adults would choose or that adults think children would like, as studies such as Rankin's [27] on Newbery award-winning books have shown.

A number of studies have revealed an increase in the number of books read voluntarily by children each year to the end of the elementary grades. Cutright and Brueckner, [6] for example, found an increase in library books withdrawn from grades three to six. In addition, they found that the number of books borrowed from libraries was directly related to the distance the pupils lived from the library.

Terman and Lima [33] found that gifted children read three or four times as many books as children of average ability. In the study by McKenzie, [23] the upper third of the class, as determined by a reading test, read twice the number of books read by the lowest third. Witty and Lehman [38] also found that the amount of voluntary reading done by bright children far exceeded that done by other children.

Summary of Reading Habits

1. The amount of reading increases up to the end of the elementary grades.
2. Girls read more than boys. (See Reading Interests)
3. Bright children read considerably more than children with a lower IQ.
4. Home influences are important in establishing reading habits. The amount and quality of reading are related to the number and kinds of books, magazines, and newspapers in the home.
5. Easy access to good school libraries and public libraries is an important influence in establishing desirable reading habits.

APPRAISAL OF RESEARCH

An analysis of the research conducted in children's reading interests, preferences, and habits, reveals certain areas of concern: definition of terms, theoretical background, materials, and research methods.

Definitions

Some investigators have not defined clearly and precisely what they mean by terms such as attitudes, interest in reading, reading interests, preferences, tastes, and habits of reading. Those who have attempted to define terms have not always used the same interpretation as other investigators. Findings from one study are then compared with others, even though the operational definition may have been quite different. This lack of standardization has led to difficulties in interpretation of results and application of findings.

Theoretical Background

The theory and practice of teaching are necessarily interrelated. Getzel claims that "the educator whose behavior is based merely on pat techniques for specific situations is operating in an intellectual vacuum. Intelligent action cannot be maximized without some guiding principles or theory, however tentatively these may be maintained." [9] Too few studies of children's reading interests, preferences, and habits have investigated problems with a theoretical background.

Materials

Perhaps the most serious criticism of all is that of the reading materials available. Can we effectively study children's reading interests and habits with limited supplies of reading materials? In interpreting research, we must consider the findings in terms of what reading material was actually available to the child. For most studies, this material would fall far short of what might and should be made available.

Research Methods

Studies of children's reading interests, preferences, and habits have generally used one or more of the following research methods: inventories, questionnaires, personal conferences or interviews, observations, analyses of pupils' records, analyses of library records, and studies of creative expression activities.

Inventories have been widely used to determine attitudes, general interests, reading interests, preferences, and habits of reading. Responses from large numbers of pupils may be analyzed through inventories, even though not all surveyed may reply or be accurate in reporting information. Inventories, however, can provide us with some general information regarding the attitudes and the likes and dislikes of children.

Studies based on questionnaires are apt to be biased. Since there is prestige attached to reading books, and since teacher and parental pressure to read is frequently a factor, pupils who read are proud of that fact and are glad to report it. Pupils who do not read books are generally not proud of it and they will either not talk about books, or they will exaggerate the number read. Moreover, there is the problem of what constitutes having "read a book." Some pupils may claim to have read a book when they have only browsed through the book, flipped the pages, skimmed a few pages, or seen a film based on the story. For these reasons, results from questionnaires tend to be biased toward pupils who are interested in books.

On the other hand, the use of questionnaires has been repeated in so many studies that it is now possible to make an assessment of changes and trends in interests over a specified period of years.

Personal conferences, or interviews, have been conducted between the investigator and children, parents, teachers, and librarians. Such a method of obtaining information may be more revealing than inventories, or questionnaires, but it is so time-consuming that numbers must be limited.

When studying the reading habits of children, observations may be used. To be effective, careful records must be kept by the teacher, and again, this procedure is time-consuming. In addition, it usually applies only to books read in school.

Another method used to study what children have read is to analyze the pupils' own records. The keeping of either formal or informal records is a widely recommended practice. Again, biased results may be obtained as in the case of questionnaires.

Some investigators have relied on library circulation figures as an index of children's reading. In a recent study in the United States, Karlin [15] found that the relationship between library-book borrowing and library-book reading was rather low. The average of books read completely by all the children was 56 percent. While this was a very limited study, it does indicate, nevertheless, that caution is warranted in interpreting studies based on library circulation figures.

Literature selections often provide the ideas which a child will portray in dramatic play, creative drama, or creative art. This method of studying children's interests may be used informally by classroom teachers but has seldom been used by independent investigators.

The methods of obtaining data are generally weak because the procedures used may have presented biased results. In addition, there is the problem of obtaining information on *all* the reading that a pupil does both inside and outside of school. Accurate and complete information has rarely been recorded for the same individuals over long periods of time—which is important in studying habits.

The problem of analyzing data is related to the definition of terms and the method of gathering data: particularly, if every time a child takes out a book, it is claimed to be a result of the operation of a particular interest, however this interest has been defined. Investigators should not assume that the interest they associate with a book is necessarily the interest that a reader has in a selected book.

The teacher needs an understanding of the interests of children generally, and his own class specifically. Since each child in a classroom will not have the same interests, we must pursue the matter further to discover the particular interests of each child. A knowledge of the general trends, as indicated by research findings, helps a teacher to anticipate the interests and preferences of pupils. Smith [31] sums it up by saying, "The reading interests with which children come to school are our opportunity, but the reading interests with which they leave school are our responsibility."

References

1. Emily L. Baker, *Children's Questions and Their Implications for Planning the Curriculum.* New York: Bureau of Publications, Teachers College, Columbia University, 1945.
2. Dan Cappa, "Kindergarten Children's Spontaneous Responses to Story Books Read by Teachers," *Journal of Educational Research,* 52 (October, 1958), 75.
3. Dan Cappa, "Types of Story Books Enjoyed by Kindergarten Children,"*Journal of Educational Research,* XLIX (March, 1956), 555-557.
4. Alice B. Coast, "Children's Choices of Poetry as Affected by Teacher's Choices," *Elementary English Review,* 5 (May, 1928), 145-147.
5. Committee on Children's Recreational Reading in Ontario. "The Recreational Reading Habits of Ontario School Children," Study Pamphlets in Canadian Education, No. Ten. Toronto: Copp Clark, 1952, 6.
6. Prudence Cutright, and Leo J. Brueckner, "A Measurement of the Effect of The

Teaching of Recreational Reading," *Elementary School Journal,* XXIX (October, 1928), 132-137.

7. Emerald V. Dechant *Improving the Teaching of Reading,* Englewood Cliffs: Prentice Hall, 1964.
8. Fannie W. Dunn, *Interest Factors in Primary Reading Material.* Contributions to Education, No. 113. New York: Bureau of Publications, Teachers College, Columbia University, 1921.
9. Jacob W. Getzels, "The Nature of Reading Interests," *Developing Permanent Interest in Reading.* Supplementary Educational Monographs, No. 84. Chicago: University of Chicago Press, 1956, 7, 5.
10. Agnes G. Gunderson, "What Seven-Year-Olds Like in Books," *Journal of Educational Research,* L (March, 1957), 509-520.
11. Albert J. Harris, *How to Increase Reading Ability.* New York: Longmans Green, 1956, 491.
12. Virgil E. Howes, "Children's Interest—A Keynote for Teaching Reading," *Education,* 83, (1962), 491-496.
13. Phila Humphreys, "The Reading Interest and Habits of 600 Children in the Intermediate Grades," *Language Arts in the Elementary School,* 20th Yearbook of Department of Elementary School Principals, 20:6 (1941), 421-428.
14. Arthur M. Jordan, *Children's Interests in Reading.* Contributions to Education. No. 107. Teachers College, Columbia University, 1921.
15. Robert Karlin, "Library-Book Borrowing vs. Library-Book Reading," *The Reading Teacher.* 16 (November, 1962), 77-81.
16. David Kopel, "The Nature of Interests," *Education,* (April, 1963), 497-502.
17. Sister M. Immaculata Kramer, "Children's Interests in Magazines and Newspapers," *I, Catholic Educational Review,* XXXIX (June, 1941), 343-358. II, *Catholic Educational Review,* XXXIX (June 1941), 348-358.
18. Nancy. Larrick, *A Teacher's Guide to Children's Books.* Columbus, Ohio: Charles E. Merrill Books, 1960.
19. May Lazar, *Reading Interests, Activities and Opportunities of Bright, Average, and Dull Children,* Contributions to Education, No. 707. New York: Bureau of Publications, Teachers College, Columbia University, 1937.
20. J. D. McAulay, "Interests of Elementary School Children," *Social Education,* XXVI (April, 1962), 199-201.
21. Ruth U. McCracken, "What Makes a Difference?" *Childhood Education* (March, 1962), 319-321.
22. Helen K. Mackintosh, "A Critical Study of Children's Choice in Poetry," University of Iowa Studies, Studies in Education, VII, No. 4 (September, 1932).
23. Edwin McKenzie, "Reading Interests of Pupils in the Intermediate Grades in the Public Schools in a Small Urban Center," *Alberta Journal of Educational Research,* 8 (March, 1962), 33-38.
24. Morton S. Malter, "Children's Preferences for Illustrative Materials," *Journal of Educational Research,* XLI (January, 1948.)
25. Inez L. Mauck, and Esther J. Swenson, "A Study of Children's Recreational Reading," *Elementary School Journal,* L. (November, 1949), 144-150.
26. George W. Norvell, *What Boys and Girls Like to Read.* Morristown: Silver Burdett Co., 1958.
27. Marie Rankin, *Children's Interest in Library Books of Fiction,* Contributions to Education, No. 906. New York: Bureau of Publications, Teachers College, Columbia University, 1944.
28. Mabel F. Rudisill, "Children's Preferences for Color versus Other Qualities in Illustrations," *Elementary School Journal,* LII (April, 1952), 444-451.
29. Herbert C. Rudman, "The Informational Needs and Reading Interests of Children in Grades Four Through Eight," *Elementary School Journal* 55 (1955), 502-512.
30. J. Harlan Shores, "Reading Interests and Informational Needs of Children in Grades Four to Eight," *Elementary English,* 31 (December, 1954), 493-500.
31. Dora V. Smith, "Current Issues Relating to Development of Reading Interests and

Tastes," *Recent Trends in Reading.* Edited by W. S. Gray. Supplementary Educational Monographs No. 49. Chicago: University of Chicago Press, 1939.

32. C. R. Stone, "Grading Reading Selections on the Basis of Interests," *Educational Method,* 10 (1931), 225-230.

33. Lewis M. Terman, and Margaret Lima, *Children's Reading: A Guide for Parents and Teachers.* New York: Appleton-Century-Crofts, 1931.

34. Robert L. Thorndike, *Children's Reading Interests.* New York: Teachers College, Columbia University, 1941.

35. Gertrude Whipple, "Appraisal of the Interest Appeal of Illustrations," *Elementary School Journal,* 53 (1953), 262-269.

36. H. J. Wightman, "A Study of Reading Appreciation," *American Schoolboard Journal,* L (June, 1915), 42.

37. Paul A. Witty, "Studies of Children's Interests–A Brief Summary," *I, Elementary English,* 27 (November, 1960), 469-475; *II, Elementary English,* 27 (December, 1960), 540-545, 572; *III, Elementary English,* 28 (January, 1961), 33-36.

38. Paul A. Witty, and Harvey C. Lehman, "A Study of Reading and Reading Interests of Gifted Children," *Journal of Genetic Psychology,* XL (June, 1932), 473-485.

39. Paul A. Witty, and Robert A. Sizemore, "Reading the Comics: A Summary of Studies and an Evaluation," *I, Elementary English,* XXXI (December, 1954), 501-506; *II, Elementary English,* XXXII (January, 1955), 43-49; *III, Elementary English,* XXXII (February, 1955), 109-114.

40. Doris Young, "Identifying and Utilizing Children's Interests," *Educational Leadership,* 13 (December, 1955), 161-165.

8. The Perceptual Basis for Learning*

JOSEPH M. WEPMAN. PH.D

Professor, Psychology and Surgery
Director, Speech and Language Clinic and
Research Laboratory
The University of Chicago

AT the Berkeley Conference on Personality Development in 1960, Roger Williams made a cogent observation about the biological approach to the study of personality which seems most appropriate to the central theme of this proceedings—meeting individual differences in reading. Speaking of personality differences, he said, in part:

> Consider the fact that every individual person is endowed with a distinctive gastrointestinal tract, a distinctive circulatory system, a distinctive respiratory system, a distinctive endocrine system, a distinctive nervous system, and a morphologically distinctive brain; furthermore, that the differences involved in this distinctiveness are never trifling and often are enormous. Can it be that this fact is inconsequential in relation to the problem of personality differences?[1]

We might begin by asking a similar question with regard to the learning of reading. Can it be that this fact is inconsequential in relation to the problem of differences in learning to read? Literally all of the systems that Williams itemizes are involved in the development of learning in children-differences not only within the systems but between them which establish the individuality of the entity, the child, with which we are concerned.

*From *Reading and the Language Arts* ("Supplementary Educational Monographs," No. 94; 1964 Chicago: University of Press, 1964), 25-33. Copyright by the University of Chicago Press. Reprinted by permission.

Author's Note.—The research reported here was partially supported by the Department of Health, Education, and Welfare, Cooperative Research Program, Office of Education, Contract No. 2225.

[1]Roger J. Williams, *The Biological Approach to the Study of Personality* (a paper delivered at the Berkeley Conference on Personality Development in Childhood, University of California, May 5, 1960 [Offprint only]).

If we grant that such differences exist, and much of this chapter is devoted to a demonstration that they do, the next and most important task is to isolate the differences of maximal importance to the act of learning to read, or stated otherwise, to identify the factors which are most likely to produce differences in children that will affect their ability to learn to read. It is the argument in this chapter that major differences do exist in children at the perceptual level of learning which may materially affect their learning; that these differences are fundamental to learning; that they underlie the conceptual level and provide the basic percepts upon which concepts are built; and that they must be understood and clarified before the conceptual level is focused upon. Too much attention, it is held—to the extent of preoccupation—has already been given to the conceptual domain, which in fact is the final stage of the learning act, and too little to the lower levels in the hierarchy. All learning, according to this theoretical position, proceeds in a hierarchical fashion from the perceptual to the conceptual level, from the decoding of an input signal below the level of comprehension before a meaningful interpretation can be placed on it through association with previously received and memory-stored percepts and concepts. The key to this integration of present stimulus with past learning lies not only in the intactness of the input transmission pathways but in the capacity of each type of signal to arouse past learning received along other modalities.

Our concern, our immediate concern, is not with the partially sighted or the partially deafened but with the child who must learn with unimpaired organs and processes. That is not to say that we should not explore in each child the adequacy of his sense organs and their capability of transmitting the signals for which they are peculiarly endowed. But assuming that they function well and transmit the sensory messages, our major attention should be directed toward understanding the individual capacity for prelinguistic perceptualization. It is this level, between absolute reception and transmission of the signal, at the point where the transmutation from signal to sign occurs, where input signal becomes translated into the alphabet of letters and sounds to form the stimulus for comprehension, that seems to be so frequently overlooked as we study the learning act. Our concern, then, lies with the differences between children in their modes of perceptualization and the effect of these differences upon their ability to learn, which stage in learning may be the very core of the reading problem.

THE MODALITY CONCEPT

Approaches to reading have stressed the gaining of comprehension directly through whatever means rather than the explication of individual differences in learning ability or the underlying processes of reading. It seems to this writer, however, that the teacher's problem lies not in the prescribed approach that is to be used with all of the children to be taught but with the approached, that is, with the child who must learn to read. What is proposed here is that the teaching of reading should be child-centered rather than method-centered; that the differences in children need to be understood to determine which methods might be most useful for a particular child or group of children. Stated differently, the question should not be whether visual sight reading or phonics or any other method is the approach to use, but which children among all of those to be taught should be taught by which method. No method should be considered incorrect for any member of a group because it has not reached all of the children. Quite to the contrary, all that the modality concept holds is that we should predetermine which child can learn best by which method. The central focus should be on the child, not on the method.

It seems time to take stock, to explore in reading what has become so evident and accepted in other fields—that to understand the group one must first understand the individuals that make up the group, that learning is an individualized process in many ways for each child. Just as he is different in personality, in intelligence, and in language ability, so, too, is he different from others in how he learns.

For this writer, much of this viewpoint is meaningful in the present context only when it is translated into the perceptual differences between children. A child's learning type—his maximal modality or pathway of learning, his differential ability to learn by eye, or by ear, or even by touch—needs to be understood before a particular approach to reading can be determined for him. Only after we have studied each child for such propensities should we think of grouping him with others and then, to the degree possible, with those others who have like propensities. That is, before we explore whether a given child or group of children should be taught by sight-recognition methods or by phonic methods, we should determine which of the perceptual building blocks he can utilize best in the integrative, conceptualizing process of gaining meaning from the printed page. It is with these prelinguistic skills that the so-called modality concept of learning concerns itself. And it is with the belief that today this determination can be made with reasonable accuracy, that we can predetermine which of the sensory input pathways each child can function with best, that we recommend this approach.

Perhaps we should cast our questions in more specific terms to avoid misunderstanding. In a previous paper, the writer isolated three functions which, for all practical purposes, are what is meant by the auditory perceptual level, and postulated that these same three functions, namely, (1) discrimination, (2) memory (retention and recall), and (3) sequential behavior or patterning, are probably of equal importance in the visual perceptual act.[2] To these should be

---

[2] Joseph M. Wepman, "Auditory Discrimination, Speech and Reading," *Elementary School Journal,* IX (March, 1960), 325-33.

added a fourth which is presently receiving a considerable amount of attention in research—intermodal transfer, or the ability to shift from one modality to another, to stimulate a given modality in recall and association through its opposing modality.

To express these ideas in even more specific terms, we might ask of a given child whether he has difficulty in auditory discrimination, in visual recall, or in the sequential patterning of either, or whether he functions adequately with each of these individual processes but cannot utilize the stimulation received along one type of pathway to arouse the necessary integrative behavior previously received along the other type of pathway.

Let us illustrate some of these questions with actual cases. Consider the child who cannot discriminate between the sounds of the language. To him, the /p/ sound in "cap" sounds like /t/; the /th/ sound is indistinguishable from the /t/ sound in the word "thin"—as just two examples of a possible host of sound discrimination confusions he may have. Such a child, it is held, should get his primary instruction in reading through the visual pathway. It has been the writer's lot to take care of many such children over the years, not initially because they were having difficulty learning to read, but because they were encountering problems in the acquisition of language and speech. One such boy comes to mind who perfectly illustrates the point.

This lad was first seen when his parents brought him to the Speech and Language Clinic at the University of Chicago when he was nearly four, with the complaint that he had not yet started to talk or that when he did try it was impossible to understand him. Examination revealed a child of adequate intelligence when assessed by non-verbal tests, without visual or auditory acuity problems. He was hyperactive, frustrated in every attempt to communicate with the adults in his environment, and said to be unusually "stubborn and mean." We found him to be relatively manageable when separated from his well-meaning but extremely anxious and demanding parents. His speech was largely jargon, but when studied, a predictable one. That is, he always substituted specific sounds for others, and when we could understand the substitution pattern, we could understand his speech. For our present purposes, let us pass over his early development of speech. With proper stimulation and understanding and especially with the passage of time and the normal course of auditory maturation, his articulation became relatively adequate. At kindergarten age, he was understandable enough, although still far from perfect in his articulation. The sounds which we know are invariably learned last by children were the sounds he produced with most difficulty. His auditory discrimination was extremely inadequate even at this time, but it continued to improve. Auditory training for discrimination seemed to help some, but without question, he acquired very little information along the auditory pathway. Since he gained most of his knowledge along the visual pathway and he was motorically adequate, he passed the usual reading readiness tests with ease. The difficult part of his schooling began in the first grade. In his school, every child was taught to read through a phonic approach. It took some time and considerable doing to convince the teachers that (1) he was not unintelligent because he couldn't learn phonics and (2) that he could learn to read if visual training methods were used.

For this child things worked out reasonably well. His school was willing to provide him with special tutoring in reading; even though the teachers continued to teach all of the other children through phonics, they permitted him to receive a sight-training program and he learned to read. We were, however, less successful in convincing the school that the other children in the first grade who were having difficulty learning to read might also need a different approach. The parents were pleased but also failed to learn from the experience. Although recognizing that the child was learning to read visually where he had failed when approached aurally, they failed to recognize that auditory imperception is not only a factor in learning to read but is, rather, a fact of life. Just recently the parents brought the child in for his yearly re-evaluation, and they brought the following inexplicable behaviors to our attention. The father complained that often when the child came to him with a question and he took the trouble to explain it to him—orally, of course—the child might nod his head as though he understood and yet five minutes later would again ask for an answer to the same question. They also found it strange that the child, who is now eight, "invariably gets confused when told something over the telephone." Both of these examples, of course, point to the auditory imperception of the child. When told something, the answer is retained only momentarily; he has notably poor auditory recall. When he receives a message over the telephone, when all of the usual visual components and clues to meaning are missing and all of the message must be understood from the auditory stimuli, he gets confused. He has continuing, and probably will have life-long, difficulty with any purely auditory stimulus. He needs, more than most children, the reinforcement of visual, tactual, and kinesthetic clues.

Teachers of such children, especially when they are in the category of the child whose problems in learning we have just reviewed, children for whom the auditory pathway is simply not functional, have two courses open to them. They can either teach them through a very directed visual approach, using auditory clues only after the child has developed that modality sufficiently through the processes of maturation so that it can be used for reinforcement, or they can approach the child visually and attempt quite separately to improve his auditory skills. When the latter approach is used, it has been our experience that the two modalities should be trained quite independently, since combining the two approaches before the child is capable of utilizing them both leads more often than not to confusion. It has also been our experience that if a child below the age of eight shows many articulatory inaccuracies in speech or oral reading because of poor auditory discrimination auditory training does him little good. Only after full maturation have we been able to see much change in such children as the result of auditory training. On the other hand, if children show auditory imperception but do not have articulatory inaccuracies, they frequently respond quite well to auditory training, even before the age of eight. The present statement is based on long standing clinical experience on this point. However, there has as yet been no carefully controlled research—and it is sorely needed.

The approach through a single modality rather than through the combined modalities receives further confirmation from our work with adult language-impaired subjects, with whom, both in speech and in reading, it was found that the multiple approach methods was often more confusing than helpful. In these adults it was also found that if the impaired pathways was separately trained, it frequently became useful for reinforcement of learning along the unimpaired pathway. It should be recognized, however, that reinforcement is only of value when it reinforces; when it confuses or takes more time than the single pathway, it may become a negative factor in learning. From this type of evidence it is argued that, in teaching reading, one should capitalize on the modality of preference, train the undeveloped or impaired pathway separately, and bring the two together when they each can add something to the other, but not before.

SHIFTS IN MODALITY

Our second question deals with the degree of limitation a given child may have along a specific pathway. Fortunately, most children have some capacity to function with both visual and auditory perception. The two abilities have their own rates of development and, when mature, most often show only approximately equal maturational levels. When a child shows his best ability to be visual and his lesser ability to be auditory, the visual approach in reading is suggested, with immediate auditory reinforcement and, in addition, auditory training to improve that capacity.

Naturally, the opposite approach would be best for the child with good auditory ability but only fair visual ability. Here it is suggested that the teacher should use a phonic approach, with strong, but secondary, sight training to bring the lesser developed pathway up to a level of major usefulness.

Parenthetically, it should be added that, although vision and audition are the major modalities discussed here, the other input sensory pathways should not be overlooked. Tactile and kinesthetic skills are for some children—fortunately very few—the best learning pathway. When they are the best approach, they should receive the same concentration of teaching attention suggested for vision and audition. They have not been stressed here in order to reduce the confusion that comes with a discussion of the multiplicity of sensory pathways and because, quite truthfully, we know much less about successful teaching of reading through other senses than vision and audition. Kinesthetic methods are available, however, and should be used. At this point, the writer must express as strongly as he can what he believes to be true—that it is the rare child of school age who needs a tactile-kinesthetic approach as the central core of his instruction. It is as wrong in the present framework to begin the teaching of reading by such an approach with any group of children who have not been previously determined as "tactile" or "tactile-kinesthetic" as it is to adopt a "visual" or "phonic" approach for any unselected group. There is no magic in any method; there are just differences in children which must be taken into account.

Our third question relates to those processes of transfer and shift from one modality to another, which for lack of a better name we call "intermodal transfer ability." In gaining comprehension from any input signal, a child must use that signal to evoke previously learned symbols received along many input pathways to form the associations necessary for comprehension. This act of arousal and integration is seen as the probable final stage of perceptual behavior before comprehension is achieved. Thus, a child who sees the printed word "dog" must evoke not only previous visual stimuli of printed forms but life forms as well; he must shift from the visual input to previously received and stored auditory patterns making up the word "dog" and perhaps to the tactile sensations of petting a dog, of his small and even his frisky movements, before the printed word has full meaning for him. Without this shift to other modal learning, little integrative meaning may be attached to the printed word. Intermodal transfer, then, seems to be vital to the learning act. Katz and Deutsch, in an extensive study of good and poor readers on a variety of perceptual tasks, concluded in part that "poor reading is associated with difficulties in shifting from one sensory mode to another."[3]

When children are suspected of having inadequacies in this phase of learning, when each modality seems adequate when studied by itself but the capacity to shift from one to another seems affected, the teacher's task seems explicit. Experience and training at cross-modal interpretation, in using each input pathway as the originating stimulus carrier and striving for the appropriate associations, is necessary for these children.

At this point we might well turn to a brief discussion of some of the suspected causes for the differences observed in the perceptual behavior of children. Extreme cases of learning problems have been described in the literature and specific causes ascribed to them, which could be overcome, the investigators suggested, by utilizing compensatory modalities. Eisenberg pointed that out very clearly in his discussion of the reading problem in brain-injured children

[3]Phyllis Katz and Martin Deutsch, *Visual and Auditory Efficiency and Its Relationship to Reading in Children,* Cooperative Research Project No. 1099 (Washington, D.C.: Office of Education, U. S. Department of Health, Education, and Welfare, 1963), p. 45.

the deficits in performance we observe may represent not at all the inherent handicap of his disease, but rather the most he has been able to accomplish in the absence of what he needed. We cannot conclude from the fact that he has not learned to read by the methods adequate for the ordinary child that he could not if attempts were made to bypass his deficiencies, by making use of other sensorimotor channels.[4]

In general, the evidence from the impaired child seems quite widely accepted. Recently, De Hirsch hypothesized a "neurophysiological immaturity" in many children with reading and language defects.[5] Katz and Deutsch have explored reading problems in the socially underprivileged, and in as yet unpublished series of reports, they have noted the explicit modality deficiencies which seem to exist above and beyond the socioeconomic and environmental handicaps from which these children suffer. They hypothesize that the auditory deficiency may be a consequence of their environment.

Individual differences in perceptual transmission and conceptual learning can be demonstrated to be along modality lines; methods for teachers or the school system to determine a given child's maximal learning modality, if they are inclined to do so, remain to be discovered.

Perhaps this is the best reason for stressing individual differences in children at this time, for during the past decade there has been a tremendous burst of interest in identification of perceptual modalities directly related to reading. While time and space forbid a complete review of the evidence, a study of the references as well as the articles themselves concerned with this factor will well repay those who are interested. It will be recalled that even some twenty years ago Monroe in her Reading Aptitude Tests (Houghton Mifflin Co., 1935) differentiated between visual and auditory functioning. Auditory-discrimination testing has been going on for almost the same length of time, and this writer as well as many others has put forth the concept that auditory-discrimination inadequacy is related not only to speech development but also to learning type and to reading disability.[6] Visual memory and matching tests have been devised and are now being standardized that will point up explicit difficulties with that facet of learning. Visual-motor tests, which have been standardized on preschool children as well as early school-age children, point to difficulties in prelinguistic function along that combination of modalities.[7] McCarthy and Kirk, building on

[4]L. Eisenberg, "Behavioral Manifestation óf Cerebral Disorders in Childhood," in *Brain Damage in Children: The Biological and Social Aspects,* ed. Herbert George Birch (Baltimore: Williams & Wilkins, 1964), p. 69.

[5]Katrina De Hirsch, Jeanette Jansky, and William S. Langford, "The Oral Language Performance of Premature Children and Controls," *Journal of Speech and Hearing Disorders,* XXIX (February, 1964), 60-69.

[6]Joseph M. Wepman, "The Interrelationship of Hearing, Speech and Reading." *The Reading Teacher,* XIV (March, 1961), 245-47.

[7]Marianne Frostig, D. Welty LeFever, and John R. B. Whittlesey, "A Developmental Test of Visual Perception for Evaluating Normal and Neurologically Handicapped Children," *Perceptual and Motor Skills,* XII (June, 1961), 383-94.

theories and models of brain function which Osgood and Wepman had independently proposed, developed a test assessing language and prelanguage levels of function along each modality; from its protocol, the language needs of children at both the perceptual and the conceptual levels can be identified.[8]

The reality of prediction is here. Its application to reading is being tried in a wide number of reading clinics and school systems throughout the country, although, unfortunately, almost solely in centers for remediation of severe learning problems. If, however, the approach seems valid for remedying reading problems, it should be equally useful for teaching those beginning to learn to read, for special reading problems are not seen as being outside the realm of the normal but as being at the extremes of the total population distribution.

The children who are easiest to identify, of course, are the so-called remedial reading problems, since they have tried and failed to achieve in the regular classrooms. How much better it would be if we were to study all children before they become problems and thus offset their lags in development—if that, indeed, is where their problems lie. Such children are, unfortunately, not the occasional child but, according to some widely quoted figures, amount to as many as 25 percent of all school children. And the remainder—the 75 percent who succeed—to what degree do they do so? How many of these children would learn more, be better able to read, find more enjoyment in reading, if they were taught by the right approach for them instead of having to learn despite the methods used?

CONCLUDING STATEMENT

It has been the writer's experience that education and educators are slow to move to new ideas, that they grudgingly adopt new approaches, but that when they do they apply them frequently without reason; whole school systems have adopted a particular new approach to reading as though a panacea had been discovered that would eradicate all the educational ills of their children. No method, no specific approach, no new text or cartoonist's illustration, no matter how apt, will solve the problems of children who are by nature as different in learning type as they are alike in anatomy. It is, for example, still not uncommon for reading readiness tests in which only visual skills are assessed to be given to whole school systems. It has also been called to the writer's attention that whole school systems have turned from vision and audition, as specific

---

[8]*Illinois Test of Psycholinguistic Abilities* (Institute for Research on Exceptional Children, University of Illinois, 1963), by James J. McCarthy and Samuel Kirk; Charles E. Osgood and Murray W. Miron, *Approaches to the Study of Aphasia* (Urbana: University of Illinois Press, 1963), p. 95; Joseph M. Wepman, "A Conceptual Model for the Processes Involved in Recovery from Aphasia," *Journal of Speech and Hearing Disorders,* XVIII (March, 1953), 4-13.

approaches to teaching reading, to kinesthetic tracing without determining which children could utilize kinesthetic skills and which could not.

It seems a wiser course to recognize that perceptual ability is the precursor to comprehension. It provides the underpinning for understanding and for generalization. It precedes and permits integration. Man has not evolved with separate visual, aural, and tactile sense receptors and a central process for integration without purpose. By determining the individual child's specific abilities and utilizing them in an organized way, reading, like all other language forms, can be acquired with a minimum of discomfort and a maximum of pleasure.

The modality approach to reading—by differentiating the perceptual levels of transmitting input signals and their ability, in the intermodal transfer, to arouse the associations necessary for integration and thus meaning—only nominates the directions of individualized training. It permits each child to function in the manner for which he is best equipped. It predicates the need for understanding each child as a total organism complete within himself. It is presented here as a challenge to every teacher—a means for assisting in the largely implausible task of making every child literate.

9. An Interpretation of Research in Reading Readiness*

ROBERT L. HILLERICH

Glenview Assistant Superintendent Public Schools
Glenview, Illinois

WE hear frequently enough these days the logical statement about the old phonics discussion: it is not a question of phonics or no phonics, but rather a question of which phonics, when, and how much. I would suggest that our current interest in early reading instruction also can not be resolved on an either/or basis; here the questions more likely are what kind of instruction and for whom.

Whether we prefer the title "reading readiness," "early reading instruction," or "kindergarten readiness," the topic is broad and difficult to delimit. On one hand we have educators such as Hymes and Sheldon saying "Touch not the little children"; at the other extreme we find O. K. Moore beating two and three year olds with typewriters (or is it vice versa?); in another direction, Fry, Mazurkiewitz, and Downing are mutilating orthography while their opposites mutilate meaning in the name of linguistics.

READING READINESS DEFINED

The present discussion will stay within the more narrow confines of the research in what we call "reading readiness" or "early reading instruction."

"Reading readiness" has been defined directly and by implication in many ways. Generally speaking, it represents progress in two areas of living: the one area is time—time for growth and development; the second is experience or training.

The element of time is reflected in such concepts as social or emotional maturity, mental age, physical maturity, and the like. These influences of the child development specialists are the predominant factors in most traditional kindergarten programs and lead to an emphasis on identification procedures as opposed to teaching methods or materials.

*From *Elementary English*, **43**, 4 (April, 1966), 359-364, 372. Reprinted with permission of the National Council of Teachers of English and Robert L. Hillerich.

The second facet of reading readiness—experience—ranges the entire gamut from a continuation of general preschool experiences to "fussing with phonics." Traditional programs in this area are developed more from logic than from research and usually lead children from concrete experiences, through verbalizing about these experiences, to gross auditory and visual discrimination activities—either in kindergarten or early in first grade. Efforts of educators who focus on this factor of experience as opposed to the time factor reveal less .concern with identification and more concern with the kinds of experiences and skills children need in order to be able to read. In such cases, "time" for adequate growth and maturity is assumed.

Whether a given school emphasizes the time or the experience factor, reading readiness may be judged successful or not in terms of the eventual success or lack of success of pupils in reading.

We live in an exciting age today as we appraise kindergarten and early first grade in terms of readiness and reading. Research today seems to deal more with skills and their placement—the experience factor—than it does with identification. In part this focus may be the tenor of the times, but in part it results from findings which negate traditional criteria.

TRADITIONAL VIEWS QUESTIONED

The mental age criterion for beginning reading instruction is an example of the traditional "time" oriented identification procedure. Investigations of this topic cluster around the 1930's and are exemplified by the Morphett and Washburne study [11].[1] It is doubtful that their study would stand up today in the more stringent "court of research." Even if we accept the study, we must still recognize that, in thirty-five years, materials, methods, and the experiences of children have changed considerably. Schramm [17], for example, reported that children who view television begin school with vocabularies about a grade higher than children who do not.

More specifically to the point, Anderson [1] compared 443 kindergarteners in an effort to determine the mental age necessary for them to use oral context and letter-sound associations in unlocking a strange word. Analysis of variance of mean gain indicated that the group with mental ages ranging from 52 to 65 months gained as much as the group with mental ages ranging from 79 to 91 months. There are a number of other studies reporting that correlations between mental age or intelligence and beginning reading or reading achievement range as low as .00.

Another aspect of the identification approach that has fallen into disrepute is the use of reading readiness tests. Regardless of tests used, correlations between readiness tests and reading achievement usually range around .40. For example, Karlin [8] reported a correlation of .36 between the

---

[1]Numbers in brackets refer to references at the end of the article.

Metropolitan Readiness Test administered in September of first grade and Gates Primary Reading Test at the end of first grade.

Bremer [3] tested readiness in grade one and reading achievement at the beginning of grade two. He found a correlation of .40 between the two tests. While 31 percent of his subjects who scored in the lowest third in readiness scored in the lowest quartile in reading, another 31 percent who were in the lowest third in readiness scored *above* the mean in reading achievement. His conclusion was that the tests might be used for diagnosis, but not for prediction.

Still another facet of the "give them time" view of early reading instruction is the concern for visual maturity. While this concern is not founded on research, it has been spoken of by Thomas Eames [5]. In reporting on the vision of five year olds he examined, he stated that the poorest in near visual acuity was quite capable of reading the usual texts. Furthermore, he pointed out that children of this age have more accommodative power than at any subsequent age.

RESEARCH EMPHASIS TODAY

Current research seems concerned mostly with content, methods, and chronological age for beginning reading instruction. The crucial questions revolve around two related points: what kind of prereading instruction is most effective, and when should formal instruction begin? The research evidence may seem contradictory in respect to this double question, but I believe a pattern is apparent.

A large number of studies have been conducted at Boston University under Durrell to isolate abilities related to success in early reading instruction. In one of these studies, Nicholson [13] tested 2,188 first graders after three weeks of school. Using the Boston University Letter Knowledge Tests, she tested pupils' ability to match lower case and capital letters prior to the teaching of those letters. Mean scores of 25.34 in matching capitals and 24.48 in matching lower-case letters suggested to her that the gross discrimination activities—distinguishing non-word forms—in traditional readiness programs are a "waste of time."

Following 1,172 of these pupils through February in first grade, Olson [14] found that knowledge of letter names and ability to write letter correlated .55 with reading achievement in February. In an unrelated study, McHugh [10] verified this relationship between knowledge of letter names and reading achievement. He found that the Boston University Letter Knowledge Tests correlated more highly with reading achievement at the end of grade one than did the Metropolitan Readiness Test. In fact, knowledge of either capital or lowercase letter names correlated more highly with reading than did the best subtest of the Metropolitan.

Lest we get the wrong idea from these studies, Linehan [9] compared the June reading achievement of 314 children who had preliminary teaching of letter names and sounds with 300 children who had not. Both groups used the same basal reading program. There was no significant difference in reading achievement at the end of the year.

While the Boston studies suggest a relationship between knowledge of letter names and achievement in reading, we cannot assume that the relationship is causal. In fact, Muehl [12] reported quite the contrary. Eighty-seven kindergarten children were assigned alternately to relevant and irrelevant groups. In each case both groups were taught to associate a group of letters as a "word" for each of three pictures. Then the relevant group was taught letter names for the letters used in the "words" while the irrelevant group was taught letter names for the same number of irrelevant letters. Muehl found a significant difference in score on the "words" in favor of the irrelevant group and concluded, from observation as well as from the data, that acquisition of letter names interferes with subsequent performance in learning words by a sight approach.

Are these studies contradictory? We recognize that only nine of our twenty-one consonants have names that begin with the sound these letters usually represent. As a result, some of the letter names could interfere with the sound association we try to develop. On the other hand, would Muehl's results have been different if, instead of the sight approach, letter-sound associations had been used in learning the "words?" A possible conclusion from these studies is that knowledge of letter names prior to teaching is a predictor of reading success not because it contributes directly to reading skill and must be taught, but because it reveals a combination of experience and ability in the child—experience or exposure to the printed form and ability to profit from or to retain that experience.

FORMAL INSTRUCTION IN KINDERGARTEN

Studies of formal programs in kindergarten and of the use of workbooks for reading readiness instruction appear to be even more contradictory. I'd like briefly to review six studies and then attempt to describe a pattern.

Blakely and Shadle [2] compared two approaches to reading readiness in kindergarten. With the same teacher, a morning section used *We Read Pictures* while an afternoon section followed a program which "grew out of children's interests." The Metropolitan Readiness Test and a Maturity Check List were used as pre- and post-tests. The test for *We Read Pictures* was also used at the conclusion of the study. These investigators concluded that girls do as well under either approach, but boys gained more following the informal program. The investigators reported teacher bias in favor of the informal approach, but several other points are important here. First, were the two approaches really different in content or only in degree of formality? Second, is the success of a reading readiness program best measured by success in readiness or in reading?

Ploghoft [16] reported a similar study with one teacher. He also used the Metropolitan Readiness Test as a criterion of success and reported no significant difference in the two approaches. The workbook, used for only nine weeks, was not named in this study.

A large scale study of reading readiness in kindergarten is still underway in Denver. Brzeinski [4] randomly assigned 122 kindergarten classes into what eventually became four treatment groups in first grade. Using a preliminary version of the McKee-Harrison *Getting Ready to Read,* he found significant differences in comparing the groups on the Gates Reading Tests. The formal program in kindergarten followed by a first-grade program adjusted for the skills taught was significantly better than any of the other three groups.

Hillerich [7], in a five-year study still underway, reported on several aspects of the *Getting Ready to Read* program in kindergarten. He compared a first-grade group of 363 children who had the formal readiness program in kindergarten with 449 who had not. Both groups had the same reading program in first grade. While the experimental group was significantly lower in aptitude on the Stroud-Hieronymous Primary Reading Profiles, they were significantly higher in reading achievement at the end of the year.

In another aspect of the same study, he evaluated the effectiveness of readiness workbooks in kindergarten, Based on teacher preference, ten sections of kindergarten pupils used the workbook with the program, while twelve sections were taught the same skills program through activities and other materials. At the end of kindergarten, mean scores on the Pre-Reading Inventory of Skills Basic to Beginning Reading indicated a significant difference in favor of the workbook group. At the end of first grade a significant difference in reading achievement between the two groups also favored the workbook group.

In addition to use of the Pre-Reading Inventory at the end of kindergarten, it was also administered at the beginning of first grade in an effort to check the amount of forgetting over the summer. There was a mean loss of 2.6 points on the 58-item test.

A recent study in California was reported very briefly in the *Phi Delta Kappan* [15]. While little information was given, indications are that 1,180 first- and second-grade pupils were compared in three treatment groups. Reports indicated that those who were taught reading in kindergarten were better readers than those who had reading readiness in kindergarten, and the latter were better readers than those who had "typical" kindergarten instruction.

We have seen a good deal of the evidence thus far, including some studies favoring workbooks and some opposing workbooks, some favoring a formal program in kindergarten and some favoring an experience approach. I would like to examine one more study because it seems to contain many of the elements which lead to this confusion of results.

Fry [6] investigated the value of reading-readiness materials in first grade. He randomly assigned eight first grades as "readiness" and "non-readiness" treatment groups. He found no significant difference between the groups on a pretest using the Metropolitan Readiness Test. The readiness group used *Before We Read* and "some" went on to use *We Read Pictures* and *We Read More Pictures* before entering the Scott, Foresman pre-primers. The non-readiness group began immediately in first grade with the Allyn and Bacon pre-primers. In mid-December both groups were tested with a 24-item Instant-Word recognition test. Results indicated that the non-readiness group's score of 12.0 was significantly higher than the readiness group's score of 10.2. A correlation of .56 was reported between the Metropolitan Readiness Test and the Instant-Word test. In conclusion, Fry questioned the value of reading readiness instruction and of reading readiness tests.

SOME CONCLUSIONS

I will depart now from the business of reporting results and enter the subjective area of concluding from these results.

First of all, since there obviously are many kinds of "reading readiness" experiences, what kinds are most helpful for success in reading? Of the representative studies examined, the programs that contribute to success are of two kinds: an experience approach appears better than a workbook approach when the latter involves interpreting pictures and/or gross kinds of discrimination; a program designed to teach the use of context and consonant-letter-sound associations seems better than an experience approach, and the use of a workbook with this kind of program was the most effective. The studies consistently separate in terms of this difference in readiness content. This division suggests to me that the traditional experience approach and the general kind of readiness workbook are teaching relatively the same thing. Neither develops specific skills, but the experience approach has the advantage of spontaneity and enthusiasm.

We might follow this conclusion with a little logic: since reading involves the discrimination of printed letters, the use of context, and the use of sounds of words, some teaching of these elements ought to be part of any prereading program. (I should hasten to add, when I talk about letters and sounds, I do not refer to a synthetic, sounding-out kind of phonics; we know the research in that area.)

A second point from these studies relates to the tests used. If reading readiness is viewed as a collection of skills or abilities, general readiness tests will not measure these skills. While a number of the studies reported did use readiness tests, the low correlation between these tests and reading achievement makes their use questionable. Furthermore, the true test of any reading readiness program lies in its contribution to success in reading. One might even speculate here that general readiness tests and general readiness programs are a circular process wherein each has helped to perpetuate the other.

Third, in any study in education there are always enough uncontrolled variables without introducing more. If readiness programs are being ·compared, the reading program following the readiness treatments ought to be the same for the treatment groups. For example, Fry was comparing groups on the effectiveness of reading readiness as opposed to no reading readiness. Yet, another variable was the use of two different reading programs with these groups.

Fourth, there seems little doubt that kindergarten children can master specific prereading skills. Anderson and Brzeinski found this to be true. Hillerich reported mastery (as measured by the Pre-Reading Inventory) by 70 percent of the kindergarten children the first year and by 83 percent the second year when workbooks were used by all children.

Finally, and by far the most important similarity in these studies, the age at which children *begin* instruction in reading seems to be a significant factor. In Fry's study, for example, the readiness work itself—or the differences in reading programs—is probably not nearly so significant as the factor of practice. At the mid-December testing, all but three of twelve readiness groups were still in pre-primers while ten of twelve non-readiness groups were already in primers.

By the same token, part of the success of the Denver and Glenview studies undoubtedly relates to this earlier start in reading instruction. In the Glenview study, children who had the readiness program in kindergarten began reading sooner in first grade and also read many more library books during the year. Once the initial skill is developed, we must recognize that children also learn to read by reading.

Some guidelines for future research are apparent from these studies. Selection of tests ought to be made in terms of what is being measured: one cannot truly evaluate the success of a readiness program with a general readiness test, nor does a word recognition test adequately measure reading achievement. Care must also be taken to control such obvious variables as the type of reading program which follows a comparison of readiness treatments. The reported differences in the success of various approaches to readiness also points up the importance of specifying the programs being compared in any study; failure to state the program used makes a research study worthless to the reader.

More longitudinal studies such as those in Denver and in Glenview are needed to investigate other programs. Are these two programs successful merely because of a running start—as many synthetic phonic programs seem to be—or will youngsters continue to progress more rapidly in reading as they advance in the grades? Success is not a short-term affair, but perhaps neither is failure. Would some of the other studies which showed no significant differences at the end of kindergarten have produced different results on a long-term basis?

Finally, comparisons of research suggest that many current arguments about early reading instruction would be deflated if we were more careful about two points. First, we cannot debate in terms of workbooks or no workbooks, readiness or no readiness, and so on. There are different kinds of these things and we need to be more specific. Secondly, in most professional articles on the subject of early reading instruction, one can tell by the dates in the bibliography whether the writer is arguing for or against formal instruction in the kindergarten. We will make little progress if we continue to pit the past against the present.

Although the issues are not resolved, we have made great strides in recent years. We can look forward to a battery of reports on early reading instruction soon, as the U. S. Office of Education beginning-reading projects are completed. Reading readiness is becoming less nebulous as we identify certain prereading skills which lead to success in reading. The old taboos are being broken down as we learn more about early reading. Yes, we live in an exciting age; youngsters today and tomorrow will reap the benefits.

Bibliography

1. D. M. Anderson, *A Study to Determine If Children Need a Mental Age of Six Years and Six Months to Learn to Identify Strange Printed Word Forms When They Are Taught to Use Oral Context and the Initial Sound of the Word,* unpublished doctoral dissertation, Colorado State College, 1960.
2. P. W. Blakely, and E. M. Shadle, "A Study of Two Readiness-for-Reading Programs in Kindergarten," *Elementary English,* 38 (November, 1961) 502-505.
3. N. Bremer, "Do Readiness Tests Predict Success in Reading?" *Elementary School Journal,* 59 (January, 1959) 222-224.
4. J. E. Brzeinski, "Beginning Reading in Denver," *Reading Teacher,* 18 (October, 1964) 16-21.
5. T. Eames, "Physical Factors in Reading," *Reading Teacher,* 15 (May, 1962) 432.
6. E. Fry, "Are Reading Readiness Materials Necessary in the First Grade?" Paper presented at American Educational Research Association meeting, Chicago, February, 1965.
7. R. L. Hillerich, "Pre-Reading Skills in Kindergarten: A Second Report," *Elementary School Journal,* 65 (March, 1965) 312-317.
8. R. Karlin, "The Prediction of Reading Success and Reading-Readiness Tests," *Elementary English,* 34 (May, 1957) 320-322.
9. E. B. Linehan, *Early Instruction in Letter Names and Sounds as Related to Success in Beginning Reading,* unpublished doctoral dissertation, Boston University, 1957.
10. W. J. McHugh, "Indices of Success in First Grade Reading," paper presented at American Educational Research Association meeting, Chicago, February, 1962.
11. M. V. Morphett, and C. Washburne, "When Should Children Begin to Read? *Elementary School Journal,* 31 (March, 1931) 496-503.
12. S. Muehl, "The Effects of Letter-Name Knowledge on Learning to Read a Word List in Kindergarten Children," *Journal of Educational Psychology,* 53 (August, 1962) 181-186.
13. A. Nicholson, *Background Abilities Related to Reading Success in First Grade,* unpublished doctoral dissertation, Boston University, 1957.
14. A. V. Olson, Jr., *Growth in Word Perception as It Relates to Success in Beginning Reading,* unpublished doctoral dissertation, Boston University, 1957.

15. Phi Delta Kappa, "Teaching Reading in Kindergarten," *Phi Delta Kappan,* 46 (February, 1965) 286-287.
16. M. H. Ploghoft, "Do Reading Readiness Workbooks Promote Readiness?" *Elementary English,* 36 (October, 1959) 424-426.
17. W. Schramm, J. Lyle, and E. Parker, "Television in the Lives of Our Children." Palo Alto: Stanford University Press, 1961.

10. Roles of Motivation in Reading*

MARION D. JENKINSON

University of Alberta

THE term "motivation" appears to have become an educational slogan, and like most slogans it has a multiplicity of meanings. Psychologists usually begin their discussion of this topic by stating their own definitions didactically, but no two definitions appear to agree. Some state that all behavior is motivated. Others contend that this definition is tautological, since to live means to be active to some degree, and activity is intrinsic in living organisms. All psychologists, however, appear to accept the notion that both internal and external stimuli urge an individual to act, though they would disagree on the precise nature of these stimuli.

There also appears to be acceptance of the idea of both physiological and psychological motives. Since reading is a cognitive act, it is proposed to limit this paper to the psychological aspects. Five aspects have been chosen which appear to be necessary to the teaching of reading at any level. They are cognitive drive, socialization, need for achievement, interest incentive, and the individual nature of reading. An understanding of these five facets appears to be essential if teachers are to set up conditions in which reading achievement seems necessary and desirable to the individual.

COGNITIVE DRIVE

Curiosity, the desire to know and then hopefully to understand, appears to be innate in human beings. It is one of the prime motivations for learning at any age. The thirst for understanding, the need to know and master the world in order to feel safe in it, is everywhere evident in child behavior. At first the baby discovers the meaning of the objects in his immediate environment through sensory exploration. He looks, listens, smells, tastes, and touches everything within his grasp. He lifts and rubs and bangs and shakes things. He is learning.

*From *Reading and the Language Arts* ("Supplementary Educational Monographs," No. 94; Chicago: University of Chicago Press, 1964), 49-57. Copyright © 1964 by the University of Chicago. Reprinted by permission.

Strange and unfamiliar objects become familiar and no longer the source of mystery that they previously were.

The development of language helps the child to organize and systematize his knowledge and to find relationships and meanings. When the child learns to read, the opportunities to satisfy his curiosity become almost limitless, since through reading he can assimilate the discoveries of others and can use their classifications and categorizations. Though individual experiences are unique, the impingement of the environment is similar, and it is possible to communicate impressions.

Words are themselves symbols of ideas, and in reading, which involves abstractions not only of overt actions and concrete objects but of covert reactions, feelings, and images, words must inevitably deal with abstractions. Moreover, as the child proceeds through the grades, the level of abstraction involved in the reading material increases greatly. The inability to deal successfully with abstraction is undoubtedly the reason for an educational phenomenon frequently noted, that while the majority of first-grade entrants are eager to learn, many adolescents appear indifferent and supercilious toward learning.

The egocentric and concrete nature of the young child's thought persists for a long period and is only gradually replaced by his ability to think logically in abstract terms. Moreover, this ability to abstract varies not only between individuals but within individuals. A high-school student may find it easier to deal with the abstractions presented in mathematics than those developed in social studies. The development of this ability tends to be erratic and does not proceed at a regular rate for any individual.

The progressive deterioration in attitude toward learning of some children cannot be disregarded. The studies in the past decade of underachievement show that there are many reasons why even students with good potential appear to be indifferent to school learning. Any attempt by a teacher to arouse cognitive drive cannot be isolated from other equally salient aspects of motivation which affect attitudes and aspirations.

Cognitive drive, then, appears to be essential for mental growth. This characterstic appears as a strong drive in intelligent people but is not so apparent in the less intelligent, at least as far as abstract concepts are concerned. This may, in fact, be a quality which differentiates levels of intelligence. Since research has long indicated the close link between reading ability and intelligence, the variation in the strength of cognitive drive is the reason for differentiating reading instruction for students of different intelligence levels.

SOCIALIZATION AND READING

A child lives not only on the growing edges of his own mind but also on the growing edges of the culture in which he is reared. Children learn directly and indirectly from their environment behaviors which enable them to become acceptable members of their culture. If a five-year-old child is asked what he is going to do when he enters school, he frequently replies, "I am going to learn to read." From the beginning, however, the process of learning to read not only relies upon the cognitive drive but also upon the level of socialization of the child. One of the major developmental tasks is to develop independence and initiate self-reliance.

For many children the experience of learning to read is their first encounter with the problem of self-reliance. Until that time, tasks which proved difficult could be abandoned without undue repercussions or would be completed by a willing adult. But in learning to read, the child has to rely entirely on his own efforts for success. Whatever devices a teacher uses will be of little avail if the learner will not or cannot put forth effort in learning.

Self-reliance is a feature not only of beginning reading but of reading development at all stages. It may be argued that this trait is a function of all learning; yet it appears to be more obvious in reading behavior, perhaps because reading is the tool of much other learning.

It seems essential, then, that at all levels and in every aspect of the reading program students should be encouraged to become independent. The habits and skills included in reading programs are usually arranged in a hierarchy which will permit this. Yet it may be that in some ways self-reliance may be inhibited. For example, the practice of reading in order to answer questions posed either before or after reading by the teacher may prevent the student from learning to formulate his own questions, and this, after all, is essential when he is using reading for his own purposes.

Self-esteem and the esteem of others are recognized as essential to gregarious human beings. Everyone needs security, success, and social acceptance. Failure of any kind tends to threaten both one's self-esteem and the esteem of others. The need for esteem must be based upon a realistic appraisal of achievement and a respect for the judgment of others. Self-esteem is closely related to the need for esteem from others but goes beyond it. Because in our culture reading is considered a developmental task, failure in reading prevents adequate adjustment, since it sabotages both types of esteem.

Many modern children in spite of their apparent sophistication have little self-confidence. Unfortunately, the reading situation frequently provides little satisfaction and little reward for the effort they expend. Reading tasks which are academically oriented and which tend to emphasize intelligence and intellectual pursuits thwart many children. Feelings of inferiority, inadequacy, helplessness, and discouragement arise, which are intensified by the social rejection. Children seldom extend full social acceptance to those they label "stupid" or "dumb." Closely linked with this problem of self- and social acceptance is that of self-actualization or self-realization—the need of an individual to do what he is best fitted for. Thus internal pressures as well as external social pressures nag reading failures. It is therefore almost inevitable that emotional adjustment problems accompany most serious reading problems.

In addition, the principle of incongruity-dissonance, suggested by Hunt, comes into play here.[1] If a child realizes there is a disparity between what he can do or what he is and what he could do or be, a cognitive dissonance occurs. He may then attempt to lessen this disparity and come close to his self-ideal. Thus it may be that his learning to read will not be motivated by rewards and punishments proffered by teachers or parents or by the acceptance of his peers, nor will it necessarily be affected by what the teacher does, but rather it will depend on what the learner feels will advance his own self-esteem or serve his interests.

Most teachers recognize that failure tends to breed more failure, just as success tends to lead to further success. Yet, how can a teacher arouse both the desire to learn and ensure adequate social and cultural adjustment for all students? Perhaps this may be achieved through understanding of achievement and aspiration and the incentives to interest.

ACHIEVEMENT AND ASPIRATION IN READING

One of the dominant themes of the North American culture is success, measured in terms of achievement. This motif is closely allied with the concept of frontier days that achievement depends upon effort. The value of those concepts may be debated philosophically, but teachers have to recognize that the ethos of achievement is fundamental. It is unfortunately true that a sense of achievement is often determined by others in an individual's group rather than by a realistic assessment of the capabilities of an individual.

Though feelings of success accompany the process of achieving a goal, they disappear quickly after attainment. Fortunately, after each success, the level of aspiration is usually raised. It is thus necessary for teachers of reading to make certain that long-term and short-term goals are realistic in terms of the individuals in a group as well as the group as a whole. The goals must seem capable of attainment to each student. Moreover, since learning appears to be facilitated when the learner is provided with a criterion by which to measure the progress he is making, periodic assessments of reading achievement should be undertaken and the results discussed with the learner.

Traditionally, reward and punishment, praise and blame, as well as group recognition and knowledge of progress have been regarded as incentives for learning. But students differ in the effects of various incentives: what is

---

[1] J. McV. Hunt, "Experience and the Development of Motivation: Some Reinterpretations," *Child Development*, XXXI (1960), 489-504.

rewarding to one may not be to another, or at least not to the same extent. While praise may be a more powerful incentive for some individuals, blame may produce more effort from others. A Russian child psychologist has suggested that censure and approval in themselves have little significance for learning; it is rather the understanding by the student of *why* his reply received a particular evaluation that is important.[2] Again we must make use of this in teaching reading.

Diagnostic teaching and diagnostic learning should become the pivot around which most effective learning rotates. As reading is being taught and learned, the teacher should observe and record what the children know and what they do not know. The teacher must scrutinize in a critical and searching manner what the children have learned and of what they are ignorant. Awareness of ignorance is the first essential of learning.

Such teaching demands both knowledge and experience. A teacher must have a thorough knowledge of what is involved in the reading process, of the total reading program, and of the content of the books, manuals, and other aids she uses in the classroom. Experience, in the sense of personal knowledge and practice, must also be part of diagnosis, which should not be based on speculation. All good teaching is diagnostic, and many teachers teach this way without being aware of it.

Conversely teachers need to teach students how to learn diagnostically. Students often can asses what they do not know accurately, but only rarely are they aware of the reasons for their mistakes. Through group discussion and by encouraging students to prove their answers by referring to the text, an understanding of *why* errors have been made can be achieved. Such an understanding is essential since patterns of mistakes in comprehension are perpetuated and reinforced if children remain ignorant of the sources of their errors.

Closely linked with the feelings generated by success are the pleasure and enjoyment derived from awareness of increased competency. Work itself may provide the enjoyment as well as the satisfaction of a job well done. Practice in the various skills of reading is necessary at all grade levels, for the repetition of satisfying acts results in the formation of habits and skills. Though increased competency leads to increased confidence, and the former is necessary for reading success, practice should not be emphasized at the expense of the pleasure.

But practice and repetition of themselves do not cause learning. Mere repetition, unless it is accompanied by insight, does not reinfore concepts. Many children experience difficulty in distinguishing or discriminating between likenesses and differences in symbols and ideas and in realizing meaningful

---

[2]N. A. Menchinskaya, "Some Aspects of the Psychology of Teaching," in *Psychology in the Soviet Union,* Brian Simon ed. (London: Routledge & Kegan Paul, 1957), pp. 190-96.

relationships. It is for this reason that the inductive teaching of word recognition has been recommended for the past two decades by reading specialists. Insights into word meaning and comprehension in general might also be more effectively developed by the teacher through skilful questions geared to the students' abilities and interests.

Philosophers have distinguished between "knowing that" and "knowing how."[3] "Knowing that" refers to the acquisition of facts, whereas "knowing how" refers to the performance of skills. This is a useful distinction for teachers as well as philosophers to make. Learning to read obviously falls within the category of "knowing how." Although agreeing with psychologists that skill depends upon practice, philosophers have distinguished further within this category between capacity and tendency. Capacity is concerned with consistency in performance, whereas tendency relates to the regularity of behavior. We frequently test children to see if they know how to read, but we still more often assume—wrongly—that once a child has acquired the capacity to read he will spend his leisure time reading. We need also to ensure that he acquires the tendency to read. To do this we must provide time within the framework of the reading program at all levels to permit leisure reading and associated library activities.

A feature of habit formation appears to be that once a habit is well formed it no longer needs to draw on other motives for energy. In the beginning, a child may learn to read because he wants to know how, or because his older brothers and sisters read, or in order to please his parents, or because other children are doing it and it is an acceptable social activity. If he becomes skilled in reading, reading becomes a secondary reinforcer and acquires a motivating force of its own. When he has learned to read, reading becomes a form of behavior which he can utilize to satisfy other needs. Reading may be used for enjoyment or for studying and thinking. It may sometimes even control behavior, if he must organize his schedule to include time for reading or must budget his finances to provide money for newspapers, magazines, or books. If the "capacity" becomes the "tendency," then he will turn to reading not only for knowledge but also to escape from the pressures of the actualities of the external world. Reading will have become an interest in itself.

INTEREST INCENTIVE

Two facets of the relationship between interest in reading need to be

[3]Gilbert Ryle, *The Concept of Mind* (New York: Hutchinson's University Library, 1949); Jane Roland, "On the Reduction of 'Knowing That' to 'Knowing How,'" in *Language and Concepts in Education,* ed. Bunnie O. Smith and Robert H. Ennis (Chicago: Rand McNally & Co., 1961), pp. 59-71; R. S. Peters, *The Concept of Motivation* (New York: Humanities Press, 1958).

examined—interest in reading itself and reading interests and tastes. Interest will determine not only whether an individual will learn to read but how well he will read, how much he will read, and in what areas he will read.

Interest has a central position in any type of learning. It has long been a psychological truism that learning is most successful when the learner has a stake in the activity being undertaken; he becomes involved cognitively or emotionally in what he is learning. Central to the function of interest appears to be the fact that it directs and focuses the learner's attention on the task in hand. This mobilization of energy may result in the formation of the important habit of concentration.

The opportunity for experience surrounds the student, but his reaction to the world must of necessity be selective. Consciously or unconsciously, he chooses what he wants to experience, and this choice is largely determined by his interests. But interest and its by-product, concentration, will only be developed if the reading matter challenges him and satisfies those needs which drove him to reading.

Attitudes and interests also appear to be closely related. The definition of interest by Getzels—*"a characteristic disposition organized through experience, which impels an individual to seek out particular objects, activities, understandings, skills, or goals for attention or acquisition"*—places the "characteristic disposition," or attitude, as the first determinant of interest.[4]

Ausubel has noted a paradox with respect to the relationship of attitude and interest to learning that is familiar to most teachers of problem readers.[5] Sometimes the best way of teaching an "unmotivated" student is to ignore his motivational state for the time being and concentrate upon teaching as well as possible. Frequently the satisfaction gained by the student from even small increments of learning develops motivation to learn more.

Meaning also appears to be closely linked with interests. If a book has little meaning for a child or does not gratify his curiosity or stimulate his thinking, he will tend to lose interest. If a book satisfies his desire to know, the very knowledge he has acquired will produce a need to know more. The knowledge has "moved or disturbed" him to the extent that further action is required to quench his cognitive drive. If reading has meaning, both interest and incentive will be generated.

Studies of reading interests, which have been numerous, reveal that sex, intelligence, and social and cultural expectancies all help to determine what a child likes to read, though his choices may shift and develop as he grows older. Preferences in reading show great variations; girls tend to read more than boys,

[4]Jacob W. Getzels, "The Nature of Reading Interests: Psychological Aspects," in *Developing Permanent Interest in Reading* ("Supplementary Educational Monographs," No. 84; Chicago: University of Chicago Press, 1956), p. 7.

[5]David P. Ausubel, *The Psychology of Meaningful Verbal Learning* (New York: Grune & Stratton, 1963), p. 226.

for example, and interest in reading appears to reach a peak in the early years of adolescence and then declines sharply in the high-school years.

Any attempt to develop reading interests must be based on the assumption that an individual can already read at a level appropriate to his mental age. Once the student has acquired some skill in reading, the teacher must be concerned with the student's development through reading. If an individual has an interest in reading, he will develop reading interests which in turn will promote his reading ability, which in turn will affect both his interest and his interests.

Though little can be done directly to teach interests, provision must be made in the curriculum for opportunities to improve interests, and the teacher must have a knowledge of interests in general. When acting as a reading counselor, the teacher must know an individual's specific interests and his reading abilities, as well as whether a recommended book has the content and style that will motivate him to read it. Even bookworms cannot be fed indigestible content.

Closely related to the problem of developing interests is that of developing reading tastes. There should be quality as well as quantity in what a student reads. Therefore, the literature and reading matter presented to students in school must be examined carefully if they are to sustain and maintain an interest in reading. Several studies have suggested that the predilection of students and adults for reading material of inferior quality may be a reflection upon and a rejection of the extensive amounts of uninteresting reading material to which they are exposed in school. Though publishers and teachers are undoubtedly aware of this, it is necessary to evaluate the content of school texts continually, in light of shifts in interests as social and cultural conditions change.

Thus through interest incentives, we should try to develop the habit of reading for all students, for our educational goal should be to ensure that individuals who can read will read.

INDIVIDUAL NATURE OF READING

Though some reading motivation springs from social and cultural needs, reading also presents an opportunity for the fulfilment of another basic human need, that of periodic withdrawal from societal pressures. Human beings need repose.

At one time children and young adults slaked their thirst for adventure, and also satisfied their imagination, largely through the medium of books. In today's world, students are in danger of becoming overstimulated. What is happening in space travel is more fantastic, more stirring to the imagination because we know it is real, than any adventure story ever written. For their craving for adventure, students have only to look at the flickering kaleidoscope of excitement presented in television programs to become satiated.

Reading, however, is a quiet business. It is a solitary activity. In this age of overstimulation we need to offer some points of repose—some time and space to think. Children and adolescents tend to be harried by activities both at home and at school. But this frenetic activity may become self-defeating in terms of the other motives discussed. There appears to be a greater danger of becoming intellectually sterile because of lack of repose rather than lack of effort. The mind is self-generated, but the generator is frequently sparked by the printed word.

In this age of mass communication, reading and reading material remain unique. The appeal of all other mass media is to the mass, to the average. Though reading material may be mass-produced, the audience is not coerced by reading as it is by television. The reader may choose his own time and place. He has an infinite number of ideas and attitudes presented in an unending variety of ways. He can select at will content which interests him or satisfies his current needs, and at all times he is responsible for his own choice. Books are still "the life-blood of the master spirits" and continue to be the prime provider of "food for the mind."

The individual nature of the reading act makes it efficacious in satisfying psychological needs. "Entertain" in its etymological sense means to "hold between," and it is with this connotation that reading can be termed entertainment. To read, the individual has to exert effort; he can never be a passive recipient. Through his exertion, he can obtain true recreation through re-creation.

CONCLUDING STATEMENT

Motivation is the prime determinant of learning and originates in external conditions as well as within the individual. It is probable, moreover, that most human acts are the result of more than one motivation, though learning appears to be most successful when attention and energy are focused upon the achievement of a single feasible goal.

Motives not only are multiple but also tend to fluctuate as goals change with age, as home and school conditions vary, and with the task undertaken. Attitudes and personality traits result in variability in both interpersonal and intrapersonal motives. Curiosity, the basis of cognitive drive, is an important collateral of intelligence and appears closely related to reading success.

Since learning to read is designated a developmental task by our culture, it influences and is influenced by the degree of socialization of the child. The goal of achievement is stimulated by intrinsic, internalized needs as well as by extrinsic cultural forces. Failure to learn to read frequently results in poor adjustment.

Interest, one of the most potent motivating drives, should occupy a central place in the reading program. Both interest in reading and reading interests need to be developed. Though reading occurs in a sociological matrix, silent reading is a solitary occupation and consequently occupies an uncommon position today.

Finally, it should be recognized that motivation is both a point of departure and an end product. The student learns to read to satisfy certain psychological needs, but through repetition of the activity, enjoyment and interest are stimulated. Reading then becomes a habit and often motivates other activities.

III

Organizational Patterns for Instruction

11. Developing Basic Reading Skills Through Effective Class Organization

EMMETT A. BETTS

HOW can basic reading skills be more effectively developed through class organization? This question is an old one, beginning with the introduction of the concept of mass education. The history of education is, in fact, the story of the rise of regimentation and subsequent attempts to break the lock-step created in our classrooms.

Of professional literature on this topic there is no shortage! Administrators have devised plans to *regiment* a whole school system into *differentiating* instruction. Other educationists have experimented with grouping and individualized instruction in the classroom. Today ardent protagonists of some plans cause many teachers to approach the problem with mixed emotions. And someone has defined mixed emotions as the feeling the young man has when he watches his mother-in-law drive over a cliff in his brand new Thunderbird convertible.

Sincere and dedicated teachers of America are raising these questions:

Should language readiness and reading readiness books be used for *all* beginners?

What is to be said for five-year-olds having a need for reading?

How do we know when a child is ready for reading?

How much reading should a child achieve before promotion?

What can we do for children who omit and substitute words, use lip movement, and finger point?

How can we group children to help slow readers? Average readers? Fast readers?

How many groups should I have in my class?

How can we take care of individual differences in reading abilities in a social studies class?

What is the best and most reliable reading test?

*Reprinted from the May, 1958 issue of *Education* (78) pp. 561-576, by permission of the publishers, The Bobbs-Merrill Company, Inc., Indianapolis, Indiana.
*From *Education,* LXXXVIII, No. (May 1958), 561-576. Reprinted by permission of the publishers, The Bobbs-Merrill Company, Inc., Indianapolis, Indiana.

How do you find the reading level of a child with a serious reading difficulty? Of an average child? Of a gifted or talented child?

Where can we get materials of a low reading vocabulary with high interest level?

Is individualized reading the best way to take care of individual differences? Can individualized reading be substituted for group reading of a basic reader? If so, how can I organize the class? How can I be sure each pupil is learning phonic and thinking skills?

These questions and variations of them reflect concern about the improvement of reading instruction through class organization, appropriate materials, and effective methods. It is quite evident that the organization of the class is directed toward the goal of providing for individual differences in the maturity of pupil skills and interests. It is equally clear that the use made of instructional materials depends upon class organization as well as the teacher's concept of the goals of directed reading-study activities. Then, too, procedures and methods are tailored to fit different types of situations. Class organization, therefore, is of necessity discussed in terms of (1) goals of instruction, (2) appropriate materials, and (3) effective methods.

LEVELS OF PROFESSIONAL COMPETENCE

The key to the problem of class organization is the professional competence of the teacher. At the lowest level are those teachers who operate at a zero level of competence—the regimenters who give all pupils in the class the same textbook and evaluate growth in terms of A-B-C-D or S-U report cards. At the top of the list are the "tenth-level" teachers who challenge all pupils in the class by means of teacher-pupil planned class, group, and individual activities. Between these two extremes are the teachers at different levels of competence—ranging from those who group primarily to help the *low achievers* to those who administer efficiently group and individualized reading programs for *all* pupils. How to help teachers at different levels of competence to improve their teaching requires differentiated supervision, in terms of individual levels of professional achievement. [8, Ch. XXV]

REGIMENTATION

In early American elementary schools, instruction was largely individual. Following the Revolutionary War a great experiment in mass education was undertaken. As the American free-school system was taking its first faltering steps, graded schools were introduced followed by graded textbooks. While the avowed purpose of these schools was to equalize educational opportunity, they fell into a lockstep and the narrow, calendar-dictated curriculum was organized on the basis of adult interests and needs. Regimentation, therefore, became—and still is!—a serious peril in education. [8, Ch. IV] [1]

ADMINISTRATIVE PLANS

About one hundred years ago, William T. Harris, Preston W. Search, John Kennedy, and other stalwarts in education began to wage a vigorous, ceaseless campaign against the lock-step in education. Their plans, however, were administrative procedures for a whole school system, including (1) the frequent reclassification of children during the school year, (2) individualized activities preceding group recitations, and (3) coaching laggards by an assistant teacher in the classroom. [8, Ch. IV]

Later—in 1913—Frederic Burk introduced an individualized plan of instruction, which is now better known as the Winnetka Plan. By 1920, the Dalton, or contract, plan of providing for individualized instruction was favorably received.

Following the introduction of the intelligence scale by Binet and Simon in 1905, special classes were organized for the mentally handicapped. Over the years, special classes have been expanded to include the physically handicapped (including the brain injured) and the gifted. More recently, clinical services have been developed to help emotionally disturbed children and the educationally retarded.

With the exception of plans for special classes, administrative plans for providing for individual differences had serious weaknesses. They tended to regiment classroom administration and promotion policies. They perpetuated a one-ladder curriculum for all children to climb. In general, they fell into disfavor because differentiated instruction is, in reality, put into operation by different teachers in different classrooms in different communities.

CLASSROOM PLANS

During the 1920's standardized test and informal inventories for evaluating reading achievement were developed and favorably received. While the standardized tests did not reveal the *wide* range of differences in the classroom, they did call attention to the *fact* that the same educational prescription could not be given to all children in the same grade.

In 1921, Fernald and Keller published their tracing technique for teaching word preception skills to certain types of non-readers. [8, pp. 381-383] Their

---

[1]Numbers in brackets refer to references at the end of the article.

use of this technique heightened interest in both remedial and corrective reading. Equally important, it called attention to the *fact* that the same methods could not be used for all children in the same class.

In the early 1930's, many challenging data were reported on retarded readers and non-readers: (1) Eighty percent had normal or superior intelligence; (2) Eighty percent were boys. At this time, twenty-five to forty percent were failed in the first grade because they had not achieved some adult standard set for them in reading. Furthermore, there was more retardation among the pupils in the upper fifty percent of the class than in the lower fifty percent. [8, Ch. 3]

The above and other events appear to have stimulated experimentation on how to develop basic reading skills through effective classroom organization. Between 1921 and 1938, three basic plans were reported: (1) grouping on the basis of achievement, (2) grouping on the basis of pupil interests, and (3) individualized reading. Most of these plans also provided for the occasional, informal grouping of children who need special help on blending in phonics, outlining, or some other specific skill. All of them emphasized the role of the teacher in providing for individual differences. Variations of these three basic plans have been reported recently in a spate of articles.

GROUPING: READING LEVELS

Since basic textbooks in reading are used in most schools, grouping children by reading levels is a generally accepted practice. In the beginning, this plan was used primarily to do something for low achievers, and slow readers. Gradually, however, the concept of helping *all* the children in the class has emerged.

There have been variations of the plan for grouping by reading levels. First, children in the primary grades and in the intermediate grades have been grouped by reading levels for departmentalized reading instruction one period a day. While this plan may be better than regimentation, it increases the chronological age range within a group, regiments the school schedule, introduces problems of the child's intergrating his school experiences, and tends to divorce reading from the language arts and the rest of the curriculum, and often underemphasizes the role of interests and motivation in learning. In reality, this plan regiments differentiated instruction in the classroom, defeating accepted goals of reading instruction.

In most schools today, however, children are grouped for reading instruction within the classroom. Three or more groups are organized to provide for the slow, average and fast readers. How many groups are organized depends upon the professional competence of the teacher, the range of pupil abilities, and other factors.

Effective grouping by reading levels embraces several important concepts:

(1) independent reading level, (2) teaching, or instructional level, (3) listening, or hearing, comprehension level, (4) interest level, (5) directed reading study activities, (6) etc. It is essential to the success of this plan, for example, that the teacher knows (1) how to estimate reading levels and (2) how to guide the group from their teaching to their independent reading levels in each directed reading activity. While the sequential skill program is built into the teaching plans for *different* basic textbooks, this plan is effective to the degree that the teacher understands these concepts.

Most teachers who group by reading levels also plan for (1) class projects, (2) free, or independent, reading, (3) small informal groups to help individuals with specific skill needs, and (4) grouping in science, social studies, and other learning areas on the basis of interests.

Some teachers have experimented with pupil leaders—monitors or helpers—of groups. Others have depended more on self-aids for groups working on study-book and other independent activities. Teacher-pupil planning is one of the keys to the successful working of other groups and individuals while the teacher is directing the reading activity of a group.

Grouping by reading levels, like all other plans, has it limitations. In the first place, there is a wide range of reading abilities and interests within a reading group. The twelve-year range in a typical sixth grade, for example, poses some very real problems regarding (1) the number of groups and (2) the availability of appropriate materials. Some teachers report they can manage no more than three groups, which, of course, does not meet the needs of all pupils in the class; other teachers can administer several groups. In addition, teachers are always searching for books, magazines, and other materials of interest to different individuals in the class. A basic reader, for example, is written for a given age level, but some retarded readers may have mature interests and a very low level of reading ability.

GROUPING INTERESTS

It is a fairly common practice to organize groups of children to pursue different interests. This is done in preparing a play, a dramatization, or a puppet show, in performing science experiments and preparing reports; in pursuing a unit of the social studies; and so on. This type of group activity extends reading into the heart of the curriculum, promotes the dynamic relationships between pupils, develops the ability to select and evaluate relevant materials and to draw conclusions, and motivates learning. Effective grouping in terms of interests usually requires considerable *class* planning and evaluation as well as *group* and *individual* activities.

When interest groups are organized, materials are made available in terms of the independent reading levels of the pupils. This requirement makes it necessary for the teacher to know the reading level of each pupil and the readability of a generous supply of books and other materials.

Pupil selection of relevant topics of interests and readable materials—of books they want to read and can read—is basic to interest grouping. For self-selection of reading materials to operate effectively, the pupil needs (1) to have a firm grasp on the reality of his own reading abilities and (2) to have clearly in mind the purposes of his contribution to the group undertaking. In other words, the group needs guidance; self-selection does not mean a laissez-faire, or "hands-off," policy is followed by the teacher.

Interest grouping, too, has its limitations:

1. Teachers need to achieve a high level of competence to administer effectively the diverse activities of groups.

2. More time is required for the teacher to plan when and how reading skills are developed and there is the ever-present possibility that skill development is haphazard rather than sequential.

INDIVIDUALIZED READING

The major goals of reading instruction are to help the child (1) mature in his interests, (2) make automatic his use of phonic and other word-learning skills, and (3) develop thinking and related abilities required for *independence in* reading and study activities. The acceptance of these goals—and they appear to be reasonable!—requires systematic planning (1) for the sequential development of interests and skills and (2) for self-selection when the child has achieved to the point where readable materials are available to him.

In the 1930's a number of plans for individualizing reading was reported in grades one to six. These plans made use of "single copies of a large number of books" on the assumption that "learning to read is an individual job." These plans provided for (1) informal estimation of reading levels, (2) records of daily or weekly progress, (3) "simple check ups" with emphasis on audience-type reading, (4) a wide range of references, fiction, and other materials, and (5) individual guidance, combined with group and class instruction.

These early plans were reported as "individualized reading," "individual guidance," "reading for enjoyment," "informal reading," and so on. The authors of these plans were not deluded into thinking that the goals of reading instruction could be achieved by a *plan* or *the* plan of individualized reading. Instead, they were deeply and justifiably concerned that individualized reading should be encouraged by definite planning. At the same time, they organized for class and group instruction to insure interest and skill development. That is, they recognized the values and limitations of individualized reading in an effective reading program.

Individualized reading is receiving increasingly popular approval. In fact, a relatively large amount of literature is now available, although the great bulk of it is an expression of opinion rather than validated facts. Probably no scholars in the psychology of pedagogy of reading, however, would recommend individualized reading as the sole basis for reading instruction. For that matter, very few teachers would go that far.

Self Selection

One of the outstanding merits of individualized reading is the emphasis on self-selection of independent reading. This emphasis can place a high value on pupil and peer motivation when appropriate group and class activities are planned around independent reading. The value is defaulted, however, when the child has to merely read to the teacher for five to fifteen minutes each week.

Recently, a cartoonist showed a frustrated master sergeant drilling recruits and yelling: "How are you going to learn to think for yourselves, if you don't do what I tell you to do!" Unlike the frustrated sergeant, master teachers do give children opportunities "to think for themselves" in setting up their purposes for reading, in selecting appropriate materials, and in evaluating what they read in terms of their purposes. But these master teachers do not confuse self-selection with aimless, unguided, and unfruitful activities of their pupils. They know that self-selection operates effectively when they give competent guidance.

Individual Development

Another significant merit of individualized reading is the opportunity, for the child to proceed at his own pace. This opportunity, too, is of high value when he is maturing in interests and acquiring the skills needed to meet those interests. But this opportunity is denied pupils when they fail to get systematic guidance in the myriad of interests and skills they need for growth in reading. The extent to which individualized reading is developmental depends upon how expert the teacher is in providing for specific learnings, either through the use of a well-planned basic reader or some other equally well-planned sequence.

Individual Attention

A third merit of individualized reading is the attention given to each child in the class. Of course, the value here depends upon the professional competence of the teacher. However, there are very real limits to the amount of time a teacher has for twenty-five to forty pupils in a class. There is also a limit to the amount of time a teacher can give to reading instruction. There is always a need to help individuals in all curriculum areas, but can reading instruction be effective when the child receives only seven to fifteen minutes of help a week?

A highly individualized plan of reading instruction requires special administrative skills on the part of the teacher. If administering three or more groups in reading has taxed her skills, she may find the record keeping and other administrative details of a highly individualzed plan overwhelming. Since small group activities are necessary to most individualized plans, this type of teacher might well perfect her skills in handling small groups before organizing her class into one-member "groups."

Leaders in education long ago emphasized the fact that *learning is an individual matter.* They also realized that teaching is concerned with a social *group* ranging in size from the total class to one member of the group. The goal of differentiated instruction, therefore, is to help each individual realize his potential, without penalizing any other pupil in the group.

Learner Needs

A fourth merit of individualized reading is the attention given to the specific needs of each pupil. In most plans these needs in word learning, thinking, and interests are idenfified in individual conferences and small group activities. Help is given to the child, who is motivated by an awareness of his needs, in both individual conferences and small groups of pupils having common needs. For this purpose, basic readers and study books, special workbooks, and informal activities are used.

How effectively individual needs are identified and provided for depends upon the professional insight of the teacher, the adequacy and systematic use of informal inventories, the sequential introduction of new learnings in the instructional material, and many other factors. Since *individualized* instruction is the goal of all plans for classroom organization, this problem of meeting individual needs is not peculair to any one plan.

Library Facilities

A fifth merit of individualized reading is the attention given to the need for a wide range of reference books, fiction, magazines, and newspapers. This wide range covers both interests and reading abilities. Since children, like adults, can read only that material which is available to them, the teacher uses all of her initiative in keeping a flow of books through the classroom from the school library, community library, homes and other sources.

Here again, library facilities are essential for individualized reading regardless of which basic plan of organization is used. Basic readers used in grouping by reading levels, for example, serve as spring boards to worthwhile independent reading.

Individual and Group Activities.

Fortunately, there are few teachers willing to depend upon individualized instruction alone. All master teachers provide for individualized reading. But they also use class activities to plan and evaluate projects. They plan for grouping by reading levels and interest areas. They know that having a child read to them only every fourth or fifth day would not make sense to an educational phychologist, a competent business man, or a parent.

OPINIONS AND FACTS

For developing basic skills in reading, class organization goes hand in hand with the use of effective methods and of appropriate materials. One of the major problems in class management is the study of and provision for individual needs in motivation, achievement, interests, word-learning skills, and thinking abilities. How this problem is handled depends upon (1) teacher competence, (2) size and composition of the class, (3) library and textbook facilities, and (4) other factors.

In recent publications on the teaching of reading a wide variety of *opinions* are expressed. There are those who sincerely believe, for example, that individualized reading, or grouping by reading levels, or grouping by interest areas or some other single plan of differentiating instruction is the *one* way for *all* teachers to teach *all* pupils in *all* classrooms. Then, too, there are those who believe that a two-book plan for the intermediate grades is an adequate solution. Though the road of progress in reading is strewn with ill-conceived, one-shot plans of improving reading instruction through classroom organization, each generation seems to breed its own variety of cultism.

Experimentation by classroom teachers needs to be encouraged, but generalizations cannot be based on one teacher's experience in one classroom in one school system. It is a well-known fact that teachers vary widely in their levels of professional competence. For this reason, supervision is differentiated to help individual teachers mature in their professional competence. For this reason, too, plans evolved in classrooms must be tested and evaluated over a period of years by scholars in the psychology and pedagogy of reading with the help of experts in statistics and experimental design.

DIFFERENCES

In a typical fourth-grade class, the children range in reading abilities from those who can barely struggle along in a pre-primer to those who enjoy the *Reader's Digest,* encyclopedias, and other materials which would challenge the best efforts of the average eighth or ninth-grader. There are those, too, with anxieties and other emotional problems which interfere with their learning. Then occasionally there is a child with a subtle brain injury which blocks his attempts at learning. Overlaying these differences are wide variations in maturity of interests, word-learning skills, and thinking abilities.

Since education increases differences, this range of achievement in attitudes, skills, and abilities is increased as the children progress (or regress!) through the fifth and sixth grades. In a typical sixth-grade, for example, there are the Johnnies who have never read a book on their own—even a pre-primer—to those who read avidly high school and even college books on meteorology, satellites, radio communication, and other areas of interest.

Yes, educating all the children of all the people has been attempted in few places on this planet. But we are committed to this task because we are firm in our belief that all citizens are born free and equal—that we must, therefore, provide equal learning opportunities for all individuals. It is to this end that a century of progress has been made. The history of this century is the story of many leaders' attempts to break the lock-step in education created by the post Revolutionary war plan for mass education.

READING LEVELS

Basic to any plan for differentiating instruction is the achievement of each individual in the class. In a fifth-grade class, for example, Johnny is unable to remember *here, the, my,* and other common words in a pre-primer. For him, self-selection of reading materials exists only in fantasy rather than in reality; he needs special help. If he has normal or superior intelligence, he may require the help of a clinical psychologist who understands language disturbances.

In the same fifth-grade class, Tommy can read a second reader on his own—without lip movement, finger pointing, substituting words, and other signs of difficulty. In a third reader, Tommy shows no signs of difficulty but he occasionally comes to a word he cannot identify or an idea he doesn't understand. He needs help from his teacher who knows how to teach him the necessary skills so that the next time he recognizes the word and can apply that skill to similar words. He also needs help from his teacher who knows how to identify and to help him with specific comprehension needs. His independent reading level, therefore, is second-reader, his teaching, or instructional, level, is third-reader.

But Tommy is not interested in reading second readers written for seven-year-olds. His fairly high intelligence, his curiosity about science and history, and his opportunities to listen in on reports and conversations have helped him to mature in his interests. He, therefore, needs books with a high interest level but a low readability level.

Mary, another fifth-grader, can read a fourth reader on her own an a fifth reader under teacher supervision. When seeking books and magazines for independent reading, she selects those at or below fourth-reader level. She has an adequate concept of her own skills in a reading situation.

Mary, along with eleven other pupils, is having an enjoyable experience in a fifth-reader story book and the accompanying study book. In each selection of the story book, Mary finds the need for new work-learning and thinking skills. At the beginning of a directed reading-study activity, the selection is at her teaching, or instructional level. After the teacher has (1) prepared the group for reading the selection, (2) guided the silent reading, and (3) given specific help on word perception and comprehension, Mary can read the selection—silently or orally— on her own. Also, on her own, she can complete the study book activities which improves her use of reading skills. In each directed reading-study activity, therefore, Mary and the rest of her group is taken from their independent reading level.

GOALS OF INSTRUCTION

Over the years a substantial amount of respectable research has been accumulated on three major goals of reading instruction:

1. The development of worthwhile *interests* which take the child to reading and which are satisfied through his increasingly effective reading-study skills. [13]

2. The acquisition of *phonic* and other word learning skills to the point where they are used automatically. [21]

3. The maturing of *thinking* and related comprehension abilities needed to solve problems and to get genuine satisfaction from reading-study activities. [16]

A comprehensive plan for the teaching of basic skills through class organization is effective to the degree that it embraces the above three goals. When any one of these goals is underemphasized or overemphasized, pupil progress is impeded.

Highly competent teachers know the interests of their pupils, understand how interests change and develop, and are alert to the need for helping children mature in them. For these reasons, they systematically use informal inventories of interest to estimate levels of maturity and to evaluate growth. [13] They confirm these estimates by systematic observation of pupil interests in different types of situations and by encouraging the self-selection of books and other materiasl for independent reading and study.

Master teachers, too, are keenly aware of the phonic and other word-learning skills of the different pupils in their classes. They systematically use informal inventories of phonic skills, for example, to estimate achievement and specific need. [14] They know that when a word, or telling, method is used, their pupils resort to saying the letters of words and to using other inappropriate skills.

To offer positive guidance, a master teacher takes these necessary steps:

1. Readability of Material

Provides appropriate materials which each child can read without signs of difficulty. [17, 18]

2. Need

Gives the child—in an individual or group situation—help on word learning when he has a need for it.

The kind of help given depends upon (1) the part of the word causing the difficulty, (2) previously learned skills, and (3) the need for learning a new skill.

3. Meaning

Insures pupil understanding of the use of the word in its context.

4. Listening

Helps the child to hear the undistorted sounds of letters and syllables in the word.

This help on listening gives the child a learning set to see the letter and syllable phonograms in the word.

5. Seeing Phonograms

Guides the pupil in relating the sounds heard in the spoken word to the phonograms representing those sounds in the written word.

This guidance requires the systematic teaching of phonic skills, beginning with the first words the child learns. It includes the sequential development of skills to deal with initial consonants, final consonants, and vowels of one-syllable words. It also includes the application of these skills to the syllables of words—without setting up for the child an artificial dichotomy between phonics and syllabication. It includes, too, the extension of phonic skills to the interpretation of pronunciation symbols in the dictionary. For the best interests of the learner there need be no trichotomy of phonics, syllabication, and pronunciation symbols; instead, his learning is facilitated by well-planned sequences of learning.

6. Blending

Takes the pupils a step further by blending the parts of two whole words to make a new one.

This includes, for example, blending the *b* of *bill* and the *l* of *left* to make the *bl* of *black*. It also includes blending the first part of one word with the rhyming part of another; for example, the blending of the *sk* of *sky* with the *ate* of *late* to make *skate*.

7. Checking Meaning

Helping the child to form the habit of making sure the word he identified by means of phonic skills fits the context in which it is used.

8. Making Rules

Helping the pupils to make generalizations about consonants, vowels, and syllables.

9. Applying Skills

Giving the pupil opportunity to apply his newly learned phonic skills to unknown words.

In addition to being keenly aware of each child's interests and phonic needs, master teachers are very much concerned with teaching children how to think. With pupil interest to motivate the reading and with the pupil's automatic use of phonic skills, the teacher is prepared to deal with the major concern of reading instruction: *thinking*.

Here again the teacher is as much concerned with specifics of comprehension as she is with specific interests and specific word-learning skills. These needs in learning how to think embrace six major concerns:

1. Purposes—felt needs—which motivate the child to read
2. Personal experiences out of which the child makes his concepts
3. Attitudes which influence the child's (1) inclination to read on a topic, (2) accuracy of interpretation, (3) recall of ideas, and (4) tendency to rationalize
4. Use of language to deal effectively with ideas (language ability includes interpretation of definite and indefinite terms, classifying, indexing, awareness of shifts of meaning, use of context clues, differentiating between language used to report facts and to influence attitudes, etc.)
5. Ability to discriminate between fact and opinion, to evaluate relevance of ideas, and to draw conclusions
6. Versatility in adjusting rate and depth of comprehension to purpose

These three goals of reading instruction—interests, word-learning skills, and thinking abilities—are inseparable essentials. These goals are ever kept clearly in mind by master teachers and conscientious authors of textbooks. To understand these goals requires a reasonable degree of scholarship in phonetics, phonics, perception, semantics, language structure, psychology of thinking, child development, differential psychology, and children's literature as well as in the pedagogy of reading. How a typical class of children with a possible twelve-year range of reading abilities is to be organized to achieve these goals has been a formidable challenge to thinking educators for more than a century.

SUMMARY

To find one plan of class organization to be executed effectively by all teachers with all children is as difficult as finding a word to rhyme with *orange*. The purpose of class organization is to provide *equal learning opportunities for all children* in the classroom-to promote better learning conditions in all curriculum areas. This *is* a worthy goal of reading instruction, but the fact remains that a few children need special services; for example the mentally limited, the brain injured, the emotionally disabled. [19]

Challenging Differences

In the first place, there is no such thing as a homogeneous group. When children are grouped by reading levels, for example, the best readers need to meet at least one new idea or word in about eighty running words in order to be challenged by new learnings. The less able children in the group may meet as many as one new word in twenty-five or thirty without showing signs of difficulty. Furthermore, differences in mental ability, verbal aptitudes, motivation, experience, etc. make occasional regrouping necessary.

Nor is there such a thing as a homogeneous group so far as interests are concerned. While master teachers can help a class or a group to develop a community of interests, nevertheless, individuals vary in the strength of their interests in a given topic.

Moreover, grouping in reading does not dictate the membership in an arithmetic or science group. Differences in the educational profile of each individual explain this fact. A given pupil, for example, may be a poor speller but a whiz in arithmetic and even in reading. This fact is both a blessing and a challenging problem in education. It is a blessing for a child to excel in art or arithmetic computation when he is a poor reader. It is an interesting challenge in a classroom to deal with the *different* needs of children and to depend upon the special contributions of different children.

Emotional Climate

Some teachers complain that poor readers have weak defenses for their egos because they stand out in contrast to their age mates. They may go to absurd extremes to conceal the reading levels of books. This is done on the false belief that children cannot and do not evaluate themselves and others.

Yet, some of these same teachers will appoint group leaders to *tell* other children words they want to know. This practice is bad for at least two reasons: (1) a word, or telling-method is notoriously ineffective for developing phonic and other word-learning skills; (2) many poor readers are not aware of their perceptual inaccuracies. Furthermore, very bad human relationships can be developed unless both leader and pupils are prepared, in attitudes, for the undertaking.

How a child feels about his low status in reading does not depend upon the class organization but upon the emotional climate in the classroom. Awareness of real achievement, the attitude of the teacher toward the pupils, and the attitude of the pupils toward each other—all these attitudes contribute to the child's self-concept. These attitudes can be developed in classroom situations where instruction is differentiated by some practical means. Of course, frustration is compounded in a regimented classroom.

High Achievers

Most teachers know that a child who either can't read or is a very poor reader is like a soldier without a gun or a baseball player without a bat. Probably for this reason the history of differentiated instruction highlights concern with mentally, physically, emotionally, and educationally handicapped children. For the same reason, low achievers tend to have higher achievement quotients than high achievers. One of the chief dangers in group or in completely individualized instruction is the tendency of the teacher to give the lion's share of her time to the low achievers.

A lay person can identify a non-reader or crippled reader, especially one who cannot remember words. But it takes a highly competent teacher to identify the child who has not learned to organize information, to draw conclusions from related facts, and do other types of thinking.

Many teachers, for example, are lulled into neglecting high achievers by the cliche: "If children enjoy books, the more they read and the better they read." While there may be a grain of truth in this platitude, there is real evidence that high achievers need as much, or more, guidance in reading as the low achievers. Nevertheless, these high achievers too often are turned loose in their classrooms or the library, without benefit of competent guidance.

Differentiated Instruction

Discussions of interests, phonics, thinking, group dynamics, and other crucial elements in education are so much prattle when the child is frustrated in a regimented classroom. Therefore, the purpose of any plan for differentiating instruction is to reach the individual in the group, where he is in attitudes and skills.

How to provide for individual differences is a problem of mutual concern to children, parents, and teachers. In no successful plan, for example, can the active participation of parents be side-stepped. The dreams of educators must face the test of reality because, in a democracy, the citizens will have the kinds of schools they want.

When the last word is written on the topic, it will be seen that differentiated instruction reflects an attitude toward the individual. In our democracy, individuals have equal opportunities to participate in government. It has long been the responsibility of teachers—dedicated to the concept of democracy—to provide equal learning opportunities for all children in the classroom.

Reference

1. *Adapting the Schools to Individual Differences.* Twenty-Fourth Yearbook of the National Society for the Study of Education, Part II. Bloomington, Illinois: Public School Publishing Company, 1925.
2. Mary C. Austin, "Organizing the Class for Effective Development of Basic Skills," *Reading in Action,* International Reading Association Conference Proceedings, Vol. II. New York: Scholastic Magazines, 1957. 89-90.
3. Kenneth D. Benne, and Bozidar Mutyan, *Human Relations in Curriculum Change.* New York: Dryden Press, 1951.
4. Emmett A. Betts, "Are Retarded Readers Dumb?" Reprinted from *Education* LXXVI, No. 9 (May 1956), 568-575. Haverford, Penna.: The Betts Reading Clinic.
5. _____. "Challenge versus Frustration in Basic Reading." Reprinted from *The Reading Teacher,* VIII. No. 1 (October 1954), 8-13. Haverford, Penna.: The Betts Reading Clinic.
6. _____. "Differentiated Instruction in Reading Activities," *American School Board Journal,* C, Nos. 5 and 6 (May and June 1940), 29-30 and 108; 27-29.
7. _____. "Equal Learning Opportunities," *New York State Education,* Vol. XXIV, No. 3 (December 1936), 212-215; 243-247.
8. _____. *Foundations of Reading Instruction With Emphasis on Differentiated Guidance.* New York: American Book Company, Revised 1957.
9. _____. *Handbook on Corrective Reading.* Chicago: Wheeler Publishing Company. Revised 1956.
10. _____. "How A Retarded Reader Feels." Reprinted from *Elementary English,* XXXIV, No. 1 (January 1957), 13-18. Haverford, Penna.: The Betts Reading Clinic.
11. _____. *Informal Inventories.* (Construction, procedures, criteria for Informal Reading, Word Recognition, and Spelling Inventories). Haverford, Penna: The Betts Reading Clinic, 1957.
12. _____. *Informal Inventory of Interests.* Haverford, Penna.: The Betts Reading Clinic, 1957.
13. _____. *Informal Inventory of Phonic Skills.* Haverford Penna.: The Betts Reading Clinic, 1958.
14. _____. "Reading and the Fourth R." Reprinted from *Elementary English,* XXXV, No. 1 (January 1958), 18-25. Haverford, Penna.: The Betts Reading Clinic.
15. _____. "Reading as a Thinking Process." Reprinted from *The National Elementary Principal,* Thirty-Fourth Yearbook, XXXV, No. 1 (September 1955), 88-96. Haverford, Penna.: The Betts Reading Clinic.
16. _____. "Signs of Reading Difficulties." Reprinted from *Education,* LXXVII, No. 9 (May 1957), 566-571. Haverford, Penna.: The Betts Reading Clinic.

17. _____ . "Success Levels for Retarded Readers." Reprinted from *Education* LXXVII, No. 7 (March 1957), 399-403. Harverford, Penna.: The Betts Reading Clinic.
18. _____ . "Using Clinical Services in the Remedial Program." Reprinted from *Education* XXVIII, No. 1 (September 1957), 27-32. Haverford, Penna.: The Betts Reading Clinic.
19. _____ . "What About Individual Differences in Reading?" *The ABC Language Arts Bulletin,* VII, No. 1. New York: American Book Company, 1957.
20. _____ . "What About Phonics?" Reprinted from *Education,* LXXV, No. 9 (May 1955), 547-559. Haverford, Penna.: The Betts Reading Clinic.
21. _____ et al. "Challenging the Learner," *Elementary English Review,* XV, No. 4 (April 1938), 149-158.
22. Jill Bonney, and Levin B. Hanigan, "Individualized Teaching of Reading," *The National Elementary Principal,* Thirty-Fourth Year Book, XXXV, No. 1 (September 1955), 76-82.
23. Doyle M. Bortner, "Pupil Motivation and Its Relationship to the Activity and Social Drives," *Progressive Education,* XXXI, No. 1 (October 1953), 5-11.
24. Alvin Broido, "Grouping by Classes for Reading," *The National Elementary Principal,* Thirty-Fourth Year Book, XXXV, No. 1 (September 1955), 67-69.
25. M. E. Broom, "Fostering Individual Progress in Reading," *El Paso Schools Standard,* XVII, No. 1 (September 1939), 10-16.
26. Harry L. Buckalew, and Mary Belle Maxwell, " Reading Levels Promote Flexibility'" *The National Elementary Principal,* Thirty-Fourth Year Book, XXXV, No. 1 (September 1955), 63-66.
27. Frederic Burk, "Breaking the Lock Step," *Journal of the National Education Association,* Vol. XIII, (April 1924), 123-124.
28. Alvina T. Burrows, "Caste System or Democracy in Teaching Reading?" *Elementary English,* XXVII, No. 3 (March 1950) 145-148, 157.
29. Alvina T. Burrows, "Individualizing the Teaching of Reading," Chapter X in *Teaching Children in the Middle Grades.* New York: D. C. Heath and Company, 1952.
30. James K. Canfield, "Flexibility in Grouping for Reading," *The Reading Teacher,* XI, No. 2 (December 1957), 91-94.
31. Esther Skonnord Carlson, and Joyce Northrup, "An Experiment in Grouping Pupils for Instruction in Reading," *The National Elementary Principal,* Thirty-Fourth Year Book, XXXV, No. 1 (September 1955), 53-57.
32. Louise G. Carson, "Moving Toward Individualization," *Elementary English* XXXIV, No. 6 (October 1957), 362-366.
33. Jeanne Chall, "Ask Him To Try On the Book for Fit," *The Reading Teacher,* VII, No. 2 (December 1953), 83-88.
34. Stuart A. Courtis, and Wendell Vreeland, *Individualization of Instruction,* Part I, "The Story of Individualization." Part II, "How to Individualize," Ann Arbor: Brumfield & Brumfield, 1931.
35. Ruth Cunningham, et al. *Understanding Group Behavior of Boys and Girls,* New York: Bureau of Publications, Teachers College, Columbia University, 1951.
36. Mary Ann Daniel, "You Can Individualize Your Reading Program Too," *Elementary English,* XXXIII, No. 7 (November 1956), 444-446.
37. Dan T. Dawson, "Some Issues in Grouping for Reading," *The National Elementary Principal,* Thirty-Fourth Year Book, XXXV, No. 1 (September 1955), 48-52.
38. Ray Dean, "A Plan for Individual Reading in the Intermediate Grades," *National Elementary Principal,* XVII, No. 7 (July 1938), 557-563.
39. Vaughn R. DeLong, "Primary Promotion by Reading Levels," *Elementary School Journal,* XXXVIII, No. 9 (May 1938), 663-671.
40. Edward W. Dolch, "Groups in Reading," Chapter XVII in *Methods in Reading.* Champaign: The Garrard Press, 1955.
41. Donald Durrell, "Grouping for Instruction," Chapter VI in *Improving Reading Instruction.* New York: World Book Company, 1956.
42. Dean N. Evans, "An Individualized Reading Program for the Elementary School," *The Elementary School Journal,* LIV, No. 3 (November 1953), 157-162.
43. Grace M. Fernald, *Remedial Techniques in Basic School Subjects.* New York: McGraw-Hill Book Company, Inc. 1943.

44. Helen A. Field, "Extensive Individual Reading Versus Class Reading," *Contributions to Education,* No. 394. New York: Teachers College, Columbia University, 1930.

45. Grace Garrettson, Beatrice Termeer, Irene Whitcomb, "Through Self-Selection – Progress Unlimited," *Reading, Bulletin,* No. 98, 23-27. Washington, D.C.: Association for Childhood Education International, November 1956.

46. William S. Gray, "Role of Group and Individualized Teaching in a Sound Reading Program," *The Reading Teacher,* XI, No. 2 (December 1957), 99-104.

47. *The Grouping of Pupils.* Thirty-Fifth Yearbook of the National Society for the Study of Education, Part 1. Bloomington, Illinois: Public School Publishing Company, 1936.

48. C. C. Grover, and Hazel Johnson, "A Plan for Group Instruction in Reading," *Fifth Yearbook of the California Elementary School Principals' Association,* V (May 1938), 92-98.

49. Tess Gurney, "My Individualized Reading Program," *Childhood Education,* XXXII, No. 7 (March 1956), 334-336.

50. Albert J. Harris, "Meeting Individual Needs in Reading," Chapter V in *How to Increase Reading Ability.* New York: Longmans, Green and Company, 1956.

51. Melva Harris, "Beginning Reading Without Readers," *Childhood Education,* XXVI, No. 4 (December 1949), 164-167.

52. Helen Hay Heyl, "Grouping Within the Classroom," *The National Elementary Principal,* Thirtv-Fourth Year Book, XXXV, No. 1 (September 1955), 83-86.

53. Kathleen B. Hester, "Grouping by Invitation," *The Reading Teacher,* XI, No. 2, (December 1957), 105-108.

54. Gertrude Hildreth, "Individualizing Reading Instruction," *Teachers College Record,* XLII, No. 2 (November 1940), 123-137.

55. Thomas L. Hopkins, "The Relations of the Co-operative Group Plan to the Curriculum," *Educational Method,* X (May 1931), 468-471.

56. Christine Hugerth, "It's Different for Each One," *Reading Teacher,* VII, No. 1 (October 1953), 5-10.

57. Leland B. Jacobs, "Let's Consider Independent Reading," *Curriculum Letter,* XI, (December 1954). Columbus, Ohio: Wesleyan University Press.

58. _____. "Reading on Their Own Means Reading at Their Growing Edges," *The Reading Teacher,* VI, No. 4 (March 1953), 27-32.

59. Elizabeth M. Jenkins, "Developing Independent Readers in the First Grade," *Elementary English,* XXVII, No. 3 (March 1950), 149-154, 170.

60. Marian Jenkins, (Compiler). "Here's to Success in Reading–Self-Selection Helps," *Childhood Education,* XXXII, No. 3 (November 1955), 124-131.

61. Marian Jenkins, "Self-Selection in Reading," *The Reading Teacher,* XI, No. 2 (December 1957), 84-90.

62. Eleanor M. Johnson, "Individualized Reading," *Curriculum Letter No. 35.* Middletown, Conn.: Department of School Services and Publications, Wesleyan University.

63. Mabel L. Johnson, "Individualized Reading Experience," *New York State Education,* XXXVIII (June 1951), 654-655.

64. William H. Johnson, "How a Large School System Meets the Problem of Individual Differences," *Educational Trends,* IX, No. 1 (January 1941), 24-32.

65. Harold Kaar, "An Experiment With an Individualized Method of Teaching Reading," *The Reading Teacher,* VII, No. 3 (February 1954), 174-177.

66. Robert Karlin, "Some Reactions to Individualized Reading," *The Reading Teacher,* XI, No. 2 (December 1957), 95-98.

67. John Kennedy, *The Batavia System of Individual Instruction.* Syracuse: C. W. Bardeen Company, 1914.

68. _____. "The Need of Individual Instruction," *National Education Association Addresses and Proceedings,* 1901, 295-303.

69. Marjorie Kingsley, "An Experiment in Individualized Reading," *Elementary English,* XXXV, No. 2 (February 1958), 113-118.

70. Margaret Kirby, "Tete-A-Tete Lessons Develop Independent Readers," *Elementary English,* XXXIV, No. 5 (May 1957), 302-303.

71. William C. Kvaraceus, and Marion E. Wiles, "An Experiment in Grouping for Effective Learning," *Elementary School Journal,* XXXIX, No. 4 (December 1938), 264-268.
72. Lois G. Lance, "Meeting Needs of Individuals," *The National Elementary Principal,* Thirty-Fourth Year Book, XXXV, No. 1 (September 1955), 70-73.
73. Nancy Larrick, "You Need Good Libraries to Teach Reading Today," *Junior Libraries,* I, No. 1 (September 1954), 4-6.
74. May Lazar, "Individualized Reading," *Education,* LXXXVIII, No. 5 (January 1958), 281-288.
75. _____. "Individualized Reading–A Dynamic Approach," *The Reading Teacher,* XI, No. 2 (December 1957), 75-83.
76. _____. et al. *Individualized Reading and the Reading Skills.* New York: Board of Education of the City of New York, Bureau of Educational Research, January 1958.
77. Murray J. Lee, "Individualized Instruction," *Education,* LXXIV, No. 5 (January 1954), 279-283.
78. "Let the Pupil Choose His Book," *Random Notes on Children's Reading.* New York: Random House Books for Boys and Girls. November 1954.
79. Josephine H. Maclatchy, and Ethel B. Beavers, "Reading for Enjoyment in the Sixth Grade," *Educational Research Bulletin,* XIV, No. 2 (February 13, 1935), 38-44.
80. Frances Maib, "Individualizing Reading," *Elementary English,* XXIX, No. 2 (February 1952), 84-89.
81. Bessie Maxey, "An Individualized Reading Program," *Instructor,* LXII, (January 1953), 47, 78.
82. Alice Miel, et al. *Cooperative Procedures in Learning.* New York: Bureau of Publications, Teachers College, Columbia University, 1952.
83. W. A. Morris, "Reducing Reading Problems Thru Organization," *The National Elementary Principal,* Thirty-Fourth Year Book, XXXV, No. 1 (September 1955), 58-62.
84. Clark E. Moustakas, *The Self-Exploration in Personal Growth.* New York: Harper Brothers, 1956.
85. Olive S. Niles, and Margaret J. Early, "Adjusting to Individual Differences in English," *Journal of Education,* CXXXVIII, No. 2 (December 1955).
86. Willard C. Olson, "Seeking, Self-Selection, and Pacing in the Use of Books by Children," *The Packet,* VII, No. 1 (Spring 1952), 3-10.
87. _____. "Self-Selection as a Principle of Curriculum and Method," *School of Education Bulletin,* XVI, No. 4 (January 1945), 52-55.
88. _____ and Sarita Davis. "The Adaptation of Instruction in Reading to the Growth of Children," *Educational Method,* XX (November 1940), 71-79.
89. Delores Cooper Palmer, *To Determine the Reaction of a Fourth Grade to a Program of Self-Selection of Reading Materials.* Master's thesis. Salt Lake City: University of Utah, 1953.
90. Helen Parkhurst, *Education on the Dalton Plan.* New York: E. P. Dutton and Company, 1922.
91. Phyllis Parkin, "An Individual Program of Reading," *Educational Leadership,"* XIV, No. 1 (October 1956), 34-38.
92. Mary C. Petty, *Intra-class Grouping in the Elementary School,* Austin: University of Texas Press, 1953.
93. Elmer F. Pflieger, "A Study of Reading Grade Levels," *Journal of Educational Research,* XLII, No. 7 (March 1949), 541-546.
94. *Reading for Today's Children.* Thirty-Fourth Yearbook, National Elementary Principal, XXXV, No. 1. Washington, D.C.: Bulletin of the Department of Elementary School Principals, National Education Association, September 1955.
95. Ruth Rowe, and Esther Dornhoefer, "Individualized Reading," *Childhood Education,* XXXIV, No. 3 (November 1957), 118-122.
96. Oswald Schlockow, "Individual versus Class Instruction," *New York Teachers' Monographs,* III (December 1900), 1-6.
97. Preston W. Search, "The Pueblo Plan of Individual Teaching," *Educational Review,* VIII (June 1894), 84-85.

98. James M. Shields, "Teaching Reading through Ability Grouping," *Journal of Educational Method,* VII (September-October 1927), 7-10.
99. Faith Smitter, "The Pros and Cons of Grouping," *The Reading Teacher,* VII, No. 2 (December 1953) 74-78.
100. Texie Smyth, "Making the Social Studies an Adventure in Individualized Teaching," *Social Studies,* XXXII, No. 6 (October 1941), 344-348.
101. W. W. Theisen, "Provisions for Individual Differences in the Teaching of Reading," *Journal of Educational Research,* II, No. 2 (September 1920), 560-571.
102. Mildred E. Thompson, "Why Not Try Self-Selection?" *Elementary English,* XXXIII, No. 8 (December 1956), 486-490.
103. T. L. Torgerson, *A Program of Differentiation in the Elementary Schools Based Upon Individual Differences.* Bulletin No. 3. West Allis, Wisconsin: Department of Educational Measurement, Public Schools, 1924.
104. A. H. Turney, "The Status of Ability Grouping," *Educational Administration and Supervision,* XVII (January 1931),21-42.
105. _____ and Hyde, M. F. "What Teachers Think of Ability Grouping," *Education,* LII (September 1931), 39-42.
106. Jeanette Veatch, "Children's Interests and Individual Reading," *The Reading Teacher,* X, No. 3 (February 1957), 160-165.
107. _____ . "Individualized Reading—For Success in the Classroom," *The Educational Trend.* Washington, D. C.: Arthur C. Croft Publications, 1954.
108. Carleton W. Washburne, *Adjusting the School to the Child.* Yonkers-on-Hudson, New York: World Book Company, 1932.
109. _____ . "Breaking the Lock Step in Our Schools," *School and Society,* VIII (October 5, 1918), 391-402.
110. Gertrude Whipple, "Good Practices in Grouping," *The Reading Teacher,* VII, No. 2 (December 1953), 69-74.
111. Harriet Wilson, "Stop Reading in Ability Groups," *Instructor,* LXV, (April 1956), 35,74.
112. Mary C. Wilson, "The Teacher's Problems in a Differentiated Reading Program," *Elementary English,* XXIV, No. 2 (February 1947), 77-85, 118.
113. Miriam E. Wilt, "Another Way to Meet Individual Differences," *Elementary English,* XXXV, No. 1 (January 1958), 26-28.
114. J. T. Worlton, "Individualizing Instruction in Reading," *Elementary School Journal,* XXXVI, No. 10 (June 1936), 735-747.
115. J. Wayne Wrightstone, *Class Organization for Instruction,* What Research Says Series, No. 13, Washington, D. C.: National Education Association, 1957.
116. _____ . "Research Related to Experience Records and Basal Readers," *The Reading Teacher,* V, No. 2 (November 5, 1951), 5-6.
117. Amy Elizabeth Yensen, "Attracting Children in Books," *Elementary English,* XXXIII, No. 6 (October 1956), 332-339.

12. Differentiating Instruction to Provide for the Needs of Learners Through Organizational Practices*

MARGARET A. ROBINSON

Toronto, Canada

DUE to the increased emphasis on education today, administrators and teachers strive constantly for new organizational patterns, new approaches, and new methods of teaching. They realize the challenge of providing for individual differences and the objective in reading instruction to develop effective and discriminating readers who will learn to have a permanent love of reading. Can organizational patterns help in achieving this objective and in solving today's reading problems? What are organizational patterns? Which one is the most advantageous? Organizational patterns are not methods of teaching but simply administrative schemes or plans of school and classroom management to help reduce the range of achievement and to enable the teacher to come closer to each pupil. To draft these plans, administrators and teachers must have understanding of the problems, organizing ability, and knowledge of child growth and educational principles.

Some organizational practices are new in the sense that we have not used them before, but they all seem to be modifications of the earliest plans of teaching. Variations of tutorial and monitorial plans of graded and ungraded classes and schools have had a long history and continue to the present day. We might say that from the tutorial plan has developed the individualized program; from the monitorial plan has developed the group system; and due to the graded classes of the past there has continued the total class approach of today. What is difficult for some of us to realize is that grades were and are artificial divisions formed for economy purposes to help the mass rather than the individual.

This paper is a brief review of current practices. For more detailed accounts I refer you to recent educational procedures, perspectives, and magazines published by the International Reading Association and to the texts of reading authorities recommended by them and others.

*An original article written for *Readings on Reading.*

Two terms used frequently in connection with organization are *homogeneous* and *heterogeneous.* Webster defines *homogeneous* as "of the same kind or nature," and *heterogeneous* as "differing in kind and nature." We know that no two children are alike and that "a homogeneous group" is a misnomer. What we really mean by a homogeneous group is a group of pupils in which the wide range of differences has been reduced. Three schemes of classroom organization, then, are: (a) an individualized program in which each pupil is taught as an individual; (b) homogeneous groups, which are either classes or smaller groups with similar ability, achievement, interests, or needs; (c) heterogeneous groups which are either self-contained classes or groups within a class. Throughout this discussion there will be references to different kinds of grouping. (1) pupil achievement, (2) mental ability, (3) special needs, and (4) pupil interests. Social and friendship groups are variations which may be called heterogeneous or homogeneous, depending on the range of differences.

Let us now briefly examine school organizations and classroom organizations.

SCHOOL ORGANIZATIONS

1. Graded Schools

The traditional method of organizing schools into a lock step system from K. to VI or VIII where pupils were promoted or failed and furniture was fixed, is one familiar to us and still with us. To meet special problems additional classes were introduced, such as junior kindergartens, kindergarten—primary or readiness classes, and opportunity classes. Later, for a time, some school organizations were based on mental ability—the ABC or XYZ plans—a form of homogeneous grouping still used in some classrooms. Another variation from heterogeneous classes was to select the brightest and slowest pupils for one class, and to place average pupils in a different class. All classes were either *High-Low,* or *Medium* and the selection was based on reading achievement. Promotion policies of the present are not quite so rigid as in the past, for most pupils are permitted to advance to the next grade each year and bright pupils may be accelerated or placed in a class or school for the gifted. The sizes of classes are gradually reduced and there are many innovations and improvements in materials, equipment, and facilities.

A form of organization which was developed late in the last century and revived today is called *departmentalization,* a system in which each teacher instructs in one subject exclusively or in related subjects. Departmentalization was an answer to the demand for more expert teaching and was used in grades five, six, seven, and eight in some areas. By the nineteen fifties educators were concluding that departmentalization had become an "artificial, mechanized instructional program." Teaching was subject-centered and, due to the demands of their many teachers, pupils could be exploited. Teachers had the responsibility of too many pupils, did not know any of them well and found the work a strain. However, semi-departmentalized programs have evolved today such as the Joplin Plan and team-teaching and these will be described under classroom organization. Even in the primary grades a semi-departmentalized structure has been tried out by having special teachers responsible for reading, art, music, and physical education. Though timetables can be adapted and more expert teaching may result, the issue is a very controversial one.

A form of homogeneous grouping now in use is called *streaming*, where principals list in order the pupils of each grade according to their reading ability and divide them into classes of decreasing size. This plan is the beginning of the ungraded school.

2. The Ungraded School

The ungraded school plan breaks the vertical lock step grade organization and removes the barriers between two or more successive grades. It is a plan of continuous progress or streaming and former "repeaters" can progress from level to level successfully and at their own rate. Sometimes there is a separation between the primary and intermediate grades but frequently all of the grades from I to VI are organized on this plan. In the primary unit plan, the basal reading material is divided into a number of units from 9 to 20 and pupils progress according to their own rate of learning. At the end of the year there is no failure of the slow readers nor acceleration of the fast readers, but each pupil continues in the unit where he can read comfortably. Some pupils may take 3 1/2 to four years to complete the work of the former first three grades. Others may move more rapidly through the units in from 2 to 2 1/2 years. In the intermediate grades the three streams are divided into classes according to the range of reading ability. Each class is subdivided into three or more groups which overlap the groups of the classes below or above. Pupils are placed in the class and group suitable for them, and may move from group to group or class to class when certain standards have been achieved. Superficial barriers of grade names are removed or temporary substitutions made (e.g., A1, A2, B1, B2; Pr. I, Pr. II; 100's, 200's . . . 600's) ·until teachers and pupils realize there is no such thing as a grade. The reading skills should be taught sequentially and systematically, and other skills, e.g. mathematics, should be developed similarly. Workshops are needed to list and study these skills and to organize them into small work-units that show a meaningful progression. Also, plans should be made not only for vertical advancement but for horizontal enrichment as well.

3. The Nongraded School

Perhaps the utopia of organizations is the nongraded school where classes are not streamed. There are no grades in the nongraded school: each child is studied as an individual and placed according to his interests, ability, and achievement. (If it seems best for an immature eight year old to be placed with a six year old, or two friends of different ages to be placed in the same class, etc., this is done.) The program for each child is planned for him. The staff is experienced. Each member has a professional scholastic background and administrative, organizational ability. Many different types of organization can be used, and also a variety of teaching methods, e.g., unit teaching, language experience approach, individualized and programmed instruction. Pupils progress at their own rate and there are no failures. The learning situation is relaxed and conducive to good mental health. The school and classes are divided into various flexible clusters. This organization is complex and requires much study before initiating it, but teachers say it is most stimulating and rewarding.

4. School Plant

Through the years the school plant has been modified to fit organizational patterns that enable the teacher to come closer to the pupil and to work out a more imaginative and flexible program. Space can be adjustable for large and small areas by having movable or collapsible walls and sometimes classrooms are provided with small glass anterooms. Resource and material centres can form the hub of the classes or schools. In one nongraded school, classrooms are arranged in complexes of two and are twice the normal size. Intermediate grade classrooms are twice as large as the primary rooms. Bookcases on rollers are used as partitions for small areas and soft cushions and carpeted floors reduce the noise and provide a pleasant atmosphere. If in the future, we have computer-assisted instruction, class size will not be an important factor and the school may appear more like a manufacturing plant. Buildings, old or modern, do not make a program, however.

CLASSROOM ORGANIZATIONAL PATTERNS

1. Total Class Approach

In the total class approach of the past one can visualize a heterogeneous group all taught from the same book by an authoritative teacher. And there are teachers today who claim they are too busy to teach individuals or groups and who continue to teach reading to the class as a whole using the same reader for all pupils. With common interests they feel they can build the esprit de corps of the class and also save preparation of many lessons. It is time-saving, they say, to teach the whole class when giving a course in phonics or using a teaching machine or projector. This traditional method takes little consideration for individual differences.

However, there are many occasions today when a class can be taught as a whole whether they are grouped heterogeneously or homogeneously. (Some educators recommend that we return to heterogeneous class organizations but that modern methods be used and the teacher's approach and attitude be changed.) The whole class can be taught poetry for appreciation, or choral reading, or short stories, or longer stories or the novel. Also the class is taught as a whole when the teacher is developing listening skills and critical thinking by reading to the class in the content area, and when having sharing periods, evaluation, dramatization, movies and T. V. lessons.

Related filmstrips projected on screen or chalkboard as an aid to basal readers are sometimes used with the whole class. It goes without saying that this highly motivated form of teaching would be even more effective if used with carefully selected groups.

2. Grouping in the Classrooms

A more common method of organization is the group system used in the self-contained classroom. The pupils may be in heterogeneous classes (i.e., with a wide range of abilities) or a modified form of homogeneous classes (i.e., with a reduced range of abilities) depending on the promotion policy of the school. The following is one example of classroom grouping.

Teacher's Plan for Daily Teaching of Developmental Reading

Date: Room:			Time 60–90 min.	
Groups	A	B	C	Ind.
Reader or Book				
Pages of Selection				
Assignment (4 min.)				
Teach C Group (20 min.+)	Skills	Skills	Directed Teaching	Skills
Check other groups (2 min.)				
Teach B Group (20 min.+)	Related Reading	Teacher Guidance	Skills	Skills
Check other groups (2 min.)				
Teach A Group (20 min.)	Directed Teaching	Skills and R. Reading	Skills	Rel. Rdg.
Check other groups (2 min.)				
Individual Guidance (10 min.)	—	—	—	Directed Teaching
Sharing and Evaluation (5 min.)				
Type of Seatwork				

In self-contained classes a teacher may have two groups or three groups or multi-groups with pupil teachers. The texts used are series of basal readers and the time spent is from one hour to one and a half hours daily. In the two-group system, one group may be on the grade level and one below the grade level, with a few gifted pupils and a few retarded pupils needing individual attention. In the three-group system one group may be on the grade level, one above, needing enrichment material and one below, needing easier material; or one group may be on the grade level and two may be below. (A deciding factor is the quartile of intelligence in which the school or class is placed.) With four groups a teacher may teach two on Monday and Wednesday, the other two on Tuesday and Thursday, and the class as a whole on Friday. When chairmen are used for small group work they must be well trained by the teacher and understand the instructions thoroughly. Often they can assist the teacher in taking up such seatwork activities as vocabulary skills. One of the criticisms of the group system is that sometimes there is a stigma attached to the "low" group and superiority to the "top" group, and this feeling leads to unwholesome attitudes in the learner. An understanding, skillful teacher using flexible grouping can do much to prevent such criticism by stimulating a pride in belonging to each group; by selling the idea that the skills learned in the third group will enable them to become much better readers; by having a (prepared) member of the "low" group visit the "top" group and contribute some background of information to their lesson; by having an absentee who, on his return, cannot keep up with his group, become a member of a lower group and so on. A comparison of learning to read with learning to jump, learning to play the piano, etc., will help the pupil understand the wisdom of belonging to the group which uses the reading material which best "fits" him.

The teacher should teach the "low" group daily for short periods and the other groups two or three times a week but she should also have daily contact with each group by examining and discussing their seatwork activities.

The teacher does not need to follow a rigid timetable but can use frequently the basal reader lesson or other lessons as springboards into dramatizations, enterprises and unit teaching. Nor does basal reading need to be taught every day, for it might be more advantageous if one day a week were kept for a library period and individualized reading, and one day for reading laboratories or programmed instruction.

There are other types of groups in a self-contained classroom. One is the temporary special *needs* group formed to teach a specific *skill*. Another type, formed when teaching projects and subjects of the content area, is the group based on pupils' *interests* as shown in selected committees and research groups. The self-contained classroom, as well as having at times the total class, frequently has a variety of other grouping, such as tutorial *individual* teaching, a "buddy system" of partners, and congenial *teams* of two or three. For example, a new pupil who cannot speak English can be helped by a capable pupil appointed to be his buddy for a stated time.

3. Cross-Grade Grouping

A plan of crossgrade or intergrade ability grouping in the intermediate grades was initiated in Joplin, Missouri and has been adopted by many areas. Pupils were grouped on the basis of scores from reading achievement tests, mental ability tests, academic status, social and emotional factors and classroom teacher's observations. No pupil could be a member of a class which was more than two grades higher than his homeroom, e.g. no grade IV pupil could go to a grade VII or VIII class. Grade barriers were removed and pupils were sent to the designated rooms for the reading period. The teacher or teachers who received the slowest readers usually have the smaller classes. The other pupils go to the rooms of the teachers who specialize on their level of achievement. In a large school teachers taught the whole class as one reading group; in smaller schools a teacher might have two reading groups. Though the range of reading achievement was lessened, special provisions still had to be made for individual pupils or small groups. Basal reading materials were used and systematic sequences followed. Periods were usually one hour in length but when increased to ninety minutes, time was given to other language arts. In some schools there were daily recreatory reading periods in the home classroom.

Some of the advantages listed for intergrade grouping are: economy of teacher effort; special emphasis on reading skills; proper adjustment of reading material and instruction; highly motivated pupils; pupils with their own classes the rest of the day. On the other hand, the organizational mechanics and movement of pupils is time-consuming; and due to the various learning rates of the pupils sub-grouping will be necessary for certain pupils. It is not advantageous to isolate the basal reader period from the language arts period in the regular classroom. Also, there are some pupils who feel unhappy if they are not in their social group.

4. Team Teaching

Another new pattern which breaks down room barriers *of the same grade* is called team teaching. It is designed to provide the advantages of departmentalization as well as retain the advantages of the self-contained classroom. Here the teachers of adjoining or connecting classrooms act as a team to plan their reading instruction cooperatively and take the responsibility of teaching the superior or the slow or the average reader. Pupils become accustomed to having two teachers (their homeroom teacher and their reading teacher) and do not feel so strange as in the vertical plan where they are not in their social groups. The slow learner can be more relaxed and cheerful when learning at his own rate, while the fast learner can be more stimulated when progressing at a rapid pace. With co-teachers, the number of groups can be lessened and the distribution of reading ability narrowed. Though one teacher may become a chairman, it is desirable that no teacher become dominant but that all teachers work together and share their findings and understanding of each pupil.

5. Individualized Reading

A fifth approach in organizational practices is the increasingly popular individualized reading program conducted usually in a self-contained classroom which can be either heterogeneous or homogeneous (but it can be used in any type of organization. Here the pupils read thousands of books (including some basal readers) under the teacher's guidance. Three or more books per child per day should be available. Each pupil has individual conferences with the teacher. The skills each pupil needs are taught him incidentally during his conference with the teacher, or sometimes in small groups.

In this program basal readers—as the core of reading construction—are removed, but may be used for independent reading. The three underlying principles frequently quoted are: (a) *seeking* (that is, the pupil has a compelling desire and drive to find a book to read); (b) *self-selection* of books on pupil's level (the pupil finds a book which satisfies him and which he can read); (c) *pacing* (the pupil is permitted to read the book at his own pace, not given a time limit). The teacher is the counsellor and, as well as using individual conferences, and some incidental group instruction, guides the class as a whole during the sharing and evaluation periods. Some advantages of this method are the high motivation and the close teacher-pupil relationship. Pupils have access to many more books and may form life-long habits of good reading. The stigma of the caste system which is sometimes felt in the "low group" is removed. One disadvantage is the teacher's inability to have sufficient conferences with each pupil, and hence, failure to develop systematic sequences of skills for each pupil. (In group or class teaching, the teacher has time to develop the skills systematically.) Much of the reading is voluntary and the fast readers read widely and fluently, but some critics think that the slow learners may accomplish little, feel inferior, and may dislike reading permanently, because they have not yet learned sufficient basic skills to read independently, and the teacher does not have enough time to teach them individually. A competent understanding teacher can overcome this problem. She must plan carefully for individual conferences, know the sequential development of reading skills, know the pupils, know the books, be able to devise forms for check lists, charts, evaluation, etc. and be able to organize the period effectively. (A suggestion follows:)

Division of Period
1. *Introduction of period* (Stimulation, motivation, teaching of skills)
2. *Selection of books* (by pupils, assisted by teachers; seating—sometimes in special groups)
3. *Individualized reading and pupil-teacher conference*

4. *Sharing time* (at the beginning or during the period)
5. *Evaluation time* (usually at the end). Simple book reports; organization activities, art activities; drama

It takes a skilled, creative, and knowledgeable teacher to guide the individualized reading program efficiently.

CRITERIA

When you wish to compare and evaluate organization patterns for reading instruction, Helen N. Driscoll (in I.R.A. *Perspectives in Reading IX* p. 31) has suggested the following guiding questions as criteria:

1. Is the plan administratively feasible?
2. Can the plan be understood by teachers, pupils, their parents and community?
3. Does the plan support what we know about the learning process?
4. Can the results of the use of the plan be measured accurately?
5. Is there evidence that the pupils have learned more effectively as a result of the plan?
6. Does the organizational plan include provision for individual differences of pupils and teachers?
7. Does the plan increase the teacher's effectiveness?

Once we decide on the form of organization we plan to use, we should believe in it and be enthusiastic about it. The pupils should be ready for the plan, too, through having acquired such good work habits as neatness, order, promptness, dependability, and consideration of others. In addition to teacher and pupil readiness for a new plan of organization, parent interest and support should be secured through letters, visits, or meetings.

Why does a teacher sometimes find that a new pupil is rated too high on his report card? Doubtless because the former teacher has used only one criterion. What criteria do we use to organize our class?

1. Consultation of accumulative record cards, conversations, inventories, and questionnaires.
2. The present teacher's observations through her daily teaching and supervision.
3. Informal tests devised by the teacher to review the work taught and to find out the pupil's needs.
4. Vocabulary sampling tests from basal readers.
5. Book-level tests based on selections in a series of basal readers. (These graded tests are sometimes called informal reading inventories and must

be prepared carefully. See I.R.A. publication Reading Aids No. 2.) Some of the standards which should be maintained by most of the members of a group are: 75% comprehension; 95% accuracy and pronunciation; freedom from tension; rhythmical reading and a conversational tone.

6. Standardized tests in reading.

Not too much emphasis should be placed on any one criterion, but to obtain a fair measure of a pupil's reading ability, combined results of several criteria should be used.

Some Tips for Teachers for Grouping

Teachers should not try a new plan of organization until they have had success in teaching the class as a whole. The following suggestions have been found helpful in grouping:

1. If inexperienced in small group teaching, begin gradually. Establish rapport and good work habits with the class as a whole before starting a two-group system. When two groups are running smoothly, then start the third. For any kind of new organizational practice, start gradually. Make a careful study of the research findings on the plan.
2. Discuss the arrangement of furniture with the class and routinize the mechanics of moving furniture early in the year. Have a "reading centre" of chairs near a chalkboard. Sit with the pupils and be a member of their group or reading club.
3. Make the "low" group feel as important as the "high" group. Help to promote an atmosphere of warmth, friendliness, pride, and willingness in each group. (Do not use such terms as *low* or *top* or *high*.) If names are chosen for the reading groups, be sure there is no association between the name and the group ability. A popular practice is to name the group after the chairman or any group member. Rotate the office of chairman periodically.
4. Have flexible grouping because of the varying rates at which some pupils progress and because of irregular attendance.
5. Be sure that directions concerning assignments are given clearly and understood by the pupils. Provide a variety of challenging and helpful seatwork activities. Check the work faithfully.
6. Confer with parents regularly by letter, report, or interview. Also, have regular conferences with teachers of your own grade and with your whole staff.
7. Draft daily and weekly plans for group activities. Give a fair proportion of time to each group and pupil.
8. Do not become discouraged. Let your reading periods be enjoyable for both you and your pupils.

THE TEACHER

1. Learning Aids and Educational Principles

The basic reading problem is not discovering the best organizational pattern but providing the pupils with an energetic, enthusiastic, conscientious and open-minded teacher, one who has professional competence and can base her methods on sound educational principles. The continuum of learning aids she understands and puts into practice. The following educational principles and others are fundamental to her instruction.

Continuum

(Concrete to)	Doing or Direct Experience	Observing or Seeing	Movies, Sound and Colour	Movies, Black & White	Three Dimensional Pictures	Flat Pictures, Slides	Diagrams, Charts, Maps	Discussion	Reading	(Abstract)

NOTE: Reading is the most difficult and abstract learning aid. Participation is the most concrete and easiest learning aid. The continuum of learning aids is of greatest value in the following order: (1) *direct experience* (doing); (2) *observing* or seeing; (3) *visual material* – television, movies, slides, pictures, maps, diagrams, etc.; (4) *discussing and telling*; (5) reading.

1. A pupil who is motivated learns more readily than one who is not. If the pupil is enthusiastic and keen, the learning will be more rapid and permanent.
2. Effective learning requires rich environment and experience in order that the pupils have understanding of the lesson.
3. Children differ. Each pupil is a unique individual with varied interests and characteristics.
4. The teacher should teach the pupil on his own reading level in order that the pupil may learn and retain more easily.
5. Each pupil has his own rate of learning marked by variability.
6. There must be teacher readiness (a knowledge of techniques; experiential background; a knowledge of pupil abilities, interests, problems, strengths weaknesses.)
7. There must be pupil readiness (physical, emotional, mental, social and language; background of information, knowledge of necessary reading skills, etc.)

8. There must be rapport between pupil and pupil; pupil and book; pupil and teacher.
9. There should be logical development in the lesson, a progression from the known to the unknown; from the easy to the difficult; from the whole to parts.
10. Provision should be made for applications of the lesson and enrichment.
11. The pupil's first reading of the lesson should be silent (unless the selection is a test).
12. Learning is more effective when the pupil participates actively rather than passively.

2. Methods

The professional competent teacher knows many methods and tries to make use of a combination of methods no matter which type of organization in her room. She tries to base her methods on many educational principles and is aware that all of the principles are fundamental to the Language Experience Approach. She might use the following combination of methods.

Organizational Patterns	Methods
Total Class Approach	Traditional
	Basal Reader Approach
	Language Experience Approach
	Poetry The Novel
Intra Grouping	B.R.A., L.E.A.
(in the classroom)	Individualized Reading
	Language Lab.
Intergrade Grouping	BRA & Skills Teaching
Joplin	(Linguistics)
Team Teaching	BRA & Skills Teaching
Individualized Teaching	Individualized Reading
	Linguistics
	Programmed Learning

3. Knowing the Skills

Not only should the teacher know the major reading skills and their sequence but she should be familiar with the sub-skills and have kits and other materials in readiness to teach them. The following list could be used as a checklist for individualized reading and other methods.

SOME BASIC READING SKILLS

1. *Vocabulary Skills (Word Recognition and Meaning)*
   a. Picture Clues–Configuration Clues
   b. Context Clues–Language Rhythm Clues
   c. Phonetic Analysis: consonants; vowels; blends; silent letters; review of phonetic analysis principles.
   d. Structural Analysis: compounds; contractions; derivatives; inflectional forms; affixes; review of syllabication principles.
   e. Glossary and Dictionary: alphabetical sequence; guide words; syllabications; accent; pronunciation (Key words and respellings, representation of consonants, diacritical marks for vowels); selection of appropriate definitions; abbreviations.
   f. Special Meanings: multiple meanings; shifts of meanings; similar meanings; idiomatic or figurative expressions.

2. *Comprehension Skills Including Critical Reading*
   a. Interpreting illustrations
   b. Following directions
   c. Finding main ideas
   d. Finding details
   e. Finding sequence of ideas
   f. Making comparisons
   g. Making inferences
   h. Drawing conclusions
   i. Predicting outcomes
   j. Differentiating facts from opinion
   k. Testing and applying conclusions
   l. Evaluating attitudes

3. *Organization Skills*
   a. Listing
   b. Sequence
   c. Main points
   d. Details
   e. Summarizing
   f. Outlining
   g. Note-taking

4. *Locating and Using Information*
   In the text, index, contents, glossary, dictionary, maps, graphs, charts, reference books, periodicals, card file, radio, and other visual aids.

5. *Related Language Skills*
   a. Correct usage: (antonyms, synonyms, homonyms, homographs; verbs, nouns, adjectives, adverbs)
   b. Punctuation
   c. Language structure: (sentence, paragraph)
   d. Creative writing: (letters, notes, records, stories, poems, plays)

6. *Appreciation*
   a. Enjoyment of humour, excitement, descriptive words, fine writing, etc.
   b. Discrimination between reality and fancy
   c. Indentifying factors which make the selection appealing
   d. Creating a desire to commit to memory or to emulate

7. *Rate of Reading*
   Adjustment of rate to purpose and type of material; skimming; fluent observational reading; self-enrichment; careful study-type.
8. *Oral Reading*
   95% correct pronunciation and accuracy; correct posture, breathing, freedom from tension; conversational tone and adequate voice projection, rhythmical and interpretive phrasing
9. *Related Skill–Purposes for Reading*
   Purposes: (preferably student's purposes and problem questions)
   e.g. broadening experience, solving a problem, appreciation, humor, guidance, verification, curiosity, escape, locating information, using information, developing a skill, etc.

4. Knowing the Child

How much should a teacher know about his pupils? Is it true that teachers pay only lip service to individual differences? Teachers can never know everything about their pupils and what they do learn will be learned gradually throughout the year. However, they can make an early start ot obtain helpful information through their study of school records; conferences with former teachers, the child's parents, school psychologist and others; daily observations; oral and written reports, testing and teaching. Some teachers jot down comments on each pupil from time to time in a notebook, using a page for each pupil. Later in the year some teachers find very useful for quick reference a class summary sheet with headings similar to the attached chart. When teaching, the teacher should consider the individual differences of each pupil but be ever mindful of the whole class. There follows a chart on child growth, individual differences, needs and interests. Teachers can use it as a guide or reference as they study the pupils in their classrooms.

SOME CONCLUSIONS

No one organizational pattern should be considered a panacea for all reading problems. The challenge is how to combine several plans—total class, inter -class grouping, intra-class grouping, individualized teaching—into a harmonious whole. In *The Reading Teacher* of December, 1967 (p. 216) Robert Karlin draws the following conclusions based on various research studies on organization.

It is evident that no clear-cut advantages of one grouping plan over another or of individual over group forms have been found. What implications, then, might be drawn from these and other studies?

A Survey of Pupils in Room

Confidential		Use Initials
Gifted (Note I.Q. whether group or individual test. Note whether non-achiever. **Note whether teacher opinion — (fast learner.)**	*Subjects* (Note whether pupil is outstanding or failure in various subjects.)	*Physical Handicaps* *Speech* *Hearing* *Sight* *Other*
Talented Violin players Piano players Choir Members Outstanding hobbies (note kind, e.g. Sciences)	*Background* (Family, home, neighbourhood) (Note whether rich or meagre. Whether extensive traveler Number of schools attended. If owner of personal library, or member of a library. If both parents working. If parents separated, etc.	*Sports* (Note if outstanding and state type.) *Behavior* (Maladjustment) (Social maladjustment, personality problems, withdrawn, nervous, etc.
Slow Learners (Note if tested by group or indiv. tests or whether teacher opinion	*Newcomers* Note country of birth. Note if language handicap.	*Misbehavior* (misconduct, dishonesty, bullying, resentful, disobedient, etc.
Work Habits (Note if poor.)		*Other Classification* (e.g. Club Member)

1. There are times when it is feasible to teach a class of children as a whole, providing all can benefit from the offering.

2. Grouping can narrow but not completely eliminate the range of reading abilities. Recognizing the difficulties in providing for individual differences, teachers might function more effectively if the range were not too great.
3. Combinations of individual and group instruction seem to be more productive than either alone. Teachers can take advantage of any organizational patterns which assist them in meeting the learning requirements of all their pupils.
4. No organizational plan will insure reading success. The "know-how" the teacher brings to the plan is what counts.

Dependence upon inter-class grouping, intra-class grouping, pupil teams, or other plans to solve instructional problems fails to take into account differences in pupils and in teachers. Some pupils and some teachers function better under one set of conditions than another. A plan of organization is not a method of teaching. It is a facilitator of method, perhaps, but no more.

There are many factors which enter into successful grouping practices and teaching, such as teacher competency and organizational ability, pupil motivation and readiness, suitability and adequacy of reading materials, type of administration, curricula, school district, etc. It would seem wise to have a broad program using all the plans which research has proven effective.

We acknowledge, then, that the success of any method of organization is largely dependent on the enthusiasm, resourcefulenss, scholarship and ability of the teacher, but the most important factor is her love for, understanding of, and faith in her pupils.

13. Groups in Reading

E. W. DOLCH

HOW should the children in a room be grouped for reading? Or should they be grouped at all? These questions are so vital both to the teaching of reading and to the children's mental health that we should look at all the possibilities and at all the problems involved before we come to a decision. A hasty answer may have grave consequences for many children.

THE WHOLE-ROOM METHOD

Many teachers still insist that there should be no divisions within a room for any reason. They believe that the room should discuss as a whole, learn as a whole, act as a whole. For most learnings, we would all go along with these teachers. The room group should be a democratic group of equals. All individuals are different, but in this country there should be no "class distinctions" of superior or inferior persons. If democracy is important in our national life, it must be learned in school life. Such a view is essential in a modern school. But what about reading?

These teachers maintain that reading can be learned in a room group, and many classrooms demonstrate that it can. Two methods make this possible. One method is the *"library method of reading"* by which all read on the same topic but in different materials. Sometimes the topics are social studies topics, and the room has books on all levels which contain material on those topics. Sometimes the units in a basic reader are the topics, with the children reading other materials both harder and easier but on the same topics used in the readers. If books of many reading series are *unitized,* that is, broken up into small booklets, each on a different topic, a library can be assembled in every room that contains reading matter on most topics at all levels. Thus each child reads material on his level and all contribute to the class discussion. This method requires (1) the

*From *Elementary English,* **31**, 8 (December, 1954), 477-484. Reprinted by permission of the National Council of Teachers of English.

assembling of materials at all reading levels, and (2) the ability on the part of the teacher to train the whole room in the habits of courteous listening, efficient contributing of ideas, and thoughtful discussion. Both of these requirements are difficult, and this is perhaps the reason there is actually little of this "library method of reading" in our schools. It is of course understood that this method needs to include class discussion of new word meanings, and class teaching of sounding of new words, since both of these tend to be neglected if children read only to themselves.

Another method used by the whole room has the whole class work on the same selection in the basic reader. This method is made possible by using the following five steps in each lesson. (1) All the children discuss the topic beforehand and the pictures in the books, all contributing to this discussion. (2) All the children learn the new word meanings in the selection either before or during the reading. (3) All the children participate in the sounding out of the hard words. (4) The selection is presented to the whole class orally by the good readers or by a reading-committee which has prepared it beforehand, that committee containing readers of all levels. (5) All the children participate in reading parts to answer questions asked either by the teacher or by the class. This plan actually uses audience reading to tell everyone what the words say, and ensures that children of all reading levels learn sight vocabulary, sounding, and word meanings.

Along with the *whole-room method* a teacher can always have *extra groups* that suit her needs. Sometimes she has an *extra group* of fast readers who go through other readers in addition to their part in working with all the children on the basic reader. Sometimes the teacher has *extra groups* that are also reading in easier readers. Sometimes there is an extra group that works only on sounding or does extra work on sounding. But these extra groups are never "separated from" the rest of the room. The room studies the basic as a unit. These other groups are *extra* or additional.

It must be remembered that along with this whole-room method will always go the individual reading period. This is an indispensable part of any plan for the teaching of reading. No kind of grouping of children will provide for the quantity of easy reading which alone will secure the fluency that will make reading easy and therefore make reading fun. It is true that when there are two or three groups, it is often said that the group at their seats "do independent reading." This is true in most schools only of the good readers. The others just waste their time because they do not have easy enough materials and because they lack incentive. The often-heard statement, "You may read when you have finished your work," also means only that the good readers get to read more. So no matter how reading is handled, there is urgent need for the independent reading period when "each reads on his interest at his level."

In addition, it must be remembered that no matter what the plan, there should be arrangement for the good readers to help the poor ones. This is managed first by seating them side by side, and then by training them in helping without making a disturbance. The poor reader can put his finger under a word and lean over to the good reader. The latter will say just the word, and that is all. It is foolish not to use the children to help one another.

THE TWO-GROUP METHOD

For many years, the two-group method for reading has been the most prevalent. Perhaps the chief reason for this has been that teachers found the whole room too large to handle in one reading group. A teacher might handle a whole room of twenty-five as one group, but how can one handle a whole room of forty that way? We do not know how powerful this factor has been because it has very seldom been given as a reason, even though it may psychologically be the chief one.

Unfortunately, the two groups in a room have usually been called the slow-group and the fast-group. This has had two very disastrous results. *First, from the child's and the parent's point of view, a stigma was put on the less able group,* since everyone resents being called "slow," since "slow" is just a kind way of saying "dumb." Adults uniformly call a stupid child "slow," and children know this. In school, the "fast group" has been called the A group, and the other the B group, making the B group secondary. Behind this system, of course, is the fact that usually the teacher liked the A group best and felt that the children in that group were more like herself and therefore the right kind of children. The teacher may never in her life have been in a B group, and hence has no idea of the point of view of that group. So the use of A and B seemed natural.

Now, however, through our interest in mental health, we are finding some of the devastating effects of treating half of the children as the "lower group." After they have been called "lower" for year after year, they do one of two things. First, they may accept themselves as lower and incapable, and quit trying. When this "lower group" reaches high school, its members make little effort. Many just "sit it out" until they reach leaving age. They have accepted their label. Others of this "lower group" resent being called second class citizens. They fight back. We are learning a great deal about this from what juvenile delinquents tell us of their school experiences. They are, as one worker tells us, ". . . bitterly resentful of the average teacher's attitude toward their weakness. They resent, too, the comparative success of their classmates. All this animosity gives rise to the oft-heard cry, 'I hate reading'."[1] One wonders which is the more damaging, acceptance of lower status, or resistance against being

[1]Helen J. Greenblat, "I Hate Reading," in *Understanding the Child,* Vol. XXI, No. 3, (June, 1952), published by the National Association for Mental Health.

given that status. But these two reactions do appear in far too many cases. In high school especially we are becoming very much aware of them.

Of course, there may be a way around this situation. Suppose we called the less capable group the A group, A meaning average. Suppose we made sure to include more than half in it, so that it is always the larger. Then we might have a smaller; faster group, who could be looked on by the others as unusual and perhaps abnormal. The children of the favored parents would be in that abnormal group and those parents would be happy in the fact. Some teachers call such a group their "Independent Readers." The children in that group could go as fast as they wanted. They might be called superior, and harm might result from that fact, but at least the other and larger group would be "average," and could hold up its head as such. To make this plan work the teacher must stoutly prefer the average group, really feeling a kinship with them and their goals, rather than rejecting them as is sometimes the case. Such a plan might manage a division on reading without harm to personalities.

The other harmful effect of the "fast" and "slow" division of a room has been that one group went rapidly through the basic reader for that grade and the slow group went slowly through that reader. This system has seemed to teachers, parents, and administrators to have unconquerable logic (and still does in some places), but, instead, the arguments against it are irrefutable. The "slow" group are not just slow; the children in it are *below grade* in sight vocabulary, in word attack, in comprehension, and in all the other skills. They need a reader for a lower grade, but they never get one. Instead, they have been given a book that was impossibly hard, and went slowly through it, with little profit. Going through a third grade reader slowly does not make it a second grade reader. Going slowly through a fourth grade reader does not make it a third grade reader. Children learn only when the task is not too hard for them, and this plan of "chasing each other through the basic" has not suited the needs of the retarded group. This is still true.

A still other handicap for the second group by this system was that they lost all interest in reading because they heard every story read and discussed by the other group first and then had to try to get enthusiastic about it some weeks or months later. The teacher also found it hard to work up enthusiasm for this rehash of the same work. In fact, every factor operated against the improvement of the "slow" group, and in consequence, this group tended to get "slower and slower" year after year.

To offset both of these difficulties, many schools have adopted different readers for the second group in a room, readers that the other group had never read and which therefore had not been "spoiled" for the second group. This has also been called the "co-basic" plan. Standard readers do differ considerably in difficulty, so that it is possible for a school system to use two separate basic readers in each room, one easy, one hard. In that case, the teacher is careful *not* to use the easy book with the faster readers, and thus to keep it as the private property of the slower group. She then can teach the book with freshness, and the children can approach it with interest. The faster readers can listen with interest also, and the slower readers can have some standing and self-respect. Such a system is imperative when two groups are used. There should never be the rehashing of the same stories by a slower group.

THE THREE-GROUP METHOD

A teacher may get a better understanding of the three group plan in the teaching of reading if she will consider what would happen if a school superintendent should divide his teachers into three ability groups. There would, of course, be the superior group into which a third or less of the teachers would be put. That placement would perhaps do them no harm, since they would know they were good teachers and since they would be too mature to be "stuck up" about their placement. Most of us, no doubt, would be in the "middle group." We would usually be satisfied since we know we are just ordinary good teachers and make no pretense to be superior to anyone. A few of us in the middle group would be a little sore that we were not recognized as superior, but we would have no real ground for complaint. Is it any disgrace to be "average"? It is the lot of merit not to be recognized in this imperfect world. So we would say nothing about it and be glad in our fellowship with other good teachers.

But what about the third group? What would happen to those teachers officially labeled as "poor teachers"? They are placed in the "below average group." Since everyone in a free country tries to think of himself as being at least average, these teachers would undoubtedly think of themselves as failures. They would be the "failure group." What would happen to them? The answer is obvious. They would quit teaching. They would give up. What is the use of trying when you are doomed to failure? Someone might try to comfort them and say they should strive to reach the average group, but they would rightly say that since there had to be a "below average" group by the three group system, they were certain to get into it. The only reasonable thing would be to stop trying.

What happens when there are three groups in reading? Is the analogy a sound one? Some would say not because they say the children at the bottom of the class know they are poor readers and recognize the justice of their placement in the "below average" group. Yes, they know they are poor readers, but does that reconcile them to being labeled publicly as failures? Does it protect them from the gibes of their classmates? Does it protect them from the sneers of their brothers and sisters, and fathers and mothers? And, most of all, does it make them work hard and do their best?

Some teachers say the poor readers are happier in their "lowest reading group" than when otherwise handled. This may be comparatively true. That is, they may be happier in a group of others like themselves *if* they had been made to feel ignorant and stupid when placed with better readers. But a skillful teacher can have a poor reader in any kind of group and make him feel happy in the situation and keep him from feeling stupid. To say that the poor readers are happier in their poor reading group means they are made unhappy when combined with the others, due to a wrong spirit among the other children.

A special case of the three group plan is the first grade. Here many children welcome being in a third group just because they would rather play than try to read. Also, the children are often unaware of any stigma attached to a third group. The teacher is tempted to use three groups especially because some children have been taught at home and thus are far ahead of those who have not been. The teacher also pleases the parents and others by having her children "rapidly get into reading." If she were more concerned with child development, social adjustment, and the expanding of experience, she would not worry about starting reading as rapidly as possible and would think more of keeping her group together than of "stretching it out," making the fastest get as far as possible ahead of the slower ones.

Some people say that the poor reader is going to be a failure in life anyway, so he might as well get used to the bottom position right now in school. This is a most cynical attitude toward the function of the school. It has been hoped that the school will get every child to do his best and will build up each child to his best possibilities. And it has been expected that the school should deal with children as "free and equal" without labeling them as superior or inferior.

There is still the objection that we need three reading levels because of the different reading levels of the children. Let us frankly face the fact that if we honestly followed the reading levels of the children we would need five or more reading groups and not three. If any teacher will give tests to her children and then check the results with her location of the children in reading groups, she will find that even with three groups she has usually two grades in each one of the three groups. That is *not* "adapting to the reading levels," and it cannot be. The adapting to reading level has to come through the teacher's manipulation of the reading lesson. We would find that the reading a child does in a reading group is seldom "reading at his level" if we know what that level is. The only possible way to have "every child reading at his own level" is through the individual reading period with books at all levels and on many interests.

Group reading is not "just reading." It is teaching by the teacher. It is "teacher help" reading, and the problem is, "How is the teacher to help?" There are words the child does not recognize. How is she to help him do so? There are words of which he does not know the meaning. How is he to be told? There is word attack to be learned. How is the teacher going to manage that learning? There is thinking about the reading matter. How is the teacher to encourage that thinking? The teacher can teach reading in a group that spreads over one grade. She can teach reading in a group that spreads over two grades, three grades, or four grades. Always there is that spread, and always she will have to teach accordingly. *Grouping does not do away with teaching reading to many levels at the same time.*

Having pointed out all the difficulties and dangers of having a third or "below average" group in reading, we must face the situation that many teachers are told to have three reading groups and so must have three reading groups. If this is the case, the teacher may take many steps to ameliorate the situation. *First,* she may throw greatest emphasis on class activities that keep all the children in one group, and not on reading which divides them. *Second*, she may promote friendship and companionship between the slow children and all the others, so that all are friends, regardless of reading ability. She can do this by committee assignments, by seating, by allowing some to help others, by reading games which bring children to all kinds of reading ability together, and the like. She may cause the better readers to "pull for" the poor readers and to be proud of their improvement. *Third,* she may get new books and attractive books for the slow readers which cause the others to envy them their attention. *Finally,* she may have three different reading series in her room, of differing degrees of difficulty, so that each group has its own readers and does not use the "hand-me-down" readers of another group. These and still other means are used by teachers who have a democratic philosophy and a real sympathy for the slow in reading so that this common plan of breaking up a room does as little harm as possible, and may even be turned into good.

THE "LEVELS OF READING WITHOUT GROUPING" SYSTEM

The latest contribution to this problem is one that has not been tried long enough or widely enough for us to learn all about it. It proposes that the children of any room in the primary grades be reading three books. Let us say one book is *Good Times* and another is *The Happy Family* and another is *Down by the River.* The teacher has a supply of each book, and all can participate in reading all the books if they wish. There are no groups. No one has to read any particular books if he does not want to. There is a library table with all levels of interesting books on it. There are work tables for making things. There are many possible activities.

The teacher begins by inviting all the children to look at *Good Times.* They like the pictures and talk about them. Then they come to the reading. It is very easy, but still the teacher takes time for it. So the best readers get tired of waiting for the others and wander off to the library table for books of their own level. Soon some other good readers wander off, but enough good readers remain so that no one feels that only the slowest are reading. Later the teacher invites them all to read *Down by the River*. Here all like the pictures and the discussion. But when they come to reading, many find it too hard and go off to the activity table. The good readers enjoy the reading, but enough poor readers remain and listen and talk so that none feel that the book is for the good readers only. The other reader, which is of middle difficulty, is read by a group that includes all levels, but always there are some who do not want to sit in and who get other occupations. The teacher never asks any child to leave, but she does invite particular children who should be in a group or who can sit in and profit. So this "invitation system" has "levels of reading without grouping."

This plan of groups of children reading at different levels without any group division naturally requires a reading method of somewhat different from the standard one. The standard basic method usually means "teach the new words, read silently first, then orally," and is built on a gradual vocabulary progression. But when children are in various groups at various levels, this cut-and-dried method will not do. Usually there is need for the "oral-silent" method[2] whereby the new material is read orally once so that all know the words, and then all read the material silently over and over to answer questions. Or the teacher may pick words to teach or choose the word attack to use according to the composition of the group in front of her. The teacher needs to know her children and to be alert to a changing situation. But the testimony is that this method avoids the "labeling" of the usual three group method.[3] We cannot know all the problems, however, until the method is widely used and until we have the testimony of very many teachers concerning it. Again, it does not take the place of an individual reading period when every child actually does read at his own reading level and on his own reading interest. No system of using basic readers will take the place of this individual reading.

SUMMARY

Reading in this country is taught by the whole-room method, the two-group method, and the three-group method. All three methods are used successfully by many teachers. But which is the *best* method?

Obviously, there is no best method for everybody everywhere. The best method has to be chosen by individual teachers for individual groups of children in individual schools. We can; however, suggest some factors which may help anyone in a decision.

First, an important factor is the number of children in the room. The smaller that number, the more likely that fewer groups will be used. Split grades

[2]Cf. E. W. Dolch, "Four Methods of Teaching Reading," *Elementary English*, 31 (February, 1954), 72.

[3]Kathleen B. Hester, "Every Child Reads Successfully in a Multiple Level Program," in *Elementary School Journal*, 53, No. 2, (October, 1952).

are a special case. When a teacher has to have two grades of children in one room, with each group a small one, she is very unlikely to split each grade into as many groups as she would in a room entirely of one grade.

Second, there is the ability of a teacher to handle a large group of children. This is a great variable, and it makes a great difference in the way teachers choose to handle groups in reading.

Third, there is the teacher's ability to handle in one group children of a wide range of reading ability. Skillful use of many techniques is involved, and teachers vary greatly in this ability. The more levels that a teacher can handle profitably in one group, the fewer groups may be used.

Fourth, there is the sensitivity of teacher and administration to the attitudes of children. At one time we ignored children's physical health, paying no attention to difficulties which are now taken care of by school nurses, visiting teachers, and so on. Similarly, some schools now ignore emotional difficulties, paying little attention to children's unhappiness in school, their resentments, their liking or disliking of school subjects. But more and more school people are becoming convinced that they must make sure that the children are happy in school and that they like the work they are doing. Schools with this attitude will weigh carefully any plan of grouping which might develop unhappiness or wrong attitudes in children.

Fifth, there is the factor of tradition to contend with. In many towns, "children were never grouped," at least not after the third grade. In other towns, "we have always had two groups in reading." In still other towns, teachers say, "Why, you cannot teach reading except with three groups." The first way to combat such tradition is, of course, to recognize that it is tradition, and not based on any scientific study or experiment. The second way is carefully to evaluate the situation, laying all prejudice aside. The final way is to experiment. Let every teacher change her grouping and see what happens. After she has given a fair trial to various ways of grouping, then she can have a sound opinion as to which grouping is best for her (but not for all others).

Finally, we must remember that whatever kind of grouping is used, there are ways of making that grouping serve the children in the best way possible. Under each plan, we have suggested such ways. If we try any method of grouping let us do it in the best way possible. *Do not compare a good way of handling one method of grouping with a poor way of handling another.* Do each in the best way possible and then compare.

14. Good Practices in Grouping*

TODAY, most basic reading activities are organized in units centering around a suitable theme of interest to the class, such as aviation, the community, wild animals, and children of other lands. Because the theme is similar for the entire class, it provides a common framework for instruction. Within this framework the reading experiences are highly diversified through group instruction. Different groups read for different purposes, use different reading materials, and receive different kinds of guidance from the teacher.

PATTERNS OF GROUPING

No single pattern of grouping is adequate. On many occasions, the children are classified into two or three groups according to their general reading attainments, with pupils shifting from group to group as needs change. For example, a child develops rapidly in many abilities, or develops special needs which can best be met in another group.

On other occasions, the children are classified according to their need for instruction in some special reading skill, for example, rapid skimming or the use of the dictionary to obtain the meaning of words. They are organized into two groups: one requiring instruction and the other having no need of it, either because the children have already mastered the skill or because they lack readiness for it.

Then, too, numerous groups are formed to give all members of the class much practice in a short time. Perhaps the children may be paired to practice oral reading, observing certain standards devised in a teacher-pupil planning period. Of course, this procedure is of value only as the reading materials are fitted to the individual child's abilities. Also the teacher should circulate among the groups giving as much guidance as possible.

*From *The Reading Teacher,* 7, 2 (December, 1953), 69-74. Reprinted with permission of Gertrude Whipple and the International Reading Association.

On still other occasions, children's interests may provide the basis for grouping. In culminating a unit on "tales of old," one fourth-grade class formed interest groups to present a story review. One group engaged in preparing story dramatizations; a second group, in writing simplified versions of stories for children in a lower grade; a third, in setting up an exhibit of books with written captions; and a fourth, in summarizing the unit on a series of bulletin boards. Interests and needs in formulating and expressing ideas in a social situation determined the classification into groups.

FLEXIBILITY IN GROUPING

Good grouping practices never form rigid lines between good and poor readers. Flexibility and tentative groupings on a variety of bases are useful in preventing rigidity. Every effort should be made to avoid, in both our speech and our attitudes toward the groups, anything which might be interpreted as segregating children because they are slow learners. We cannot afford to be insensitive to the effects of children's opinions. When we imply that certain of the children are slow, the implication is harmful not only to the children so designated, who may easily develop feelings of inferiority, but also to the rapid learners because they are prone to conclude that they can succeed without diligently applying themselves.

Another way to avoid undesirable distinctions involves planning some activities to be shared by all groups. These may be story telling, dramatizations, book-sharing programs, individual reports, display of construction and art work, and almost any of the activities designed to introduce or to culminate a unit of reading. In such activities all the children are encouraged to contribute.

PURPOSEFUL SELF-DIRECTED ACTIVITIES

If the class is organized so that the teacher works with some of the children while one or more groups work alone, the teacher has an opportunity to encourage those working independently to take responsibility and to be sensitive to the rights of others. By using positive incentives she can help her pupils decide for themselves how best to act when others are busily at work. After much practice the children can learn to move around the room as necessary and even to talk over problems with one another without disturbing other groups.

The teacher will need to provide for enjoyable and purposeful independent activities. Much of the effectiveness of her instruction will depend on her avoidance of meaningless seatwork or busy work.

There are many possible types of worthwhile independent activities for children. One kind is the free reading of books on the unit that is underway. Of course, this activity taxes the teacher to assemble enough suitable books. The children using library and work tables can gather around numerous attractive books and become absorbed in reading them.

Examining pictures on the unit to see what can be learned from them is always helpful. In the middle grades children may be invited to write a statement giving one new fact learned or even a paragraph summarizing ideas gathered from a whole collection of pictures which can be passed easily from child to child. Also composing captions for pictures to be posted in the classroom is a good language-arts activity. Of course, all such written work should be carefully evaluated by children and teacher.

Instead of giving the conventional list of questions to be answered *after* reading, why not ask the children to try to answer fact questions *before* reading and then to check their answers by reading? One class attempted this with much pleasure in connection with a factual selection on the habits of squirrels. The teacher gave no clues as to whether or not the oral answers preceding the reading were accurate. Instead, after replies had been given to all the questions, she indicated that some answers were excellent but that others were either incomplete or wrong. She then encouraged the children to read the story in order to verify their own information.

Other types of independent activities are many and varied. In the very early grades, for example, the children may finger paint, observe or care for pets, cut and paste pictures into a booklet, decorate boxes they are planning to use for some purpose, model with clay, make birthday cards or decorations and materials for a party, and look at picture books, children's magazines, and illustrated catalogs. In Grade 3 and above independent activities include: writing the last three lines of a poem when given the opening line; writing an original fable after reading and discussing many fables; matching poems with pictures in preparation for making an illustrated book of poems; copying new words learned in "my own vocabulary book"; working on scrapbooks; preparing labels for exhibits; copying experience stories or group compositions to take home; preparing articles for the class or school newspaper; writing at the blackboard; and looking through books to find stories on a given topic and stacking the books for use.

Variety is essential. If children are expected to carry on the same type of independent activity day after day, they find it monotonous and tend to fritter away their time, and fail to think. This is just the opposite of the attitude for which we should strive—one of thinking actively, choosing, experimenting, judging, reasoning, and imagining.

ACTIVITIES UNDER DIRECT TEACHER GUIDANCE

In working with groups it is desirable that the teacher take a leisurely approach. She should not feel hurried to get to another group since the introductory activities determine to a large extent the value of the subsequent reading activities.

Whatever the school grade, whether Grade 1 or Grade 8, the teacher's aim in introducing new reading material is the same. She is endeavoring to relate the content to the child's experiences, foster interest in it, establish motives for the reading, and anticipate and overcome difficulties, including those presented by unfamiliar words. Often in a stimulating introduction to a story, the teacher will refer to the pictures in the book, and will build up on the board questions that the children in the group wish to have answered. Before oral reading she will perhaps encourage the children to devise suitable standards, e.g., "try to interest everyone in what you are presenting," "read loud enough for everyone to hear."

Sometimes the group activity will be concerned with the outcomes of rereading. In a seventh-grade class, for instance, a group had reread a vividly written selection to identify sound pictures (e.g., the galloping of horses, the clatter of plates); color pictures (e.g., through the bleached silver grass); odor pictures (e.g., the mellow smell of coffee); action pictures (e.g., tramped steadily, turned an expert somersault); and descriptive pictures (e.g., towering cliffs). In the class period that followed, sentences and paragraphs were read aloud and comments made to identify and support the students' choices of word pictures.

A further important activity consists in appraising work carried out by the children independently. If they have illustrated some portion of what they have read, time should be devoted to having the group evaluate the illustrations in light of the context. This is an excellent activity for improving comprehension and interpretation of material read. In the case of written work, evaluative activities will lead the children to appraise their spelling, handwriting, and expression. The appraisal ought to place emphasis chiefly upon the choice of the best ideas met in reading and upon good clear expression that others will understand.

Building a group composition which utilizes the ideas the children have gained through silent reading is a useful activity. The composition may be either creative or informational. If, for example, the group has been perusing poems about dogs such as Winifred Welles' "Dogs and Weather," with the teacher's guidance the children may develop on the board a poem about the dog they would like to walk with. On the other hand, in informational composition, the children may wish to make a summary record of what they have learned or to prepare explanations of articles they are placing on display in the room. Together the children may decide on the ideas to be included, on the order of presenting them, and on the specific statements to be made, as the teacher or a capable child records these on the board.

Perhaps no use of the teacher's time with the children is more significant than that spent in guiding discussions based on silent reading. Here we must remember that children require help in language arts other than reading. The children should be led to do most of the talking. The teacher should give enough guidance to insure that the discussion has real educational value for all those concerned—the slow, reticent pupil as well as the bright pupil in the same group. (Grouping, of course, does not equalize needs but merely reduces the range of individual differences in some few respects.) As soon as possible, children ought to learn to follow the rules of courtesy so well that the raising of hands is unnecessary. Standards to guide the discussion may be developed on the board by the group with the help of the teacher. Examples:

> *We try to say something worth hearing.*
> *We give everyone a chance to talk.*
> *We listen carefully to what others say.*
> *We ask someone to explain anything we do not understand.*
> *We talk only when no one else is talking.*
> *We keep to the subject.*
> *We talk so that others can hear easily.*

Whenever working with a group of children, then, the teacher stresses purposefulness, child activity, participation by every child in the group, and the integration of reading with the other language arts.

GUIDANCE THROUGH GROUPING

Good grouping in the classroom enables the teacher to help the child develop his capacities to the fullest extent. With fewer children to work with at a time, she can give greater attention to the individual child's needs. Recognizing that his progress in reading is dependent on many factors, she can acquaint herself with his intellectual, emotional, and environmental responses. She is then in a position to adapt instruction to the particular child and thereby to prevent maladjustment.

One of the big outcomes we are striving for today through the reading activities is success and satisfaction. This has become an outstanding goal because of the fact that personality problems are frequently associated with reading failure. Therefore, in our group activities, let us note at once any child who seems immature, restless, worried, discouraged, retiring, overly ambitious, or unusually aggressive. Would it not be wise to ask ourselves: Why does this child act in this way? How shall I interpret his responses? In terms of our best answer we can then create in school the best possible situation for freeing the child of tensions, worries, or wrong attitudes either toward himself or toward his classmates. Let us connect with group reading a maximum of fun, enthusiasm, and individual group success. Thus, grouping aids in the development of the child's personality.

However, grouping cannot achieve everything desirable in the classroom. It is no panacea for all ills. Rather it helps us to carry on as nearly individual work as possible in a fairly large class. It enables us to meet children's needs much better than if we gave instruction to the class as a unit. The degree of success achieved through grouping will depend largely upon the energy, understanding, and skill of the teacher. The good teacher will read such reports as those contained in this issue of *The Reading Teacher*, will experiment, and will develop further those procedures which prove successful.

SUPERVISION FOR BETTER GROUPING

Grouping is most likely to succeed when supervisors and administrators facilitate the teacher's efforts. Among her needs is an adequate number and variety of reading materials for her pupils. Thus the school administrator interested in improving grouping should order many individual books, sets of supplementary books, and a supply of basic readers at the children's reading levels. He should not mechanically order a reading textbook for the given grade in numbers sufficient to supply each pupil with a copy.

Also, the school leader will need to determine the difficulties which the teachers face in using grouping to the best advantage. He may invite teachers to describe their handicaps, then follow with definite help in overcoming these. This will consist, perhaps, in short meetings where teachers exchange ideas and share the good techniques they have worked out, in aid to the individual teacher in grouping her pupils and fitting the reading materials to their abilities, in arranging visits for teachers to observe the reading activities of other classes, and in preparing concrete bulletins of suggestions based on superior practices in schools the country over.

15. Does Homogeneous
Grouping Give Homogeneous Groups?*

IRVING H. BALOW

HOMOGENEOUS grouping for reading instruction in the elementary schools is often based on several assumptions. One assumption is that homogeneous groups are secured by classifying pupils on the basis of their scores on achievement tests and by limiting each group to a narrow range in test scores. According to this assumption, once pupils have been placed into such groups individual differences in achievement have been severely limited. Hence the teacher will need to provide only one set of materials and prepare only one lesson to teach the group. In short, the teacher can concentrate on the entire group rather than on individuals in the group.

A second assumption made by many advocates of homogeneous grouping is that increased achievement is an automatic result of homogeneous classes. That is, homogeneous grouping automatically leads to greater gains in reading achievement than heterogeneous classes that have a wide range of reading ability. The grouping itself is assumed to be the significant factor.

The study reported here was concerned with testing these assumptions. More specifically, the study was directed to answer the questions: Are homogeneous groups homogeneous? Do homogeneous groups make greater gains in reading achievement than heterogeneous groups?

In October, the principal of a school in southern California, in consultation with his fifth-grade teachers, decided that homogeneous grouping for reading instruction would result in greater gains for the children and would make the teaching of reading easier for the teachers. It was decided that a comprehensive test of reading achievement should be administered to the four fifth-grade classes and that the composite score would determine which group the child would enter.

In November, Form AM of the Iowa Silent Reading Tests, New Edition, was administered to the ninety-four fifth-graders. The median grade equivalent for the children on the total test ranged from 2.0 to 9.0.

*From *The Elementary School Journal* 63, 1 (October, 1962), 28-32. Copyright © 1962 by the University of Chicago. Reprinted by permission.

160

The children were divided into four classes on the basis of their grade equivalent. Children in Class A had grade equivalents that ranged from 5.7 to 9.0. Grade equivalents of children in Class B ranged from 4.6 to 5.6, in Class C from 3.6 to 4.6, and in Class D from 2.0 to 3.6.

Table 1 shows the number of children in each homogeneous class, the range in grade equivalent for each class, and the median grade equivalent for each class.

TABLE 1. *Median and Range in Grade Equivalent in Reading for Four Fifth-Grade Classes after Homogeneous Grouping*

	Class A	Class B	Class C	Class D
Number of pupils	21	29	26	18
Range	5.7–9.0	4.6–5.6	3.6–4.6	2.0–3.6
Median	6.7	5.2	4.0	3.3

Table 1 suggests that this organization resulted in more homogeneous classes. Under heterogeneous grouping each class would have had a range of seven years (2.0 to 9.0) in reading ability. Under homogeneous grouping, two classes had a range of one year; another, a range of one and a half years; and the last, three and a third years. But such data reveal only a small part of the picture.

The Iowa Silent Reading Tests consist of eight subtests that measure rate, comprehension, directed reading, word meaning, paragraph comprehension, sentence meaning, alphabetizing, and use of index. Table 2 shows the range in each homogeneous class for each subtest.

TABLE 2. *Range in Grade Equivalent in Reading for Four Homogeneous Fifth-Grade Classes That Took the Eight Subtests of the Iowa Silent Reading Tests*

Subtest	Class A	Class B	Class C	Class D
Rate	2.1–12.7	1.8–12.7	1.8–12.7	1.8–7.4
Comprehension	3.8–11.1	2.5–11.1	2.0– 6.5	2.0–6.0
Directed reading	2.5–11.8	1.8– 7.0	1.8– 5.7	1.8–5.2
Word meaning	4.5– 8.5	2.9– 7.9	1.9– 6.1	1.9–3.8
Paragraph comprehension	3.7–10.2	1.9– 9.4	1.9– 8.6	1.9–5.6
Sentence meaning	4.4–10.3	2.9– 8.4	1.9– 7.5	1.9–9.5
Alphabetizing	3.1–12.4	3.1– 8.1	3.1– 9.8	3.1–5.9
Use of index	4.7–11.3	1.9– 8.0	1.9– 6.5	1.9–6.0

As Table 2 shows, on any one subtest there was a tremendous overlap in scores from one homogeneous class to another. In fact, on most of the subtests classes B, C, and D have grade equivalents from second-grade level to sixth-grade level.

In Class A, the "above grade level" class, the smallest range (four years) is on word meaning and the greatest range (ten years and six months) on the rate test. On rate, the children in this class ranged from more than three years below grade level to almost seven and a half years above grade level. On the word meaning test, the scores in Class A ranged from more than a half year below grade level to more than three years above grade level. On each of the eight subtests, some children in Class A scored below grade level.

In Class B, the smallest range in grade equivalent was five years, and this range was found in the alphabetizing tests; in each test the scores ranged from almost two years below grade level to more than three years above grade level. The greatest range was on the rate and the comprehension tests. On the rate test, children ranged from more than three years below grade level to almost seven and a half years above grade level. On the comprehension test, scores ranged from more than two and a half years below grade level to almost six years above grade level.

Classes C and D had more restricted ranges, but the scores in each class were so divergent that only by stretching the term could any of these classes be considered homogeneous with respect to any of the subtests.

Table 2 presents evidence that groups designated as homogeneous in reading ability may in fact be extremely heterogeneous. Classification on the basis of standardized test scores does not necessarily result in homogeneous groups.

The second assumption tested in this study is that once the pupils have been grouped, the problem of teaching reading is solved and greater gains in reading achievement will result.

To test this assumption, the sixth-grade classes in three other schools in this community in southern California were tested. One school was using homogeneous grouping for reading instruction for the second year. The experience of the previous year had been evaluated informally, and the teachers were convinced that the children had made greater gains in reading as a result of homogeneous grouping. The sixth grades that served as the control group were selected because no special grouping methods had been used in these schools. Each sixth-grade teacher had a random selection of the sixth-grade children in the school.

In October, Form B, Intermediate Battery-Complete, of the Metropolitan Achievement Tests, was administered to all the children in the two groups. The results of this test were immediately given to the teachers of the experimental group so the scores could be used for grouping.

In the school that used homogeneous grouping three groups were organized. The pupils whose scores were above grade level went to one teacher for an hour each day for reading instruction. Pupils whose scores in reading were average went to the second sixth-grade teacher. Pupils whose scores in reading were below average went to the third sixth-grade teacher.

In January, the California Short-Form test of Mental Maturity was administered to all children in the two groups, and the intelligence quotients were secured. In June, Form A, Intermediate Battery–Complete, of the Metropolitan Achievement Tests, was administered.

The average intelligence quotient for the homogeneously grouped classes was 103.5 and for the control classes, 103.9. The variance of the intelligence quotients of the two groups was tested, and no statistically significant difference was found. A *t* test of the difference between means resulted in a *t* value of .175, which has a probability greater than .80 with 164 degrees of freedom. These findings strengthened our assumption that the two groups of pupils were of equal intelligence at the beginning of the experiment.

The variances of the reading test scores at the beginning of the experiment were tested and found to be statistically equal for the two groups. The mean raw score of the homogeneous group was 23.80 and of the control group, 20.97, a difference of 2.83 points. When this mean difference was tested by using the *t* test, a *t* value of 2.64 was found, a value which is significant at the 1 per cent level of probability. The hypothesis that the two groups were equal in reading abilities at the beginning of the experiment was therefore rejected. At the start of the study, the reading achievement of the homogeneous group was significantly higher than the reading achievement of the control group.

Growth in reading from October to June was determined by subtracting the October score from the June score for each child in the study. The difference was the gain as measured by the Metropolitan Achievement Tests–Reading. The mean gain for the children in the homogeneous groups was 5.078 points and for the children in the heterogeneous groups, 5.157 points. The variances of the growth scores for the two groups were tested and found to be statistically equal. The mean difference was tested using the *t* test and a *t* value of .10 was found. The probability of a *t* value of .10 with 164 degrees of freedom is greater than .90. Consequently, the hypothesis of no difference in growth between the two groups was accepted.

The first assumption, that a homogeneous group may be secured by classifying children according to a reading test score, would seem to be untenable. The evidence presented here tends, instead, to substantiate the belief that reading growth, in all its aspects, varies with each child. Reading ability is made up of many skills. The child in the fifth-grade who secures a grade equivalent of 4.5 on a reading test may be scoring below grade level because he is poor in word analysis. He may use context clues well, have high intelligence, and answer all questions on the test. Another child with the same score may be very good at word analysis, but he may not comprehend well and he may read too slowly to complete the test. These two children cannot be considered equal in reading skills even though they received the same score in reading. If test results are used as the basis for grouping, however, these two children would be placed in the same homogeneous class.

The second assumption, that greater gains in achievement will necessarily result from homogeneous grouping, was also rejected by the evidence presented in this study. The difference in mean growth scores was in favor of the control group, not the homogeneous groups, though the difference was not significant. The results show, however, that in this study the homogeneous grouping did not lead to greater measured gains.

There may be advantages which accrue to classes that are homogeneously grouped for reading instruction, but these advantages are not automatic. Procedures more sophisticated than achievement testing are required to secure a reasonably homogeneous class. But homogeneity is not enough. Once homogeneity is secured, to justify the grouping, a program must be devised that will result in greater reading growth.

16. In Defense of Individualized Reading*

JEANNETTE VEATCH

DR. Paul Witty's article, "Individualized Reading: A Survey and Evaluation,"[1] needs to be questioned from several points of view.

Dr. Witty describes "developmental reading" as that which combines the "best features of both individualized and group instruction." This statement gives support to the use of basal readers. It does not make clear the differences between the individualized, self-selection approach and the ability-grouped, basal reader approach so long dominant in educational practice.

I am heartened and encouraged to read[2] that "The good reading program is one in which the so-called basal materials are recognized as no *more basal* than additional printed materials which provide for development and wide application of skills" and that "One should recognize the limitations in some basal materials."[3] This hardly comes to grips with some of the controversial issues at stake. Later on we are told, " . . . an efficient reading program includes both 'individualized' and group activities. Moreover [it] is developmental in approach and . . . 1) aims to cultivate the skills . . . 2) recognizes various purposes and needs for teaching . . . 3) depends on other experiences and activities in association with reading . . . 4) seeks the fulfillment or extension of interests . . ."[4]

This is an admirable statement about an efficient reading program. I think it says just what an individualized program should stand for. But the next paragraph continues:

"A *defensible* reading program *accordingly* recognizes the value of systematic instruction.[5] (italics mine). What is meant by "systematic

---

*From *Elementary English,* 37, 4 (April, 1960), 227-234. Reprinted with the permission of the National Council of Teachers of English and Jeannette Veatch.

[1](Assisted by Ann Coomer and Robert Sizemore.) *Elementary English,* (October, 1959).

[2]*Ibid.,* 411.
[3]*Ibid.,* 410.
[4]*Ibid.,* 413.
[5]*Ibid.,* 450.

instruction"? Does he mean what I mean by that term? A thoughtful re-reading of the total concluding statement reveals that "systematic instruction" will include the use of a basal text as the " dependable guide and efficient plan for insuring the acquisition of basic skills."[6]

Here I must part company with Dr. Witty. I believe in systematic instruction, but of the type that develops with each child as he reads through increasingly challenging materials. Because of these and other reasons I submit that Dr. Witty's article is incorrectly titled. The questions that I raise deal with the inadequacies of both its "survey" and its "evaluation" aspects.

What, then, would I have Dr. Witty do to meet my criticism?

MORE DEFINITION OF CLASSROOM PRACTICE NEEDED

I think, first, that a more complete definition of individualized reading is needed. The historical background is well done, but the description of actual classroom practice is limited. Several good references are cited, but the addition of something like the following would be helpful:

1

Individualizing a reading program means that pupils personally choose the books and materials by which teachers instruct each one in reading. These books must number roughly triple the class size in different titles. They must include more than the varied and changing interests of every pupil. There must be enough titles at all achievement levels to guarantee a valid, honest selection by each child. The teacher selects the book supply, but the child chooses his own book—perhaps with help and guidance—but with honest respect for his preferences.

2

Individualizing a reading program includes group organization on *other* bases than general achievement or ability. As each teacher confers with each pupil on his self-selected material, the diagnosis of the specific difficulty is more easily discernible than under any other condition. When two or more children have a common difficulty—or interest or purpose—the teacher groups *them* and provides immediate help on that specific item. The teacher dissolves the group when she sees no necessity of working further. It is then replaced by a new one with *other* pupils having *other* problems in common. There is no permanent group of any kind for any child.

[6]*Ibid.*, 410.

As the days roll by, the reading period is divided roughly in half, the first portion devoted to individual conferences, the latter to group meetings. The teacher plans the group meetings from the private individual records of the preceding day where notations are kept of difficulties, problems, and challenges.

3

Individualizing a reading program means a personal teaching period for each child of at least five minutes about every three days. The interrogation and observational skills of the teacher, as always, determine the value of that conference. There is no manual to tell her *what* questions to ask, but there are sources which tell a teacher what *kind*[7] of questions to ask. But we know that the intensity of learning resulting from the intimacy of this personal contact is a powerful motivation for children to read *independently*. Even if the amount of time spent in oral reading were the same in both approaches, the high level of pupil-teacher interaction, facilitated by the *structure* of the one-to-one relationship, greatly increases the will to learn, as compared to that found in the low-level interaction of a ten-to-one situation. When a child has his teacher all to himself, the feeling that "somebody cares" easily develops.

But the time spent on reading for each child is *not* the same in an individualized program as it is in an ability-grouped program. Under the former, each child's silent reading is markedly increased over the latter approach. The amount of oral reading in each is about the same, although more intensive opportunities occur under a self-selection program than under any other type. For example, under the traditional program of ability grouping, 30 children are divided up into about three groups of ten each. Each group has about one-third of the hour of an hour-and-a-half long reading period, or 20 to 30 minutes for each group. This figures to about 2 to 3 minutes per child per day. *But*, the conventional five-step lesson plan requires 1) motivation for the story, 2) vocabulary study (on unknown words not as yet met in the basal reader), 3) preliminary silent reading with skill and comprehension building—*all* of which take place *before* any child reads orally to his teacher.[8] What then happens to the amount of time spent on oral reading in a 20-30 minute reading period? Obviously it is drastically reduced. A child is lucky if he reads orally every *other* day. Time allotments looked at in this way show why a child reading every third day to his teacher in an individual conference has equal or more actual oral reading than his conference in an ability-grouped pattern.

Another aspect of the individual conference is so unique as to merit emphasis. The oral reading of children under a basal plan usually consists of

[7] J. Veatch, *Individualizing Your Reading Program*, p. 53, New York: G. P. Putnam, 1959.

[8] It might be noted that No. 1 and No. 2 are quite unnecessary in an individualized program.

material that the teacher has heard so many times that boredom must be fought, and concentration on the children's efforts is difficult. When the material has been chosen by the child, his personal commitment to its meaning is of such high level that teachers find themselves easily caught up in the content of the material. I have been told by many teachers that they learn to know many trade books in a surprisingly short time, simply because they become interested in the stories that the pupils discuss with them and read to them during these individual conferences.

THE IRRECONCILABLE MUST BE FACED

What else would I have wished Dr. Witty to include in his article?

I would have hoped that a listing, and discussion, of those issues which are irreconcilable between basal reader systems and self-selection programs would have been included. These are two *opposing* approaches to reading instruction, and to pretend otherwise is not to understand the full import of one or the other. Dr. Witty does seem to feel that the "good" aspects of individualization can be incorporated in a "developmental" program, which, you recall, he defines as *including* basal readers. I think he is wrong. I think the inclusion of the unique practices of an individuated program would *destroy* a basal, ability-grouped program, and high time, too.

But what are some of these controversial, irreconcilable issues? Let me list some, and hope that they will be dealt with more deeply in some future publication.

1

To what degree do the teacher-made assignments in teacher-chosen (i.e. administration-publisher-chosen) books and materials affect the desire of the child to learn to read?

2

To what extent does the current conventional ability-grouping affect the mental health of our nation's children?

3

To what extent does the individual's own choice of activity, differing from any of his peers, promote or retard mental health and social growth?

4

To what extent does the use of the manual and the year-in-year-out repetition of its lessons in infrequently-revised textbooks affect the dynamic and creative character of the teaching?

5

To what extent do the skills that one child needs in learning to read coincide *in any aspect* with needed skills of other children in the peer group?

6

To what extent does the systematic instruction using basal texts enhance or retard the application of the right skill to the right child at the right time?

7

To what extent should all skills be taught to all children—or more than two at a time—in identical sequence?

8

To what extent does self-selection differ in principle when used in an individualized program and when used in the extended-reading phase of a basal program?

9

What is the difference between the *teacher-assignment* type of individuation (the heart of the Dalton and Winnetka plans) and the pupil *self-assignment* type which is the heart of the approach under discussion?

10

To what extent does the personal individual conference, and the fluid special-needs grouping, affect the learning climate of a given classroom?

11

To what extent do identical assignments for a group or class compare in learning effectiveness to self-assignments under teacher guidance?

Ruth Strickland raised other questions that merit inclusion.[9]

Question 1.   Why have we, in our effort to build readiness for reading worked it thru more and more mechanical means, and departed even farther from the way in which children most naturally learn?

Question 2.   Why have we simplified and still further simplified the material we put in beginning readers until the sentences children are to read bear little resemblance to the sentences they speak?

Question 3.   How do we justify the vocabulary of the present day readers and the conviction that vocabulary *alone* (italics mine) determined level of difficulty?

. . . .

Question 6.   Why must we start all children in the same or similar books?

These are but some questions to which all educators interested in reading instruction must address themselves far more assiduously than they have in the past. In my opinion, these are the questions which proponents of basal texts must answer if they are to work towards improvement in reading practice.

I feel that these questions are indeed appropriate to include in an article entitled "Individualized Reading: A Survey and Evaluation," since they raise issues between two basically differing patterns. Basal reader proponents cannot have their cake and eat it, too. These issues cannot be dodged forever. They must be faced.

A SECTION ON RESEARCH

Another area that I would have wished Dr. Witty to include in his article would have been the important and best investigations now available. It is indeed puzzling to figure out why he omitted so many of the best. Perhaps it is because the majority are, as yet, unpublished. It is hoped that this mention will speed the day when they will appear in print.

MORE RESEARCH NEEDED

Since the first national push in the direction of self-selection type individuation did not come until 1952-53, it is a wonder that we have as much data as now exists. That much of these data gives us a fairly large picture of the pattern is fortunate, particularly in the light of the curious lack of interest in this

---

[9]Allen J. Figurel (ed.), *Reading in a Changing Society,* pp. 162-164; 1959 Proceedings, International Reading Association, Vol. 4. New York: Scholastic Magazines.

new departure and new idea in the specialized field of reading. The International Reading Association, for example, has not *programmed* a single paper at its national conventions on the subject of individualized reading since 1957. There seems to be a kind of boycott or censorship of the subject even though discussion from the floor in 1958 and 1959 meetings was not lacking.

For that matter, in spite of thousands of studies on reading, we still know little about the total value of *any* major reading practice. What well-controlled studies, for example, with durability measurement, support the hoary practice of segregating children in remedial reading classes? And what about Dr. Witty's pattern of developmental reading? Traxler[10] found " . . . . after two decades the term developmental reading is not standardized in common usage. There was *little actual research* of (it) during this period" (italics mine). I wonder why Dr. Witty is so demanding of full-blown research of the infant practice of individualized reading when that practice which he espouses is considered neglected in one of the major research volumes on reading?

WHAT DO STUDIES SHOW?

The first two studies I would like to mention are largely descriptive and observational in character. But within the limitations of their structure they give us valuable information on the subject, "What about the skills?" "Are the skills really taught?"

Constance Carr[11] found that teaching skills and developing abilities were an integral part of an individualized program. She investigated 20 third and fourth grades using such an approach to discover what skills and abilities were developed. Comparing her observations with recommendations made by six authors of major texts on the teaching of reading, she found the teachers strongest in teaching those skills which all authors said were important, and weakest in those about which there was some controversy as to their importance. Dr. Carr's study raises questions as to the conventional sequence of time and place of certain skills, yet verified that skills actually were taught.

The Board of Education of the City of New York[12], in an initial survey of this practice in 20 schools, notes:

[10]A. E. Traxler, et al, *Eight More Years of Research in Reading,* p. 38. New York: Educational Records Bureau. 1955.

[11]C. Carr, *Individual Development of Abilities and Skills in Reading.* Unpublished Ed. dissertation, Teachers College, Columbia University 1958.

[12]Board of Education, City of N. Y. *Individualized Reading: Interim Report* 1956-57 Mimeographed.

(Readers will be interested to know that all of the New York City Material now in mimeographed form will be available in a monograph in Spring, 1960. It has long been the most comprehensive treatise in a bibliography now reaching over a hundred items. Statistical data is being prepared for inclusion.)

... teachers are more aware of the skills than they have ever been before.

... Teachers are developing the skills with more insight than heretofore.

... Teachers, *rather than reading manuals,* are assuming responsiblity for teaching the skills ...

Not every step of every skill needs to be taught to every child.

Gertrude Hildreth,[13] in discussing the experimentation in New York City, where hundreds of teachers are now individualizing their reading instruction, notes in her book: "Teachers have discovered that all free choice reading of a primary pupil develops his skills *so long as the child has assistance when he requires it"* (italics mine). This is not a study, of course, but an observation by a major figure in the field of education.

There are references to the matter of skill teaching in the innumerable articles about the practice. But the above, particularly the first two, I believe, serve as at least tentative substantiations that skills most assuredly *do* get taught in an individual program. As with every aspect of all reading programs, we need more and more detailed work.

Let us move to another type of study. There are several that should not be excluded from the presentation. The following depend, to greater and lesser degrees, upon experimentation with controls built into the investigation. These are a far cry from those which worried Constance McCullough with their reports of "cheerful miens and numbers of books." (I trust she has by now regretted *that* statement.)

The findings of the following studies cover so many facets of reading instruction that it is exceedingly difficult to organize them under any one category. Thus I will proceed to describe each study separately, and report on what I consider to be pertinent findings.

I feel that the best research (*i.e.,* with the best controls) is that of Antoinette McChristy.[14] She matched 8 second grades on 1) year's attendance and age; 2) mental status; 3) socio-economic class; 4) reading grade status; 5) teacher background, experience, and competence; and then compared the results of the experimental self-selection pattern with the conventional basal reading pattern. She reports that:

1. Mean grade achievement, total reading gain, and vocabulary were significant statistically in favor of the experimental groups.
2. On results of the regular testing program (California Reading Test, forms

[13]G. Hildreth, *Teaching Reading,* p. 257. New York: Henry Holt, 1958. [2]Quoted on p. 410 of the article.

[14]A. McCristy, *A Comparative Study to Determine Whether Self-Selection Reading Can Be Successfully Used at Second Grade Level.* Unpublished master's dissertation. University of Southern California, 1957.

BB & CC) 59% of the experimental subjects gained 2 years or more, while 24% of control subjects gained 2 years or more.

She concluded that this approach could be used successfully in the second grade and would yield results superior to the conventional three ability grouped, basal reading pattern, and the children *could* choose materials that would promote their reading growth.

From a study by Cyrog[15] of a self-selection program by seven elementary teachers over a three year program, I note in part that:

1. Individualized reading over a two or three-year period produces better than average results.
2. Individualized reading can be used successfully in first grade.

The "halo" or Hawthorne effect was minimized but not entirely eliminated, by such measures as equal time spent in experimental and control classes in the reading period, uniform class size, equal consultant assistance, and equal administrative emphasis.

Philip Acinapuro[16] in a controlled study of three pairs of middle grade classes found statistically significant differences favoring the individuated groups in 1) silent reading comprehension, 2) total silent and oral achievement.[17] He found individualized reading is equally effective as a three-ability group approach in the development of reading vocabulary.

As this is one of the best controlled studies available, I think it noteworthy that his data revealed his experimental subjects reading more both in and out of school. This, I should think, should give pause to those who do not find pupils reading much outside of school. Is not something wrong when children don't like to take books home? Is it true that basal readers are, perhaps, not intended to be enjoyed until *after* all skills are learned? Acinapuro shows that skills and the "cheerful miens" went along together.

Sam Duker[18] reports on a study which, among other things, should allay the charge that "only master teachers can individualize successfully." He set up a situation in which student teachers carried the brunt of the experimentation and

[15] Francis Cyrog, "A Principal and His Staff Move Forward in Developing New Ways of Thinking About Reading," *California Journal of Elementary Education,* 27 (February, 1959) 178-87.

[16] Philip Acinapuro, *A Comparative Study of the Results of Two Instructional Reading Programs: An Individualized Pattern and 3-Ability Group Pattern.* Unpublished Ed. D. Dissertation. Teachers College, Columbia University, New York 1959.

[17] Tests used were: Gray's Standardized Oral Reading Paragraphs, C. A. Gregory Co., Indianapolis, Indiana. Iowa Every Pupil Tests of Basic Skills. Boston: Houghton-Mifflin.

[18] S. Duker, "Research Report: Effects of Introducing an Individualized Reading Approach by Student Teachers," *Research in Action*; p. 59, 1957. Proceedings International Reading Association.

were compared against experienced teachers following a conventional basal program. Ten fourth, fifth, and sixth grade classes were involved. Dr. Duker leaned over backward in avoiding unwarranted assumptions. Yet, in spite of some minor structural flaws, this work does give us new insights into its area of investigation. He found statistically significant gains in achievement and vocabulary improvement (Stanford Achievement Tests used) and, as with Acinapuro, markedly improved attitudes towards reading and lessening of problems of discipline.

These are several, among many available, that I believe need inclusion in a presentation such as this. In my opinion, each of these uses much better research techniques than those in this article. Dr. Witty failed to point out the weaknesses in those cited of Kaar, Walker, Bohnhorst and Sellars, Anderson, *et al.* Therefore, I felt constrained to comment that the best investigations were omitted from the article.

There are many, many *reports* in the bibliography[19] that, while informative, are not well-grounded, research-wise. In most of them the "halo" or Hawthorne effect is obvious and has quite correctly been pointed out by Dr. Gray, McCullough, and others. These report teacher experience and observation with self-selection. The lengthy bibliography includes so many that space permits mention of only a few: Lucy Polansky,[20] Ethel M. Schmidt,[21] from the same source as Dr. Duker's report. Those by Willard C. Olson, Frances Maib, Grace Garretson, Mabel L. Johnson, June McLeod, Bessie Maxey, Jill Bonney and Levin Hanigan, and Mildred E. Thompson[22] are some more that should be noted. Except to those who wish to disprove the effectiveness of an individuated program, these reports have not served as *research references* so much as needed *sources* for eager and experimentally minded teachers. I personally feel that these articles and reports are more like case studies and are more wisely used as examples of classroom practice.

There are undoubtedly many more studies which have not come to my attention. I would be happy to be informed of any others.

Baltimore County, Maryland, has set up a controlled research project involving eighteen classrooms in which children are matched as to age, grade, reading achievement, and intelligence, and teachers matched as to experience. Six classes are using the complete traditional basal reader approach; six classes are using a modified, part basal, part individualized approach; and six are on a completely individualized approach. However, the six classes on an

---

[19] I will be happy to send a bibliography to those who request it, *c/o* Penn State University, University Park, Pa. Enclose a long, self-addressed stamped envelope.

[20] *Research in Action,* Proceedings of the International Reading Association, 1957, p. 59, 167.

[21] *Ibid.,* p. 169.

[22] All reprinted in J. Veatch, *Individualizing Your Reading Program.* New York: G. P. Putnam, 1959.

individualized pattern are interpreting it as one which *excludes any* grouping. This is unfortunate because, if not corrected, an accurate evaluation will not occur.

There are several doctoral studies now in progress. I happen to know of one by Sperry at Los Angeles State College, Kelly and Braidford at New York University, Bretlinger at the University of Arizona, and Carline, Bird, Stine, and Mattera at Penn State. These vary in design from survey type to controlled experimentation.

In addition to these several doctoral studies, Dr. Lyman C. Hunt of The Pennsylvania State University, under a U.S. Government grant, is conducting a TV experiment using 15 half-hour programs on the teaching of reading in which individuation bears a major part. This should culminate in some important findings later in the year.

May I again point out that there is no doubt that much, much more research is needed. But it must, as I believe these I have described do, come to grips with more of the fundamental issues. We must move on from that classic study on reading disability, *Why Pupils Fail in Reading,* by Helen A. Robinson[23] (a great step forward in its day), which makes no mention of the possibility that pupils fail in reading because they so dislike that which *is given them* to read by teachers—namely, the basal readers. New investigations must explore *this* territory. What is the role of pupil choice of material in learning to read? Where is the reserach which shows that children *like* to read basal books exclusively? Is this as important as teachers who have used the self-selection principle in their classroom think it is? Sperber[24] asks: "Have you ever seen . . . children in your class fight over a basal reader?" Is he alone?

In concluding my discussion of research, may I repeat that all we now know about individualized reading is still inadequate, even though we do see some major guidelines. It seems to me that we should welcome a new and challenging approach—even if it is the first serious threat to a decades-old system. I am appalled at the finality with which Dr. Witty and other able, well-known people have pre-judged or incorrectly judged this developing practice as 1) unimportant, or 2) a "fad," or 3) something good teachers have always done.

Individualized reading is but the beginning of a renaissance in which teaching is returned to the teacher. It is what Alexander Frazier calls "open learning"—in which all children progress at their own speed regardless of that of their peers.

Ours is a wide and free country, and difference of opinion is to be cherished—but let us differ on fundamental issues, not on inadequate information.

[23]Chicago: The University Chicago Press, 1943.

[24]Robert Sperber, "Individualizing a Third Grade Program," from *Individualizing Reading Practices* by Alice Miel, p. 34. Teachers College, Columbia University, 1958.

17. Individualized Reading as Part of an Eclectic Reading Program*

W.PAUL BLAKELY

Professor of Education in the College
of Education, Drake University, Des Moines, Iowa

BEVERLY MCKAY OSIER

formerly teacher in the Public Schools,
Nevada, Iowa

ALTHOUGH some of the more partisan advocates of Individualized Reading have presented it as an all-or-nothing program, there have been expressed authoritative opinions that it may contribute rewardingly, along with elements of other recognized types of reading instruction, to an eclectic reading program. Witty wrote,

> It seems that a defensible program in reading will combine the best features of both individual and group instruction in reading. . . . A defensible reading program . . . recognizes the value of systematic instruction, utilization of interests, fulfillment of developmental needs, and the articulation of reading experience with other types of worthwhile activities.[1]

Likewise, Strang raised the question whether it is necessary to choose between individualized and basal reader approaches, and identified the effective teacher as one who, whatever the major approach used, introduces all the necessary features of a successful reading program.[2] Artley, Robinson, and Barbe are among the other specialists who could be cited to the same effect.[3,4,5]

*From *Elementary English,* 43, 3 (March, 1966) 214-219. Reprinted with the permission of the National Council of Teachers of English and W. Paul Blakely and Beverly McKay.

[1] Paul Witty, "Individualized Reading—a Summary and Evaluation," *Elementary English,* 36 (October, 1959) 450.

[2] Ruth Strang, "Controversial Programs and Procedures in Reading," *The School Review,* 69 (Winter, 1961) 420-21.

[3] A. Sterl Artley, "An Eclectic Approach to Reading," *Elementary English,* 38 (May, 1961) 326.

[4] Helen M. Robinson, "News and Comment: Individualized Reading," *The Elementary School Journal,* 60 (May, 1960) 411-20.

[5] Walter B. Barbe, *Educator's Guide to Personalized Reading Instruction.* Englewood Cliffs, New Jersey: Prentice-Hall, Inc., 1961, pp. 223-4.

To give further substantiation to these opinions, and to provide a source of guidelines for schools and teachers wishing to use individualized reading in an eclectic reading program, the authors undertook the following investigation during the school year 1962-63. It was the purpose of the investigation to discover what means are being used to supplement a basal reader program with individualized instruction in grades four, five, and six.

The investigation was carried out by means of a questionnaire which was constructed for the purpose and sent in the quantity of five copies each to the elementary supervisors or comparable officials in fifty Iowa school systems. The school systems were selected arbitrarily and subjectively, with geographic distribution within the state and elimination of very small systems being given consideration. Each of the fifty officials was requested to distribute the five questionnaire to teachers of grades four, five and/or six whom he believed to be using individualized reading procedures along with a basal reader program.

A return of 124 questionnaire of the 250 thus distributed, was received. The return percentage of 49.6 should be interpreted bearing in mind that some officials may have had no teachers in their systems eligible to receive the questionnaires under the terms specified, and others may have had fewer than the five for whom questionnaire were supplied.

Of the 124 questionnaires returned, eleven answered negatively the first question, "Do you use individualized reading as part of your reading program, *along with basal reading series?"* (This happened in spite of the stipulation in the accompanying letter to the elementary supervisor or other official which was intended to prevent it.) This comparison of eleven with 113 (total, 124) in no way represents the prevalence or scarcity of the practice being investigated, of course.

Individualized reading was identified in the first question as follows:

> Individualized reading is not new! It refers to the procedures involved when reading time is spent by children reading materials which they themselves select, with teacher guidance when necessary, and the activities associated with such reading: pupil record-keeping, individual teacher-pupil conferences, and individual or group instruction in reading skills when need arises.

Two respondents of the 124 described a program which was more or less strictly individualized reading rather than a use of it in combination with the basal reader program. This left a population of 111 respondents who indicated that they did use individualized reading along with a basal reading series, and on whose answers the following analysis is based.

THE ROLE OF INDIVIDUALIZED READING IN THE ECLECTIC PROGRAM

In the questionnaire, the respondent was offered four possible procedures among which to indicate the one she was using; or, in case none of the four was appropriate, a fifth choice, "Other." An examination of Table 1 shows that the use indicated most frequently was that of a supplement to the basal reader, used regularly regardless of whether or not the basal reader has been completed. Other uses indicated with considerably less frequency were (in descending order) a special approach for retarded readers, to fill out a year or semester for any group which finishes basal readers, miscellaneous "other" uses, and to fill out a year or semester for only the superior group. (The percentages in the tables do not necessarily total 100. A respondent might indicate more than one response to most questions.) Among the "other" practices reported were use of individualized reading in a program of interclass grouping ("Joplin Plan"), use of the Science Research Associates Reading Laboratories, use of individualized reading for twelve weeks followed by the basal reader program, and use of individualized reading as a special approach for both the retarded and the superior readers. One teacher reported an individualized reading group which children might join when they demonstrated that they had acquired certain skills.

TABLE I Method of Incorporating Individualized
Reading into the Reading Program Selected
Iowa Schools, 1963

Method	Teachers Indicating	Percent of Total
To fill out a year or semester for only the superior group	11	10
To fill out a year or semester for any group which finishes basal readers	24	22
As a special approach for retarded readers	30	27
As a supplement to the basal reader, used regularly even though the basal reader has not been completed	88	79
Other	19	17

BASIS OF STUDENTS' BOOK SELECTIONS

Respondents were asked, "How do students select books?" An analysis of the responses, which were not structured on the questionnaire, is shown in Table II. The basis mentioned most frequently was interest, while teacher guidance, selection from a group which the teacher has selected as being at his level and suitable, and selection on the basis of relation to reading and other subject units being studied were mentioned less frequently. Miscellaneous other bases, mentioned from one to eight times each, were availability, appearance and physical characteristics, recommendations of friends, guidance of librarians, individual ability, and selection from books and stories suggested in the basal reader.

TABLE II Basis of Students' Book Selections in Reading Programs Selected Iowa Schools, 1963

Basis	Teachers Indicating	Percent of Total
Interest	77	69
With teacher guidance	25	23
From group teacher has selected as being at his level and suitable	25	23
Relation to reading and other subject units being studied	20	18
From books and stories suggested in basal reader	8	7
Individual ability	8	7
Guidance of librarian	6	5
Recommendations of friends	4	4
Appearance, physical characteristics	2	2
Availability	1	1

SOURCES OF BOOKS AVAILABLE TO CHILDREN

Ranking high as sources of books used by children in individualized reading, as mentioned by the 111 respondents, were the school central library, the public library, and the classroom library. Less frequently mentioned were the county library (in Iowa, usually associated with the Office of the County Superintendent of Schools) and the children's homes. Other sources, mentioned by a few respondents, were book clubs, the teacher, the S. R. A. Laboratory (a misinterpretation of the question), and the library service of the Iowa State Education Association (a sales, not a lending agency). The information concerning sources of books is presented in detail in Table III.

TABLE III Sources of Books Available to Children Selected Iowa Schools, 1963

Source	Teachers Indicating	Percent of Total
School central library	82	73
Public library	73	65
Classroom library	67	60
County library	24	22
Home	22	19
Book clubs	7	6
Teacher	6	5
S.R.A. Reading Laboratory	4	4
I.S.E.A. Library Service	1	1

TYPES OF MATERIALS USED

Table IV shows that the most frequently mentioned types of materials used in the individualized reading part of the eclectic reading program were fiction trade books, non-fiction trade books, various basal readers, periodicals, and content texts. The S. R. A. Reading Laboratory was mentioned by five percent of the respondents, while newspaper and comic materials were mentioned in three responses. It should be noted that fiction and non-fiction trade books were both mentioned by a large majority of the respondents.

METHODS OF KEEPING RECORDS OF CHILDREN'S READING

The variety of methods of keeping records of children's reading associated with individualized reading is shown in Table V. Mentioned most frequently were filing cards, student notebooks, charts, and written reports. Thirteen percent of the respondents said that no records were kept. Mentioned once or no

TABLE IV Types of Materials used in Reading
Programs Selected Iowa Schools, 1963

Type	Teachers Indicating	Percent of Total
Fiction trade books	102	92
Non-fiction trade books	99	88
Various basal readers	83	75
Periodicals	73	66
Content texts	67	60
S.R.A. Laboratory	5	5
Newspapers	1	1
School newspapers	1	1
Comic-type	1	1

more than four times were the S. R. A. record-keeping procedure, graphs, check sheets, cumulative folders, and questionnaires.

Of the teachers reporting no record keeping procedure, one said, "I do not keep a chart or file. I believe if a child will read for enjoyment and not because of a star or a check, he is on the way to a life of reading, and not just a year or twelve years."

TABLE V Methods of Keeping Records of Children's
Reading Selected Iowa Schools, 1963

Method	Teachers Indicating	Percent of Total
Filing cards	33	30
Student notebooks	29	26
Charts	28	25
Written reports	22	20
No records	14	13
S.R.A. procedure	4	4
Graphs	3	3
Check sheets	3	3
Cumulative folders	2	2
Questionnaires	1	1

TYPES OF TEACHER-PUPIL CONFERENCES

One of the elements that usually distinguishes individualized reading from simple "free reading" is the provision for definite individual discussion and instruction involving the teacher and the pupil. Table VI shows that only twenty-five percent of the respondents indicated the use of individual conferences, while twenty-four percent indicated the use of small group conferences, and thirty-five percent, a combination. Twenty percent indicated that they held no conferences.

TABLE VI Types of Teacher-Pupil Conferences in
Reading Programs Selected Iowa Schools,
1963

Type	Teachers Indicating	Percent of Total
Individual	28	25
Small group	27	24
Combination of above	35	31
No conferences	21	20

ACTIVITIES THAT TAKE PLACE
DURING TEACHER-PUPIL CONFERENCES

Table VII indicates that the activity taking place most frequently in the individualized reading conferences in the respondents classrooms was the child's telling the story in his own words. Oral reading and question-answer sessions were mentioned by fifty-one and forty-one percent of the respondents respectively; while fewer mentioned checking for comprehension and vocabulary and helping in correcting difficulties, and discussion of story, characters, incidents, etc. Activities mentioned by one to six percent of the respondents were discussion of book to be read next, discussion of written report, pupil evaluation of his own achievement, taping of oral reading or reporting, and dramatization. Three respondents said they varied the activities to meet the needs of the children. The fact that a large number of the respondents mentioned several activities indicates that many teachers follow this practice, which is, of course, necessary for true individualization of reading instruction.

OCCASIONS FOR GROUP INSTRUCTION

The inclusion in Table VIII of thirteen categories derived from answers to the question, "What occasions, if any, are used for *group* instruction specifically related to the individualized reading part of the program?" indicates the wide variety of such occasions. Those mentioned most frequently were need of the group for help with a particular skill, opportunity for individual ideas or discoveries with the class, opportunity for oral book reviews, need to prepare the class to select and evaluate books, a number of student's having chosen the same or related material, need for the whole class to plan for a particular activity, need to introduce new concepts, and need to stress reading skills in teaching the content areas.

TABLE VII Activities Which Take Place During
Teacher-Pupil Conferences in Reading
Programs Selected Iowa Schools, 1963

Activity	Teachers Indicating	Percent of Total
Child telling story in own words	68	63
Oral reading	56	51
Question-answer session	45	41
Check for comprehension, vocabulary, etc. and help in correcting difficulties	13	12
Discussion of story, characters, incidents, etc.	12	11
Dramatization	6	6
Taping of oral reading or reporting	3	3
Activities varied to meet needs of children	3	3
Pupil evaluation of own achievement	2	2
Discussion of written report	1	1
Discussion of book to be read next	1	1

Group instruction or sharing provides an opportunity for interaction among students and the bringing together of ideas, opinions, and concepts gained from their independent reading experiences. Instruction provided in groups, where common need or readiness warrants it, is also more economical of teacher time than individual instruction and thus more efficient.

TABLE VIII Occasions for Group Instruction Specifically Related to the Individualized Reading Part of Programs Selected Iowa Schools, 1963

Occasion	Teachers Indicating	Percent of Total
Group needs help with a particular skill	19	17
Sharing individual ideas or discoveries with class	18	16
Oral book reviews	9	8
Preparation of class to select and evaluate books	9	8
Number of students choose same or related materials	8	7
Planning by whole class for a particular activity	6	5
Introduction of new concepts	5	5
Stressing reading skills in teaching the content areas	5	5
Follow-up activities	3	3
Wide interest shown in some phase of work	2	2
Oral reading to class	2	2
Panel discussions	1	1
Word building and analysis	1	1
None	27	24

GOALS OF THE INDIVIDUALIZED READING PART OF THE PROGRAM

As shown in Table IX, and as might be expected because of the nature of individualized reading, the most frequently mentioned goals of the individualized reading part of the eclectic reading program were love of reading and broadening interests. It is significant, however, that four of the next five items in rank have to do with skills of reading: increased comprehension, enriched vocabulary, greater independence in work, and mastery of skills. Skills areas mentioned less frequently are improved fluency and speed, improved self-expression, improved research skills, independent application of word attack skills in context, and development of ability to select materials wisely. Mention by several respondents of increased knowledge and broadened background indicates another potential contribution of individualized reading.

TABLE IX *Goals of Individualized Reading Part of*
Programs Selected Iowa Schools, 1963

Goal	Teachers Indicating	Percent of Total
Love of reading	37	33
Broadened interests	36	32
Increased comprehension	22	20
Increased knowledge	20	18
Enriched vocabulary	19	16
Greater independence in work	14	13
Mastery of skills	13	12
Adoption of reading as a leisure activity	11	10
Development of literary appreciation and taste	10	9
Improved fluency	10	9
Increased speed	10	9
Increased amount of reading	8	7
Reading of wider variety of materials	8	7
Improved self-expression	8	7
Improved research skills	7	6
Independent application of word attack skills in context	7	6
Broadened background	5	5
Development of ability to select materials wisely	4	4

TEACHER OPINION OF THE VALUE OF INDIVIDUALIZED READING AS PART OF THE READING PROGRAM

It is probably not surprising, in view of the selection process used in getting respondents in this investigation, that 108 of the 111 were favorable toward the use of individualized reading in conjunction with the basal reader program. Individual comments included the following: "Interest has been established within the slower group to stimulate their seeking the help needed." "In my opinion, the basic text does not provide very much challenge to the better readers and by individualizing the program you can make these people stretch their minds." "I feel that each child is progressing at his own rate and developing interests." "Individualized reading is essential! It is a self-motivator for application of skills taught. It removes the temptations of poor work-study habits, dawdling, and mischief. It provides for repetition of skill teaching. Its content leads children into joyful experiences with reading."

CONCLUSION

The results of the investigation reported here, based on questionnaire responses of 111 middle-grade teachers, give credibility and meaning to the assertion that individualized reading procedures may enrich and strengthen an eclectic reading program, offering contributions that complement the basal reader series.

IV

Human Variation in Reading Performance

18. Reading Abilities of Bright and Dull Children of Comparable Mental Ages*

EMERY P. BLIESMER[1]

IN a recent study by Kolstoe [2],† the usefulness of mental age as a unit of measurement was investigated by comparing the mental abilities of bright and dull children of similar mental ages. In general, his results revealed only minor differences in the traits measured. The present investigation is a companion study which involved essentially the same samples of bright and dull children as those employed by Kolstoe. Its purpose was to determine the extent to which children of equal mental age but markedly different in chronological age and IQ tend to be alike with respect to achievement in reading. This was done by comparing bright and dull children with approximately equal estimated true mental ages with respect to each of several abilities involved in reading comprehension. The criterion for 'dull' was an estimated true Standford-Binet IQ of 84 or below; the one for 'bright' was an estimated true Stanford-Binet IQ of 116 or above. Thus the minimum separation between the two groups was approximately two standard deviation units along the IQ continuum. Estimates of the true IQ's and MA's were obtained by applying the standard formula for correction for regression to the obtained IQ's and MA's, with the reliability coefficients used in the formula being those reported by Terman and Merrill for various IQ levels.[2]

Results of the extensive investigations of Lewis [3] and of McGehee [4], earlier studies by Almack and Almack [1] and by Van Wagenen [8], and a later study by Thomas [6], suggest that, in general, bright children achieve below, and dull children achieve above, levels consistent with their indicated mental ages. One might expect, therefore, that a direct comparison of the achievement of bright and dull children with approximately the same mental ages would show

---

*From the *Journal of Educational Psychology,* 45, 6 (October, 1954). Reprinted by permission of Abrahams Magazine Serivce, Inc., 56 East 13th Street, New York, New York.

†Numbers in brackets refer to references at the end of the article.

[1]This article is based on the writer's Ph.D. dissertation. The work was done at the State University of Iowa under the co-direction of Professors A. N. Hieronymus and J. B. Stroud.

[2]L. M. Terman and M. A. Merrill, *Measuring Intelligence,* Boston: Houghton Mifflin Co., 1937, p. 46.

results favoring the latter. The fact that the older, low IQ children have been in school longer and have been exposed to instruction in certain specific reading skills not taught in the lower grades would also lend support to such an hypothesis. On the other hand, most of the investigations of the relationship between brightness and over-and under-achievement have failed to take into consideration regression effects resulting from lack of reliability in the mental age measures, which would account for some of the observed differences. Ceiling and floor effects, and procedures used in extrapolating age and grade scales on standard reading tests may also be responsible for finding very little over-achievement among high IQ groups and under-achievement among groups of low IQ pupils. Thus, assuming equal variability of reading age scores and mental age scores, it is virtually impossible for a pupil at or near the 99th percentile on an intelligence test to 'over-achieve' or a pupil near the first percentile to 'under-achieve'.

In a study by Ramaseshan [5], ninth-grade pupils of similar mental ages *(Chicago Tests of Primary Mental Abilities)* were grouped according to chronological age. Children with similar mental ages but different chronological ages (and, consequently, differing IQ's) were compared on the subtests of the *Iowa Tests of Educational Development.* Her bright group was found to excel on all of the subtests of the ITED, but differences were statistically significant for only three of these subtests. Of some pertinence to the purposes of the writer's study is the fact that no significant differences were found on the three subtests measuring the ability to read and interpret material in specific content areas.

Unsicker [7] equated groups according to mental age by matching groups of bright third- and fourth-grade pupils with groups of dull seventh- and eighth-grade pupils, first on the basis of *Kuhlman-Anderson Intelligence Test* scores, then on the basis of *California -Tests of Mental Maturity* results. When the groups matched on the basis of Kuhlman-Anderson MA's were compared with respect to reading comprehension scores earned on the *Iowa Tests of Basic Skills,* Unsicker found significant differences favoring the bright group. Differences between the groups matched on the basis of California MA's were not significant.

In addition to the fact that different criterion tests were employed, the present study differs from most of those in which the problem has been investigated previously in that estimated true scores were used in the matching procedure, individually administered intelligence tests rather than group tests were employed, and the criterion tests were of an appropriate level of difficulty so that ceiling and floor effects did not operate to bias the means.

PROCEDURE

Method of Sampling

In order to measure a wide range of comprehension abilities, it was decided to employ test materials which are appropriate at the fourth- to fifth-grade level of reading ability. Considering the IQ criteria for 'bright' and 'dull' (lower and upper IQ limits of 116 and 84, respectively), and studying the overlap of MA's at various CA's for these bright and dull criteria, it was decided to use a mental age range of from ten years, seven months, through twelve years, six months, and to restrict the bright group to children with CA's of ten years or less and the dull group to children with CA's of fourteen years or above.

Children in the dull group were selected from regular eighth- and ninth-grade classes and some special education classes in two junior high schools, and children in the bright group from regular third- and fourth-grade classes in three elementary schools, in the public school system of a large Iowa city. For identification of pupils likely to meet sample specifications, the cumulative record folder of each child in the two junior high schools, and in third and fourth grades in the three elementary schools, was studied. A list was made of all the junior high pupils' who were fourteen years of age or older and for whom IQ's of 90 or below had been obtained with group intelligence tests which had been administered by the schools in previous years. In the elementary schools, a list was made of all third- and fourth-grade pupils who were ten years of age or younger and for whom IQ's of 110 or above had been obtained with group intelligence tests in previous years.

From the list of pupils indicated as likely to meet specifications for the dull group, pupils were selected randomly and the *Revised Stanford-Binet Scale,* Form L, was administered until there were obtained twenty-nine pupils who met the following specifications:

1) Estimated true IQ's of 84 or below.

2) Estimated true MA's of from ten years, seven months, through twelve years, six months.

From the list of third- and fourth-grade pupils indicated as likely to meet sample specifications for the bright group, pupils were selected randomly and the *Revised Stanford-Binet Scale,* Form L, was administered until there was obtained a sample of pupils meeting the following specifications:

1) Estimated true IQ's of 116 or above.

2) Estimated true MA's of from ten years, seven months, through twelve years, six months.

3) As many bright children in each of four six-months mental age intervals or levels (which constituted the two-year range indicated in the preceding specification) as there were dull children in that interval.

In the process of obtaining enough bright cases in each level to match the number of dull cases in that level, extra cases were obtained for some of the levels. For purposes of statistical analysis, extra cases in each level were later discarded randomly. The final sample contained twenty-eight children in each group, dull and bright, one case originally selected for the dull group having been lost because of incomplete data. In the dull group, there were fifteen boys and thirteen girls; thirteen in Grade 8, six in Grade 9, and nine in special classes. The bright group was composed of sixteen boys and twelve girls; fifteen in Grade 3 and thirteen in Grade 4. A summary of information relative to the dull and bright groups in the sample is presented in Table I.

TABLE I. Characteristics of the Samples

	Groups	
	Bright	Dull
Range of CA's	8–7 through 9–10	14–2 through 16–3
Mean CA	9–2.5	15–5.4
Range of MA's (est. true)	10–8 through 12–6	10–8 through 12–6
Mean MA	11–3.2	11–3.0
Range of IQ's (est. true)	116 through 138	72 through 84
Mean IQ	126.5	79.5

Selection of Comprehension Abilities Investigated

A survey of the professional literature, teachers' manuals accompanying series of readers, standarized tests, and reported results of factorial studies was made for suggestions of specific abilities involved in reading comprehension. Consideration was also given to availability of measuring instruments for these specific abilities, the possibilities of adapting available instruments to the purposes of this study, and the purported importance of given abilities. This resulted in the selection of the following abilities for inclusion in this investigation:

1) Word Recognition (the ability to recognize given words 'on sight').

2) Word Meaning (the ability to understand or recognize the particular meaning of a word as it is used in context).

3) Memory for Factual Details (the ability to recall specific facts which have been definitely stated in a selection).

5) Perception of Relationships among Definitely Stated Ideas (the ability to recognize or to formulate an idea which is not explicitly stated in a selection but which is contained in the selection when two or more definitely stated ideas are considered together).

6) Recognition of Main Ideas (the ability to recognize the central thought or main idea of an entire selection, a paragraph, or a specific part of a paragraph).

7) Drawing Inferences and Conclusions (the ability to recognize, or to formulate, an idea which is not stated in a selection but which is dependent upon the combination of an idea (or ideas) which is (are) definitely stated in a selection and one which is outside the selection and within the informational or experiental background of the individual).

In addition to these abilities, measures of reading rate and listening comprehension were also obtained. Reading rate scores were secured not only because comparisons between the groups were of some interest in themselves, but also because marked differences in rate could be responsible for differences in comprehension abilities, even though the tests were untimed. The measures of listening comprehension were obtained in order to determine whether differences in general comprehension ability exist when unencumbered by possible difficulties with mechanical skills in reading.

Criterion Tests Used

Eighty words from the Flashed Word Recognition and Word Analysis Test of the *Durrell Analysis of Reading Difficulty,* and twenty more difficult words from various forms (Q through T) of Part II (Vocabulary) of the Reading Comprehension Test, Advanced Battery, of the *Iowa Tests of Basic Skills,* were included in the Word Recognition Test. These one hundred words were arranged in lists of twenty each and were presented tachistoscopically for a duration of approximately one second. Only results obtained with the last four lists (eighty words) were included in the analysis of results.

The Word Meaning Test was a multiple response test consisting of a representative sample of fifty items chosen from various forms (Q through T) of Part II (Vocabulary) of the Reading Comprehension Test, Elementary and Advanced Batteries, of the *Iowa Tests of Basic Skills.*

A test of Comprehension Abilities was made up of nine reading selections and one hundred and thirty items which were adapted from the Reading Comprehension Test of the Elementary and Advanced Batteries of the *Iowa Tests of Basic Skills,* Forms L through T. Five subtest scores, each based on from twenty-five to twenty-seven items, were obtained as measures of these five specific abilities: Memory for Factual Details, Location or Recognition of Factual Details, Perception of Relationships among Definitely Stated Ideas, Recognition of Main Ideas, and Drawing Inferences and Conclusions. The reading selections were chosen on the basis of relative difficulty, apparent interest value, and the extent to which items accompanying selections represented the specific abilities named above. To obtain subtests of approximately equal length and difficulty, a number of original items were eliminated and additional ones were constructed when necessary.

A Listening Comprehension Test was constructed in a manner similar to that for the Test of Comprehension Abilities, except that items for Location or Recognition of Factual Details were not included. The test consisted of four reading selections and forty-two items. The test booklets contained only the questions related to the selections. The selections and the test items were read aloud to the subjects by the examiner; and subjects marked their chosen responses to each question after it and its answer choices had been read.

The Reading Rate Test consisted of a selection of approximately fifteen hundred words of fourth- to fifth-grade level of difficulty. Subjects were instructed to read the selection once "at the same speed as you usually read." They were told before they began that there would be questions over the material read. A short comprehension test, consisting mainly of items measuring memory for details, followed the reading of the selection. The rate score was a complement of the number of complete ten-second intervals which had elapsed during the reading of the selection.

All of the criterion tests were administered by the writer during an eight-day testing period. All were administered as group tests, without time limits, with the exception of the Word Recognition Test, which was administered to each subject individually. All test items, except those for the Word Recognition Test, were of the four-choice multiple-response type. Except for the Reading Rate Test rate scores, all scores used in the analyses of results represented the number of items answered correctly.

Analysis of Results

An analysis of variance design, 'group-by-levels', was employed in the analysis of results.[3] The bright and dull children represent the 'groups,' and the intervals of six months in the two-year mental age range used in the study constitute the 'levels.' A schematic presentation of the groups-by-levels design as it applies to this study is shown below.

MA Level	MA (Es'd True)	Criterion Scores	
		Bright Group	Dull Group
I	12–1 to 12–6	n = 7	n = 7
II	11–7 to 12–0	n = 9	n = 9
III	11–1 to 11–6	n = 7	n = 7
IV	10–7 to 11–0	n = 5	n = 5

In the case of each ability investigated, the null hypothesis was tested, *i.e.,* that the means of the populations of which the dull and bright groups were representative samples were the same. To test this hypothesis, the ratio of the mean square for groups to the mean square for within cells was employed. This ratio yields a value which is distributed as F, provided that the hypothesis is true

---

[3]E. F. Linquist, *Design and Analysis of Experiments in Psychology and Education.* Boston: Houghton Mifflin Co., 1952.

and that certain conditions are met. A five per cent coefficient of risk, selected in advance of the analyses, was employed in rejecting the null hypothesis.

RESULTS

A summary of the obtained results is presented in Table II. The table includes the mean and standard deviations for each group, the differences between the means, and the F-values obtained in the tests of the significance of the differences between the means of the bright and dull groups. Positive differences favor the bright group.

TABLE II. Summary of Results: Mean Scores for Each Group, Differences Between Means, and F-Values, for Each Ability

Ability	Bright		Dull		Differences (MB–MD)	F*
	Mean	SD	Mean	SD		
Word Recognition	58.6	11.8	56.2	13.0	+2.4	0.499
Word Meaning	30.4	6.1	30.8	6.1	−0.4	0.076
Memory for Factual Details	17.4	4.0	15.1	4.8	+2.3	3.678
Location or Recognition of Factual Details	15.8	3.6	12.7	3.3	+3.1	10.126**
Perception of Relationships among Definitely Stated Ideas	15.4	3.6	14.0	3.6	+1.4	2.058
Recognition of Main Ideas	16.3	4.1	13.9	3.9	+2.4	5.319**
Drawing Inferences and Conclusions	14.9	3.1	12.9	3.7	+2.0	4.628**
Total Comprehension Abilities	79.8	15.1	68.4	16.7	+11.4	7.922**
Listening Comprehension	30.6	3.6	23.6	4.7	+7.0	47.574**
Reading Rate (rate score)	61.6	17.9	55.4	15.9	+6.2	1.602
Reading Rate (comprehension score)	10.7	2.4	9.8	3.4	+0.9	1.444

Obtained differences between the mean scores of the two groups favored the bright group with respect to all of the abilities except Word Meaning. In the case of this one exception, the difference was not only nonsignificant, but also less than one raw score unit. The analyses of variance yielded significant differences with respect to the following five abilities: Location or Recognition of Factual Details, Recognition of Main Ideas, Drawing Inferences and Conclusions, Total Comprehension Abilities, and Listening Comprehension. While not significant at the required level, differences between the mean scores for Memory for Factual Details and for Perception of Relationships among Definitely Stated Ideas were substantial, and further investigation with respect to these two abilities seems warranted. Differences with respect to Word Recognition, Word Meaning, and Reading Rate were not significant.

The Test of Listening Comprehension was included in anticipation of the possible event that the group which was found significantly poorer on most of the abilities would be found to be significantly better with respect to listening comprehension. Then such results might have been interpreted in terms of possible difficulty with mechanical skills in reading rather than in terms of differences in intellectual abilities or specific comprehension abilities. However, the bright group, which excelled on nearly all of the abilities, also excelled significantly on the Listening Comprehension Test. Similarly, if a significantly higher rate had been found for the group also found to be significantly poorer with respect to most of the abilities, the poorer showing might have been attributed, in part, to tendencies to read carelessly and too hastily. However, no significant rate difference was found between the two groups and analysis of the reading rate comprehension check indicated that the two groups had read the reading rate selection with comparable degrees of understanding. These findings with respect to reading rate and listening comprehension tend to further indicate that superiority in reading comprehension involves superiority in intellectual functions rather, than in the more mechanical skills.

Tests for interaction between groups and levels were also made. No significant interaction effects were found for any of the abilities tested, thus satisfying one of the necessary conditions or underlying assumptions involved in the particular design of the study.

Inspection of the frequency distributions for the various abilities involved in this study revealed that, in general, obtained scores did not closely approach the maximum possible at the upper end of the distribution or the 'chance' scores at the lower end. Thus, neither ceiling nor floor effects operated to bias the results.

CONCLUSIONS

In the strictest sense, the sample studied may be regarded as a representative sample only of hypothetical populations that show the same relative distribution of MA's, IQ's, and CA's as the groups in the sample itself; and generalizations based upon obtained results should be restricted to these hypothetical populations. However, since no significant interaction effects between groups and levels were found, restrictions upon extending generalizations to real populations may be lifted to a considerable extent. Therefore, generalizing to a population of dull and bright children with widely differing IQ's but approximately equal MA's within the MA ranges found in this study and with reference to the various comprehension abilities as defined operationally, the following conclusions seem warranted:

1) Bright children are significantly superior to dull children of comparable mental ages with respect to total reading comprehension and the following specific abilities: locating or recognizing factual details, recognizing main ideas, and drawing inferences and conclusions.

2) It seems probable that bright children are also superior to dull children of comparable mental ages with respect to memory for factual details and perception of relationships among definitely stated ideas.

3) Bright children are superior to dull children of comparable mental ages with respect to listening comprehension.

4) Reading rates of bright and dull children of comparable mental ages appear to be approximately the same when comparable degrees of understanding of material read are attained, with a wide range in rate being found in both groups.

5) Bright and dull children tend to be alike with respect to ability in word recognition and word meaning. Bright children are significantly superior to dull children of comparable mental ages with respect to the relatively more complex, and intellectual, comprehension abilities.

6) It would seem that levels of expectation with respect to the more complex comprehension abilites should not be as high for dull children as for bright children of comparable mental ages.

References

1. John C. Almack, and James L. Almack. "Gifted pupils in the high school." *School and Society,* 14: 227-8, September 24, 1921.
2. Oliver P. Kolstoe. "A comparison of mental abilities of bright and dull children of comparable mental ages." *Journal of Educational Psychology,* 45: 161-68, March, 1954.
3. W. Drayton Lewis. *A Study of Superior Children in the Elementary School.* George Peabody College Contributions to Education, No. 266, George Peabody College for Teachers, Nashville, Tenn., 1940.
4. William A. McGehee. *A Study of Retarded Children in the Elementary School.* George Peabody College Contributions to Education, No. 246, George Peabody College for Teachers, Tenn., 1939.
5. Rukmini S. Ramaseshan. "A Note on the validity of the mental age concept." *Journal of Educational Psychology,* 41: 56-58, January, 1950.
6. G. I. Thomas. "A study of reading achievement in terms of mental ability." *Elementary School Journal,* 47: 28-33, September, 1946.
7. Willard D. Unsicker. *A Psychological Study of Bright and Dull Children with Comparable Mental Ages,* unpublished Doctor's dissertation, State University of Iowa, Iowa City, Iowa, 1950.

8. M.J. Van Wagenen. "A comparison of the mental ability and school achievement of the bright and dull pupils in the sixth grade of a large school system." *Journal of Educational Psychology,* 16: 186-92 March, 1925.

19. Sex Differences in Reading Ability*

ARTHUR I. GATES
Teachers College
Columbia University

WHICH are better readers—boys or girls? This study of sex differences in reading ability was based on the test scores of 13,114 pupils—6,646 boys and 6,468 girls in Grades 2 through 8.

Each child included in the study took all three of the Gates Reading Survey tests: Speed of Reading, Reading Vocabulary, and Level of Comprehension. The tests were given in the spring of 1957 in twelve school systems in ten states.

The group that took part in the study was approximately typical in intelligence or scholastic aptitude, socioeconomic level, and other pertinent respects.

Since the children in the school systems selected for the study were required to repeat grades relatively infrequently and since the results for each grade were analyzed separately, any distortion of the facts of sex differnces in reading because of grading practices would be revealed.

As Table I shows, in each of the twenty-one comparisons the mean raw score for the girls is higher than the mean raw score for the boys, and most of the differences are significant. Even in Grade 2, for which the tests are so difficult that they are not recommended, the girls obtained higher scores on all three tests.

One question of interest is whether the superiority of the the girls varied from grade to grade. When the data for Grade 2 were omitted and the data for each of two successive grades from third through eighth were combined, the following differences in mean raw scores in favor of the girls were secured:

Test	Grades 3 and 4	Grades 5 and 6	Grades 7 and 8
Speed............	1.43	1.59	1.29
Vocabulary........	2.7	2.22	2.38
Comprehension	1.36	1.42	1.00

*From *The Elementary School Journal*, **61**, 8 (May, 1961). Copyright ©1961 by The University of Chicago Press. Reprinted with the permission of The University of Chicago Press and Arthur I. Gates.

TABLE I. Means and Standard Deviations of Raw Scores of Boys and Girls on Three Reading Tests

Test and Grade	Number	Mean	Standard Deviation	Test and Grade	Number	Mean	Standard Deviation
Grade 2:				*Grade 4:*			
Speed*				Speed*			
Girls	888	8.43	5.73	Girls	1,177	17.38	7.99
Boys	938	7.37	5.11	Boys	1,171	16.39	8.38
Difference	.....	1.06	0.62	Difference	.....	0.99	−0.39
Z test	.....	4.17	.....	Z test	.....	2.93	.....
F test†	.....	.....	1.26	F test†	.....	.....	1.10
Vocabulary				Vocabulary			
Girls	888	11.26	6.99	Girls	1,177	23.19	8.58
Boys	938	9.41	7.18	Boys	1,171	21.02	10.10
Difference	.....	1.85	−0.19	Difference	.....	2.17	−1.52
Z test	.....	5.58	.....	Z test	.....	5.61	.....
F test†	.....	.....	1.06	F test†	.....	.....	1.39
Comprehension				Comprehension			
Girls	888	8.66	5.97	Girls	1,177	19.47	7.56
Boys	938	7.05	6.06	Boys	1,171	18.07	9.20
Difference	.....	1.61	−0.09	Difference	.....	1.40	−1.64
Z test	.....	5.72	.....	Z test	.....	4.03	.....
F test†	.....	.....	1.03	F test†	.....	.....	1.48
Grade 3:				*Grade 5:*			
Speed*				Speed*			
Girls	1,037	13.01	6.94	Girls	933	20.94	8.25
Boys	1,030	11.15	6.95	Boys	1,027	19.63	8.69
Difference	.....	1.86	−0.01	Difference	.....	1.31	−0.44
Z test	.....	6.09	.....	Z test	.....	3.42	.....
F test†	.....	.....	1.00	F test†	.....	.....	1.11
Vocabulary				Vocabulary			
Girls	1,037	17.35	8.13	Girls	933	28.16	9.04
Boys	1,030	14.99	8.89	Boys	1,027	26.36	10.63
Difference	.....	2.36	−0.76	Difference	.....	1.80	−1.59
Z test	.....	6.30	.....	Z test	.....	4.05	.....
F test†	.....	.....	1.20	F test†	.....	.....	1.38
Comprehension				Comprehension			
Girls	1,037	14.41	7.50	Girls	933	23.64	7.43
Boys	1,030	12.69	8.44	Boys	1,027	22.60	9.20
Difference	.....	1.72	−0.94	Difference	.....	1.04	−1.77
Z test	.....	4.90	.....	Z test	.....	2.76	.....
F test†	.....	.....	1.27	F test†	.....	.....	1.53

TABLE I. *Continued*

Test and Grade	Number	Mean	Standard Deviation	Test and Grade	Number	Mean	Standard Deviation
Grade 6:				Boys	786	33.45	11.80
Speed*				Difference	.....	2.30	−1.42
Girls	818	17.14	7.67	Z test	.....	4.12	.....
Boys	848	15.18	7.24	F test†	.....	.....	1.29
Difference	.....	1.96	0.43				
Z test	.....	5.09	.....	Comprehension			
F test†	.....	.....	1.12	Girls	804	28.91	7.37
				Boys	786	27.76	8.65
Vocabulary				Difference	.....	1.15	−1.28
Girls	818	31.66	10.01	Z test	.....	2.85	.....
Boys	848	29.02	11.30	F test†	.....	.....	1.38
Difference	.....	2.64	−1.29				
Z test	.....	5.03	.....	*Grade 8:*			
F test†	.....	.....	1.27	Speed*			
				Girls	811	21.49	7.62
Comprehension				Boys	846	20.07	7.84
Girls	818	26.22	8.00	Difference	.....	1.42	−0.22
Boys	848	24.42	9.40	Z test	.....	3.74	.....
Difference	.....	1.80	−1.40	F test†	.....	.....	1.06
Z test	.....	4.22	.....				
F test†	.....	.....	1.38	Vocabulary			
				Girls	811	39.60	10.72
				Boys	846	37.15	11.90
Grade 7:				Difference	.....	2.45	−1.18
Speed*				Z test	.....	4.41	.....
Girls	804	19.43	7.46	F test†	.....	.....	1.23
Boys	786	18.27	8.05				
Difference	.....	1.16	−0.59	Comprehension			
Z test	.....	2.98	.....	Girls	811	31.33	7.22
F test†	.....	.....	1.16	Boys	846	30.49	8.21
				Difference	.....	0.84	−0.99
Vocabulary				Z test	.....	2.21	.....
Girls	804	35.75	10.38	F test†	.....	.....	1.29

*The time allowed for this test is six minutes for Grades 1 through 5 and four minutes for Grades 6 and above.

†F (∞, 1000) .05=1.08 .01=1.11; F (500, 400) .05=1.16 .01=1.24.

When these differences in raw scores were converted into differences in reading grades, based on grade norms, it was found that in both speed and vocabulary the girls were superior by about 0.2 reading grade in Grades 3 and 4, by about 0.3 in Grades 5 and 6, and by 0.4 in Grades 7 and 8. But the corresponding figures for comprehension were 0.2, 0.3, and 0.2.

The means of these differences are 0.2, 0.3, and 0.33; they show a slight increase from the lower to the higher grades. When the nine differences in raw scores were converted into standard scores, no consistent trend was found; the average for all grades (Grade 2 excluded) and all tests showed a superiority of slightly less than 0.2 standard deviation for the girls.

The variability of test scores for boys and girls in each grade is indicated by the standard deviations in Table I, which also shows the results of the F test. The standard deviations for the boys are greater in all cases except in speed in Grades 2, 3, and 6. In the case of vocabulary and comprehension, tests in which speed is not a factor, the variability of the boys is greater in all comparisons. The difference is significant in all greades except Grade 2—a grade in which variability is not reliably measured by these tests.

Finally, the boys outnumbered the girls in the three lowest scores in all the tests by about 2 to 1 in Grades 3 and 4 and by gradually decreasing proportions thereafter. The boys made the highest scores slightly more often than the girls, but their superiority was too inconsistent from test to test and from grade to grade to be reliable. The greater variability of the boys seems therefore to be due primarily to the fact that a greater proportion of boys got low scores.

Taken together, the findings have some bearing on several of the many explanations of the fact, strongly confirmed by this study, that on the average girls' reading abilities excel boys'.

The usual explanation for the girls' superiority in reading is that they mature earlier. The explanation seems unlikely, for the superiority of the girls appears to be, on the whole, as great in the upper grades as in the lower.

The distribution of scores obtained on tests of reading ability differs from that obtained on non-reading intelligence tests. The distribution of scores on tests of reading ability shows that a relatively large proportion of boys obtained the lowest scores without a corresponding increase in the number obtaining top scores.

The present data suggest an environmental rather than a hereditary explantion. It is possible that more girls than boys pursue a kind of life in which more respect, more incentives, and more opportunities for reading appear earlier and persist longer. Contrariwise, more boys than girls may find little or no early need for learning to read. These boys fall behind the girls at the beginning, and a relatively large number of them remain in the conspicuously poor reading group throughout the grades.

If this thesis is valid, it explains the results of the study: the boys' lower mean scores in reading ability throughout the grades, the greater variability of the boys' abilities, and their predominance at the bottom of each grade group without a corresponding accumulation at the top.

20. Are Fast Readers the Best Readers?–A Second Report*†

J. HARLAN SHORES

Professor of Education
University of Illinois,
Urbana, Illinois

WHETHER fast readers are the best readers depends in large part upon what is meant by reading rate; that is, upon how rate is measured. Reading rate is ordinarily measured as an original reading time (*i.e.,* the words read per minute during a single reading and not including the time taken to answer comprehension questions), or it is measured as a total reading time including both the time for a single original reading and the time taken to answer comprehension questions. Most rate measures either do not permit rereading or discourage this practice even though some reading, such as keeping a long series of ideas in mind in proper sequence or following precise directions, obviously requires rereading even by proficient readers.

It is at once apparent that a single rapid reading for superficial comprehension is a different measure from one that also included time to answer questions. The question-answering task is often as time-consuming as is the actual reading. It is also apparent that neither of these tests is the same as a measure of the amount of time taken to read and use these materials for whatever comprehension purpose the reader has in mind.

The fact that experiments with reading speed have differed in what is measured as reading rate probably accounts in large part for the somewhat conflicting findings. Realizing that some readers go through the materials once rapidly and then reread all or part of the material for the specific purposes set by the comprehension questions, an adequate measure of reading rate must provide three scores—an original reading rate, a time for reading the questions, rereading the materials, and answering the questions; and a total time which is the sum of the previous two.

The question then, "Are fast readers the good readers?" needs to be broken down into several questions. Defining a "good reader" as one who

*This study was conducted with the assistance of a reasearch fund provided by Spencer Press, publishers of *Our Wonderful World, Childrens Hour,* and *The American Peoples Encyclopedia.*

†From *Elementary English,* **XXXVIII**, 4 (April, 1961), 236-245. Reprinted with the permission of the National Council of Teachers of English and J. Harlan Shores.

comprehends well, we need to ask, " Are good readers those who read rapidly during an initial reading?" Do the good readers read rapidly when dealing with the study-type comprehension questions and when rereading to answer the questions? Are the good readers those who take less time in total to read, reread, and answer questions? A single answer is not adequate for these three questions and they in turn give rise to others. Are the fast readers the good readers on each of these measures regardless of the difficulty of the material and the purpose for reading? It is to these questions that this article is directed.

In the January, 1950, issue of *Elementary English* this author and Kenneth L. Husbands reported an investigation concerned with the relationship between reading speed and comprehension [5] [1]. The general conclusion of this study was that there is no relationship between reading speed and comprehension when the task is difficult. The fast reader was not the best reader when he was reading biological science material in order to solve a problem. In fact, under these conditions the efficient and able reader slowed his rate to that of the inefficient reader.

STUDENT AND ADULT POPULATIONS

The present study, like the earlier one, was conducted with sixth-grade students. However, in the current study data were also collected from a group of able adult readers, and more adequate instrumentation was employed throughout.

All forty-six sixth graders of a K-12 consolidated school on the Southeastern coast of the United States comprised the student population. Even through the "tourist trade" was the largest industry, each of the children included was a permanent resident of the country. It is apparent from Table I that the children were of average age in grade and were somewhat above average in intelligence and reading achievement. In terms of their mental ability the group may have been slightly under-achieving. Table I also indicates that the two sixth-grade groups reading for different purposes were closely equivalent in chronoligcal age, mental age, and measures of general reading abilities.

The adult group was taken from several advanced undergraduate and graduate unversity-level courses dealing with the teaching of reading. A few of these were junior and seniors in the program preparatory to teaching in the elementary grades. The majority were experienced teachers and administrators working toward graduate degrees.

---

[1]Numbers in brackets refer to references at the end of the article.

TABLE I. *Equivalence of Groups Reading for Main Ideas and for Ideas in Sequence Expressed in Raw Scores*

Measure	Group A (Main Ideas)		Group B (Sequence)		Group A plus B	
	Mean	SD	Mean	SD	Mean	SD
C.A. (months)	137.48	4.28	135.83	6.51	136.65	5.41
M.A. (months)	151.57	26.88	147.61	22.92	149.59	24.78
California Reading*						
Comprehension	29.26	6.80	27.87	6.11	28.57	6.43
Total Score	104.43	14.97	103.65	15.19	104.04	14.92
Iowa Silent Reading†						
Comprehension	69.87	22.88	71.13	21.73	70.50	22.07
Rate	26.70	8.23	26.57	10.16	26.63	9.14
Total Score	122.26	35.23	124.91	36.16	123.58	35.32
Combined Scores—California plus Iowa						
Comprehension	99.13	28.53	99.00	26.22	99.07	27.09
Vocabulary	100.43	16.85	103.00	16.67	101.72	16.62

*Ernest W. Tiegs and Willis W. Clark, *California Reading Test,* Los Angeles; California Test Bureau, 1950.

†H. A. Greene and V. H. Kelley, *Iowa Silent Reading Tests,* Yonkers on Hudson, N. Y.; World Book Co., 1956.

TESTS USED

With the sixth-grade students four reading rate measures provided ten rate scores, and five comprehension measures provided eleven comprehension scores. The Iowa Silent Reading Tests [2] gave one rate score based on a portion of original reading time. Three tests developed by the author, each measuring an aspect of the reading of science materials, provided three rate scores each—a measure of original reading time, a measure of rereading and question-answering time, and a measure of total reading time.

Each of the rate tests provided one or more measures of comprehension and the California Achievement Tests [7] provided additional comprehension measures. Whenever sub-tests of the Iowa and California tests were measuring in the same area these scores were combined for a more adequate measure. Thus the following scores were available from these two reading tests: California comprehension, Iowa comprehension, combined comprehension, combined vocabulary, combined directed reading, combined references, combined interpretation, Iowa rate (California does not provide a rate score), California total score, and Iowa total score.

Mental ages were derived from the California Test of Mental Maturity, Non-Lanuage Section [6], and the Sequential Tests of Educational Progress [4] were used to measure achievement in science.

After the standardized tests were administered, three unpublished tests developed by the author of this study were used. One of these, called *Reading for Problem Solving in Science,* is a forty-item test measuring ability to do directed reading for the solution of problems in science. The comprehension reliability of this test with the Kuder Richardson formula is .83. The rate reliability with the split-half method and the Spearman-Brown correction was .56 for original reading time, .43 for question answering time, and .39 for total time.

This was followed by the Directed Reading of Science Materials Tests administered in twenty successive sessions during which the 23 pupils in each sixth-grade group read a science passage of from 200 to 400 words that had been drawn from *Our Wonderful World* [8] and was at that time unfamiliar to them. Group A was instructed to reach each passage for the main idea while Group B was instructed to read the same passage to keep the ideas of the passage in mind in their proper sequence. Different passages were employed for the different "tests." There was a total of twenty questions to be answered by those reading for main ideas and eighty questions for those reading for ideas in sequence. Three rate scores (original reading time, rereading and question-answering time, and total time) were taken for each of the twenty "tests." The split-half reliabilities of these tests of rate and comprehension are shown in Table II [1].

Fifty-one advanced undergraduate and graduate students read five of the same twenty selections from the *Direct Reading of Science Materials Tests* read by the sixth graders Twenty-eight read for Purpose A (main ideas) and twenty-three read the same five selections for Purpose B (to keep ideas in mind in sequence). The adults were checked on comprehension and speed for each passage in the same manner as the sixth graders. The difference in the treatment was that the adults responded to all five passages at a single sitting whereas the children responded to only one passage at a sitting.

The adult population was deliberately chosen as a group of able readers. Most of the group were practicing elementary school teachers. A few were administrators and a few were advanced students (juniors and seniors) in a program preparatory to teaching. It may be that success in a field requiring much reading is better evidence of ability to do work-type reading than is any test now available. At any rate successful teachers and good students in teacher education programs probably can offer evidence of adequate reading skills.

As further proof of reading ability the adults scored well on the *Directed Reading of Science Materials Tests.* Their average accuracy level was 92 per cent when reading for main ideas, as contrasted with 56 per cent for sixth graders.

When reading for the more difficult task of getting ideas in sequence the adult average accuracy level was 80 per cent whereas the sixth grade level was only 42 per cent. On the test of *Reading for Problem Solving in Science* the average adult accuracy level was 90 per cent and the average sixth grade level was only 63 per cent.

TABLE II. Reliability of Scores on Directed Reading of Science Tests

Measure	Mean	Standard Deviation	Coefficient of Reliability*
Type A—			
Main Idea			
Comprehension	11.70	4.29	.80
Original Rate	443.74	126.99	.97
Question Rate	119.22	40.62	.82
Total Rate	567.35	138.48	.95
Type B—			
Ideas in Sequence			
Comprehension	36.34	10.73	.90
Original Rate	462.57	159.42	.96
Question Rate	449.87	177.68	.93
Total Rate	916.78	193.54	.98

*The split-half method and the Spearman-Brown correction were used with all scores.

It is apparent then that the adult group used in this study are quite effective readers. It is then altogether likely that the relationships between speed and comprehension scores exhibited by this group more nearly represent the kind of relationships that are optimum than do those of sixth-grade students.

Early in the plans for the study serious consideration was given to the question of whether it would be appropriate to use the same measures and materials with able adult readers as are used with sixth-grade students. It is likely that literature or even "story type" material from science or the social studies that would be suitable and interesting to sixth-grade students would have little appeal for educated adults. However, the descriptive science materials used were thought to be suited to adults and of interest to them. This premise was strengthened by the fact that most of the adults indicated on an anonymous questionnaire that the materials were interesting. There is little question but that the materials made realistic adult demands upon the reading skills.

STATISTICAL METHOD

In order to substantiate that the two sixth-grade groups were not significantly different from one another in chronological age, mental age, science achievement, and general reading ability, the t test of significance of difference between means was used [1]. The values of t ranged from .004 to .222 indicating that the slight differences between the two groups in these characteristics could easily be explained by chance factors.

Analysis of the data was made with product moment correlations [1] between the various rate and comprehension scores. These correlations for the sixth-grade population are set forth in Table 3. For the adult population the correlations between rate and comprehension are given in Table 4.

Comparisons between sixth-grade and adult populations were based upon the rate and comprehension correlations and upon mean comprehension and rate scores.

FINDINGS—SIXTH-GRADE STUDENTS

Fast readers are the best readers when rate is measured by the Iowa Silent Reading Test. In Table III the correlations between Iowa rate and the various comprehensions range from .39 to .82 with an average correlation of .58, significant at the one per cent level. The Iowa rate score does not correlate as strongly with the tests of science comrephension as with most of the Iowa and California tests of comprehension.

On the Reading for Problem Solving in Science Test, fast readers are not the best readers. With this type of reading there is little relationship between rate of initial reading and various measures of comprehension. The highest correlation (see Table III) was .29 with combined interpretation and the lowest was − .09 with combined references. Although most of these show a low positive relationship between rate of reading and comprehension, all of them are low enough to be explained by chance factors.

Those who read rapidly during a single reading of the Directed Reading of Science Materials Tests also comprehend well on tests of general reading abilities. These correlations (see Table III) were generally significant ones for both the group reading for the main idea and for the group reading for a sequence of ideas. There are, however, notable exceptions for each group. The rapid readers for main ideas are not those who comprehend well when Reading for Problem Solving in Science where a low negative correlation was found. It is also interesting to note that the correlation between speed of reading science materials and comprehension in general reading abilities as measured by the Iowa and California tests is higher than is the correlation between speed and comprehension when reading the science materials for main ideas (.29).

TABLE III. *Coefficients of Correlation Between Measures of Sixth-Grade Reading Rate and Comprehension**

Rate Measures	Calif. Total	Iowa Total	Calif. Comprehension	Iowa Comprehension	Comprehension Measures Combined Comprehension	Combined Directions	Combined Interpretation	Combined References	Rdg. Problem Solving Sci.	Directed Rdg. Sci.—Main Ideas	Directed Rdg. Sci.—Sequence	Average Correlations¹
Iowa Rate	.56	.82	.50	.71	.70	.54	.66	.41	.38	.46	.39	.58
Reading Problem Solving Science												
Orig. Rate	.26	.27	.09	.21	.19	.16	.29	-.09	.20	.19	.19	.18
Ques. Rate	.01	.23	.02	.28	.23	.24	.12	.23	-.28	-.22	.16	.09
Total Rate	.18	.37	.10	.37	.33	.32	.30	.16	-.09	.31	.16	.25
Directed Reading Science (Main Ideas)												
Orig. Rate	.50	.62	.31	.61	.57	.62	.49	.30	-.03	.29		.45
Ques. Rate	-.06	.20	-.10	.19	.13	.04	.17	.08	.07	.07		.08
Total Rate	.41	.57	.24	.57	.52	.52	.45	.30	-.03	.26		.39
Directed Reading Science (Sequence)												
Orig. Rate	.58	.68	.45	.55	.56	.27	.72	.19	.39		.06	.47
Ques. Rate	-.02	.16	-.12	.10	.05	-.15	.23	-.09	-.13		-.46	-.05
Total Rate	.29	.47	.16	.36	.34	.07	.52	.04	.13		-.25	.22

*The signs of all correlations have been converted to a common base. No sign indicates a positive relationship between speed of reading and comprehension.
¹Average correlations were calculated in terms of Z equivalents.

Exceptions to the generality that those who read rapidly during a single reading of science materials for the purpose of keeping a series of ideas in mind in proper sequence are also those who comprehend well on tests of general reading abilities are found with two of the general reading abilities. Positivie correlations but low enough to be explained by chance factors are found with the factors of use of references and following directions. Thus those who read science materials rapidly for sequence are not necessarily those who use references and follow directions well. It is rather strange to find a positive correlation at all between any measure of rate of reading and these somewhat meticulous types of reading comprehension, and, at least for use of references, the correlations with rate do tend to be generally low. However, comprehension of combined directions correlates well with original rate of reading on the Iowa test and on the Directed Reading of Science Tests for main ideas.

It is also interesting to note that the fast readers are not the best readers when both speed and comprehension are measured on the Directed Reading of Science Tests for sequence of ideas. This correlation (.06) is so low that one can say that there is no relationship between rate and comprehension for this relatively difficult reading task.

For both Directed Reading of Science Tests the correlations between original reading rate and the various comprehension measures average in the upper forties (significant at the five per cent level). The average correlation between original reading rate on the Reading for Problem Solving in Science Test and the various measures of comprehension was positive but low (.18) enough to be possibly explained by chance factors.

In view of the generally strong correlations between each of the measures of initial reading time and most of the various measures of general reading comprehension, it is interesting to note that this same result is not found between comprehension scores and time taken to reread and answer questions. Invariably the correlations are low or negative between comprehension and rate of question answering, which includes rereading. In other words those who read general reading test materials rapidly on a first reading also read well, but those who reread and answer questions rapidly are not necessarily those who read well. These correlations between comprehension and rereading and question-answering time ranged from +.24 to −.28 with average correlations for the three measures (See Table 3) of +.09, +.08, and −.05.

The total rate score is a combination of the original reading rate and the question-answering rate, and it really is not as meaningful as is either of the two scores from which it was derived. However, the correlations between the various comprehension measures and the total rate scores were as high as +.57 between the Iowa comprehension test and the Purpose A (main ideas) total rate scores and as low as −.25 between comprehension and total rate on the Purpose B (sequence) test. The average correlation was not significant at the five per cent level with any of the three tests deriving a total rate score.

FINDINGS—ADULTS AND CHILDREN COMPARED

The reader will recall that while the correlations between rates of original reading and comprehension of general reading abilities in the sixth-grade group were generally high, this was not true between rate and comprehension with the measures of the reading of science. While data for adults was not available regarding general reading abilities, it was possible to relate speed and comprehension measures for each of the three measures of the reading of science materials. Each of these correlations (see Table IV) was low — generally somewhat lower than it was with the children. Fast readers, even among adults, are not the best readers when reading scientific materials to solve a problem, to get the main idea, or to keep a series of ieas in mind in sequence.

A case was made earlier for regarding the fifty-one adult readers as a select group of fairly efficient readers on the basis of their professional and academic accomplishments as well as on the basis of their comprehension scores on the Directed Reading of Science and Reading for Problem Solving in Science Tests. How then do these relatively efficient readers differ from the sixth graders? It would seem that the efficient reader would adjust his rate downward, shift gears so to speak, when he was dealing with either more difficult materials or a more demanding purpose. Did the adults slow down for the more demanding tasks? Did the children?

Comparing the average comprehension score of the sixth-graders with that of the adults (see Table V) the children scored 8.35 to the adults 15.91 (52 per cent as well) on the Purpose B (sequence) task. On the other hand the children scored 2.78 to the adults 4.60 (60 per cent as well) on the Purpose A task, and did 70 per cent as well on the RPSS (Reading for Problem Solving in Science) Test. Using these relative comprehension percentages as an index of difficulty the Purpose B task was most difficult, then Purpose A, and the RPSS Test was the least difficult.

Looking at the Original Rate — Words Per Minute column of Table V, it is apparent that both groups slowed their rate somewhat for the more demanding tasks. The adults read the relatively easy RPSS Test at 291 words per minute. They slowed for Purpose A to 213 w.p.m, and for the more difficult Purpose B they read at only 182 w.p.m. The sixth graders also slowed somewhat as the materials became more demanding. They read the relatively easy RPSS Test at 153 w.p.m, for Purpose A at 138 w.p.m. and for the more difficult Purpose B at 137 w.p.m. But note the difference. Where the adults slowed 78 words per minute between RPSS Test materials and Purpose A and slowed another 31 words per minute between Purpose A and Purpose B, the children slowed only 14 w.p.m. between RPSS and Purpose A and only 1 w.p.m. between Purpose A and Purpose B. Even taking into account the fact that the children were reading more slowly and therefore each word per minute slower is a larger percentage of their actual rate, it is readily apparent that the adults are adjusting their rate to the difficulty of the task much more than are the children.

*TABLE IV. Coefficients of Correlation Between Measures of Adult Reading Rate and Comprehension **

Rate Measures	Comprehension Measures		
	Directed Bdg. Sci. Main Ideas	Directed Rdg. Sci. Sequence	Reading for Problem Solving in Science
Directed Reading of Science Main Ideas[1]			
Orig. Rate	.03		
Ques. Rate	.10		
Total Rate	.07		
Directed Reading of Science Sequence[2]			
Orig. Rate		.04	
Ques. Rate		−.13	
Total Rate		−.09	
Reading for Problem Solving in Science[3]			
Orig. Rate			.26
Ques. Rate			.14
Total Rate			.23

*The sign of all correlations have been changed. No sign indicates a positive correlation between speed of reading and comprehension.

[1]N equals 28
[2]N equals 23
[3]N equals 19

One way of noting this flexibility of rate on the part of the adults is that they read for Purpose A only 73 per cent as rapidly as they read the RPSS Test, and they read for Purpose B only 86 per cent as rapidly as they read for Purpose A. The children, on the other hand, read for Purpose A 86 per cent as rapidly as they read the RPSS Test, and they read for Purpose B 99 per cent as rapidly as they read for Purpose A.

Another way of noting the increased flexibility of reading rate among the adults is by comparing the average reading time for adults and sixth-graders on each of the three reading tasks. The children read the relatively easy RPSS Test materials only 52 per cent as rapidly as did adults. However, they read for the more difficult Purpose A at 65 per cent of the adult rate and for the most demanding Purpose B, they are reading at 75 per cent of the adult rate. It is likely that this trend to read relatively more rapidly as the task becomes more demanding should be reversed for most efficient sixth-grade reading.

This pattern of less difference between child and adult rates with relatively difficult materials than with relatively easy materials is even more obvious with rereading and question answering time than it is with rate of original reading. The children answered the relatively easy RPSS Test questions 78 per cent as rapidly as did the adults, but they answered the more difficult Purpose A materials at 87 per cent of the adult rate and they went through the most difficult Purpose B materials at 98 per cent of the adult rate. The adults are markedly adjusting their rate to the requirements of the task—slowing down and rereading when it is needed—whereas the children are making relatively minor rate adjustments as the reading demands increase.

TABLE V. Mean Comprehension Scores and Reading Rates for Adult and Sixth Grade Testees*

Group	Compre- hension	Original Rate	Original Rate—WPM	Question Rate	Total Rate
Adult—Purpose A	4.60	73.28	213.15	32.25	105.53
Sixth—Purpose A	2.78	113.04	138.00	37.21	150.25
Adult—Purpose B	15.91	85.56	182.35	126.13	211.69
Sixth—Purpose B	8.35	114.17	136.62	128.30	242.47
Adult—Reading for Prob. Solv. Sci.	35.89	60.63	291.48	207.74	268.37
Sixth—Reading for Prob. Solv. Sci.	25.10	115.58	152.85	267.54	383.13

*Except for Original Rate—WPM (words per minute) the rate scores are in terms of number of five second intervals. Adult and sixth-grade scores are based upon the five passages read by both age groups.

CONCLUSIONS

1. Fast readers are the good readers when reading some kinds of materials for some purposes. When reading other kinds of materials for other purposes there is no relationship between speed of reading and ability to comprehend. In general the fast readers are the good readers on the reading tasks presented in the standardized tests of general reading ability. There is no relationship between speed of reading and comprehenion for either sixth-grade children or well-educated adults when reading scientific materials for the purpose of solving

a problem, getting the main idea, or for keeping a series of ideas in mind in sequence.

2. When either adults or sixth-grade children read the same materials for two different purposes and when the purpose for reading is set for the reader in advance of the reading, the purpose for reading influences the speed with which the reading is done. This finding is supported in Roossinck's study [3] of the reading of scientists and sixth-grade children.

3. There is no relationship for either adults or sixth-grade students between comprehension and rate of the work-study reading involved in responding to the comprehension questions. In other words those who work rapidly on the rereading and question answering are not necessarily the best readers.

4. Efficient adult readers are much more flexible in adjusting reading rate to the demands of the task than are sixth-grade students. In comparison to the adults, the children read relatively more rapidly as the task becomes more demanding with a consequent loss in relative comprehension. The efficient adult slows his rate and rereads as necessary in keeping with the demands of the task. Sixth-grade students need to develop this type of rate flexibility.

5. Inasmuch as there are different relationships between rate and comprehension when rate is measured as an original reading time and when rate is measured to include rereading and question-answering time, it is important to define what is meant by reading rate. This finding also suggests that authorities in the filed of reading would do well to attempt to standardize a practice for measuring reading rate. Since rereading and reorganizing what is read is both necessary and time consuming when reading for some purposes, the most meaningful measure of rate would be one which offered both an original reading time and a time for rereading and answering questions. The total time, which is a sum of these two, destroys some of the specificity of the composite parts and is useful only as an indication of the total amount of time taken to complete a work-study reading task.

Bibliography

1. Downie, N. M. and R. W. Heath, *Basic Statistical Methods.* New York: Harper and Brothers, 1959.
2. Greene, H. A. and V. H. Kelley, *Iowa Silent Reading Tests.* Yonkers-on-Hudson, N. Y.: World Book Co., 1956.
3. Roossinck, Esther P., *Purposeful Reading of Science Materials by Scientists and Children.* Doctor's Thesis. University of Illinois, 1960.
4. *Sequential Tests of Educational Progress.* Co-operative Test Division, Educational Testing Service, Princeton, N. J., 1957.
5. Shores, J. Harlan and Kenneth L. Husbands, "Are Fast Readers the Best Readers?" *Elementary English,* 27 (January, 1950). 52-57.

6. Sullivan, Elizabeth R., Willis W. Clark, and Ernest W. Tiegs, *California Test of Mental Maturity, Non-Language Section.* Los Angeles: California Test Bureau, 1951.
7. Tiegs, Ernest W., and Willis W. Clark, *California Achievement Tests.* Los Angeles: California Test Bureau, 1950.
8. Zim, Herbert S., Editor-in-Chief, *Our Wonderful World.* Chicago, Ill.: Spencer Press, 1961.

21. A Balanced Reading Program for the Gifted*

PAUL WITTY

Professor of Education
Northwestern University
Evanston, Illinois

ON the opening day of the school year six-year-old Bill arrived carrying under his arm a book—*All-About-Electricity*. At recess the principal of the school, who had noticed the book on Bill's desk, commented to the boy: "That's a good book. Are you enjoying the pictures?" "Yes, it is a good book," Bill answered. "I've read about two-thirds of it. I like the pictures too."

Bill's language development was really exceptional. Although he was barely six years of age, his vocabulary was outstanding. He was able to read and comprehend third or fourth grade materials readily. He had already completed a rather large number of children's books, and he was presently finding out all he could about electricity.

Bill could read before coming to school. He was not *taught* to read. He had learned, his mother said, by asking the names of the words he saw on signs and in newspapers, magazines, and books. Soon he was able to read phrases and short sentences.

There is a considerable number of such very intelligent children. In Bill's own classroom in a suburban area there were two other pupils who on entering school were able to read primary grade materials successfully. In the second grade of the same school, there was Mary, who exceeded the average of pupils in the sixth grade on tests of reading ability.

These children are clearly to be classified as "gifted." There is of course no clear-cut line of distinction between the gifted and others, although educators have for many years been inclined to refer to children as gifted if their I.Q.'s were 130 or higher [12].[1] At one time, such children were thought to comprise about 1 per cent of the elementary school population. Today, estimates are usually somewhat higher. For example, J. J. Gallagher indicates that 2-4 per cent of the general school population will have I.Q.'s of 132 and over and may be referred to as "gifted." In favorable socio-economic communities the percentage may be 6-12 [6].

*From *The Reading Teacher,* **16** (May, 1963), 418-424. Reprinted with the permission of Paul Witty and the International Reading Association.

[1]Numbers in brackets refer to references at the end of the article.

CHARACTERISTICS OF THE GIFTED

One of the most noticeable characteristics of the gifted child is his remarkable language development. Thus, C. C. Miles states: "Approximately half of the California gifted children learned to read before starting to school. In Witty's group 38 per cent learned to read before the age of five; and of Terman's children, 20 per cent learned at this age, 6 per cent before three" [8].

Early precocity in vocabulary development continues in the typical gifted child. For example, one ten-year-old child studied by the writer said that *flaunt* meant "to show or display with intent to show": *Mars* was defined as "a planet, God of War, also a verb."

Another characteristic of gifted children is the rapidity of their learning. They usually complete assignments in less than half the time allotted to them. On examinations such as the Stanford-Binet, they sometimes finish in a few seconds tests for which a minute is permitted.

By the time the typical child in the writer's early study was in the fourth grade, he had displayed knowledge and skills on tests which equalled the norms for children two grades above him [15]. Many were the equals of pupils in grades three or four years above them.

The verbally superior child can be identifed readily by the use of intelligence tests. There are other children, however, whose ability and promise are also outstanding who cannot be discovered in this way. These children, too, should be found and encouraged to make full use of their abilites. Perhaps it would be desirable to consider the gifted child as one whose performance in a potentially valuable line of human activity is consistently or repeatedly remarkable.

Educators must be concerned about all types of gifted and talented children, but attention will be given in the first part of this article to pupils of high abstract intelligence. There is evidence that this group is frequently neglected. Moreover, such pupils are found in almost all classrooms. And every teacher can do much to enrich their experience and to encourage their full development. Perhaps the greatest possibility for enrichment lies in the field of reading and language development.

It is evident that guidance of gifted children should begin at home. Parents should read aloud to them and answer their numerous questions about the names of letters and words and phrases they see. Under such conditions and without formal instruction, some gifted children learn to read. Books on various topics should be made availabe to them, and they should be encouraged to read, without exploitation [1, 16].

It is important that the gifted child's ability and rate of learning be fully recognized when he starts school. Teachers, therefore, should have knowledge of the results of intelligence and aptitude tests. They should make an appraisal, too, of the child's reading status at the time he enters the first grade. If a gifted child who already can read is required to follow routine textbook assingments and is forced to "read" highly repetitious and largely meaningless materials, he will often develop unfortunate attitudes and habits. From the first, reading materials should be made available which will challenge the gifted child's abilities, extend his interests, and present context in a meaningful way [17].

Although some gifted children learn to read before they start school, many others require instruction. In these cases it is essential for the teacher to recognize the rapidity of their learning. With such children it is usually desirable to bring with experience charts and then move rapidly into the reading of primers such as *Friskey the Goat or Peanuts the Pony* from Our Animal Story Book Series. There should be a correlated use of reading materials from such series as The True Books, I Want To Be Books, and others [10]. Children's literature should be a part of a balanced reading program [7].

The provision of valuable experiences perhaps proceeds with fewer obstacles when grouping is practiced, as in Cleveland's Major Work Classes. Partial segregation, as followed in the Colfax Elementary School of Pittsburgh, is also highly successful in enabling the gifted child to advance rapidly in accord with his ability and interests. But how is the teacher in the typical heterogeneous class of the primary grades to offer such children appropriate opportunities and motivation? In the first grade the problem is especially perplexing and difficult. A crucial factor in determining the success of such a program resides in the availability of sufficient materials of instruction to satisfy the pupils' varied needs. Since a few gifted children will be able to read upon entering school, a wide assortment of books encompassing various topics and levels of difficulty should be provided. Children's encyclopedias, dictionaires, magazines, and weekly papers are also desirable. Plans should be made by the teacher for individual conferences with each child to offer the guidance many superior pupils require to gain skills in reading and develop resourcefulness and self-direction in selecting and using books.

To provide for skill development, standard tests of oral and silent reading may be administered to an entire class of primary grade pupils. Then the pupils may be assigned to small groups for the acquisition of needed skills. Appropriate practice materials or devices such as the Reading Laboratory may be used to offer the specific help some individuals may need, while the teacher gives additional help to other individuals encountering difficulties. If the gifted pupil needs little or no help in skill building, he may employ his time in independent reading or in other types of suitable, constructive endeavor to be shared later with his classmates [2, 5].

There are several kinds of group endeavor which are especially suitable for entire classes of pupils who vary widely in ability. Through suitable group endeavor the gifted pupil may receive appropriate attention. The writer has stressed the value of using certain films and their accompanying books in such efforts. For example, the film "Shep the Farm Dog" and others in the It's Fun to Find Out Series were shown and the books were read by pupils in second grade classes [18]. Discussion followed, and opportunities were made for the pupils to explore each topic further in children's books.

The results of testing showed that under these conditions gifted pupils as well as others made significant gains in the acquisition of reading skills. Similar results have also been obtained in classrooms in which film-strips such as "The Little House" have been shown and the text on the filmstrip has been followed in books.

The following type of grouping has also been employed successfully in attempts to meet the needs of the gifted classes enrolling pupils of widely varying ability. Interest inventories are administered and the results are used to set up small flexible groups to explore each area of interest considered to be worthwhile and appealing. Reading materials related to each topic are then made available on varied levels of difficulty. In these interest groups the gifted child is able to participate and contribute from his own individually challenging reading. Such opportunities are not only profitable for the gifted pupil; they have been found of value in motivating other children to read books of greater difficulty than they ordinarily might be expected to read. This type of grouping is often effective in science and social studies.

As has already been indicated, the importance of interests should be fully recognized [4]. Studies have shown that most gifted children have rich and varied interests. They often have a few strong interests, but usually are versatile. They may collect stamps or specimens of various kinds. They are often enthusiatic observers of birds, flowers, the stars, and animal life. But there are some whose home backgrounds are impoverished and in whom wholesome interests are few. To ascertain the extent and nature of the pupil's background and interests, it is desirable for the teacher to administer an interest inventory informally to each child. Worthy interests should then be identified and associated with reading materials whenever possible. In case interests are few or are deemed unsuitable, efforts should be made to create new patterns through direct experience, the use of films and filmstrips, and other activities. One of the chief responsibilities of the school is to provide for the gifted learner wide and suitable reading experience throughout the primary grades.

In the middle grades an effort should be made to provide a balanced program of reading according to the unique nature and needs of each child. Extensive reading in the subject fields is desirable for the gifted child, who should be encouraged to adjust his rate of reading according to his purposes and the type of subject matter.

Despite this promising picture, there are many gifted pupils who need greater help and guidance. In fact, each gifted child requires careful study to determine his particular nature and his needs. As L. M. Terman and M. H. Oden [13] have pointed out:

Gifted children do not fall into a single pattern but into an infinite variety of patterns. One can find within the group individual examples of almost every type of personality defect, social maladjustment, behavior problem, and physical handicap; the only difference is that among gifted children the incidence of these deviations is, in varying degrees, lower than in the general population.

One problem teachers encounter in dealing with some gifted children is their tendency to concentrate too much reading in a single area, to become too specialized in their reading interests. This tendency sometimes appears in an area such as science, in which a gifted child may want to read to such an extent that his pattern of reading lacks balance. In this case, encouragement of wide reading is especially desirable, although special interests should be recognized. In many instances balance in reading is achieved when the teacher and the librarian work together in efforts to help gifted pupils become increasingly proficient in selecting and using books independently.

Some gifted pupils require assistance and guidance in acquiring reading skills. They should receive appropriate instruction geared to their needs. These children are sometimes regarded as "underachievers" and may display personality irregularities and emotional problems traceable to factors such as unfavorable home conditions and unfortunate previous school experience. Attention to these conditions should accompany reading instruction.

To engage successfully in encouraging the gifted child's reading, the teacher should have information about each child's ability and his status in silent and oral reading. The results of standard tests will be helpful. But the teacher should be able to employ other techniques of child study to obtain additional information. It has been pointed out that from interest inventories clues may be obtained which will help the teacher understand pupils' attitudes, problems, and needs [9]. Similarly, anecdotal records and other forms of observation may yield data of value. Occasionally, such study will simply make it clear that the teacher's major problem is to help pupils develop more varied or worthwhile patterns of interest.

A balanced program provides the gifted pupil with opportunities to satisfy some of his personal and social needs through reading. An identification with a character in a story is sometimes beneficial. Thus, a gifted boy recovering from rheumatic fever experienced great personal satisfaction by reading Marguerite De Angeli's *Door in the Wall*, a narrative laid in seventeenth-century England, which portrays the ways in which Robin, the son of a noblemen, stricken on the eve of departure for the contests, overcame his affliction and won the king's recognition. Similarly, Eleanor Estes' *The Hundred Dresses* proved of value to an insecure girl through her discovery of the successful course followed by another girl in obtaining group sanction. Elizabeth Yates' *Amos Fortune: Free Man,* a story of a boy's rise above his enviornment, tells of the problems faced and overcome by an African prince sold into slavery. His devotion to the needy and his many sacrifices provide a heartening picture of what man can be at his best. This book has proved a source of inspiration to many boys.

In the excellent biographical literature now available gifted pupils may find additional inspiration as well as a sound basis for the formation of an ideal of self that is in keeping with their outstanding abilities and promise. Regional books like Loise Lenski's *Strawberry Girl* and *Cotton in My Sack* and family stories such as Eleanor Estes' *Ginger Pye* may also help some gifted children understand people better. Many other books contain materials suitable for fulfilling varied needs.

Muriel Crosby has described a number of situations in which books have served admirably in enabling pupils to make wholesome indentifications [3]. She states:

> All children, like all adults, have problems. Books will not by themselves solve children's problems or adults' problems. But books may help. Books often tell of the problems children may sense but not fully recognize as their own. Books often bring to light a problem which a child cannot bring himself to talk about.

READING FOR THE CREATIVE STUDENT

Many of the foregoing suggestions concerning reading guidance apply not only to the verbally gifted, but also to pupils of outstanding promise in art, music, creative writing, and other fields. Such pupils may also be superior verbally. We cannot anticipate, however, that all gifted pupils will be located through the use of intelligence tests. In fact, E. P. Torance states that "about 70 per cent of the top 20 per cent on measures of creativity would have been excluded from gifted groups which were selected on the basis of intelligence only" [14].

Since the coefficients of correlation between measures of verbal ability and proficiency in art, music, and other creative pursuits are relatively low, there will probably be found a considerably larger number of poor readers among creative pupils than among the verbally gifted. It is desirable, therefore, that creative students be identified and that a thorough appraisal be made of their reading ability and needs. Necessary skills should then be cultivated through the use of appropriate materials.*

If some talented children we may find reading limited to a narrow specialization, while in others there may be only a meager interest shown in reading. In still others, reading may be seldom engaged in because of unfortunate

*The Reading Laboratories of Science Research Associates and other skill-building materials may often be used independently by many of these pupils.

attitudes concerning its value. Attention to interest and motivation is essential if unfortunate habits and attitudes are to be altered. In this effort inventories may be employed to disclose interests that may often be profitably associated with reading experience. There is also the possibility of helping the creative child find suitable reading in the area of his talent.

That the need for guidance of the creative student is great may be seen by reference to the work of E. P. Torrance, who has pioneered in making suggestions for rewarding creative activity. In a provacative article on creative thinking [14] he states:

> Many of the highly creative individuals are disturbing students in classroom groups in elementary schools. The problem of teachers and guidance workers resolves itself into one of helping highly creative individuals maintain those characteristics which seem essential to the development of creative talent and, at the same time, helping them acquire skills for avoiding, or reducing to a tolerable level, the peer sanctions.

Like the verbally gifted, the creative child often has a need for experience in reading that will enable him to meet personal and social problems and help him build an appropriate and individually suitable ideal of self. Reading for these purposes may prove even more effective for creative pupils, whose need for assistance appears to be so great. Of course, reading alone is not enough. But reading related to experience and accompanied by discussion may prove quite rewarding.

It will be noted that in this paper the suggested program in reading is essentially developmental in nature and may be recommended for all pupils. One of the great values of such an approach is the pleasure to be found by pupils in "the wonderful world of books." This statement certainly applies to gifted children who, when they have an opportunity to read materials of interest to them, turn joyfully to reading for information and recreation. Their lives will be enriched greatly as their satisfactions are enhanced through books.

References

1. Abraham, Willard. *Common Sense about Gifted Children,* New York: Harper, 1958.
2. Barbe, Walter. *Educator's Guide to Personalized Reading Instruction.* Englewood Cliffs, N. J.: Prentice-Hall, 1961.
3. Crosby, Muriel. "Reading for Human Relations," *The Packet,* 16 (Winter 1961-62), 13.
4. Darrow, Helen F., and Howes, Virgil M. *Approaches to Individualized Reading.* New York: Appleton-Century-Crofts, 1960.
5. Draper, Marcella K., and Schwietert Louis H., revised and edited by May Lazar. *A Practical Guide to Individualized Reading.* New York: Board of Education, Publication No. 40, Oct. 1960.

6. Gallaher, James J. *Analysis of Research in the Education of Gifted Children.* State of Illinois: Office of the Superintendent of Public Instruction, 1960.
7. Larrick, Nancy. *A Teacher's Guide to Children's Books.* Columbus, Ohio: Charles E. Merrill, 1960.
8. Miles, Catherine Cox. "Gifted Children," Chapter 16 in *Manual of Child Psychology,* 2nd edition, edited by Leonard Carmichael. New York: John Wiley, 1954.
9. *Northwestern University Interest Inventories.* Evanston, Ill.: Northwestern University.
10. *Our Animal Story Books.* Boston: D. C. Heath. *The True Book Series.* Chicago: Children's Press. *I Want to Be Books.* Chicago: Children's Press. *The Walt Disney Story Books.* Boston: D. C. Heath.
11. Stauffer, Russell G. "Individualized and Group Directed Reading Instruction," *Elementary English,* 37 (Oct. 1960).
12. Terman, Lewis M., and Oden, Melita H. *The Gifted Child Grows Up.* Stanford, Calif.: Stanford University Press, 1947.
13. Terman, Lewis M., and Oden, Melita. "The Stanford Studies of the Gifted," in *The Gifted Child* (edited by Paul Witty), p.25. Boston: D. C. Heath, 1951.
14. Torrance, E. P. "Exploration in Creative Thinking," *Education,* 81 (Dec. 1960).
15. Witty, Paul A. *A Study of 100 Gifted Children.* Lawrence, Kansas: University of Kansas Press, 1930.
16. Witty, Paul A. *Helping the Gifted Child.* Chicago: Science Research Associates, 1952.
17. Witty, Paul A. "Reading Instruction—A Forward Look," *Elementary English,* 38 (Mar. 1961).
18. Witty, Paul A., and Fitzwater, James P. "An experiment with Films, Film Readers, and the Magnetic Sound Track," *Elementary English,* 32 (Apr. 1955).

22. Auditory Discrimination and Visual Perception in Good and Poor Readers*

C. P. GOETZINGER
D. DIRKS
C. J. BAER

Departments of Otorhinolaryngology
and Hearing and Speech, Kansas University
Medical Center, Kansas City, Kansas

AUDITORY discrimination and acuity as factors related to under-achievement in school have received attention by investigators in the field of education. Programs to evaluate the hearing acuity in particular of school children are becoming increasingly more widespread, and are tending to encompass even the pre-first grade classes.

Although hearing acuity for pure tones is usually regarded as a good index by which to evaluate auditory capacity, and hence to rule out hearing as a reason for poor school achievement, nevertheless, the other important aspect of hearing, namely, auditory discrimination, perhaps deserves more attention than has hitherto been supposed. That the problem of auditory discrimination however has not been entirely neglected, is attested to by the fact that several diagnostic reading batteries, such as the one by Monroe, [1] include sections for assessing this dimension of hearing. In addition, reading programs at the elementary level as well as remedial reading procedures are constructed to provide training in learning to listen.

Bond [2] in 1935 compared good and poor readers in auditory acuity, discrimination and memory span. He found statistically significant differences in favor of the good readers in all three areas. Later, Kennedy [3] investigated reading in relation to acuity for pure tones, but found no significant correlations except at the tenth grade level. She also studied auditory discrimination with the Seashore Pitch Test records and with nonsense syllables. In addition, the Western Electric 6-B pure tone audiometer was utilized in an attempt to measure the frequency difference limen. She concluded with reference to auditory discrimination that, " . . . the silent reading groups differ significantly as this factor was tested with the Seashore records on the 4-C audiometer." There were no differences, however, between good and poor readers on the frequency difference limen test. [3]

---

*From *Annals of Otology, Rhinology and Laryngology,* **69**, 1 (March, 1960), 121. Reprinted by permission.

[1]Numbers in brackets refer to references at the end of the article.

Robinson [4] found acuity loss to be an infrequent cause of reading disability. Auditory discrimination and memory span were more frequently associated with a reading problem.

Henry [5] showed significant differences in reading scores between subjects with normal hearing and those with high frequency losses.

More recently, Poling [6] administered the Monroe-Sherman Group Diagnostic Reading Aptitude and Achievement Tests to 58 boys and 20 girls within the age range 8 to 13 years. This investigator did not find significant differences between good and poor readers either in auditory acuity for pure tones or auditory discrimination. In regard to auditory memory span, she concluded that it ". . . accounts for some of the failure in learning to read." [6]

It is apparent, therefore, that the research relative to auditory discrimination and reading ability is in conflict. That variables such as the influence of speech reading were not always adequately controlled was apparent from the review of the literature. Furthermore, test materials, varying in difficulty, could account for discrepancies in the results. It would appear, therefore, that further research is needed in the area of auditory discrimination and reading problems.

Reading is primarily a mental function. It is commonly mediated, however, through the visual channel. Obviously then, a disturbance of the sensory conducting mechanism resulting in seriously reduced visual acuity, or some other difficulty severely hindering impulse transmission would be expected to interfere with reading accomplishment. But, disregarding the cases of blindness or near blindness contingent upon acuity reduction, a myriad of investigations through the years have failed to uncover significant relationships between persistent reading disabilities and such deviations as esophoria, exophoria, hypermetropia, myopia, etc. Nevertheless, Poling [6] has identified several factors which appear to be related to poor reading such as near-acuity and binaural vision. She emphasized the point, however, that her findings for selected subjects should not be generalized, but required further research on an unselected sample.

Thurston [7] reported a factor analysis study of visual perception concerned with the identification of central rather than ocular factors. In addition to the major area of study, the battery of visual perceptual tests, such as various illusion tests, Hidden Pictures, Circles Test, Street Gestalt Completion, the Gottschaldt Figures, etc., was administered to a group of fast and slow readers at the college level.

Along with other results, Thurston reported a low positive correlation between reading rate and reading comprehension. He concluded, therefore, that his subjects could not be considered as either good or poor readers except as the terms related to speed of reading. In summarizing the results of the experiments with fast and slow readers, Thurston wrote. [7]

Fast and slow readers should be studied carefully as to their perceptual differences in order to identify the perceptual functions which differentiate them. ... It is quite likely that the purely ocular functions, such as accommodation and convergency, are marginal to this problem. Sensory acuity is also likely to be of secondary significance. With this admission, there has been a tendency to ignore completely the perceptual functions which can be distinguished from the more restricted ocular functions. By "perceptual functions" we mean here the central processes that are initiated by sensory stimulation as distinguished from the physiological functions of the eye as such. ... Too much attention has been probably given to the cultivation of reading interest and to personality adjustment in reading problems. The problem should be investigated more intensely in what seems to be the obvious direction.

The primary purpose, therefore, of this study was to investigate auditory discrimination and visual perception in good and poor readers, and to explore the relationship between such factors and reading achievement.

Specifically, the questions for study were as follows:

1. Do good and poor readers matched for I.Q., C.A., and sex show statistically significant differences in auditory discrimination as measured by the recorded W-22, the recorded Rush Hughes and the non-recorded Wepman tests?

2. Is there a statistically significant difference between the "difference scores" of good and poor readers? (The "difference score" refers to the magnitude of the difference between scores obtained on the W-22 and the Rush Hughes tests. The concept will be discussed in the paper.)

3. Do good and poor readers, matched as described, show statistically significant differences on the Raven's Progressive Matrices, the Gottschaldt Figures, and a Figure-Ground test? (The Raven's Test is a nonverbal intelligence test. The Gottschaldt and the Figure-Ground are tests of visual perception.)

4. What are the relationships between some of the variables and reading?

SUBJECTS

Thirty male subjects ranging in age from 10 years 7 months to 12 years 9 months inclusive, were selected for study from a Kansas City, Missouri, public school. The experimental group consisted of 15 poor readers who were attending a reading clinic class. The control group of good readers were selected from the regular classes of the same school. The subjects were matched for chronological age within six months, and for Stanford-Binet I.Q., Form L, within 6 points. The I.Q. range for the 30 subjects was from 94 to 119. All were reported to have 20/20 vision as determined by the school nurse. Two of the control subjects wore glasses with correction to 20/20. The experimental group, in addition, had been referred for a complete ophthalmological examination. No visual defects were found. Specific socio-economic data were not collected on the subjects. The school, however, was located in a middle-income-group neighborhood, and teachers' estimates placed the subjects within the middle range.

EQUIPMENT

The recorded tests of auditory discrimination (W-22 and R. H.) were administered monaurally with a Beltone 12-A speech and pure tone audiometer. The assembly is portable. It consists of the audiometer, a matched pair of TD-39 earphones mounted in MX-41 AR cushions, and a turntable. The equipment was calibrated to National Bureau of Standard Norms for sound pressure, frequency and linearity of attenuators, and was checked periodically for sound presssure output with an Allison artificial ear, Model 3A.

The test chamber was an unoccupied storage room (20 x 20 ft.) on the second floor of the two story school building. The ambient noise level of the room during the tests did not exceed 50 db on the C-Scale of a General Radio Sound Level Meter, Model 1551-A. The enrollment of the school was 250 students so that recess periods were at a minimum. Furthermore, no child was tested during recess. As the school was located a considerable distance from thoroughfares, relatively no traffic noise was experienced.

The tachistoscope employed in the study was manufactured by the Keystone View Company. Essentially, it consisted of an overhead projector and a flashmeter to control exposure time. The projector, as the name implies, is used to project 2x2-inch 35-mm projection slides on a screen. The Flashmeter provided exposure durations of 1/100, 1/50, 1/25, 1/10, 1/5, 1/2, 1 second and unlimited. A beaded motion picture screen, 50x50-inch, was located 11 feet from the subject's chair. The slides were projected on an identical area at the center of the screen during the tests.

THE TESTS

Auditory discrimination was measured with the Rush Hughes recordings of the Harvard PB (phonetically balanced) word lists, the C.I.D. W-22 records and the Wepman Test. The Rush Hughes and the W-22 tests (8) consist of 50 monosyllabic words in each list. The lists are balanced phonetically containing the sounds of the English language in approximately the same proportion as they would occur in a sample of ordinary speech. The W-22 lists, however, are much less difficult than the Rush Hughes Recordings. This is apparently due to distortion in the Rush Hughes recordings as well as the clipped and speedier method of presenting the words. In clinical practice discrimination scores obtained with the Rush Hughes records are about 20 per cent poorer than those obtained with the W-22 records. In scoring the tests a value of two points is credited for each word correctly heard. Since there are 50 words in each test-list, a score of 100 per cent would be credited if there were no errors.

Both tests (the W-22 and the Rush Hughes) are in general use in Hearing Clinics throughout this country, and represent the best available measures of general discrimination ability. The tests are administered at an intensity level sufficiently above threshold to assure a maximum score. Each test consists of several lists which are essentially equivalent as to difficulty. There are, therefore, several forms of the W-22 as well as of the Rush Hughes tests. For this study, the Rush Hughes recordings of test lists 7 and 8, and the W-22 recorded lists 1E and 2E were used.

The "difference score" or simply the difference between a subject's scores on the W-22 and on the Rush Hughes tests, is experimentally employed in diagnosis in the Kansas University Hearing Clinic. [9] As mentioned above, a subject will usually score 20 per cent higher in discrimination on the W-22 than on the Rush Hughes test. This difference score, however, appears to be relatively constant and independent either of degree of acuity loss or discrimination loss as indicated by the W-22 test. Clinically, we have observed that an abnormally large difference score is frequently associated with hearing dysfunction at the cortical level as indicated by an abnormal EEG and by neurological examination. The difference score is, therefore, of interest in this study.

The Wepman Test [10] of auditory discrimination consists of 40 paired words. Thirty pairs are identical words and 10 pairs are different words. The subject, back turned to the examiner, is required to designate whether the paired words as spoken by the examiner are the same or different. In scoring the test, the number of right responses are recorded separately for pairs of words which are the same or different. In this study, however, correct responses from each category were totalled, and differences between groups analyzed from the composite scores.

The Raven's Progressive Matrices, 1938 version [11] is an English nonverbal test of intelligence which is described by the author as: "...a test of a person's capacity at the time of the test to apprehend meaningless figures presented for his observation, see the relations between them, conceive the nature of the figure completing each system of relations presented, and, by so doing, develop a systematic method of reasoning." [11,1]

The test consists of five sets of twelve problems. The initial problem in each set is practically self-evident with succeeding problems becoming progressively more difficult. There is no time limit for the test. Correlation with the Terman-Merrill Scale is reported to be .86. Norms for the group test on school children range from 8 to 14 years inclusive. There are also norms for adults. The scoring of the test is simply the number of problems correctly solved. Indices of mental capacity for children are determined by percentile points at half-year intervals. The test was of interest to us because of the extent to which visual perception might enter into the solution of the problems.

The Gottschaldt Test requires the subject to find a relatively simple geometric figure which is embedded within a more complex design. Teuber and Weinstein [12] have reported that brain-injured subjects do poorly on the task. The test is divided into two parts, section A and B, with the latter containing the more difficult figures. The method and time limits for the test as described by Thurston [7] were used. In scoring the test, the total number correct solutions for the two parts as well as in each part separately was utilized for statistical comparisons.

The Figure-Ground Test consisted of a series of nine slides of common concrete objects such as a cup, hat, penknife, boat, milkbottle, bird, hand with pencil, iron and basket. The objects were imbedded in homogenous backgrounds of wavy lines and squares. [13] The objects as well as the backgrounds were done with black India ink. The slides were projected on the screen by means of the tachistoscope for exposure durations of 1/5, 1/2, 1 second and unlimited time. The scoring involved the types of responses, (whether foreground, background or mixed) for the series at each exposure rate. The test is utilized to measure foreground-background disturbance, particularly in brain-damaged subjects.

In conjunction with the preceding battery, the scores from the California Reading Test (Form X), which had been administered to the entire school system during the month of May, were made available to us. A composite score of reading comprehension and vocabulary was used by us in the statistical treatment of the data.

PROCEDURE

All testing was conducted in the previously described room during a six weeks' period in April and May. The total test time per subject was about one hour and a half excluding the reading test which was administered by the school system. The battery was administered individually (with the exception of the Raven's Test where groups not exceeding four were taken) during three sessions.

In the first session, the hearing acuity and auditory discrimination tests were completed. The order of presentation of the tests was: pure tone thresholds, the W-22, the Rush Hughes and the Wepman. For the monaural tests (pure tone, W-22 and Rush Hughes) the right and the left ears were alternately selected as the first test ear to counter-balance possible order effects.

The clinical ascending method was used to determine the pure tone threshold. The W-22 and the Rush Hughes tests were administered at a comfort level setting above threshold as determined during a short practice session. The practice session which preceded each test in each ear consisted of having the subject listen to five practice words from a different recorded list to ascertain his comfort level as well as to accustom him to listening over earphones. For the W-22 test the comfort level was always 40 db or slightly greater above the average speech reception threshold for the equipment, and 50 db or slightly greater for the Rush Hughes test.

For the Wepman test (the non-recorded test) the subject sat at a distance of one meter from the experimenter with back turned to control the factor of lip-reading. After the practice session as provided in the manual, the experimenter clearly enunciated the paired words, monitoring his presentation level at about a 70 db level as measured by the C-Scale of the General Radio Sound Level Meter. Following the subject's response the next pair of words were spoken and so on until the test was completed.

In session two the Raven's Test was completed, in groups not exceeding four, following standard procedure.

In the final session, the subjects received the Gottschaldt Figures, and the Figure-Ground Test. The Gottschaldt Test was administered as described by Thurston. [7] In the Figure-Ground Test the nine figure-ground slides were presented, following a practice session with five slides, the figures of which were on white backgrounds. The subject sat at a distance of 11 feet from the screen in a darkened room. A 25 watt desk lamp to the rear of the experimenter provided sufficient illumination to write the responses. The slides were presented only once at exposure rates of 1/5, 1/2; 1 second and unlimited time in that order. All slides were presented at the exposure rate of 1/5 second, then 1/2 second, etc. Responses were recorded verbatim by the examiner.

In the statistical analysis of the data, t tests, F tests for homogeneity of variance and product-moment correlations were computed. [22]

RESULTS

The results of the pure tone threshold tests for the experimental group revealed normal hearing in both ears. As a matter of fact only two subjects deviated from the norm by as much as 15 db, and in both cases at only 4000 cps in one ear. A primary pre-requisite for a control subject had been normal hearing for pure tones. Therefore, no subject was considered for the control group unless the threshold test had indicated normal hearing in each ear for the frequencies 500, 1000, 2000, and 4000 cps. Statistical analysis of the data showed that the two groups were not different in threshold sensitivity. Other preliminary statisitcs indicated that there were no statistically significant differences between ears either on the W-22 or the Rush Hughes discrimination tests. Therefore, the scores for the two ears were averaged, and the data treated accordingly.

In Table I are shown the basic statistical computations for the two groups as well as mean differences and the t test results of these differences. The F tests had indicated that the groups were homogeneous as to variance at the .05 level, and are therefore not recorded in the table.

Inspection of the last column of the table shows that the groups did not differ significantly either in Binet I.Q. or chronological age. That the two groups were highly dissimilar in reading ability is evident not only from the statistically significant t test, but from the fact that there was no overlapping of ranges. It will be also noted from the last column that the Rush Hughes, Wepman and the difference score differentiated the groups at the .01 level of confidence. Conversely, the difference between the W-22 scores was non-significant. It will be recalled that the W-22 is an easier test of auditory discrimination than the Rush Hughes test. To determine the extent to which intelligence could be a factor in the results, product-moment correlations were computed between the W-22 and I.Q., the Rush Hughes and I.Q., the Wepman and I.Q., and the Difference Score and I.Q. for each group as well as for the combined groups. The correlations ranged from .08 to .15 and are statistically nonsignificant. Apparently, none of the discrimination tests is related to intelligence as measured by the Binet Scale at this age level.

TABLE I. *Means, Standard Deviations and Ranges of Chronological Age, and the Test Scores for Experimental and Control Groups. Also Shown are Mean Differences Between Groups and T Test Results*

| | Experimental Group | | | Control Group | | | | |
	M.	S.D.	Range	M.	S.D.	Range	M/Dif.	T*
C.A.	140.92	6.71	153–127	140.60	7.80	155–130	.32	.33
I.Q.	104.46	7.27	117– 94	107.66	6.20	119– 97	3.22	1.25
Read.	124.52	10.54	140–109	162.28	8.61	178–150	37.76	10.37**
W-22	93.80	3.64	98– 88	94.27	1.81	97– 90	1.53	.56
R.H.	68.73	5.58	79– 60	75.13	5.19	84– 63	7.60	3.15**
D.S.	25.70	5.27	36– 15	19.20	4.74	32– 11	6.50	3.44**
Wep.	34.40	2.64	38– 28	37.67	1.25	40– 35	3.27	4.36**
Rav.	29.00	16.41	38– 18	41.31	10.63	55– 20	12.31	3.66**
Gott.	19.40	8.24	29– 6	25.93	8.67	38– 6	6.53	2.05
G.A.	11.20	5.48	20– 2	14.00	4.38	21– 3	2.80	1.78
G.B.	8.20	3.37	20– 3	11.93	4.24	20– 3	3.73	2.57*
F.G.	6.00	1.30	8– 3	6.27	.97	8– 5	.27	.63

C.A. in months
Reading in months of reading age   *df. at .01 level = 2.763
**df. at .05 level = 2.048

Next, correlations were computed between the auditory discrimination tests. As might be expected, the W-22 and the Rush Hughes tests were significantly related at the .01 level, (r was .58). No relationship was found between either of these tests and the Wepman (r was .043; r was .169). It would appear from these results that different aspects of discriminatory ability are being measured by the PB lists. One wonders whether or not the Wepman test is related to auditory memory span.

Correlations were then computed between reading and auditory discrimination. Correlations of .564, - .545, 589 and .079 were obtained respectively between reading and the Wepman, the difference score, the Rush Hughes and the W-22. The first three correlations are significant at the .01 level, and the last is not significant. The negative relationship between reading and the difference score means that as the reading score improved the difference score decreased. There is, therefore, a low positive relationship between auditory discrimination and reading as measured by the Rush Hughes, the Wepman and the difference score tests. None of the relationships is sufficiently high to predict reading achievement from discrimination ability.

By referring to the last column of Table I again, it will be seen that the Raven's test significantly differentiated the groups (t was 3.66) at the .01 level. The t results for the total Gottschaldt (t was 2.05) and the figure-ground (t was .63)* were statistically nonsignificant. As a next step t tests for differences between groups were computed separately for section A and B of the Gottschaldt. The former did not differentiate the groups (t was 1.78). The latter t test differentiated the groups at the .05 level. In other words, on the more difficult section B of the Gottschaldt test the good readers were superior in performance to the poor readers at the .05 level. Correlations were then computed between the total Gottschaldt and the Raven's test, the total Gottschaldt and Binet I.Q. and the total Gottschaldt and reading. The resulting correlations were respectively: .489, .305 and .262. Only the r between the Gottschaldt and the Raven's test, therefore, was significant at the .01 level of confidence. Although the ability to disembed a figure from a more complex design is inherent in the Raven's test, its presence is too weak to predict performance on the Raven's from the Gottschaldt test. That the ability is not related either to reading performance or I.Q. as measured by the Binet test, is indicated by the non-significant correlations.

Finally, the raw data for the Rush Hughes, the Wepman, the Raven's and reading were converted to T scores. A composite score for the two auditory discrimination tests and the Raven's test was correlated then with the reading test. The correlation obtained from this procedure was .731. In view of the small number of cases in the study as well as the nature of the data the computation

---

*The figure-ground t of 6.3 is for the exposure rate 1/5 of a second. Since the t results for slower exposure rates were even smaller, they were not recorded in the table. Only foreground correct responses received a credit of one. There were only two background responses and two mixed responses for each group. Hence, the groups were homogenous as to their response patterns.

of multiple correlations did not seem justified. Although generalizations as to the predictability of reading achievement from the above mentioned battery of tests should not be made from our selected data, nevertheless, the results appear to offer promise and hence, merit investigation on a larger unselected sample.

COMMENT

The results of this investigation offer confirmatory evidence for previous research which has indicated that poor readers are significantly inferior to good readers in auditory discrimination. A further finding of the study is that the discrimination inferiority of the poor readers is a function of the level of difficulty of the test, which is not, however, correlated with intelligence per se as measured by the Binet scale. The two auditory discrimination tests (the Rush Hughes and the Wepman) which differentiated the groups (the experimental and control groups) were not related, and thus appear to be measuring different aspects of auditory discrimination. Past research is in agreement that poor readers manifest a deficit in auditory memory span. Whether or not the Wepman Test reflects this particular facet of discrimination cannot be determined from the data.

As we have noted in this paper, the W-22 and the Rush Hughes tests are phonetically balanced monosyllabic word lists, which are employed extensively in hearing clinics to measure discrimination ability. Poor ability in auditory discrimination is a relatively common occurrence in individuals with hearing losses even after their acuity deficits have been overcome through amplification. Such disturbances in auditory discrimination are particularly apparent in cases of Ménière's disease which is of cochlear origin, of tumors of the VIII nerve, and of tumors of the temporal lobe of the brain. Decreased auditory discrimination is also a common observation in old people, even though their acuity losses for pure tones may be relatively inconsequential. In other words, decreased acuity as a result of perceptive deafness is usually accompanied by a decrease in ability to discriminate speech clearly. In old people, however, discrimination disability is frequently much greater than would be expected on the basis of their actual acuity loss for tones. That the poor discrimination in such cases is attributable at times to a reduction in the spiral ganglion cells and fibers of the VIII nerve appears well established, especially in view of the work of Schuknecht et al. [14,15,16,17] That poor discrimination at other times is due to central factors is clear from the research of Bocca. [18,19]

During the past year at the Hearing Clinic of the University of Kansas Medical Center research has been in progress as to whether or not auditory discrimination tests, varying as to level of difficulty, might be utilized to differentiate primary cortical discrimination dysfunction from dysfunction resulting either from auditory tract or from cochlear lesions. We have observed,

[9] for example, that old subjects with similar hearing loss for pure tones and similar W-22 scores not infrequently manifest marked dissimilarity on the Rush Hughes test. It was suggested by Goetzinger and Rousey [9] that a large difference score between the tests might be indicative of primary auditory-cortical area dysfunction superimposed upon the normal difference between the tests. For many old subjects as well as young subjects reduced discrimination on the W-22 test, as a result of perceptive hearing impairment, is common. Their Rush Hughes scores are also reduced. The difference score, however, is usually about 20 to 24 per cent. When this difference score increases markedly, cortical dysfunction is suspected. By cortical dysfunction is meant a disturbance in the primary auditory perception areas of the temporal lobes. It does not imply a disruption in language formulation or in the processes associated with an auditory symbolic disturbance as in sensory aphasia. Furthermore, it does not refer to mental deterioration. At the present time we are attempting to collect supporting data for the hypothesis of the difference score from EEG tracings. As with all research the results have not been without disappointment. However, the findings have been consistent enough to warrant continued pursuit of the technique.

Of particular interest has been the consistency with which a large difference score in one ear has been associated with an abnormal EEG in the contralateral hemisphere. Bocca [18, 19] has demonstrated an absence of summation for speech in cases of temporal lobe tumors in the ear contralateral to the tumor under certain conditions of binaural stimulation. In view of the fact that each ear is represented bilaterally in the brain, that pure tone tests of hemispherectomized patients show no difference in pure tone sensitivity between ears, that unilateral differences associated with the reception of speech do appear to occur in the contralateral ears of temporal lobe tumors, the importance of the auditory decussation fibers for discrimination and in particular, their terminal endings in the primary temporal-cortical areas, is suggested. We have had only one hemispherectomized patient (a child of ten years) among our patients. Although her pure tone threshold was normal in both ears, the difference score was 20 per cent larger in the ear contralateral to the removed hemisphere.

In terms of the present study, therefore, the statistically significant larger difference score for the poor readers might suggest a reduction in function at the primary auditory-cortical level.

As indicated in our results the good readers were significantly superior to the poor readers on the Raven's test. Visual perception as measured by the Figure-Ground test at the designated exposure rates did not differentiate the groups. The difference between the groups on section B of the Gottschaldt test was, however, significant at the .05 level of confidence, with the good readers evincing a superiority. A correlation of .489, significant at the .01 level, was found between the total Gottschaldt and the Raven's test. Although a low positive relation appears to exist between the tests, nevertheless, it is clear that the inferior performance of the good readers involves much more than the ability measured by the Gottschaldt. Other tests of visual perception might provide more fruitful results.

Socio-economic status of the subjects had not been specifically investigated. Teacher estimates classified the subjects within average limits. That this is an important variable of the Raven's test has recently been demonstrated by Sperrazzo and Wilkins. [20] Another variable frequently mentioned is the effect of emotional disturbance on the test. Kasper [21] reported that the Raven's test did not consistently differentiate psychiatric adults from the norms. Although we have not included emotional disturbance as a major point of research in this paper, we administered the battery with the exception of the visual perception tests (the Gottschaldt and the figure-ground) to 12 boys and 3 girls in a school for emotionally disturbed children. The average score for the Raven's test was only slightly below the norm for their age. Furthermore, their auditory discrimination scores were not different from the control group of good readers. This study will be reported in a subsequent paper.

SUMMARY AND CONCLUSIONS

Fifteen poor readers from a public school reading clinic were matched with 15 good readers from the same school on the basis of Binet I.Q. and chronological age. All were males. The subjects were administered a battery of tests which included the W-22, the Rush Hughes and the Wepman auditory discrimination tests, the Raven's Progressive Matrices (1938), the Gottschaldt Figures, the Figure-Ground Test and the California Reading test, Form X.

In terms of the questions posed for study, first as to whether the groups differed significantly in auditory discrimination; second, as to whether they differed significantly on the difference score; third, as to whether they differed significantly on the Raven's test and the Visual Perception tests; and fourth, as to the relationships between some of the variables and reading, the findings were as follows:

1. The W-22 test did not significantly differentiate the groups. The good readers were significantly superior to the poor readers at the .01 level on the Rush Hughes, the Wepman and the difference score. The latter findings support past research which indicates that good readers have better discrimination than poor readers. The former finding (W-22) points up the consideration of the level of difficulty of a test. In other words, a relatively easy discrimination test such as the W-22 does not differentiate good and poor readers. In addition to these findings no correlation was demonstrated between any of the auditory discrimination tests and Binet I.Q. A positive correlation of .58, significant at the .01 level was found between the W-22 and the Rush Hughes tests. Neither of

these tests nor the difference score correlated significantly with the Wepmen test. Apparently, the Wepman test measures a different aspect of auditory discrimination than the PB tests. The Rush Hughes and Wepman tests correlated with reading at the .01 level. The respective correlations of .589 and .564 are too low for predictive purposes. The W-22 did not correlate with reading.

2. The statistically significant difference between groups on the difference score (.01 level) plus the lack of correlation between the difference score and intelligence possibly is suggestive of a primary auditory-cortical dysfunction in poor readers. Implications relative to this possibility were discussed.

3. The difference between groups on the Raven's test was significant at the .01 level of confidence. Neither of the visual perception tests differentiated the groups. When, however, the two sections of the Gottschaldt test were analyzed separately, section B, the more difficult part, differentiated the groups at the .05 level. The correlation between the total Gottschaldt test and reading was .305, a nonsignificant relationship. Positive correlations (.01 level) were found between the Gottschaldt and the Raven's tests, and between the Raven's tests and reading. When a T-score combination of the Rush Hughes, Wepman and Raven's tests was correlated with reading, a correlation of .731 was obtained. Generalizations based upon these correlations should not be made because of the nature of the data. The findings with a combination of tests appear promising, and suggest further research with a larger unselected sample as well as with other tests.

References

1. Monroe, M.: *Children Who Cannot Read.* Chicago: University of Chicago Press, 1932.
2. Bond, G. L.: *The Auditory and Speech Characteristics of Poor Readers.* Teachers Coll., Columbia Univ., Contrib. to Educ., No. 657, New York, 1935.
3. Kennedy, H.: "A study of Children's Hearing as It Relates to Reading," *J. of Exper. Educ.* 1:238-252, 1941.
4. Robinson, H. M.: *Why Pupils Fail in Reading.* Univ. of Chi. Press, 1953.
5. Henry, Sibyl: "Children's Audiograms in Relation to Reading Attainment: I. Introduction to and Investigation of the Problem," *J. of Gen. Psychol.* 70:211-231, 1947.
6. Poling, Dorothy L.: "Auditory Deficiencies of Poor Readers." *Supp. Educ. Mono.* 77:107-112, 1953.
7. Thurstone, L. L.: *A Factorial Study of Perception.* Univ. of Chi. Press, 1944.
8. Hirsh, I. J.: *The Measurement of Hearing.* New York: McGraw-Hill Book Co., 1952.
9. Goetzinger, C. P., and C. L. Rousey,: "Hearing Problems in Later Life," *Medical Times* 87:771-780, 1959.
10. Wepman, J. M.: Auditory Discrimination Test. Chicago, 1958.
11. Raven, J. C.: *Standard Progressive Matrices.* London, H. K. Lewis and Co., 1958.
12. Teuber, H. L., and S. Weinstein,: "Ability to Discover Hidden Figures after Cerebral Lesions," *A.M.A. Arch. Neurol. and Psychia* 76:369-379, 1956.
13. Myklebust, H. R., and Brutten, M.: "A Study of the Visual Perception of Deaf Children," *Acta Oto-Laryngol. Supp.* 105, 1953.

14. Schuknecht, H.: "Presbycusis," *Laryngoscope* 65:402-419, 1955.
15. Schuknecht, H.: "Techniques for Study of Cochlear Function and Pathology in Experimental Animals," *Arch. Otolaryngol.* 58:377-397, 1953.
16. Schuknecht, H., and Woellner, R. C.: "An Experimental and Clinical Study of Deafness from Lesions of the Cochlear Nerve," *J. of Laryngol. and Otol.* 69:75-97, 1955.
17. Schuknecht, H., Neff, W., and Perlman, H. B.: "An Experimental Study of Auditory Damage Following Blows to the Head," *Annals of Otology, Rhinology and Laryngology* 60:273-289, 1951.
18. Bocca, E.: "Clinical Aspects of Cortical Deafness," *Laryngoscope,* Special Issue, International Conference on Audiology, 68:301-309, 1958.
19. Bocca, E.: "Binaural Hearing: Another Approach," *Laryngoscope* 65:1164-1171, 1955.
20. Sperrazzo, G., and Wilkins, W. L.: "Further Normative Data on the Progressive Matrices," *J. of Consult. Psychol.* 23:273-274, 1959.
21. Kasper, S.: "Progressive Matrices (1938) and Emotional Disturbance," *J. of Consult. Psychol.* 22:24-25, 1958.
22. Walker, H., and Lev, J.: *Statistical Inference.* New York: Henry Holt and Co., 1953.

V

Reading for the
Culturally Deprived

23. Dialect Barriers

to Reading Comprehension*

KENNETH S. GOODMAN

Associate Professor of Education
at Wayne State University
Detroit, Michigan

THE task of learning to read is not an easy one. But it's a lot easier to learn to read one's mother tongue than to learn to read a foreign language, one which the learner does not speak. Actually each of us speaks a particular dialect of a language. Each dialect is distinguished from all other dialects by certain features as: some of its sounds, some of its grammar, some of its vocabulary. The dialect which the child learns in the itimacy of his own home is his mother tongue. All physically normal children learn to speak a dialect. Whatever happens to his language during his life, however fluent and multilingual he may become, this native dialect is his most deeply and permanently rooted means of communication.

Since it is true that learning to read a foreign language is a more difficult task than learning to read a native language, it must follow that it is harder for a child to learn to read a dialect which is not his own than to learn to read his own dialect.

This leads to an important hypothesis: *The more divergence there is between the dialect of the learner and the dialect of learning, the more difficult will be the task of learning to read.*

This is a general hypothesis. It applies to all learners. If the language of the reading materials or the language of the teacher differs to any degree from the native speech of the learners some reading difficulty will result. To some extent also there is divergence between the immature speech of the young learner and adult language norms in the speech community. Children have mastered most but not all of the sounds and syntax of adult speech. A further divergence reflects the fact that older members of any language community are less influenced by language change than are the youth. Thus the teacher may cling to language which is obsolescent in form or meaning. Books particularly lag behind language change since they freeze language at the date of composition. Though this paper is mainly concerned with gross dialect differences it must be

*From *Elementary English,* (December, 1965), 853-860. Reprinted with the permission of the National Council of Teachers of English and Kenneth S. Goodman.

remembered, then, that the reading problems discussed apply to some extent to all learners because minor dialect differences are features of even homogeneous speech communities.

THE DIVERGENT SPEAKER

For purposes of discussion we'll call the child who speaks a dialect different from that which the school, text, or teacher treats as standard, *the divergent speaker*. Divergence, of course, is relative and there is by no means agreement on what standard American English is. Divergent is a good term however, because it is neutral as a value term and it is important, perhaps critical, in considering the problems of the divergent speaker to avoid labeling his language as bad, sloppy, or sub-standard. We need to keep clear that, though some dialects may carry more social prestige than others, they are not necessarily more effective in communication. Gleason has said, "It is a safe generalization to say that all languages are approximately equally adequate for the needs of the culture of which they are a part." Dialects represent subcultures. Therefore it can similarly be said that all dialects are equally adequate for the needs of the subculture of which they are a part.

Every child brings to school, when he comes, five or six years of language and of experience. His language is closely intertwined with the culture of his community; it embodies the cultural values and structures the way in which he may perceive his world and communicate his reactions to others.

His language is so well learned and so deeply embossed on his subconscious that little conscious effort is involved for him in its use. It is as much a part of him as his skin. Ironically, well-meaning adults, including teachers who would never intentionally reject a child or any important characteristic of a child, such as the clothes he wears or the color of his skin, will immediately and emphatically reject his language. This hurts him far more than other kinds of rejection because it endangers the means which he depends on for communication and self-expression.

Things that other people say sound right or funny to a child depending on whether they fit within the language norms of his dialect. He has become exceedingly proficient in detecting slight, subtle differences in speech sounds which are significant in his dialect and he's learned to ignore other differences in speech sounds that are not significant. He uses rhythm and pitch patterns of his language with great subtlety. He enjoys puns on language which employ very slight variations in relative pitch and stress. By the time divergent speakers are in the middle grades they have learned to get pleasure from the fact that an in-group pun based on their common divergent dialect is unfunny to an outsider like their teacher who doesn't share the dialect.

All children develop vocabulary which falls generally within the vocabulary pool of their speech community. Through repeated experience common for their culture they have begun to develop complex concepts and express them in their mother tongue.

In every respect the process of language development of the divergent speaker is exactly the same as that of the standard speaker. His language when he enters school is just as systematic, just as grammatical within the norms of his dialect, just as much a part of him as any other child's is. Most important it is a vital link with those important to him and to the world of men.

There are some differences between the problems of the divergent speaker in an isolated rural community where a single dialect is the common speech and has been for several generations and the problems of the divergent speaker in the center of one of our great cities. This latter child may live in a virtual ghetto, but his friends and neighbors represent a variety of language backgrounds. Transplanted regional dialects become social class dialects. As the city-dweller grows older he comes into increasing contact with the general culture and its language. In the home community the idiolects, the personal languages of individuals, will cluster closely around a dialect prototype. But the dialects of urban divergent speakers are much more varied and shade off from distinct divergent dialects to standard speech. Variables such as family origin, recency of migration, degree of isolation from influences outside the subculture, attitudes toward self, personal and parental goals are some of the factors which may determine idiolect.

DIVERGENT LANGUAGES OR DIALECTS

Language diversity among divergent speakers complicates the task of understanding the literacy problems which they have. The basic problems will be the same but the specific form and degree will vary among individuals.

Teachers need to give careful consideration to the separate characteristics of several kinds of language divergence. They need to first differentiate immature language from dialect-based divergence. Language which is immature is always in transition toward adult norms. Teachers need not worry too much about immaturity in language since desired change is virtually inevitable. On the other hand whatever the teacher does to speed this change is in the direction the child is moving. He can confirm the teacher's advice in the speech of his parents. But if the teacher "corrects" the dialect-based divergent language, this is at cross purposes with the direction of growth of the child. All his past and present language experience contradicts what the teacher tells him. School becomes a place where people talk funny and teachers tell you things about your language that aren't true.

Another point that needs to be clarified is the difference between standard regional speech and some imaginary national standard which is correct everywhere and always. No dialect of American English ever has achieved this status; instead we have a series of standard regional dialects, the speech of the cultured people in each area.

It's obvious that a teacher in Atlanta, Georgia, is foolish to try to get her children to speak like cultured people in Detroit or Chicago, just as it's foolish for any teacher to impose universal standard pronunciations which are not even present in the teacher's own speech. I'm referring to such hypocricies as insisting that *u* before *e* must always say its own name and therefore *Tuesday* is /Tyuzdey/. Cultured speech, socially preferred, is not the same in Boston, New York, Philadelphia, Miami, Baltimore, Atlanta, or Chicago. The problem, if any, comes when the Bostonian moves to Chicago, the New Yorker to Los Angeles, the Atlantan to Detroit. Americans are ethnocentric in regard to most cultural traits but they are doubly so with regard to language. Anybody who doesn't speak the way I do is wrong. A *green onion* is not a *scallion*. I live in Detroit not Détroit. I can carry my books to work but not my friends. *Fear* ends with an *r* and *Cuba* does not. Such ethnocentrisms are unfortunate among the general public. They may be tragic among educators. Too often we send children off to speech correction classes not because their speech needs correction but because it isn't like ours. Pity the poor child who finds himself transplanted to a new and strange environment and then must handle the additional complication of learning to talk all over again. And, of course, if the child is a migrant from the rural South to the urban North, his speech marks him not only as different but socially inferior. He is told not just that he is wrong but sloppy, careless, vulgar, crude. His best defense is to be silent.

In his classroom the divergent speaker finds several kinds of language being used. First is the language or bundle of idiolects within dialects which he and his classmates bring with them as individuals. Represented in their language or dialect is the language or dialect of their parents and their speech community. Next there is the language of the teacher which will exist in at least two forms. There will be the teacher's informal, unguarded idiolect and his version of correct standard speech; the way he says things off guard; the way he strives to speak as a cultivated person. Another version of the standard language will be the literary form or forms the child encounters in books. To this we must add the artificial language of the basal reader. Artificial language is not used by anyone in any communicative situation. Some primarese is artificial to the point of being non-language, not even a divergent one.

THE CONSENSUS OF LANGUAGE AND
THE UNIFORMITY OF PRINT

Two things are in the divergent child's favor. First, all speakers have a range of comprehension which extends beyond the limits of their own dialect.

All of us can understand speech which differs from our own, particularly if we are in frequent contact with such speech. As they grow older, urban children are in increasing contact with a number of dialects other than their own. Secondly, the English orthography has one great virtue in its uniformity across dialects. No matter how words are pronounced printers across the country usually spell them the same. Though we get some mavericks like *guilty* and *judgment* we spell *pumpkin* the same whether we say *pəŋkin* or *pəmpkən* and *something* the same whether we say *səmpthin* or *səmpm*. This standardization of print for a multidialectial speech suggests that part of the problem of learning to read for divergent speakers could be eliminated if teachers let children read in their own dialects and if teachers got rid of the misconception that spelling determines pronunciation. One child asked his teacher how to spell /ræt/ . "R-a-t" she said. "No, ma'am" he responded. "I don't mean rat mouse, I mean right now."

POINTS OF DIVERGENCE AMONG DIALECTS

Now if we examine the areas in which dialects differ we can perhaps shed some light on the barriers divergent readers face. Let us start with sound.

Sound Divergence

Intonation.
Dialects differ in intonation. Perhaps what makes an unfamiliar dialect most difficult to understand is its unexpected pitch, stress, and rhythm. Teachers often complain when they first begin to work with divergent speakers that they can't understand a word. But after a short time they seem to tune in on the right frequency. They catch on to the melody of the dialect. Since intonation is essential in understanding oral language, it is logical to assume that it must be supplied mentally by readers as they read in order for comprehension to take place. How much comprehension is interfered with if the teacher insists on intonation patterns in oral reading which are unnatural to the divergent reader can only be conjectured at this time. But there is no doubt that this is a source of difficulty to some extent.

Phonemes
Phonemes are the significant units of speech sounds which are the symbols of oral language. All American dialects share more or less a common pool of phonemes. But not all dialects use all these phonemes in all the same ways. They pattern differently in different dialects. Since phonemes are really bundles of related sounds rather than single sounds, it is likely that the range of sounds that compose a particular phoneme will vary among dialects. Vowel phonemes are

particularly likely to vary. Even within dialects there are some variations. Good examples are words ending in -og, such as /dog/, /fog/, /frog/, /log/; or are they /dɔg/, /fɔg/, /frɔg/, /lɔg/? In my own idiolect I find I say /frɔg/, /fɔg/, /dɔg/, /lɔg/, but I also say /cag/, /bag/, /smag/.

Obviously phonics programs which attempt to teach a relationship between letters and sounds cannot be universally applicable to all dialects. The basic premise of phonics instruction is that by teaching a child to associate the sounds which he hears in oral language with the letters in written language he will be able to sound out words. But a divergent speaker can't hear the sounds of standard speech in his nonstandard dialect because he does not have them or because they occur in different places in his dialect than other dialects. The instruction may be not only inappropriate but confusing. When he reads the lesson he may then be forced to sound out words which are not words in his dialect. To illustrate: Take a child who normally says /də/ rather than /tə/ and /nəfin/ rather then /nəθin/. Teaching him that the digraph <th> represents the first sound in *the* and the medial consonant in *nothing* makes him pronounce words not in his dialect and throws a barrier across his progress in associating sound and print.

NEW READING MATERIALS AND
SOUND DIVERGENCE AMONG DIALECTS

Recent attempts at producing beginning reading materials which have regular one-to-one correspondence between letters and phonemes will not solve this problem and may actually compound it since there will be a tendency for teachers to assume that the matched correspondence of sound and letter is to be uniform throughout the reading materials. For example, they might assume *frog* and *log* to have the same vowel sound and so teach the sounds to be the same when a student might well use /a/ as in *father* in one and /ɔ/ as in *caught* in the other. The matched phonemic-graphemic books assume that there is a uniform spoken set of sounds that can by ingenuity and counting of data be inscribed with a uniform written alphabet. This is not true, when the spoken language is viewed as a national-international phenomenon or when it is viewed as a local phenomenon in a heterogeneous cultural country as one of our urban centers.

Transcription of the sound language in ITA faces the same problems. It has a wider alphabet and can therefore transcribe more literary and sensible English than the limited lexicon of the American linguistic readers. The British ITA materials, however, cannot be read literally except with the "received pronunciation" of the BBC. When as an American I read about "levers" in an ITA book I must say /liyverz/. The principle that spelling is the same across dialects is sacrificed and ITA spelling requires pronunciation narrowed to one special class dialect. Teachers using these materials need to make some adjustments for the dialects used by themselves and their students. There may be, no doubt is, a spoken language in common but it is not so uniform as is the common spelling system.

Another place where sound divergence among dialects affects the handling of reading materials is the traditional sets of homophones. Homophones, words that sound alike, will vary from dialect to dialect. *Been* and *bin* are homophones in my speech. In another dialect *been* would sound the same as *bean* and in still another *Ben* and *been* would be sounded alike. Bidialectal students may bring up new sets of homophones. One teacher asked her class to use *so* in a sentence. "I don't mean sew a dress," she said. "I mean the other so." "I got a *so* on my leg." responded one of her pupils.

Grammar Divergence

The Suffix

Inflectional changes in words involve using suffixes or internal changes in words to change case or tense. In certain dialects of American English speakers say *He see me* rather than *He sees me*. They are not leaving off an *s*. There isn't any in their dialect. Similarly, plurals may not use an *s* form. *I got three brother,* is common in Appalachian speech. One teacher reported to me that her pupils could differentiate between *crayon* and *crayons* as written words and respond to the difference by selecting plural and singular illustrations, but they read the words the same, one crayon, two /kraeyən/. The problem is not an inability to see or say the *s.* It doesn't seem to belong in the pronunciation of *crayons.* The inflectional ending *s* to indicate plural is not in the grammar of this dialect.

Most Americans will add /əz/ to form plurals of words ending in /s/ /z/ /š/ /ž/ /č/ as in *busses, mazes, washes, colleges, churches,* but in the Blue Ridge Mountains this ending also goes with words ending in /sp/, /st/, /sk/ as in /waspəz/ /pohstəz/ /tæskəz/ (H. A. Gleason, *An Introduction to Descriptive Linguistics,* New York: Holt, Rinehart and Winston, p. 62). This kind of difference will be reflected in the child's reading. The differences are systematic within the child's dialect. In terms of the school and teacher they may be divergent, or as we say, incorrect, but in terms of the reader and his speech community they are convergent, that is, correct.

Not only suffixes vary, but also verb forms and verb auxiliaries. When a child says, "I here teacher," as the teacher calls the roll he is not being incomplete. No linking verb is needed in this type of utterance in his dialect. There is a difference in the syntax of his dialect and other American English dialects. Fortunately such differences are minor in American English. One area of difference seems to be the use of verb forms and verb makers. *We was going, They done it, We come home* all are examples of this phenomenon.

Vocabulary Divergence

An area of dialect divergence that people are most aware of is vocabulary. Most people are aware that *gym shoes* in Detroit are *sneakers* in New York, that in Chicago you may *throw* but in Little Rock you *chunk,* that a Minnesota *lake* would be a *pond* in New Hampshire. Perhaps there is less awareness of words which have similar but not identical meanings in different dialects. All words have a range of meaning rather than a single meaning. This range may shift from place to place. The meaning of *carry* may be basically the same in two dialects but some uses will be correct in one dialect but not in the other.

Vocabulary differences among dialects may cause reading difficulty and must be compensated for by the teacher who uses texts printed for a national market.

I've dealt primarily here with the barriers to learning how to read that result when the readers have divergent languages. There are of course other important problems which grow out of the differences in experience, values, and general subculture of the divergent learners. Readers can't comprehend materials which are based on experience and concepts outside their background and beyond their present development.

THE READING PROGRAM FOR DIVERGENT SPEAKERS

Let's address ourselves to a final question. What is currently happening as the divergent speaker learns to read? I've found that divergent speakers have a surprising tendency to read in book dialect. In their oral reading they tend to use phonemes that are not the ones they use in oral language. Their reading often sounds even more wooden and unnatural than most beginners. There is some tendency to read their own dialect as they gain proficiency, but in general it appears that teachers are more successful in teaching preferred pronunciations than reading. What is lacking is the vital link between written and oral language that will make it possible for children to bring their power over the oral language to bear on comprehending written language.

There seem to be three basic alternatives that schools may take in literacy programs for divergent speakers. First is to write materials for them that are based on their own dialect, or rewrite standard materials in their dialect. A second alternative is to teach the children to speak the standard dialect before teaching them to read in the standard dialect. The third alternative is to let the children read the standard materials in their own dialect, that is to accept the language of the learners and make it their medium of learning. The first alternative seems to be impractical on several counts. Primarily the opposition of the parents and the leaders in the speech community must be reckoned with. They would reject the use of special materials which are based on a non-prestigious dialect. They usually share the view of the general culture that their speech is not the speech of cultivation and literature. They want their children to move into the general culture though they are not sure how this can be brought about.

The second alternative is impractical on pedagogical grounds in that the time required to teach children who are not academically oriented to another dialect of the language, which they feel no need to learn, would postpone the teaching of reading too long. Many would never be ready to learn to read if readiness depended on losing their speech divergence in the classroom. The problem is not simply one of teaching children a new dialect. Children, the divergent among them, certainly have facility in language learning. The problem involves the extinction of their existing dialect, one which receives continuous reinforcement in basic communications outside of the classroom. Labov's research in New York indicates that divergent speakers do not seem to make a conscious effort to use language forms which they recognize as socially preferred until adolescence. Younger children may hear differences but lack the insight to realize which forms are socially preferred. Of course, teenagers may deliberately avoid preferred forms, too, as they reject adult ways and adult values.

In essence the child who is made to accept another dialect for learning must accept the view that his own language is inferior. In a very real sense, since this is the language of his parents, his family, his community, he must reject his own culture and himself, as he is, in order to become something else. This is perhaps too much to ask of any child. Even those who succeed may carry permanent scars. The school may force many to make the choice between self-respect and school acceptance. And all this must be accomplished on the faith of the learner that by changing his language he will do himself some good. As one teenager remarked to me, "Ya man, alls I gotta do is walk right and talk right and they gonna make me president of the United States."

The only practical alternative I feel is the third one. It depends on acceptance by the school and particularly by the teacher of the language which the learner brings to school. Here are some key aspects of this approach:

1. Literacy is built on the base of the child's existing language.
2. This base must be a solid one. Children must be helped to develop a pride in their language and confidence in their ability to use their language to communicate their ideas and express themselves.
3. In reading instruction the focus must be on learning to read. No attempt to change the child's language must be permitted to enter into this process or interfere with it.
4. No special materials need to be constructed but children must be permitted, actually encouraged, to read the way they speak. Experience stories must basically be in their language.
5. Any skill instruction must be based on a careful analysis of their language.
6. Reading materials and reading instruction should draw as much as

possible on experiences and settings appropriate to the children. While special dialect based materials are impractical, we may nonetheless need to abandon our notion of universally usable reading texts and use a variety of materials selected for suitability for the particular group of learners.

7. The teacher will speak in her own natural manner and present by example the general language community, but the teacher must learn to understand and accept the children's language. He must study it carefully and become aware of the key elements of divergence that are likely to cause difficulty. Langston Hughes has suggested an apt motto for the teacher of divergent speakers: "My motto as I live and learn, is dig, and be dug in return."

My own conviction is that even after literacy has been achieved future language change cannot come about through the extinction of the native dialect and the substitution of another. I believe that language growth must be a growth outward from the native dialect, an expansion which eventually will encompass the socially preferred forms but retain its roots. The child can expand his language as he expands his outlook, not rejecting his own sub-culture but coming to see it in its broader setting. Eventually he can achieve the flexibility of language which makes it possible for him to communicate easily in many diverse settings and on many levels.

I'd like to close with a plea. You don't have to accept what I've said. I don't ask that you believe or that you agree with my point of view. My plea is that you listen to the language of the divergent. Listen carefully and objectively. Push your preconceptions and your own ethnocentrisms aside and listen. I think that you'll find beauty and form and a solid base for understanding and communication. And as you dig you'll find that you are indeed dug in return.

24. Reading for the Culturally Disadvantaged*

MILDRED B. SMITH, Ph.D

Area Director, Elementary Education,
Flint Community School, Flint, Michigan

> Every teacher and probably every parent knows that it is imperative for boys and girls to learn to read adequately.—Paul McKee

EDUCATORS have been talking about a high quality of education for all children for many years. Most would quickly agree that every boy and girl should benefit from quality education tailored to his or her particular needs; yet the door to opportunity is not easily made available to every child.

One of the problems currently receiving considerable attention, particularly in urban centers, is how to cope with the deficiencies that burden too many children when they begin school. This paper suggests that a different approach is needed to teach culturally disadvantaged boys and girls to read.[1]

Reading, as we all know, opens the door to learning. Reading unlocks the portals to world splendors, to adventure, to all the fascinating knowledge about people, animals, places, things. Yet, reading does not do this for the disadvantaged youngster. For him, the first experiences of reading can present fear and ego-shattering barriers to all future learning. Such a child requires what we know to be good instruction—*and something more.*

It is the content of this "something more" that puzzles and all too often baffles educators. Before proceeding on this topic, let us examine the social-psychological setting of the disadvantaged, which creates the need for attention.

THE SOCIALIZATION PROCESS

The good teacher knows that a child's behavior is learned through the

*From *Educational Leadership,* 22, 6 (March, 1965), 398-403. Copyright © 1965 by the Association for Supervision and Curriculum Development. Reprinted with permission of the publisher and Mildred B. Smith.

[1]In this context, the term "culturally disadvantaged" refers to the many children who lack the necessary environmental motivation to achieve. Reading, for example, has not been made to seem important for them and they, therefore, do not "want" to read.

socialization process, one of the inevitable functions of our society.[2] Chief among the socialization agencies in our society are the home and the school, each of which shares an essential role. The family, however, exerts the first and perhaps the predominant social influence upon the child. As a primary group, the family defines the basic ideas, values and emotions that are to influence the child throughout his life span.

If a child's family members read extensively in his presence, the child soon realizes that learning to read is important. No other communication is necessary for this value to be transmitted to the child. Similarly, an uneducated father can indicate to his son the importance of a college education by admiring in his presence a friend who attends college. Working-class parents who demonstrate interest in books or formal education transmit their values to their children. Other parents can limit their children's values to areas of entertainment-satisfaction or possessing a car. As the child interacts with members of his family group, he internalizes the expectations of these "important" people, and their values become his.

Although it is the first socializing agent, the family is not the only one for the child. When the child enters school, the teacher becomes for him an additional important person. It is at this stage that the expectations of both parents and teachers influence the attitudes, values and aspirations of children.

Culturally disadvantaged children who are underachievers possess characteristics that are usually identifiable. This under-achieving child invariably exhibits a poor attitude toward classroom work as well as unsatisfactory work habits.

This child is frequently without pencil or paper, but is likely to have an assortment of gum or candy wrappers in his desk. His notebook (if he has one) is untidy. He can be described as "working with one eye on the teacher and the other on his paper." He may talk to and poke other students the moment the teacher turns his back to write on the chalkboard. He plays with gadgets kept in his pockets or desk, and spends considerable time eating candy, pretzels and the like. The disadvantaged child (a) is not interested in his school work; (b) sees little value in it; and (c) finds himself forced into a strange and often a hostile environment.

On the other hand, the child who comes to school from a home in which he is required to complete a job on time, is rewarded for doing it well; sees his parents reading books and magazines; and is encouraged by his parents; has a good chance for success in reading. This student is motivated from within to

---

[2]*Socialization* is referred to as the process of inducting the individual into the ways of the group. For further discussion of this concept, see W. B. Brookover, *A Sociology of Education,* New York: American Book Company, 1955; Bernard Barber, *Social Stratification: A Comparative Analysis of Structure and Process,* New York: Harcourt and Co., 1957; and Mildred B. Smith, "Interpersonal Influence on the Occupational Expectations of Sixth Grade Students," unpublished Ph.D. dissertation, Michigan State University, 1961.

achieve. He acquires the determination, desire and ambition to learn. These qualities seem to contribute as much as native ability to success in reading.

The importance of the home environment as a factor in reading achievement should be understood by the educator. The sympathetic teacher understands that the culturally disadvantaged child is severely handicapped by an environment which he did not request and over which he has no control. Such a child may read and perform in other subjects at a level far below that he is capable of achieving.

The Reading Program

All children require good basic instruction in reading. However, additional motivation techniques and material must be employed in such instruction to compensate for the deficiencies that are inherent in the disadvantaged child's environment. Ideally, motivation should come not only from the teacher, but from the parent as well. Since many parents of disadvantaged children are unaware of the importance of stimulation, it becomes the task of the teacher and the administrator to bring this to their attention so that together, educators and parents can provide the child with the kinds of experiences that will encourage him to want to read.

Prereading Experiences

The disadvantaged child often enters school with a subnormal vocabulary which severely retards his reading progress. An effective, well-designed pre-school program can enhance intellectual stimulation and greatly improve verbal language ability.

What causes the experience void of these children? In most cases, parents do not challenge their boys and girls to explore their environment—by asking questions, answering questions, and calling attention to details. Such parents overlook obvious points: (a) differences in colors of objects, "red chair," "blue ball," "blue and green boxes"; (b) differences in sizes of things, "large chair," "small box"; (c) differences in shapes of things, as "square table," "round ball"; (d) words that express how objects feel, "damp cloth," "soft sponge," "heavy iron," "fuzzy chicken."

Educators will agree that disadvantaged children need a variety of experiences but it should be noted that these children, however, do not *intellectually experience* their present environment because they are not challenged to "see," to "distinguish," to "know about" it. Many of these children frequently relocate both within the city and from city-to-city—frequently moving to other sections of the country. Yet, all they can say about such traveling is an expression such as, "we went south." They are unable to identify cities, buildings, animals, highways, rivers, and historical landmarks along the route. This situation occurs because parents, brothers, or sisters have not encouraged the children to examine their surroundings for detail. They are not asked, "Did you see . . .?", and "Did you notice . . .?"

This "pattern of thinking" or behaving is learned at an early age through interaction with adults and older siblings. A good preschool program should not only help the child develop this "pattern of thinking," but should help to unlock the child's door to intellectual experience about his total environment.

Experience and Vocabulary

Closely allied with intellectual stimulation about things, places and ideas, is vocabulary. If the child observes detail and "tests his experiences" by talking about them, he then learns specific vocabulary.[3] In this manner, the child enlarges his speaking and listening vocabularies. Both types must be developed. It is not enough for the teacher to say the appropriate words. The child must say them also; and he will be reluctant to do so when such words are never spoken in his home. The teacher must realize that the child is experiencing a language that is "foreign" to him.[4] At this point, he must teach it as a foreign language (for example, using the word in a sentence and having the child repeat it).

In summary, disadvantaged preschool children need (a) to build ideas and concepts through intellectual stimulation and (b) to develop oral language facility. An effective program must include both direct and vicarious experiences. Direct experiences would include trips to such places as the grocery store, drug store, hardware store, zoo, library, fire station, farms (fruit, vegetable, animal), and horticultural gardens. Vicarious experiences would include the use of filmstrips, recordings, storybooks, and imitation realia, as toy fruits, vegetables, flowers, and animals, all of which can help build concepts and vocabulary.[5]

INVOLVING PARENTS IN PRESCHOOL PROGRAM

A parent education program is an indispensable part of any preschool program for disadvantaged children. Parents not only can assist the teacher on field trips, but should be encouraged to learn along with the children. Parents

---

[3]It is believed that this kind of learning and behaving causes children to earn a higher score on standard intelligence tests. If this assumption is correct, intelligence tests do not adequately reflect the potential of culturally disadvantaged children.

[4]Since so much of the language spoken by the teacher is foreign to the disadvantaged child, English should be approached in this setting for what it is—a foreign language to the child.

[5]It is not uncommon for these children to be unable to identify common fruits and vegetables, even though they may frequent the grocery with parents (an indication that parents are not calling their children's attention to details in their immediate environment).

can be taught the finger plays, songs, and games their children are learning, allowing for carryover experiences in the home.

All parents need to be encouraged to read daily to their children, and many need to be taught how to do this.[6] A take-home library that is managed by volunteer parents can provide read-aloud materials for the entire family.

School and Home Reading Experiences

The prereading program described earlier, emphasizing ideas, concepts and vocabulary development, should be continued in the kindergarten and primary years.

It is important that children not be forced into formal reading instruction before they are ready. However, undue emphasis must not be placed upon "waiting" until they are "ready to read." Instead, action is best directed toward getting children ready to read and providing materials that are meaningful in relation to their life experiences. Real-life stories which utilize the culturally disadvantaged child's own experiences and vocabulary make excellent beginning-to-read material.

Typewriters are ideal for creating interest in reading. The teacher types stories of children's experiences as told by them. These then are distributed as "reading stories." Children not only enjoy reading about their own happenings, but get an extra incentive from seeing their thoughts in print. Classrooms equipped with typewriters facilitate this teaching method. Children should also be encouraged to use the typewriter.

The regular reading program can be augmented by many good trade books. Children should be motivated to read trade books both at school and at home. Since many disadvantaged children are poor readers, additional techniques are very helpful. One technique is to begin a Bookworm Club, offering every child an incentive to read trade books. Another idea that usually works is to take the time following a library period to allow each child to get started reading the story. Otherwise, boys and girls are likely to forget the book soon after taking it home. With the reading of the story started at school, they are already interested in it and more apt to continue reading once they are at home.

The teacher should frequently read to the class and see that there always are many interesting books in the classroom. The teacher who reads books for her own enjoyment lets the students know that their teacher likes to read.[7] It is

---

[6]A booklet, "How to Help Your Child with Reading," has been used at parent meetings to explain techniques of reading aloud to parents in Flint, Michigan. (It should be noted that an illiterate parent can encourage his child to enjoy books by looking at storybooks and discussing the pictures with him. The very fact that this parent takes time with a book "shows" that he values reading and wants the child to learn to read.

[7]It is a paradox that the person who teaches reading and who is constantly encouraging children to "enjoy books" is seldom if ever seen doing the same by the students.

important that the teacher set a time for sharing reading experiences with the students. In this way, the teacher becomes a member of the learning group, sharing in the excitement and interest.

Children who already have experienced failure with a standard reading program find the basal reader most formidable. Such materials may be eliminated in lieu of some type of multilevel self-help reading materials. These consist of short stories which can be completed during a single reading period. This approach gives the child immediate reinforcement and a feeling of accomplishment. A typical result is that children like the self-help reading material because it "puts us on our own more and the teacher does not have to tell us what to do all of the time."[8]

Parents and Reading Achievement

Parents may be invited to the school to help in many ways. A successful involvement can be achieved by invited parents during the library period. In addition to assisting the teacher with clerical chores, mothers show their children that they not only want but *expect* them to learn to read.

Fathers, too, can provide this encouragement by taking turns with library duties as well as reading to the class during the library period. They thus demonstrate to their children, particularly boys, that men value reading. Culturally disadvantaged boys especially need this type of masculine approval, since most prodding to achieve is normally associated with mothers or female teachers. All too often boys look upon their chums who take school work seriously as "sissies."

Mothers can help, also, by making single-story reading booklets. The child who finds thick hard-covered books difficult to "read for fun" will be delighted to discover he can finish a thin booklet and he gets the added satisfaction of reading several books. One mother simply cut up outdated reading books into individual stories under the teacher's direction. They then added covers.

Underachieving students require special help with vocabulary development. A file box of word cards enables the child to keep his own record of words that cause him difficulty. He can study these words at school, and also take them home for study. Again, teachers should instruct parents so they can help by flashing the word cards.

The following are suggested study steps that can be explained to parents as a guide for helping their child study reading words. The child should:

1. Look at only one word at a time. Think about how it begins and ends.
2. Say it softly. Think about how it sounds.
3. The meaning should be in *your own words.*

[8]A quotation from a Flint, Michigan, elementary class.

4. Your sentence should be a good sentence—it should make sense.
5. Check to see that you have given the correct meaning and have used it in a sentence.

Another suggestion is to encourage parents to provide dictionaries and other reference books for home study. This produces an academic atmosphere in the home, facilitating the desire to learn. A quiet period in the home every evening can be managed by parents. Such a reading and study period helps all the children in the home to complete their homework, to read, write, or play games quietly. Parental support of this kind strengthens the school program, instilling interest in reading beyond the regular school day.

Summer Reading Activities

Summer carryover of reading experience is very important in maintaining interest, fluency, and vocabulary. For this reason, summer reading activities that parents can manage are suggested. Suggestions[9] for parents may include: (a) continuing the daily "quiet time" in the home for individual reading, reading aloud to children, and playing quiet games; (b) having educational materials available—trade books, educational records, encyclopedias, dictionaries, and newspapers; (c) taking children to the library regularly; (d) encouraging children to make out grocery lists from newspaper advertisements; and (e) while riding in the car, encouraging children to read road signs and posters and see how many states they can identify by recognizing license plates.

A New Role for the School

As this article has emphasized, culturally disadvantaged children require special programs, teaching techniques, and materials to compensate for the areas of lack in their life experiences. This cultural lack, attributable in part to their homes and in part to their community environment, calls for stepped-up educational efforts if achievement is to match individual potential.

It is important to point out that such a realization does *not* mean that the school should simply take over and do everything for the child, thereby assuring his educational development to a satisfactory level. In the first place, the school, as structured in our society, cannot assume such control over the child. Secondly, no outside agency, school or otherwise, should assume the proper role of the parent.

Rather, the rightful role for educators is seen to be that of teaching and of assisting parents to assume their responsibilities, and of assuming their

[9]A more comprehensive list of suggestions could be printed for distribution or could be explained to parents at meetings during the last month at school.

obligations to the public for the educational development of all children. The ideal and productive relationship, then, is the cooperative sharing of mutual responsibilities by the parents and the schools, working together to bridge the cultural gap with purposeful planning and educational programing.

25. Teaching Reading to the Culturally Different Child*

JOSEPHINE T. BENSON

University of Pittsburgh

THE culturally different child may be the product of many different environments. There are: (1) the transient child who moves often from one school to another within the city; (2) the child of migrant workers; (3) the child who moves from a rural community to the city where life is much more complicated; and (4) the bilingual child to whom English is a second language, little used and poorly spoken.

Teachers must recognize that just as there are wide differences among children in general, so also are there many differences among the culturally different. They differ in mental ability and reading, in motivation, and in interest and tastes as well as personality. Their cultural and educational backgrounds may be very different. Some children who have the ability to read well prefer not to because they may be excluded from their neighborhood gang. Other children are not necessarily culturally deprived. They may recently have come from another country whose language they speak and read easily, but are just beginning to learn English.

There is no easy solution to these problems. What is good for one is not necessarily good for all. We must accept each child as an individual with his strengths and weaknesses. Different techniques must be used for maximum learning. As we develop better understanding of the individual child, reading programs will improve giving each child a better opportunity to more nearly reach his potential.

The culturally different child usually comes from a home atmosphere in which there is very little furniture, few pictures and toys, if any. His parents have very little education, work at unskilled jobs or "go on welfare". They have little ambition and no hopes for the future. Consequently, these children are not motivated and have no one to emulate. Their homes are void of any intellectual stimulation such as books, magazines or even a newspaper.

*From *Progress and Promise in Reading Instruction* in A Report of the 22nd Annual Conference and Course on Reading. Pittsburgh, 1966, 140-151. Reprinted with the permission of the author and Donald L. Cleland.

259

MOTIVATION

For these children a good learning atmosphere is imperative. They need a classroom atmosphere which will attract and hold their interest through its many "on-going" activities.

Many books on different grade levels and on various subjects will help to spark an interest. Building libraries with a trained librarian are excellent, but, if we want children to be attracted to books, there must also be books in the classroom where the child can reach for one if, and, when, he desires to do so. Attractive bulletin boards and pictures; a poetry corner; science and social studies displays; a sand table; a listening corner equipped with a sound recorder, a tape recorder and ear phones add interest. A special-interest table or corner for the display of rock collections, sea-shells, a piece of coal or stalagmite, etc. will stimulate oral discussion. Every classroom should have a magnifying glass and a small inexpensive telescope for exploring. A well-equipped classroom should include picture dictionaries for first grade and possibly second and regular dictionaires as soon as the children are ready for them. Encyclopedias, maps, and a globe are helpful to children who have acquired the skill to use them. The classroom newspaper should be included in all classroom activities.

To further stimulate these children, many of whom tend to be apathetic and passive, some teachers make posters with slogans and appropriate illustrations such as "Put a Tiger in Your Reading" or "Put Your Reading in Orbit". It could be even more effective, providing they were able to have the older children decide upon a slogan for the group and an illustration and then have them elect one or two of the members to make the poster.

ORAL LANGUAGE

By the time the child comes to kindergarten his language patterns are set. He has already learned to speak and use language as he has heard it in his neighborhood and home. This may be the vernacular of the region in which he lives, a combination of English and the foreign language of the parents or the language of the street. He experiences difficulty in school because the language that he hears there, and is expected to use, is different from the language that he has learned at home. This is not only confusing but is also frustrating.

An investigation of the oral language patterns of culturally different children, conducted by Dominick Thomas from the Detroit Public Schools, showed that these children used shorter sentences with fewer words and less variety than children from higher social status groups. It also showed a deficiency in the amount, correctness; and maturity of their oral expression. Furthermore, he found that children living in low socio-economic urban areas used approximately only 50 per cent of the words found in three leading basal first grade readers. These same children made no use of approximately 20 per cent–50 per cent of such word lists as the International Kindergarten Union, Dolch, Gates, Rinsland and Thorndike. [1] [1]

We know that a child's progress in learning to read depends to a great extent upon his previous experience with oral language. We also know that a child finds it easier to recognize words in print if they are already a part of his speaking vocabulary. The culturally different child has an extremely limited vocabulary. Parents of these children have little communication with their children. Their own vocabularies are very meager. These children speak in phrases rather than in sentences, make many grammatical errors, and often mispronounce words and enunciate poorly. Therefore, it is most imperative that oral language should be a major part of the readiness program both at kindergarten level and first grade.

Children can be given rich experiences by taking them to visit a farm, a circus, an airport, a fire and police station. Since many of these children never have an opportunity to go any farther than a few blocks from their homes, the teacher should not overlook many possibilities for extending experiences within walking distance of the school. Even the experiences they have encountered usually have very little meaning because there was no one to discuss these experiences with them. They are lacking in the conceptual foundations needed to build new concepts.

Language development should not be limited to the primary grades. Many of the older children could profit by first hand experiences commensurate with their abilities and interests. Many of them have never seen a movie or eaten in a restaurant. They should have opportunities to ride on buses, streetcars, trains and in taxicabs.

There should be much free and spontaneous conversing; sharing and relating experiences; talking on a toy telephone; playing they are on radio or television; manipulating puppets, especially finger puppets; and, dramatizing and choral reading.

Culturally diadvantaged children should be given opportunities to tell stories from pictures. At first they may only be able to enumerate objects seen in the picture. Later they should be able to interpret the picture. After they learn to tell a story from a single picture, they should then be able to tell stories from two or more pictures in sequence. Along with this experience in interpreting pictures a child should be given the experience of telling a story by means of pictures he has painted or drawn. Since the child, when drawing or painting a picture, often has much more in mind than appears in the finished product, he should be given the opportunity to tell his story from his picture.

Their speaking vocabularies increase as they learn the words to their songs,

[1]Numbers in brackets refer to references at the end of the article.

and through the stories and poems told or read to them by their teacher. Children in first and second grade love the Nursery Rhymes and ask to repeat them again and again. Dr. A. F. Watts, an Englishman, maintains that forty nursery rhymes introduce four hundred new words. [2]

A Kindergarten teacher may play this game with her reading readiness group of culturally disadvantaged children. She takes a small object from her desk. Holding it in her closed hand she asks the children, "What do I have in my hand?" The various children ask, "Do you have a ball in your hand?" etc. The teacher replies, "No, I do not have a ball in my hand," etc. The idea is to encourage and aid the children to talk in sentences and the teacher refuses to answer anyone who does not.

SENSORY EXPERIENCES

Because of limited verbal ability and inadequate experiential background, the culturally different child learns best through concrete and visual experiences. He needs much practice in the use of descriptive adjectives. These children have very few toys, if any, and are not familiar with many ordinary objects found in middle class homes. As a result, the tactile skills are not fully developed. They should be given every opportunity to identify numerous objects by shape and texture, noting if they are smooth or rough; hard or soft; round or square. In the classroom, many opportunities are present for developing better tactile skills. Primary children are always interested in the teacher's clothes and in each others. What kind of fur is on the collar of the teacher's coat? How does it feel? Is Billy's coat made of wool? Is it smooth like silk? A box containing samples of velvet and satin ribbon, velveteen, wool, cotton, and silk, which the children could feel, would be useful. Another box might contain a miscellaneous collection of objects which they could handle to feel the differences in textures such as: a sponge, a piece of coal, wood, cotton, stalagmite, a pebble. Ask children to describe how they feel; also have them make a game of it by having individual children close their eyes and identify an object handed to them.

The other senses of taste, smelling, seeing and hearing must also be developed. The sense of "seeing" is probably their best developed sense. They have a certain awareness of their environment. They see the river but, as mentioned previously, it has little, if any, meaning to them because they have never had an opportunity to ask questions and to voice their thoughts about the river. These children need to become more conscious of some of their surroundings.

Some afternoon ask the children to report the next morning on all the things they observed on the way to school. The assignment must be given in advance otherwise the teacher will find they are aware of very little in their environment. They must be taught to be observant. On other occasions they should be directed to listen for different sounds, or to report on different odors such as bread baking, coffee, fruit, gasoline, spices, etc. Let them taste white and brown sugar; maybe vanilla, molasses, chocolate and ginger cookies. Several books about the five senses have been published by Crowell Company recently for reading to the children. [3]

LISTENING

For many years teachers were so absorbed in teaching children written language that little attention was directed towards speaking and listening. It was taken for granted that children acquired these abilities before they came to school. With the advent of the radio and television, the emphasis has shifted to oral communcation. Children who live in crowded homes in slum areas where the radio or television is rarely turned off have learned to tune out many of the noises surrounding them. As a result, their attention and memory spans are limited. They cannot distinguish slight differences in sound and therefore possess little auditory discrimination. Reading research tells us that the ability to note differences and similarities in words and the ability to hear separate sounds and be able to blend them into a known word are essential. Teachers should impress upon children the importance of careful listening. It will be just as important to them when they are adults as now. Both listening and reading are dependent upon the learner's ability to understand words quickly and meaningfully. Children should be taught specific skills for listening and how each is necessary for a particular purpose or kind of listening such as reading for information, for critical evaluation, and for appreciation. Good listening habits need to be developed at all grade levels.

These children need an abundance of auditory readiness to prepare them for phonic skills. Have them listen for rhyming words in nursery rhymes and other poems. Have them listen for the two words that rhyme out of three words given; such as: "man, pan, book". Vary the exercise by asking for the word that does not rhyme with the other two words. Have the children divide a paper in two columns and write the words you say beginning with "p" in the first column and the words beginning with "t" in the second column. The same exercise could be used with words beginning or ending with "m" and "n", "b" and "d".

Children like to listen to recorded music and interpret the sounds. Mendelssohn's *Spring Song*, Herbert's *March of the Toys, The Blue Danube Waltz* by Strauss and *The Carnival of the Animals,* by Saint Saens, among others are good for listening skills. [4]

READING

When the teacher feels that the children are ready for reading she then has the task of helping them to acquire a reading vocabulary while continuing to help them to enlarge their speaking and hearing vocabularies. Words which are already in their speaking and hearing vocabularies will be easier to learn when met in print.

Children can learn the names of nouns through pictures. Pictures can be cut from old reading readiness books or mail order catalogues and pasted on 3 x 5 cards with the name printed below the picture and on the back of the picture. The name should be cut off the card. The pictures can then be matched with the words. These can be self-checked by turning over each picture to see if the word on the back matches the word placed under the picture.

Picture dictionaries help children to recognize words. In addition, each child should have a picture dictionary which he has made up for his personal use by cutting pictures from magazines, catalogues.

Some teachers like to label various objects in the room to aid in word recognition and meaning.

Make a small shoestring chart (9' x 12") with blocks of various colors on one side and the names of the colors on the opposite side in a different order. Use a black shoelace or colored yarn to connect the color with its name. This can be used by individuals who need practice.

Since culturally different children have poor auditory discrimination, they need much practice in phonic analysis. Sound games such as Dolch's Consonant and Vowel Lotto are more popular than work-book exercises. [5]

Many different word games should be used with these children. They like the element of suspense that games offer. Games not only create interest but also hold attention. They give a child a chance to win even if someone else knows more words and this builds self confidence which these children need.

By the time the culturally different child has reached the fourth grade, he is more than likely to be approximately one and one-half years retarded in reading. He often has a language of his own through which he communicates with his friends. It is very different from the language of the classroom. For example, these children may say they had to "carry" a brother to school where we would use the word "take". They may talk about a "shoe bite" when they have a blister on a foot or they ask if they can "hush" out the light. They often use prepositions incorrectly when they comment that they went *by* a friend's house when they actually went *to* his house. To help children overcome this, have them play a game with prepositions in which they are asked to put an object on, in, under, around, beside, on top of, or behind a table, etc.

Many words have double meanings and children sometimes make a game out of them. Teachers should encourage this by calling attention to the fact that cartoonists draw heavily from these words for many of their cartoons. Encourage the children to watch for these cartoons and to bring them to school to share with their classmates. Interest in words may be heightened by asking children to watch for articles on the origin of words and on certain expressions which often appear in the newspaper. A recent article on the origin of "blue jeans" and another on the origin of "OK" should have interested them. Ask the children to draw a picture of the following: a home run, a ghost writer, a horse doctor, raising cats and dogs, etc.

Dictionary readiness should be introduced in the primary grades and dictionary skills in the third or fourth grade depending on when the children were ready. Many exercises are available in dictionaries, teachers' manuals and workbooks to give practice on these very important and useful skills. To encourage the use of the dictionary set aside a prominent corner of a blackboard for writing a provocative question such as: "If someone said you were agile, would you be insulted?" or "Is this true? If you are pugnacious you are quarrelsome."

What kind of reading program can we plan for this culturally different child whose different speech patterns cause him to distort certain words such as "iron" which he pronounces "arn"; whose recognition and understanding of words is so meager that he too often meets words in print which are not in his understanding or speaking vocabulary? Some teachers are using the Language-Experience Approach and finding it more effective than using standard reading books. While this approach is versatile and informal, it must be carefully and thoughtfully planned. It must be preceded by an adequate readiness program as described earlier in this paper. Provision must be made for teaching word-attack skills and the various comprehension skills. The topic of discussion should reflect the interests and experiences of the entire group. The lesson may be the aftermath of a field trip or a project or some vicarious experience such as a film or filmstrip. The Language-Experience Approach does not differentiate between reading and other language activities. Each child is encouraged to share his ideas with the other children. He quickly develops a writing vocabulary and soon can write his own stories independently. Books are a vitally important part of this type of program. The children read many books and use them as a source for their writing.

The teacher stimulates discussion and acts as a source person in locating and supplying needed information; she also records and aids the children in organizing the material.

Through the Language-Experience Approach these children can identify with the reading material and are highly motivated to read it because it is their experiences, and, therefore, something they can understand. Their writings give them a feeling of accomplishment and to add to their self-esteem. This approach provides an excellent opportunity for children to learn to take notes, to outline, to organize and to read critically.

While the Language-Experience Approach is more often thought of as a reading approach for the primary grades, there is no reason why it could not be just as effective in the intermediate grades.

Teachers who use the basal reader approach will find that experience charts can be a very helpful supplementary aid in teaching reading to all children.

A study by Dr. Brazziel gives additional proof of the close relationship between reading deficiency and the below-standard language usage of school children.[6] The children in the intermediate grades are overwhelmed with the great number of new words introduced in the content subjects. These technical words are often very abstract. Sometimes it is better for the teacher to introduce fewer concepts in the content subjects and to explain and teach them more thoroughly. Using a topical unit approach may be more satisfactory because each child could be given reading material on his reading level. Sometimes trade books can be substituted for textbooks in Social Studies. These may help to clarify the concepts in the history text. Books like Laura Ingalls Wilder's, *Little House in the Big Woods* give a clearer and more interesting account of pioneer life than some history books. The content fields provide rich experiential background as well as good material for the development of thinking skills.

Culturally different children should have ample time for recreational reading so that they can make individual choices of what they want to read. Since these children are usually lacking in motivation, there must be available many books on various subjects at all grade levels to stimulate and satisfy their interests. Taste for good literature must be developed gradually. Children who read nothing but the "comics" can not be expected to jump from that type of reading to a "Junior Great Books" Selection. The change must be very gradual.

In middle class communities, the number of children retarded in reading averages between ten and twenty per cent while in low socio-economic areas it may range as high as eighty per cent. These children have double problems. Their lack of self-esteem and experiences, low motivation and low acceptable verbal facility is further accentuated by their reading failure. A thorough testing program is needed to ascertain mental ability and to diagnose their difficulties. They must then be given reading material on their reading level. Motivation is a real problem. Although we now have a number of books which are known as "High Interest—Low Vocabulary Series" these books do not include multiracial groups nor is the reading material something with which they can identify. A modified language-experience approach where the child dictates to the teacher his reactions to an experience or incident, etc. can be typed and used as reading material for him. *Ten Great Moments in Sports, The Deep Sea Adventures* and *The Morgan Bay Mystery Stories* will satisfy their taste for sports, mystery and surprise endings. *The American Adventure Series* are popular with children who are reading retardates. Many children enjoy the ridiculousness of the Dr. Seuss books. *The Reading Skill Builders* contains a variety of short selections. Reading games, vocabulary and phonics skills, mentioned previously, should also be included in this program.

In the past few years much concern has been shown in the large cities for the culturally different child. The Detroit Public Schools are presently developing the *City Schools Reading Series* for grades one through three. The project was started in 1959 under the direction of Dr. Gertrude Whipple. The program follows the basal reader methodology and includes teachers' manuals, workbooks and word cards, etc. Five pre-primers have been published instead of the usual three, but the books are shorter so that they may be completed more rapidly and thus give a feeling of accomplishment earlier. The books show children of multi-racial groups in urban settings to give the children an opportunity to identify themselves with characters that are familiar. The environment shown in these books is not that of the tenement or housing development type, but is one to which culturally different children might reasonably aspire. The illustrations used in the books are large and colorful with one center of interest and no unnecessary details. The stories are humorous or have a surprise ending to sustain interest. The vocabulary was carefully chosen to meet the needs of these children and much repetition of words has been provided. An evalaution of the first three pre-primers showed the City Schools Series to be significantly more effective in stimulating interest in reading and word recognition than the regular basal series.

The *Bank Street Readers* prepared by the Bank Street College of Education in New York City is also an "urban-centered" series of eight books for grades one through three. A reading readiness program is followed by two pre-primers. Since sixty percent of Americans live in cities these readers are designed for children of all economic social and cultrual background and not just for the culturally different. The publishers of the Bank Street Readers claim they have broken with tradition by including such forms of literature as vignettes, poems, stories, dialogues and essays for greater interest. The vocabulary used is taken from the children's speech rather than from established word lists.

Another new reading series is the *Skyline Series*. Recommended by the publisher as a co-basal series in grades two, three and four or with remedial pupils through the junior high level, these books are also about urban life. There is only one teacher's guide to the three books, but specific suggestions are given for each lesson. The authors and artists of this series are from mixed racial and cultural backgrounds and the stories are reflections of their own experiences. The brief sentences and the natural phrasing are typical of the culturally deprived city child. These stories could also be used with children who were not culturally deprived to give them a better understanding of how other children live. This program was developed for the St. Louis Public Schools.

The *Chandler Language-Experience Readers* are being developed to use with culturally deprived children in the San Francisco Public Schools. Knowing that many more boys than girls have reading problems, they have made a special effort to develop experiences which will foster their interests. Like similar series, they have built their stories on familiar experiences of urban, culturally deprived multi-racial groups and have developed the vocabulary from the childrens' speech. All pictures used in the books are actual photographs of culturally different children participating in familiar experiences. The program is to extend gradually through grade six. It includes six paperback pre-primers and, at the present time, extends only through second grade. An added feature is the five (4 minute), 8mm. color films which are integrated with the series.

The *Urban Education Studies Albums* consist of eight basic albums each of which has twelve 18 x 18 inch photographs to be used to develop basic languages skills and responsible citizenship. Special City Albums, each containing twenty-four photographs of New York, Denver, Detroit, Washington, D. C., Los Angeles and San Francisco have been designed for use not only in those cities, but also by any one interested in the growth of large cities. Prepared with the aid of Ford Foundation funds, these albums have been used in the New Haven, Connecticut schools with much success. A detailed teacher's guide accompanies each album.

These are only a few of the many programs that are being developed throughout our country to motivate and to interest the culturally different child in learning to read.

References

1. Dominic Thomas, "Oral Language of Culturally Disadvantaged Kindergarten Children." *Reading and Inquiry.* J. A. Figurel (ed.) I. R. A. Conference Proceedings. Volume 10. Newark, Delaware: International Reading Association, Inc. 1956. pp. 448-450
2. A. F. Watts, *The Language and Mental Development of Children.* London: George C. Harrap and Company, Ltd., 1964, p. 40; p. 31.
3. Paul Showers, *Find Out by Touching.* New York: Thomas Y. Crowell Publishing Company, 1961.
4. Lillian Logan, *Teaching the Young Child.* Boston, Massachusetts: Houghton Mifflin Co., 1960. p. 216.
5. Edward W. Dolch *Dolch Games.* Champaign, Illinois: Garrard Publishing Company, 1948.
6. Brazziel, Wm. F., Report given at the American Educational Research Associations Meetings, Atlantic City, New Jersey, February, 1962.

Resource Material

1. *Ten Great Moments in Sports.* University Park, Pa: Penn's Valley Publishers, Inc., 1961.
2. *The Deep Sea Adventure Series.* San Francisco, Calif.: Harr, Wagner Publishing Company, 1959 and 1962.
3. *The Morgan Bay Mystery Series.* San Francisco, Calif.: Harr, Wagner Publishing Company, 1962.
4. *The American Adventure Series.* Chicago, Illinoise: Wheeler Publishing Company, 1948.
5. *Dr. Seuss.* New York: Beginners Books, Inc., Random House, Distributors, 1958.
6. *Reading Skill Builders.* Pleasantville, New York: Reader's Digest Services, Inc., Educational Division, 1958.
7. *Cities Schools Reading Program.* (Writers' Committee of the Great Cities School

Improvement Program of the Detroit Public Schools—Gertrude Whipple, Chairman). Chicago, Illinois: Follett Publishing Company, 1964.

8. *Bank Street Readers*. New York: The Macmillan Company, 1965.
9. *The Skyline Series*. New York: Webster Division, McGraw-Hill Book Company, 1965.
10. *Chandler Language-Experience Readers*. San Francisco, Calif.: Chandler Publishing Company, 1964.
11. *Urban Education Studies Albums*. Betty Warner Dietz, Editor. New York: The John Day Company, 1965.

VI

Development of Reading Skills

26. What Research Tells Us About Word Recognition*

NILA BANTON SMITH

New York University

WORD recognition, or "word perception" as we often call this phase of reading, is the most fundamental of the reading skills. Without ability to recognize words, the reading process cannot proceed. Important as word-recognition skills are, experimental research did not concern itself with this aspect of reading until rather late in our history.

Delving into historical research, we find that during the beginning centuries of reading instruction children were taught to read by the alphabet method, and the only technique which they were expected to use in attacking an unrecognized word was simply to spell it. By some mythical process, spelling the word was supposed to tell an individual how to pronounce it.

The writer [19] [1] found that the use of phonics did not enter American reading instruction until after the Revolutionary War, and then it came in as a patriotic, rather than a pedagogic, measure. Noah Webster, who wrote the first series of American readers and who was highly activated in terms of patriotic motives, sought some means of unifying the diversity of dialects which existed in the United States following the Revolutionary War. Unity was an essential aim at that time because on it depended the future existence of the young nation. The idea of teaching all children in the country to give the same sound to each letter and to each of the important groups of letters occurred to Webster as a means of teaching all young Americans to pronounce words in the same way. And so phonics was introduced vigorously in his *Blue Back Speller* and taught for many years for the purpose of unifying spoken language in America.

Eventually, however, the patriotic emphasis on teaching phonics subsided, and teachers discovered that learning the sounds of letters aided children in recognizing words in reading. Patriotism and phonics parted ways, and pedagogy took over where patriotism left off. Pedagogy gave phonics a new function, that of helping children to attain independence in attacking new words while reading, and in this role, phonics has been continued in classrooms down to the present time.

*From *The Elementary School Journal* 55, 55 (April, 1955), 440-446. Copyright © 1955 by the University of Chicago. Reprinted by permission.

[1]The numbers in brackets refer to references at the end of the article.

The years between 1840 and 1860 constituted a period of vigorous protest against the A-B-C method by educational leaders, and in some quarters against the method of teaching the sounds of letters. During these years, Bumstead [4] and Webb [26] began publishing readers based on the word method. Many school people were intrigued by the startling discovery that children could recognize whole words without knowing the letters and began using this method. The majority of schools, however, continued to use the phonic method in teaching children to read.

So much for the historical research in regard to word recognition. Although it is only in comparatively recent years that experimental research has begun to invade this area of reading, there are several studies which can be reported. These studies seem to fall mainly under four headings: "How do we recognize words?" "Is phonics effective?" "When should phonics be taught?" "What elements should be emphasized?"

HOW DO WE RECOGNIZE WORDS?

The earliest experimental studies in word recognition had to do with perception. They were conducted for the purpose of ascertaining the general nature of the word-recognition process. While not directly concerned with phonics, these studies certainly pointed toward word analysis.

Huey [14], a pioneer in investigating this problem, concluded some four decades ago that, in the case of the fluent reader, the general form or outline of the word is a sufficient visual cue to its recognition:

> The aid supplied by the context tips the balance in favor of the unitary recognition of the word. . . .With very familiar words, the letter recognition is checked in its incipiency. . . .With new words, the recognition of certain letters may quite complete itself before the whole word is known [14:103].

Hamilton [11] and other early investigators agree with Huey. Several years later, Vernon [24] also concluded that both the total word form and its distinguishing characteristics are important aids to recognition. She further concluded that children in the process of learning to read are influenced more by significant parts of words than are adults with mature reading habits.

These and several others who have investigated perception seem to agree that, in the majority of cases, the general characteristics of a word are the clues by which it is recognized but that, when some unfavorable condition arises or when the words are strange or difficult, additional distinctions within the word are required. As early as 1925, the following aids to word recognition were identified: the context, the total configuration of a word, significant details of words, phonetic analysis, and use of the dictionary [10]. At the present time we teach children the use of all these methods of attack plus another one just recently added, the study of word structure. Phonics, however, is the only one of these which has been the target for much research. The effectiveness of teaching phonics has been challenged by many investigators.

IS PHONICS EFFECTIVE?

Among the earliest studies reported in regard to the effectivness of phonics were those conducted by Currier and Duguid from 1918 to 1923. After five years of experimentation with different primary-grade groups, Currier reported:

1. Phonetic drills have a very real value but are not essential to every child as a part of the daily program in primary grades.
2. Phonetic drills should at all times be employed with discretion and adapted to the needs of the individual child or special group.
3. Word-pronunciation drills have proved to be of much value [6: 452].

Another early study was the Newark phonics experiment conducted by Sexton and Herron [18]. The experiment involved nearly a thousand pupils in Grades I A and I B, who were also followed through Grade II. Some of the groups were taught phonics; others were not. The results favored the teaching of phonics strongly. Nevertheless, they showed that there was less difference between phonic and nonphonic groups than between groups having different teachers. Good teachers obtained unusually good results whether or not they taught phonics, and vice versa.

Garrison and Heard [8], working with four classes of children during their three primary years, concluded that children having phonics learned greater independence in pronunciation than did the no-phonics group.

Agnew [1] carried on some rather extensive studies with primary-grade children in Raleigh, North Carolina. His conclusions indicate that, while comprehension in silent reading was not affected by isolated phonics, longer periods of phonetic study did increase word recognition and pronunciation as checked in oral reading. Tate [20] also concluded that isolated phonics instruction increased ability to recognize words but that it did not affect comprehension.

Other investigators have found positive correlations between phonics and comprehension. In the study of Tiffin and McKinnes [23], the correlations between scores on a phonic test and three silent-reading tests varied from .55 to .70. Russell [17] also found that phonics contributed to comprehension.

Templin [22], who investigated phonic knowledge as related to reading and spelling in Grade IV, concluded that a substantial amount of phonic knowledge had been acquired by fourth-grade pupils. He also found that, in unfamiliar test situations, the poor spellers and poor readers applied their phonic knowledge less well than did good spellers and good readers, while the difference was not significant when phonic knowledge was measured in familiar words. This may indicate a real difference in the ability of children of similar intellectual level to transfer what they know from one situation to another. On the other hand, it may be related to the various methods of teaching. One wouldn't expect that isolated methods of teaching phonics would transfer as much as related methods.

Gates and Russell [9] conducted a study with three groups of pupils. Group D received the smallest amount of phonics or word analysis; Group E were given moderate amounts of informal, newer-type word analysis, comparisons, and the like; and Group F was provided with large amounts of conventional, phonetic drill. Pupils in Group E, who were given moderate amounts of informal, newer-type word analysis work, exceeded those in the other two groups in all tests of word recognition and comprehension.

Tate, Herbert, and Zeman [21] also found that incidental teaching of phonics, in connection with children's needs in working out words encountered in their reading, was superior either to the teaching of isolated phonics or no phonics instruction.

House [13] studied the effect of a program of instruction on pronunciation skills in the middle grades. The results of his experiment showed a distinct superiority of pupils who were given specific training with carefully prepared instructional materials over those who received no such training. This investigator pointed out that word-analysis skills can be taught more effectively not only when systematic instruction is given but also when the functional use of what is taught can be integrated with such instruction.

To sum up these conclusions, it appears that we have a considerable body of evidence to the effect that phonics instruction is valuable but that its greatest value is realized only when it is closely related to children's needs and is given direct application to words which cause them trouble in their daily reading.

WHEN IS PHONICS INSTRUCTION MOST VALUABLE?

In years gone by, phonics instruction was begun on the children's first day in Grade I, and intensive instruction in learning the sounds of letters and combinations of letters was continued all through the early and later first-grade period. At present the trend seems to be to provide some kind of phonics readiness program in Grade I but to delay more intensive phonics instruction until Grades II and III.

The research done on phonics would seem to justify this delay. Sexton and Herron [18], in the Newark phonics experiment previously cited, drew the conclusion that the teaching of phonics functions very little or not at all during the first five months in Grade I but begins to be of some value during the second five months and is of great value in Grade II.

Dolch and Bloomster [7] found many individual differences in regard to the mental age at which children were able to work profitably with phonics. Their general conclusion, however, was that a mental age of seven years was necessary for a child to make the best use of phonics. Garrison and Heard [8], mentioned previously, also concluded that much of phonics instruction should be deferred until Grade II or Grade III.

All these studies point toward a delay of phonics instruction for the average child until Grade II. I find nothing in research, however, which indicates that we should not provide for the development of phonics readiness in Grade I so that those children who need phonics will be prepared to work with it when a more intensive phonics program is offered at the second-grade maturity level.

WHAT SHOULD BE TAUGHT IN A PHONICS PROGRAM?

A summary of research on phonics would not be complete without a mention, at least, of studies which have been made to determine phonic content. A pioneer study to determine the relative importance of phonics elements was conducted by Vogel, Jaycox, and Washburne [25], who analyzed the vocabularies of readers and standard vocabulary lists to find out which letter groupings occur more commonly. An early study of Cordts [5] also analyzed primary reader vocabularies for phonetic elements. Two more recent studies have been reported by Black [3] and by Oaks [16] in regard to frequency of consonant and vowel sounds, respectively, in primary reading vocabularies. The length of the lists from these studies prevents their presentation in this article.

MISCELLANEOUS STUDIES

A few studies, broader in scope than the phonics studies, have been made. Bennett [2], for example, conducted an analysis of word-recognition errors made by children. The analysis was concerned with 37,274 errors made by retarded readers at about the third-or fourth-grade level in school placement. The errors which she found had to do with the final letters, the initial letters, median vowels, reversals of initial consonants, reading of a whole word or part in right-to-left sequence, final -s errors, and substitutions.

Hester [12] checked the word-recognition ability of 130 pupils referred to a reading clinic, all of whom were below third-grade level. She found that 18 of the pupils had no difficulty with the letter names, sounds, or blends. One hundred and twelve of the pupils lacked partially or entirely the knowledge of phonics essential for independent word attack. She concluded that, whereas configuration clues and context clues are essential in good reading, failure to teach the child the sounds of letters will leave him unable to attack new words independently when the other methods fail.

In recent years we have been hearing a great deal about auditory perception and visual perception, both of which are fundamental factors in word recognition. One study in this area; that of Murphy and Junkins [15], is well worth noting. It involved three groups of children: an experimental group of pupils which was given thirty audiotry discrimination lessons as a part of the regular reading instruction, a second experimental group which was given visual-discrimination lessons, and a control group that continued its regular program of instruction. Auditory and visual discrimination tests were given to all groups at the end of six weeks. As would be expected, the group with auditory training excelled in this type of perception, while the group with visual training excelled in visual perception. The most important result was the gain in the number of words retained of those taught. The experimental groups doubled their capacity, while the control group made little progress. Later experiments indicated that reading failures in the first grade were greatly reduced when a combination of training in both auditory and visual perception was provided.

SUMMARY

In conclusion, we might say briefly that research tells us:

1. It cannot be assumed that *all* children need phonics.

2. Phonics is effective with children who need word-recognition help, but its greatest effectiveness is attained when it is taught functionally and is related to children's reading needs.

3. It is advisable to delay intensive phonics instruction until a child has attained a mental age of seven years.

4. Phonics instruction is most valuable at the second-and third-grade levels.

5. The use of configuration clues and context clues should be supplemented with phonics.

6. It would be well to give more attention to both visual and auditory discrimination in teaching all types of word recognition.

Bibliography

1. AGNEW, DONALD C. *The Effects of Varied Amounts of Phonetic Training on Primary Reading*, pp. 8–50. Duke University Research Studies in Education, No. 5. Durham, North Carolina: Duke University Press, 1939.

2. BENNETT, ANNETTE. "An Analysis of Errors in Word Recognition Made by Retarded Readers," *Journal of Educational Psychology,* XXXIII (January, 1942), 25-38.
3. BLACK, ELSIE BENSON. "A Study of the Consonant Situations in a Primary Reading Vocabulary," *Education,* LXXII (May, 1952), 618-23.
4. BUMSTEAD, JOSIAH F. *My Little Primer,* Boston: Perkins & Marwin, 1840.
5. CORDTS, ANNA D., and McBROOM, MAUDE MARY. "Phonics," *Classroom Teacher,* II, 427-29. Chicago: Classroom Teacher, Inc., 1927.
6. CURRIER, LILLIAN BEATRICE. "Phonics and No Phonics," *Elementary School Journal,* XXIII (February, 1923), 448-52.
7. DOLCH, E. W., and BLOOMSTER, MAURINE. "Phonic Readiness." *Elementary School Journal,* XXXVIII (November, 1937), 201-5.
8. GARRISON, S. C., and HEARD, M. T. "An Experimental Study of the Value of Phonics," *Peabody Journal of Education,* IX (July, 1931), 9-14.
9. GATES, ARTHUR I., and RUSSELL, DAVID H. "Types of Materials, Vocabulary Burden, Word Analysis, and Other Factors in Beginning Reading," *Elementary School Journal,* XXXIX (September and October, 1938), 27-35, 119-28.
10. GRAY, WILLIAM SCOTT. *Summary of Investigations Relating to Reading.* Supplementary Educational Monographs, No. 28. Chicago: University of Chicago, 1925.
11. HAMILTON, FRANCIS. *The Perceptual Factors in Reading.* Columbia University Contributions to Philosophy, Psychology, and Education, Vol. XVII, No. 1, pp. 52-53. Lancaster, Pennsylvania: Science Press, 1907.
12. HESTER, KATHLEEN B. "A Study of Phonetic Difficulties in Reading," *Elementary School Journal,* XLIII (November, 1942), 171-73.
13. HOUSE, RALPH W. "The Effect of a Program of Initial Instruction on the Pronunciation Skills at the Fourth-Grade Level as Evidenced in Skills Growth," *Journal of Experimental Education,* X (September, 1941), 54-56.
14. HUEY, E. B. *The Psychology and Pedagogy of Reading,* pp. 102-16. New York: Macmillan Co., 1912.
15. MURPHY, HELEN A., and JUNKINS, KATHRYN M. "Increasing the Rate of Learning in First Grade Reading," *Education,* LXII (September, 1941), 37-39.
16. OAKS, RUTH E. "A Study of the Vowel Situation in a Primary Vocabulary," *Education,* LXXII (May, 1952), 604-17.
17. RUSSELL, DAVID H. "A Diagnostic Study of Spelling Readiness," *Journal of Educational Research,* XXXVII (December, 1943), 276-83.
18. SEXTON, ELMER K., and HERRON, JOHN S. "The Newark Phonics Experiment," *Elementary School Journal,* XXVIII (May, 1928), 690-701.
19. SMITH, NILA BANTON. *American Reading Instruction,* pp. 69-70. Newark, New Jersey: Silver, Burdett & Co., 1934.
20. TATE, HARRY L. "The Influence of Phonics in Silent Reading in Grade I," *Elementary School Journal,* XXXVII (June, 1937), 752-63.
21. TATE, HARRY L., HERBERT, THERESA M., and ZEMAN, JOSEPHINE K. "Nonphonic Primary Reading," *Elementary School Journal,* XL (March, 1940), 529-37.
22. TEMPLIN, MILDRED C. "Phonic Knowledge and Its Relation to the Spelling and Reading Achievement of Fourth Grade Pupils," *Journal of Educational Research,* XLVII (February, 1954), 441-54.
23. TIFFIN, JOSEPH, and McKINNES, MARY. "Phonic Ability: Its Measurement and Relation to Reading Ability," *School and Society,* LI (February 10, 1940), 190-92.
24. VERNON, M. D. *The Experimental Study of Reading.* Cambridge, England: Cambridge University Press, 1931.
25. VOGEL, MABEL; JAYCOX, EMMA; and WASHBURNE, CALRETON W. "A Basic List of Phonics for Grades I and II," *Elementary School Journal,* XXIII (February, 1923), 436-43.
26. WEBB, RUSSEL. *Webb's Normal Readers.* New York: Sheldon, Lamport & Blakerman, 1856.

27. A Study of the Techniques of Word Identification*

H. ALAN ROBINSON

Director of the Reading Conference
and a member of the reading staff
at the University of Chicago

THE purpose of this study was to determine the relative effectiveness of various techniques for the identification of unfamiliar words met in reading. The following hypotheses were proposed:

1. Context clues alone will not be sufficient for the successful identification of unfamiliar words by average fourth grade readers.

2. Word configurations, in addition to context clues, will not add materially to the fourth grader's success in identifying unfamiliar words.

3. Phonic and/or structural elements in initial positions added to context and configuration clues will enable fourth graders to identify unknown words.

4. When context, configuration, and phonic and/or structural elements in initial positions are not of sufficient help, the addition of phonic and/or structural elements in final positions will permit successful identification of the unfamiliar words.

5. When context clues plus configuration and phonic and structural analysis fail, analysis of the words in their entirety will result in successful identification.

A review of the literature indicates that mature readers use context and configuration clues in perceiving words [4].[1] When the words are familiar, these clues suffice, but when the words are unfamiliar more detailed analysis seems necessary [5]. It appears that children who are still learning how to read are more influenced by significant parts of words than are mature adult readers [10], although this tendency may be related to the techniques they have learned rather than to natural inclination. According to studies of word perception, when analysis does take place, the first part of the word appears to be more significant for word perception than the end [6].

This study endeavored to discover what the fourth grade reader actually does in attacking unfamiliar words. Toward this end it became necessary to devise two instruments, one for ascertaining the words unfamiliar to a given

*With the aid of Carol Hostetter, research assistant.

*From *The Reading Teacher,* **16** 4 (January, 1963), 238. Reprinted with permission of H. Alan Robinson and the International Reading Association.

[1]Numbers in brackets refer to references at end of article.

population, and the other for the presentation of those words in a reading framework in which the subjects would attempt to identify the words through a variety of identification techniques.

MATERIALS

1. *Sight Word Test*

The test words were chosen from those words familiar to 50 per cent or more of pupils in grade six, based on the Dale-Eichholz study [3]. This test was designed to screen out those pupils who could identify two-thirds or more of twenty-two test words. The twenty-two test words were randomly scattered through a list of forty-five words making up the Sight Word Test.

2. *Test Passage*

Five forms of a selection were designed to measure the ability of fourth grade subjects to identify the twenty-two test words through different techniques of word identification. The passage was below fifth grade reading level excluding the test words, and approximately sixth level including the test words, based on the Dale-Chall readability formula.

Form I of the. test passage used blank spaces instead of the twenty-two words in order to assess the subjects' use of context clues alone.

Form II of the same test passage used configurations of the twenty-two words to assess the use of context plus configuration.*

Form III of the same test passage used context and configuration clues plus beginning elements of each of the twenty-two unfamiliar words.

Form IV of the test passage contained context and configuration clues plus beginning elements and final elements of each of the twenty-two unfamiliar words.

Form V of the same test passage contained each of the twenty-two words completely exposed.

PRELIMINARY INVESTIGATION

In order to validate the tests, the investigator and a research assistant conducted a pilot study with twenty-five pupils in a private school in Chicago. The tests appeared suitable for pupils reading at fourth grade levels. The actual study was conducted in May 1962 with fourth graders in a nearby suburban school system where the population was closer to "average" than in a private school.

*In presenting the configurations of words alone each letter in the word was filled in so that the actual letters were represented but could not be identified as such.

PROCEDURE

1. The words on the Sight Word Test were presented in rapid succession to each of eighty-eight subjects. Sixty-one subjects failed to pronounce correctly two-thirds or more of the twenty-two test words and, as a result, were chosen as the subjects for the experiment. They returned the following week to read the five forms of the Test Passage.

2. Each of the sixty-one subjects individually read Form I silently, or orally if the subject desired, and stated the words he thought should be placed in each of the twenty-two blank spaces. Subjects were helped to pronounce any words other than the test words if they asked for such help. They were encouraged to think about what they were reading.

3. Subjects were then given the subsequent forms, one at a time. They were asked if they wanted to alter any of their decisions or suggest words for those they had not responded to at all.

4. The number of correct responses for each subject on each of the Test Passages were totaled, and means and standard deviations were computed for forms III through V. Correct responses for forms I and II were so few that statistical treatment would have been meaningless.

5. The number of correct responses for each of the twenty-two words was tabulated, and percentages of words correct on each form were computed.

FINDINGS

Hypotheses one and two may be accepted as valid for this population.

Hypothesis one proposed that average fourth grade readers would not find context clues alone sufficient for the successful identification of unfamiliar words. Through context clues alone about one-seventh of 1 per cent of the test words were identified, and only about 14 per cent of the responses were meaningful synonyms. Two of the sixty-one subjects correctly identified one word each, while fifty of the subjects mentioned meaningful synonyms. Of the 1,342 responses possible (number of subjects—61 times number of words—22), there were 188 responses, including the two correct identifications.

Hypothesis two stated that the presence of word configurations, in addition to context clues, would not add materially to the fourth graders' success in identifying unfamiliar words. When word configuration was added to context clues, about one-fifth of 1 per cent of the test words were identified, and again about 14 per cent of the responses were meaningful synonyms. Three of the sixty-one subjects correctly identified one word each, although two of them had identified the same words correctly using only context clues. Forty-eight of the subjects mentioned meaningful synonyms; two subjects withdrew estimates they had made using context clues alone. Of the 1,342 possible responses, there were 185 meaningful responses including the three correct identifications.

Hypotheses three through five must be rejected for this population.

Although the subjects were more successful in identifying unfamiliar words when using phonic and/or structural elements and through analyses of the whole word, no single subject succeeded in identifying all the words. Percentages of correct responses for each of the twenty-two words ranged from 0 to 21 per cent (M, 6.4) on Form III (context-configuration-initial elements); 2 to 36 per cent (M, 17.8) on Form IV (context-configuration-initial elements-final elements); 10 to 61 per cent (M, 35.8) on Form V (context and entire word).

Hypothesis three proposed that the addition of phonic and/or structural elements in initial positions to context and configuration clues would enable the fourth graders to identify unknown words. Correct responses on Form III ranged from 0 to 6 per cent with a mean of 1.41 and a standard deviation of 1.66. Obviously, out of a possible twenty-two words correct, the addition of initial elements to context and configuration resulted in little success for this group of subjects or any one subject in the population.

Hypothesis four stated that when context, configuration, and phonic and/or structural elements in initial positions were not of sufficient help, the addition of phonic and/or structural elements in final positions would permit successful identification of the unfamiliar words. Correct responses on Form IV ranged from 0-16 with a mean of 3.93 and a standard deviation of 3.28. Although two subjects were able to identify 50 per cent or more of the words, the addition of final elements did not result in successful identification for the total population.

Hypothesis five proposed that if context clues plus configuration and phonic and structural analyses failed, analysis of the words in their entirety would result in successful identification. Correct responses on Form V ranged from 1-19 with a mean of 7.95 and a standard deviation of 4.58. Approximately one-quarter of the sixty-one subjects could identify 50 per cent or more of the words when viewing the total word in context.

DISCUSSION

An obvious conclusion is that no word identification technique was used very successfully by this group of subjects. No subject correctly identified all the words. On the other hand, the study had certain limitations. The test words were in the listening vocabularies of the pilot population, but this information was not ascertained for the final test population. The school in which the pilot study was conducted is attended by an exceptionally able group of pupils. A limitation might also lie in the test passage, which may not have been constructed well enough to provide the kinds of context clues helpful to fourth grade subjects. Since the results of a study of word identification ought to be cumulative, that is, each word identification technique needs to build on and incorporate the preceding one, another limitation of this study is the single ordering of techniques. This study started with context, added configuration, then beginning elements, then final elements, and finally presented the whole word. Perhaps different results would be achieved if beginning elements were presented before the total configuration of the word, or final elements before beginning, et cetera.

Actually, a case could be built for devoting more attention to any one aspect. It appears that these subjects, for instance, would profit from instruction in the use of context clues. Even when confronted with context clues alone and no word form, the selections of words which could complete meaning were meager and inaccurate. When parts of the word form were presented, most subjects seemed to concentrate all effort on sounding the parts without regard to context. On the other hand, it was impossible to determine the role of context when subjects correctly identified words in the final test passage where the whole word was viewed in the contextual setting.

Nevertheless, it does seem reasonable that these subjects reading at approximately fourth grade level should meet with a greater degree of success in the identification of unfamiliar words than was reflected in this study. Perhaps average fourth grade readers need an intensification of instruction in the synthesizing of word identification techniques. Since it appears that most success in identification occurs when many techniques are used, pupils may need to learn how to marshall these forces.

Perhaps an additional step needs to be taken in the designing of programs aimed at helping pupils identify words. After the pupils have learned to apply the techniques of identification to familiar words, we should not assume that pupils will on their own transfer this skill to unfamiliar words. Probably many pupils similar to the subjects involved in this study need guidance and direction in applying word identification techniques to unfamiliar words.

Further study of average fourth grade readers using the tests of this experiment in a number of permutations could add interesting and valuable evidence to the present results. Additional experimentation of this kind with readers at a variety of grade levels might help to explain the results of this study. This small piece of research only offers a testing method and results for a specific population. Further research along these lines, or even replications of this study, might eventually contribute to the development of significant insights into instructional practices and the construction of instructional materials.

References

1. Anderson, Irving H., and Dearborn, Walter F. *The Psychology of Teaching Reading.* New York: Ronald Press, 1952. Chapter 5.

2. Dale, Edgar, and Chall, Jeanne S. "A Formula for Predicting Readability," *Educational Research Bulletin, Ohio State University,* 27 (Jan. 1948), 11-20.
3. Eichholz, Gerhard, and Dale, Edgar. *Children's Knowledge of Words.* Columbus: Bureau of Educational Research and Service, Ohio State University, 1960.
4. Gray, William S. "Reading" in *Encyclopedia of Educational Research* (edited by Chester W. Harris). New York: Macmillan, 1960. Pages 1098-99.
5. Hamilton, Francis. *The Perceptual Factors in Reading.* Columbia University Contributions to Philosophy, Psychology, and Education, XVII. New York: Science Press, 1907.
6. Huey, Edmund B. *The Psychology and Pedagogy of Reading.* New York: Macmillan, 1908. Chapters 4 and 5.
7. Porter, Douglas. "The Instrumental Value of Sound Cues in Reading." Unpublished paper presented at Annual Meeting of American Educational Research Association, Feb. 17, 1960.
8. Tinker, Miles A. "Visual Apprehension and Perception in Reading," *Psychological Bulletin,* 26 (Apr. 1929). 223-40.
9. Vernon, M.D. *Backwardness in Reading.* Cambridge: Cambridge University Press, 1957. Chapters 2 and 3.
10. Vernon, M.D. *A Further Study of Visual Perception.* Cambridge: Cambridge University Press, 1954.
11. Vernon, M.D. *The Experimental Study of Reading.* Cambridge: Cambridge University Press, 1931. Chapters 5-7.
12. Woodworth, Robert S. *Experimental Psychology.* New York: Holt, 1938. Pages 23 and 28.

28. An Inductive Approach to Word Analysis*

CONSTANCE M. McCULLOUGH

Associate Professor of Education
San Francisco State College

WHEN I was on the threshold of my teens, I went to visit some friends on a farm. City-bred, I thought that horses that were white were older than horses that were gray. There was a lot for me to learn in those two weeks.

One experience of that visit impressed me more than any other. I helped to bring in the cows one night, and the next night asked for the privilege of bringing them in all by myself. Not realizing the density of the ignoramus with whom he was dealing, my host consented.

I went out alone, down to the pasture along the strip of woods, rounded up the cows, and got them started up the lane toward the barn. My bosom swelled with pride in my accomplishment and with affection toward the beasts that were cooperating so well. Full of confidence, I began to stride ahead of the herd. But when I reached the barn and looked back down the lane, I could see the swinging tails of cows headed for the pasture again.

I never think of the teaching of word analysis without remembering those cows, for they told me more in a short time about the relationship between a teacher and a group of learners than a good deal of the research in reading. With all due apology to proud parents and fond teachers, I must report that children are much like cows. You never can tell where they are in their thinking if you get ahead of them. You have to prod with questions and let them take the lead. Otherwise, chances are good that you will lose them and arrive at the barn-the end of the lesson or the end of the book-without them.

The essence of an inductive approach to teaching word analysis is just that. The teacher fences off the desired area and the children go up the lane; the children are the first to discover; the teacher encourages from the rear until everyone gets to the barn.

AUDITORY EXERCISE

Take the problem of teaching the sound of the initial consonant *b*. First,

*From the May, 1955, issue of *Education,* Reprinted by permission of the publishers, The Bobbs-Merrill Company, Inc., Indianapolis, Indiana.

the teacher has to make sure that the children can discriminate between the sound of *b* and the sound of other letters. She says, "I am thinking of the name of a person in this room. It begins like *Billy* and *Bobby*. What do you suppose it is?" She hopes that someone will say *Betty* or *Bernard* or *Bonita*. But perhaps little Milly will say, "Peter". The teacher will say, "Let's listen. Do these words begin alike: *Bill, Bobby, Peter?*" Milly, reading the teacher's face better than the sound of the initial consonant *b*, says, "No," but she's really not sure.

The teacher must spend a good many little game periods with Milly and her kind until Milly's batting average is championship level. It won't help if the teacher says, "Look, Chum: *Billy* and *Bobby* begin with the same sound as *Betty, Bernard,* and *Bonita*. Now, remember this." Milly will be memorizing instead of listening to initial sounds. No, the teacher must stay behind the cows. "I'm thinking of something that begins like *ball* and *bat* and it's a game." "I'm thinking of something that begins like *box* and *bag* and it is on the table." Something to eat, comething to wear, whatever it is, the teacher must keep after the group until the children catch on. Perhaps the teacher can work this into a game that reinforces some other learning—reminds the children of facts they are learning in other subject areas.

As seatwork, the children may draw pictures of words that begin with that sound. A chart may be made of such pictures. In meaning for the children, such a chart is superior to a chart the teacher makes of commercial pictures.

If the initial sound is *s* and a child says that *circus* begins like *see* and *say*, the teacher should accept this offering in the ear training exercise, for these words do, indeed, begin alike in sound.

VISUAL EXERCISE

When the children can hear the initial sound of *b*, they are ready to look at words containing that initial sound, and to determine the letter which makes it. Notice that the *ear* training *precedes* the *visual* lesson. Now that the children have proved that they can distinguish the initial consonant sound *b* from other sounds, the teacher takes them on to the visual exercise.

Since children learn a new task better if that task involves known facts, it is better to use in the visual exercise, words the children have in their reading vocabulary—sight words familiar to them. This implies three things: (1) The visual exercise will not be undertaken unless and until the children have mastered by sight two, but preferably three or four or five words that start with *b*. (More words are preferable to fewer words because the more examples the children have of the principle they are trying to discover, the easier it will be to observe.) (2) Even though, on occasion, children who are invited to engage in the visual exercise are operating at different vocabulary levels, there will be an attempt on the part of the teacher to keep the vocabulary at the sight vocabulary level of the poorest reader in the group. Otherwise, the poorest reader will be not only the poorest reader but the one for whom the exercise is made deliberately more difficult by the use of words he does not know. Perhaps this suggests that, ordinarily, the first visual lesson should be administered to a relatively homogeneous group—a group reading at the same level of sight vocabulary—and that only later visual exercises should involve mixed groups. (3) Obviously, the children will have been reading for some time before such a visual exercise is undertaken, since the limited vocabulary of the beginning reading books does not start with a cluster of *b* words, such as: "Billy bumped his buttons on the back bench." When parents complain that their children are not learning phonics, this is the teacher's answer. The ingredients for the lesson are not yet assembled. One might just as well say, "Why haven't you baked that three-egg cake today?" Answer: "Not enough eggs yet."

Since children forget something they do not use, two other precautions should be taken in the use of the visual exercise: (1) The visual exercise should be introduced when it will be useful in the solution of new words. If the next story the children are to read will contain a *b* word, it is a good time to introduce the visual exercise. Then, (2) in introducing the next story the teacher will not tell the children the word. She will, rather, present it with a picture or put it into a revealing context: "The *baker* makes bread and cake," and let the children guess from the picture or verbal context, and from the initial consonant, what the word must be. By her encouragement of the use of the new learning, the teacher does not let it rust out.

The visual exercise goes something like this: The teacher says, "I am thinking of some words you have been reading. They begin like *ball* and *boy*. What are they?" As she says *ball*, she writes *ball* (in manuscript if the children are accustomed to manuscript) and stands so that all can see the word as she writes it. As she says *boy* she writes *boy* under *ball,* so that the *b's* are in a column, directly under one another:

ball

boy

This means that, as the teacher writes the *b* in each word, the children hear that sound in the teacher's pronunciation of *ball, boy,* or whatever word it is; the sight and sound of the letter occur simultaneously.

Jimmy volunteers *"Box."* The teacher says and writes *box,* immediately under *boy.* " Now, let's all say these words and listen to hear whether Jimmy is right." The group says, *"Ball, boy, box."* "Does *box* begin with the same sound as *boy* and *ball?"* They agree that it does. Bobby offers, *"Baby,"* and the teacher goes through the same procedure as with *box.*

When four or five words are in a column on the blackboard, the teacher decides to see whether or not the children are arriving at the barn. "Let's say the words over together and listen to the beginning of each word again." The children look and listen. "Does anyone notice anything alike about the way the words *look?"* Algernon will say that they are all short words. He is still in the pasture. But, if the teacher is lucky and the children are ready, Joe will say, "They all begin with the same letter." The teacher looks at him as at a diamond stick-pin on the floor of the supermarket. "Say that again!" Joe sticks out his chest two more inches and says it again. "How many of you think you see what Joe sees in these words?" Those who see and those who are good politicians indicate that they do. Algernon tries hard to come out of the pasture, but he may not make it that day.

"Who would like to come up to the blackboard and draw a line under the letter in the first word?" Joe had better have the honor. "Who would like to draw a line under the letter in the second word?" Some children who have not caught on up to this time may be helped by this stress. Meanwhile, the opportunity to go up and find the right letter gives Joe and his like a great deal of satisfaction. (A variation of this which emphasizes form is to overlay the initial *b* in each word with colored chalk, different children doing this.)

GENERALIZATION AND APPLICATION

Now to close the barn door: "Who can tell me what he knows from this? When a word begins with this letter, what do we know about its sound?" John, the philosopher, may come through: "When a word begins like that, I know it begins like *ball* and *boy* and *box* and *baby,"*. Perhaps, to dramatize the statement, the teacher will write a *b* above the words in the column on the blackboard. She may, in addition, engage the children for a few minutes in proving their point by finding other words beginning with *b,* on charts and signs about the room. Young children enjoy the physical relief of this field trip off the chairs.

But, before she dismisses the group, she says, "Let's see whether we can use what we know. I shall write a sentence on the blackboard. Read it to yourselves and see whether you can recognize the new word." She writes a sentence in which all the words are known to the children by sight except the new *b* word: "Pony's home is in the barn." After time for silent reading, Martha is selected to read the sentence. "How did you know, Martha?" Martha says, "I knew because Pony's home *is* in a barn and because *barn* begins with the same letter as *ball."*

The follow-up can be one of several tasks. The teacher may have other such sentences, which the children are to read, in which they are to underline the *b* in the strange word, and for which they are to draw a picture representing the new word. She may have sentences. with the *b's* left out, for the children to insert. She may have them find sentences in their readers containing *b* words. She may have them make up their own sentences containing *b* words. She may have them make a list of all the words they know that begin with *b*. She may have them trace over the *b's* that begin certain words, using a bright color. Some of these exercises are better than others, in that they stress meaning as well as form. The exercises in which the children write or trace over the *b's* are good because of the tactile experience with the shapes of the letters.

The next day the teacher may appear with a chart, which the children may call their *ball* chart:

b—   *ball*
           boy
           box
           baby

As the children learn new *b* words, they will add them to the chart.

SPECIAL PROBLEMS

If, in the course of the visual lesson, a child offers a word that does not begin with the consonant under discussion (say, *circus* for the *s* sound in *see* and *say*), the teacher will write the word to one side, not in the column with the other words. After the generalization has been made that words beginning with that sound begin with that letter (*s*), she will point out that *circus* begins with the same sound also, and that there are other words which begin with the same letter as *circus* and begin with the sound in *see* and *say*.

Notice that, in all this discussion, it has not been necessary to name the letter or to attempt to sound it alone—"buh." The reason the name of the letter has been avoided is that it is easy for the children to confuse the name of the letter with the sound the letter makes, and they may try to sound out a word by spelling it out. The reason the consonant sound has not been given in isolation is that it is impossible to sound the consonant without some sort of vowel accompaniment. This makes the blending more difficult. (This is not true in the case of vowel sounds. One may say, "The *a* sound in *cake* and *say*," without confusing the listener.)

SYLLABICATION

The inductive approach may be applied to all phases of word analysis. In syllabication, for instance, the first job is ear training, the child's own discovery of the number of syllables in different words. "Let's tap out these words as I say them. How many taps can you give to beat out the word *return?*" Ultimately, the teacher says, "These beats are called *syllables.*" She writes *syllables* as she says, "Syl-la-bles. Let's all say it." One fine day, she puts several words of different lengths but of one syllable on the blackboard, directly under each other:

catch
go
mitt
bat

She asks how many syllables are in the first word, and so on, and after each word she has a child indicate the number of syllables. Then she asks how many vowel sounds they hear in each word. The blackboard record becomes:

Word	Syl.	Vowel
catch	1	1
go	1	1
mitt	1	1
bat	1	1

"Can you tell the number of syllables in a word by something else besides tapping out the words?" "Yes;" someone says, "there is a syllable for every vowel." The teacher wants, "There is a syllable for every *sounded* vowel," but the exercise does not warrant that conclusion. Another day can be devoted to words like *came, strange,* and *toe;* another day to words like *tail* and *fear,* and still another to words like *boil* and *mouth.* In *came,* the *e* is silent; in *tail,* only the *a* is sounded; and in *boil* and *mouth,* the two vowels from a single, new sound. As children mature, the generalizations which they make about word analysis may well be expressed on the charts they make recording their knowledge of word parts.

MATERIALS IN KEEPING WITH THE INDUCTIVE APPROACH

Teachers who appreciate the soundness of the inductive approach to the teaching of word analysis use the children's sight vocabulary to construct exercise materials. They use suggestions from the manual and workbook of the basal reader. While they may gather ideas from other books, they always translate them into the sight vocabulary of the children. They are careful, too, to avoid materials which make the discoveries for the children, taking the initiative for learning out of their hands. If the printer has already shown which parts of the words are alike, by use of colored inks or bold type, the child is a willing follower in practice but a doubtful follower in thought, and there is no telling how many cows are headed back toward the pasture. (Is he thinking, "Color all the see-aitches," or is he really associating sight and sound?) The efficient teacher of word analysis is one who keeps clearly in mind the processes through which children must go in the accomplishment of the tasks she sets, and one who lets neither improperly constructed commercial materials nor pied pipers lure her away from her position of encouragement from the rear.

29. Phonics in the Reading Program—A Review and an Evaluation*

PAUL A. WITTY

Professor of Education
Northwestern University

ROBERT A. SIZEMORE

Director, Instruction in Language Arts,
Toledo City Schools, Toledo, Ohio

RECENTLY Rudolph Flesch aroused considerable concern among parents and teachers by the publication of *Why Johnny Can't Read.* (12)[1] In this book he contends that Johnny can't read because phonics is not taught in the modern school.

Mr. Flesch, we believe, has over-simplified the problem of reading instruction in a manner similar to that of writers who have sometimes placed the blame for juvenile delinquency on a single factor such as the reading of comic magazines. (29 and 33)

Controversy concerning phonic instruction is neither new nor unusual. In other countries as well as in the United States this issue has been debated for a long time. In recent years interest in phonics has centered upon how, when, and by what methods phonics should be presented. It is of special interest to note the intensity with which this issue has been debated in England as late as 1954. Proponents for and against phonics issued some extreme statements and a moderate point was presented by others. Some newspaper writers have presented rather unbiased points of view based on research.

In America, the recent intemperate views have been set forth by some newspaper reporters and by a journalist. However, Dr. John McDowell, the Assistant Superintendent of Schools, Diocese of Pittsburgh, comments sagaciously

> the revival of this strict phonetic approach to reading has been viewed with alarm by some and joy by others; all, however, have shown considerable interest and concern. Some have vigorously maintained that the phonetic

*From *Elementary English,* (October, 1955), 355-371. Reprinted with the permission of the National Council of Teachers of English and Paul A. Witty and Robert A. Sizemore.

[1]Numbers in parentheses refer to references at the end of the article.

method is not only *a* way of teaching reading, but *the* way. Some write about it as though it were a new discovery never before attempted, or as if phonetic training has never had any role whatever in primary reading. (18, p.506)

In order to clarify certain aspects of this issue, the writers propose in this paper to review available research studies pertaining to the use of phonics in reading programs.

One of the first studies was that of Edmund J. Gill. (16) In 1912, Gill reported in the *Journal of Experimental Pedagogy* that he had studied three groups of children from three different schools. One, group X, consisted of children whose average age was six and one-half years and who had been in the process of learning to read for two years. The second, group Y, averaged seven years, two months of age and had also been engaged in learning to read for two years. The Y group had been taught by a phonic method while the X group had used a modified "Dale" method of phonics instruction. The third, group Z, had been taught by the method of wholes—a "Thought or Sentence" method, a procedure in which one learned "to recognize the visual wholes of words in meaningful groups." These children had an average age of seven years, three months and had had sixteen months of instruction in reading.

In his experimental procedure, Gill selected "two paragraphs of equal length . . . from a reading book used in the upper classes of an infant's school. These were printed separately on cardboard, in type similar to that used in the book from which the extracts were made, but without punctuation or spacing." The pupils read these selections aloud to the experimenter. Gill concluded that:

> Comparing the reading times for the three schools, a striking similarity throughout is shown at those two (X and Y) using phonic methods of teaching to read, thus suggesting the two variations of the one method to be of equal practical value. Their reading times are, however, more than double those than the children at Z, who, in fluency and intelligence of reading, also were equally superior. Further, questions which were asked to find out to what extent the extracts had been really 'read,' i.e., understood, served to confirm the impressions formed by a comparison of the different reading times, of the relative values of word and phonic methods.
>
> It is also worth noting that the mean variation in the case of Z is relatively smaller than the mean variation of the other two cases. The shortness of the average time for the class is not due to a few exceptionally good pupils, but the work was very uniform. . . . The results of the above investigation indicate the greater practical value of the sentence method of teaching to read, as compared with the phonic. (16, p.245)

Gill pointed out further that a comparison of the good readers with the poor readers in his groups indicated that the former groups tended to read by wholes, attending to the word rather than to parts or to letters.

The results [of Gill's study] confirm the views expressed by Claparede in the *Psychologie de l'Enfant et Pedagogue Experimentale:* "The mind proceeds from the simple to the complex; the fact that the child sees the whole before perceiving its parts does not contradict this statement. For the child, the whole, not being a collection of parts, but on the contrary a block, a unity, to go from the simple to the complex is to proceed from the whole to its part." (16)

In 1912, Dumville reported in the *School World* on "The Methods of Teaching Reading in the Early Stages." (10) As reviewed by Sister M. Dorothy Browne (5), Dumville "firmly believed that words should be learned as wholes and not in isolated sound parts." He taught upper elementary and secondary school pupils to read by means of a phonetic alphabet. "The control or 'look-and-say' groups were given complete lists of the words occurring in the test, presented in phonetic transcription and regular spelling. The students in this group were told to learn the words as wholes to prepare for a test. The 'phonic' groups were instructed in the powers or sounds represented by the phonetic symbols and then told to apply these to the lists so as to prepare for a test." Following thirty minutes of study "a prose selection containing the words studied was given individually to each student." The author concluded that "there was little difference in the achievements of the elementary school groups, but the students from the secondary school who received phonic instruction were much superior . . . [and] that perhaps both groups used both methods of word attack while studying."

A year later, in 1913, C.W. Valentine (27) reported a comparison of the "Look and Say" method with a phonic approach. In a preliminary test he selected two classes of twenty-four students each in the Training College, Dundee, Scotland and taught them "a passage of English prose written in Greek characters." One group used a phonic approach; the other, a "look-and-say method." After testing, he concluded that "in every test. . .the Phonic method proved superior."

Following this preliminary testing, Valentine subjected two groups of children—ages six-and-one-half to eight years—to similar but improved experimental procedures. From these experiments he concluded:

There seems to be nothing so inherently difficult, even for little children, in the synthetic work involved by the Phonic method as has been asserted by some of its critics. Such synthesis was done readily by infants of six years of age. . . . Children taught by the Phonic method do better than those taught by the "Look and Say" method, both in reading words previously seen and words previously unseen. . . . There seems to be some evidence, however, that for very dull children the "Look and Say" method is more efficient. (27, p.108)

In discussing the two methods of teaching, Valentine questioned the contention that the look-say method "gains and holds the interest of the children more readily." For "interest in the matter is not lost in slowly plodding through the words letter by letter . . . [and] it may be seriously questioned whether such interest in the matter is always essential at the earliest stages of reading. . . . Too great an interest, indeed, in the story which is being read seems undesirable from a psychological point of view, even when the 'look-and-say' method is being used. [A footnote here explains as follows: "I refer, of course, to reading lessons in school where it is desirable that the child shall be storing up a knowledge of words that he will be able to apply when reading alone."] It may tend to divert attention from the words themselves and cause, not only wild guessing and misreading of words, but also such a very fleeting attention even to words properly read that they are not remembered on future occasions. One does not advance one's knowledge of a foreign language best by reading highly exciting novels in that tongue. . . . At the point at which the interest of the child seems to be failing it is doubtless well to seek to hasten the reading. The ideal plan with the average child would seem to be an alternation of the two methods. . . ." (27, pp.111 f.)

In commenting on his belief that the look-and-say method is better for very dull children, Valentine states that "it may be the only possible method. No doubt it is also the better method for the very dull teacher." (27, p.112)

In 1914, Mabel Hassell and Lillian Varley (17) selected two schools—one in which phonic analysis was taught, and another in which the sentence method was employed, (a procedure wherein the "words are never taken singly but always in sentences, and the sentence has always a message for the reader.") An oral reading test was given to the one hundred forty-five, seven-year-old children in these schools. The teachers kept records of individual errors and total reading time. The results disclosed that nine boys in the non-phonic school did attempt "phonetic analysis" while thirty-three boys and six girls in the phonics school did not use such analysis when the need arose. Also a phonic attack often caused the reader to lose "grip of the selection." Whole word readers, too, in both schools completed the selection much more quickly.

In another study, the first and second graders of Tilton, New Hampshire public schools were utilized by Lillian B. Currier and Oliver C. Duguid. (7) "Two classes of equal size and equal average ability were formed" in each of the two grades. One class in each grade was given phonetic drills; the other "had no knowledge whatever of phonics. Words were developed by quick-perception and sense-content methods."

As a result of observations made during the year the writers reported:

The phonic classes so concentrated upon letter sounds that the attention was diverted from the sense of the paragraph to word pronunciation. This brought about lack of interest and fatigue and destroyed the pleasure which the story should yield. The reading was generally less smooth, slower, and the idea confused.

The classes having no phonics were found to enjoy reading for the sake of the story. From the story they got the sense-content. They were less careful and less correct than the phonic classes in regard to word pronunciation. Keeping the sense in mind, they often substituted words from their own vocabulary for difficult or unfamiliar words in the text. They read more swiftly and with more expression. Fatigue was reduced, because curiosity in the story held the interest and caused the attention to be focused upon the outcome of the story. (7, p.286)

A final test for these classes in June of 1916 indicated there was little difference among pupils in attacking new words whether they were phonetically trained or not. Those who were foreign born or who had speech impediments or poor pronunciation habits were helped by phonetic procedures, while the expressionless, the hesitant, or the habitually slow readers were helped by non-phonetic training.

Seven years later, in 1923, Currier (8) reported that she had continued experimentation with third and fourth grade groups throughout a five-year period. Based upon her observations during this five-year period, she drew the following conclusions:

1. "Phonetic drills have a very real value but are not essential to every child as a part of the daily program in the primary grades."

2. "Phonetic drills should at all times be employed with discretion and adapted to the needs of the individual child or special group."

3. "Word pronunciation drills have proved to be of much value." However, they may prove to be only a very good device.

4. "Much careless oral reading and failure to get the idea from the printed page come from poorly or carelessly supervised silent reading."

5. "It is of greatest importance to arouse, hold, strengthen, and develop the interest of pupils."

6. A single phonic system should not be used for every pupil. What is food for one may be poison for another. The needs of different pupils should be ascertained and the best method for meeting particular problems should be employed. (8, p.452)

During a period of years from 1905 to 1924 experiments were conducted in methods of teaching beginners to read in English schools. W. H. Winch proceeded in the belief that the values of various methods of teaching reading differ. (30) In a monograph, published in 1925, he describes his efforts to determine the relative values of teaching reading by the look-and-say method, by an alphabetic method, by an "ordinary" phonic method, and by a special phonic method called the "phonoscript" method. In the phonoscript method "marks are placed without and within ordinary literal characters which give to ever letter a definite and invariable sound. The last proposition is not a reversible one; the same sound is represented, not by one definite shape but by various shapes." Although Mr. Winch set out to "survey the relative success of phonic, look-and-say, and alphabetic methods of teaching reading in its very early stages," his study became "in consequence of the superiority of phonoscript readers in early stages with their own form of print, an evaluation of this system as against an ordinary phonic method." For the early experiments children in the poorer economic levels in London suburbs were chosen. Groups were equated according to their "potentiality to begin to learn to read." The Readiness tests were devised by Mr. Winch. The average ages of the groups of children at the beginning of the experiments were under six years. Mr. Winch concludes:

> Phonic and look-and-say methods are put in practice and compared. The result is a victory for the phonic method. A phonic and an alphabetic method are compared. The result is a victory for the phonic method. The most recent phonic system, Mr. Hayes' *Phonoscript*, is compared with an ordinary phonic system; the result is a victory for the phonoscript method. (30, p.174)

Winch also comes to the conclusion that "no phonic method (including phonoscript) produces adequate correctness in spelling." He closes with this recommendation:

> . . . English children, under our conditions of school organization, may quite profitably begin definitely to learn to read at an average age of 5 years 3 months the normative age in London for the commencement of the second half of our Grade II educational year. In schools where the children are well-born and of good environment, they may begin earlier; in schools attended by very poor children, later. (30, p.176)

Grace Arthur (2) in 1925 reported a study of one hundred seventy-one first-graders in seven public schools of Chisholm, Minnesota. These children were given standardized tests prior to entrance into the first grade and again near the end of the first grade. Arthur concluded:

> It would seem from these data that time spent in teaching phonetic methods to children with a mental age of less than five and a half years is largely wasted, since a median score of zero is not impressive as the result of a year's faithful effort. Children with mental ages from 5.5 to 6.4 evidently do gain something from the teaching of phonetics. Yet the increase in efficiency for the next higher mental-age group, 6.5-6.9, is so great as to suggest that age as the better one at which to begin the teaching of reading by this method. (2, p.178)

In the *Journal of Educational Psychology* for April, 1927, Arthur I. Gates (14) reported two studies of the results of phonic training in beginning reading. The first study was made in the Horace Mann School. Pupils underwent daily practice in phonics from November, 1923 to May, 1924. In the other study, four groups of New York Public Schools had training from October 1925 to April 1926. These groups were compared with others equated on the basis of CA, MA, IQ, and "abilities shown in several tests of word recognition, word perception, knowledge of the alphabet and reading."

The groups receiving phonetic instruction were provided with materials which "may be considered as representing the superior types in which phonetic analysis and blending are related as closely as possible to real reading situations." The non-phonetic groups used "exercises arranged wholly to stimulate reading to secure the thought. . . to emphasize comprehension. . . to demand accurate discrimination of words and phrases in order correctly to indicate or express the thought." (14, p.220)

Gates concluded that:

> The results of both studies show slight differences between the two groups in gross achievement in the recognition and in the pronunciation of isolated words although differences in methods of attack were apparent. Both groups showed ability to recognize elements in new words and both showed a degree of independent ability to work out the recognition of unfamiliar word forms. . . In tests of rate and accuracy of pronunciation in oral reading, the two groups were about equally competent in general, although the non-phonetic pupils in the second experiment had had less oral reading experience than the phonetic and probably less than was advisable. In this work the non-phonetic pupils usually showed a greater disposition to depend on the context and to attack the larger word units or features of configuration; the phonetic groups resorted more to detailed analysis of the new words encountered.
>
> *In general efficiency in silent reading comprehension, the non-phonic pupils demonstrated markedly superior attainments.* If this type of ability is admitted to be the main objective of reading instruction, the non-phonetic training showed a clear advantage. In the second and longer study, the non-phonetic pupils were superior in silent reading by 35 per cent; in the first study their advantage was also marked. (14, p.225)

In 1928 Elmer Sexton and John Herron (23) reported that nearly one thousand pupils took part in a "controlled experiment to test the value of phonics in the teaching of beginning reading." The experiment was started in 1925.

Pupils in eight schools of "various types" from different sections of Newark, New Jersey were divided into phonic and non-phonic instructional groups. At the end of five months of training and again at the end of ten months the pupils were tested by means of a number of reading tests. Results for those children who had had uninterrupted instruction were compared. Further tests were made on four hundred twenty-six pupils who continued in controlled groups through the first half of the second grade.

The results, Sexton and Herron state:

> clearly indicate that the teaching of phonics functions very little or not at all with beginners in reading during the first five months. It begins to be of some value during the second five months but is of greater value in the second grade.
>
> Although the experiment was conducted "to test the value of phonics in the teaching of beginning reading," the results show conclusively that there is immeasurably less difference between classes taught with and without phonics than between different schools. Where results were unusually good in a class taught by a teacher using phonics, they were unusually good when the same teacher taught without phonics. On the other hand, poor results were secured in both phonic and non-phonic groups taught by the same teacher. . . .the outcome of the experiment tends to favor some phonetic instruction, beginning in the second half of the first year. . . . (23, p.701)

Raymond M. Mosher (19) in March 1928 indicated "some results of teaching beginners by the look-and-say method." He had selected previously twenty-six first-graders in the Demonstration School of New Haven State Normal School and employed look-say procedures with them. Vocabulary accomplishments ranging from zero to 1,455 words for different pupils were indicated.

Later, in 1930, Mosher and Sidney Newhall (20) compared a phonics and word approach, using seven classes of first graders in three public elementary schools of New Haven, Connecticut. The children were equated according to intelligence test results. Each group contained children of superior, average, and below average intelligence. After two years' training the pupils were tested for frequency of eye fixations, speed on easy and difficult material, and comprehension.

The authors concluded that:

> 1. The measures of speed, fixation pauses, and comprehension seem to show, both individually and collectively, no essential difference in the results of the two training methods compared, at least at the end of the second year.
>
> 2. If these measures comprise a valid index of reading proficiency then the supposed advantages accruing to phonic training are negated. Look-and-say children under the experimental conditions maintained in the schools are able to read approximately as quickly and effectively as phonic children.
>
> 3. In general, our results suggest that added time devoted to phonics

would not appreciably increase reading skill, and that therefore phonic training is not especially to be recommended as a device for that purpose. (20, p.506)

S.C. Garrison and Minnie Heard (13) began an experiment in September, 1927 which continued through May, 1930. No child was included "who had any knowledge whatsoever of reading or spelling." "Equivalent group techniques. . . in regard to children, teachers, and teaching conditions" were used. One hundred eleven children were divided into two groups—those of 100 IQ or more, and those below 100 IQ—and placed in four classrooms. One class in each of the two categories received phonetic training during the first and second year but not in the third. Phonetic training was not given to one class in each of the two categories during the same years.

Every effort was made to keep teaching conditions alike except in a fifteen minute period each day, during which the phonetic group received instruction in phonetics. . . . The non-phonetic group during this period used what Gates called the *intrinsic* method—[exercises] arranged to teach children to discriminate accurately between words and to stimulate thought. (13, pp.9-10)

At various times during the three-year period the children were checked by standardized tests. Garrison and Heard stated:

From the data collected in this study, the conclusions stated below appear to be indicated; however, it must be remembered that in many cases the P.E. of the difference between the Phonetic and non-Phonetic is not significant.
1. Training in phonetics makes children more independent in the pronunciation of words.
2. Children with no phonetic training make smoother and better oral readers in the lower grades.
3. . . bright children seem to be helped more by training in phonetics than are dull. *For all children, phonetic training seems to be more effective in the latter part of the primary grades.* (Italics not in the original.)
4. In the teaching of reading it seems probable that much of the phonetic training now given should be deferred till the second and third grades. It appears that work in meaningful exercises which are planned to increase comprehension and to teach discrimination of words is more important than phonetics.
5. Children who have had training in phonetics have some advantage in learning to spell over children who have had no such training. Training in phonetics would be well worth while for spelling alone if for no other reason.
6. First grade children with no phonetics training seem to lose less during vacation than do children with such training. Apparently, phonetic

training makes a young child, particularly a young dull child, dependent upon a device of word analysis which is more difficult to retain than is his own particular method. With the older children, children at the end of the second grade, phonetic training seems to be an aid in retention during vacation. (13, pp.13 f.)

Herbert Carroll in 1931 (6) attempted to assess "through the medium of spelling, the effect of intelligence upon phonetic generalization." Carroll selected words from a list by Gates and tested bright and dull fourth and fifth grade children in Public School 210 of Brooklyn, New York. The results of his testing indicated that the bright children transferred phonetic generalizations more readily and hence made more misspellings since the rules did not apply to many words. He concluded that "a phonetic-nonphonetic classification of the misspelled words shows that the bright are much more likely than the dull to err phonetically." (6, pp.180 f.) This study suggests the necessity of stressing the exceptions to phonic rules.

For eight weeks—from March 2, 1936 to April 24, 1936—Harry L. Tate (24) experimented with first grade pupils in the Eli Whitney School of Chicago. Dividing the class of 73 into two groups, Tate subjected one group to a phonetic approach—"both in the supplementary and in the basic reading the emphasis in attacking new words was placed on the phonetic method. However, none of the other elements that enter into proper teaching of reading were neglected." While no phonics instruction was given to the control group, exercises devoted to word and phrase recognition, and recognition of the sense of a selection including exercises requiring dramatic action, completion exercises, and exercises requiring oral response were employed. After standardized tests were given, Tate declared:

> Phonics instruction and drill. . . is far superior to the look-and-say method in developing ability to recognize words. The results. . . give a slight indication that the look-and-say method is superior to phonics instruction and drill in developing the ability to comprehend sentences. Results obtained. . . show conclusively that the look-and-say method is superior to phonics instruction and drill in developing the ability to comprehend paragraphs of directions. The use of as many as thirty minutes daily for special phonics instruction and drills leads to an unbalanced development of the abilities to comprehend words, to understand sentences, and to grasp the meaning of paragraphs. Other deductions that do not rest directly on the data and therefore do not have the weight of conclusions are:
>
> 1. Regular periods for phonics instruction and drill are not desirable.
> 2. Phonics should be used by the pupil as a tool and not as subject matter to be mastered for its own value.
> 3. Overemphasis on phonics hinders rapidity and thoroughness of comprehension. (24, pp.762-763)

Edward Dolch and Maurine Bloomster (9) reported in 1937 that they had studied children in the first two grades of a school "in which the teaching of phonics had been uniform for at least two years and in which phonics had had some emphasis, though not an unusual amount." The children were tested in May, 1935 and again in May, 1936 with standardized intelligence tests and a Word-Attack Series of Dolch-Gray. Dolch and Bloomster commented on their measurement of the pupils' mental development and phonic attainment as follows:

> When consideration is given to the difficulty of accurate measurement of young children in both the fields concerned, the relation between mental maturity and the use of phonics is remarkably high. The scattergrams made from the scores show a further significant fact: children of high mental age sometimes fail to acquire phonic ability but children of low mental age are certain to fail. The scattergrams seem to show the thing in which we are perhaps most interested, namely, the minimum age for phonics readiness. Children with mental ages below seven years made only chance scores; that is, as far as this experiment indicates, a mental age of seven years seems to be the lowest at which a child can be expected to use phonics, even in the simple situations provided by these two tests.
>
> It has always been known that some first-grade pupils learned to use phonics; but it is also known that many children reach a mental age of seven years before the end of grade I. Most of the others, though not all, reach the mental age of seven years in grade II. These results seem therefore to check with school experience. They do not tell, however, exactly when the teaching of phonics should be started. Ear-training, which is the basis of phonics, may begin early. Children may be taught to notice the similarities between sounds some time before they are expected actually to use sounding generalizations. This study does suggest, however, that the schools are perhaps expecting results from phonic-teaching far too soon. (9, pp.204-205)

A research study of college students was reported in 1938 by Maurine Rogers (21). This investigator attempted to determine the relationship between mispronunciation and comprehension, as well as the effects of phonic training upon certain aspects of reading. Seventy-two poor silent readers of the freshman class at the University of Iowa were divided into two groups. One group was given phonic training (a modification of Anna Cordts system) while the other served as a control group.

From her results Rogers concluded that

> ... Mispronunciation of a word and lack of comprehension of its meaning often go together. On the average, 78 per cent of the mispronunciations in this study were accompanied by inaccurate comprehension. (21, pp.386 f.)

She also found a high frequency of repetitions, substitutions, and omissions in the reading of these freshmen. Thus any instruction in oral reading should involve training to overcome repetitions and omissions. The high frequencies of these errors justifies more practice in oral reading than in phonics, although the latter should be included if mispronunciations are common in the student's oral reading.

At the college level phonic training is an effective technique for the improvement of pronunciation, oral reading, and reading vocabulary.

The value of phonics in pronunciation in contrast to more sight training lies in the fact that the student is given a tool which will enable him to attack new and unfamiliar words while sight training would improve only the particular words studied. Although it is an aid in oral reading and vocabulary, it should not be used exclusively. Improvement in vocabulary should also include training in suffix and prefix cues, motivation in using the dictionary and any other helpful devices. The value of this research has been to indicate that phonic training is one technique which may be used in the improvement of vocabulary at the college level. (21, pp.387 f.)

In the *Elementary School Journal* for September and October of 1938, Arthur Gates and David Russel (15) considered the "types of materials, vocabulary burden, word analysis, and other factors in beginning reading."

Three hundred fifty-four pupils, "fairly representative of the population of New York City," in nine classes of four Manhatten schools were equated for mental age and assembled into groups. In one phase of the experiment, three groups were accorded differing types of phonic training. Group D "received the smallest amount of phonics or word analysis." Group E was "given moderate amounts of informal, newer-type word analysis, comparisons, etc." Group F "had substantial or large amounts of conventional phonetic drill."

At the end of the training period, Gates and Russell concluded:

In the case of the scores for the entire groups, although the differences were not marked nor highly reliable, Group E had the highest scores in all the tests of word recognition and comprehension, and Group D exceeded Group F slightly in two of the four, being equal in the other two. The activities used with Group E were, in the main, examples of more recent, informal exercises in comparing, studying, and analyzing word forms. It is significant that the scores of the pupils in that group exceeded those in the groups employing the more conventional or formal phonetic drills by slightly more than one-tenth of a grade in the Gates standardized tests of both comprehension and word recognition. A program including little or no phonetic or word analysis activities in the first year is not as good as the informal program but is at least as good as one containing large amounts of formal phonetic work.

In the case of the group highest in reading—readiness scores, the moderate, modern program of word analysis gave the highest average scores in reading and word recognition, but it barely exceeded the minimum word-analysis program, which in turn had a very slight advantage over conventional phonics. Since the differences have low reliability, the indication is that it matters little which type or how much phonics is taught to the ablest pupils during the first year but that a moderate amount of the newer, more informal types of word analysis is most promising. The average pupils (those of intermediate reading-readiness scores) appear more clearly to secure greater benefit from this type of experience and to profit best from the conventional, formal phonics. The pupils of lowest reading readiness scores show this trend still more clearly. A moderate amount of informal word analysis is helpful; very little of this type seems to be better than large amounts of formal phonetic drill. The latter apparently does not 'take' well when taught to children of low readiness scores. (15, pp.122 f.)

In 1939 Donald Agnew (1) reported the results of another widely-quoted study. He attempted to determine the relative effects of large and small amounts of phonetic training. Two hundred thirty pupils in Grade III A of Raleigh, North Carolina were chosen as subjects. To these pupils were given a number of tests, both group and individual. In order to determine the extent of the phonetic training the subjects had undergone in grades I, II, and III, a questionnaire of twenty-five questions was submitted to each teacher who previously had taught them.

The study of the pupils in Raleigh yielded inconsistent results:

> The comparisons made failed to reveal a significant advantage or disadvantage (in terms of reading test scores) arising from different amounts of phonetic experience. . . [When the subjects had] large amounts of phonetic experiences in grades I and II, [there appeared] to be a tendency [for reading abilities] to be affected adversely [by the training.] [Yet,] large amounts of phonetic experiences in grades I and III [appeared] beneficial. . . . (1, 33 f.)

"In order to check the results obtained in the Raleigh investigation," and "to provide new data on the effects of larger and more consistent amounts of phonetic experience than found in Raleigh," Agnew undertook a second investigation. He selected one hundred ten pupils in two schools of Durham as subjects. "In the selection of these schools, two principles were borne in mind: first, it was desirable to obtain subjects who had experienced large amounts of phonetic training; and second, it was desirable to obtain a distribution of subjects comparable to those used in the Raleigh investigation." (1, 36) These children were tested and then eighty-nine from the Raleigh group were compared with eighty-nine from the Durham group.

From the second investigation Agnew concluded:

> The comparatively large and more consistent amounts of phonetic training received by the Durham pupils seem to have resulted in greater phonetic abilities. . . .

Not only were the Durham pupils "superior to the Raleigh pupils in word pronunciation ability" but also seventy per cent of the Durham pupils "used phonetic methods of word pronunciation," while only thirty per cent of the Raleigh subjects did so. "Comparatively little difference [appeared between the two groups] . . . in the silent reading abilities measured." The Durham group, moreover, had a larger vocabulary, was slower but more accurate in oral reading, and had a greater eye-voice span than the Raleigh pupils. Mr. Agnew inferred that these were the results of the phonic training given the Durham group. (1, pp.42 f.)

Sixth grade pupils who "had received their early training during a period when phonics were in disrepute and training in them was not generally given" were selected by Sister M. Dorothy Browne as suitable subjects for a remedial program using phonics. (5) Three hundred twenty-six pupils from parochial schools in Chicago, Detroit, and the District of Columbia were divided into four experimental and four control groups. The groups were equated on the basis of reading age and intelligence. For approximately a school year, the experimental groups were given daily ten-minute phonic drills preceding the regular reading lesson. The phonic program followed the approach of Anna Cordts in which "the phonetic elements are studied in words, phrases, and sentences." At intervals during the experimental program the subjects were given standardized reading tests. From these tests, Browne concluded that:

1. Progress in reading in the sixth grade may be aided by a carefully planned series of lessons in phonics.
2. Children with low IQ's are as likely to profit from phonic instruction as those with higher IQ's.
3. Children with IQ's below 100 make more progress in reading as a result of phonic instruction than those with higher IQ's.
4. The study of phonics is helpful not only to the pupil who is deficient in reading, but it is even more effective in stimulating the better reader to further growth.
5. The greatest gain in favor of phonetic training for children with initial reading ability of average and above grade is evidenced in groups with IQ's between 90 and 109. (5, p.42)

Sister Browne comments that "the significant progress made by subjects with IQ's below 90 is not a denial of the conclusions drawn by Dolch (9), but seem to confirm the assumption that the ability to apply phonic analysis depends upon the attainment of a certain mental age, rather than the possession of a particular intelligence quotient. Dolch considers a mental age of seven years as the lowest level for phonic readiness and the lowest mental age in the present study was nine years and five months." (5, p.38)

She maintains that:

In general, the findings of this study evidence a specific value to reading achievement in simple systematic phonic lessons when these lessons are used as one of a number of aids to accurate word recognition. This conclusion may be reconciled with the opinions of those who oppose the use of phonics in beginning reading as well as with the opinions of those who reject any but a meaningful analytical approach. Since the study of phonics produced results as a remedial measure in reading, it would seem that they have a proper place in a primary reading program. A timely correction of method instead of the complete abandonment of misused educational practices would do much to obviate the necessity of great amounts of remedial teaching. (5, p. 39)

In *School and Society*, February 1940, Joseph Tiffin and Mary McKinnis (26) reported their study of one hundred fifty-five pupils from the fifth through eighth grades of the Langlois School in Lafayette, Indiana. In an attempt to determine the relationship between phonic ability and reading ability they gave these pupils Roger's individual phonic ability test of "one hundred nonsense words utilizing most of the letter combinations found in the English language," the Iowa Silent Reading Test, and the new Stanford Reading Test. The following correlations were computed:

Reading Criterion	Correlation with Phonic Ability
New Stanford Reading Test	.70±.027
Iowa Silent Reading (Comprehension)	.66±.030
Iowa Silent Reading (Rate)	.55±.038

"These correlations show with reasonable certainty that phonic ability is significantly related to reading ability among the pupils studied." (26, p. 191)

Tiffin and McKinnis pointed out further:

For the 155 pupils studied, representing an age range from 9 years 11 months to 15 years 9 months, there was practically no relation between phonic ability and chronological age. The coefficient of correlation was −.08−.055. (26, p. 191)

In concluding, the authors commented:

Though the present investigation shows that a functional mastery of the isolated principles of phonics is significantly related to reading ability, the authors do not conclude that reading should be taught by drill in the isolated principles of phonics or that drill should necessarily be given in all cases of retarded reading. But it is felt that a program of reading instruction which does not, by direct or indirect instruction, yield a mastery of the principles of phonics is not accomplishing its full purpose. . . . It seems highly probable that cases found to be markedly deficient in phonic ability and not markedly deficient in other important characteristics, may be profitably treated by instruction and drill in the specific principles of phonics. . . .Such cases are obviously rare. It is not often that the source of the difficulty in a retarded reader can be traced so directly to a single causative factor. Yet the existence of even a few such cases, coupled with the evidence of the present study that phonic ability is related to reading ability. points to the conclusion that the pendulum may have swung too far and that we have been too much neglecting this phase of reading. (26, p. 192)

David Russell (22) reported in December 1943 a diagnostic study of spelling readiness among four classes of one hundred sixteen pupils when they were in the first grade and early part of the second grade. In two of the classes the teachers employed phonics while in the other two classes little phonics was used in the reading programs. These Vancouver, British Columbia pupils were tested in May, June, and November of 1941 with seven individual and six group tests.

Russell stated:

The results support the findings of Agnew and others that considerable phonics instruction in the first grade has a favorable influence upon achievement in word recognition and accuracy in reading. They indicate that some of the habits of attention to parts of words, of seeing similarities and differences in words, and of recognizing common phonograms in words, or other habits developed in phonetic analysis, apparently are of value in early attempts at spelling English words. The results do not establish, however, a clear pattern of cause and effect relationships between phonetic instruction and successful visual and auditory perception. It is important to note that the teachers of the 'phonics' group used more than a phonetic method with an exclusive reliance on the sound of words. Accordingly it is not possible to say definitely that work in phonics improves visual and auditory perception as measured by the tests used, or that practice in visual and auditory techniques necessarily is the cause of good phonetic analysis and high early spelling achievement. It would seem rather that the visual and auditory techniques are part-and-parcel of the program of phonetic instruction in the classes studied, and that separation into cause and effect is unwarranted. The chief point probably is that primary pupils may acquire a group of basic word skills which are necessary for success in reading, spelling, and other language activities. (22, pp. 278 f.)

In October 1953 The Reverend John McDowell (18) reviewed data from a study of ten parochial schools in the diocese of Pittsburgh. Five schools were recommended by a supervisor as schools in which the phonetic method was in use. The school office of the diocese selected five schools of comparable "intelligence and socio-economic levels" in which a "diocesan-approved" program "included phonetic training, as a subsidiary word-attack skill which is introduced gradually and developed through analysis of meaningful material." (18, p. 507)

The pupils were given a series of tests during the fourth grade. Ten fourth grades were selected including 550 students. Computation of data, however, included "only those whose entire primary work was uninterrupted in either the phonetic or regular reading programs. . . ." (18, p. 509)

One hundred forty-two fourth graders who had used the phonetic method and a comparable number who had used the "diocesan" method from the beginning of their entry into the first grade were compared on the results of the Iowa Silent Reading Test. Dr. McDowell concluded:

> The group following the diocesan program, . . .reads faster, understands words, comprehends paragraphs, uses the index, and, in general, reads better than the phonetic group. The latter, however, is better at alphabetizing. . . ."On Directed Reading and Sentence Meaning [parts of test] the groups are about the same." (18, 510)

The results of the Metropolitan Reading Test of 128 pupils in each group indicated that "the trend on the reading and language usage tests strongly favors the diocesan program," although the results were not statistically significant.

> on the spelling test, however, those following the phonetic program were clearly superior to the other group and the difference is very significant . . . That the phonic group is doing superior work in alphabetizing and spelling should not be suprising. From the very beginning, training in the alphabet and spelling is stressed . . . Children who are taught to spell from the beginning should excel in these skills. The strange thing is that they are not better at such skills. The fourth graders following the phonetic method had a 5.4 grade equivalent in alphabetizing and a 5.3 grade equivalent in spelling. The group following the diocesan program had a 4.7 in alphabetizing and a 4.9 in spelling. The norm for both groups is 4.5 since the tests were administered in January of the fourth year. (18, p. 513)
> . . . for the phonetic group, their word meaning grade equivalent was 4.5 and their grade equivalent for paragraph comprehension and sentence meaning was 4.1. It is not difficult to see what must be sacrificed in a program that is oriented toward pronouncing and spelling skills. (18, p. 513)

The group following the diocesan program had [a] grade equivalent for word meaning . . . [of] 5.1; it was 4.6 for Paragraph Comprehension and 4.4 for Sentence Meaning . . . There is a more rounded and harmonious development of reading skills and nothing is sacrificed. One can hardly complain about children midway through the fourth grade being able to spell at the level of children who are completing that grade. (18, pp. 511-514)

McDowell also matched 56 pupils who had missed the first semester (5 months) of the phonetics program with 56 pupils who had had the entire phonetics program. He concluded:

> Apparently after three and a half years, it makes little difference whether the child had those first five months of extensive drilling in the mechanics of pronouncing and rhyming. In fact, the Phonics B group [group that missed the first five months] did about as well in alphabetizing as the Phonics A group [group which had the total program.] On those skills so fundamental to reading, Phonics B group is doing slightly better work. (18, p. 515)

When McDowell compared "the performance of children in the best phonic program [64 pupils] . . . " with all 142 pupils using the diocesan method, he stated: "The conclusion should be obvious. The phonetic method, even under ideal conditions, is not accomplishing the results that it is said to accomplish." (18, p. 516)

Three hundred eighteen pupils in five Minneapolis public schools were tested near the end of their fourth grade by Mildred Templin. (25) She reported in February 1954 that her study was

> concerned with the relation of phonic knowledge irrespective of how it was acquired, to spelling and reading achievement. [Specifically] it was designed to investigate: (a) the level of phonic knowledge of fourth grade pupils, (b) the relation between phonic knowledge and reading and spelling skill at this grade level, and (c) what differences, if any, exist in the phonic knowledge of good and poor spellers and of good and poor readers. (25, p. 441)

Phonic tests were constructed and administered over a two weeks period. Reading tests were also given as a part of the regular school testing program.

The tests established that a "substantial amount of phonic knowledge" was acquired by these fourth grade pupils and that phonic knowledge was somewhat more highly related to spelling than to reading. Further, the pupils had higher scores when the test item was a familiar word rather than a sound or nonsense-word. These pupils did not apply phonic knowledge "equally in all of the recognition tests. . . . For the experimental sample there are real differences in the degree of application of phonic knowledge by fourth grade pupils under various conditions." (25, pp. 445, 448, 453)

That the poor spellers and poor readers applied their phonic knowledge less well than good spellers and good readers in the unfamiliar test situations while the difference was not significant when phonic knowledge was measured in familiar words in an intriguing finding. The degree of understanding of sound-symbol association differs for the upper and lower deviate groups although the measured scores show little difference in the familiar test situation. This may indicate a real difference in the ability of children of similar intellectual level to transfer what they know from one situation to another. On the other hand, it may be related to the various methods of teaching used with these children or to the particular testing procedure used in this study. (25, p. 454)

For a doctoral study at the State University of Iowa, Louise Beltramo (4) formulated an alphabetical approach* "for helping first grade children develop independent word-attack skills useful in identifying words in their everyday reading." An experimental group of five classes of one hundred twenty first grade children received an extra period of "word recognition instruction" for twenty minutes each day during the first semester and twenty-five minutes three times each week during the following semester. The control group of eighty-six children received only the regular program. "The teachers carried on the entire reading program in their usual manner, which it was assumed would exemplify the emphasis and practices provided for fostering independent word recognition in the average classroom."

The groups were tested before and after the experimental training period. From her study, Beltramo concluded that children taught by this experimental procedure made higher reading scores but that the results were not statistically significant. The "children who ranked in the upper third of the class" were definitely helped in reading achievement. Further, she stated, "First grade children can learn the phonic readiness skills as well as the basic phonic skills. For most children, systematic instruction is important for gaining proficiency in these skills." Spelling ability was also helped by the experimental procedures. (4, p. 2290)

Mary Watkins (28) in a recent (1953) doctoral dissertation compared the reading proficiencies of children who were progressing normally through school with children of the same IQ and reading level but who were "retarded readers." She selected "third grade children making normal progress in reading and children of grades 4, 5, and 6, reading at the third grade level." Sixty-four pairs were selected from among these children. Each pair consisted of one retarded and one normal-progress pupil. These were matched for mean reading grade, IQ, and sex. After testing these children with standardized tests, Watkins stated: "Retarded readers seem to possess more phonetic knowledge

---

*No explanation was given as to the nature of this "alphabetical approach" in the abstract of the dissertation which the writers read. Beltramo does refer to "phonic readiness skills."

than the normal-progress group but the retarded readers do not apply this knowledge." (28, p. 644)

In the spring of 1954, Ralph Bedell and Eloise Nelson (3) reported results of a study involving regularly enrolled fourth, fifth, and sixth graders of the middle school of the National Cathedral School for Girls, Washington, D.C. Working with these sixty pupils of "superior intellectual ability and of high socioeconomic level," the investigators gave the experimental group (one-half of the students) instruction in three kinds of word attack—"meaning involving the use of context clues and expectancy of words and concepts; visual, involving visual characteristics of words (identification of known parts within words, use of syllabification, use of prefixes, suffixes, and root words); sound attack, sounding of vowels, consonants, vowel and consonant combinations, and use of other methods of phonetic analysis." Instruction was offered for thirty minutes a day for fifteen days. In all other respects the experimental and control groups had similar training. Tests were given before and after the training period. In addition, pupils in the experimental group wrote daily self-evaluations of each exercise.

Bedell and Nelson state that the experimental group was superior and that "net changes in total scores received by the combined fourth, fifth, and sixth grades on the pre-test and post-test were found to be statistically significant at the .05 level of confidence." (3, p. 173) They concluded that the procedures used in their study produced superior results and could be used with other elementary school children advantageously.

In 1954 Lloyd Dunn (11) reported a study of certain aspects of the reading of mentally normal and mentally retarded boys of the same mental age. Dunn selected boys of mental age 8-10 and tested them by means of various standardized tests.

From the test results, Dunn concluded that

as to qualitative aspects of the reading process, clear-cut differences appear to exist between mentally retarded and normal boys of the same mental age in ability to use context clues; retarded boys are very inferior in this skill. While reading, they tend to make more faulty vowels and ommissions of sounds than mentally normal boys; they make, significantly, fewer repetitions. There would appear to be no differences between the two groups of boys in tendency to make reversal errors, in handedness, in mixed lateral preference, or in speed of recognition of phrases and words.

A number of other factors probably do contribute to the general reading disability of mentally retarded boys. As compared with mentally normal boys of comparable mental ages, they tend to have an excessive number of hearing and vision difficulties. On the basis of teacher ratings, they appear to be more maladjusted, and to come from inferior home backgrounds; parent-child relations in the homes of handicapped children tend to be particularly poor. (11, p. 300)

CONCLUDING STATEMENT

In this paper the writers have reviewed research concerning the place and value of phonics in a reading program. From this review one may conclude that the nature and amount of phonic instruction to be given is still a debatable question. Adherents to any one of a number of positions may find justification for their views in published sources from the devotees of the doctrine of "no phonics" to the advocates of a highly artificial approach. Despite this fact certain trends do appear and certain recommendations may be made tentatively.

A readiness program for phonics can safely be recommended, since research studies substantiate the need for phonic readiness. Moreover, many phonic systems appear to be difficult for most five and some six year old children. Such children frequently become hopelessly confused and discouraged after exposure to involved systems of phonics instruction. Mental age and other factors are important in determining the propriety of using a phonics approach. Hence phonic readiness should be ascertained before instruction is offered. In this respect, the findings of the research studies are in accord with the experience of teachers.

Phonic systems may develop a tendency in children to recognize words piecemeal. This emphasis results, particularly when the method is used apart from a meaningful approach in very slow reading. The child is often so hampered by his attempts to sound out each part of a word that he fails to react to natural, larger perception units in oral and in silent reading. The research studies indicate this limitation of phonic systems.

Another limitation of phonics instruction is that it does not utilize other techniques that bring about quick, accurate word recognition. Children and adults often recognize words quickly, as wholes, and often recognize groups of words with rapidity too. The good reader does not see each letter or all the letters. He may, for example, respond to the total form of the word and thus be aided in recognition of it. Accordingly, a soundly conceived program of word recognition is not limited to phonic procedures. Instead, it is a broad program associated with meaningful reading; it utilizes phonics as only one part of the total approach. Again, the research studies point to the merits of this broader program of word recognition.

Many children do need help in the mastery of phonic skills although some appear to have made satisfactory progress in reading without formal instruction Therefore, a system of careful diagnosis of individual needs should precede the introduction of instruction in word analysis at all levels. Many workers believe that phonic instruction is particularly effective with some disabled or very retarded readers. It is, however, not the only procedure employed nor the sole procedure used with such readers.

The value of phonic approaches with very poor readers is suggested by the work of one of the writers in association with Norma Olson (32) In this study, work began with experience charts. After a basic stock of sight words was mastered, phonic exercises were introduced. These exercises were designed to give practice in the application of principles formulated by the pupils themselves. With older pupils this approach proved particularly successful. Several of the research studies agree with these findings.

It is well to remember that many basal reading programs give attention to phonics adequate to meet the needs of most children. If children fail to acquire competency under such a program, it is perhaps desirable to introduce some special approach. However, this work should always be articulated closely with the basal program and care should be taken to make the entire approach individually appropriate and meaningful. Phonetic study should begin with known words and an auditory-visual emphasis should be employed.

The research studies do *not* substantiate the contention of Flesch and others that we can have perfect readers by using a phonics approach at an early age. Some shortcomings "in our total instructional program—for which the causes are not in our methods but in our lack of teachers, classrooms and adequate supplies and equipment" (31, p. 35) affect our teaching of reading. To obtain better results, we need better prepared teachers, more adequate and improved instructional materials, and closer cooperation between homes and schools. There are other needs too. But these needs do not include another system of phonics to be employed by parents with children at age five on the assumption that the use of this system will solve our reading problems. (31)

References

1. Agnew, Donald C. *The Effect of Varied Amounts of Phonetic Training on Primary Reading.* Duke University Research Studies in Education Number 5. Durham, N.C.: Duke University Press, 1939.
2. Arthur, Grace. "A Quantitative Study of the Results of Grouping First Grade Classes According to Mental Age," *Journal of Educational Research,* Vol. XII (October, 1925), pp. 173-185.
3. Bedell, Ralph and Nelson, Eloise S. "Word Attack as a Factor in Reading Achievement in the Elementary School," *Educational and Psychological Measurement,* Vol. XIV (Spring, 1954), pp. 168-175.
4. Beltramo, Louise. "An Alphabetical Approach to the Teaching of Reading in Grade One." *Dissertation Abstract,* Vol. XIV, Part 3 (1954), p. 2290.
5. Browne, M. Dorothy. *Phonics as a Basis for Improvement in Reading.* Washington, D.C.: The Catholic University of America, 1939.
6. Carroll, Herbert A. "Effect of Intelligence upon Phonetic Generalization," *Journal of Applied Psychology,* Vol. XV (April, 1931), pp. 168-181.
7. Currier, Lillian B. and Duguid, Oliver C. "Phonics or No Phonics" *Elementary School Journal,* Vol. XVII (December, 1916), pp. 286-287.
8. Currier, Lillian B. "Phonics or No Phonics," *Elementary School Journal,* Vol. XXIII (February 1923), pp. 448-452.
9. Dolch, Edward and Bloomster, Maurine. "Phonic Readiness," *Elementary School Journal,* Vol. XXXVIII (November, 1937), pp. 201-205.

10. Dumville, Benjamin, "The Methods of Teaching Reading in the Early Stages," *School World,* Vol. XIV (1912), pp. 408-413.

11. Dunn, Lloyd M.C. "A Comparative Study of Mentally Retarded and Mentally Normal Boys of the Same Mental Age on Some Aspects of the Reading Process," *Dissertation Abstracts* Vol. XIV, Part Number 2 (1954).

12. Flesch, Rudolph. *Why Johnny Can't Read and What You Can Do About It.* New York: Harper and Brothers, 1955.

13. Garrison, S. C. and Heard, Minnie T. "An Experimental Study of the Value of Phonetics." *Peabody Journal of Education,* Vol. IX (July, 1931), pp. 9-14.

14. Gates, Arthur I. "Studies of Phonetic Training in Beginning Reading," *Journal of Educational Psychology,* Vol. XVIII (April, 1927), pp. 217-226.

15. Gates, Arthur I. and Russell, David H. "Types of Material, Vocabulary Burden, Word Analysis and Other Factors in Beginning Reading." *Elementary School Journal,* Vol. XXXIX (September and October, 1938), pp. 27-35; 119-128.

16. Gill, Edmund J. "Methods of Teaching Reading," *Journal of Experimental Pedagogy,* Vol. I (1911-1912), pp. 243-248.

17. Hassel, Mabel and Varley, Lillian. "A Reading Test," *Journal of Experimental Pedagogy,* Vol. II (1914), pp. 298-301.

18. McDowell, John B. "A Report on the Phonetic Method of Teaching Children to Read." *The Catholic Educational Review,* Vol. LI (October, 1953), pp. 506-519.

19. Mosher, Raymond M. "Some Results of Teaching Beginners by the Look-and-Say Method." *The Journal of Educational Psychology,* Vol. XIX (March, 1928), pp. 185-193.

20. Mosher, Raymond M. and Newhall, Sidney M. "Phonic Versus Look-and Say training in Beginning Reading," *The Journal of Educational Psychology,* Vol. XXI (October, 1930), pp. 500-506.

21. Rogers, Maurine V. "Phonetic Ability as Related to Certain Aspects of Reading at the College Level," *Journal of Experimental Education,* Vol. VI (June, 1938), pp. 381-395.

22. Russell, David H. "A Diagnostic Study of Spelling Readiness," *Journal of Educational Research,* Vol. XXVIII (May 1928), pp. 690-701.

23. Sexton, Elmer K. and Herron, John S. "The Newark Phonics Experiment," *The Elementary School Journal,* Vol. XXXVII (June, 1937), pp. 752-763.

24. Tate, Harry L. "The Influence of Phonics on Silent Reading in Grade I," *The Elementary School Journal,* Vol. XXXVII (June, 1937), pp. 752-763.

25. Templin, Mildred C. "Phonic Knowledge and Its Relation to the Spelling and Reading Achievement of Fourth Grade Pupils," *Journal of Educational Research,* Vol. XLVII (February, 1954), pp. 441-454.

26. Tiffin, Joseph and McKinnis, Mary. "Phonic Ability: Its Measurement and Relation to Reading Ability," *School and Society,* Vol. LI (February 10, 1940), pp. 190-192.

27. Valentine, C. W. "Experiments on the Methods of Teaching Reading," *Journal of Experimental Pedagogy,* Vol. II (1913-1914), pp. 99-112.

28. Watkins, Mary. "A Comparison of the Reading Proficiencies of Normal Progress and Reading Disability Cases of the Same IQ and Reading Level," *Dissertation Abstract,* Vol. XIV, Part Number 4 (1954), p. 644.

29. Wertham, Frederic. *Seduction of the Innocent,* New York: Rinehart and Company, Inc., 1953, 1954.

30. Winch, W. H. *Teaching Beginners to Read in England: Its Methods, Results and Psychological Bases.* Journal of Educational Research Monographs, Number 8. Bloomington, Illinois: Public School Publishing Company, 1925.

31. Witty, Paul "Public is Mislead on the Meaning of Reading," *The Nation's Schools,* Vol. LVI (July, 1955), pp. 35-40.

32. Witty, Paul and Olson, Norma. "Non-Readers in the High School—Two Case Studies," *Exceptional Children,* Vol. XVIII (March, 1952), pp. 161-167, 186.

33. Witty, Paul and Sizemore, Robert A. "Reading the Comics," *Elementary English,* (December, 1954 and January, 1955).

30. Development of Reading Skills*

HELEN ROBINSON

IN the past two or three years we have witnessed more interest in the teaching of reading skills than in any comparable period within my memory. The press, radio, television, parent groups, and professional meetings have brought to the fore many controversial issues in this area. This interest in the teaching of reading is indeed encouraging if those of us in schools maintain a calm and inquiring attitude, appraising carefully the values and the limitations of the techniques we use. But defense of the status quo is no substitute for scrutiny of our practices. Therefore the most urgent challenge to schools today is to take stock of the methods actually used by teachers, to appraise the results achieved, and to strengthen our reading programs in every possible way. Only after this is done can we interpret to the public, with confidence, our current practices in teaching reading. In this article I can do no more than highlight certain trends in the teaching of reading skills in the elementary and the high schools.

READINESS FOR READING

The first trend I wish to emphasize relates to reading readiness. We now strive to promote readiness for reading rather than leaving its development to time and chance. In the past, teachers frequently waited for children to become more mature in language skill, in intellectual ability, in social and emotional control, in visual and auditory discrimination, and even in their interest in learning to read.

Today, teachers know that language ability can be developed through experiences, provided they converse with children about the experiences. It is essential that pupils be given opportunity to express their own ideas so as to encourage the understanding and use of an ever increasing number of words. Many opportunities to share ideas, to discuss activities, and to explain how

*From *The Elementary School Journal,* 58 (February, 1958), 269-274. Copyright © 1958 by The University of Chicago Press. Reprinted by permission.

315

things come to be, accompanied by concrete demonstrations, enrich the meanings of words.

Research has shown that a stimulating environment can promote maximal use of intelligence and can actually increase scores made by pupils on intelligence tests. All children need direction and assistance to develop their intellectual potentialities, but this assistance is especially needed by children who score at the lower ranges, by underprivileged children, by those who come from lower socioeconomic levels, and by pupils in whose homes a language other than English is spoken.

Visual discrimination, essential to the perceiving of the intricate details of our words, can be increased through consistent attention to forms, shapes, likenesses, and differences in pictures and drawings. Subsequently comparisons of word forms are essential. Auditory discrimination can be sharpened through detailed study of words that rhyme, that begin with the same sound, that have the same number of sounds, and the like. All this attention is given to spoken words in preparation for associating them with printed symbols.

Finally, the desire to read can be quickened through reading aloud stories and factual materials on topics which interest young children. Many pupils come from homes where little use is made of printed materials. Hence teachers should seize every opportunity to demonstrate the wealth of pleasure and information available in books.

We cannot safely assume that all the reading abilities are ready to be tapped at age six. Indeed, the army literacy program of World War II showed that these readiness skills may not be mature by age eighteen or over; many servicemen failed to learn to read until a readiness program was instituted (1). It is clear, then, that we cannot wait for years of living to bring readiness for beginning reading. Instead, good teachers hasten children's progress in all aspects of readiness through well-planned programs to meet the specific needs of large and small groups and of individuals within each group.

Today, the notion of reading readiness has extended upward throughout the elementary school and the high school. All teachers are faced with the problem of evaluating the readiness of each pupil to read the books that are to be used in class. Many years ago when children were promoted from grade to grade, or to high school, only after they had reached a specified level of reading achievement, readiness was assured. But the promotion policies today consider the welfare of the whole child, and consequently reading achievement differs widely in any class. Some pupils are ready to read with ease the books normally allocated to their grade or class. Selected pupils are ready for more difficult materials, while others are far less mature in reading. Thus each teacher must not only ascertain the readiness of his pupils but must also develop the skills necessary to enable pupils to make continuous progress.

GETTING THE MEANING

The second skill I wish to emphasize is that of getting thought from printed or written symbols. This concept of reading for comprehension is not new, but it is of paramount importance.

Recent controversies have brought to the fore many misconceptions in the minds of laymen, selected teachers, and even some persons who claim to be reading specialists. Most of us realize that parents judge the reading ability of their children by the facility with which they pronounce the words in their readers. Few parents stop to question their children's facility in silent reading. They are frank in admitting their inability to determine whether their children get meaning from print. Thus it is not surprising that parents are inclined to distrust teachers who cannot clearly explain how they teach this skill or how they appraise pupil progress in this area. Today, then, school personnel from kindergarten through high school must be certain that they are teaching children to secure maximal meaning from printed and written materials. And they must also be prepared to demonstrate and explain their goals and procedures to the lay public.

In the primary grades, books and teacher-prepared materials are designed to take account of the realm of experience and understanding of children. This does not imply that we can ignore meaning. Instead, it becomes easier to show children that there is a literal meaning and that, in addition, meanings are implied. The person writing certain lines may mean to be humorous or serious, may feel happy or sad. To understand the intention of the writer requires reading beyond the literal meaning, reading more than the words themselves. Stories have sequence, so that the ordering of events and the selection of important events in a story can lay the foundation for finding main ideas and for outlining. Common words may have several meanings, and a single meaning may be expressed by more than one word. Books appropriate to the primary-grade level may contain conflicting information, and consequently children can learn early to decide which is correct.

At the middle-grade level, pupils move forward and read about experiences less familiar to them. This is the time when teachers must be certain that their pupils have some understanding of what it is like to live in Alaska or China or Mexico in order to comprehend what they read about these faraway peoples. It is the time when children must learn about the differences between living today and in the early years of our country. Children must be made sensitive to the background of the writer in order that they may accurately determine whether he is attempting to convince the reader, to explain an idea, or merely to state a fact.

At the middle-grade level the literal meaning should be made clear, but implied meanings are also stressed. Recognition of the feelings and convictions of writers is essential for this purpose. Evaluation for accuracy becomes prominent. The application of the information read is demonstrated in solving arithmetical problems, following science experiments, making articles in the shop, using a recipe, and in a multitude of other situations.

At the upper-grade levels, pupils have developed sufficient maturity to begin to examine, through reading, some of the simpler social and political problems of the times. Of course they are still gaining a background of our culture and that of others, of our scientific knowledge and how it came to be. But teachers need to challenge hasty conclusions and to foster in the reader the habit of getting information and evaluating it.

Students in high school may be getting their terminal education or be preparing for college. For students of either type, the meaning conveyed by print must be stressed. Now abstract words and concepts are met and should be understood. It is most important that young people who are terminating their formal education be truly prepared to read, with understanding, newspapers and magazines, as well as books. If these future citizens are not prepared to evaluate what they read and to reach reasonable decisions, they will be unable to take their places in our democracy and to preserve it.

To sum up, reading must be conceived as a process of comprehending ideas and securing information from written and printed materials. This skill must be developed consistently from the kindergarten through the high school.

RECOGNIZING THE WORDS

Important as meaning may be, it cannot be obtained without word recognition, which is the third trend I shall discuss. While a few children learn to recognize words before they come to school, and some others will learn to do so by trial and error, all children can profit from learning a variety of means for recognizing words.

Today, the majority of schools are committed to the technique of beginning with an idea that is vital to children and progressing to the printed word that conveys this idea. The word is later broken down into its basic sound elements, and the letters standing for the sounds take on names, just as people do. Still later, the names and the sounds of the letters and combinations of letters, the shape and form of the word, and the meaning of the context in which it appears serve as clues to identify an unknown word.

However, teachers who are dedicated to the exclusive use of one method or another can truly claim success. Studies have shown that proficiency in the various skills that combine to make up reading is achieved by different methods of teaching. For example, undue stress on the phonic method of word recognition leads to slow and accurate recognition of words and to more precise oral reading, but it results in slow silent reading and less skill in understanding what is read (2).

In contrast, the experience approach achieves a higher level of comprehension at a more rapid rate but gives limited skill in pronouncing words accurately and in unlocking unfamiliar words. Indeed, word-form and context clues are the chief resources of children taught in this manner, and these are not enough. For this reason the reading curriculums developed by most schools today include the use of many means for recognizing words.

However, if we face facts squarely, we recognize that, in spite of the prescribed curriculums, some teachers emphasize one or another approach to word recognition and may not systematically develop others to the level where they are useful. Hence some of the public criticism has served to sharpen our awareness of the assets and the liabilities of different methods for teaching word recognition and may result in more systematic teaching.

Another fact has been overlooked by many of us. While we recognize that children differ in a myriad of ways, we do not always take this knowledge into account when we teach word recognition. Some children learn more rapidly from the things they see, and others from the things they hear. Studies of retarded readers reveal that some have well-developed visual aptitudes, with poorly developed auditory aptitudes, and vice versa. We are prone to overlook these differences and to make exclusive use of the methods which prove most effective for the vast majority of children. We need more research to determine means for identifying those children who will learn to read more effectively by stressing one or another method. Furthermore, we must prepare teachers, both in teacher-training institutions and through in-service training, to adjust their methods to the needs of pupils. Perhaps a more penetrating insight on the part of teachers into why and how various methods operate, and less attention to following a pattern or a model, might achieve this goal.

Finally, teachers at every level, primary grade, middle and upper grades, or high school, are faced with the necessity for teaching word recognition. Retarded readers and slow learners are often kept with their age mates in the modern school. Average readers need practice to develop word recognition quickly and accurately. They need instruction to insure that they can unlock unfamiliar words independently. Our critics are right when they state that we cannot, and must not, teach by sight every single word a person is to meet. But in teaching word recognition, we must avoid failing "to see the forest for the trees." In more precise terms, let us remember that the ultimate goal of word recognition is to provide a basis for obtaining the author's message as he intended to convey it, with an understanding of the time and the setting in which it was written.

WORD MEANINGS

As children and young people learn to use structural analysis and context clues as aids to word recognition, the same techniques should be applied to obtaining the meanings of words. Learning to use the dictionary is also an invaluable asset. Too often, children have to learn to use the dictionary in a trial-and-error fashion.

Introduction of the picture dictionary in the primary grades lays a good foundation for teaching efficient use of an easy dictionary in the middle grades. In the upper grades a good junior dictionary can be used, but in high school the students should be taught how to use an unabridged dictionary. Not only should they become proficient, through motivated practice, in locating the unknown word, but they should learn to pronounce it from the pronunciation key. Most important is skill in selecting the meaning appropriate to the context.

But few students, just as few of us adults, are motivated to look up all the words they need to learn. That is why direct instruction to increase the breadth and depth of vocabulary is essential, and it should be given in every subject of the curriculum. Studies have shown clearly that vocabulary growth is more rapid when direct instruction is given than when the instruction is only incidental. Hence all teachers at all academic levels should locate words unfamiliar to their class, usually before making the reading assignments. Experiences and discussion will serve to clarify meanings for the pupils.

Furthermore, individuals sometimes fail to get meaning from selections because of distortion of, or unfamiliarity with, word meanings. Such incidents should never go unnoticed, and individual instruction should be given to correct the misconceptions. In addition to unfamiliar words, many known words take on different meanings in specific fields. It is essential that such meanings be made clear to all pupils.

It is true that we cannot teach the meanings of all words that our pupils will encounter in life. Hence we need to promote independence here, as in all reading skills. Familiarity with the use of the glossary, the dictionary, encyclopedias, and other resources is needed. Also, a knowledge of the common prefixes, suffixes, and root words increases independence in securing word meanings.

New words should always come from their natural setting, that is, from context, and should be returned to this setting rather than being taken from a list, which is meaningless to the learner. At the high-school level, an interest in word origins can usually be developed. Knowledge of how words came to have their present meanings helps students to be alert to future changes in a language such as ours, which is far from static.

RATE OF READING

The fourth trend I see is toward so-called speed reading. This great desire to read faster and faster may be a symptom of our rushing social scene, or it may be a result of the demands made on most of us to keep up with the ever increasing flow of printed materials. Whatever the cause, elementary schools, high schools, colleges, and many adult programs are currently teaching people to read more rapidly. Before this stress on reading speed becomes a fad and destroys the major objective of understanding what we read, educators should weigh carefully some of the information available. Let us examine a few factors which should be considered in relation to rapid reading.

First, if we are agreed that reading is a process of thinking, then a person can read no more rapidly than he can think. Some children and adults have a rapid tempo, while for others it is slow. The person who reacts slowly cannot hope to read at top speeds. Thus it is not realistic to attempt to teach everyone to read at any given speed. We must expect individual differences in this skill just as in any other.

Second, the rate of reading must depend on the reader's purpose. If he is reading to secure the general idea of a selection, he may read very rapidly. However, if he wishes to get a clear grasp of all the facts presented, to weigh each fact in relation to others, or to evaluate what he reads, he may need to move very slowly.

Third, the degree of familiarity with the topic treated in a given selection influences reading rate. If the words and the concepts are fimiliar and readily understood, a more rapid rate is justified.

The foregoing considerations imply that a good reader has at his command a wide range of reading speeds. He selects the speed appropriate to his purpose and to the materials, just as an automobile has several speeds which we use for various purposes. My experience with people who read slowly is that they have only "low gear." The danger in teaching them to read more rapidly is that they will eventually have only "high gear," which, for many purposes, is totally inadequate. To avoid this dilemma, those who teach rapid reading must be sure that the material and the purpose justify a rapid speed. In addition, teachers must check regularly to be sure that the learner is able to move to slower speeds as they are needed. A continuous evaluation of comprehension appropriate to the reader's purpose is essential whenever reading rate is stressed.

But the silent-reading rate should increase gradually from the primary grades into adult life. Good teachers at every developmental stage and in all subject area should clarify the purpose for reading each assignment—whether it is to be read slowly and thoughtfully, or rapidly for a general idea of the contents. If this plan is followed, our next generation will acquire a flexibility of reading rates which should eliminate the need for a large portion of the adult speed-reading programs in current use.

MAINTAINING INTEREST IN READING

Of course proficiency in one or all of the reading skills is of no consequence if the process of teaching these skills destroys the learner's interest in reading or fails to give him satisfaction as a result of reading. Therefore the application of the reading skills is of vital importance in producing a literate population.

To get pupils to use their reading skills, we must rely on feeding children's interests. Finding the right book at the right time for any pupil will do the trick. This is no easy task, and it implies that we teachers must become familiar with the dominant interests of each child—not just what he will take without objection, but what he will pursue eagerly. A "good" book concerned with this interest, written on a level at which he can read without faltering, gives the child pleasure. If he finds pleasure and profit in reading, he will read more.

Let us not spoil the child's fun in free reading by "questioning him to death" on what is read. Instead, let us find out why the child liked the book, what he considered the most exciting part, what he disliked, and, finally, what he would like to read next.

If we consistently teach reading skills, and if we are always certain that children are getting pleasure from reading, we may be sure that tomorrow's adults will be better readers than those of today.

References

1. Goldberg, Samuel. *Army Training of Illiterates in World War II.* Teachers College Contributions to Education, No. 966. New York: Bureau of Publications, Teachers College, Columbia University, 1951.
2. Gray, William S. *The Teaching of Reading and Writing: An International Survey,* chap. vi. Monographs on Fundamental Education, X. Paris: United Nations Educational, Scientific and Cultural Organization, 1956. (Distributed in the United States by Scott, Foresman and Company, Chicago 11, Illinoise.)

31. How to Develop Concepts
and Their Verbal Representations[*]

MARY C. SERRA

Illinois State University,
Normal, Illinois

THE attempts to define the word "concept" have been many, but as yet there has been little agreement on an adequate definition. For empirical purposes, however, Dewey's definition is commonly accepted: "Concept" is defined as a "meaning sufficiently individualized to be directly grasped and readily used, and thus fixed by a word" (7:60).[1]

Concepts exist at all levels of complexity. A concept can be based on one experience with an object or upon a multitude of experiences, and it will increase in complexity with the amount of experience. It can be based on varying degrees of relationships among objects. Concepts of increasing levels of complexity are based on a hierarchy of concepts dealing with objects and their relationships. Concepts are also symbolized and verbalized by the individual, and the symbols or words in themselves become new concepts with a new hierarchy.

Verbalization, however, is not essential to indicate the existence of a concept. Behavior may demonstrate the acquisition of a concept. It is obvious that the fourteen-month-old toddler who, having once touched a hot stove, thereafter avoids all stoves has a well-established concept of a hot stove. He has in no way, however, the ability to verbalize his experience with a stove.

READING CONCERNED WITH VERBALIZED CONCEPTS

Research that attempts to deal with concepts as related to the reading process is concerned with verbalized concepts. The investigator must realize that any printed statement of a concept is only one expression out of an almost unlimited number that the author might have used. Hence, failure of a child to acquire the concept through reading may arise from poor choice of expression by the author rather than from weakness in the child.

[*]From *The Elementary School Journal*, 53 (January, 1953), 275-285. Copyright © 1953 by The University of Chicago Press. Reprinted by permission.

[1]Numbers in parentheses refer to references at the end of the article.

The approach beginning with printed material becomes involved in word meaning. Through general agreement, certain sounds, symbolized in writing by certain combinations of letters, are called "words," and certain meanings are attached to certain words. The question is simply whether a child is aware of, and in accord with, the common agreement concerning each word. But most words have multiple meanings; that is, they symbolize different concepts. All concepts that have been verbalized can be expressed in many ways, through the use of different words and of different syntactical devices. There is a distinct tendency for research dealing with concepts to bog down into investigations of word meanings.

Numerous experimenters investigating the area of concepts have been interested in determining best teaching procedures rather than in establishing principles of how to develop concepts. Inferences drawn from research into the way concepts develop and from the factors that influence their development provide the needed principles.

DIRECT EXPERIENCE

Findings from a review of research on factors influencing concept development indicate that the more direct the experience on which the concept is built, the greater will be the individual's knowledge and understanding of that concept.

Experience is necessary in order to build concepts. It is impossible, however, for any person to develop all the concepts needed in modern life on the basis of direct experience alone. Vicarious experience must be utilized, much of which will be received through the medium of language. When verbal symbols are added to the stock of established concepts, it is essential that these initial concepts be formed on the basis of direct experience. In order to build concepts, then, it is necessary to provide experience in order to establish the simple concepts that will be subsequently combined and manipulated to form the more complex concepts. Concepts that can be traced back only to verbal language or to symbols acquired through language result in mere verbalism.

Margaret Bedwell's investigation (2) established the fact that it is possible to have verbal or factual knowledge without having a functional concept. Using twenty-one third-grade children, she determined their comprehension of the number of concepts they read in their geography and history books. Actual experience, as she pointed out, is the most important factor in concept development.

Sister M. B. Herbers (13) investigated the comprehension difficulties of thirty third-grade pupils as they used third-grade readers. This study indicated that concrete materials and personal experiences are necessary to overcome verbalism. Herbers' findings were substantially as follows:

1. Pupils revealed inadequate and incorrect concepts of words, phrases, and sentences.

2. Materials which were used by the pupils with facility showed hazy and erroneous concepts.

3. There was a lack of understanding of all items to which there were correct responses in the yes-no or multiple-choice test.

Osburn, Huntington, and Meeks (22) experimented with vicarious experience between the levels of direct experience and of verbalization. The population for this study included sixty-seven kindergarten children. A series of exercises composed entirely of pictures, illustrating various relationships between the pictures, was used. The findings were that experiences with pictures, illustrations, models, and the like should be used to make concrete the relationships implied in language.

Phipps (23), too, pointed out that concrete experience is important in the development of concepts. His subjects were in five sixth-grade classes. An experimental group was given an overview of the material presented orally by the teacher; visual aids were used; and important words were posted and used in drill. The control group was not drilled on vocabulary. No check was made to find whether the children actually understood the concepts that they used in their history readings. This was a study to determine whether history-reading ability was improved through special attention to development of readiness for vocabulary and aid in use of vocabulary. Phipps concluded that adequate preparation through concrete experience is a necessary component for units of classwork.

Sachs (25) made the point that children do not acquire concepts by merely meeting words in context. He worked with 416 Freshmen in college to determine the extent of their meaning vocabulary. His study shows the limitations of the reading method of improving vocabulary. The work of Sims (28) emphasizes that the role of experience is of utmost importance in the development of concepts, and Stolte (29), working with geographical concepts, drew the same conclusions. Wiedefeld (34), in the field of history, concluded that building concepts necessitates the providing of experiences.

VOCABULARY DEVELOPMENT

Much of the research devoted to determining the most effective means of increasing vocabulary assumes that enlargement of vocabulary is in itself a virtue, without questioning the dimensions of the concepts with which words are associated. In that direction lies verbalism. In the mass, however, this research demonstrates that vocabulary is increased by experiences of two kinds: (1) experience with the raw materials of the concepts for which given words are symbols, that is, experience with objects and processes and with lower-level concepts on which the required concepts are built; and (2) experience with the given word itself, that is, hearing the word, speaking the word, and reading and writing it. Experience with the raw materials of concepts develops the concept; experience with the word associates word and concept.

Dunkel's conclusion (8) that the ability to determine the precise meaning of a word is related to the ability to read with comprehension gives the clue to the reason for the great number of investigations of word meaning and vocabulary development. He constructed a new type of vocabulary test because he was dissatisfied with the conventional test which assumes a "core meaning" or "sphere of meaning" for each word. These tests, he felt, did nothing to test the student's interpretation of the precise meaning taken on by a word used in a particular situation. In Dunkel's test, each word tested was used in a paragraph and then in five sentences. Subjects were to mark the item which had the same meaning as the word in the paragraph. This test was administered to subjects in Grades X, XII, and XIV. Dunkel concluded, in effect:

    1. The ability to determine the precise meaning of a word is related to the ability to read with comprehension.
    2. Education and maturity lead to development of the ability to determine the precise meaning of a word.

The studies cited below (in chronological order of publication) are among the more conspicuous of those dealing with vocabulary building.

Haefner (12) found that it seemed possible to improve the vocabulary of a group of adults by merely exposing them for a few minutes each day to a new word. Vocabulary is acquired, in part, by casual learning. Vocabulary can also be acquired by formal drill. Newburn's study (21) of the relative effect exerted by two methods of vocabulary drill on achievement in history gave evidence to this effect. Liddell (15) confirmed Newburn's findings. She also found that, as children encounter unknown words in their reading, different methods of word drill vary in effectiveness. She investigated the relative effectiveness of four methods of teaching word meanings to 236 pupils in Grades IV and V:

    1. The "telling" method was most effective. In it, the teacher and the children discussed the "unknown" words, gave definitions, illustrative sentences, and synonyms.
    2. The "context" method, in which the children figured out meanings from context and the teacher checked the results following class discussion, was second in the order of effectiveness.
    3. The "picture" method, in which children attempted to determine meanings of words from appropriate illustrations, was third in order of effectiveness.
    4. The "dictionary" method, in which the children attempted to

determine meanings from dictionaries, was the least effective of the four methods.

Liddell's study indicates that class discussion under teacher direction is the most effective method of vocabulary drill. In this investigation, however, the children were not necessarily acquiring new concepts but were, in most instances, merely associating words and concepts.

Gray and Holmes (11) studied exhaustively the development of meaning vocabulary. In a series of studies involving subjects in Grade IV, they investigated methods of developing meaning vocabularies in reading. The experimental groups were offered specific vocabulary help to form clear, vivid associations between word meanings and the written symbols. In the control group no guidance was given except as the children asked individually for help. The conclusions were:

1. *a)* Specific, direct help in developing meaning brings greater vocabulary growth then incidental learning of meaning.

b) Stock of "sight" words may be greatly expanded by encountering new words in material read.

c) Growth is stimulated if the author makes frequent use of defintions, illustrations, etc., in explaining meanings.

d) Discussions attendant on a unit tend to expand and enrich meaning associations with words.

e) Pupils with limited vocabularies are not able to grasp meanings of new words readily without specific help.

f) Specific guidance in vocabulary development is of particular value with pupils of limited initial achievement and limited mental ability.

g) Context is the chief aid to development of meaning when specific guidance is not given.

h) When direct guidance is given in learning meanings, gains are uniform for verbs, nouns, and adjectives.

i) When children are not taught word meanings, verbs are learned most readily, nouns next, and adjectives least readily.

2. *a)* Direct methods of vocabulary development are helpful in improving students' use of new words in written composition.

b) Direct methods of vocabulary development result in greater fluency in oral discussion than does the incidental method.

3. Direct methods of vocabulary development bring greater improvement:

a) in accuracy of word recognition than does the incidental method.

b) in fluency in silent reading (fewer fixations, shorter fixations, etc.).

c) in detail and accuracy of comprehension, grasp of relationships, and organization of ideas obtained from reading material.

Using a population of sixty-eight sub-Freshmen of a junior high school,

Traxler (30) concluded that reasonably permanent gains in vocabulary can be made through drill. He found that word meaning is learned by studying the definitions, by reading, and by making sentences using the word. Mere reading of a word was not particularly effective.

Waring (32) investigated the relative values of the intensive and the incidental methods of teaching vocabulary to thirty-four high-school students. Her research produced some pertinent findings: (1) Intensive training in vocabulary using specific words leads to greater gains in general vocabulary than does the incidental method of word study. (2) Intensive training in vocabulary leads to greater gains in knowledge of specific words than does the incidental method. The findings of Waring's study imply:

1. Intensive training makes pupils "word-conscious" and leads to gains in general vocabulary.
2. Specific training in prefixes, suffixes, and roots adds definitely to general vocabulary gains.
3. Studying a word in context and building as many settings for it as possible help to fix the word in mind, give the symbol a frame of reference, and sharpen its meaning.
4. It would appear that pupils in the first quarter gain the most from intensive vocabulary study.

For one hundred junior high school pupils, Waters (33) found that thorough study of meanings and uses of specific words improves comprehension of the words studied. Her experimental group was given instruction requiring the use of the dictionary; engaged in class discussion of "new" words; used exercises in selecting most accurate, vivid, and colorful words, and the most specific words; and kept vocabulary notebooks. The control group received no special training in vocabulary. Waters concluded:

1. Pupils did not accept the responsibility of becoming acquainted with words they did not know.
2. Pupils did improve slightly in word knowledge as a result of their everyday contacts, even though they received no special training on the words.
3. Systematic "drill" evidenced greater effectiveness than mere incidental treatment of vocabulary.

At the sixth-grade level, Phipps (23) concluded that wide experience with words and with the concepts they symbolize is essential to the improvement of the reading of history materials. Readiness for reading history materials is achieved by building concepts and making vocabulary meaningful.

Curoe and Wixted (5,6) found that a short period of direct instruction in word study will result in enriching the vocabulary of college Seniors. Blair (3) drew similar conclusions from an experiment with college Juniors as well as Seniors.

Studying the reading vocabularies of fifth-grade pupils, Sanderson (26) found that many children lack adequate understanding of words met in their informational reading. She concluded that direct instruction in developing and clarifying meanings of words will increase the reading vocabulary and, in addition, will be an aid in general language development.

The study of Bradley, Cahill, and Tate (4) using fifth- and eighth-grade pupils demonstrated that clarification of meaning is an important factor in acquiring a reading vocabulary. It further pointed out that composing sentences with new words added no further meanings to those previously learned.

From the conclusions of the Shannon and Kittle (27) research, word study alone is not enough. Using 336 pupils from Grades VIII–XII, inclusive, they attempted to determine whether pupils remember the meanings of words when intensive word study is required. They found:

1. Vocabulary cannot be taught effectively by cramming. Although considerable immediate vocabulary learnings may result from cramming, they are not permanent.

2. Pupils who are told the meanings of words by their teachers, or by means of glossaries, learn more than those who look the words up in dictionaries.

3. When the purpose of a learning exercise is vocabulary development, the placing of a large number of words in continuous context has no advantage, and it is more helpful to underline the words in context than to leave them for the pupils to seek the meanings of without such motivation [27:6].

Shannon and Kittle did not determine the extent to which concepts existed prior to the attempt to learn the meanings of new words. It can be conjectured that at the secondary-school level the experimenters selected as "new" words many that required the building of new concepts as well as the association of words and concepts.

Sachs (25) demonstrated that it is possible for adolescents to have encountered words in their reading many times without having learned their meanings. Something more than wide reading is necessary for vocabulary-building.

MULTIPLE MEANINGS OF WORDS

Related to, but somewhat opposed to, the research in vocabulary-building is the research in semantics. The investigator in vocabulary meaning assumes that the more words the child knows, the more readily will his concepts be formed.

The semanticist says, "Words do not mean what they say." But through semantics, another factor influencing concept development is recognized, namely, the multiple meanings of words.

The real significance of multiple meanings arises from the fact that we must receive so many of our concepts through stimuli in the form of words, spoken or written. For the reception of spoken or written language, there must be agreement upon the meanings of words. When words may have from one to a score of accepted meanings, the recipient is faced with a large sorting task with each sentence he reads or hears. Let him fail to sort out the intended meaning of a word, and the concepts he forms may be totally wrong.

A growing mass of research deals with the multiple meanings of words. A brief review of the pertinent work in this area will establish the fact that multi-meaning is a factor influencing concept development.

Foster (9) found that words possessing the largest number of meanings tend to be used more often with more different meanings than those possessing a smaller number of meanings. He gathered 1,976 compositions on 500 topics from pupils in 38 school systems in 13 states. His purpose was to determine the "socially" important meanings with which 100 selected words of high frequency usage were used in a wide and representative sampling of written composition. Words were placed in the following four groups (examples of the words listed are included here):

1. Group I.—Words with 45 or more meanings: *(a) point*, 110 meanings; *(b) take*, 106 meanings; *(c) cut*, 108 meanings.
2. Group II.—Words with 27-44 meanings: *(a) bed, (b) board, (c) small.*
3. Group III.—Words with 15-26 meanings: *(a) book, (b) church, (c) picture.*
4. Group IV.—Words with 13 or fewer meanings: *(a) act, (b) boy, (c) fear* [9: 294].

He concluded that (1) the number of meanings with which the check words in the study are used is more dependent upon the number of meanings the word has than is the frequency with which the word occurs; (2) approximately half of the total meanings with which multi-meaning words are used appear to be socially important; (3) the socially important meanings of the large majority of the words bear 70 per cent or more of the total usage of the word; and (4) words with the largest number of meanings tend to be used with a larger number of socially important meanings than do words possessing a smaller number of meanings.

In her study on the meaning load of two books, Bachmann (1) found that 1,291 words had more than one meaning: (1) 676 had 2 meanings, (2) 327 had 3 meanings, (3) 107 had 4 meanings, and (4) 181 had 5-25 meanings. She found that emotional experiences become associated with meanings and senses of verbal symbols just as surely as with more concrete objects and symbols of environment. Meaning is a function of the ideational and emotional experiences of the interpreter and user of verbal symbols. The kind of thought or idea that the reader gets from the printed page is not identical with that of the writer, nor will it be identical among a group of readers even with a homogeneous background.

Lobby (16,17) found that many meanings and shades of meanings are derived from the same material even though the individuals are in the same group under the same instructor. A selection was taught very thoroughly to a group of seventy-seven sixth-grade subjects. The passage that was taught was then used as a basis for understanding a second and a third passage from the same book. The second and third selections were developed through silent reading. The subjects were tested on the second and third passages. The findings were:

1. Children had difficulty in expressing their thoughts in writing.
2. Median scores on the tests averaged 64 per cent.
3. Children understood slightly more than 60 per cent of the words encountered in their reading.

In an investigation conducted by Richards (24) it was found that meanings tend to be dependent upon the multiple contexts in which they occur. Appropriate meanings at any given time depend upon the total context or setting. When words out of living context are considered in the classroom, relevance to the child's experience is lost, and the word is therefore drained of meaning.

Lange conducted an investigation to determine, "through analysis of language situations and responses, the extent to which certain terms in educational psychology have common meanings for lecturers and students in an undergraduate core course in the psychology and practice of teaching (14:642). *Curriculum* and *individual differences* are examples of the terms selected. His findings are paraphrased below:

1. From one semester's study of word meanings, 45 important terms in education did not have meanings in common for 168 students and the instructors.
2. Meanings of the terms remained relatively unchanged.

Lange concluded that there are vague, varied, and contradictory meanings for terms which name important concepts. Thus, there is reason to question the effectiveness of current instructional practices in the area of psychology and the practice of teaching.

Strong (30) found that pupils use different meanings for words of high frequency on lexical counts. She conducted a study on the meanings used for 50 high-frequency words by 490 subjects in Grade V. The words were selected from 4,073 spontaneous writings of pupils in 12 curriculum fields. Examples of words used are *make* and *pocket.* Strong found that a comparison of the occurrence of individual check words indicated that the range of occurrence was from 1,439 times for *make* to five times for *pocket.* The total number of running words was 353,641. Her conclusion was that the range of frequency and occurrence for the different meanings of the check words used by the pupils was large. Fifth-grade pupils made use of 17 per cent of the 2,849 meanings for the words selected in this study.

Fries and Traver (10) found that the 850 words of Basic English represent 12,425 meanings in the *Oxford English Dictionary,* with 5,991 added senses not separately numbered.

In his study of the multiple meanings of words, Lorge (18, 19) found that the assumption that words of high frequency are readily understood is erroneous. Words like *game,* which appears among the first thousand words in Thorndike's list,[1] may be used with as many as fifteen meanings. Many of the most frequently used words are multi-meaning in value. No grading of vocabulary load can be made without reference to meaning. It will be discovered that the vocabulary load, even in primers, is not a function of the number of different words so much as it is a function of different meanings that pupils must understand and use.

Using college students, Lovell (20) conducted a study to determine the "Interrelations of Vocabulary Skills: Commonest vs. Multiple Meanings." He found that (1) 43 per cent of the common basic words have multiple meanings and (2) that the average number of multiple meanings known by students was 145 out of a possible 222. Apparently intensity, or richness of vocabulary, is fairly closely related to extensiveness, or knowledge of single most common words; for general purposes one may be estimated from the other.

One means of developing concepts is through extending vocabularies. The investigations of Blair (3), Curoe and Wixted (5, 6), Gray and Holmes (11), Haefner (12), Liddell (15), Newburn (21), Sachs (25), Sanderson (26), Shannon and Kittle (27), Traxler (31), Waring (32), and Waters (33)—all point out that direct study of words and their meanings is productive in extending vocabulary.

SUMMARY

A review of research indicates that concepts are better developed when these conditions are present.

---

[1]Edward L. Thorndike, *A Teacher's Word Book of the Twenty Thousand Words Found Most Frequently and Widely in General Reading for Children and Young People.* New York: Bureau of Publications, Teachers College, Columbia University, 1931.

1. Provision is made for a wide range of experiences, vicarious as well as direct.

2. Careful instruction in word study should be provided to extend vocabularies and knowledge of word meanings. In this instruction, high-level concepts should be related to those at lower levels, and careful differentiation must be made between mere verbalism and established concepts.

3. The multiple meanings of words provide a means of developing concepts based on vicarious experiences received through language. It must be recognized, however, that high-frequency words are not readily understood, although many of the most frequently used words are multi-meaning in value.

References

1. Bachmann, Helen. "Semantic Study of Books of Two Authors Dealing with Classical Antiquity," *The Graduate School Abstracts of Theses,* pp. 16-27. University of Pittsburgh Bulletin, Vol. XL, No. 3. Pittsburgh, Pennsylvania: University of Pittsburgh, 1944.
2. Bedwell, Margaret. "Comprehension of Concepts of Quantity in Third Grade Social Studies Reading Material." Unpublished Master's thesis, University of Iowa, 1932.
3. Blair, Glenn Myers. "An Experiment in Vocabulary Building," *Journal of Higher Education,* XII (February, 1941), 99-101.
4. Bradley, Martha H., Loretta A. Cahill and Harry L. Tate. "Acquisition of a Reading Vocabulary," *Elementary English Review,* XVIII (January, 1941), 19-21, 32.
5. Curoe, Philip R. V. "An Experiment in Enriching the Active Vocabularies of College Seniors," *School and Society,* XLIX (April, 1939), 522-24.
6. Curoe, Philip R. V., and William G. Wixted. "A Continuing Experiment in Enriching the Active Vocabularies of College Seniors," *School and Society,* LII (October, 1940), 372-76.
7. Dewey, John. *How We Think.* Boston: D. C. Heath & Co., 1910.
8. Dunkel, Harold B. "Testing the Precise Use of Words," *College English,* V (April, 1944), 386-89.
9. Foster, Harry Kittredge. "The Semantic Variations of Certain High Frequency Words in Written Composition of Eighth Grade Pupils" *Journal of Experimental Education,* XI (June, 1943), 293-97.
10. Fries, Charles C., with the co-operation of A. Aileen, Traver, for the Committee on Modern Languages of the American Council on Education. *English Word Lists,* pp. 73-93. Washington: American Council on Education, 1940.
11. Gray, William S., and Eleanor Holmes. *The Development of Meaning Vocabularies in Reading.* Publications of the Laboratory Schools of the University of Chicago, No. 6 Chicago: University of Chicago Press, 1938.
12. Haefner, Ralph. "Casual Learning of Word Meanings," *Journal of Educational Research,* XXV (April-May, 1932), 267-77.
13. Herbers, Sister M. B. "Comprehension Difficulties in a Third Grade Reader," *Elementary English Review,* XVI (February, 1939), 53-57.
14. Lange, Philip C. "Study of Concepts Developed by Students in an Undergraduate Course in the Psychology and Practice of Teaching," *Journal of Educational Research,* XXXVI (May, 1943), 641-61.
15. Liddell, Glenda Lucille. "An Experimental Investigation of Methods of Teaching Word Meanings." Unpublished Master's thesis, University of Southern California, 1931.

16. Looby, Ruth. "The Meanings Derived by Children from Words and Phrases in Literature." Unpublished Doctor's dissertation, University of Iowa, 1937.
17. Looby, Ruth. "Understandings Children Derive from Their Reading," *Elementary English Review,* XVI (February, 1939), 58-62.
18. Lorge, Irving. "The English Semantic Count," *Teachers College Record,* XXXIX (October, 1937), 65-77.
19. Lorge, Irving. "Word Lists as Background for Communication," *Teachers College Record,* XLV (May, 1944), 543-52.
20. Lovell, George D. "Interrelations of Vocabulary Skills: Commonest vs. Multiple Meanings," *Journal of Educational Psychology,* XXXII (January, 1941), 67-72.
21. Newburn, Harry K. "The Relative Effect of Two Methods ot Vocabulary Drill on Achievement in American History," Unpublished Doctor's dissertation, University of Iowa, 1934.
22. Osburn, W. J., Mirriel Huntington, and Viola Meeks. "The Language of Relativity as Related to Reading Readiness," *Journal of Educational Research,* XXXIX (April, 1946), 583-601.
23. Phipps, William Rodgers. *An Experimental Study in Developing History Reading Ability with Sixth Grade Children through the Development of History Vocabulary.* Johns Hopkins University Studies in Education, No. 28. Baltimore: Johns Hopkins Press, 1940.
24. Richards, I. A. *How to Read a Page.* New York: W. W. Norton & Co., 1942.
25. Sachs, H. J. "The Reading Method of Acquiring Vocabulary," *Journal of Educational Research,* XXXVI (February, 1943), 457-64.
26. Sanderson, Marion. "An Experiment in the Developing of Meaning Vocabularies," *Studies and Summaries,* pp. 31-35. Prepared by HUGH S. BONAR, Manitowoc, Wisconsin: Public Schools, 1941.
27. Shannon, J. R., and Marian A. Kittle. "An Experiment in Teaching Vocabulary," *Teachers College Journal,* XIV (September, 1942), 1-6.
28. Sims, Ruth Lytle. "Concept Analysis of Primers and Preprimers," *Elementary English Review,* XV (December, 1938), 302-5.
29. Stolte, Helen B. "The Ability of Fourth Grade Children to Comprehend Certain Geographical Concepts." Unpublished Master's thesis, University of Iowa, 1935.
30. Strong, Laverne. "A Study of the Meanings Used for Certain High Frequency Words by Fifth Grade Pupils." Unpublished Doctor's dissertation, Pennsylvania State College, 1947.
31. Traxler, Arthur E. "Improvement of Vocabulary through Drill," *English Journal,* XXVII (June, 1938), 491-94.
32. Waring, Doris Vivian Adams. "An Evaluation of Extensive and Incidental Methods of Teaching Vocabulary." Unpublished Master's thesis, University of Michigan, 1939.
33. Waters, Betty. "A Teaching Project in Language Vocabulary Enrichment." Unpublished Master's thesis, University of Iowa, 1939.
34. Wiedefeld, M. Theresa. *An Experimental Study in Developing History Reading-Readiness with Fourth Grade Children.* Studies in Education, No. 31. Baltimore: Johns Hopkins University Press, 1942.

32. Spurs to Reading Competence*

LAURA ZIRBES

INCREASING competence in reading can be fostered and developed, but it takes more than instruction and training. Competence requires more than specific habits and skills. It is not a mere matter of rate and comprehension as measured by tests, nor is it something to be gained by drill lessons or formal practice exercises. Increasing competence is rather a matter of measuring up to ever more challenging reading situations as they arise in the course of experience—a matter of intelligent initiative and effective self-direction in the uses of reading as a resource, wherever it serves a need or purpose in living and learning, wherever it contributes to the satisfactions, meanings, and values that vicarious experience extends.

Reading competence is much more than a composite of techniques. It is a creative process of adaptive situational adjustments to emergent cues, a continuing quest, in which successive steps are inferred from what went before and projected situationally, as promising ways ahead—as alternatives to be tried and evaluated in action.

Now, it must be clear from what has been said so far that "all this" is contingent on interactive situational guidance that is not only insightful and flexible, but *dynamic* in its challenges to individuals and groups. Such guidance must provide the impetus to high endeavor and full involvement. It must provide access to suitable resources, and intrinsic incentives to inquiry and effort. Lessons and assignments are too didactic to suffice. No single text, no stereotyped procedure will serve as an adequate spur to the optimal level of involvement so characteristic of wholehearted developmental learning.

The first spur is the challenge to "note," to inquire, to discover. Creative guidance sets conditions that are the spurs to active attention, inquiry or discovery—to finding *out*, finding *why* or finding *how*. It seeks to *create* the questing concern, and provides it with conditions and resources that have promise of leading on, at whatever level.

*From *The Reading Teacher*, **15**, 1, 14-18. Reprinted with permission of the International Reading Association.

Competence in *beginning* reading is spurred by the realization that what has been "said" orally can also be "said" in print; that reading not only recovers what has been said orally and said in print, but can also recover what has been done or experienced, or put into oral or visual language, or expressed pictorially or in action.

Some *group* experiences are spurs to types of reading which contribute richly to competence. To illustrate, the following bona fide instances are cited:

A sudden devastating spring flood became an absorbing topic of spontaneous discussion in a school assembly. Subsequently the kindergarten group played it out with large blocks on the floor. The first grade dramatized the rescue scenes described in radio reports and pictured in newspapers. An intermediate grade was so impressed by the discussion that it undertook a study of *Great Rivers of the World,* and an upper grade projected a whole series of inquiries and reports on "Water—What Man Does With It, and What it Does to Man."

At a subsequent school assembly session several weeks later, these groups and others contributed in ways which illustrate how direct experience can become a real spur to increasing competence in reading. Children stopped to note titles of the flood pictures that had been posted in the school corridor by the upper primary groups. The lower intermediate class that had studied great rivers of the world presented several series of slides, each of which was about one of the world's great rivers—the Amazon, the Rhine, the Nile, the Ganges and the Mississippi. Panels of children interpreted the groups of slides, and exhibited the books which they had used as sources of information.

This program was a spur to several individual inquiries. The books, maps, travel folders, and copies of *National Geographic Magazine* that were used in these studies were assembled for an exhibit, during which each young exhibitor made a report and answered other children's questions. There were illustrations and reports on the following topics: Kinds of Bridges, Famous Bridges, Great Dams, Rapids and Waterfalls, River Stories. The story about log rafts led to the development of a study of the "History of Papermaking." This involved a great deal of purposeful selective reference reading as well as responsible proofreading in the preparation of a mimeographed class booklet to which individuals contributed.

In another school, an upper-grade report of a news item led to a discussion of colonialism. A boy said he wanted to read several versions of the history of Colonial America, one of which was written by a colonist. He said he was interested in what might be revealed by the differences between *that* account and *others* that were written at least a hundred years later. His interest was a spur to group thinking which led to the formulation of the following questions for study.

1. What evidences of Spanish exploration and colonization remain where American cities, mountains, or rivers have Spanish names?

2. What remains as evidence to indicate that other European nations had a part in colonizing America?

3. What were the issues which led the American colonist to fight the war for independence?

4. How is all this related to attitudes toward colonialism today?

It should be clear that satisfactory answers to such questions required competent reading, and that the experience of locating, selecting, and reporting pertinent information was a spur to increasing competence.

How different it would have been to read to answer ready-made questions succinctly stated on a blackboard or in a single required test, with a view to getting set for a recitation! It is interesting to consider how barren and uneducative this latter approach is, in comparison to the challenging spur to competent reading when inquiry itself is guided by a genuine data-gathering quest and a maturing concern for the location, selection, and cumulative consideration of pertinent information. The spurs to such reading are the dynamic factors which make for carry-over. The interactive consideration of findings is far more educative than the choice of alternatives in so-called "objective tests." The spurs to high scores on such tests should not be confused with spurs to broader, fuller competence in reading!

Effective teaching does much more than emphasize specific techniques, for it is a process contingent on creatively adaptive reading, fluid mind sets, judgments, and continuities of forward adjustment and needs. To develop competence, functional guidance and creatively adaptive interaction do what they can to foster fluid continuities of concern, flexibly responsible mind sets, judgments, and commitments. The quality of teaching at every level can be judged by its developmental consequences and effects. Hence instructional expectations which encourage dependence on direction, and which fail to provide the spurs to the self-reliant use of books, are to that extent responsible for incompetent reading.

Any teacher should realize that reading interests can be cultivated, that the school can provide contacts and experiences which give free access to the literary heritage with which today's children are blessed, and with the types of life enrichment which juvenile literature offers. The actual spurs to intelligent selection and free reading can be identified by sensitive evaluation which takes account of more than comprehension and rate! Objective scores on tests and diagnostic data on remedial needs can be personalized and supplemented to foster maturing experiences in self-direction, resourcefulness in the location and purposeful use of reference materials, competence in the interpretation and organization of findings, and in their creative use.

All of this assumes a considerable measure of insightful concern for reading competence on the part of teachers, librarians, and parents, but that can be developed and fostered by responsible democratic leadership.

A competent reader carries on a continuity of activities like the following, without needing or wanting direction. An experience or a comment may start the process. An example follows:

Someone referred to paper being manufactured from rags. The teacher was ready with several possible comments from which she selected one or two to try out as "starters." She said: "I thought some paper was made from wood." . . . "is *all* paper made from rags?" . . . "Manufactured means made. Paper is *made* from rags." She asked, "Where did you get that information?" . . . "How did you come to know that?" She said, "Perhaps we could make paper." . . . "I wonder where the people who make paper get enough rags?" . . . "It would be interesting to know *how* paper is made." The teacher's comments started conversation. She listened and entered in without shutting others out. Talk went on for a few minutes, most of it relevant, but some of it clearly irrelevant. Instead of referring critically to the irrelevance of some suggestions, the teacher picked up leads to further group discussion, and worked toward fuller participation. One child asked, "Where do you suppose we could go to see paper being made?" Another child said, "Maybe we could find out how it is done and make some paper ourselves."

One measure of the reading competence of that group was the intelligent self-directed use of several reference books to locate information on papermaking, but the *spur* to that activity was the prospect of making paper and the need for the information.

The next day the children's reports on what they had found in reference books were used as the basis for planning. The steps were set down and referred to as plans progressed. Paper was made and used for Mother's Day greetings. There was zest and zeal in the whole process.

Children's interests can be a spur to wide and extensive reading and the very amount of it contributes to fluency. The cumulative impact of vicarious experience in pictures and print not only aids imagery, but provides cues to word recognition and spurs to the concern for meaning.

Any teacher should recognize the signs that reading is being freely used as a resource for finding out. Any teacher should realize that children's questions can be useful as spurs to fuller involvement. Once the process of inquiry is under way, guidance can provide reading resources, encouragement and interaction to foster and sustain it. No stereotyped routine or lesson plan will do what needs to be done to develop the initiative and judgment that carries individuals and groups along on the way to increasingly self-reliant competence in reading. Nothing short of that is needed for ever more effective independent study on successive levels of personal, educational, and social maturity.

Directive assignments may "cover the ground," but guidance which concerns itself with the optimal fulfillment of every pupil's potential competence sets itself to proceed developmentally.

The school should not do less than launch every child on a lifelong, life-related, life-wide course, as a fully literate, competent user of reading. Suppose, instead, that the school settles for less, limiting its curricular concerns in reading to required material covered, to stereotyped lessons from required texts, to formal training in reading habits and study skills. Would that suffice to ensure reading competence? No more formal instruction in oral or written language would suffice for the free and effective uses of language in communication—much less for the flowering of the language arts in literary appreciation and expression.

Now it remains to make very explicit—perhaps by contrast, and by recourse to illustrations—just how teaching which provides spurs to reading competence differs from low-level pedantic instruction, which dulls the edge of learning, and disregards the developmental potentialities of reading competence as the key to ever more literate living.

Whereas a directive assignment expects compliance, it is not as conducive to the development of competence as one which is a challenge to self-reliant situational judgments, projected into purposive courses of action.

Reading can be experienced as a quest in which self-directed next steps are considered, selected, initiated, projected, consummated and evaluated in a continuity of purposive action—a dynamic self-directed search for meanings, guided by an emergent sequence of inferences, insights, judgments and action projected, paced, and evaluated as inquiry.

Competence is developed by guided experience in this process. Well-conceived reading programs provide challenging experiences in which the satisfactions and responsibilities of independent study, as well as the potentialities of free access to generous and varied reading resources, are explored. Lives that are not enriched by reading not only miss the values of the literary heritage; they miss the vicarious experiences which might provide enrichment and identification with current concerns and opportunities. Without competence those who have acquired reading and study skills are less likely to find satisfaction and challenge in books, less likely to be intelligently selective and mature in their interpretation of the "printed word," less judicious in their reactions to propaganda, less informed and less liberal in their outlook. These are values well worth considering and well worth fostering. They should serve as spurs to a fuller realization of the need for forward adjustments in the reading programs of today's schools. Those who for any reason counsel education to forego the implications of expanded reading resources and deepened insights into learning in favor of a narrow emphasis on required texts and directive instructional practices are regressive. Their counsel cannot be trusted for guidance on the way ahead.

Children who have access to several books about animals—or several books about homes around the world—or to a collection of references related to any challenging problem, are likelier far to read more and to read more intelligently, more competently, than those who are limited to turn-taking in a prescribed reading text.

Browsing which culminates in selection and then develops into the thoughtful preliminary perusal of a particular book as an orientation to actual reading is a developmental engagement. It not only leads to self-directive commitment, but to active adaptation of pace and procedure to whatever serves to engage the reader's purposes, and it instigates coordinated visual and mental processes that are sufficiently satisfying to favor further reading. Persistence in the responsiveness to such opportunities develops competence in extensive reading. Teachers can widen the array of reading materials, and guide by cultivating interest and by interacting to foster values which contribute to dynamic attitudes.

Children can learn to *care* about good books by having the advantage of satisfying opportunities for selection and free use.

The teacher whose guidance does not foster competence may find it easier and more congenial to follow mass methods, requiring conformity and discouraging initiative. But conformity to directive mass management is not conducive to the reading competence toward which developing individuals should be headed on their way to maturity. Whatever his level, the student who expects to be told exactly what to read and what to do with what he is "required to read," has been seriously retarded and diverted from the way to reading competence. It should go without saying that the reorientation of such students is every teacher's responsibility.

33. Critical Reading in the Elementary Schools*

INEZ E. BISHOP

Northern Illinois University

EDUCATORS recognize that critical reading is a skill which must be taught to students in our elementary schools. Scrutiny of this reading ability continues to make it a favorite topic for debate and discussion. However, such debate and discussion has not lead to common agreement on the definition of critical reading, on the basic underlying skills, nor on the particular place critical reading should hold in the sequential development of the reading program.

To consider any of the above questions, the urgent need to teach students to read critically must be understood. Although we now communicate through many forms of mass media (fiims, television, radio, audio and video tapes) written references are the basic resource used to develop messages channeled through these media. Also, several of these media combine the presentation of a picture and the spoken word with written material which is flashed to the audience. Today, children encounter communication from all sources at an early age. We are surrounded, then, by the need to teach students in the elementary schools to read critically.

The three areas of disagreement mentioned in the first paragraphs are as follows:

1. What is critical reading?
2. What are the basic underlying skills?
3. Where should critical reading be taught in the sequential development of the reading program?

Critical reading is defined by some as the ability to detect certain specific propaganda techniques such as card stacking, name calling, status appeal, scapegoating. Others interpret reading critically as the ability to analyze literary works in depth, evaluating the style, ideas, and philosophical focus of the author. A third definition equates critical reading with critical thinking. This last definition implies the testing of the hypothesis set forth by the author on the basis of objective evaluation by the reader.

*An original article written for this book of readings.

A more inclusive definition of critical reading, which cuts across the three just described and adds another necessary element, is the following. Critical reading is the reconstruction of the message of the author as the reader interprets it. In this reconstruction of the purpose of the writer, the critical reader must include a summary question which he asks the author and then answers for himself. The question is as follows: "What would the result or outcome be in relation to this topic if your philosophy or viewpoint were developed?" This definition of critical reading can be applied to propaganda articles, to literary works, to scientific treatises, and to all other written material.

The need for critical reading has been established. A more inclusive definition has just been described. The question of the basic underlying skills must be answered next.

In current literature on the teaching of critical reading, discussion of the underlying skills assumes that these skills (analysis of plot, style, philosophical approach, or propaganda techniques) start with consideration of a story or an article. This approach bypasses the much earlier teaching and learning of the basic vehicle through which the author tells his story and by which the reader reconstructs the message of the author.

Words, words, words! In any analysis of written material, words in all their semantic variations and the connotations and denotations thus associated with these words is the key to critical reading. Words with their impact upon the intellect and emotions are the blocks upon which thought units, sentences, and paragraphs are built. It is through and by the semanticism of words that an author sets the stage, develops the thesis, and woos the reader to come with him to the conclusion of a literary work, a scientific treatise, or a propaganda article. Also, it is through the analysis of the meanings of words in various contexts that a reader critically evaluates written material, reconstructs the purpose of the author as he interprets it, and answers the following question: "What would be the result if the philosophy of the writer were developed?" The skills underlying critical reading, then, are those of understanding words in all their semantic variations and the meaning associated with words in many and varied contextual settings.

The last question to be answered is the following: "Where shall we teach critical reading in the sequential development of the reading program?" Actually, critical reading is being learned long before we teach children to detect the inferred meaning in literary passages or in propaganda articles. Critical reading begins with the first word a child hears. He associates various meanings to these spoken symbols because of the tone, the bodily gestures, and the facial expressions used by the speaker. As his social experiences increase word meanings are also increased and modified. The responses he gets from his peers and from adults as he verbalizes his reactions to the world around him establish additional semantic meanings to words. Since it is through and by the semanticism of words that an author develops the theme of his story, critical reading is being learned from the time a child first hears words and later verbalizes his reactions to his environment. Thus, the learning and teaching of this skill has been placed for us in the sequential development of the reading program at the time children first listen to words and then verbalize spoken symbols.

What do the answers given to the three basic questions previously listed mean for the teaching of critical reading in the elementary school? First, children who enter school with great deficits in listening and speaking experiences need teaching emphasis on these skills. Second, if critical reading is accepted as the reconstruction of the purpose of the author as the reader interprets it, to teach reading is to teach critical reading. Teachers then must accept the fact that this skill should be emphasized at the time students begin to read and this emphasis continued throughout the later phases of the reading program. Another part of this same focus will be to help students understand the how and why of different interpretations given by their classmates. Each student will enrich his individual communication with authors by understanding the interpretation of others in the class. Third, if the skills basic to critical reading are understanding words in all their semantic variations and understanding words in different contextual settings, word study should be a vital part of the entire reading program. This means not only from the standpoint of phonetic and phonic analysis, but a rich, varied study of the meaning of words as they are used in language situations such as dramatic activities, written activities, verbal experiences, and the study of word meanings used in communication through audio-visual devices and techniques. Word study as a vital part of the reading program also means analysis of the ways in which words have come into our language, ways in which words continue to become a part of our language, and why the meanings of words have changed, historically. Through this continued and directed vocabulary study and during all phases of the sequentially developed reading program, students will analyze the reasons for certain words having highly charged meanings and the reasons for certain words appealing to our emotions, to our senses, to our intellect. On the basis of this varied, semantic, linguistic study of words, students can then read critically and analyze thought units, sentences, paragraphs, stories, and articles.

Last, knowing that children bring to school meanings which they associate with words because of the context in which they first heard them and later verbalized them, teachers of reading need to recognize the interrelatedness of all the language skills. Reading skills are built upon and also build towards effective communication in all language situations. Critical reading relates to critical listening, critical writing, and effective speaking. In the total language program (listening, speaking, reading, writing) many activities should be included which lead students to evaluate the changes in the meaning of words because of the language context in which they are used. For example, students might write about a topic and then record this story on tape to note the changed meaning of certain words because of linguistic clues which are used in speaking-juncture, stress, and pitch. The same words used in written material may carry different meanings because of the absence of these linguistic signals. Additional language experiences in this context include listening to a report on television and then rewriting the same report to share with others in class. Differences in meaning of the spoken and written word can again be studied. Also, students might translate a poem into prose to evaluate the various meanings the same words have when written in each of these literary forms.

Eventually, in teaching critical reading, a teacher asks students to evaluate literary works to understand the plot of the story, the style of the author, the philosophical focus of the material. Also, students need to read propaganda articles to detect techniques such as card stacking, scapegoating, status appeal, and the bandwagon approach. However, words are the building blocks of thought units, sentences, paragraphs, and stories. It is through and by the meaning of words that the theme in all written material is developed. The critical reader analyzes word meanings in all their semantic variations and in different contextual settings. This analysis begins at the time a child first listens to words and later verbalizes reactions to his environment. A rich study of these semantic word variations and the meanings of words in many contextual settings should be a vital part of teaching critical reading. It is the basis upon which the more complex techniques of critical reading are built.

VII

Reading in the Content Areas

34. Sequence in Reading in the Content Areas*

GERTRUDE WHIPPLE

READING in the content areas makes demands upon the reader which are in striking contrast to those of general, assimilative reading such as that commonly carried on in an English class. For general or basic reading, a preponderance of literary fiction is used; for content reading, a preponderance of informational material, scientific, mathematical, or social. For basic reading, authors of textbooks elaborate their ideas; for content reading, a considerable part of the reading matter is of a highly condensed type. Many basic reading selections offer spontaneous interest value, whereas few selections in subject-matter textbooks are immediately appealing. For basic reading, ideas are comparatively easy to assimilate and recall if the reader thinks while he reads; for content reading, the ideas demand concentrated study. In basic reading, comparatively few specialized terms appear, while content material abounds in technical words and symbols. Finally, the content areas present not only illustrations, as in general reading, but also diagrams, maps, charts, and tables. In view of these characteristics of content reading, the pupil faces difficult problems in comprehension, interpretation, recall, and use of the ideas, especially in solving problems.

In helping pupils meet the requirements of content reading, there is probably nothing more important than to fit the reading task to the pupil's maturity and to increase its difficulty gradually. This can be done only if the teacher knows the chief factors that govern sequence in developing reading abilities. This paper discusses a few of these factors and points out their significance in the program.

THE CONCEPTS AND GENERALIZATIONS FORMING THE FRAMEWORK OF INTERPRETATION

Each content area has its unique framework of interpretation, which

*From *Reading Instructions in Various Patterns of Grouping* ("Supplementary Educational Monographs," No. 90; Chicago: University of Chicago Press, 1964), 124-129. Copyright © 1960 by the University of Chicago. Reprinted with permission from The University of Chicago Press and Gertrude Whipple.

consists of the basic concepts and generalizations of that area. In each field specialists have tried to lay these out in sequential fashion, proceeding from simple to complex and from concrete to abstract. If the teacher lacks an awareness of these basic concepts and generalizations, reading in the subject-matter area descends to vague description.

Equally disastrous is the promotion of obsolete concepts. An illustration of such a concept from geography is the old idea of temperate-zone climate. Latitude is thought of as the sole determinant of climate, to the neglect of other factors. Among these are altitude, rainfall, its distribution, ranges of temperatures as well as averages, duration of the frost-free period, and directions and velocities of the winds. By the secondary grades and certainly in college, students should have gradually extended their framework of interpretation of climate sufficiently to avoid any oversimplification. The student who has not done so can interpret reading matter about climate only in a superficial manner.

Concept-building is quite different from mere teaching of facts, no one of which can give the child a concept. He must draw from his experiences a general idea apart from the particulars he has noted. As in the case of concepts, no one can give the child a generalization. He can acquire it only if he possesses the concepts on which it is based, and gains new insight concerning their relationships.

Concept-building ought to be begun in the kindergarten, and continued all the way through the school to the end of the twelfth grade. The concepts to be built at first are indicated chiefly by simple words. The word form is usually familiar, but it is used with a new meaning such as *out-of-doors* used to mean in its natural state, *change* referring to money, and *big, bigger,* and *biggest* as used in arithmetic.

In the early grades, a new concept ought never to be introduced to the child in its printed form. Rather it should be developed through other means such as firsthand experience, observation, visual aids, demonstration, illustration, and explanation. Reading the printed page can then help to establish and clarify the concept developed orally so that it will become the child's own and can then be used in interpreting more difficult ideas.

By the intermediate grades, the reading materials in the content areas include literary words, figurative words, abstract words, words signifying the passage of time, and words remote from the child's experience. Unfortunately, in this period when the child's reading rapidly broadens, teachers often begin to expect the pupil to acquire new concepts chiefly through written communication. Far too often they neglect the informal, developmental, discussion type of teaching before the reading. At the secondary level, teachers sometimes follow this practice of expecting pupils to gain new concepts independently through the process of reading. When this is done, the student is soon "in over his head."

Of course, the teacher's aim should always be to make the pupil increasingly able to learn through his reading and to help him become less and less dependent upon another's help. However, the teacher will need to insure either that the pupil already has the conceptual background assumed by the reading matter or that he will be able to develop that background through self-help methods such as the use of a dictionary, the study of pictures or diagrams, or the performance of an experiment. Always we should remember that only a mature reader is able to develop new insight through the act of reading.

PROBLEMS TO BE SOLVED

A second factor that determines sequence in content reading is inherent in the methodology of the subject. For example, in arithmetic he reasons, thinks through a verbal problem situation, to distinguish known factors from unknown. Having identified the relationships, he applies his reasoning ability to determine the computations which need to be made to reach a solution; then he applies his computational skills.

In science the successful worker initiates a problem, he observes real things, maybe non-living as well as living, he experiments, and he checks and rechecks his findings. This last task is done partly or wholly through reading. Even though firsthand experience is the chief method of learning in science, reading is indispensable. As a result of reading and other activities, the mature worker explains objects and events not previously clear to him, he predicts what is likely to happen under given conditions, and he plans and carries on other activities to solve the new problems that arise.

In social studies an excellent description of how a mature reader proceeds has been given by Rudisill.[1] She says he goes to his reading with a purpose that determines his procedure. For many years social-studies specialists have advocated that this purpose should often be to obtain the solution of a particular problem. Usually the reader refers to a variety of reference materials. He compares facts from these sources, notes discrepancies, checks the qualifications of authors and the sources of their data. He makes sure he knows the arguments on both sides of controversial issues. He interprets map and globes for certain ideas not conveyed in the verbal presentations, since maps are the unique tools of the social studies. Frequently he reads related literature for enjoyment, thereby making his concepts clear and concrete and clarifying and enriching his experiences. Constantly he differentiates between the fictional and factual.

[1]Mabel Rudisill, "What Are the Responsibilities of Social Studies Teachers for Teaching Reading?" *Improving Reading in the Junior HIgh School,* pp. 91-97. Proceedings of Conference, December 13-14, 1956, Department of Health, Education, and Welfare, Office of Education (Secondary Schools Section). Bulletin 1957, No. 10. Washington, D. C., 1957.

As defined by Russell, "A problem is a task which a child can understand but for which he does not have an immediate solution."[2] Problem-solving is the process by which one goes from the task or problem to a solution which seems reasonable. Problem-solving is quite different from concept formation. It is directed toward a definite goal or around an obstacle, whereas a concept may be built up over a period of years, or even be the by-product of other learning. The search for clues to the solution of a problem leads to selective reading. In other words, not all ideas in the reading matter are given consideration, but only those which appear to have a bearing upon the solution.

A particular issue can be a problem to a child only if he can understand the task. A teacher needs to be sure that what he considers a problem is really a problem for the child. Also, the same learning situation may create a problem for one child but not for another.

In problem-solving in the content areas, reading can be an important aid, but it is seldom the sole method used in reaching a solution. Clues and needed information are obtained also by experimenting, seeing demonstrations, taking excursions, using audio-visual materials, interviewing, listening to others, and the like.

Different investigators have laid out varying methods of attack in problem solving. Those enumerated by Dewey in 1910 consist of five steps, namely, (1) "a felt difficulty," (2) "its location and definition," (3) "suggestion of possible solution," (4) "development by reasoning of the bearings of the suggestion," and (5) "further observation and experiment leading to its acceptance or rejection."[3] From time to time other writers have presented lists of steps, but all of these seem to lean heavily upon Dewey's. Today it is known that problem-solving is not a single clear-cut process and that the various steps reported are simplified versions; they omit the difficulties, emotional upsets, and blind alleys that are met during the process.[4] In reality there is no definite pattern for the discovery of solutions to problems.

Most of the problems that children meet in the content areas demand an understanding of the situation, perception of the relationships, a search for ideas and information from many related sources, distinction of the pertinent ideas and the way they are related, and achievement of some sort of reorganization of the material to obtain insight and a solution. Here again is a somewhat simplified version that more nearly resembles the method of the disciplined adult mind than that of the child.

Ability in problem-solving is, of course, influenced by age and general intelligence. Of even greater importance, according to the research, are several other factors—the nature of the problem and the motivation and mind-set of the

[2]David H. Russell, *Children's Thinking,* p. 251. Boston: Ginn & Co., 1956.
[3]*Ibid.,* p. 256.
[4]*Ibid.,* p. 257.

solver. Problems presented in concrete, immediate situations can be solved even by preschool children, whereas those involving intricate relationships and requiring logical reasoning are better adapted to older students.

The difficulty of the problem should always be matched to the maturity of the child. The teacher should engage the interests of the child in solving the problem and encourage the proper mind-set: an open-minded attitude, willingness to explore the possibilities, and a critical attitude toward the various solutions entertained.

Problem-solving experiences appropriate for the preschool child should be continued for the school child. As he grows older, he is able to grasp concepts that are less concrete. He comes to verbalize with increasing ease and can state the problem better in words. Now he should use reading as an aid in problem-solving in the content areas. As he advances from elementary school to college, he should become more versatile in devising solutions, should consult a larger number of sources, should utilize more varied approaches to reading for clues, and should be more critical of the solutions that suggest themselves.

Reading in problem-solving must always be undertaken in a larger setting. For example, in the social studies the children must first be led to recognize and clarify the problem through discussion. Before anything can be done toward a solution, they must become concerned about the problem and interested in solving it. Group planning is a second step: Where shall we obtain the needed information? How shall we divide up our responsibilities? At this point reading enters in as one means of securing information. During the course of the next step, evaluating and verifying information, the children should grow in ability to locate sources, to compare the views of different writers, to check these views against past experiences, and to test solutions to see whether or not they work. Later the reader organizes his ideas obtained from various procedures such as reading, map-study, experimentation, and interview. In the light of all the evidence, the group makes its decision, since it has a broader background of experience than any individual.

THE RESEARCH TECHNIQUES REQUIRED

A third factor governing sequence in reading relates to the skills required in study-type reading, note-taking, and the utilization of libraries. In first grade, for instance, science and social studies books closely resemble the basic readers for the grade. As we advance to higher grades, the textbooks present more specialized knowledge until, by the later years of high school, many of them can be interpreted by mature readers only.

Even the primary child must learn to locate needed material within a book. This involves examination first of the table of contents, for few textbooks include an index below Grade III. It also involved learning to skim material in science and social studies in order to find the part that answers a given question; the child must be taught to hold the question in mind as he skims and, having located the information, to read it selectively in terms of his question.

It is imperative in subject-matter fields to distinguish between fact and fiction as one reads. Such disrimination is easy to cultivate if the teacher, conscious of its importance, takes steps to promote it.

The primary-grade child must learn to interpret short, easy materials in the curricular fields. From the beginning, the teacher should emphasize that a good reader tries to remember what he knows about a subject before he reads. After many such experiences children should acquire the habit of recalling important related ideas as a background for understanding. Equally important is encouragement to reflect on what is read and to establish the habit of rereading when necessary.

The primary-grade child should become skilful in reading orally to an audience for purposes such as presenting new ideas, proving a point, and answering a question.

By the intermediate grades, the child should be introduced to certain new reading skills as well as helped to maintain and extend those he acquired earlier. During this period, he should learn to use an index and list of maps, to make use of simple bibliographies in locating material, and to find needed references on shelves in a children's library. Special attention should be given to the use of children's encyclopedia. More and more he should be led to appraise a book in terms of the purposes for which he needs it; "Does it give enough material to satisfy my purpose or must I look further? How recent is the material? What questions does it leave unanswered?"

At this level the child should grow in ability to understand reading material of increasing difficulty. Especially important to promoting understanding is following the logical organization of the material presented. The teacher should help his pupils note topic headings, see paragraph organization, and recognize the progression of ideas. In these grades note-taking during study reading should also be introduced.

By the secondary level there is urgent need for the integration of skills during reading activities. The secondary teacher, more than any other, ought to engage in diagnostic teaching. If he proceeds too rapidly or too slowly, his pupils will suffer losses.

At the secondary stage the student must be taught to use efficiently atlases, handbooks, yearbooks, and other types of references peculiar to the subject. He must acquire new library skills such as the use of the standard card catalog, special indexes to locate biographies, plays, and other types of material, and adult periodicals to obtain current information on a topic. At this stage, too, teachers should cultivate skill in detecting propaganda, and in synthesizing information from various sources, classifying the pertinent ideas in logical order.

In all the content fields, research in books must be closely related to other means of learning—to seeing, asking, setting up experiments, gathering data, compiling records, computing, and making maps and diagrams. The more efficient the child is in reading, the more likely he is to excel in these skills, and vice versa.

SUMMARY

The first two of the three main factors, namely the interpretive framework and the nature of the problem to be solved, are inherent in the given subject matter. Thus the teacher must have a good subject-matter background if he is to insure the child's growth in reading abilities. He himself must know the chief concepts to be promoted at each stage in these cumulative subjects. Without such understanding, the teacher is unable to insure the gradual development of new skills and the maintenance of old ones.

At all stages there is great value in diversification of the reading materials. Wide reading of every kind of suitable material available in a content area furnishes concrete details, gives varied points of view, and raises further questions for research. Fortunately, today a wealth of literature is offered for teachers and children to choose from in science, social studies, and arithmetic, and even more specialized fields.

35. Special Reading Skills Are Needed in Social Studies, Science, and Arithmetic*

E. ELONA SOCHOR

MORE and more teachers are recognizing the importance of reading skills in all areas of the curriculum. Gone forever is the belief that the ability to read all materials can be adequately evaluated or developed in a basal reader or an English class.

Reading has no content of its own. It is a process used for acquiring information, for solving a problem, or for recreation and enjoyment. It is a means to an end.

Therefore, in order to read, we must read some type of content material. What is commonly called "reading" in the school is the comprehension of stories or other types of literature such as are found in basal readers or anthologies.

The present trend is to include in such textbooks a greater variety of materials with a sampling of selections from social studies and science. However, these selections remain a mere sampling. Sufficient ability to read all the types of content materials necessary in school activities cannot be developed by using any one textbook. Nor can the development of these abilities be left to chance.

THE PRESENT PROBLEM

The importance of adequate reading ability in the various areas of scholastic achievement, even at the elementary level, has long been recognized. (13, 16).[1] Educators have accepted the fact that a child unable to read materials at his interest and maturity levels is denied one vital aid to learning.

Reading skills are basic in our present-day schools if a child is to achieve in all curriculum areas at a level commensurate with his capacity. Moreover, it is the direct responsibility of every teacher to see that each pupil is able to capitalize on his potentialities. She should contribute what and how she can toward this end.

*From: *The Reading Teacher,* **6**, 4 (March, 1953), 4-11. Reprinted with permission of the International Reading Association." Author deceased.

[1] Numbers in parentheses refer to references at the end of the article.

Teachers at the elementary school level commonly recognize the effect of reading deficiencies when a child attempts to read particular social studies, science, or health books, even though as teachers they may do little to remedy the situation. The recognition of a child's inability to read and interpret an arithmetic problem, however, seems to be less apparent.

In contrast, many secondary school teachers are just becoming aware of the fact that "reading" is an integral and necessary part of learning in their classes. These teachers still assume too frequently that the development of all reading abilities should be completed when a child leaves the sixth grade.

Yet it is at the secondary level that the need to read adequately in specific content fields is more pronounced. The content becomes more specialized. As a result, the "reading" becomes more difficult if the skills characteristic of and necessary for the particular area are not developed.

Another common assumption of secondary school teachers is that all the necessary reading skills can be developed in an English or special "reading" class. Thus, since concepts are basic to reading comprehension, the teachers of these classes must develop historical, mathematical, and scientific concepts with the students referred to them. The fallacy of such as assumption is obvious.

Likewise, at the elementary school level, the development of reading skills is frequently not included in specific subject matter learning activities. The teacher assumes that the time spent on developing reading skills in the daily "reading period" is sufficient. She assumes further that a child will be able to read all materials if he can read his basal reader well or achieve satisfactorily on a standardized, "general" reading test.

The basic premise underlying the use of such procedures at any grade level, however, has been refuted by research.

THE COMPLEXITY OF READING

At one time, reading was considered a "general ability." It was assumed to be the same regardless of the material being read.

The development of skills was limited to a period reserved for "reading instruction." Reading achievement was appraised solely by means of a "general" reading test. If a child succeeded in these situations, the teacher concluded that the child was a "good reader" in all materials.

In view of what was known about the reading process, such practices were justified thirty-five years ago.

More recent investigations, however, have indicated otherwise:

1. Reading is not a "general" ability. Rather it is a complex of many skills and abilities. (7).

2. Reading comprehension in any subject matter area can be broken down into many skills and abilities. (12, 14, 19, 20).

3. The ability to interpret what is read requires a different pattern of comprehension skills in each content field. (4, 12, 19, 21).

4. A student may be able to comprehend satisfactorily in one content area and not in another. (12, 15).

5. The ability to grasp the "facts" does not guarantee the ability to do higher level, or critical, interpretation. (1, 8).

6. One reading test, standardized or teacher-constructed, cannot appraise reading ability in all reading situations. (4, 12, 19, 21).

7. While there are reading skills common to the various areas of the curriculum, there is enough difference in the nature and pattern of the skills characteristic of each area to warrant specific instruction. (12, 15, 19).

TEACHING IN THE CONTENT FIELDS

The conclusions listed above have definite implications for teaching in the content areas.

First, since reading comprehension is not a "generalized" or "unitary" ability, all teachers should teach specific reading interpretation skills systematically in the subject matter areas. This is best accomplished when and as reading is required for learning.

Certain skills appear to be relatively basic to all areas of the curriculum. These skills can be introduced in the basal reader program or in any other textbook. However, the use and application of these same skills in interpreting other content materials read must be guided and encouraged by the teacher. Sufficient transfer of training in most cases will not occur automatically, probably because the varying nature of the concepts among the subject matter areas requires different ways of thinking.

Skills suggested as basic to reading comprehension in all materials are:

1. Interpreting the facts accurately.

2. Grasping the general idea or meaning of the selection.

3. Identifying the sequence, whether chronological, logical, or arbitrary.

4. Organizing the ideas, which involves recognizing the central theme, the main ideas, the significant details related to the main ideas, and the coordinate value of main points and details.

5. Reaching a conclusion or generalization.

6. Solving problems of various types; i.e., personal, social, scientific, or mathematical.

7. Evaluating ideas for relevancy, authenticity.

8. Interpreting pictorial materials, such as graphs, maps, diagrams.

9. Following directions.

In addition to the ability to use the above skills with facility, there are two other factors important to learning in subject matter areas when reading is involved. These, like the skills, should be included in the learning activities.

The first is the development of an adequate reading vocabulary in each content area. Words that are typical of and frequently used in subject matter materials must be thoroughly understood by the reader if he is to comprehend the materials. Another aspect is that the same word may be used in a different manner or with different meanings in the same text. Readers should be guided into appreciating the significance of word meanings basic to adequate interpretation of printed materials.

The other factor is the reader's habit of relating what he is reading and learning to previously learned knowledge. Reviewing or referring to information already known, using a concept developed in the past, determining the significance of the "new" ideas as compared with the related "old" ones, classifying facts to get an "over-view," reorganizing or summarizing a unit; these are some of the ways through which boys and girls can acquire the habit of utilizing their backgrounds.

A second implication drawn from the studies on reading comprehension applies to verbalism, the repetition or use of words and phrases without understanding their meaning. The evil is pronounced in schools today, particularly at the secondary school level and in the content fields.

Requiring more adequate comprehension, discouraging the memorization of factual material or an author's terminology and phrasing, encouraging the expression of ideas in personal language patterns, and stressing the development of concepts will help to combat this unfortunate and critical situation.

Most effective is placing emphasis upon those comprehension skills in the subject matter areas which necessitate a higher level of "thinking." (9). Mere interpretation of facts is not sufficient. More adequate ability in and use of such activities as applying facts, organizing and evaluating ideas, and solving problems will provide the solution.

A third implication is that the reading ability of every student should be appraised in each content field with materials taken from that field. In view of the lack of tests designed to measure specifically reading comprehension skills, teachers should construct informal tests (2, Chapter XXI) using subject matter selections to determine the needs of pupils. Daily observation and evaluation by the teacher of a child's performance when reading subject matter textbooks or discussing information acquired are also helpful.

Such appraisal should also determine the level in the content field at which the child is able to work independently and the level where he needs teacher guidance. (2, Chapter XXI). The fact that a pupil is achieving successfully in a third basal reader, for example, does not mean the same pupil is necessarily ready to read a "third level" science book.

The child may lack background of information for those particular science topics. He may be frustrated by the number or the nature of the science concepts included. The language may be too difficult for him to interpret.

The same situation may occur in any other subject matter area and at any "grade" level.

In content fields particularly, teachers are vitally interested in the pupils' acquisition of usable knowledge and understandings basic to living. It is true that reading is but one aid to learning. However, reading is still the most widely used aid.

When reading is used as a tool for learning, there must be adequate comprehension. What is not understood cannot be learned readily; and what is not well learned cannot be retained. Reading comprehension skills in all areas are necessary to learning.

Beginning with the child "where he is" applies to the use of arithmetic or history texts as well as to a basal reader. Instruction must be initiated at the appropriate level of difficulty. Guidance should be supplied in terms of the child's individual needs in particular content material.

In order to do this, the teacher must know the skills necessary for interpreting subject matter textbooks or other materials which are used in learning activities. She needs an appraisal instrument with which she can evaluate the achievement and needs of the students in the area. Then she must provide systematic guidance at the pupil's level of development.

DIFFERENCES AMONG CONTENT FIELDS

To give guidance in the development of reading skills necessary for a particular content field, any teacher must know which comprehension skills are peculiar to that field. The reading process in the different curriculum areas varies. As mentioned earlier, certain concepts and ideas are characteristic of each subject matter field. These are represented by the so-called "technical vocabulary." The word form as well as the meaning of specialized words must be mastered.

The desired understandings and learnings differ in the various areas because of the basic nature of the content. In social studies, for example, the social aspects of our culture are emphasized; in science, the scientific aspects. The recognition of cause-effect relationships is important in both areas, though the understandings are derived differently.

Each area has a background of information that is essentially its own. The organization of this background is one type for mathematics, another for English.

Ideas are not evaluated in the same manner. Emotional reaction to poetry is desirable in English; lack of objectivity, undesirable in science.

Thus, the pattern of thinking necessary for acquiring knowledge in one of these areas, let us say science, differs in varying degrees from each of the others. Moreover, that same type of thinking is required to interpret and evaluate printed materials in science.

The ability of students to think cannot be assumed to be present in spite of intelligence, maturation, or normal school progression (14, 20). This is especially true of critical thinking in content fields.

In addition to these differentiating factors, each subject matter area utilizes its own specialized devices, such as maps, graphs, tables, thermometers, formulas, diagrams, symbols, and signs. Frequently, accurate interpretation of such devices is closely related to the comprehension of the printed materials.

Thus, regardless of which subject matter field is considered, the teacher guiding the learning activities is in the most strategic position to develop the necessary understandings, abilities, and habits—the background of information, the concepts and the vocabularly, the organization of ideas, the skills in interpreting specialized devices, and the ability to think critically with and about the facts and knowledge acquired.

She will know more about the content being explored, and she will understand the needs of her students better than anyone else can in that particular situation. Moreover, she can develop the above through normal classroom activities as needed.

SPECIFIC SKILLS BASIC TO READING
IN THE CONTENT FIELDS

The relative importance of specific skills varies among the content areas. For example, it is more important to be able to follow directions and to visualize what is read in science than in social studies.

On the other hand, identifying the central theme and the mood, tone, and purpose of the author tend to be more significant in social studies.

Problem solving is more specific and utilizes facts more directly in science and mathematics. However, the ability to solve problems of another type is just as important in social studies.

The interpretation of figurative language is an important factor in literature and in many social studies materials. Science materials tend to be written more directly, thus requiring the ability to note details carefully.

The ability to locate information and to discriminate between fact and opinion appear to be more important in social studies than in science.

Differentiating between relevant and irrelevant facts is important in both social studies and mathematics. However, in mathematics certain facts are more significant than others in the solution of problems. These must be recognized. Moreover, thinking in mathematics is highly quantitative, and much depends upon the grasp of mathematical concepts and vocabulary.

In the reading of literature materials, the reader's purpose is most frequently one of enjoyment and pleasure. This requires the use of sensory impressions and the reader's projection of himself into the situation; for example, feeling the rain on his face, hearing the crackle of the fire, seeing the beauty of the waterfall, and experiencing emotionally the joy at receiving a much desired pet.

Too involved and overly critical analyses of an author's style, character development, descriptive passages, etc., do not help to develop literary interests and tastes or to broaden pupils' experiences. In fact, the opposite may result.

The specific reading comprehension skills, both literal and critical, that are vital to each content field should be developed systematically. And provision should be made for an adequate supply of necessary concepts and a rich background of information.

In order to determine what concepts, understandings, and skills are basic, the teacher has merely to refer to professional texts on reading or the subject matter itself. (5, 6, 10, 11, 17, 22). The majority of such sources discuss some aspects of these topics. A compilation from several sources would probably be superior to a listing from one source.

Additional and valuable information can be derived from a careful analysis of what pupils do as they (1) study and acquire knowledge, (2) develop and apply comprehension skills, and (3) experience difficulty with reading comprehension or application of what is read.

The lack of space prohibits a complete survey or reproduction of the concepts, understandings, and abilities basic to each subject matter area. For purposes of illustration, possible listings of specific comprehension abilities basic to reading and understanding social studies and science materials are presented:

1. Social Studies
   Grasp the general meaning of a selection.
   Interpret figurative language.
   Understand the many abstract and complex ideas.
   Locate information.
   Organize and summarize.
   Discriminate between relevant and irrelevant material.
   Differentiate between fact and opinion.
   Recognize the mood, tone, or intent of the author.
   Interpret maps, graphs, and other pictorial representations.
2. Science
   Note details carefully.
   Read analytically.
   Interpret formulae, tables, charts, diagrams, etc.
   Perform a specific problem.
   Follow directions.
   Recognize the steps in an experiment.
   Visualize what is read.
   Identify cause and effect relationships.
   Classify ideas.

The above abilities are characteristic of the particular curriculum areas named. Typical reading comprehension skills basic to all content fields were presented earlier in this discussion. Both are necessary to adequate reading ability in subject matter fields.

SUMMARY

The foregoing discussion on reading comprehension in the content fields points out:

1. Since reading is a basic tool for learning, the inability to comprehend printed materials adequately interferes with a student's ability to achieve in content areas.

2. The reading process is a highly complex one, consisting of many skills and abilities. Some are more or less common to all content fields while others are more specific to particular content areas. Therefore, one reading test is not adequate for appraising the comprehension skills necessary to all reading activities.

3. Reading skills should be developed and applied systematically in every content field at all school levels. Daily learning activities with subject matter materials provide the best opportunity for developing these skills.

References

1. Bedell, Ralph Clarion. *The Relationship Between the Ability to Recall and the Ability to Infer in Specific Learning Situations.* Unpublished Doctor's Dissertation. Kirksville, Missouri: University of Missouri, 1934.
2. Betts, Emmett A. *Foundations of Reading Instruction.* New York: American Book Co., 1950.
3. Bond, Elden A. *Tenth Grade Abilities and Achievements.* Contributions to Education, No. 813. New York: Bureau of Publications, Teachers College, Columbia University, 1940.
4. Bond, Eva. *Reading and Ninth Grade Achievement.* Contributions to Education, No. 756. New York: Bureau of Publications, Teachers College, Columbia University, 1938.
5. Bond, Guy L. and Eva Bond. *Developmental Reading in the High School.* New York: Macmillan Co., 1941.
6. Craig, Gerald S. *Science for the Elementary School Teacher.* New York: Ginn and Co., 1947.
7. Davis, Frederick B. *Fundamental Factors of Comprehension in Reading.* Unpublished Doctor's Dissertation. Cambridge, Massachusetts: Harvard University, 1941.
8. Dewey, Joseph C. *A Case Study of Reading Comprehension Difficulties in American History.* Unpublished Doctor's Dissertation. Iowa City, Iowa: State University of Iowa, 1931.
9. Glaser, Edward M. *An Experiment in the Development of Critical Thinking.* Contributions to Education, No. 843. New York: Bureau of Publications, Teachers College, Columbia Univeristy, 1941.
10. Gray, William S., Editor. *Improving Reading in Content Fields.* Supplementary Educational Monographs, No. 62. Chicago: University of Chicago Press, 1947.
11. Horn, Ernest. *Methods of Instruction in the Social Studies.* New York: Charles Scribner's Sons, 1937.

12. Humber, W. J. *An Experimental Analysis of Selected Reading Skills as Related to Certain Content Fields at The Univeristy of Minnesota.* Unpublished Doctor's Dissertation. Minneapolis, Minnesota: University of Minnesota, 1942.

13. Lee, Dorris Mae. *The Importance of Reading for Achieving in Grades Four, Five, and Six.* Contribution to Education, No. 556. New York: Bureau of Publications, Teachers College, Columbia University, 1933.

14. Maney, Ethel S. *Literal and Critical Reading in Science.* Unpublished Doctor's Dissertation. Philadelphia: Temple University, 1952.

15. Robinson, Francis P. and Prudence Hall. "Studies of Higher-Level Reading Abilities," *Journal of Educational Psychology,* XXXII (April, 1941), 241-52.

16. Rudolf, Kathleen B. *The Effect of Reading Instruction on Achievement in Eighth Grade Social Studies.* Contribution to Education, No. 945. New York: Bureau of Publications, Teachers College, Columbia Univeristy, 1949.

17. Russell, David H. *Children Learn to Read.* New York: Ginn and Co., 1949.

18. Salisbury, Rachel. *A Study of the Transfer Effects of the Training in Logical Organization.* Unpublished Doctor's Dissertation. Madison, Wisconsin: University of Wisconsin, 1934.

19. Shores, J. Harlan. *Reading and Study Skills as Related to Comprehension of Science and History in the Ninth Grade.* Unpublished Doctor's Dissertation. Minneapolis, Minnesota: University of Minnesota, 1940.

20. Sochor, E. Elona. *Literal and Critical Reading in Social Studies.* Unpublished Doctor's Dissertation. Philadelphia, Pennsylvania: Temple University, 1952.

21. Swenson, Esther J. *The Relation of Ability to Read Materials of the Type Used in Studying Science to Eighth Grade Achievement.* Unpublished Master's Thesis. Minneapolis, Minnesota: University of Minnesota, 1938.

22. Wesley, Edgar B. and Mary A. Adams. *Teaching Social Studies in Elementary Schools.* Boston: D.C. Heath and Co., 1946.

36. Methods and Materials for Teaching Reading in Mathematics*

MAURICE L. HARTUNG

THE relation between instruction in mathematics and the ability to read is today more in the focus of attention than ever before. Mathematics instruction is undergoing rapid changes in content and in method. Moreover, the changes are taking place at all levels in the educational structure from the first grade to and including the freshman year of college. As the new programs emerge, it is easy to see that they involve an attitude toward the role of reading in mathematics that differs in important respects from the one that has been dominant in the past. We will analyze these changes and their implications for both instruction in reading and in mathematics.

As is well known, in the past teachers of mathematics have relied on reading to a very limited extent. There are several reasons for this. At the elementary level, the materials were not written so that a genuine understanding of arithmetic could be obtained by reading them. The result was that the teacher and pupil made no effort to read anything but the lists of verbal problems, and often those were neglected. The books were actually a set of directions on "how to do it." They told the pupil what operations were to be done, and how to write the work on paper, but for the most part left the reasons for doing things unexplained.

In such circumstances one might expect that the teachers would orally supply the missing explanations and the theory. However, the overwhelming majority of them were not in possession of the explanation themselves, or were not convinced of the desirability of passing it on to the pupils. They too relied upon "how to do it" methods supported by unceasing drill upon the techniques of calculation. They seldom taught the pupil how to read a mathematics book. They depended upon imitative behavior—the teacher worked a problem on the chalkboard, and the pupils worked others in the same way.

Moreover, it was thought necessary to break down each major learning task into a sequence of "bonds" to be formed, as specific habits to be acquired.

*From *Reading Instructions in Various Patterns of Grouping.* Supplementary Educational Monographs, No. 90. Chicago: University of Chicago Press, 1960. Reprinted by permission.

In the process of multiplication, for example, the pupil was taught to multiply a two-digit number by a one-digit number first without "carrying," and then "with carrying." He was taught what to do if a zero occurred at the end of the numeral of the number being multiplied, as in 360, or if it was "internal," as in 306. Arithmetic was thought of as consisting of hundreds of "specific habits" of this sort which the pupil was to make automatic by practice. For example, in the 1930's, one prominent authority published a long article on the subject "Making Long Division Automatic" which described at length only a part of the habits to be learned for this process.

As the pupil advanced to the junior and on into the senior high school the situation was little better. The commonest complaint of the teacher was that the pupils did not know how to read—or, at least, to read materials from which they were expected to learn mathematics. The same pattern of learning and teaching persisted. The situation was of course, relieved somewhat after the ninth grade because mathematics became an elective subject. The greater selectivity of the students enabled them to read directions and problems better, but relatively little was done to develop understanding, or to help the students understand mathematics as the modern mathematician views it.

READING IN NEW MATHEMATICS PROGRAMS

We have sketched the situation as it was—and still is in the vast majority of schools. Let us now look at the emerging programs. This time we will begin our examination at the secondary level and will later consider the elementary programs, since this reverse sequence has been followed in all but one of the emerging programs.

When we examine the new programs from the point of view of reading, a notable difference appears at once. The student is expected to do some reading. The method is usually straightforward exposition designed to develop understanding. Expository materials sometimes continue for several pages before they are followed by exercises designed to develop further understanding and skills. It is true that the explanations are often quite informal, but they are nevertheless aimed at the development of fundamental concepts and principles of mathematics.

Let us take, as an example, a development of the distributive principle; that is, $a(b+c) = ab + ac$. Formerly, an explicit discussion of this principle was ignored, or at best treated very superficially. In a modern program it is explained with care. Its role in the theory of algebra is discussed, and its uses are illustrated. Special topics of algebra that formerly received extended treatment, such as "combining like terms," and "factoring," are shown to be merely applications of this general principle. All of this will ordinarily require considerable exposition in the textbook, and it is assumed that the pupil can read this exposition and understand it.

The current emphasis upon mathematical concepts and principles is the result of the participation of mathematicians in the preparation of textbooks. While this participation is long overdue and is welcome, it has involved a notable change in learning theory. The mathematicians are interested in having students acquire generalizations. They have little faith in the formation of specific habits as a method of learning, although this rejection is based more on personal experience than on knowledge of psychological findings. They are accustomed to learning mathematical generalization by methods that are primarily deductive. They want to get far and get there fast. The result is that they *write about mathematics.* They expect the student to learn the material relatively fast, largely by reading, and then to apply it to the solution of problems or in further learning.

There is, however, a considerable group of teachers who hold a somewhat different view. They are deeply interested in having the pupil "discover" the facts and generalizations. Their methods, and the materials they produce for student use, tend to be much more inductive. Nevertheless, the methods call for much more learning through reading than is true in the traditional programs.

Following these all too brief comments on the secondary programs, we may ask what is going on at the elementary level. Here the story is far from clear. Informal experimentation is going on in a number of different centers. The effort seems to be directed toward teaching in the elementary schools concepts which have until recently not even been introduced in the high schools. Much of the work seems ill-conceived, for even if one demonstrates that it is possible to introduce certain concepts much earlier than we have thought possible, it still remains to prove that it is *desirable* to do so. We must take care lest we exchange the essential concepts and skills of arithmetic for a superficial treatment of a loose collection of ideas presented before the pupil is ready to use them in any fundamental way. It is too early to determine the future of these experimental programs. It is not likely, in any event, that they will become part of the curriculum of many schools for a few years.

The main stream of the elementary program will probably continue in the channel which has been cut during the last ten or fifteen years. An effort will be made to make arithmetic more meaningful, and the method used will rely upon the use of objects and other visual aids. Since this method tends to make very little use of reading, it tends to produce a discontinuity in the program of the elementary school and the rapidly emerging program of the secondary school. On the other hand, the elementary schools are relying less upon reading and more upon visual and concrete materials. On the other hand, the secondary schools, are embarking on programs that rely more than ever before on the ability to gain ideas from the printed page. The remainder of this paper will be given to a discussion of the issues that thus arise, and to suggestions for their resolution.

PROBLEMS IN READING IN MATHEMATICS

In the first place, we must recognize that mathematics consists of concepts and principles. The ideas are all abstract from the beginning. Mathematical ideas cannot be seen, or heard, or touched. They have no color, or weight, or size or texture. They are of the mind. At the same time, we have need to communicate these ideas to others. We also have need to record them in writing so that we can examine several together, or the same idea at later times. We do this by means of symbols. Some of the symbols we use are those of ordinary discourse—words and punctuation marks. Others are specialized symbols for the mathematical ideas. The pupil in school must learn to read both kinds if he is to succeed in mathematics. Moreover, he must learn to read in the fullest sense of the word. Merely pronouncing the words and naming the signs is not enough. They must communicate meaning to him.

We must also recognize that in the earliest stages of learning mathematics pupils acquire these meanings inductively through concrete experience. In the later stages, after they have acquired a stock of meanings and some ways of relating them, they can learn meanings directly from the printed page. Thus the use of objects to represent the idea of number becomes the keystone of method. Since the pupil must learn to gain ideas from books as well as from objects, the book presents him with pictures of objects, but the purpose remains the same. As the groups become larger, the pupil in the traditional programs virtually learned by rote the number names associated with them. In a modern program he is shown how the principles of the base ten system of numeration provide a systematic yet simple way of compounding the names or numerals so that only a few basic ones are required. This system is also presented by using objects and pictures of objects along with the words so that the pupil is, at the outset, constantly associating the words he uses with their meaning.

From this simple beginning knowledge of mathematics is built step by step. The meaning of addition and subtraction may be associated with action by using movable objects, and pictures of objects that move. Thus the signs plus (+) and minus (−) are associated with the combining and separating of groups. The reasons for the various steps in the processes may be shown. In the elementary stages every new concept and process may be pictured, and the pupil can become accustomed to develop an understanding of the symbols by which it is represented.

As we undertake to teach arithmetic by this method, we find that as the concepts become more complex it becomes more and more difficult to present them pictorially. However, this need not concern us unduly. The purpose of our method has been, in the last analysis, to teach the pupil to gain mathematical ideas from their written expression. At the beginning the pupil is helpless, but as we continue systematically to present mathematics in ways he can understand, and deliberately teach him how they are expressed in writing, he gains in both these abilities. Gradually, the concrete representations can be reduced and the symbolic forms increased until he is able to learn from the latter alone.

Many teachers have not grasped this important point. They use the visual aids for the development of concepts, but they fail to make the transition from the concrete to the symbolic form so that the pupil learns to read. It is, of course, a distinct improvement over the older programs to develop understanding, but it is a serious mistake to leave the pupil relatively helpless to learn on his own through reading. Moreover, it is especially important that he learn to read mathematics at a time when the curriculum of the secondary schools is turning away from imitative behavior and toward the learning of principles through reading.

In addition to the systematic use of concrete and visual aids, a few other principles of method deserve comment. One of these is that the vocabulary should be carefully controlled. The mathematics class should not be burdened with teaching of a large general vocabulary. Instead, it should concentrate on the essentially mathematical terms and see that they are taught thoroughly. The general vocabulary should be held to the minimum number of words necessary to describe the concrete situations.

Another important point is that symbols should be introduced wherever they can aid thought. One such place occurs in the teaching of problem-solving. The pupil should be taught to express what is happening in equation form. This focuses his attention upon analyzing the *structure* of the situation, rather than upon the details of the computational process. Only when he has analyzed the situation and expressed it in equation form should he turn his attention to the computations involved. This means, among other things, that instead of avoiding the use of symbolic expression on the grounds that it is too difficult, the pupil must be taught to read and write symbolic expressions (such as the equation) because actually they make his task easier.

Finally, the writing of mathematics needs to be carefully considered. On the one hand, the book needs to encourage "discovery" at every stage and to avoid, as far as possible, telling the pupil what or how to think. On the other hand, no book can allow the pupils to make all the false starts, to wander down the various side roads, to explore and reject all of the irrelevant ideas that are characteristic of the genuine method of discovery. Moreoever, it would be impossible, even if it were desirable, for the pupils really to "discover" many of the ideas and processes of arithmetic that are the refinement of the thinking of wise men through the ages. Consequently, the materials of mathematics should seek to lead the student onward while partially but not completely controlling his thinking. They must strive for a method of "controlled" discovery. In the past, mathematics books have not been written in this way. They have told, or they have asked. They have not sought to guide the student in the same heuristic way that a skilled teacher guides him.

Needless to say, as we seek to develop such materials, we must rely on the ability of pupils to read. At the same time, as we teach through successive stages of such materials, we are continually increasing this ability. This is vastly different from the sort of method which assumes that the pupil can already read mathematical exposition or, going to the other extreme, leaves reading virtually out of the picture entirely.

Finally, it is also important that we have this kind of writing so that teachers can use the new materials without special preparation. We cannot wait to introduce new materials until the teachers are trained to teach it. Teachers can and must learn along with students.

CONCLUDING STATEMENT

A new program in mathematics, guided by modern learning theories, and leading pupils from concrete experience into the abstract world of mathematics, is coming into being. Reading will have a very important role to play in it, but this will not be by accident. It will come as a result of a deliberate effort to prepare materials in such a way that pupils can learn mathematics through reading.

37. Methods and Materials for Teaching Reading in Science*

GEORGE G. MALLINSON

THE problems associated with reading in the content areas have been studied more extensively for science than for any other subject-matter field. Among the earlier studies was the major investigation by Curtis[1] in which he summarized the results of more than one hundred investigations in the problems of vocabulary related to science teaching. The findings of his investigation were supplemented by those from a series of studies by Mallinson *etal*[2] in which other dimensions of reading difficulty in science books, in addition to vocabulary load, were analyzed. More recently, the studies of Herrington[3] and the reviews of research on problems in reading by Mallinson and Lockwood[4] have enabled textbook authors and publishers to be more effective in developing textbooks of science with levels of reading difficulty appropriate for the students for whom the books are designed.

All these studies were concerned, directly or tacitly, with two basic aims: (*a*) the development of science vocabularies suitable for the science topics being studied, and (*b*) the sequential growth of reading skills for better understanding of science. The efforts of the workers, however, were beset by problems, unique

*Supplementary Education Monographs: Ed. by Helen M. Robinson: *Reading Instructions in Various Patterns of Grouping.* 22nd Conf. on reading 1960, Vol. 22, (90) pp. 145-149. Reprinted with permission of The University of Chicago Press. Copyright 1960.

[1] Francis D. Curtis, *Investigations of Vocabulary in Textbooks of Science for Secondary Schools.* Boston: Ginn & Co., 1938.

[2] George Griesen Mallinson, "Textbook and Reading Difficulty in Science Teaching," *Science Teacher,* XXV (December, 1958), 474-75.

[3] Roma Lenore Herrington, "An Investigation of the Consistencies with Which Readability Formulas Measure and Reading Experts Estimate the Reading Difficulty of Materials for Elementary Science," pp. iii-41. Unpublished Master's thesis, Western Michigan College, Kalamazoo, Michigan, May, 1956. Roma Lenore Herrington *et al.,* "An Investigation of Two Methods of Measuring Reading Difficulty of Materials for Elementary Science," *Science Education,* XLII (December, 1958), 385-90.

[4] George G. Mallinson and J. Bryce Lockwood, "Reading Skills for Effective Learning in Science: Research on Problems in Reading Science," *Reading for Effective Living,* International Reading Association Conference *Proceedings* (1958), III (edited by J. Allen Figurel), 172-73.

to the field of science, that produced results considerably less rewarding than had been sought.

PROBLEMS WITH READING IN SCIENCE

The preparation of reading materials for science, and the development of methods for using the materials, are hampered by four major difficulties:

1. The recent explosive growth in the fields of science has accelerated the obsolescence of scientific vocabulary. Annually vast numbers of terms drop from common scientific use and many new ones are added. Thus lists of scientific vocabulary need constant modification.

2. One of the major concerns with science teaching is the overlap of science topics that are taught at different grade levels. Also, from one grade level to another, as well as from one specialized science subject to another, there is little continuity. Hence, the development of sequence in reading with science material is severely handicapped. Obviously, subject matter that suffers from lack of sequence is not conductive to the development of materials and methods for sequence in reading subject matter.

3. The sophistication of the materials of science with which students have contact is increasing daily. The scientific ideas that interest the students are becoming increasingly complex. It is indeed difficult to utilize a "one-syllable-word" vocabulary for developing a "ten-syllable" science concept.

4. There is great disagreement among authors and publishers concerning the level of reading difficulty with which science books should be written. Some espouse the viewpoint that the development of sequential reading skills with these materials should be congruent with growth in science knowledge and in the understanding of science concepts. Thus a textbook designed for science courses at the ninth-grade level should have a ninth-grade level of reading difficulty.

Others believe that the efforts of a student in using science materials should be devoted to "learning the science" and not dissipated in struggling with the problems of developing reading skills. The lack of resolution of these conflicting viewpoints is evidenced by analyses of the reading difficulty of different science textbooks. The findings indicate that competing textbooks are written with levels of reading difficulty below, at, and above the grade levels of the students for whom the books are produced.

Despite the foregoing problems publishers do seek to surmount these obstacles and "build sequence" in the reading materials they market for courses in science.

TECHNICAL VERSUS NON-TECHNICAL VOCABULARY

The words that are used in writing textbooks of science fall in two categories. In the first category are those words that are part of the common vocabulary of the student. They are regularly used whether or not the material in question is scientific in nature. These terms constitute the non-technical vocabulary. Among such words would be "the," "begin," "house," and "follow." In general, except where it is impossible to do otherwise, authors and publishers use only non-technical words whose grade levels of difficulty are below that of the students for whom the book is designed. In general, it is assumed that the student has learned the terms prior to studying the science content. Such words are found in many of the well-known word lists. If it is necessary for an author to use a *difficult* non-technical word, for example, "incapacitate," in a sixth-grade science textbook, the word is treated like a term in the technical vocabulary.

The second category of words, namely the technical vocabulary consists of those terms that are unique to science and which are used for developing scientific understandings. Such words may or may not be difficult, depending on whether they have been introduced and used in earlier science courses. Ordinarily students will not use such terms in their conversation or encounter them in general reading materials. Among such words are "mammal," "photosynthesis," "proton," and "convection."

The technical vocabulary may be handled in several different ways:

It is well-known that the ability to learn new words increases with maturity. Thus, the vocabulary load of technical terms in science books increases as the grade levels of the books increase.

In books designed for the third grade or below, the number of scientific terms introduced is ordinarily 40 or less. The material in books for the lowest level is practically non-verbal. Technical terms are introduced only where they are clearly related to illustrations and their meanings are evident. In the upper elementary grades, from 50 to 75 new technical terms are introduced at each grade level. In the seventh and eighth grades the number increases to about 125, and in the ninth and tenth grades, to about 175. In books designed for juniors and seniors, as many as 250 technical terms may be introduced. There is little tangible research evidence that such increases in vocabulary load are justifiable. Apparently the logic is based on empirical evidence.

Beginning with Grade IX, a new dimension of vocabulary is found in some textbooks. In addition to the "essential," "key," or "required" vocabulary, a second group of "desirable" terms may be included with illustrations, supplementary activities, or in sections that are optional. The number of desirable terms may equal those in the "essential" list.

Nearly always, the technical terms are brought to the attention of the students when they first appear in the text. This may be accomplished by using boldface type, by italicizing the term, or by footnoting. If the term is difficult, or above the level of the students, in addition to being technical, its phonetic spelling may be included following the term in the text or in the footnote. If the meaning of the term is not completely explained in the text, its definition may also be included in the footnote. For example, the word "microscopic" is technical, and at a certain grade level, may be difficult for the students. Since it is an adjective and ordinarily would not be explained in the text, the definition might be included in the footnote. A difficult non-technical word appearing in the text is usually treated in the same way as a difficult technical term.

In most textbooks for science the technical terms, and the difficult non-technical terms appear in lists at the ends of the chapters in which they are introduced and in the glossary with their definitions.

In general, the newer vocabulary lists are prepared by modifying and reanalyzing some of the earlier lists such as those prepared by Curtis[5] and Mallinson.[6]

THE GESTALT OF READING DIFFICULTY

Although the measures taken for developing graded vocabulary lists for science, for keeping the lists up-to-date, and for properly introducing technical terms are indispensable they alone are not sufficient to provide for the sequential development of reading skills, or assure the proper level of reading difficulty of the text material. The pattern, or *Gestalt,* of the presentation is equally significant.

A sentence consisting of ten non-technical, easy words is obviously not difficult to understand. However, a sentence of fifty non-technical, easy words, with several dependent clauses, and obtuse phrases is likely to be more difficult than one that contains a few technical terms. With such difficult sentences, it is unlikely that sequence can be attained.

Authors and publishers of science textbooks seek to eliminate these road blocks to sequence. The obtuse phraseology, or just plain "bad writing," is ordinarily eliminated in the standard editing procedure. The length and complexity of the sentences are controlled by continuous inspection of the material as writing progresses. In general, the materials are measured for these dimensions of reading difficulty with one of the common reading formulae.

Generally, the publishers seek to establish the level of reading difficulty on the basis of *Gestalt,* about one-grade level below the students for whom the book is designed. Measurements of books published recently compared with those of books published about ten years ago indicate some improvement with respect to this aspect of reading difficulty. However, many publishers have not been able to resolve the problem of increasing the level of sophistication of science materials without increasing the reading difficulty of their materials. In some cases, the reading difficulty has increased markedly.

[5]Curtis, *op. cit.*

[6]George Greisen Mallinson, "The Development of a Vocabulary for General Physical Science," *Twelfth Yearbook of the National Council on Measurements Used in Education,* Part II, 1955, pp. 6-8.

USING MATERIALS TO DEVELOP
SEQUENCE OF READING SKILL

The extent of attainment of direct, compared with that of concomitant, objectives has been sufficiently established to warrant little or no discussion here. However, suffice to say, the less direct the efforts are toward exploiting the attributes of a material, the less it is likely that a student will profit from using the material. If the "built-in" qualities of reading materials for science are to be optimally useful, both the teacher and the student must be aware of the qualities and use the materials accordingly. A few suggestions are here made.

In nearly all science textbooks there are introductory sections called "To the Student," "To the Teacher," or some similar name. In these sections are discussed the ways in which the technical and non-technical vocabularies are treated. These sections should be considered initial assignments for the students. In general, without such attention, students are likely to be unaware of, or prone to ignore, bold-faced or italicized terms, phonetics, definitions, and other similar devices designed for sequence in growth of reading skills.

Training should be given to the student in examining all emphasized terms, in using the phonetics and in checking the glassary in which the meanings of the terms are further amplified.

The lists of key words at the ends of the chapters should not be studied *before* the materials in the chapters are covered. Otherwise, the student will acquire a number of atomistic definitions that are out of context. The relationships between words and their contexts and the development of reading skills need no amplification here. These lists may well be suitable for post-testing, but hardly for pre-study.

The process of reading the science materials, however, demands some examination. There have been a few, not completely conclusive studies undertaken that suggest that certain special skills beyond the general reading skills, need to be developed in order to read science materials with understanding.

In general, these studies indicate that extensive reading of science material in and of itself does not yield significant increments in learning science. However, these studies indicate also that where direction and effort is applied in such reading toward the development of science understandings, there is a significant increase.

The implementation of such general findings is best expressed by Culver in this statement:

Certainly the student should not expect to read a science textbook as rapidly as he reads a book of science fiction or simply written biography. Neither should he expect to read a textbook for the purpose of finding the steps for proving an experiment as rapidly as he reads a textbook just for pleasure. Nevertheless, many a student makes little adjustment in his reading rate. Of all content fields, science requires the most accurate reading. There are, of course, times when skimming may be utilized, as in locating specific items of reference, and rapid reading is usually preferable in reading science fiction or biography of scientists. When, however, a student reads to find details, to learn the steps for an experiment, or to locate information to help him form a generalization, he must read at a rate which will allow him to be accurate.

The science teacher can help a student vary his reading rate by providing class drills which will show the appropriate rate for various materials. To point up the difference between skimming and a slower rate of reading required for accuracy, follow the skimming exercise with one in which the student reads a selection and is then given a detailed comprehension test.[7]

CONCLUDING STATEMENT

It may be said that one of the best criteria for the development of reading skill using science materials is growth of understanding of the science material. Measurements of the accumulation of scientific facts may serve some objectives. However, the results of the measurements are not indications of understanding any more than the ability to parrot dictionary definitions is a measure of general reading ability. Thus, since a criterion of the development of reading skill is the students' level of understanding of the science, evaluation in science should take cognizance of this dimension.

[7]Mary Kay Culver, "Materials and Procedures to Develop Reading Efficiency in the Sciences: In Grades Seven through Nine," *Promoting Maximal Reading Growth among Able Learners,* pp. 111-12. Edited by Helen M. Robinson. Supplementary Educational Monographs, No. 81. Chicago: University of Chicago Press, December, 1954.

VIII

Reading Disabilities

38. Reading and Reading Difficulty:

A Conceptional Analysis*

MORTON WIENER
WARD CROMER

IN trying to impose some coordinating conceptual framework upon the phenomena subsumed under reading and reading difficulty, we believe with T. L. Harris (1962) that "the real issues arise from different conceptions of the nature of the reading process itself and of the learning processes, sets and principles to be stressed" (p. 5). In the present paper we will specify and discuss a number of issues which we believe must be considered to develop a more adequate conceptual framework. The issues are derived from an analysis of the diversity of definitions of reading and the variety of explanations offered to account for reading difficulty. Once the issues are clearly defined, a coordinating framework may be possible. We will spell out what we think to be one such conceptualization of reading and reading difficulty. Four interrelated issues emerge from an examination of the many definitions of reading. Discussion of these issues may help clarify some of the present ambiguity and confusion about reading.

Indentification versus Comprehension.

The first issue is, what behaviors define reading? Some definitions focus primarily on the identification of the stimulus configurations (letters, letter patterns, words, clauses, sentences) appearing on the printed page, while others emphasize the comprehension of the material. When identification skills are emphasized, the defining attribute of reading is the correct "saying" of the word. Comprehension, on the other hand, implies the derivation of some form of meaning and the relating of this meaning to other experiences or ideas.

The assessment of identification is restricted to some evaluation of what and how words are "said." (How the word is to be pronounced and the variability permitted are both based on some implicit consensus.)

*From *Harvard Educational Review,* **37**, 4 (Fall, 1967), 620-643. Reprinted with permission of *Harvard Educational Review,* and Morton Wiener and Ward Cromer.

*The authors wish to thank Dr. Joachim F. Wohlwill, Dr. James M. Coffee, and the other colleagues and students who read the manuscript in one or more of its revisions and who made helpful suggestions and criticisms. The time to write this paper was made possible in part by Grant M-3860 from the National Institute of Mental Health, United States Public Health Service.

Comprehension, on the other hand, is assessed by such criteria as the ability of the reader to paraphrase, to abstract the contents, to answer questions about the material, or to deal critically with the contents. Comprehension can also be inferred partly from the relative quality of identifications, i.e., by the tone, inflection, and phrasing of the identifications. However, the inability to demonstrate comprehension in any of these ways may be a function of restricted language, restricted experience, limited intelligence, or combinations of these three, rather than a function of a reading difficulty. If comprehension is used as the criterial behavior of reading, then these other possible antecedents of noncomprehension must be ruled out before the problem can be called a "reading difficulty."

When both kinds of behaviors are included in definitions of reading, the question arises whether these are solely a matter of empasis on two parts of one process, or whether different activities are implied? At first glance, it would appear that these differences are matters of emphasis only. For those holding a single process view, identification can be considered a necessary antecedent to comprehension. Closer examination of the relationships between identification and comprehension shows, however, that rather than this one relationship, several are possible.

Although both identification and comprehension require some discrimination process (i.e., to identify or comprehend the reader must be able to distinguish among words), comprehension and identification do not necessarily imply each other. One example of the occurrence of identification without comprehension is the child who may be able to read (i.e., "say") the words printed in a scientific journal with some facility without having any notion of the meaning of the words. Another example is an American or a Frenchman who, with only a limited amount of training, can pronounce most words in Italian (a language which has a high relationship between spelling and sound), without knowing the meanings of the words. Whether these instances are considered reading depends upon the definition. We recognize that there may be differences between the saying aloud of material by individuals who do not comprehend and by those who do. Comprehension can sometimes be inferred from inflections, tone, and pauses, all of which may be derived from the context of the material read rather than from the sentence construction. These differences, when present, are often both subtle and difficult to denote reliably.

The occurrence of comprehension without identification, on the other hand, is less evident and examples are somewhat more difficult to cite. The best single example is given by Geschwind (1962) in his work with aphasics. He finds that some aphasic patients are able to respond appropriately to the meanings of a written communication, but apparently are unable to identify the words, i.e., to say them. As we understand it, some aphasics may be able to follow printed instructions without being able to "say" them aloud. A more subtle example can be found in "speed reading" which appears to exemplify nonidentification in that the very speed required makes identification unlikely. To acquire speed reading the individual must learn to eliminate persisting identification patterns. We hold, first, that the behavior occurring in speed reading is similar to that of more typical fast readers and, second, that in the advanced stages of reading, the presence of certain identification activities may interfere with the speed of reading and may result in less than maximum comprehension. Once reading skills have been acquired, reading may go from the discrimination of stimuli directly to comprehension without concomitant identification. Further, in good readers identification occurs primarily for novel or difficult material where there is an attempt to achieve some auditory or other discriminations which can be the basis for comprehension[1] (e.g., by sounding out an unfamiliar word).

Acquisition versus Accomplished Reading.

A second issue emerging from comparisons of definitions of reading is, does reading refer to the behavior occurring during acquisition of skills or to the behavior manifested after these "skills" have been achieved? Investigators who define reading in terms of accomplished reading often imply that certain other skills are present without spelling them out. Those who emphasize the acquisition of reading give definitions which focus on the skills that need to be mastered, often without stating what constitutes the end-product.[2]

Definitions of reading generally associate acquisition with identification behavior on the one hand, and comprehension with accomplished reading on the other. An emphasis on problems associated with the acquisition of skills most often implies a focus on identification skills, while a focus on accomplished reading often implies a stress on comprehension activities.

The failure to distinguish between acquisition and accomplished reading in definitions partially accounts for the confusion about the *relationship* between identification and comprehension. In the acquisition of reading skills, identification may be a necessary *antecedent* to comprehension (as we will discuss in more detail below, word meanings are typically available to the child primarily in auditory form). But identification, which is essential in the acquisition phase for comprehension, may be irrelevant for the skilled reader who already has meaning associated with the visual forms and who may go directly from the written forms to the meaning without identification: that is, without an intermediary "verbal-auditory" transformation. Put another way,

---

[1]We will attempt later to make a distinction between visual and auditory comprehension as components in the acquisition of reading.

[2]The research literature on reading difficulties reflects these same differences in emphasis. Some researchers focus on difficulties that can be considered as problems of acquisition, e.g., difficulty with word recognition or phonetics, etc. (Budoff, 1964; Elkind, 1965; Goens, 1958; Robeck, 1963; Goetzinger, 1960; Marchbanks; 1965). Others focus on difficulties that occur after acquisition is relatively complete, e.g., advancement of comprehension skills, critical reading, or enhancement of experiences (Robinson, 1965; Woestehoff, 1960; Chapman, 1965; Emans, 1965; Gray, 1960).

although some form of identification (saying a word either aloud or subvocally) may be essential for comprehension during acquisition, its nonoccurrence is not a problem for an experienced reader. Thus, the final product of reading need not include components that went into its acquisition. To draw an analogy, many of the components that go into the acquisition of good driving skill disappear as the driver becomes more proficient. In early learning there is much more cognitive behavior associated with the sensory-motor behavior, while in the later phases operating a car is almost totally sensory-motor.

Relative versus Absolute Criteria.

Another source of ambiguity for conceptualizing reading is the different implicit criteria used for designating "good" reading. Sometimes, reading skill (and reading difficulty) is defined in terms of absolute or ideal criteria, but more often in terms of relative criteria. Both approaches present problems. When absolute or ideal criteria are used, a good reader is typically specified as someone able to read a certain number of words at a given rate with some particular level of comprehension. Insofar as ideal criteria are arbitrary, standards can be designated which include differing proportions of the reading population. Using absolute criteria, children during the acquisition of reading skill would not be considered good readers.

A relative definition of reading skill invokes criteria which specify, either implicitly or explicitly, some normative group. The implication of a relative criterion is that the same kind or level of skill may be called "good or bad reading" depending on who is doing what and when. For example, a second-grade child who has difficulties in phonetic skills (such as blending of sounds into words, which may be a necessary precursor of auditory comprehension) is not considered a reading problem when relative criteria are used, while a child in the sixth grade who lacks this skill is labeled as having a reading difficulty. In both instances, the same skill is missing. In this context, a sixth-grader may be defined as a poor reader, yet a third-grader behaving the same way (as far as we can determine) might be considered a good reader. It becomes evident that very little information can be communicated by statements about good or poor readers unless they are accompanied by clear specifications of the normative group's behaviors. Further, unless the relative criteria are made explicit, there can be no basis for comparing two "poor readers" since they might have been defined as such by different criteria.

The most important problem raised by a relative point of view is that very different behaviors may be given the same label. Having been given the same label, these different behaviors may later be treated as if they were the same phenomenon. The reading-research literature gives evidence that this danger is real in that poor reading is used as a generic term, apparently without the recognition that different investigators may be talking about very different forms of behaviors.

Research approaches and inferences are influenced by whether a relative or an absolute point of view is assumed. These different viewpoints implicitly specify the groups to be studied (those who are taken to be poor readers) and, more importantly, what is considered to be the appropriate control group for the study (the normative baseline against which the experimental group is to be compared). If the criteria are not made explicit, inappropriate control groups may often be established. For example, if a third-grader with an IQ of 75 is compared with other third-graders, he may be defined as a poor reader. Yet if he is compared with other children with IQ's of 75 in the third grade, he may be labeled a good reader by some relative criterion. In the former case, what is at issue may be relevant to intelligence, not to reading.

It may be more useful to specify the "ideal" case of reading and what its components or essential behaviors are. Having spelled out the ideal case, different people can be compared in terms of the presence or absence of these specifications, independent of distinctions between a person learning to read and an accomplished reader, and independent of evaluative statements as to how "good" the reading is.

Reading versus Language Skills.

Investigators vary in the extent to which they emphasize the role of already present auditory language (i.e., knowledge of word meaning and the availability of grammatical forms) either as a separate skill or as one included in reading. There may be little or no concern with previously acquired auditory language capabilities when reading is considered as identification. When reading is considered as comprehension, some investigators (Fries, 1962; Lefevre, 1964; Bloomfield, 1961) deal explicitly with the role of language in reading. The majority of research is less explicit, even though comprehension implies the utilization of meanings already available in some other (usually auditory) form. In studying reading difficulty, Milner (1951) explicitly notes the differential experience with verbal language skills in children from middle and lower socioeconomic backgrounds and its relationship to reading skill. Bereiter and Engelmann (1966) also consider this issue a major one as evidenced by their attempt to train culturally deprived children in language skills before introducing reading. A failure to be explicit about the relationship between reading and previously acquired auditory language often leads to ambiguities as to whether a particular difficulty is a reading problem, language problem, or both.

Examination of Specific Definitions.

Having noted some issues, we can now examine specific definitions[3] of reading in order to demonstrate their varying degrees of emphasis on: (a)

---

[3]The particular definitions offered here are not meant to be exhaustive but were chosen primarily because they appear to exemplify the different emphases with which we are concerned.

discrimination, identification, and comprehension; (b) acquisition versus the final product of accomplished reading; (c) absolute versus relative criteria for good reading; and (d) the relation of language skills to reading skills.

The first definition reveals an emphasis on the acquisition of reading skills without specification of the attributes of an accomplished reader. More particularly, it focuses on the development of identification processes with comprehension skills noted only incidentally:

> There are several ways of characterizing the behavior we call reading. It is receiving communication; it is making discriminative responses to graphic symbols; it is decoding graphic symbols to speech; and it is getting meaning from the printed page. A child in the early stages of acquiring reading skill may not be doing all these things; however, some aspects of reading must be mastered before others and have an essential function in a sequence of development of the final skill. The average child, when he begins learning to read, has already mastered to a marvelous extent the art of communication. He can speak and understand his own language in a fairly complex way, employing units of language organized in a hierarchy and with a grammatical structure. Since a writing system must correspond to the spoken one, and since speech is prior to writing, the framework and unit structure of speech will determine more or less the structure of the writing system, though the rules of correspondence vary for different languages and writing systems. . . .
> Once a child begins his progression from spoken language to written language, there are, I think, three phases of learning to be considered. They present three different kinds of learning tasks, and they are roughly sequential, though there must be considerable overlapping. These three phases are: learning to differentiate graphic symbols; learning to decode letters to sounds ("map" the letters into sounds); and using progressively higher-order units of structure. (Gibson, 1965, pp. 1-2)

In that the above definition focuses on acquisition, we can infer that a relative scale would be used for designating individuals who are not progressing adequately. What is most noteworthy is that there is also some ambiguity in this definition as to whether the development of language skills is part of reading or prior to and/or independent of reading.

In contrast to Gibson, Geschwind (1962, p. 116) working with aphasics, offers a definition which focuses only on the accomplished reader and comprehension and which makes no reference to identification behaviors or processes in acquisition of reading:

> The word *read* is used in the narrow sense of "ability to comprehend language presented visually" and not at all in the sense of "ability to read aloud."

By this definition, any reading without comprehension would be designated either as non-reading or as a reading problem, though it does not require "saying" for "reading" to occur. The definition makes no reference to the role of discrimination of the printed stimuli, which we assume must occur in order for comprehension to take place. Further, no explicit statement is made about either the relative or the absolute amount of comprehension which must be present for an individual to be designated a good or poor reader.

The following definition is ambiguous about the relationship of identification to comprehension:

> ... reading involves ... the recognition of printed or written symbols which serve as stimuli for the recall of meanings built up through the reader's past experience. New meanings are derived through manipulation of concepts already in his possession. The organization of these meanings is governed by the clearly defined purposes of the reader. In short, the reading process involves both the acquisition of the meanings intended by the writer and the reader's own contributions in the form of interpretation, evaluation, and reflection about these meanings. (Bond & Tinker, 1957, p. 19)

The word "recognition," as used here can be taken to mean either discrimination or identification; both usages are incidental to the role of comprehension. Further, this definition refers almost exclusively to the activities of the accomplished reader without apparent concern for the activities necessary for acquiring reading skills (other than the acquisition of meaning). By this definition, most children could be designated as having reading difficulties in that they have not yet acquired the "recognitions" nor the "meanings intended by the writer." This definition also makes little distinction between reading and language skills, thereby making it possible to confuse a language deficiency with a reading difficulty.

In contrast, the next definition makes an explicit distinction between language usage and reading.

> The first stage in learning the reading process is the "transfer" stage. It is the period during which the child is learning to transfer from the auditory signs for language signals, which he has already learned, to a set of visual signs for the same signals. This process of transfer is not the learning of the language code or a new language code; it is not the learning of a new or different set of language signals. It is not the learning of new "words," or of new grammatical structures, or of new meanings. These are all matters of the language signals which he has on the whole already learned so well that he is not conscious of their use. This first stage is complete when within his narrow linguistic experience the child can respond rapidly and accurately to the visual patterns that represent the language signals in this limited field, as he does to the auditory patterns that they replace.
>
> The second stage covers the period during which the responses to the visual patterns become habits so automatic that the graphic shapes themselves sink below the threshold of attention, and the cumulative comprehension of

the meanings signalled enables the reader to supply those portions of the signals which are not in graphic representation themselves.

The third stage begins when the reading process itself is so automatic that the reading is used equally with or even more than live language in the acquiring and developing of experience—when reading stimulates the vivid imaginative realization of vicarious experience. (Fries, 1962, p. 132)

This definition is also more explicit than most in distinguishing between acquisition and the accomplished reader, the relation of identification to comprehension, and the difference between language skills and reading skills. It does not, however, specify the forms of behaviors which would constitute reading difficulty, except those skills necessary for adequate "transfer" to occur.

The next definition focuses on the sequential development of reading from identification to comprehension. It does not make explicit the role identification plays in the skills which develop later. It also exemplifies the relativity of definitions of reading when it states that what constitutes reading skill depends upon the level of the learner as he progresses from acquisition to accomplished reading.

We may define reading as the act of responding appropriately to printed symbols. For the beginner, reading is largely concerned with learning to recognize the symbols with represent spoken words. As proficiency in reading increases, the individual learns to adapt and vary his method of reading in accordance with his purpose for reading and the restrictions imposed by the nature of the material. As the learner achieves skill in the recognition side of reading, the reasoning side of reading becomes increasingly important. The nature of the reading task, therefore, changes as the learner progresses from less mature to more mature levels; reading is not one skill, but a large number of interrelated skills which develop gradually over a period of many years. (Harris, A. J., 1948, p. 9)

These examples should make evident the diversity of emphases, the ambiguity and confusion in definitions of reading. Further, this discussion has shown that investigators, with few exceptions (e.g., Fries), have not made distinctions between reading activities and language activities, or if so, they have been ambiguous as to the independence or interdependence of language and reading. All definitions that focus on meaning or comprehension imply language as an antecedent, but do not necessarily offer a basis for identifying poor reading as a reading difficulty rather than as a language difficulty.

AN ANALYSIS OF READING DIFFICULTY

The issues raised thus far have been related to different usages of the term "reading." Other issues emerge when the term "reading difficulty" is examined. An analysis of the usages of the term "reading difficulty" indicates that four different assumptions are used to account for reading difficulty and its etiology. Each of the four models implies particular kinds of remediation.

The Assumption of Defect.

Investigators who hold that reading difficulty is attributable to some malfunction, i.e., something is not operating appropriately in the person so that he *cannot* benefit from his experiences, exemplify what we call a defect model. This approach generally implies that this impairment is considered to be relatively permanent. Defect explanations typically involve sensory-physiological factors. For example, Reitan (1964) discusses "reading impairment . . . and its relationship to damage of the left cerebral hemisphere" (p. 104). Some investigators appear to assume a defect whenever there is a reading difficulty. We hold that while an assumption of defect may be appropriate for some instances (e.g., cases of visual, hearing or other sensory impairment) there is no evidence that an assumption of defect accounts for all reading difficulties. Further, investigators holding a defect view often do not distinguish between the implications of a defect during acquisition of reading skill and after acquisition has taken place (e.g., blindness, brain damage). This type of explanation also implies that for "normal" reading to occur in individuals with a defect, change must occur (e.g., brain surgery) relatively independent of reading, or a different sequence in the acquisition must be utilized (e.g., teaching a blind person to read through the use of the tactual modality).

The Assumption of Deficiency.

Other investigators have argued that reading difficulty is attributable to the *absence* of some function, i.e., a particular factor or process is absent and must be *added* before adequate reading can occur. Most attempts at remedial reading instruction are based on this interpretation of reading difficulties. The child must learn something he has not yet learned (e.g., phonetic skills, language skills, etc.) in order to make up his deficiency. In contrast to the defect explanation of reading difficulty, reversibility is almost always assumed.

The Assumption of Disruption.

A third type of model used to account for reading difficulty assumes that the difficulty is attributable to something which is *present* but is *interfering* with reading and must be *removed* before reading will occur. For example, if a child is "anxious," "hyperemotional," or has "intrapsychic conflicts," he may be unable to learn to read (cf., Koff, 1961). An assumption of disruption is implicit in investigations of so-called neurotic learning disabilities. It is also implicit in any approach which maintains that using the wrong methods to teach reading will disrupt and interfere with the learning that takes place when the correct teaching method is used. Occasionally the assumption of disruption operates jointly with the deficiency assumption, the notion being that first the interference must be removed and then the missing components must be added.

The Assumption of Difference.

Lastly, various researchers assume that reading difficulty is attributable to *differences* or mismatches between the typical mode of responding and that which is more appropriate, and thus has the best payoff in a particular situation. This model assumes that the individual would read adequately if the material were consistent with his behavior patterns; thus, a *change* in either the material or in his patterns of verbalization is a prerequisite for better reading.

Cromer and Wiener (1966) posit that poor readers have evolved different response patterns; i.e., they elaborate "cues" in a manner different from that of good readers. Within their framework, both good and poor readers "scan" and derive partial information from the printed stimuli; the specific difference between the good and poor readers is that poor readers generally elaborate these cues by responding more idiosyncratically than do good readers, either because they have not learned consensual response patterns or because they have learned idiosyncratic patterns too well. In this framework, reading difficulty is expected to occur when there is a mismatch between the material being read and the response patterns of the reader.

An example of a mismatch is when auditorally- and visually-presented languages are discrepant, as might be the case for a lower-class child who speaks a neighborhood "slang." The child may not be able to elaborate the cues in "formal language patterns." He does not read well because he does not draw from the same language experiences as does the middle-class child for whom a typical reading test is written; there is a mismatch between the reading material and his typical pattern of responding. If, however, the material were presented in the same form as his spoken language, we posit that he would then be able to read more adequately. This child would not be considered a reading problem but rather a language problem in that he does not draw from the same language experiences as the middle-class child for whom a typical reading text is written.

Still another example of a mismatch involves the reading of highly technical material. An individual may have difficulty because he (in contrast to an expert in the same area) has sequences which are less likely to match the reading input. A psychologist reading a physics book or a physicist reading a psychology book would be slowed down, would show more errors in his reading, and would have less comprehension than when each reads in his own field. In this instance, there are differences in reading abilities, depending on the material being read. It does not seem meaningful, however, to consider these differences in skill as reading problems. Thus no pathology is posited for a "reading difficulty" stemming from a mismatch.

Associated with each of the assumption models are implicit differences in the kinds of factors—sensory-perceptual (physiological), experiential-learning, and personality-emotional (psychological)—assumed to account for reading difficulty. Pointing to physiological factors generally implies a defect; i.e., something other than the behaviors involved in reading must be changed or in some way dealt with before improved reading can occur. When the focus is on experience or learning, either a deficiency or a difference is implied; i.e., the individual has not learned a particular skill or has learned a different one. On the other hand, explanations that focus on psychological factors imply a disruption and/or a deficiency. In sum, not only are there different assumptions to account for reading difficulty but in addition, each assumption model implies a particular set of operative factors and a particular form of intervention or remediation.

Models for Conceptualizing Reading Difficulty: Antecedent-Consequent Relationships

Another source of confusion in the literature is the form of explanation offered to account for "reading problems." Some investigators refer to single "causes" of reading difficulty while others state that multiple "causes" need to be invoked. Applying a formal or logical analysis to these kinds of explanatory statements reveals additional conceptual problems. This task can be facilitated by reformulating and extending a model developed by Handlon (1960) to spell out possible forms for explaining schizophrenia.[4] We have substituted the term "reading difficulty" where in Handlon's original application the term schizophrenia appears. We will try to "explain" reading difficulties by relating the variables associated with reading (antecedents) to the variables associated with reading difficulties (consequents).

1. Model One

(in Handlon's form of explanation) states that reading difficulty "is a class with a single member, this member having a single radical cause." In our conditional form, Model One is "If A, then X," where A is a single specific antecedent and X is a class ("reading difficulty") in which each instance of a reading difficulty is considered equivalent.

An example of Model One is Carrigan's (1959) synaptic transmission (chemical) theory of reading disability. She maintains that disabled readers are part of a population of slow learners characterized by atypical production of two chemicals, ACh (acetycholine) and ChE (cholinesterase). Although the

---

[4]Handlon, in his model called Single-Multiple Causal Factors uses the terms "cause" and "effect"; with our philosophical bias we prefer the terms "antecedent" and "consequent." These terms will be used here in a conditional ("If, then") rather than a causal form. The conditional statement is not meant to imply either a spatial or temporal relationship, but a relationship in a formal-logical sense, We thank Dr. Roger Bibace who brought this article to our attention.

balance and concentration level of these chemicals is affected by environmental (anxiety producing) factors, it is the chemical factor itself which is seen to underly reading disability, that is, reading disability is presented also as if it were a single member class. Another example of Model One, Delacato's (1959) theory of "central neurological organization," attributes reading difficulty to a lack of cerebral cortical dominance.

Although logically possible, Model One does not seem very promising. Most investigators reject both the notion that a single antecedent accounts for all reading difficulties, and the notion that reading difficulty is in fact a class with only a single member.

2. Model Two

states that reading difficulty is "a class with a single member, that member having multiple factors constituting the radical cause."[5] In our conditional form, Model Two is "If A or B or C . . . , then X," where A, B, etc. are particular and independent[6] antecedents, and, as in Model One, X is a class with a single member called "reading difficulty."

Rabinovitch (1959) appears to use a Model Two form of explanation. He defines reading retardation as reading achievement two or more years below the mental age obtained on performance tests and then goes on to list three subclasses of antecedents of reading difficulty (exogenous, i.e., cultural and emotional factors; congenital brain damage; and endogenous, i.e., biological or neurological disturbances). Similarly, Roswell and Natchez (1964) in their treatment of reading disability argue for a multi-causal model and describe a series of antecedents that can "cause" reading difficulty (e.g., intellectual, physical, emotional, environmental, educational, and growth factors). Investigators using this model might *consider* reading difficulty as different for the different "causes," but they do not *specify* nor delineate these differences; that is, they seem to treat reading difficulty as if it were a single member class.

Although this form of explanation may also be logically tenable, we are convinced that the assumption that reading difficulty is a class with a single member is unacceptable. Our belief is that reading difficulty is a multiple-member class and that Model Two forms of statements might better be changed to "If A, then X_1"; "If B, then X_2"; "If C, then X_3" where X_1, X_2, X_3 are particular and independent manifestations within the class reading difficulty

---

[5]We will consider this statement only in the form "If A or B or C, then X" rather than the form "If A and B and C, then X," since the latter is logically reducible to "If A, then X," where A stands for a conjunctive category.

[6]By using the symbols A, B, C . . . and X_1, X_2, X_3, etc., there is a possible implication that these symbols may be treated as an ordinal series, with the later implying the earlier. In each model except for Model Six (see below), these symbols are used only in the sense of a nominal scale (Stevens, 1951) and could be written in the form "If alpha, then X_{alpha}; if aleph, then X_{aleph}; etc."

(Model Five, see below). We maintain that if an investigator looks carefully enough, he will find different members within the class X which might better meet the criteria of a class with a single member associated with a particular antecedent, and that it is incumbent on investigators to explore their "single consequent" in a multiple-antecedent/single-consequent model to determine whether the consequent is in fact a class with only a single member.

3. Model Three

states that reading difficulty "is a class with several members, all members having the same single . . . cause." This statement can be represented in the following form: "If A, then X_1 or X_2 or X_3 . . . " where A is a particular antecedent and X_1, X_2, etc. are particular members of the class called "reading difficulty." To the extent that investigators have not labeled the specific forms of reading difficulty (that is, different members of the class reading difficulty), then they would be unlikely to apply a model using a single antecedent and multiple consequents. In fact, no appropriate examples of Model Three were located in the literature. Those that appeared at first to be examples of Model Three were found to be more appropriately assigned to Model One, which treats the consequent as a single-member class.

4. Model Four

states that reading difficulty "is a class with several members, each having single or multiple causes that are not necessarily unique to that member." In other words, there are many antecedent variables and many manifestations of reading difficulty (consequents) and the relationships between these antecedents and consequents are unspecified or unspecifiable. This model can be represented in the form: "If A and/or B and/or C . . . , then X_1, or X_2, or X_3 . . . "

This form of explanation appears to be most popular in the current literature; for examples one can turn to almost any comprehensive book on the "diagnostic teaching of reading" (e.g., Strang, 1964; Bond and Tinker, 1957; Bryant, 1963). These textbook approaches list all the possible "causes" of reading difficulty and then discuss techniques for remedial instruction. The relationships between the many antecedents and the many consequents are never clearly specified. The problems inherent in this approach are exemplified most clearly in a study reported by Goltz (1966). Working with "individual remedial reading for boys in trouble," he advocates the simultaneous use of five basic approaches to the teaching of reading (sight word, phonics, combination, linguistic, experiential) in the hope that one will work (he draws the analogy of shotgun pellets). The results of this approach were "some astounding successes and remarkable failures." The need for a theoretical rationale for relating possible difficulties and specific types of intervention is obvious. Again, we argue that it is incumbent on investigators to attempt to locate the particular antecedent and its relationship to a particular consequent.

5. Model Five

appears to be the most acceptable form for explaining the phenomenon called reading difficulty. It states that reading difficulty is "a class with several members, each member having a single, unique cause. This statement can be represented in the form: "If A, then X_1; or if B, then X_2; or if C, then X_3 ... " where the X's represent different particular patterns of less-than-ideal reading. This model says that there are many antecedent variables and many manifestations under a general rubric "reading difficulty"; and the relationships between the antecedents and the consequents are, at least in theory, specifiable. Both Model Five and Model Four have multiple antecedents and multiple consequents. Model Five, however, associates a different antecedent with a specific consequent. For example, de Hirsch (1963) attempts to distinguish between two groups of adolescents with language disorders by suggesting that the etiology of each is different. Kinsbourne and Warrington (1963) note that two syndromes of developmental cerebral deficit seem to be associated with different forms of reading difficulty.

6. Model Six

assumes that each of the manifestations of reading difficulty (i.e., the X's) is a member of the general class called reading difficulty and that each of these forms is independent. It may be, however, more meaningful to conceptualize the manifestations within the class, reading difficulty, in a model which includes a notion of sequence. This kind of model is not considered by Handlon; we will elaborate it as *Model Six*. This model can be represented in the following form: "If A, then X_1" and "If X_1, then B" and "If B, then X_2," and "If X_2, then C" and "If C, then X_3 ... X_n." If, for example, C does not occur nor does X_3, then X_n, the particular form of behavior defined as reading, would not be expected to develop (X_n being defined as a class with a single member, a particular form of reading which is the end-product of the sequence and can be considered as an indicator on an absolute scale). Model Six explicitly includes the notion of an ordinal series and implies that if any member of the sequence were missing, further evolution of the sequence would not be expected, or at least not in the acquisition phase of learning to read. If the sequence has already evolved and there is a disruption, then depending on the point in the sequence where disruption occurs, later forms of reading may be present, even though some or all earlier forms are absent. This kind of formulation can account for differences in the kinds of reading difficulties noted when a disruption is present during acquisition or occurs in an accomplished reader (e.g., the reading of brain-damaged adults who were previously good readers versus the reading of brain-damaged children during the acquisition phase). Another implication is that the arbitrarily designated end point of a sequence specifies the antecedents and prior sequences to be included.

A CONCEPTUALIZATION OF READING AND
READING DIFFICULTY

We pointed out earlier that some investigators treat reading as identification while others treat it as comprehension and that this difference has implications for what was defined as reading difficulty. In an effort to integrate these seemingly disparate approaches, reading will be conceptualized and discussed as a two-step process involving first identification and then comprehension. During the discussion, the antecedents for identification will be considered first and then comprehension will be considered.

Identification

Identification will be used to mean "word-naming," in the context of a transformation of stimuli.[7] In the discussion that follows, our formulation comes from an analysis of visual-to-auditory transformation; similar analyses could be derived for other transformations. We assume a physiological substrate which is adequate for "normal" functioning to occur.

"Discrimination" constitutes one set of antecedents to identification. Prior to discrimination, however, a child must attend to the stimulus to make sensory input possible. Given sensory input, the child must then be able to make form discriminations. By discrimination, we mean the ability to make proper focal adjustments; to distinguish figure-ground, brightness, lines, curves, and angles; and to respond to differences in the amount of white space surrounding the forms (this latter discrimination is involved in the delineation of word units). These forms of discrimination are antecedents of identification.

Given the ability to discriminate, the child can begin to identify by distinguishing on the basis of angles and curves ("man" from "dog") or word length ("dog" from "good"), by responding to variations in relations among letter sequences ("on" vs. "no"), and by responding to spatial orientations of visual stimuli (left/right and up/down). These antecedents not only make

[7]Identification presupposes a discrimination of one graphic symbol from others, discrimination of auditory symbols from others, and a transformation of these symbols from one form (usually visual) to a second form (usually auditory). The original visual forms and the transformed auditory forms are considered to be equivalent, differing only in that the referents are represented in different modalities. The two symbol forms are considered equivalent in that they contain the same information for members of a communication group. Essentially, then, the major critical antecedents of identification are the discriminations among the original symbols, the discriminations among the transformed symbols, and a "knowledge" of the principles of transformation from one form to the other. Implicit in this conceptualization is that the transformed symbols (i.e., words as said aloud) can become an input for another individual. Implied also is that there is some consensual basis to assess the adequacy of the identification, with consensus meaning only that there is agreement within the group using the particular language or dialect.

possible new identifications but also make earlier forms of identification easier because the reader can respond to more of the available and co-occurring cues. For example, "dog" and "good" can be discriminated on the basis of word length, and the orientation of the first and last letters.

Using discriminations among sequences and general configurations, the child can now learn to identify a relatively large number of words solely by discriminating the first and last letters in an otherwise similar configuration (e.g., length, round vs. angled, internal letters, etc.). Although this discrimination may be adequate in the early stages of reading acquisition, the child must later learn to discriminate other components in the word such as internal letters ("bat" vs. "but" vs. "bet" vs. "bit"), sequence of letters ("there vs. "three"), additions of letters ("smile" vs. "simile"), etc. In these cases, to increase speed, it would appear that the child has to learn to respond to the variety of available cues and the order of their importance as the basis of discrimination of words within his language.

Antecedents for the identification of words in isolation are not sufficient for reading words in a sequence such as a phrase or a sentence; the individual must learn to say the words in the order given, although he does not necessarily have to "look" at them in that order. A knowledge of language and language sequences will facilitate the discrimination of words in a sequence insofar as the co-occurrences of words can become an additional basis for discrimination, e.g., "the horse's mane" vs. "the horse's mine."

The antecedents discussed thus far are associated with learning to read using the "look-say" approach, which is essentially how one learns to read an ideographic language. Both this approach and languages requiring its use present special difficulties in that the reader must maintain a great many specific forms in his memory. Although he can discriminate new from old words and even among new words, he has no readily available way of identifying ("saying") the new words. If it were possible for a child to have a source of identifying words the first time he encountered them (e.g., via another person reading it or a speaking typewriter), and if he had the ability to store and recover the words as presented and as said, then the "look-say" method would be sufficient for reading. However, if new or novel words occur and there is no external source for initial identification, then a skill for identifying by oneself is required.

There are at least three different ways in which identification of new words occurs. They can be ordered by degree of explicitness for relating visual to sound forms. First, the individual may respond to some similarities among graphic forms, and he may also respond to some of the patterns of similarity among associated auditory forms. For example, the word "mat" looks like "man" and "hat," such that one approximation of the sound of "mat" could be the combination of the first part of "man" and the last part of "hat." The first sound approximated might not have exactly the same form as if it were emitted in the presence of the object. It could be corrected, however, by the reader's recognizing that the word as said sounds like some other word he had said at some other time.

The second way is like the first in that the reader uses similarities among graphic forms to aid his identification. In the first case, however, this response to similarity is incidental; in the second, it is systematic. An example of a systematic approach is the use of what linguists (such as Fries, 1962) call "spelling patterns." The individual is taught to look for similarities among visual and auditory forms by systematic exposure to various types of possible patterns, their variations, and their associated sounds. For example, if the individual learns to identify the words "man," "ban," "hat," and "fat," he will be able to identify the word "mat." Other examples of spelling patterns are mane/bane/hate/fate; and mean/bean/heat/feat. Thus, the possible similarities among visual forms, among auditory forms, and between visual and auditory forms are made somewhat more explicit by example.

In contrast to these two ways where similarity among graphic configurations is the basis for identifying new configurations, the third way requires the reader to know more explicit rules for transforming specific visual configurations into specific sounds, i.e., phonetics, to use Fries' terminology. For example, there is a "rule" that says when there is only one vowel in a word and it comes at the beginning or middle of a word, it is usually short ("hat," "and," "bed," "end"). These rules also include the notion that various locations and combinations of letters are associated with different sounds. One example is the "rule" that a vowel when followed by an "r" is neither long nor short, but is controlled by the "r"; e.g., "fur," "bird," "term."[8] One major difference between the phonetics approach and the other two is that identification of new words does not require previous experience with similar old words. However, the use of phonetics requires one additional ability, that of ordering letters from the beginning through to the end of a word. This skill, called "scanning," involves systematic eye movements from left to right and an organization of the input in that order.

Knowledge of co-occurrence of letters and words within a language will increase the rate of reading. Because not every word can come at a particular point in a sequence, the individual can identify words or groups of words rapidly even from very brief scanning of the material. Thus, "knowledge" of language or word sequences independent of visual input will reduce the amount of information required from scanning for identification to occur. At later stages, the reader may even be able to skip some of the words in a particular sequence, yet respond adequately with this decreased information. We propose that the ability to respond to this partial information, that is, the "elaboration" of these cues, can be based on learned patterns of sequential occurrences or what has

[8]In this context, ITA (cf., Downing, 1964; Downing, 1965) is seen as a procedure for simplifying acquisition; that is, for decreasing the number of "rules" the child must learn during acquisition of reading.

been called "previously learned co-occurrence probabilities" (Kempler and Wiener, 1963). Differences among readers in their ability to identify a sequence correctly may be explained by differences in response availabilities rather than by differences in visual inputs. Since response patterns may be differentially available among individuals, given specific reading materials, a reader may "respond" to the same material with differing degrees of adequacy depending upon the availability of appropriate response patterns, even assuming the "same" input.

Comprehension

If comprehension[9] is now included in the definition of reading, additional antecedents must be considered. In our usage, comprehension refers to the addition of some form of meaning associated with the identifications or discriminations, i.e., the words elicit shared associations, or consensual indicator responses to or about the referent, or a synonymous response. At least during acquisition, comprehension can occur and be examined at any point at which identification can occur; once the visual forms are transformed to auditory forms, there is a possibility of comprehension, given the presence of appropriate language skills. These language skills can be learned either before or along with the acquisition of identification skills. Language can include not only meaning but also those subjects typically dealt with by linguists (patterns, grammar, sequences, meaningful units, and so on). To the extent that these structural components are critical for meaning, these forms must also have been mastered or, alternatively, they must be learned during the acquisition phase.

It has been implied that meaning is available primarily through language as it occurs in the auditory form. We also have assumed implicitly that once there is a transformation from the visual to the auditory form, comprehension would follow. If the reader's auditory transformaiton (identification) corresponds to his already available auditory language forms, then meaning can be associated with the visual forms. For example, if a child in his identification says the word "ball" in the same way as he has heard it or as he says it in the presence of the referent object, then meaning can be transferred to the visual form. The assumed sequence has been: discriminations among input forms and output forms; transformation; identification; comprehension—all of these being required.

In all of the discussion thus far, individual differences have not been considered. Yet recognition of individual differences may be highly relevant in accounting for differences in forms of discrimination, identification, or comprehension. For example, individuals with low intelligence or with restricted language skills or restricted experiences might better be considered as having "problems" in these particular areas rather than in reading *per se*. Similarly,

[9]A concern with the definition of comprehension and meaning would take us too far afield, even if we were competent to deal with this complex problem.

there are other instances of non-reading which might better be attributed to the conditions under which reading occurs, the content of the material being read, or the "motivation" of the individual reader and his interest in the material. In these instances, a reading problem cannot be assessed until learning has been tried under more "ideal" conditions with materials of more significance to the reader.

We can now note some instances: (a) where auditory transformations may not lead to comprehension although the reader ostensibly uses the same language as is used in the printed material; and (b) where comprehension facilitates or even makes possible identification which would not otherwise occur.

A first instance of an identification without comprehension is when the reader has had either insufficient or no previous experience with the referent so that it is not part of his meaning-vocabulary. For example, a story about children playing with a kite may elicit no referent (and no meaning) in an individual in a subculture where no one plays with kites. A second instance of identification without comprehension can occur in individuals who have had experience with the referent, but in circumstances where these referents are typically communicated in nonverbal forms such as gesture or tone. This problem is likely to occur in individuals who use what is sometimes called "expressive language" or nonverbal rather than verbal language. For example, a child could point and say "ball" in a particular tone as a substitute for saying, "I want this ball!" or "May I please have the ball?" or "Give me the ball" (cf. Bereiter and Engelmann, 1966; Bernstein, 1965; Deutsch, 1962). For comprehension to occur in these instances, the individual must be taught to use verbal language or at least to recognize that the "message" he communicates gesturally can also be communicated through words. A third way identification can occur without comprehension is when the sounds of the words as read are different from the sounds of the words as they occur in the reader's vocabulary. For some rural Southern children "y'all" may be the commonly heard and said form of "you." If a reader identifies (says) the word "you," he may not transfer the sound "you" to the meaning of "y'all." Another example is a child from a lower-class background who may not "say" the words in the same way or in the same sequence as his middle-class teacher; and therefore, if he makes his transformations into the teacher's language, comprehension may not occur. A fourth instance of identification without appropriate comprehension is when there is a lack of correspondence between the reader's auditory language and that of the material being read. For example, not how difficult it is to read and comprehend the following passage, which is a description of Harlem.

On School: "Everyone shouting and screaming and nobody care about what they is going on. But at least it somewhere to stay away from when they make you go." And on the purpose of fighting gangs: "In this bizness you got have a place of your own and a chain of command and all that. Everything go by the book. Then you get a name. And when you get the name maybe you can stay live a while. Thas why most men get in gangs. To stay live. Thas why the gangs form in the first place." (*Time* Magazine, February 24, 1967, p.96)

In the third and fourth examples, there is a discrepancy between the language of the material being read and the reader's own language. This discrepancy can be resolved either by "correcting" the reader's language so that it matches the written form or by modifying the written material to correspond to his language patterns. As Labov (1967) notes, however, if the teacher is to locate the source of the difficulty and take appropriate remedial steps, he should "know" the child's nonstandard language. Labov spells out in some detail the possible discrepancies between the disadvantaged students and their teachers in their pronunciations and uses of grammar. He also discusses some of the implications of such discrepancies in the teaching of children who speak a nonstandard dialect.

One further way in which identification can occur without comprehension is when the particular meaning of the graphic material is different from the meaning typically elicited in the individual (e.g., slang, idiomatic expressions, and poetry), all of which depend on less consensual meanings. An example is a foreigner trying to read a popular detective story which uses slang and colloquialisms. Another example would be an accomplished reader reading James Joyce, where the words have highly personalized referents.

On the other hand, comprehension can facilitate identification if the reader has highly advanced language skills available, e.g., vocabulary, sequences, appropriate generating grammar (In Chomsky's, 1957, sense). To the extent that each of these skills facilitates identification by decreasing the range of possibilities of what is likely to occur in the written material, less information is necessary from the visual input to elicit the whole sequence. Thus, there are a number of ways in which knowledge of language in terms of both meaning and structure may aid identification and even make possible specific identifications which otherwise would not occur. First, the context and meaning of the material already read may generate and/or limit new forms of identification via the individual's understanding and elaboration of the material being read. For example, all other factors being constant, two scientists will differ in the rate and understanding of specific scientific material if they have a different familiarity with the subject matter. A second way in which language aids identification is through the structure of the language which limits the possible types of words or sequences which can occur at any given point. Further, comprehension may make possible identifications which otherwise might not occur. A beginning reader who has not learned phonics but who has a good vocabulary and uses language as it typically occurs in written form may be able to "guess" a word he has not previously identified. He can identify the word on the basis of his comprehension of the context, or familiarity with the structure of the language, or both. To exemplify how the structure and context contribute to identification, all one needs to do is to remove words randomly from a story (Cloze technique, Taylor, 1953) and note the limited number and types of word insertions which occur. Third, extensive language experience facilitates speed of reading. Having learned (and being familiar with) possible elaborations, the reader requires fewer cues for a particular response to occur; the assumption here is that the requirement of fewer cues is associated with more rapid scanning, e.g., speed reading of familiar material. Fourth, comprehension facilitates the recognition of errors in reading when there is a mismatch between any of the three possible sources of information mentioned above and the identification as "said." For example, when the word elaborated from the cues is not congruent with later elaborations—it does not fit the content, context, or sequences as previously experienced—the reader will experience the possiblility of an error and "check" the input for more cues.

Once reading is defined as comprehension (which we hold can occur only after basic identification and language skills have been mastered), then identification becomes secondary and may eventually be eliminated except for identifying new words. As noted earlier, an individual with good language (meaning and structure) skills can, in the case of speed reading, go directly from the discrimination to the meaning without the intermediate step of (auditory) identification. Typically, readers use identification in "reading" (here "reading" is being defined in terms of comprehension) in the following ways: first to make the words auditorally overt (i.e., saying the words aloud so they can be understood); second, to make the words covertly auditory (i.e., lip moving); then, implicit identification (i.e., the reader experiences the words as if they were said aloud but there is no evidence of overt saying); and, finally, identification is eliminated when the reader goes directly from the visual configurations—without experiencing the words as auditory forms—to their associated meaning, e.g., speed reading. Theoretically, at least identification (in contrast to discrimination) is not necessary and, in fact may not occur in the accomplished reader. It is even possible that a method could be devised for teaching reading (i.e., comprehension) without the intermediate step of auditory identification. If, for example, we could evolve principles for understanding how a child learns his original language—which includes the transformation of the experience of objects into words in auditory form—we might begin to understand how a child might learn to go from an original visual form directly to meaning without an intermediate auditory "naming."

We hope this attempt to impose some order on the diversity of phenomena included under reading or reading difficulty will be of heuristic value to other investigators. Recognizing that we have only touched on the complexities of reading behavior, we hope others will bring to bear other coordinating principles to this area of investigation.

References

Bereiter, C. & Englemann, S. *Teaching disadvantaged children in the preschool.* New York: Prentice-Hall, 1966.

Bernstein, B. A socio-linguistic approach to social learning. In J. Gould (Ed.), *Social science survey.* New York: Pelican, 1965.

Bloomfield, L. & Barnhart, C. L. *Lets read.* Detroit: Wayne State Univer. Press, 1961.

Bond, G. & Tinker, M. *Reading difficulties: their diagnosis and correction.* New York: Appleton-Century-Crofts, 1957.

Bryant, N. D. Learning disabilities in reading. Mimeo.

Budoff, M. & Quinlan, D. Reading readiness as related to efficency of visual and aural learning in the primary grades. *J. educ. Psychol.,* 1964, **55** (5), 247-252.

Corrigan, Patricia. Broader implications of a chemical theory of reading disability. Paper presented at Amer. psychol. Assn. Meeting, 1959.

Chapman, Carita. Meeting current reading needs in adult literacy programs. In H. A. Robinson (Ed.), *Recent developments in reading.* Supplementary educ. Monogr., Univer. of Chicago Press, 1965, No. 95.

Chomsky, N. *Syntactic structures.* The Hague: Mouton & Company, 1957.

Cromer, W. & Wiener, M. Idiosyncratic response patterns among good and poor readers. *J. consult. Psychol.,* 1966, **30** (1), 1-10.

De Hirsch, Katrina. Two categories of learning difficulties in adolescents. *Amer. J. Orthopsychiat.,* 1963, **33**, 87-91.

Delacato, C. H. *The treatment and prevention of reading problems.* Springfield: Charles C Thomas, 1959.

Deutsch, M. The disadvantaged child and the learning process: some social, psychological and developmental considerations. Paper prepared for the Ford Foundation "Work Conference on Curriculum and Teaching in Depressed Urban Areas." New York: Columbia Univer., 1962.

Downing, J. A. *The initial teaching alphabet.* New York: Macmillan, 1964.

Downing, J. A. *The i.t.a. reading experiment.* Chicago: Scott, Foresman, 1965.

Elkind, D., Larson, Margaret, & Van Doorninck, W. Perceptual decentration learning and performance in slow and average readers. *J. educ. Psychol.,* 1965, **56** (1).

Emans, R. Meeting current reading needs in grades four through eight. In H. A. Robinson (Ed.), *Recent developments in reading.* Suppl. educ. Monogr., Univer. of Chicago Press, 1965, No. 95.

Fries, C. C. *Linguistics and reading.* New York: Holt, Rinehart and Winston, 1962.

Geschwind, N. The anatomy of acquired disorders of reading disability. In J. Money (Ed.), *Progress and research needs in dyslexia.* Baltimore: Johns Hopkins Press, 1962.

Gibson, E. J. Learning to read. *Science,* 1965, **148**, 1066-1072.

Goens, Jean T. *Visual perceptual abilities and early reading progress.* Suppl. educ. Monogr., Univer. of Chicago Press, 1958, No. 87.

Goetzinger, C. P., Dirks, D. D., & Baer, C. J. Auditory discrimination and visual perception in good and poor readers. *Annals of Otology, Rhinology, and Laryngology,* March 1960, 121-136.

Goltz, C. Individual remedial reading for boys in trouble. *Reading Teacher.* **19** (5).

Gray, W. S. The major aspects of reading. In H. A. Robinson (Ed.) *Recent developments in reading.* Suppl. educ. Monogr., Univer. of Chicago Press, 1965, No. 95.

Handlon, J. A metatheoretical view of assumptions regarding the etiology of schizophrenia, *AMA Archives of gen. Psychiat.,* January 1960, 43-60.

Harris, A. J. *How to increase reading ability.* London: Longmans, Green, 1948.

Harris, T. L. Some issues in beginning reading instruction. *J.educ. Res.,* 1962, **56** (1).

Kempler, B. & Wiener, M. Personality and perception in the recognition threshold paradigm. *Psychol. Rev.,* 1964, **70**, 349-356.

Kinsbourne, M. & Warrington, E. K. Developmental factors in reading and writing backwardness. *Brit J. Psychol.,* 1963, **54**, 145-156.

Koff. R. H. Panel on: Learning difficulties in childhood. Reported by E. A. Anthony, *J. Amer. Psychiatric Assn.*, 1961, **9**.

Labov, W. Some sources of reading problems for Negro speakers of nonstandard English. In A. Frazier (Ed.), *New directions in elementary English*, Nat. Council of English, 1967.

Lefevre, C. A. *Linguistics and the teaching of reading.* New York: McGraw-Hill, 1964.

Marchbanks, Gabrielle & Levin, H. Cues by whicl children recognize words. *J. educ. Psychol.*, 1965, **56** (2), 57-61.

Milner, Esther. A study of the relationship between reading readiness in grade-one schoolchildren and patterns of parent-child interaction. *Child Devel.*, 1951, **22** (2), 95-112.

Rabinovitch, R. D. Reading and learning disabilites. In S. Arieti (Ed.), *American handbook of psychiatry.* New York: Basic Books, 1959.

Reitan, R. Relationships between neurological and psychological variables and their implications for reading instruction. In H. A. Robinson (Ed.), *Meeting individual differences in reading.* Suppl. educ. Monogr., Univer. of Chicago Press 1964, No. 94.

Robeck, Mildred. Readers who lacked word analysis skills: a group diagnosis. *J. educ. Res.*, 1963, **56**, 432-434.

Robinson, Helen M. Looking ahead in reading. In H. A. Robinson (Ed.), *Recent developments in reading.* Suppl. educ. Monogr., Univer. of Chicago Press 1965, No. 95.

Roswell, Florence & Natchez, Gladys. *Reading disability: diagnosis and treatment.* New York: Basic Books, 1964.

Strang, Ruth. *Diagnostic Teaching of reading.* New York: McGraw-Hill, 1964.

Stevens, S. S. (Ed.) *Handbook of experimental psychology.* New York: John Wiley and Sons, 1951.

Taylor, W. "Cloze procedure": a new tool for measuring readability. *Journ. Quart.*, 1953, **30**, 415-433.

Woestehoff, E. Methods and materials for teaching comprehension—in corrective and remedial classes. In Helen Robinson (Ed.), *Sequential development of reading abilities.* Suppl. educ. Monogr., Univer. of Chicago Press, 1960, No. 9.

39. Personality Characteristics
of the Disabled Reader*

JACK A. HOLMES

PSYCHOLOGISTS and teachers alike have been well sensitized to the fact that emotional factors should, and perhaps do, play a vital and important role in the reading life of every child. Just how they play that part however, has remained a mystery. In his classical review, in 1941, Gates [1] [1] reported that in cases where personality difficulties occur together with reading difficulties, they may be causes, concomitancies, or results. Furthermore, he virtually wrote off the importance of emotional factors when he stated that there is no single personality-pattern characteristic of reading failure; and there is no proved one-to-one relationship between any one type of adjustment difficulties and type of reading difficulties.

Undaunted by Gate's authoritative statement however, the profession has continued to pursue the search. But I can assure you, from my review [2] of the pertinent literature from 1953 through the summer of 1959, published recently in the *Review of Educational Research,* that in the main, the same general conclusions arrived at by Gates are, but for slight modifications still applicable. Since 1953, approximately one hundred experimental studies in the area of personality and reading have been completed, half of which are unpublished doctoral dissertations. Actually, a few investigations reported significant differences for specific personality traits between good and poor readers but unfortunately, many such differences tended to be nicely counterbalanced by other studies which reported significant differences in *exactly* the opposite direction.

In this paper, I propose to do three things: First, I shall try, by taking a fresh point of view, to give some perspective in a field where the evidence first blows hot and then cold, but never blows very hard in either direction; second, I shall pose a few critical questions and then bring to bear on them some unusually revealing evidence from our own laboratories; and finally, I shall present some new concepts which I boldly suggest may provide a better

*From *Journal of Developmental Reading,* **4** (Winter, 1961), 111-122. Reprinted with permission of the International Reading Association. Author deceased.

[1]Numbers in brackets refer to references at the end of the article.

theoretical frame of reference for understanding some of the dynamics of the personality-school-learning problem than some of the concepts now in use.

Let us first, then, address ourselves to an analysis of some of the more consistent findings in the recent literature. Using different populations rating scales, and projective tests, Malmquist, [3] Meyer, [4] and Hallock, [5] working in the *primary* grades, found that lack of self-confidence and self-reliance. instability, and timidity were characteristic of poor readers.

Sociometric and questionnaire methods used by Tabarlet [6] Norman and Daley, [7] and Bouise [8] at the *elementary* level showed that poor readers had greater withdrawing tendencies and were less popular with their classmates than were the good readers.

But, at the *intermediate* level, studies by Cutts, [9] Karlsen, [10] Veltfort, [11] and Wynne [12] produced *no* significant differences in the personality factors of good and poor readers when the Rorschach, Bender, Goodenough, Finney Aggressive Content Scale, and items rewritten for children from the Minnesota Multiphasic Personality Inventory were used.

At the *junior high school* level, Granzow [13] and Bauer [14] found that poor readers were less well-adjusted to school rulings and not so well-accepted by their peers as good readers. In contrast, studies by Blackham [15] and Bauer indicated that the good readers had better mental health, self-expressiveness and drive for achievement, but were more introverted than the poor readers.

At the *high school* level, Zohary [16] and Holmes [17] using the Minnesota Multiphasic Personality Inventory, Rorschach, Thematic Appreception Test, Johnson Temperament Analysis, Heston, and SRA Youth Inventory, were, in general, not able to find significant differences between the fast and the slow readers or the powerful and the non-powerful readers

Finally, at the college level, Voas [18] and Holmes [19] in two studies, utilizing the Minnesota Multiphasic Personality Inventory, Guildford-Zimmerman Temperament Survey, Johnson Temperament Analysis, Bell Adjustment Inventory, and the California Test of Personality, *again* were not able to establish significant and convincing differences for any of these personality subtests between fast and slow, or powerful and non-powerful readers.

If one hopes for consistent grade-to-grade findings in these results one is bound to be disappointed. However, and this is my first point if one takes a *developmental approach,* one discovers that relationships between reading and personality found at the primary level become inconsistent at the intermediate and junior high school grades, and so far as the evidence is concerned, seem completely to disappear at the high school and college levels. Of course, there may be many possible explanations, such as the increased selectivity of students, the unreliability and use of different types of tests etc. There is perhaps, a more useful explanation, which, however, seems thus far to have been overlooked: that is, (a) there may be, in fact, an actual "gradient shift" in the relationship between personality factors and reading disabilities as children advance through the grades; but (b) because of the fact that personality tests tend to be standardized on gross differences in clinical samples, the personality subtests in general use today may be assessing personality traits at too superficial a level; and further, (c) the cross-sections of personality which are tapped may be simply inappropriate characteristics to be related to school learning.

Under a United States Office of Education contract, we are now engaged in an analysis of a reading study. Although the analysis is not complete, some preliminary findings can be reported. From a representative sample of 400 high school students, the 108 fastest and the 108 slowest readers were selected. Figure 1 presents the contrasting mean scores earned by these two groups on 54 independent variables. It should be understood that the raw means were transmuted into standardized Z-scores based on the total sample, so that they are comparable across the board from test to test.

Figure 1 clearly shows that for Speed of Reading, our fast-reading group made an average Z-score of 60. In contrast, our slow-reading group made an average Z-score of only 40. The great difference in these two Speed of Reading scores can be appreciated better, perhaps, if it is realized that they are comparable to obtaining scores approximately equal to the 90th and 12th percentile, respectively, on norms established on the total group of 400. It will also be noted that this differential tends to hold in areas assessed by the Primary Mental Abilities Test: verbal, spatial, reasoning, and word fluency.

Likewise, large differences are evident in the linguistic area, such as Vocabulary in Context and Isolation, Range of Information, Phonetic Association, Word Sense, Homonymic Meaning, Prefixes, Suffixes, Latin and Greek Roots, and Spelling Ability. The differential continues to hold in the visual perceptual area, that is in Dot Embedded Figure-Ground, Cue-Symbol Closure, Word Embedded, and Perception of Reversals. Figure 1 also illustrates that these fast and slow readers can also be differentiated on Auding [20] and certain auditory factors, such as Tonal Memory, Tone Quality, Tone Intensity, Tonal Movement, Rhythm, Pitch, and Musical Taste.

It also should be noted that except for Academic Adjustment and Morale, indicated by Variable No. 31, small and insignificant differences were found on the Study Methods Test. In dramatic contrast to the wide separation shown in the intellectual and linguistic areas, the differences between the profiles of the fast and slow readers virtually collapse on the subscales of the Kuder Preference Record and the SRA Youth Inventory. Furthermore, although the evidence will not be presented in this paper, a similar situation was obtained for powerful versus non-powerful high school readers on these same fifty-four variables.

As previously mentioned, Mrs. Zohary intensively pursued this question by trying to find a relation between reading and personality, using such personality tests as the Minnesota Multiphasic Personality Inventory, Rorschach, Thematic Apperception Tests, Heston Adjustment Inventory, and the Johnson

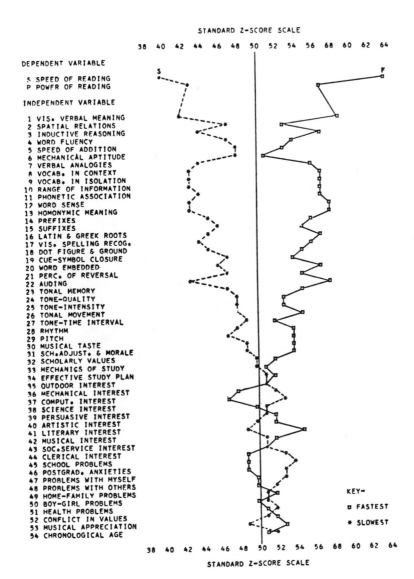

FIG. 1. FASTEST VS. SLOWEST READERS. PROFILE COMPARISON OF CO-OPERANT ABILITIES, INTERESTS, AND PROBLEMS MANIFESTED BY THE 108 FASTEST AND 108 SLOWEST READERS IN TOTAL SAMPLE OF 400. ALL MEAN-GROUP SCORES EXPRESSED IN STANDARD Z-SCORE FORM DETERMINED FROM TOTAL SAMPLE.

Temperament Analysis, but her findings were essentially the same. Her results were very disheartening and frustrating to a young lady who had come all the way from Israel to get her degree and so I encouraged her to go one step further and have the respective mothers of the fast- and slow-reading girls rate their daughters on each of the items in the Johnson Temperament Analysis. This she did.

Table I compares the profiles and self-ratings with the *mothers'* ratings of their fast-reading daughters. The most impressive thing about the comparison is the remarkable congruency of the two profiles.

TABLE I

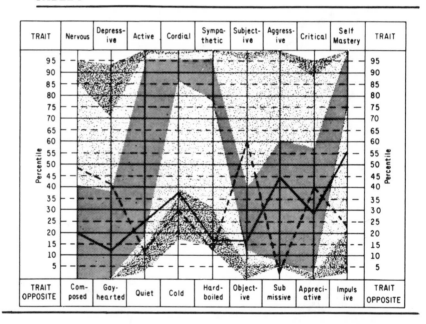

TRAIT	Nervous	Depress-ive	Active	Cordial	Sympa-thetic	Subject-ive	Aggress-ive	Critical	Self Mastery	TRAIT
TRAIT OPPOSITE	Com-posed	Gay-hearted	Quiet	Cold	Hard-boiled	Object-ive	Sub missive	Appreci-ative	Impuls ive	TRAIT OPPOSITE

In marked contrast, Table II reveals that the mothers of the slow-reading girls rated their daughters not only quite differently from the manner in which these girls had rated themselves, but in such a way as to make their daughters appear much less socially acceptable than did their daughters' self-ratings. That is, the mothers rated their slow-reading daughters as more nervous, depressive, quiet, cold, hard-boiled, subjective, submissive, critical, and impulsive than the daughters had rated themselves.

My second point, then is this: discrepancies between parental attitudes about their children and children's self-attitudes may be more important for school learning than the child's attitudes about himself.

TABLE II

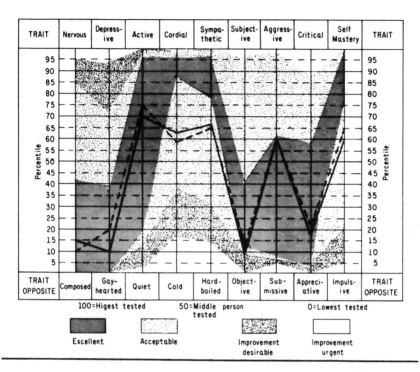

TRAIT	Nervous	Depress-ive	Active	Cordial	Sympa-thetic	Subject-ive	Aggress-ive	Critical	Self Mastery	TRAIT

| TRAIT OPPOSITE | Composed | Gay-hearted | Quiet | Cold | Hard-boiled | Object-ive | Sub-missive | Appreci-ative | Impuls-ive | TRAIT OPPOSITE |

100=Higest tested   50=Middle person   0=Lowest tested
                              tested

Excellent   Acceptable   Improvement   Improvement
                                        desirable   urgent

In November of last year, the University of California Press published a monograph [21] which illustrates a methodology and way of conceptualizing a new set of personality dimensions called *mobilizers.* In this particular study the relationship between personality and spelling ability in 1599 college students was examined. The method of successive sample analysis was used, first to select out of some thirty-three personalities *scales* (including both the clinical and added scales of the Minnesota Multiphasic Personality Inventory, the Johnson Temperament Analysis, and the Heston Personality Inventory) only those scales which were consistent from sample to sample in making significant contributions to the variance of spelling and, second, to select out of an original 1,018 personality items only those items which were consistent from sample to sample in differentiating the best from the worst college spellers for each of the sexes. Our results were as follows:

For men, successive analyses or cross-validations in samples I through VII reduced the thirty-three original personality *scales* to just one: lack of confidence, with self-mastery functioning as a suppressor variable. However, lack of confidence accounted for only 9.2 percent of the variance of spelling ability. Likewise, successive item analyses on Samples I through VII reduced the original 1,018 items to twenty-four, which were still discriminating the best from the worst spellers. Now, if we extract the essence of these items, we are able to describe tendencies.

Space allows us only to illustrate the types of items that survived. For *men,* the *best spellers* reported that they felt– that there are really *few things worth living for,* that they are dedicated to a life of duty, tend to brood a greal deal, resent criticism, do not want to be controlled by customs, do not consider themselves go-getters, often pause just to mediate and philosophize concerning the *purpose* of life, enjoy work which makes them think, dislike the idea of belonging to several clubs, consider themselves fast learners, are hard to please, prefer reading to conversation as a help in formulating their ideas, admit to periods of great restlessness, and finally, say they certainly feel useless at times. Recall that these tendencies are for the *best* men spellers.

The *worst* men spellers, on the other hand, had a syndrome which reflected opposite points of view; that is, they did not place a high value on intellectualism and dedication. In fact, without the benefit of philosophical concern, they seemed to accept *life as something to be enjoyed.*

A similar analysis for college *women* indicated that only 3.6 percent of the variance of spelling could be ascribed to personality factors, and out of the original 1,018 items, only sixteen survived the successive cross-validations. Generalizations based upon these items indicate that the *best women* spellers tend to be more intellectually efficient, composed, confident, *and* critical, but less gregarious than those college women who are the worst spellers.

To put the question bluntly, then, a positive relationship between personality and achievement in specific school subjects either exists, or it does not exist. The very meagerness of all these findings strikes at the claims of those who proclaim that the major cause of school failures is the maladjustment of the personality. The situation is particularly poignant in the case of men. Trends throughout the entire spelling study testify that, for *men,* success in spelling at the college level is more closely related to what standard personality scales would call "maladjustment" rather than "good adjustment!" These trends belie the importance of endeavoring to bring every child into line with some "normatively" derived concept of good adjustment in order that he may learn the better. The *re*-consideration of what is meant by good adjustment is needed by people concerned with personality-theory and school-learning.

Our third major point, then is: *"Personality adjustment for whom and for what purpose?"* If the notion that different personal-*values* are requisite to the achievement of outstanding success or failure in different areas of learning is tenable, then it would be more realistic and informative to speak of a "spelling-value charactertistic," a "reading-value characteristic," or perhaps an "arithmetic-value characteristic," instead of an adjusted or maladjusted personality, per se. In the spelling study, the evidence points (but, only points) to the suggestion that, in general, the so-called more *mal*adjusted men are, in fact, better adjusted to the task of learning to spell than are the more adjusted "via the norms" and socially confident ones.

Psychology and education have not yet come to grips with the problem of trying to understand the psycho-educational importance of a variable (such as a spelling-value personality characteristic) which itself makes relatively little or no direct contribution to the success or failure of a criterion (for example, spelling) but which, nevertheless, facilitates the functional powers of those independent variables, i.e., I.Q., phonetic, etc., that do. The mobilizer concept, therefore, opens the way for a serious consideration of this problem.

What is about to be hypothesized is *not* a suppressor phenomenon. A *mobilizer,* although at this time a hypothetical construct, is defined as a deep-seated value system, the presence of which facilitates the functional organization of those sub-skills underlying success in a higher, more complex ability. By selecting and marshalling such necessary subskills into an "intracerebral communications system," mobilizers unify and press them into active service in accordance with the purposes of the individual—the total manifesting itself as a higher, more complex ability. In other words, psychocatalytic mobilizers act to coalesce or integrate the available and pertinent subskills and thus bring a person's problem-solving potentials into focus on the problem at hand, be it spelling, reading, writing, arithmetic, or the like.

Mobilizers, as here postulated, then, are to be differentiated from motivators and interest factors. More related to concept-integration than concept-formation, mobilizers must play their major roles as the fundamental value-systems from whence spring the many and specific attitudes a person holds toward the *purpose and worth of life, duty, criticism, customs, adversities, society, intellect, and the self.* In short, success depends not only on what one knows, but the way in which one marshals what he knows.

In conclusion, let us take the liberty to theorize a bit more and try to draw together the main points we have made.

Experimental attempts to establish a relationship between certain personality traits and success in reading or spelling have yielded inconsistent results—positive at the lower grade levels, negative at the high school and college levels. Our gradient shift hypothesis explains these inconsistencies and gains further credence if we picture these developmental changes as a gradual process of *internalizing* into deep-seated value systems what was initially, in the child, merely a superficial role-mask or *persona* guide for behavior.

However, out of such childhood notions of what one's self-image ought to be, develop deep-seated value-convictions called *mobilizers*. These, in turn, govern which of one's total mental resources will be marshalled in order to pursue the task at hand.

Mobilizers, as deeply ingrained stabilizers of behavior, soon become inaccessible to the usual type of personality test-item in use today. This is so, not because of some repressive or resistive mechanisms within the individual, but simply because present-day personality scales are not constructed along the dimensions appropriate for assessing such mobilizing traits of the personality.

When self-fulfilling behavior is reinforced, the child is able to mobilize more and more of his energies for the purposive-pursuit of his task, but when such behavior is in conflict with authoritative and parental notions of what the child ought to be doing, then the converse would tend to be true. Finally, we may expect that when such conflicts appear, they would tend to be especially disruptive to school achievement during the formative years when the child is striving to establish the basic concepts in which he can believe, the purpose and worth of his own most appropriate self-image, and the mode of behavior that will most likely lead to its realization. [22]

References

1. Arthur I. Gates, "The Role of Personality Maladjustment in Reading Disability," *Pedagogical Seminary,* LIX (1941), 77-83.
2. Eli M. Bower and Jack A. Holmes, "Emotional Factors and Academic Achievement," *Review of Educational Research,* XXIX (December, 1959), 529-544.
3. Eve Malmquist, *Factors Related to Reading Disabilities in the First Grade of the Elementary School.* ACTA Universitatis Stockholmiensis, Stockholm Studies in Educational Psychology No. 2, Stockholm: Almquist and Wiksell, 1958.
4. George Meyer, "Some Relationships Between Rorschach Scores in Kindergarten and Reading in the Primary Grades," *Journal of Protective Techniques,* XVII (December, 1953), 414-425.
5. George A. Hallock, *Attitudinal Factors Affecting Achievement in Reading.* Unpublished Doctoral Dissertation. Detroit: Wayne State University, 1958. Abstract: *Dissertation Abstracts,* XVIII (1958), 2061-2062.
6. Bobby E. Tabarlet, *A Study of the Mental Health Status of Retarded Readers.* Unpublished Doctoral Dissertation. Baton Rouge: Louisiana State University, 1958. Abstract: *Dissertation Abstracts,* XIX (1958), 735.
7. Ralph D. Norman and Marvin F. Daley, "The Comparative Personality Adjustments of Superior and Inferior Readers," *Journal of Educational Psychology,* L (February, 1959), 31-36.
8. Louise M. Bouise, "Emotional and Personality Problems of a Group of Retarded Readers," *Elementary English,* XXXII (December, 1955), 544-548.
9. Warren G. Cutts, Jr., *A Comparative Study of Good and Poor Readers at the Middle Grade Level.* Unpublished Doctoral Dissertation. Syracuse, N. Y.: Syracuse University, 1956. Abstract: *Dissertation Abstracts* XVI (1956), 1855.
10. Bjorn Karlsen, *A Comparison of Some Educational and Psychological Characteristics of Successful and Unsuccessful Readers at the Elementary School Level.* Unpublished Doctoral Dissertation. Minneapolis: University of Minnesota 1954. Abstract: *Dissertation Abstracts,* XV (1955), 456-457.

11. Helene R. Veltfort, *Some Personality Correlates of Reading Disability.* Unpublished Doctoral Dissertation, Palo Alto, Calif.: Stanford University, 1956. Abstract: *Dissertation Abstracts,* XVI (1956), 1947-1948.
12. Robert L. Wynne, *The Relationship Between Reading Ability and Personality Inventory Responses in Elementary School Children.* Unpublished Master's Thesis. Berkeley: University of California, 1955.
13. Kent R. Granzow, *A Comparative Study of Underachievers, Normal Achievers, and Overachievers in Reading.* Unpublished Doctoral Dissertation. Iowa City: State University of Iowa, 1954. Abstract: *Dissertation Abstracts,* XIV (1954), 631-632.
14. Edith B. Bauer, *The Interrelationships of Personality and Achievement in Reading.* Unpublished Doctoral Dissertation. Berkeley: University of California, 1956.
15. Garth J. Blackham, *A Clinical Study of the Personality Structures and Adjustments of Pupils Under-Achieving and Over-Achieving in Reading.* Unpublished Doctoral Dissertation. Ithaca, N.Y.: Cornell University, 1954. Abstract: *Dissertation Abstracts,* XV (1955), 1199-1200.
16. Dvora Zohary, *Reading Rate and Personality.* Unpublished Master's Thesis. Berkeley: University of California, 1955.
17. Jack A. Holmes, *Significant Differences in the Substrata Factor Patterns Which Underlie Reading Ability in Known-Groups at the High School Level.* Preliminary report: U. S. Office of Education Contract, 538-8176, 1959-1960. (Full report in preparation.)
18. Robert B. Voas, *Correlates of Reading Speed and the Time Required to Complete Personality Inventories.* U.S.N. School Aviation Medicine Research Report No. NM 001 108 100; Report No. 16,ii, 1956.
19. Jack A. Holmes, "Factors Underlying Major Reading Disabilities at the College Level," *Genetic Psychology Monographs,* XLIX (February, 1954), 3-95.
20. Auding is a technical term used to differentiate the hearing and understanding of human speech from hearing in general; that is, auding is to hearing, as reading is to seeing.
21. Jack A. Holmes, *Personality and Spelling Ability.* University of California Publications in Education, Vol. 12, No. 4, Berkeley: University of California Press, 1959.
22. Jack A. Holmes, "Emotional Factors and Reading Disability," *Reading Teacher,* IX (October, 1955), 11-18.

40. Characteristics of Dyslexia and Their Remedial Implication*

N. DALE BRYANT

REMEDIAL procedures for dyslexia are implicit in the general characteristics of the reading disability as those characteristics are revealed through diagnostic measurements, including errors made in reading and difficulty in accomplishing certain simple learning. Dyslexia is not a simple entity since there is considerable variability in degree and nature of the impairment. However, much of this variability arises from associated and secondary factors, and there are certain common characteristics that form the core of the disability. This paper will attempt to outline some of these characteristics and point out a few remedial cues to be gained from them.

Dyslexia must be differentiated from other reading difficulties, such as problems of reading comprehension, lack of adequate reading instruction, attentional problems, or "emotional blocking," even though in some cases these may also be present, thus complicating the symptom picture. Dyslexia is concerned with word recognition, and the term "word-blindness" used by some neurologists to popularly identify the dysfunctioning is descriptive of the extreme difficulty in learning to recognize words. The term dyslexia implies a neurological dysfunctioning if only because of its similarity to the neurological condition alexia, which represents a loss of ability to read resulting from damage to the association areas and connections in and around the angular gyrus of the dominant cerebral hemisphere. However, while alexia is a traumatic disruption of existing skills and memories, dyslexia represents a developmental inefficiency in functioning that handicaps learning. Certainly, in some cases, damage, prenatal complications or genetic factors have been causally associated with dyslexia. In most cases, however, a neurological disorder is merely inferred from the nature of the dysfunctioning and associated symptoms. In many cases, it is also apparent that emotional and educational factors are contributing to the learning problems of the child, regardless of whether or not neurological factors are primary.

*From *Exceptional Children* **31**, 4, (December, 1964), 195-199. Reprinted with permission of *Exceptional Children* and N. Dale Bryant.

410

ASSOCIATED CHARACTERISTICS

Dyslexia first becomes evident as a child reaches kindergarten and first grade, though it is often not recognized until much later and, indeed, is frequently never recognized for what it is.

The child is usually a boy although the reason for this is not unquestionably established. Explanations include: (a) greater vulnerability of males to prenatal and other sources of brain damage; (b) sex linked or sex influenced genetic factors; (c) slower maturation of males; (d) different social expectations and activity levels for males. It is probable that, at least in some cases, each of these factors contribute individually or in combination to the higher frequency of dyslexia in males.

Dyslexia is not a broad defect in general intelligence; IQ's tend to be in the normal range and occasionally reflect very superior ability. However, certain indices of intellectual performance are usually found to be relatively low, e.g., the Coding subtest of the Wechsler Intelligence Scale for Children.

While the primary symptoms are not apparent until school age, many associated symptoms occur with much greater frequency than in the normal population. Usually associated with reading difficulties is confusion when quickly identifying left or right. There is a good chance that the dyslexic boy has some confusion about months, seasons, and judgment of time, direction, distance, and size. On a test of motor development and coordination, he is likely to score low, frequently below the norms for his age. He is much more likely than a normal child to have had speech difficulties and some difficulties may still remain. Similarly, he may have poor auditory discrimination in spite of his adequate auditory acuity. He is more likely than the normal child to have male relatives with similar difficulties in learning to read, and he is also more likely to have been premature or to have survived some complication of pregnancy. The dyslexic child will probably not show gross defects on a neurological examination and will not necessarily appear immature on pediatric examination, although both of these conditions are not infrequent. As in all cases of children with difficulties, he is likely to feel inadequate, stupid, and guilty because of his disability and his repeated failures.

PRIMARY CHARACTERISTICS

With the exposure to reading instruction, the primary characteristics of the disability become apparent. In spite of learning to recognize some words, he has extreme difficulty in associating the sounds with the visual symbols of letters. This disability is apparent in the confusion of letter sounds, particularly the vowels which have several interfering sounds. Even in the simplest situation of remedial instruction, the stability of sound association in word recognition is many times more difficult to establish than for the normal child. In the classroom situation, children are expected to abstract the common sound elements associated with letters when words containing different letters and sounds are presented. For the dyslexic child this compounds the associational problems. Either because of interference between the various associational pairs or because of a defect in the ability to abstract in this area, the dyslexic child has great difficulty in learning sound associations as they are commonly taught in the classroom. This is a key point in designing remedial instruction for dyslexia. Remediation is almost doomed to failure if it merely repeats the classroom procedure requiring the child to abstract and associate common visual and sound elements when several associations are to be learned at once.

A second primary characteristic of the dyslexic reader is his tendency to ignore the details within words and, instead, to base word recognition on initial letter, length of word, and a few other insufficient cues. This is not due to a simple defect in visual discrimination since adequate discrimination can be made when two words are presented together; rather, the defect comes in the utilization of memory of word shape wherein the details and sequences of letters within the word are often undifferentiated. Thus, a dyslexic boy is likely to accept the word "postal" and even, in an extreme case, a letter combination such as "peistad" as being the word "pasted." No other memory difficulties may be apparent though the inadequacies of most memory batteries make this very hard to determine. Lack of sound association may contribute to the dyslexic's inadequate use of details in word recognition since sound association helps identify and sequence a perception of separate letters within a word. However, the converse may also be true and poor differentiation of details in the visual memory of words may contribute to the difficulty in learning to associate sounds with the letters in those visual memory images. It is evident that classroom or remedial procedures which do not focus attention on the details within words are unlikely to overcome this disability.

A third primary characteristic is a spatial confusion most obvious in the child's inability to consistently differentiate between reverse images such as letter pairs like "b" and "d." Sometimes, up and down reversals add "p" to the b-d confusion. Since this confusion of reversed images is often associated with confusion of the child's own left and right and, because proper differentiation depends entirely upon subjective cues, not merely greater discrimination of shape variations, this is one of the confusions most resistant to remediation. Since the subjective cues of left and right are based upon kinesthetic experience, remedial procedures need to use kinesthetic factors.

These three primary characteristics are probably manifestations of basic defects in neurological functioning. However, for purposes of describing the consistent symptoms of dyslexia, these characteristics may be adequate even if not all inclusive. These same characteristics are normally seen in children just beginning to read but they are rapidly overcome without special help. The dyslexic child persists in these characteristics as he grows older. It is as if dyslexia represents a massive unreadiness for reading. The maturational process, that, in conjunction with experience, produces reading readiness in beginning readers seems to lag for dyslexic youngsters even though there is some slow improvement apparent as the child grows older. Improvement with age in a dyslexic boy who had not been helped by years of remediation may reflect maturation. However, in addition, it may also reflect the fact that remedial procedures often confuse and obscure the very learning they are attempting to bring about. As he grows older, a child with moderate dyslexia may develop considerable reading ability, even though he is still far behind his age-mates. His recognition of familiar words increases, but his errors in reading are likely to reflect the same characteristics described. While his reading may be at fourth grade level, most of his errors are likely to be simple ones, more typical of the reading performance of a child reading at first or second grade level. Simple words are correctly identified in one sentence and incorrectly recognized in a later one because of poor differentiation of details within the words. Vowel sounds are inconsistent if the word is the least bit unfamiliar and reversals of letters (and sometimes words or word parts) are still frequent.

REMEDIAL IMPLICATIONS

First of all, it is essential to understand that the dyslexic child's inability to abstract when several associations are presented together makes it necessary to simplify tasks that he is asked to perform so that only one new discrimination or association is made at a time. Furthermore, this discrimination or association must be made repeatedly until it is automatic for the child. Thus, if a child confuses the letters "m" and "n," he needs to differentiate them alone. Once this is done, differentiation should be made in words where no other discriminations or associations are required, e.g., when he knows that one of the two words shown him will be "map" or "nap." Correct differentiation of perhaps a dozen trials for each pair of words would prepare the child for correct differentiation of "m" and "n" in pairs and then groups of words of gradually increasing complexity until the child is recognizing the "m" and "n" in words he knows but doesn't expect to be presented. In this way, a dyslexic child may learn to discriminate "m" and "n" in a matter of fifteen minutes and may never have trouble with that discrimination again. The same child might go for years having his "m" and "n" errors pointed out to him without learning to correctly and consistently differentiate between them because there were too many other discriminations and associations that he was attending to at the same time.

Similarly, the dyslexic child will probably never learn vowel sounds when they are thrown at him all together. However, practice with a single vowel and a single sound for that vowel (preferably the more common short sound) when no other discriminations or associations are required is likely to establish an association that will become automatic. Later, when another vowel or another sound for the previously learned vowel is introduced, the automatic association is likely to be retained without either interfering with the new learning or causing a loss of established association.

Thus, an essential procedure in remedial instruction for dyslexia is to simplify a confusing task to a single discrimination or association that can be correctly made by the child and then to practice it in recognition tasks of increasing complexity until it is well established as an automatic response. In this manner, the dyslexic's inability to abstract from a complex situation can be circumvented. Identifying letter-sound associations that the child confuses and working in the manner described helps overcome the difficulties in associating symbols and sounds.

There are several procedures suggested by the primary characteristic of ignoring details within words. Obviously, the child's attention needs to be called to the details. The usual teaching by the "whole word method" which is adequate for the normal child who will attend to details on his own, is not adequate for the dyslexic child. Writing a word is useful, not only because of kinesthetic feed-back, but because each letter must be remembered and reproduced even when the child has to look at a copy of the word immediately before he writes it. If he cannot write it, tracing it and copying it can prepare him for writing it. Filling in missing letters in a word is another way of forcing attention to the details and, perhaps, sharpening the visual memory image. Regardless of the procedure used to call attention to the details of each word learned, once the word is learned, it should be differentiated from other words with which it is likely to be confused. For example, if a child learns the word "then," he should practice differentiating it from "thin," "there," "their," "than," etc., even though he may not be able to identify the other words except that they are not "then" which he has just learned. This child, dyslexic though he may be, is unlikely to confuse these words later but without such discrimination practice, he would be almost certain to confuse some of them.

Confusion of reversed images as in "b" and "d" particularly need to be approached in as simple a task as possible because of the great difficulty in overcoming this confusion. If the child is also confused about his own left and right, this should be worked on, perhaps by using a ring, watch, or bracelet on the dominant hand and by providing kinesthetic practice for the dominant side. An important procedure in kinesthetic practice is writing or tracing one of the confused letters. Each day a large letter (i.e., "b") should be traced and words such as "bab" pronounced as it is traced. (A tracing poster on the door of the child's room at home can encourage frequent practice.) The letter should be traced or copied in various sizes on blackboard, paper, and in the air. Variations of this practice should proceed until the child can differentiate "b" from "d" when the letters are presented alone. Subsequently the same procedures can be followed that are described above for overcoming confusion between "m" and "n;" that is, from "b" and "d" presented alone, a child can go on to practice wiLh pages of words like "dog" and "bog." These more complex words should be gradually introduced with the child tracing each of the "b's" on a page and saying the word. As he establishes correct differentiation of the letter "b," he can begin to trace the letter "d," always saying words containing that letter. The steps in increasing the complexity of the task should be so small that he is never allowed to make a mistake because a few errors can disrupt a great deal of previous learning and re-institute confusion. Thus, the characteristic of letter reversals suggests a procedure for using kinesthetic practice and discriminating tasks of gradually increasing difficulty. Experience suggests short practice periods separate from other remedial work, very gradual steps when increasing difficulty, and massive distributed practice.

SUMMARY

Dyslexia is a complex syndrome with considerable variability in degree of reading disability and nature of associated characteristics. Secondary factors, as well as emotional and educational factors, increase the apparent complexity of the disorder. However, there are at least three characteristics that are so consistent as to be considered primary to the disability. These are: (a) difficulty in simple learning of associations between letter symbols and letter sounds (particularly multisound vowels). This difficulty is related to trouble in abstracting common elements from complex experiences; (b) use of insufficient word recognition cues by attending primarily to initial letter, length, and general shape while tending to ignore cues of details within words; (c) confusion of left-right reversals in letters of similar shape (i.e., "b" and "d").

These primary characteristics suggest procedures that might help overcome the disability. Each discrimination or association problem that causes repeated errors in material even below the child's reading level should be worked with by itself until the difficulty is overcome. The simplest and most basic discriminations or associations should be established first. Each new word should be taught by some procedure involving writing the word or filling in missing letters so that attention is directed to details within the word. In addition, it is essential to provide discrimination training between each new word and words of similar shape. Confusion in left and right reversals of letters requires distributed kinesthetic practice and discrimination training with materials of gradually increasing difficulty. No other discriminations should be required during the practice in discriminating left-right reversals. In contrast with the standard, but relatively ineffectual, remedial procedure (of having a dyslexic child read "at his level" with correction of errors), the above procedures consistently work to improve the dyslexic's reading ability because they help overcome specific disability characteristics.

References

Bryant, N. D. Reading Disability: Part of a syndrome of neurological dysfunctioning. In J. A. Figurel (Ed.) *Challenge and Experiment in Reading* 1962 Yearbook of the International Reading Association, New York: Scholastic Magazine Press, 1962, 7, 139-143.

Bryant, N. D. Learning disabilities in reading. In J. A. Figurel (Ed.) *Reading as an Intellectual Activity* 1963 Yearbook of the International Reading Association, New York: Scholastic Magazine Press, 1963, 8, 142-146.

Bryant, N. D. Some principles for remedial instruction for dyslexia. Reading Teacher. In press.

Hermann, K. Reading Disability. Springfield, Illinois: Charles C Thomas, 1959.

Money, J. (Editor) Reading disability. Baltimore, Maryland: Johns Hopkins Press, 1962.

Pasamanick, B. and Knobloch, H. Epidemiologic studies on the complications of pregnancies and the birth process. In G. Kaplan (Ed.) *Prevention of Mental Disorders in Children*. New York: Basic Books, 1961. Pp. 74-94.

Rabinovitch, R. Reading and learning disabilities. In Sylvano Arieti (Ed.) *American Handbook of Psychiatry*. New York: Basic Books, 1959. Pp. 857-869.

41. Instructional Causes of Poor Reading*

WALTER B. BARBE

THERE are, of course, many causes of a child's difficulty in learning to read. To single out any one cause, regardless of how important it may be, tends to create the impression that it is *the* cause. Early research in the field of reading reflected the attitude that particular factors were the cause of all reading problems. But as one author attempted to show that poor reading was due to one factor, another author attempted to lay the blame elsewhere.

An examination of current research in the field of reading disability clearly indicates that the multiple-causation belief is most prevalent today. This means that not only are there many various factors which cause reading problems, but within each case itself there is possibly more than one cause. The very combination of causes sometimes creates a problem, although the single causative factor may not have been important enough alone actually to cause a reading problem of any serious nature.

The reason for so much attention to the cause of reading problems is two-fold. First of all, if the reason for the reading difficulty can be determined, the cure is more readily achieved. The second reason, however, has more far-reaching effects. It has to do with preventing additional problems from occurring. By understanding what has caused reading problems, there is more likelihood of preventing future problems from developing. It is in this phase of .any remedial reading program that the greatest value actually exists. To be continually correcting problems is a never ending task, involving the expense of far more money per pupil than any school system can justify. If the expense of both time and money on these particular children results in a better reading program so that future problems are avoided, then there can be no complaint against the diagnostic and remedial reading program.

The most commonly mentioned causes of reading difficulties are physical factors. Poor vision and hearing, generally poor health and low intelligence are all mentioned as being the underlying cause of reading problems. Emotional

*From *Education,* **77** (May, 1957), 534-540. Reprinted with the permission of the Bobbs-Merrill Company, Inc., Indianapolis, Indiana, and Walter B. Barbe.

417

factors have, of late, come to receive their full share of attention as causes of reading problems. But less frequently mentioned, and certainly as important, are reading difficulties due to instructional problems.

Children having difficulties in reading due to an instructional cause are in a peculiar position. With any of the other causes of reading problems, there can be little actual blame. It is no one's fault that a child could not see well enough to learn to read, even though it could perhaps have been avoided if early and proper diagnosis had taken place. But in any event, there are no guilt feelings attached to a child's failure to learn to read because of a physical problem. Exactly the opposite is true with respect to instructional causes. The very mention that the child's problem may be due to something within the school and not within the child threatens us as teachers. It is perhaps for this reason that we have not examined carefully enough those reading problems which have as their origin flaws in the instructional program.

It seems likely that the child who is having reading problems as a result of nothing within himself, but something within the school program, falls into one of two categories. Either the child has received (1) *inadequate instruction* or (2) *improper instruction.* At first reading they may be one and the same thing; but they are definitely separate and distinct instructional causes of reading problems.

INADEQUATE INSTRUCTION

Critics attacking the public schools have directed far too much attention to inadequate instruction as a cause of reading problems. While it is true that many reading problems are caused because of this, it is not true that this is the single reason for reading problems. As teachers, we are all trying to improve, and the ability to recognize that we are making mistakes and want to do something about them is the hope that fewer and fewer reading problems will develop as a result of inadequate instruction.

Lack of Skill Instruction

In considering inadequate instruction, it is necessary to realize that some children have not been taught to read. This may be because the teacher does not believe in teaching the skills, or it may be that her program has failed to reach particular children. Overcrowded classrooms would be one explanation of this, and too wide a range of ability in a single room would be another explanation. Frequent changing of teachers or schools interrupt the program and may cause problems. The reason which most teachers would be first to mention, however would be the cutting down of time in which they can teach by needless interruptions and special activities.

The most important question to be asked when inadequate instruction is mentioned is, "Has the child been taught to read, or has he been left to learn on his own?" Now it is a fact that many children will learn to read with or without the help of the teacher. Some children actually reach a certain level of maturation when the ability to read comes as naturally as did the ability to walk and talk. But with the majority of children, this almost miraculous stage is never reached if it is left to maturation alone. The teacher, or the parent, must give the maturation process a helping hand. If this is not done, many children will not learn to read well.

While merely placing books in front of some children will so stimulate them to want to read that they will learn in spite of our instructional method, certainly not because of it. This is a fine method for those children with whom it works. It is a deplorable method for all the others.

Is reading a subject or a skill? Perhaps it would be more nearly correct to say that it is a skill after it has been learned; but until that time of mastery, it can be little more than a subject. As a subject, there are certain skills that have to be learned. Too many children are not learning these skills, and are unable to read.

Incidental teaching has been highly praised, but the teacher who believes that incidental teaching means to teach those things when and if she stumbles on to them is not in the group that deserves the praise. Incidental teaching means teaching all the basic skills of reading as the need arises. The skillful teacher sees that the need does arise for all the necessary skills. The teacher who confuses incidental teaching with accidental teaching fails to give the children certain basic skills in reading that they will need when they progress to a high level of reading material.

Children must be taught to read. They learn to read as a result of this teaching. They cannot be expected to learn to read without the benefit of guidance from the teacher. The few children who are exceptions to this are better off for having been exposed to the skills, for later on they may need to use these skills even if they do not at the particular moment see the need. An inadequate coverage of the basic skills in reading is a major cause of reading problems.

Inflexible Program

The teacher may teach the skills necessary for reading, but not reach all of the children. In a classroom in which there are too many students, some children are victims of inadequate instruction. There are just too many children for the teacher to reach every child. Classrooms of thirty, forty and sometimes even fifty are not unheard of. In such instances, it is a certainty that some reading problems are being developed because the instruction is inadequate for some of the children. They simply need more teaching than they can possibly get under such circumstances. It is no fault of the teacher that all such children are not taught, but is instead an administrative fault brought about by the unfortunate notion that large classes are economical.

Even within a class with a normal pupil load, it is still possible that the range of abilities is so great that the teacher is unable to give adequate instruction to all levels. It is not uncommon for a class to contain children reading on as many as eight different reading levels. Actually, the higher in school the children go, the greater is this spread. It is little wonder that teachers do not provide instruction when they are expected to teach skills to children who range in reading ability from the first through the twelfth grades, all within the same room and expected to learn at approximately the same rate.

Changing Teachers

Another reason why a child may have a reading problem due to inadequate instruction is the change in teachers. Probably even one year with a particular teacher of reading is not enough, but certainly less than one year is too short a time. The teacher must devote too much time learning the particular child, to have him leave at less than a year. The learning about the child which the teacher has done is the child's best hope for success. When this is wasted by either the teacher's leaving, or the child's moving, instruction cannot be as effective.

In this period of learning the child, the teacher is following a program of presenting the skills. She is establishing channels by which she can teach the child. She is developing attitudes which will make the child receptive to her particular type of teaching. Only in rare instances, therefore, should the program be interrupted. This stresses the need for requiring teachers to respect their contracts to teach throughout the year, in all but the most urgent circumstances. By the same standard, signing a contract without intending to complete the school year is nothing less than fraud and should not be treated lightly for the children suffer as a result of such action.

Even one move may put a child into the position that he learns little of the actual content material of a particular grade. The three and four shifts, which are not uncommon even within a single city, doom the child to inadequate background of skills. Where it is at all possible, the child should be transported to the school in which he was originally registered, rather than transferred to the new school which may be closer.

This may appear as undue concern about what teacher a child may have, but it actually is more important today than ever before. Schools of some years ago followed rigid curriculum guides, and it made relatively little difference into which room the child might go. Changing from one teacher to another meant probably little more than a difference in personality of the teacher. But today, when strict adherence to a curriculum guide is recognized as ineffective teaching for all children, a change in teachers may well mean a completely different approach with different stressing of skills. While it would not be desirable to return to the rigidity of earlier days, it might nevertheless be wise to have flexible curriculum guides, particularly in areas in which there is a mobile school population.

Interruptions in Program

Interruptions in the class period may well account for many children failing to learn to read. Children are scheduled to spend approximately six hours a day in school, or approximately thirty hours a week. When lunch periods and recesses are subtracted from this, there is probably from twenty to twenty-four hours left for instruction each week. (This is the same amount of time that researchers are reporting that children watch T.V. each week.) Classroom routine, such as calling the roll, collecting money, and many other expected tasks, takes more of this time. If a teacher is not careful, there will be no time left for instructional purposes. It is a certainty that many reading problems exist for no other reason than that the children have just never been taught. In spite of the value of the many enrichment activities being carried on in the modern school, when they take on more importance than the regular instructional program they need to be curtailed.

These are certainly not all of the reasons for inadequate instruction, but they are the more important ones. The hope that can be seen in this situation is that none of them are things which must continue.

IMPROPER INSTRUCTION

It sometimes hurts us to recognize that in this day of better trained teachers, more adequate psychological services and more and better methods and materials for teaching reading, that there can still be reading problems. There are these problems, however, and some of them are due to improper instruction.

Of importance to all people concerned with helping children is the number of children who are reading problems because of improper instruction. This cause of reading problems may be due either to the teacher or the parent. It may be because the teacher simply has not been taught how to teach reading, or because she isn't interested enough in teaching to use what she knows. It may be that the teacher is too rigid to adapt the program to each particular child. If none of these, improper instruction may be caused by either a wrong diagnosis of the child's difficulty, or no diagnosis at all.

Untrained Teachers

Because of the tremendous increase in the birth rate in the past fifteen years, the schools are now packed to capacity with eager youngsters who want to learn to read. But along with this desire to read, is also a desire to watch T.V. and look at the comics. If the learning process is too difficult, the child will forego the pleasure of learning how to read and turn to other less difficult medias of communication for gaining information.

Along with the sudden upswing in the birth rate a sudden upswing in the enrollment in teachers colleges did not come. While the enrollment in colleges has gone up, the number entering teaching has been alarmingly low. As a result of this, schools which have had hordes of children descend upon them must find someone to teach these children. Ideally, the schools would like to raise the standards of their teachers. But when no one applies for the vacancy, the school can hardly demand that any standards be met, much less that higher than ever standards be reached.

Recognizing this problem, many states have lowered their standards to those of a generation ago. No longer is the four year degree a requirement to teach. In some states only two years college work is required for a certificate, and in special instances there are beginning teachers with only a high school diploma. It is hardly a solution to bring untrained people into the classroom for, even though many may actually make a good teacher, there will be many who actually harm the children by not knowing what they are trying to teach nor how to go about teaching it.

Teaching reading is not just a matter of having the children read page after page, but this is the technique that is being used by many untrained teachers. Unlike the medical profession that has constantly raised its standards, even though there have not been enough doctor's available, the teaching profession has been forced to lower the standards required for teachers. It is certainly questionable whether this is a wise move, for it has resulted in lower pretige for teachers. This, in turn, has resulted in more capable students turning to other professions in alarmingly large numbers.

Teaching children to read by the wrong method is the beginning of a problem which will be a costly one if it is to be corrected. The hiring of sub-standard teachers, who do not know how to teach reading, is no solution to the teacher shortage but is instead only adding to the problems of education.

No Systematic Program

The need for systematic reading instruction must not be minimized. Instruction in the skill of reading in a haphazard, hit and miss fashion results in far too many reading failures for it to be considered an effective method. There are certain sequences which should be followed in teaching the skills involved in learning to read. These sequences are as important as the more obvious sequences involved in learning to use arithmetic. Just as the child cannot be expected to be able to multiply before he can add, neither should the child be expected to read new words before he has been taught the skills of word attack.

And by the same measure, the child who cannot read second grade material in his reader, certainly should not be expected to read fourth or fifth grade material in the content areas.

The skills involved in learning to read, while not rigidly set as they are in some areas, are logical. Research studies show, for example, that teaching initial consonant sounds before initial vowel sounds is a better practice. But if the danger is that neither will be taught, then the teacher should be allowed to teach either first. The tragedy is that trained teachers know these things; untrained teachers do not know them. Is it fair to the pupils that they must try to learn the difficult task of reading from an untrained, unskilled person?

Single Method of Instruction

The great danger of a so-called "new" method of teaching reading is that so much attention is directed to this single method that the teacher may fail to recognize that no one method will work for all children. It is going from one extreme to the other that has characterized educational philosophy as an indefinite, always uncertain field. Actually, every teacher can do a better job of teaching reading, and it is the constantly changing program that insures the child of the best possible education. But there needs to be caution exercised against going from one extreme to the other because not all children learned by one particular method. Not all children will learn by any one method, and the teacher who tries to teach all children by exactly the same method is doomed to failure before she starts.

Some children learn to read most easily by a phonic approach. They hear sounds clearly, can distinguish between sounds without difficulty, and enjoy the developing of words out of sounds. Phonics help them so much that this is the method by which they should be taught. But within the very same classroom there will be children who not only can't hear the sounds, but can't seem to learn them. In the school or class in which the teacher is convinced that she has discovered *the* way to teach reading, these individuals will fail. It is true that in some select communities, special single method programs appear to be successful. But the question arises whether these same children would not have been just as successful with any program in which the teacher put so much faith.

Other children learn by a sight method, far better than by a phonic approach. These children need to be taught by the method with which they have the greatest success. But even those children who have one particular way in which it is easiest for them to learn, under some circumstances an appeal to another sense will aid in the learning. Some children, and they are usually the ones who have the greatest difficulty in learning to read, can be reached by neither a visual nor an auditory approach. With them the teacher must use the kinesthetic or tactile sense.

In identifying children who have reading difficulties because of a single approach in their teaching, it is frequently necessary to know something about the school in which the child is enrolled and the teacher he has. The symptom of such improper instruction is usually total failure in reading, with the knowledge of some skills which can be recited but which cannot be used in the reading situation.

Inadequate Understanding of Child

Before an adequate reading program can be carried on, the child needs to be understood by the teacher. Certainly not all children will need diagnosis, of a more highly specialized nature than the teacher can provide but those who do should receive the best possible. No diagnosis of the child's problems can lead to a much more severe reading problem; as well as to other types of personal and social maladjustment. An inadequate or incorrect diagnosis can have the same effect.

Frequently specialists in reading see so many cases of poor reading due to a particular cause that they are inclined to believe that they have found the cause of all reading problems. About the time that this happens, the specialist is in danger of then making the case fit what he already believes, instead of finding out what the problem actually is. There are, of course, many symptoms which are quite common in reading disability cases. But these symptoms are only symptoms, and should not be considered causes of the problem itself.

Until the teacher knows what the problem is, there is little chance of success in treating the problem. Therefore, adequate diagnosis is essential for a successful reading instruction.

There can be little doubt that some reading problems are actually caused by some phase of the instructional program. Because as teachers we have the responsibility of doing as much as possible to improve reading instruction, it is necessary for us to examine ourselves and our procedures in order that we will profit by our mistakes. There has been too much of this by the journalist, eager to produce sensational material. But there has perhaps been too little by teachers, who are not concerned with the profits to be made by sensational expose. This discussion of where we as teachers have failed is intended only to make us more aware of how we can improve our reading programs, and is not meant to be an attack on those who are doing a better job of educating all children than ever before in the history of American education.

IX

Linguistics

42. Linguistics and Reading*

EMMETT A. BETTS

EFFICIENT reading is a process—basically a thinking process—which requires the *automatic* use of word-perception skills. Reading is a process of decoding writing which symbolizes speech sounds that are used to encode messages. Hence, reading is two steps removed from the message—a fact which appears to be unrecognized by some reading specialists, some linguists, and some psychologists.

Equally important, reading is done by organisms with frontal lobes—by individuals who vary considerably in motivations, perceptual skills, and thinking abilities. These individuals *learn* to listen, talk, read, and write. Because they *learn* to encode and decode spoken and written language signals, their verbal behavior is studied by psychologists. Hence, reading instruction has a psychological as well as linguistic basis.

Furthermore, there is substantial progress being made today on the sociological as well as on the psychological basis of differentiated reading instruction. Differences among pupils in levels of achievements, language facility, learning rates and the like have been recognized by the vanguard of reading instruction. But, today, more emphasis is being given to the needs of superior learners. And, today, culturally deprived pupils are being discovered—their motivations, their control over the phonological and grammatical levels of language, their cognitive structures, and so on.

FACETS OF READING INSTRUCTION

For several generations an enormous stumbling block in reading instruction has been the fruitless attempt to regiment reading instruction—to assume that all pupils are prepared to learn to read upon admission to school, to use the same textbook with all pupils of that fiction called a grade. In today's

*From *Education*, **86** (April, 1966), 454-458. Copyright © 1966 by The Bobbs-Merrill Company, Inc., Indianapolis, Indiana. Reprinted by permission.

reading instruction, however, there is evidence that individualized and group instruction is superseding the iniquitous regimented instruction of the past.

At each succeeding level of reading achievement, therefore, pupils present greater ranges of reading achievement and perceptual and conceptual needs. For example, in a typical fifth grade the range is from those who need help in beginning reading to those who do read so-called twelfth-grade materials of interest to them. It appears that the more efficient the reading instruction the greater is the range. But no competent teacher would attempt to teach all the pupils of a grade the same word-perception skills and the putting perception in word perception. When maximum use is made of the conclusions gleaned from both linguistics and psychology, the teaching of word-perception skills is taken far beyond the ineffective "grunt and groan" phonics of yesteryear.

In general, linguists who have either dabbled or made serious attempts to prepare beginning reading materials have found themselves trapped by (1) their lack of understanding of the psychology of word perception, (2) their lack of experience in the teaching of reading, and (3) their failure to evaluate word perception in relation to the intonation of efficient reading. They have not published, for example, a systematic treatise on either the linguistic basis or the psychological basis of word perception.

In the past, educators have been concerned with phonic rules. For example, the "short" vowel rule has been stated: If there is only one vowel in a stressed syllable and it is followed by a consonant (e.g., *at, hat*), the vowel is usually "short". This statement, it will be noted, stresses the whole word, the word pattern, rather than the vowel alone.

Furthermore, educators have studied the application/exception ratios for these rules and have found that the above-mentioned rule applies to 53 per cent of the "closed" syllables in beginning reading and to 71 per cent at the third-reader level. However, many of these words, especially function words, are said one way when stressed as isolated syllables and another way in phrase stress (e.g., *can* as/'kan/ and /kən/).

Under the leadership of Leonard Bloomfield, the linguists, too, have concerned themselves with patterns of relationships between sounds of words and the letters of words. Instead of phonic rules they deal in spelling patterns, especially those spelling patterns (e.g., *it-sit*) which consistently represent patterns of sounds. Although Bloomfield recommended the use of consistent spelling patterns in beginning reading, he was undoubtedly aware of the many pitfalls of writing materials using closed syllables only and ignoring intonation, especially phrase stress. He, therefore, recommended "either to postpone other graphs [irregular spellings] until the elementary habit has been fixed, or else to introduce them, in some rationally planned way, at earlier points" (p. 501). It is the second part of his statement that has been violated by zealots of the word-pattern idea.

EIGHT VALID STATEMENTS

To summarize this situation, the following statements appear to have validity:

1. The word pattern includes both consonants and vowels; therefore, consonants are introduced as systemically as vowels are.
2. There are not three basic patterns emphasized by some linguists but more than twenty basic patterns.
3. Pattern 1 (*at-sat, set-pep, it-lip, not-stop* and *us-but*), which has intrigued linguists, is for the pupil really five patterns. As a general pattern it is ambiguous for the pupil, because he does not have the linguistic sophistication to make the required over-all generalization.
4. A valid word pattern has value to the degree that it functions not only for identifying one-syllable words (e.g., *sat*) but also for identifying embedded patterns in the stressed syllables of multisyllable words (e.g., in *satisfaction*).
5. A word pattern is serviceable to the degree that it has a high application/exception ratio, or batting average.
6. Many irregular spellings tend to pattern, as in *right, sight, might,* and *light.*
7. Word perception as an automatic part of the on-going reading process requires an awareness of both syllable stress and phrase stress.
8. Both word pattern cues and phonogram cues are used to identify words, as the *oi* in the unpatterned word *noise.*

PERCEPTUAL LEARNING

Furthermore, the perception of words, as the structuring of stimuli, is a psychological process. Perceptual learning is:

1. *Category learning.* The pupil learns word-pattern and phonogram categories.
2. *Cue learning.* The pupil learns to identify the unknown part of a word (e.g., the *ar* of *cart* or the *Ne* syllables of *Neanderthal*) as a cue to be learned or previously learned.
3. *Probability learning.* The pupil learns, for example, that the usual sound of the vowel is /ī/ in *by, my, why, sky, try.* On the other hand, he learns that the *ow* in *cow* or *crow* probably stands for the sound /aù/ or /ō/.
4. *Relationship learning.* The pupil learns the relationships between regular spellings and sounds and between irregular spellings and sounds. In learning a new skill, he is taken from the spoken word to the written word. When the pupil applies his word perception skill, he "feeds back" from the written word to the spoken word.

5. *Generalization learning.* The pupil learns to make generalizations regarding the relationships between the sound patterns and letter patterns of words and of phonograms.

6. *Mediation response learning.* The pupil learns to use obscure and unoberservable processes that operate between the stimulus and the response. For example, in responding to the word *hat* the beginner may call on pre-established associations with *at* and *cat.* In responding to the word *redound* or *retaliate,* the experienced reader may call on one or more pre-established associations, depending on which part is unknown: the number of places in which he sees vowels as indicative of the number of syllables, the relationship between the phonogram *ou* and the sound /au/, awareness of syllable stress, and so on.

SIGNIFICANT FACTORS

The perceptual process of decoding writing into speech is dependent upon a number of conditions and factors:

1. Motivation, e.g., the attitudinal factor *need* to identify the unknown part or parts of a particular word
2. Attention as a powerful selector of stimulus information to be processed and as a constant feature of perceptual activity
3. Set, a determiner of perception, which, among other things, causes the pupil to regard reading as a poverty-stricken word calling process or as a thinking process
4. Grouping of stimuli into recognizable syllables, phonograms, and other patterns for making optimum use of a limited span of attention
5. Meaning, both structural and referential, needed for the closure of perception
6. Contrast, such as the contrastive letter patterns which represent contrastive sound patterns
7. Feedback, a circular process, from the examination of letter groupings of the written word to the sounds of the spoken word; for example, the *application* of word perception skills to the written word during the silent reading
8. Closure, as in the identification of the word *noise* after the usual sound represented by *oi* is recalled
9. Kinesthesis, as it operates in inner speech and in word learning.

IN CONCLUSION

Generally speaking, linguistics is a source of content for the teaching of reading and psychology supplies information on which to base methodology.

These two disciplines have not been wedded as a new discipline, psycholinguistics, but substantial progress has been made to demonstrate they are not out of ardor!

The key to improvement in reading instruction is not only materials which are built on sound linguistic and psychological bases but also the teacher. The chief problem is convincing teachers of teachers and certifiers of teachers that well-defined courses in psychology and linguistics are essential prerequisites to a methods course—that competence is achieved by a firm grasp of the basic disciplines rather than a proliferation of courses on methods.

References

Betts, Emmett Albert, "Excellence in Contemporary Reading Instruction." (Boston, Massachusetts: New England Reading Association, September, 1965).

———. "Linguistics and Reading: A Critique," pp. 130-140 in *Innovation and Experiment in Modern Education.* Report of the Twenty-ninth Educational Conference, Educational Records Bureau. (New York: American Council on Education, 1964).

———. "A New Area: Reading and Linguists," *Education,* Vol LXXXIV, No. 9, (May 1964), pp. 515-520.

———. "Reading: Linguistics," *Education,* Vol. LXXXIII, No. 9, (May 1963), pp. 515-526.

———. "Report on Phoneme-Grapheme Relationships: Dictionary," Coral Gables, Florida: Reading Research Laboratory, University of Miami, 1964.

———. "Word Perception Skills For Tomorrow," *Education,* Vol LXXXV, No. 9, (May 1965), pp. 523-528.

Black, Elsie Benson. "A Study of the Consonant Situations in a Primary Reading Vocabulary," Education, Vol. LXXII, No. 9, (May 1952), pp. 618-623.

Bloomfield, Leonard, *Language* (New York: Henry Holt and Company, 1933).

Oaks, Ruth E. "A Study of the Vowel Situation in a Primary Vocabulary," *Education,* Vol LXXII, No. 9, (May 1952), pp. 604-617.

43. Linguistics, Psychology, and the Teaching of Reading*

CONSTANCE M. McCULLOUGH

I.

WITH every contribution and every criticism from relevant disciplines, the teaching of reading has the opportunity to improve. All you have to do to realize this is to see what happens in classrooms in which there are poorly-informed teachers as compared with classrooms in which well-informed teachers continuously reassess their practices in the light of new information. Historically and hysterically, as these contributions and criticisms have come, we have tended to go overboard, doing too much of the new thing or applying it in ways and at times that are not best or even desirable for reading growth. Materials have appeared which stress the new, and completely ignore some very worthwhile elements in the total reading program. They are welcomed like manna from heaven. Sometimes I wonder which is worse—to be poorly-informed or to be caught in the hysteria of the new bit-though ordinarily I try not to say this aloud.

The thing we must learn as teachers is that there is no perfect contribution or perfect material; there is only a perfect teacher; and that perfect teacher is the one who evaluates each contribution to see what it can be and mean in an entire program which consists of much more than any one contribution.

As teachers we have been trained in the application of psychological principles to classroom procedures. We might be said to be amateur psychologists. Certainly we have had a great deal of help from psychologists in the teaching of reading. But most of us have had little training in the linguistic concepts which now clamor to be recognized. We have been flying on one wing. Somehow, now, in mid-air, we must assemble that other wing-of appropriate size and shape and timing to provide balance and efficient progress in flight.

Dr. McCullough is a Professor of Education at San Francisco State College. This article is based on the Fifth Edith P. Merritt Memorial Lecture, given at the College in June, 1966.

*From *Elementary English,* **44** (April, 1967), 353-362. Reprinted with the permission of the National Council of Teachers of English and Constance M. McCullough.

It is interesting to note that when children have difficulty learning to read, we tend to blame material or method, and a critic comes along and says, "Do *more* of *this*." More phonics, for example. Actually, instead of doing more of what we have been doing, we should be exploring for the missing parts that we haven't known and haven't used. This is what Marianne Frostig did in developing her tests and materials for the identification and improvement of subskills in visual perception, and what Samuel Kirk did in developing his tests of psycho-linguistic abilities in young children. There are plenty of parts still missing in our knowledge of language. There is much still to explore. And I believe it will be only when the teacher of reading informs herself of the new findings in linguistics and psychology, and studies the possibilities of their congenial application, that a program superior to the ones currently used will emerge. It is in that belief that I present this paper.

II.

At the recent Dallas meeting of the International Reading Association, I had the good fortune to hear a paper by Lee Deighton of Macmillan Company. Deighton is an editor and author who explores the problems of language and learning, and as you probably know has made some very helpful contributions to vocabulary development.

In his paper he reminded his audience that, while the reading eye progresses in a series of pauses and movements, from left to right, in the case of English, it cannot during any one pause take in more than about an inch of print. On many occasions it may not view a whole word in any one pause. It may even see the back end of one word and the front end of another. The speed at which the eye performs in this manner is relatively limited, especially in unfamiliar material in which guesswork about the words the eye has skipped can be fatal to meaning.

The brain, meanwhile, is champing at the bit. It must assemble all of this garbage into something meaningful. While the eye trots earnestly along, the nerve impulses which process its findings may be going at as great a rate as 200 miles an hour. Various estimates have been given by various sources. For the nerve impulses it must be worse than wiping dishes for a meticulous washer. But the point that Deighton made is that the brain has a chance to do a thorough job of mulling over meanings, a chance to be right and wrong several times about the author's meaning. He speaks of it as a circular movement, though I am not sure that "circular" exactly describes it and I suspect he is not either.

But with the example of an expression like "the little white house," he shows that the ideas of "little" and "white" are modified when the eye comes to "house," for a little house has not the littleness of a little dog, and the whiteness of white paint is not the same as the whiteness of feathers in a little white feather, or the whiteness of a stone in a little white stone. Therefore, Deighton believes that the mind holds in abeyance certain ideas as it explores the effect of other ideas upon them.

Let's see how Deighton's theory works on a sentence which I shall now read. My first word is *In*. I shall continue slowly to add words, and you as a listener try to determine what adjustments your thought has to make to grasp the meaning of this sentence: "In . . . its . . . hose-like . . . gray . . . trunk, . . . the . . . little . . . figure . . . on . . . the . . . matchbox . . . carried . . . a . . . Republican . . . banner."

The word *In* has several different meanings, such as that referring to time, place, manner, or state of being. *Its* suggests possession by an inanimate either in a previous sentence or in the current one. Linguists call *its* a noun determiner and expect a noun to follow it sooner or later. *Its* confirms the fact that *In* is being used as the beginning of a phrase. *Hose-like* has an attributive form implying that a noun is soon to come, but is puzzling in meaning because there are. several kinds of hose. *Gray* is another attributive form which still does not identify the hose. *Trunk* is a surprise, for the usual trunk into which one puts things is not shaped like a hose of any kind and is not ordinarily owned by an *it*.

My pause, which is here signaled by a comma, marks the end of the phrase, and gives hope for the coming of a noun. *The,* indeed, signals that coming. *Little,* another attributive word, is again a puzzler, this time because littleness is relative. *Figure* qualifies as a noun and as an inanimate; *its* must refer to *figure*. But *figure* has several meanings, too. Does a figure eight have something in a hose-like gray trunk? Or is the word *figure* used as a general term for a shape of some kind? If *hose-like gray trunk* has suggested *elephant* to the listener, the reference to a little figure is indeed baffling. The listener feels still worse when he hears that the little figure is *on the matchbox,* for now the size is whittled down to nothing like an elephant.

Carried follows the noun phrase in the expected position for the verb in a Noun-Verb-Noun type of basic sentence (NVN), and confirms this hunch with its *d* ending. But there are different meanings for *carry* too. The listener must settle for the idea that this *carry* is used in the sense of "hold in a stationary position," for you can't go far on a matchbox. *A* denotes the coming of another noun. *Republican* is in either an adjective or noun position. The sentence could stop there. But *banner* proves that *Republican* is an adjective, and the listener does not have to imagine what kind of square a Republican would have to be to fit on a matchbox. *Republican* confirms the hunch that the figure is an elephant after all; the trunk belongs to the elephant. The *In* at the beginning of the sentence means the trunk was curled around. It is an embracing *In*. The listener must imagine what the banner may have on it, who might own such a thing, whether the little figure is a statue or a picture, upright or prostrate, attached or unattached, and so forth.

The listener who had had no experience with the Republican emblem would not get the meaning of this sentence at all. Or if, in listening, he did not catch the word *Republican*—if, in reading, he skipped over it—he would be mystified. The African listening to this and knowing the Republican emblem might still see in his mind an African elephant; an Indian, an Indian elephant.

Now, what did you smart people have to be able to do to get this message clearly? You had to listen carefully. It is said that we catch seventy-five percent of the sounds we could hear, and that we then add the missing links by context or situation, to realize the intended words.

You had to note the similarity of my Indiana English pronounciation to that to which you were born or are accustomed. You had to invest these spoken symbols with the meanings your experience has given them. You had to group into meaningful English units—that is, words, phrases—the stream of sounds you heard. Intonation and pauses peculiar to the English sentence helped you. In reading, of course, you would have had to reinvest the *symbols for sound* with intonation and pauses.

Familiarity with the structure of the English sentence helped you. The little words, like *in* and *on* and *the*, were important clues, also. You had to know what they signaled and what they might mean if they were words of multiple meaning. You had to catch the signal for the past tense of the verb *carry*, in order to know the time of this observation. You had to know the function of a pronoun and be able to reason that *its* referred to *figure* and not to *matchbox* or *banner*.

If this sentence had carried an emotional intent, you would have had to be sensitive to that, also. As it was, if you are a Democrat, you simply had to restrain yourself.

III.

The English language is literally laced with signals, or lacily littered with signals, however you like it. In a composition of ten sentences, it is quite possible that an *it* in the last sentence refers clear back to a noun in the first sentence. Phrases and synonyms echo one another from one sentence to another, the same meaning sometimes serving even different functions.

Our study of meaning, therefore, cannot be confined to one word or one phrase or one clause or one sentence or even one paragraph. The meaning and even the pronunciation of some words depend upon the purpose of the speaker or author. Some of the things which we have thought of as niceties—perhaps to be observed and taught, and perhaps not—such as the style or mood of the speaker or author—even deliberate ambiguities—cannot be optional if, as in many cases, clear reception of meaning cannot be gained without them.

What I have been saying is that all of these skills and knowledges, all of these dimensions of concepts, are the concern of teachers of reading. The readiness of the young child for reading, the readiness of the college student for a science text assignment, depend upon such preparation. And in passing I should like to observe that what Robert Lado has done for the understanding of the language needs of a Spanish-speaking child in learning English, what Claude Wise and others have done to compile the linguistic needs of children from still other backgrounds, must be put in a form readily useful to teachers. Houghton Mifflin's *Introducing English* for the reading readiness of Spanish-speaking children is a step in the right direction. But *is* it not possible to produce comparable material with suggestions and additions to accommodate the needs of children of other language groups as well?

IV.

Meanwhile, back at the ranch, psychologists and educators have tried to extend their understanding of the reading process. You probably know of the work of Irving Lorge at Columbia University, who investigated certain vocabulary problems with Thorndike, and on his own developed a formula by which the difficulty of reading material could be roughly determined. His formula was one of several, such as the Flesch, the Dale-Chall, and the Spache, by which school systems and teachers can estimate the difficulty of textbooks and tradebooks perpetrating them on youngsters.

Lorge was aware that elements were missing from the formula. Obviously conceptual difficulty was one. But he believed that organization of material was also a potent factor. From John Carroll, the well-known linguist at Harvard, he obtained some paragraphs from essays written for College Board Examinations. He selected passages of equal length and difficulty according to his formula. The vocabularies, the sentence length and complexity, the topic treated, were the same. The only apparent difference, as far as Lorge could tell, lay in organization and in clues to organization. He tested students on the meaning of these passages and found that they were better able to answer questions on passages well-organized *and* bearing clues to organization.

I read his unpublished paper on this experiment in, I believe, the fall of 1960, and it so aroused my interest that I have really never recovered from the fascination of this problem.

It led me back to the work of James McCallister at Chicago Teachers College thirty-five years ago, in which he identified nine different kinds of paragraph organization which students should learn to recognize to facilitate their reading of textbooks. I studied a set of textbooks in science for the elementary school and found two kinds of pattern throughout the series—one in which an illustration is followed by a statement of principle, and one in which the steps in an experiment are enumerated. In a tenth-grade chemistry text I identified twelve different patterns of paragraph organization.

The problem, as I saw it, was to make teachers aware of these patterns and of ways to teach them so that students would not read everything the same way and come out with the main idea every time—sometimes useful and sometimes not so useful. You know, we have hypnotized our students and ourselves for years by stopping with "the main idea and a few significant details" instead of considering the author's trend of thought.

Of course, the flaw in my thinking at the time was that I hoped to find comparable patterns in every text, whereas the truth is that each author tends to have a habit pattern of his own. The teacher must be able to recognize the patterns the author habitually uses if she is to help students to recognize and use them. The problem is to find the units of thought, composing patterns.

Unaware of Bloom's now famous taxonomy or of Guilford's now famous cube of cognitive processes, I produced empirically from my observations of textbooks in science and social studies a schema of the cognitive ingredients which are expressed in such material. To distinguish it from the creations of other great geniuses throughout history, I entitled it "McCullough's Excelsior"—referring, of course, to the analogy someone once made, likening the action of ideas in the brain to the dumping of a raw egg into a box of excelsior. A linguist will tell you that this schema may be true of English speakers and not of speakers of some other languages, and so as I describe it you must realize that I am a prisoner of my own language.

Here it is: The brain of a human being receives sensory impressions of objects and living organisms in patterns of events and situations, modified by his own thought-and-feeling predispositions and reactions. He becomes conscious of various relationships: whole-part, cause-effect, sequential, comparison-contrast, and coordinate-subordinate. From these he can develop certain products of the mind: theories, laws and principles, generalizations, summarizations, definitions, classifications, and procedures. These, in turn, he can support with examples, elaboration, and application.

The order in which he does any of these things is individual.

This schema does not include processes, such as induction or deduction, because I was concerned about what was on a printed page, not about how it got there. Neither does it include such topics as evaluation or analogy, for they are special cases of existing categories.

When you think of *words*, in connection with this schema, you see many more possibilities for the development of concepts and vocabulary relationships than we have ever used before. Dictionary definitions begin to look extremely sick, by comparison—as indeed they must be if the book is not to weigh a ton.

You also begin to see that if reading is thinking, then we should be sure that a child cannot only *speak English* but think in the various ways in the English language before we expect him to *decipher the print* and think in it. And if the child is to keep fresh the various ways of thinking, then our daily activities should offer this variety over a period of time. For example, what happens to other thought patterns when some preschool and kindergarten programs emphasize the use of context clues? This is good, but what is being done about other elements?

And if, in word-analysis, we use a set of cards on which the child must analyze words and then put them under headings, such as "toys" and "food," what are we doing to balance this with experiences in which *he* must decide the heading under which certain words he selects might belong; and what are we doing to give him equal exercise that is not simply a classification experience? You begin to see that in giving the child fifteen minutes of this and ten minutes of that in the classroom all of these years, we have been making decisions without knowing it—decisions that distort his readiness to meet the thought challenges of the reading task.

As I tried to identify the types of thought in sentences within paragraphs, I discovered for myself some very important facts about language in habitat. Let me give you an example. Take the sentence, "He ran." This is a statement of fact. It does not reveal the situation in which "he" is. Now add, "As he looked back over his shoulder he could see that the bear was still after him." This second sentence does a lot. It suggests why he ran and tells what he did next:

> The bear came after him.
> He ran.
> He looked over his shoulder.
> The bear was still coming.

So "He ran" is not only a statement of an event but also a statement of the effect of a cause.

If, instead, the sentences read, "He ran. Each step was the biggest he could possibly take," the second sentence describes the way he ran, elaborating the first. The first sentence may be a summary or generalization of the series of descriptive sentences to follow.

If, instead, the sentences read, "He ran. She skipped after him," you have two statements of event, one event following another, and providing a contrast. You don't know the human motivation for this—whether they were both going toward the candy store, whether she just liked him, or whether he had learned early to stay away from women.

The upshot of this is that, just as the linguists have discovered that the sound of a letter depends upon the situation of the letter in the word—"back, bake, bark, balk"—and as Deighton found that the meaning of a word is altered by its relationships with other words—"The bare branch could bear the bear no longer"—so I found for myself that the meaning of a sentence, the contribution of a sentence, the classification of a sentence, depends upon its surroundings.

The student who reads sentences like a string of beads, each at its isolated face-value, is headed for trouble. The teacher who confines her help to only what she considers the new, hard words, is missing many of the serious problems that confront the student. The elements of language are not islands. They create a fabric whose very open spaces are significant.

V.

Another fascinating observation you can make if you *study* language instead of just using it, is that a second sentence seems sometimes to put a spotlight on a word or phrase in the preceding sentence. In "He ran. She skipped," the contrast of *he* and *she*, *run* and *skipped*, stresses both of these elements. But in "He ran. Each step . . . ." "Each step . . . ." features the *ran*. In some paragraphs you can follow the author's progress in stressing first one dimension, then another, as though you were watching fireflies on a summer night. Language also contains an echo effect:

> August was a very *dry* month.
> The *thirsty* cattle stood by the *empty troughs*.
> Farmers looked for *clouds* in the *blazing* skies.
> But *no rains* came.

Listening activities can sharpen a student's sensitivity to types of ideas. I have enjoyed considerable enlightenment from listening activities myself. There is a person who has always reduced me to utter silence. I realize now that she has an intimidating habit of sounding like God but with less wisdom. Her emphatic judgmental statements about everything render further comment unnecessary if not unwelcome. I have also followed conversations in which the same person tells the same story to a succession of different people. With one partner who attempts to placate him, comment by comment, he becomes disgusted at what he interprets as lack of sympathy. With another partner who adds fuel to his fire—"How outrageous! . . . Well, I never! . . . *etc.*"—he is more angry at the end than he was at first. Students can learn a good deal about *sources of ambiguity* in language by recording conversations in which remarks have been misunderstood and misinterpreted. They don't have to leave home to get ample evidence for analysis in class.

Hilda Taba, as you know, in her effort to encourage the use of higher thought processes in class discussions, has charted the level of challenge of teacher questions and the quality of student comments, with some very insightful results. And Hayakawa has shown how the insertion of certain loaded words can trigger feelings and reactions.

VI.

Now, how can we help students gain some mastery over the linguistic problems in reading? If you wish to prove to your students that there is no telling where an author will go from one sentence to the next, give them a sentence and ask each student to say or write what might sensibly come next. In spite of the unpredictability of an author's next step, students must form hunches about what the author will do. You can give them a typical opening sentence for a paragraph of classification or comparison or cause and effect or illustration of a principle or definition or description or interpretation, and ask them to say what may happen next and why they think so.

Students of limited English background are not ready for the many ways in which English can express a single thought. They need experience in listening and reading to find duplication of thought in different wording.

If you wish to prove to your students how dependent they are on signal words, word order, and word endings in unfamiliar material, you may be inspired by Lewis Carroll or C.C. Fries to give them a sentence like this: "The lorks of the inksy anks glom sterb stonk by co-glickent gunding." They'll never guess that the atoms of the common gases form diatomic molecules by co-valent bonding, but they will know something about the relationships of the words and the nature of the statement.

Carl LeFevre in his helpful book, *Linguistics and the Teaching of Reading* (McGraw-Hill), gives lists of signal words. What he does not tell you is the frequency with which they don't signal what you expect. For example, "both . . . and" are coordinates in the sentence, "He was both clever and wise." But in the sentence, "They were both clever and wise," "both" may be referring to *they*, signaling backwards instead of forwards to "clever and wise." The language is full of untrustworthy characters. Take the word *since*: "Since you left the company, much has happened." Is the *since* causal, with the meaning that nothing could happen as long as a bottleneck like you was around, or is it temporal, indicating only the passage of time? And what about the word *by*, an innocent-looking word which we have often passed over as we dwelt upon the rare noun which followed? "Come by ten o'clock. Come by train. Come, by the way. Come by the house. Come by sometime." The dictionary lists ten uses of *by* as preposition alone, and several more as an adverb. In unfamiliar material the student should be cautious—should hold in abeyance, as Deighton says, his decision about its meaning.

For years we have told students that the word *however* signals a change of direction, a reversal; but it doesn't always. In written material, the questions, "However did you do it?" and "However, did you do it?" show their different intent only by the presence of the comma. And in many sentences, *however* adds to or limits the preceding idea rather than controverting it. We have had students look up hard words in the dictionary. Sometimes we should have them look up the easy ones to see the many meanings that are well established, not to speak of those which may be gathered in time.

How can we tell when "you were" is singular and when it is plural and when it is condition contrary to fact? How can we tell that a question in a textbook is a question even before we come to the mark at the end? How can we tell the passive voice is being used and the subject is not the actor? What are the signals for the remote past that help us sense flashbacks and time change?

If the author uses signals such as *first, next, finally, on the other hand, besides, another point, in summary,* his organization is easy to follow. That is, it is easy if the student recognizes the signals. But if an author just as well-organized does not give these helpful signals, the reader has to sense them. How can the student sense that a new point is being made, not just an addition to the old? How can he tell that a subordinate point is being made? How can he tell that now the author is telling all the negative things about a topic, having just told all the positive things? How can he tell the flavor of a generalization from a specific fact, a definition from a statement of function, a principle from an illustration? By ear training and by visual analysis, students must learn how to detect such differences: but if we ourselves do not know the points to be observed, we cannot teach students to follow the ideas of the author.

A characteristic of English is the use of pronouns or alternate words instead of repetition of the same word. What proof is there that the pronoun refers to *this* word and not to *that*? What tells the reader that two words are being used synonymously?

Some nouns like *reindeer* and *fish* have the same form for singular and plural. In what situations do these dual purposes create reading difficulty and a dependence upon signals?

VII.

I do not have to tell you that this kind of learning can be done only by children who are well-acquainted with the English language. We should expand our idea of the disadvantaged to include all of us: children who do not speak English, children who do not recognize "book English," children unready for the concepts in assigned texts, and teachers unready to help them decode the meanings they encounter.

The reading act requires the decoding of written symbols into the sounds which those symbols rather inaccurately represent. The decoding of written symbols into sounds gives the reader the original speech-symbol for an idea. The interaction of these ideas, appraised by a knowledge of the order of English, the signals of relationship, and the possible meanings each word or phrase or clause may have in a variety of contexts, gives the reader what, from his experience, the author has meant to say. If the reader stops here, he will be fair game for any propagandist and will never produce ideas of his own. Now he must use his thought processes upon what he has observed and gathered, to develop products of his mind stimulated by this reading. The last step in the reading act is the use or expression of these ideas, these products, and the testing of them to see their validity.

In this paper I am concerned mainly with the second step, the decoding of meanings. But it is only one part of the total process. We should never magnify it to the exclusion of other important parts. Neither should we neglect it, either as teachers or as students of the language.

One wonderful contribution that this study of meaning can make is that it can vitalize some of the erstwhile deadly parts of the English program, those whitened bones set in orderly rows on the blackboard, defying utility and interest. Who hasn't hated the so-called irregular verbs: *drink, drank, drunk; see, saw, seen*? But Archibald Hill in his classification of verbs in his book, *Introduction to Linguistic Structures* (Harcourt, Brace), shows fifteen or more patterns in which verbs are found. One realizes that the so-called irregular verbs are friends in disguise, with built-in signals to tense, whereas a verb like *cut*, which we have always appreciated for its dependability, gives no clue. We can realize the "signal" advantage to the child-who-*sounds* these endings or internal changes *correctly*.

The structural approach to English, used by many teachers with foreign students and the disadvantaged, is notoriously dull. Here is a who-dun-it I wrote in India, in structural English: "This is a man. This is a robber. This is a knife. This is a murder. This is a jail." I couldn't get a publisher. But if children can make discoveries about verbs, about structure, about the ways language works—in listening, speaking, reading, and writing activities—the language arts program will get a better Hooper rating. Curiosity will supplant lethargy, and discovery will replace boredom and inefficiency in learning. Practice will have more meaning.

I believe that we are on the verge of a great awakening in the language arts. (Perhaps it is niggardly of me not to say "REawakening.") There are more reasons for thinking this than I have time to convey. If we inform ourselves about the nature of our languages, if we are curious and interested ourselves, neither we nor our children will need the artificial stimulus of color on letters, or the evasive crutches by which we first teach a symbol for the symbol of a symbol, and then the symbol of a symbol that the symbol for the symbol stands for.While some linguists would have us start with the alphabet, others with "Nan can fan Dan," and others with children's natural language, we should be good enough specialists in the teaching of reading to know that none of these alone is sufficient.

Let the linguist tell us about the language in his orderly way. Let the psychologist tell us how children learn. Let us then use this information to make a more suitable program for learning than either can conceive. Let us be curious about our own language so that the zeal created by our own efforts of discovery will electrify our classrooms. Let us have the restraint not to impose the fruits of our discoveries in dull little lists or artificial sentences upon children whose being cries to express itself. Rather, let us set the stage so that the discovery can be theirs and the learning confirmed by the intensity of their attention at the moment of insight.

Twenty-three years ago I reported the discoveries my college students had made about seven types of context clues to the meaning of unfamiliar words. *My* thinking stopped with theirs. I realize now that we were seeing only the top of the iceberg. Nine-tenths of the signals suggestive of meaning were hidden by our ignorance of other supportive linguistic clues. Those context clues are still valid. But think how much more you and I can do today to give our children power through insight.

References

1. Bloom, B. S., ed., *Taxonomy of Educational Objectives.* New York: McKay, 1956.
2. Booth, A.D., *et al.,* "Aspects of Translation," *Studies in Communication 2.* London: Secker and Warburg, 1958.
3. Context Clues, entire issue, *The Reading Teacher,* volume 11, April 1958.
4. Enkvist, Nils E., *et al., Linguistics and Style.* London: Oxford University Press, 1964,
5. Firth, J. R., *Papers in Linguistics 1934-51.* London: Oxford University Press, 1957.
6. Fries, C. C., *Linguistics: The Study of Language.* New York: Holt, 1962.
7. ---, *The Structure of English.* New York: Harcourt, 1952.
8. Frostig, M., *Developmental Test of Visual Perception.* Los Angeles: the author, 1961.
9. Gleason, H. A., Jr., *Linguistics and English Grammar.* New York: Holt, 1965.
10. Halliday, M. A. K., et al., *The Linguistic Sciences and Language Teaching.* London: Longmans, 1964.
11. Harper, Robert J. C., et al., *The Cognitive Processes.* Englewood Cliffs, N. J.: Prentice-Hall, 1964.
12. Hayakawa, S. I., *Language in Action.* New York: Harcourt, 1941.
13. Hill, Archibald A., *Introduction to Linguistic Structures.* New York: Harcourt, 1958.
14. Hunt, Kellogg W., *Grammatical Structures Written at Three Grade Levels.* Champaign, Illinois: National Council of Teachers of English, 1965.
15. Kirk, Samuel A. and James McCarthy, "The Illinois Test of Psycholinguistic Abilities: An Approach to Differential Diagnosis," *American Journal of Mental Deficiency,* 56 (November 1961) 399-412.
16. Lado, Robert, *Linguistics Across Cultures.* Ann Arbor: University of Michigan Press, 1957.
17. ---, *Language Teaching: A Scientific Approach.* New York: McGraw-Hill, 1964.
18. LeFevre, Carl, *Linguistics and the Teaching of Reading.* New York: McGraw-Hill, 1964.
19. Loban, Walter, *The Language of Elementary School Children.* Champaign, Illinois: National Council of Teachers of English, 1963.
20. McCallister, James, "Reading Ability of Junior College Freshmen," *Chicago School Journal,* 18 (1936) 79-82.
21. National Council of Teachers of English, *English for Today.* New York: McGraw-Hill, 1962.
22. Newsome, Verna, *Structural Grammar in the Classroom.* Oshkosh: Wisconsin State College, 1962.
23. Roberts, Paul, *English Sentences.* New York: Harcourt, 1962.

24. Russell, David H., *The Dimensions of Children's Meaning Vocabularies in Grades Four Through Twelve.* Berkeley: University of California Press, 1954.
25. Shuy, Roger, ed., *Social Dialects and Language Learning.* Champaign, Illinois: National Council of Teachers of English, 1964.
26. Strang, Ruth, "Secondary School Reading As Thinking," *The Reading Teacher,* 13 (February 1960) 194-200.
27. Whorf, Benjamin L., *Language, Thought, and Reality.* Cambridge, Massachusetts: M. I. T. Press, 1964.
28. Wise, Claude, *Applied Phonetics.* Englewood Cliffs, N. J.: Prentice-Hall, 1957.

44. A Comprehensive Linguistic Approach to Reading*

CARL A. LEFEVRE

Professor of English
Temple University
Philadelphia, Pennsylvania

I.

INTRODUCTION: THE NEED FOR A SYNTHESIS OF LINGUISTIC APPROACHES

We often hear such questions as these: What do you think of the linguistic approach to reading? Just what is the linguistic approach to reading anyhow?

Such questions are off point because at present no single linguistic approach merits the use of the noun marker or determiner *the,* which would signify the one and only. Bloomfield and Fries have given their names to spelling and word methods of teaching beginning reading, and despite all denials, reading teachers will consider both methods as part of phonic word analysis because both deal with relationships of sound and spelling; they do not even venture into *structural* word analysis. The veneration that these men have earned by their other work in linguistics hardly justifies the use of the exclusive term, "the linguistic approach," to designate their narrow methods. Possibly no single method ever will deserve it.

This is true for a number of reasons. Primarily, our present knowledge is so far from closed that it is commonly said to be exploding; this is true in linguistics as in other disciplines. Moreover, in no age has progress been achieved through blind or myopic imitation of what has already been done. Quite the contrary. Modern linguistics is both a revolution in and a continuation of the study of language. When we break eggs to make our omelet, we do not lose the eggs.

What must inevitably come, in my opinion, is a synthesis of linguistic approaches to reading: a synthesis developed, controlled, and corrected by

Dr. Lefevre is the author of *Linguistics the Teaching of Reading* and many articles on reading published in the professional journals; he is also co-author with his wife, Dr. Helen E. Lefevre, of *Writing by Patterns* and *English Writing Pattern* (grades 2-12).

*From *Elementary English,* **42,** 6 (October, 1965) 651-659. Reprinted with the permission of the National Council of Teachers of English and Carl A. Lefevre.

means of an interdisciplinary attack on reading problems, bringing to bear all pertinent knowledge; a synthesis in line with the best experience of teachers of reading and the English language arts, and in line with the best experimentation these teachers are capable of. Such a synthesis must move far beyond spelling and word attack and into reading processes at the sentence level *even in beginning reading;* eventually it should range into problems of reading extended discourse, not only of exposition but the many forms of literature. This is something of what is meant by "a comprehensive linguistic approach to reading."

II.

LINGUISTIC PHONICS: PHONEMES AND SPELLING

Leonard Bloomfield

If Leonard Bloomfield's son when he entered school had not encountered a "far-out" exponent of the kind of phonics Bloomfield derided as "the hiss and groan method" of teaching reading, the development of linguistics applied to reading might have been quite different. As it was, Bloomfield invented an approach to beginning reading that limits instruction during a long introductory period to a rigid alphabetical principle—single phoneme by single letter—applied to a language whose spelling is notoriously inconsistent with its phonemes. It is hard not to feel that Bloomfield's method was the result of an impassioned effort to straighten out some of the worst kinks of bonehead phonics. However it was, his introductory method featured such so-called sentences as "A man ran a tan van," and "Can a fat man pat a cat?"

Unfortunately, this kind of ingenious but un-English material not only bears the great name of Bloomfield, but it has been hailed as "*the* linguistic method of teaching reading." Bloomfield's followers among linguists are too many to be counted; his work has been the source of numerous graduate theses; the imitative materials based upon it are too numerous to be cited. All this is a bit like "The Emperor's New Clothes."

C. C. Fries

Recently C. C. Fries, the present dean of American linguists, has presented an extension of the Bloomfield method of teaching beginning reading. If the Bloomfield method is a spelling approach at the level of single letters and phonemes—and it is—the Fries method is a spelling approach at the level of one-syllable words. Fries himself admits that it is a specialized word method; it generates such un-English sentences as these, presented all in capital letters: "PAT A FAT CAT" and "A CAT BATS AT A RAT." It is difficult to detect any qualitative difference between Bloomfield's "Can a fat man pat a cat?" and Fries' "A CAT BATS AT A RAT." It is the misfortune of both methods to present, among *the very first lessons in reading,* tongue twisters and jawbreakers far removed from the language of children.

I understand that Mrs. Rosemary Wilson and her associates, however, in consultation with Professor Fries, are making adaptations and additions in classroom experiments with these materials.

Some Important Distinctions

We seem to have been so blinded by our ritual of thinking of handwriting and print as spelling that we have come almost to equate both writing and reading with spelling, though we know better. Correct spelling has become a shibboleth, even in the very beginning stages of teaching reading and writing: too many children have a traumatic fear of misspelling. (The elimination of this fear is no doubt an important reason for whatever successes may rightfully be claimed for ita, along with the ita emphasis on *writing.*)

Let us make some important comparisons and contrasts among the operations of *spelling, writing,* and *reading.* As linguistic operations, spelling and writing are active in a sense that reading is not. Spelling requires recognizing and producing single letters and single words; writing, however, requires the creation of meaning-bearing patterns of words, using the sentence as the basic building block of composition. Thus we see that writing, not spelling, is seriously concerned with communication. Now consider reading: reading involves no active production of letters, words, or sentences at all; what reading requires is recognition and interpretation of the graphic counterparts of entire spoken utterances as unitary meaning-bearing patterns; *this is reading comprehension.* These considerations may help us to evaluate the role of spelling in reading and in reading instruction.

Sooner or later all the letters in all the words, and all the words laid end to end, line after line, and page after page, must reach not from here to eternity in the child's eyes; all words must pattern themselves into sentences. The sentence is the fundamental unit both for written composition and for reading comprehension; with patience and skill, sentences may indeed be skillfully put together in interesting ways to compose all the larger language constructs—but not in the primary grades. The first lesson is that each sentence begins with a capital letter and usually ends with a period. Let the children take it from there, with no more initial emphasis on spelling than the reading process itself requires.

III.

READING IN TERMS OF THE REQUIREMENTS OF THE ENGLISH LANGUAGE SYSTEM

Reading as a Language-Related Process

Because our writing system ultimately represents the spoken language, any attempt at a *direct* interpretation of the grapnıc symbols laid out in neat rows on the printed page is not the best approach to reading. We must go first from writing to sound, and then from sound to message; even the most rapid reading probably involves both steps in virtually simultaneous succession. Written and printed communications not only can be read aloud, but when they are read visually, or "silently" as we say significantly, the mental ear still picks up, be it ever so fleetingly, the sound track of the same utterances in speech. It is this echo of the sound of speech, more than mere punctuation, that groups and orders English words into meaning-bearing patterns. When the pattern does not come off right, we go back and reread until it "sounds right."

The process of going from print to sound to meaning is rather more than what is often meant by so-called inner speech, suggesting stammering, inefficient comprehension. It involves the process of though itself, "a silent flow of words," as Sapir phrased it. Or in Vigotsky's penetrating statement, remarkably pertinent to reading comprehension: "Thought is not expressed in words, but comes into existence through them." Thus, to approach visual reading as the direct interpretation of a set of graphic symbols, like the Morse code in print, would be quite superficial, and very seriously misleading. What is needed now in reading is an approach in depth, and approach to, and through, the basic language itself.

Since writing and print represent graphic counterparts of spoken language patterns, the natural and best way to read is precisely in those terms. English language patterns have been described by linguists as composed not only of the basic individual sounds—*phonemes;* not only of basic meaning units, words and word parts—*morphemes;* but normally of sentences, which in turn have components that may be arranged in an infinite variety of patterns and orders—*syntax.* Beyond this trilevel structure, the sounds of language, and this is true of English in a very significant way, include the overall melodies and rhythms of patterns longer and more complex than words, phrases, and clauses. In beginning reading these patterns would be sentences predominantly.

Reading Sentence Patterns

Introductory treatments of descriptive and structural linguistics usually suggest common English kernel sentences, note some of the possibilites of expansions, substitutions, and inversions, and give an indication of passive and other transformations. In his method of "sector analysis," Robert Allen is developing an interesting approach to reading and writing sentences by analyzing out the important sentence parts. My own book, *Linguistics and the Teaching of Reading* (McGraw-Hill, 1964) is the first work to attempt a comprehensive application of linguistic data to reading and writing processes with primary emphasis on the sentence. This is an introductory book, of course, and makes no attempt to be comprehensive. *Writing by Patterns,* a collaboration of Helen and

Carl Lefevre, is a work text that applies structural grammar to writing problems in grades 11-14, depending on the students' needs; much of the material is applicable to reading, and the two are treated somewhat as cross related. This book was published in April, 1965, by Alfred A. Knopf, Inc.

The great virtue of descriptive and structural grammar is its objectivity, its clear focus on the structure of the code as the means of carrying the message. This virtue is not found in the recent transformational and generative grammars, which, under the banner of "deep grammar," enter the subjective realm of the message. They also admittedly hark back to traditional grammar and school grammar. While these new-old grammars represent a legitimate effort to penetrate the relatively unknown area between language structure and psychological meaning, they will not necessarily help the native English speaker read and write his language. No one any longer defends the old grammars on these grounds.

Transformational or generative grammar attempst to formulate all the "rules" according to which it is assumed the native speaker can invent new sentences of his own and interpret new sentences invented by others. It is questionable whether these subjective, "internalized" rules will prove helpful in teaching native speakers to read and write, however, because teachers and pupils alike possess native linguistic intuition and intelligence enabling them to invent and interpret new sentences unconsciously, without recourse to rules for invention and interpretation. For teaching the skills of literacy, it hardly seems necessary to codify native linguistic intuition and intelligence. On the contrary, these invaluable traits should be exercised freely and creatively, rather than self-consciously analyzed. On the other hand, a clear, objective consciousness of the structural patterns themselves and their common transformations, available through study of structural grammar, can improve the pupil's understanding of his language as a code, and hence liberate his creative energies to develop his skills of literacy.

Reading Paragraphs and Extended Passages of Exposition

Up to now, linguistic analysis of reading problems has been largely confined to structures below the level of syntax: phonemes and morphemes. We have seen, however, that applications of syntactical data have already begun to yield some results, and it seems probable that similar and related data and principles can be extended into the analytical readings of longer passages. Making this extension is an important next stage in linguistics and in English linguistics applied to teaching the skills of literacy. Some work has already been done and more is in progress.

So far as I know, Zellig Harris was the first modern linguist to make a tentative entry into rigorous "discourse analysis"; his student and colleague,

Noam Chomsky, has given some further consideration to this topic. Current applications of Kenneth Pike's "tagmemics" and experimental investigations by some of his students into extended language patterns and forms give promise of producing interesting new insights into the structure of both expository prose and literature. It seems possible that tagmemics may have the potential of relating language patterns to particle, wave, and field theories.

An obvious first consideration in analyzing the "organic" structure of well-written paragraphs is the use of structural joints and connective tissue not only *withing* sentences, but *between* and *among* sentences. For example: simple pronoun references, both to the usual persons and to "things" and abstractions; similarly noun references; similarly by structural extension references by means of other word-form classes, such as verb cross references by means of derivational prefixes and suffixes added to the same base.

Also, referring ahead or back to a noun, an adjective, or an adverb having the same base; parallel syntactical patterns including elliptical constructions, that constitute structural references to each other; the use of all structure words, such as the coordinating conjunctions, *and, but, for, nor, or, yet, so;* and especially the subordinating conjunctions, such as *although, because, however, moreover, nevertheless, since*—the whole set; and the correlatives, such as *if . . . then, not only . . . but also, while . . . still,* and so on through the list. These are some of the syntactical devices that extend into paragraph construction and into longer passages of well-knit prose.

Reading Literature as Syntax

Structural resources of english such as we have just been considering in expository passages also lend themselves admirably to imaginative writing. Creative writers are fertile in their production of structural inventions and manipulations of language patterns; an extended treatment would require detailed discussion of many points of linguistic interest in literature that can only be mentioned here, however.

For example: what I call structural puns, the unconventional substitution of a member of one word class for another, such as a noun for a verb, and then using grammatical inflections with the substituted word (Ciardi, Keats, Wordsworth); unusually long and involved sentence patterns running to many lines (Browning, Chaucer, Faulkner, Shelley, Steinbeck); extended syntactical patterns treated as sentences, but that are "fragments" according to school grammar (Blake, Coleridge, Dickens, Keats, Shelley, Whitman, Wordsworth); myriad special sentence patterns, apostrophes, commands, inversions, prayers, wishes, apposition, compounding of elements, ellipses, parallelism of ellipses, parallelism of certain word forms, or of word groups and clusters, phrases, clauses (writers far, far too numerous to mention).

The point in a discussion of reading is that to fully comprehend literacy passages having unusual, or as often as not unique structure, the reader must absorb the entire meaning-bearing pattern as a whole. He may do this either by an automatic, unconscious, and intuitive process which is the fruit of long experience, or he may do it by means of a direct analysis of each author's peculiar and characteristic uses of language resources. Direct linguistic analysis is an excellent means of breaking an author's code and so involving pupils in an appreciative study of literature in their early and formative years. In time they should automatically respond to the meaning-bearing structures as wholes, each one having its overriding intonation pattern, or tune; in this respect, literary passages are comparable to the phrasing of music, building toward larger movements.

IV.

READING IN TERMS OF INTONATION:
REQUIREMENTS AND OPTIONS

Intonation in Visual, or Silent, Reading

The English graphic system partially represents the important sounds of the language system far beyond the presentation of phonemes by graphemes, beyond the representation of morphemes by spellings, even beyond the representation of sentence patterns by capitalization, word order, and punctuation. The *part* in the term *partially* stands for intonation, both in single elements and in overall patterns of the melodies and rhythms of English.

Merely to pronounce words having two or more syllables requires correct accent; in linguistic parlance, *accent* is called *stress* and is defined as "loudness"; stress is a very important grammatical and syntactical feature of intonation. "He puts the emphas'is on the wrong syllab'le" is a hoary linguistic joke that makes the point. Putting the emphas'is on the wrong syllab'le betrays the speaker as either non-native or a half-educated fool, the latter being a lot more fun.

The difference between *con'tract* and *contract'* distinguishes noun from verb in a whole set of contrasting pairs. This grammatically important distinction is not signaled by any specific feature of the writing system; only the distribution of such words in larger patterns gives the clue. And yet no literate native speaker of English misses the point. The same use of stress difference also distinguishes a set of pairs of nouns and verb-adverb groups, as in *set'up* and *set up'*; and still another set, pairs of compound nouns and noun groups, as in *black'board* and *black board* .

Many, though not all, punctuation marks correspond to decisive points of intonation in equivalent spoken language patterns. The period always, and the semicolon usually, are signals for a special way of dropping the voice, indicating that the preceding meaning-bearing pattern has been completed; conversely, the absence of a period normally indicates that the voice should *not* be allowed to drop in the end-signaling way between the opening capital letter and the closing semicolon or period. Persons who use this "fade-fall terminal" within sentences in oral reading are reading either by single words—word calling—or by fragmentary word groups that do not bear meaning. This kind of reading, all to common in the elementary school, destroys the unity of the unitary meaning-bearing pattern. It is a dangerous practice, because, unchecked, it may lead to a habitual internalized word-and-fragment-seeing procedure in silent reading, deadly to reading comprehension

The fade-fall terminal also occurs at the end of many questions in English, notwithstanding the popular falsehood, "A question always ends with a rising inflection." For example: *Who won the game? Where are the keys? Who was it?* A rising inflection on these questions changes their meaning completely, the point being that the difference between a fade-fall and a fade-rise terminal in such questions is the only structural signal we have for a qualitative difference of intent. There is no graphic symbol for it at all. The fade-fall terminal would be the high-frequency choice in such questions.

The rising inflection may be used to terminate other questions also: *Where did you say my notebook is? Did you tell me that this is your car?* The one hard rule for the fade-rise terminal to signal a question in English applies to statements converted to questions solely by this terminal. It is often used ironically in such questions as "you call this a ball game?" The rising inflection is the only spoken signal we have that this is a question rather than a statement.

A rising tone is commonly used within sentences where commas occur and usually in counting and in listing: *one, two, three, four, five; wood, glue, nails, cloth, paint.* The fade-fall is used only at the end of the last item.

The foregoing comments are concerned only with gross obligatory features of English intonation, those features that native speakers normally produce with intuitive ease and that foreigners find extremely difficult to master. In primary teaching of reading to children who are native speakers, all we have to do is see to it that they read orally (in order to hear silently with the mental ear) intonation patterns that are indigenous to their speech communities. This is all we have to do about intonation—but it is exceedingly important that we do it unfailingly and very well.

Intonation in Oral Reading and Interpretation

Many linguist designate all that we call "tone of voice" as *paralanguage;* it includes such effects as whining, laughing or crying while talking, or talking with overtones suggestive of these; talking with relish or gusto; talking with distaste or disgust; using rasping, whispering, oversoft, or overloud tones; and all like effects. Paralanguage is often referred to as an "overlay" of subjective interpretive characteristics on the basic code pattern required for communication; the point is that every speaker must use the required features of the language code, but he may exercise various intonational options as well. His options must never violate the code, however, except for a deliberate communicative purpose.

Some linguists designate as *kinesics* all those non-lingual actions that accompany speech, often more important in communication than all that could possibly be communicated by the bare linguistic structures themselves. *Kinesics* includes all bodily gestures, nudges, nods, finger, hand, and arm signals, shrugs, and facial gestures such as winks, smiles, sneers and leers—the whole gamut of expressive actions, so important in acting and interpretation.

All these rich resources of human communication should be brought to bear on the oral reading of literature, for the sheer joy of it, but also in order to develop associations that may carry over into the individual pupil's visual or silent reading of literature.

Oral reading "with expression" is interpretive reading that builds upon but far outreaches obligatory intonation features and patterns; with sufficient practice oral reading can develop into a fine art, closely allied with acting. So long as the interpreter observes the requirements of the intonation system, he is limited only by the dictates of good taste and judgment. Keen interest in both written composition and in silent reading can be stimulated by the teacher's skilful involvement of the children's creative imagination and vivacity in oral interpretation.

Reading Literature as Language and Form

Sensitivity to the nuances of language, appreciation of dialects, access to poetry, responsiveness to the forms of literature—all can best be cultivated on the basis of *the whole sound of the piece* when well read aloud. Not every reader need be an artist in oral interpretation—a producer; every child has his own potential, however, worthy of a little classroom attention. Surely every child should have many opportunities to hear and attend to, good oral interpretations of literature—to be a consumer. If the child has the authentic sound in his ear, his eye then in silent reading can help his mental ear tune in on the mnemonic sound track by association with other pieces; but if he has never had the authentic sound in his ear, his mental ear will be deaf to the graphic presentation, no matter how beautifully done.

Professional readings, movie, television, and radio presentations, are all excellent sources of enrichment, but the audio-visual device of choice is the classroom teacher, or a parent, in everyday, seemingly casual interpretive readings. No one loves literature because he was assigned to love it; no one can possibly feel in his heart that it is great, just on his teacher's say-so. The best approach, not only to drama and fiction, but above all to poetry, is to hear it live and flowing sweetly on the tongue. A parent at home or a teacher in your schoolroom is not an artist way off on a high pedestal somewhere, but someone you know and can touch.

The arbitrary division of poems into lines, and rigid notions of meter, present problems that often baffle and finally discourage the young hopeful trying to appreciate poetry. The line of verse is a visual rather than an auditory unit; even when an elaborate rhyme scheme is followed, the echoing of the rhyme is contained within meaning-bearing structures. Stanzas and other verse forms are overlaid often very skillfully, on patterns of English syntax. In poetry as in prose the good old sentence is still the basic building block of English. Nothing is more destructive of good verse than a ding-dong metrical reading, line by line, with a fade-fall terminal at the end of every line. (A mechanically repeated fade-rise terminal would be no better.) Every sentence should be read as a sentence, with syntactical terminals where they belong according to English syntax—not according to lines, or to rhymes.

Any attempt to read English poems with a uniform two-stress meter is foredoomed and absolutely fatal to poetry, because English is a four-stress language. This four-stress system itself is a structural part of the language system as a whole, not an interpretive option of the speaker or oral reader; the interpreter does have options but his options fall within the English four-stress system. This stress system and the meter of any poem can be reconciled if the presumed two stresses of the meter are regarded as relative rather than absolute stresses. That is, certain stresses are regularly heavier than the others, but the heavy stresses are not equally heavy.

For an example, let's take a look at Stevenson's "Requiem," a simple poem in two stanzas, having an *a a a b, c c c b* rhyme scheme. The *a* and *c* lines have four beats, or heavy stresses, each; they begin and end with a beat. The *b* lines begin with two weak stresses (the equivalent in certain respects on one heavy stress or beat), and then have three more beats. Taking fade-fall terminals as the chief clues, the poem is written in four sentences: (1) lines 1-2; (2) lines 3-4; (3) lines 5-6 (4) lines 7-8. Visually, the second stanza is punctuated as a single sentence with a colon at the end of the first line.

Below, the poem is presented twice: first marked for a uniform two-stress metrical rendition; second, marked with suggestions for a reading that observes the meter, but follows the four-stress system. The stress notations are: ´ for heavy stress; ˆ for medium stress; ˋ for light stress; ᴜ for weak stress, Instead of two stresses, one strong and one weak, we use heavy, medium, and light for strong, reserving the weak stress of the four-stress system for the weak stress in the two-stress metrical reading. Thus we preserve the contrasts of the meter without killing the poem.

Requiem

Under the wide and starry sky
Dig the grave and let me lie.
Glad did I live and gladly die,
And I laid me down with a will.
This be the verse you grave for me:
Here he lies where he longed to be:
Home is the sailor, home from the sea,
And the hunter home from the hill.

Requiem

Under the wide and starry sky
Dig the grave and let me lie.
Glad did I live and gladly die,
And I laid me down with a will.
This be the verse you grave for me:
Here he lies where he longed to be:
Home is the sailor, home from the sea,
And the hunter home from the hill.

The mistaken effort to achieve equality of beat and uniformity of meter throughout this or any poem cannot help producing, a metronomic, rocking-horse effect. The deadly soporiferous sequel is too well known. Children don't naturally hate poetry; they love it. But given too much poetry read in a rocking-horse jog, they will either learn to ignore it if they are normal, or kill it with kindness if they are teacher's pets. A few will go to college and major in English in spite of all.

A final point. Longer language constructs, such as poems, essays, sonnets, short stories—especially those literary forms that can be read at one sitting, as Poe suggested for the proper length for a short story—probably have overall melodic and rhythmic contours, embracing all components into an organic form so as to create a sense of completion when the piece has run its course. That is, the various forms of writing, particularly creative writing, are not static forms, but intricate linguistic processes, events patterned through time. The graphic form of these processes or events is the permanently organized embodiment of the writer's original creative experience: this I take to be the essence of literary form. In performing the piece, as it were, either silently or orally, the reader recreates for himself the writer's experience in the form he has shaped it to, but with appropriate nuances and overtones of the reader's own.

In all this, literary forms resemble songs or sonatas; longer works may well resemble concertos, symphonies, operas. This is not mere imagery. Musical notation and all the forms of music have developed within cultures of men who speak; the analogies and interrelationships of speech and song, of language and longer forms of music, make a fascinating subject for study.

45. A Global Theory of Reading—and Linguistics*

JANET W. LERNER

THE need for a comprehensive theory of reading has been recognized as critical by a number of scholars who study or teach reading (Gray, 1960; Kingston, 1966; Robinson, 1966). One major advantage of such a global framework is that it would provide an effective way of incorporating new information generated by such related by such related disciplines as linguistics. Benjamin Bloom (1966) has emphasized that every piece of research must have a place within a larger conceptual framework.

The purpose of this paper is twofold. First is to discuss a global theory of reading; that is, what are the major aspects of the field called reading, and what are the elements that should be considered within each of these major aspects? The second is to discuss the role that linguistics can play within such a global theory; that is, at what points can linguistic findings be applied.

It is difficult to formulate a global theory of reading for there is no agreement about the meaning of such basic terms or concepts as phonics, sight words, or traditional method. In fact, there is no agreement as to the meaning or framework of the term *reading*. In spite of its difficulty, it seems clear that such an integrated theory would be useful. It would encompass the various splintering branches of reading and place the contributing components into some perspective. It could help to order and simplify knowledge so that both research and instruction could proceed in a more orderly fashion. It would help to sort and evaluate the bewildering deluge of new materials and techniques, machines and gadgets, and methods and mediums confronting us.

Moreover, theory building can be useful in separating and distinguishing what we *know* from what we *believe* or infer. John Dewey contended that theory is the most practical of all things; it widens the range of attention; it puts confusing components into meaningful order, and it provides a more scientific approach to a field of learning.

Helen Robinson (1966) has devised a useful framework to view the field of

*From *The Reading Teacher*, **21**, 5 (February, 1968) 416-421. Reprinted with permission of Janet W. Lerner and the International Reading Association.

457

reading. After analyzing a number of theoretical models of reading, she concluded that there is confusion among three separate aspects or systems in the attempts at model building. Robinson viewed the total reading picture as having three major aspects or systems: 1] distinct reading skills and abilities; 2] reading-learning process of the child; and 3] actual teaching of reading in our schools. This total view of reading can be pictured as three concentric circles, increasing in size and adjacent at a single point.

Although the aspects or systems are considered as conceptually separated so that they can be analyzed and described, the three systems are not in reality separate entities. They are, in fact, intimately interdependent and intertwined. The impact of one system upon the other is indeed of the essence in understanding reading.

System 1, the reading skills and abilities is concerned with *what* the child should achieve; system 2, the reading-learning process, is concerned with *how* the child acquires these reading skills; and system 3, the teaching of reading, is concerned with the larger picture of the impact of teacher, class, and the entire school environment on the child's process of acquiring reading skills.

SYSTEM 1. SKILLS AND ABILITIES IN READING

Robinson has suggested a model of the first system, skills and abilities used in reading. This work is based upon an earlier model developed by William S. Gray (1960), but modifications were incorporated from the recent work in the substrata factors of reading by Holmes (1965), as well as work in theoretical models of reading by others. The five areas included in this revised model of reading skills and abilities are 1] word-perception, 2] comprehension, 3] reaction, 4] assimilation, and 5] reading rate. Robinson (1966) further suggests that abilities in reading for different purposes and skills in oral and silent reading might be included. The model is not concerned with the process for achieving these goals.

Within this first system, there are two places where linguistic findings are being applied. The first place is within the element of word perception. Word perception includes both word recognition and word meaning. The linguistic approach to reading of the Bloomfield-Fries type is concerned only with word recognition through the decoding of the phonemegrapheme relationship. Their linguistic tool is phonology, the sound system of the English language; and their approach is through selecting only those words that have a consistent and regular spelling pattern for beginning reading (Fries, 1963).

A second area of possible linguistic applicability within this first aspect of reading is within the comprehension element. Lefevre (1964) suggests that for comprehension of the written language, children need ability in what he calls "sentence sense." The skill is one of translating the written language or graphic symbols back into primary form, spoken English, so that the child will understand the meaning of the sentence. The linguistic tool for accomplishing this is called "intonation," which consists of pitch, stress, and juncture. This intonation accounts for the rhythm and melody of American English and must be supplied by the reader in order to capture the meaning of the sentence.

The linguists, then, who have concerned themselves with reading, have staked out these two rather narrow foundations for reading instruction within this aspect of reading skills and abilities. It is interesting to note that in many ways these two linguistic approaches to reading are diametrically opposed. One is concerned only with the phonology or sound system of the English language, with the skill of decoding written phoneme symbols to spoken sounds of English, and with the selection of consistent and regular spelling patterns for words used in teaching beginning reading. Decoding the *sound,* not the meaning, is their chief concern. The other approach is concerned with the structual melody of English, and emphasis is on putting meaning into the written language.

SYSTEM 2. THE READING—LEARNING PROCESS

The second system of reading within the global framework outlined above deals with the processes the child uses in learning the skills and acquiring the abilities outlined in system 1. For information and knowledge in this area, students of reading have borrowed heavily from a number of related disciplines such as psychology, exceptional education, and sciences dealing with language and cognitive growth and maturation.

The field of psychology has been the source for many so-called principles of reading. Many contributors of these principles of reading were educated in the field of psychology and made direct application to the reading-learning process. More recently, work in learning theory, operant conditioning, creativity, and discovery techniques have added to the understanding of the reading-learning process. Special education, particularly work in the field of learning disability, as well as recent work in such fields as vision, neurology, and psycholinguistics, is also broadening concepts of the reading-learning process.

Linguistics, the science of language, has an important potential contribution to make in description and analysis of the reading-learning process. The linguists have re-emphasized that reading is a language-related process. Linguistics is the study of the nature of language, in general, and the nature of the English language, in particular. It seems obvious that to develop a theoretical system of the reading-learning process, one must look at the English language. The linguist's percepts of how a child learns to speak his native language and the linguist's construct of the nature of the English language should be vital to any theory of the reading-learning process. In this second major aspect of reading, linguistics has possible and potential applicability, but it remains to be worked out more specifically.

SYSTEM 3. THE TEACHING OF READING

The third system of the global framework is the teaching of reading. The reading skills and abilities and the child's process of attaining these skills do not occur in a sterile laboratory or a vacuum. They occur in the vital on-going situation of a real classroom, and the classroom is part of the dynamic organizational environment of the school. To develop an understanding of this process and the impact of this larger setting requires help from the fields of educational administration, organizational theory, and certain branches of sociology. The relationship of these disciplines to the teaching of reading is analogous to the relationship between the reading-learning process and psychology. Perhaps it is because not enough credence has been given to this third major aspect that research results in reading do not give a clear and continuous picture which permits theory building.

Most research in reading is controlled experimentation. An experimental group using method "A" is compared to a control group using method "B." According to the typical research design in reading the two groups are to be the same in all respects except for the single variable being tested. In a sense, then, both groups are intended to be *controlled* groups. The amount of freedom, innovation, and creativity is intended to be curtailed to test or vary only the reading method or the material being researched. However, the active, on-going school situation is not, in fact, the carefully controlled environment of experimentation. The particular reading method under study does not remain "pure" as if it existed in a vacuum, but it is necessarily modified and shaped by the functioning organization of the school. The impact of all the facets of the organizational structure and the decision-making process direct the reading method to be what it *is* rather than what the author of the method thought it *ought* to be. Time and time again investigations by authors of reading methods as well as other objective observers revealed that reading methods under study were not the ones actually being carried out in the classroom (Lerner, 1967).

Moreover, it is a remarkable finding that frequently the experimental group does significantly better than the control group. In almost all of the twenty-seven studies of beginning reading sponsored by the United States Office of Education last year, the experimental populations made significantly greater gains than the control populations (Stauffer, 1966). These results can only mean that uncontrolled factors, or intervening variables, must be operating. A number of authors have recognized that the Hawthorne effect and "reading drive" are contributing, but uncontrolled and unmeasured, factors in experimental research. Perhaps another overlooked variable is the school's organizational environment.

One of the few conclusions reached as a result of research in reading, such as these twenty-seven studies on beginning reading, is that the teacher is a key factor—more important, it appears, than the method, material, or media (Clymer, 1967). However, the teacher functions within a schoool environment, and the administrative and supervisory relationships and attitudes toward the teacher also affect the reading program. Teachers probably do not function in the same way under different organizations.

Perhaps the study made by Robert Rosenthal (1963) has bearing on this point. Two groups of rats of equivalent ability in running certain types of mazes were arranged. One group of rats was described as a batch of "rat geniuses;" the other as a bunch of "stupid rats." Two groups of laboratory assistants undertook to teach the two groups of rats to run an identical maze by identical methods. The results? The rats described as geniuses learned noticeably better than the equivalent rats which had been called "stupid." Do teachers function differently in different administrative atmospheres? Should these differences in administrative atmospheres be taken into account in analyzing research findings?

The Harvard Report of Reading in Elementary Schools (Austin, 1963) revealed that central administrative officers frequently are unaware of what is occurring in the reading programs of their own schools. Consequently, a gap exists between what they believe their reading program to be and what it actually is. Field researchers found that for the most part administrators did not have the interest, training, nor inclination to take an active interest in a well-planned reading program. Is it any wonder, then, that the spark of interest shown by administrators in a well-publicized research project puts a teacher and reading instruction into high gear?

The science of linguistics seems to have little that is applicable to this third major aspect, the teaching of reading. Fields such as organizational theory, sociology, and educational administration seem most promising in developing a theory of this aspect of reading, the actual teaching of reading within the school.

SUMMARY

In summary, what place does linguistics have, at present, in the total picture of reading? It has possible applicaiton in a few specific places. In the first major aspect, skills and abilities, there are two spots of possible applicability. First, in the word perceptional element, phonological skill in phoneme-grapheme relationships may be helpful in decoding the printed symbol. Second, in the comprehension element, the skill of "sentence sense" is important. Intonation is the linguistic ability which helps to translate the secondary printed sentence back to the primary oral form of English. In the third system linguistics has little to contribute.

Within the second major aspect or system, the reading-learning process, linguistics has something to contribute, but it has not as yet been incorporated within a theory of the reading-learning process. Linguistics can help the reading teacher develop new attitudes and perspectives toward the English language itself and the integral role of language in the developmental and thinking processes of the child. It can help teachers develop a new respect for various dialects and an acceptance of a variety of language levels. The linguists have made it clear that a child's own native language is as close to him as his skin, and it is one of the most important links he has with the outside world. Most essential, however, for the reading teacher, is the realization that the child's own language provides one of the few available starting points in the educative process.

References

Austin, Mary C., and Morrison, C. *The first r: the Harvard report on reading in elementary schools.* New York: Macmillan, 1963. P 239.

Bloom, B. S. From the president. *Educational Researcher,* 1966,5.

Clymer, T. What do we know about the teaching of reading? *Educational Leadership,* 1967, 389.

Fries, C. *Linguistics and reading.* New York: Holt, Rinehart & Winston, 1963.

Gray, W. S. The major aspects of reading. In Helen M. Robinson (Ed.) Sequential development of reading abilities. *Supplementary Educational Monographs* No. 90. Chicago: University of Chicago Press, 1960, 8-24.

Holmes, J. A. Basic assumptions underlying the substrata-factor theory. *Reading Research Quarterly.* 1965, 5-28.

Kingston, A. J. (Ed.) The use of theoretical models in research in reading. *Highlights of the Pre-Convention Institutes* No. V. Newark, Delaware: International Reading Association, 1966.

Lefevre, C. A. *Linguistics and the teaching of reading.* New York: McGraw-Hill, 1964.

Lerner, Janet W. A new focus for reading research: The decision-making process. *Elementary English,* 1967, 236-242.

Robinson, Helen M. The major aspects of reading. In H. Alan Robinson (Ed.) Reading: seventy-five years of progress. *Supplementary Education Monographs* No. 96. Chicago: University of Chicago Press, 1960, 22-36.

Rosenthal, R., and Fode, K. L. The effect of experimenter bias on the performance of the Albino rat. *Behavioral Science,* 1963, 183-189.

Stauffer, R. G. The verdict: speculative controversy. *The Reading Teacher,* 1966, 563.

46. Applying Linguistics to Remedial Reading*

MRS. ROSEMARY G. WILSON
H. G. LINDSAY

HAVE you ever had the following experience in working with a retarded reader? The pupil sits before you looking intently at some common word, such as "where" or "once" or "said," but is quite unable to recognize and read it. Not wishing to prolong his suffering, you finally pronounce the word, and perhaps, use it in a sentence. His face lights up as he exclaims, "Oh, is that what the word is? I know that."

During fifteen years of working with severly retarded readers at all grade levels, the experience described here has happened literally hundreds of times. For a while we coped with the problem it presented in various accepted ways, but always with that feeling that there was something missing. The real significance, however, eluded us until an increasing interest in and study of the field of strucutral linguistics began to shed light on many problems which had been troubling us in working with retarded readers. Since the scope of this paper is limited, we shall discuss and illustrate only those aspects of this vast field of the scientific study of language which have particular application to the problems of the pupil in need of remedial reading help. No more than a mention can be made at this time of the importance of certain aspects of linguistics in the field of beginning reading. As times goes on it may be that the contributions of linguistics to the regular reading program will help us to achieve our goal of the prevention rather than the remediation of reading problems.

What special assistance, then, does linguistics offer in solving the problem of the type of pupil described at the beginning of this article? The answer to this question lies in the principle emphasized by both Leonard Bloomfield and Henry Lee Smith in discussing the relationship of linguistics to reading, that "meaning is not derived directly from the printed symbol (or word) but rather from the printed symbol put back into speech, either vocal or sub-vocal." For example, in the case of the pupil described earlier, no amount of looking at the word "once" will result in his knowing it and, therefore, getting meaning from it. Upon

*From *The Reading Teacher,* **16**, 6 (May, 1963), 452-455. Reprinted by permission of the International Reading Association and Rosemary G. Wilson.

hearing the word said, however, the pupil immediately recognizes it and understands its meaning since it is a word that he has used in his own speech for a long time.

The three words used in the illustration "where," "once," and "said" were chosen because of the difficulty which such irregularly spelled words present to the reader who has not learned them early in his school career as sight words. Even more tragic are his struggles with regularly spelled words which, with a minimum of skill in phonetic analysis, he should be able to figure our and pronounce for himself. Therefore, the plan which we worked out for use in the class described in this article was based upon the research contained in the publication *Let's Read,* by Leonard Bloomfield and Clarence L. Barnhart, Wayne State University Press, 1961. The regular, systematic, and sequential nature of the program set forth in this book seemed to have real value for the type of pupil in our experimental group.

THE EXPERIMENTAL PROGRAM

The setting for our work was a junior high school in a congested area of the city, in which half of the seventh and eighth grade pupils had reading scores three or more levels below the city median. The principal's concern about the reading situation had finally resulted in the initiation of an experiment to find out whether something could be accomplished with a small group of selected pupils. This experimental group was made up of thirteen seventh grade boys and girls whose test scores indicated that they were reading at or below second grade level. The guidance of the Central Curriculum Office of the city school system over a long period in presenting the values and techniques of the linguistic approach resulted in our decision to use as background for the experiment the Bloomfield material mentioned previously.

No commercial material for carrying out this program was available, and it was necessary, therefore, for us to prepare all the materials to be used in the experimental group. Because of the time·and energy required, the pupils were involved in this phase of the work and they participated in the construction of various kinds of teaching materials, such as flash cards, word charts, sentences, and story booklets.

In accordance with the suggestions of Bloomfield, the experiment started with the alphabet as a background for all the rest of the work. Although the pupils in the experiment were in the seventh grade, there was no child, at the outset, who had complete mastery of the alphabet. After the alphabet, lists of words were presented in regular, sequential patterns, beginning with three letter words containing vowels which are commonly called "short." One vowel was presented at a time and *complete mastery* of the word based on that vowel was demanded before words with a different vowel were presented. The words used were those which were already a part of the hearing and speaking vocabulary of the class. Flash cards of the words were prepared on three-by-five cards for class use, and small flash cards of the same words were used by individual pupils. A very limited number of high frequency sight words was added to both sets of cards. Additional sight words were introduced as the experiment proceeded.

Charts were made, also, to include the lists of words being studied in order that the patterns of rhyming words might be fixed firmly in the minds of the pupils from both the auditory and visual approaches. After several patterns of rhyming words were firmly fixed in the minds of the pupils, a more complex and, for these particular boys and girls, a more difficult chart was prepared. The original lists of word patterns were combined and arranged so that the patterns of similar endings (that is, the same vowel and final consonant) would be arranged vertically and the patterns of similar beginnings (same initial consonant and vowel) would appear horizontally.

man	mat	map
can	cat	cap
ran	rat	rap
Nan	Nat	nap

The pupils used their individual flash cards to construct sentences. The use of the flash cards automatically restricted the sentence vocabulary to those words already mastered, and limited the difficulties to the patterns already studied. The sentences were then copied in notebooks so that the writing might be another facet to reinforce the learning. Furthermore, material would thus be provided for reading practice. The sentences were combined and compiled into a booklet, the pupil's own reading book. The boys and girls seemed to enjoy the challenge of constructing sentences out of limited word lists and to appreciate their increasing word power. Group stories also evolved, and finally some individual stories appeared which represented an interesting degree of creativity.

As a next step, and in accordance with Bloomfield's suggestion, nonsense syllables were added. These proved of value in pure auditory and visual discrimination since the factor of meaning was completely removed. The use of one color for words and a different color for syllables on the word chart helped the pupils to differentiate readily and accurately.

So that all pupils could be actively and profitably occupied as much as possible, a system of partners was set up. Materials such as individual flash cards, sight word lists, writing materials, group sentence booklets, and easy reading books were arranged in the pupils' desks so that there could be independent cooperative learning going on a maximum part of the time. Word games, such as Word Lotto, were also constructed by the group.

The pupils were quick to discover that the small, regular words and nonsense syllables were actually parts of longer words, familiar through sound. Much work on auditory discrimination accompanied the teaching of the word lists, and it followed naturally that some highly regular polysyllabic words should be presented visually as well. Practice in blending discernible parts into a whole which represented an already familiar auditory experience brought many expressions of astonishment and pleasure.

The first semester included only the beginnings of practice of the highly regular three-letter words based on the short vowels. It was decided to continue the work into the following year by using the Bloomfield material in the suggested order. Since much work had been done orally with initial and final consonant blends and consonant digraphs, it was hoped that this material could be presented visually early in the new semester.

As a result of this short experiment with the group of thirteen seventh graders and through repeated experiences with individual pupils who are severely retarded, certain conclusions seem to be evolving. There is obviously great interest on the part of the pupils in a program of reading that is built on the known and familiar, is so logical and orderly, so unencumbered with extraneous difficulties, and so well organized. Pupil participation that started as an expediency developed into an outstanding contribution to the work since it released pupil creativity and initiative. The program has definitely become the pupils' own program. Sentences and stories which seemed stilted at the outset later proved amusing to the boys and girls. The fact that it was possible to build so much so readily on something known, such as on the word "man," seemed to bring new hope for the future in reading. The speed with which a list of words could be learned gave a sense of accomplishment and of power that was a new experience to these severely retarded readers.

Success is contagious, and as a result of the experimental work in this junior high school remedial reading teachers at all levels of the school system are employing this approach to some degree. Traditional phonics workbooks which are so unsuitable for use with older pupils and, in many instances, so linguistically unsound have disappeared from the classroom. Much work still needs to be done by ourselves and others in this field, but just to have one ninth grade boy say that "this is the first time reading has made any sense to me" is proof to us that we are at least heading in the right direction.

X

Innovation and Technology in Reading

47. Progress Report on i.t.a.*

JOHN DOWNING, Ph. D.

No one can read the preceding report without recognizing that we now know far more about the processes of reading and of learning to read than we did before the experiments were undertaken.

Thus comments Sir Cyril Burt in his review of the British i.t.a. research in *The i.t.a. Symposium* published by the National Foundation for Educational Research in England and Wales on January 31, 1967. It is the results of this research that have caused many teachers to wish to find out more about i.t.a. This article is designed to answer the questions of teachers who may be taking their first look at i.t.a. as well as for those who have been following the progress of this approach since it was first launched some seven years ago.

WHAT IS i.t.a.?

The i.t.a–Initial Teaching Alphabet–belongs to a group of approaches which in the science of linguistics would be termed *simplified and regularized writing-systems.* 'Writing-system' denotes a system of written or printed characters in the medium of ink which represents the system of sounds of the spoken language in the medium of air. The traditional orthography (t.o.) of English is, of course, a writing-system also, but it is complex and irregular in contrast to the simplified and regularized systems of the i.t.a. kind. Other systems like i.t.a. are, for example, Malone's UNIFON, Laubach's English the New Way, Wijk's Regularized English.

WHAT ARE THE CHIEF FEATURES OF i.t.a.?

i.t.a. has three main characteristics:

1. It is an augmented alphabet. Figure 1 shows i.t.a.'s 44 characters. This

*From *The B C Teacher,* **47** (December, 1967), 100-105. Reprinted by permission from the British Columbia Teachers' Federation.

number is made up of 24 letters from the conventional Roman alphabet (q and x
are omitted as redundant) and 20 new characters for those phonemes (sound
units) of English which have no single letter of their own in t.o.

Figure 1.

2. i.t.a. has regularized spelling. For instance, the words 'one' and 'done'
are written 'wun' and 'dun' in i.t.a. to match the regularity of the spelling pattern
in words like bun, fun, run, sun.

3. i.t.a. is a transitional writing-system. The i.t.a.alphabet and its use in
i.t.a. spellings are designed deliberately to facilitate the change from i.t.a. reading
to t.o. reading.

WHAT IS THE EDUCATIONAL AIM OF i.t.a.?

i.t.a.'s essential purpose is to clarify the structural relations between the
visual stimuli of written or printed English and the auditory stimuli of spoken
English. This clarification of structure is obtained by i.t.a. in three main ways:

1. By reducing the number of alternative visual signals for words and for
phonemes. Each word has only one visual form in i.t.a., e.g., 'dab' only (not
DAB, Dab, etc.). Also, most (though not all) phonemes are printed one way only
in i.t.a. For example, the vowel sound common to tie, mine, mind, sigh, guy, by
is always written ie, thus tie, mien, miend, sie, gie, bie in i.t.a. The structure then
stands out clearly within normal English sentences because regular relationships
between the visual and auditory stimuli occur much more frequently in a wider
variety of words.

2. By removing most multiple-letter representations of single phonemes. A single phoneme is usually coded with a single i.t.a. character; e.g., the word 'through' has just exactly three i.t.a. characters (but seven t.o. letters) for this word's three phonemes, ᚦrω and this one-for-one relationship again clarifies the structure.

3. By abolishing gross irregularity from the code. In i.t.a. the spelling of a word does not conceal the structure, as t.o. spelling often does. For example, in the t.o. forms of gone, done, bone, one, the child's search for structure is frustrated by the ambiguous use of letter o. In i.t.a.'s gon, dun, bœn, wun, the different phonemes are clearly different in their visual representation.

WHAT EDUCATIONAL BENEFITS CAN BE OBTAINED WITH i.t.a.?

Four major educational benefits have been found in the British schools which have participated in the wide-scale trials of i.t.a.:

1. Children more rapidly perceive and understand the structural relations of written and spoken English. As a result, during the first year of school, they generally develop a much wider reading vocabulary in i.t.a. then can be attained in t.o.

2. Self-expression in creative writing can be much more satisfying to children and their teachers with the help of i.t.a.

3. Children have greater self-confidence in their own problem-solving abilities because their hunches are so much more certain to be right in i.t.a., with its more regular code.

4. Because all words in i.t.a. are equally 'phonetic' in their i.t.a. spelling, all the above advantages can be gained without artificial selection of vocabulary. This permits us to put i.t.a. to work to enrich children's experiences of their cultural heritage.. For example, children's literature becomes accessible to first-hand experience by the young child at an earlier stage in the business of learning to read.

However, these benefits from i.t.a. are not automatic. It matters very much how i.t.a. is taught.

WHAT TEACHING METHODS ARE BEST WITH i.t.a.?

As Sir James Pitman, the designer of the i.t.a. alphabet, has pointed out so modestly, i.t.a. itself is merely a set of characters—not a teaching method. It must also be admitted that i.t.a. is not inevitably associated with any particular method of teaching. As a matter of fact, quite a wide range of different teaching approaches are currently available in the different i.t.a. programs of various publishers. Teachers must apply their professional training and experience to choose the particular i.t.a. program they believe will help them to use their own special talents and professional skills in bringing out the fullest possible educational benefits from i.t.a.'s potential.

We should note that several of the well-established t.o. series have been transliterated into i.t.a., e.g., *Janet and John*, published by Nisbet in England, was the series put into i.t.a. for the original British i.t.a. experiments. Another well-known series now available in i.t.a. as well as t.o. is the *Beacon* series of Ginn in England. Mention should also be made of *The Griffin Readers* (publisher, E. J. Arnold) and the *Through the Rainbow* series (publisher, Schofield and Sims) which have i.t.a. and t.o. versions. In this category also is the American series, the *New Basic Readers* published by Scott, Foresman Company. Teachers who know the good points of such well-known series may find them equally valuable in their teaching methodology in their i.t.a. classrooms. They now have the additional value of being in the i.t.a. writing-system.

Several series of readers have been written especially for i.t.a. The first i.t.a. series written deliberately to exploit the benefits of i.t.a. was the *Downing Readers* (publisher Initial Teaching Publishing Co. London and Toronto. Also available from i.t.a. Publications Inc., New York). These books are based on the original British research on i.t.a. and were written only after several years of experience in the experimental i.t.a. classrooms. Thus they are geared to proven values in i.t.a. They have a carefully graded vocabulary chosen to permit young children to discover the structure of English within natural language as they experience it in listening to the everyday speech of their parents, brothers and sisters, friends, T. V., radio, etc.

The i.t.a. teaching methodology of the *Downing Readers* also places much emphasis on children's self-expression in their own creative writing. Letter-formation, handwriting, or spelling are relegated to a secondary position, and creativity has priority in the free-writing period. In this the *Downing Readers* approach to i.t.a. is similar to that known in America as 'the language experience approach.' This series also stresses the need for individualized teaching in i.t.a.

The *Downing Readers* were designed not only specifically with i.t.a. in mind, but also as an international series for all the English-speaking world. The care taken to make them equally valid for other countries as well as Britain has led to their being used quite widely in Canada, Australia and the United States.

A second series published in i.t.a. only is the American *Early-to-Read* i.t.a. series by Mazurkiewicz and Tanyzer (publisher, i.t.a. Publications Inc., New York). This series was written before the American i.t.a. research and demonstration program began, so it was available for the large scale i.t.a. study in Bethlehem, Pennsylvania. Judging from the lengthy review by Ohanian in *Elementary English* (Vol. 43 pages 373-380; 1966), the *Early-to-Read* i.t.a. series has a very different educational approach from that used in the i.t.a. *Downing Readers*. Ohanian, referring to the *Early-to-Read* series, calls it 'a phonic approach' because 'learning phonic clues precedes the learning of word wholes.' Unlike the *Downing Readers,* in this other American series 'a basic sight word list is not an important consideration.'

This difference in methodology appears to arise from the contrasting educational theories on which the two different series are based. Whereas the *Downing Readers* have the guided discovery approach as their essential basis, Ohanian's review of i.t.a. as taught in the *Early-to-Read* series states that 'the mode of teaching and learning is largely through telling and being told respectively and much less through guided discovery.'

The writing aspect of teaching i.t.a. also appears to be somewhat different in the *Early-to-Read* series. According to Ohanian, there is a particular order for teaching children to write the i.t.a. characters when the *Early-to-Read* series is used. In the *Downing Readers* approach, the only correct order for learning to write the i.t.a. characters is that determined by the words which the child wants to write in his own creative work.

Thus, already within i.t.a. teaching methods one can discern the two extremes of current educational theory represented in these two different series. Just recently, a third new series especially designed for i.t.a. teaching has been made available by the Educational Research Council of Greater Cleveland in Ohio, and doubtless in the next few years other alternative i.t.a. programs will be written and published as educators obtain more experience and research information on i.t.a.

IS TRANSITION REALLY 'EASY'?

The transition from i.t.a. to t.o. has always been the first question in teachers' minds when considering whether or not to use i.t.a. Teachers in the British i.t.a. research frequently commented that there was 'no difficulty' in the transition stage. Nevertheless, the results of tests in the research did show some slowing down in the children's progress in this transition phase. But it must be remembered that the children tested were in the original i.t.a. experiment in Britain, in which no special teaching materials or methods were available for the transition stage, and the teachers were the pioneers who had never taught i.t.a. previously.

Now, the *Downing Readers,* the *Early-to-Read* series, and the materials of the Educational Research Council of Greater Cleveland all have special materials and methods for the transition stage. But, again, they do not agree in their methodology of the transfer process. After the final i.t.a. book in the *Downing Readers,* come two books, T1 and T2, printed entirely in t.o.—but with a graded introduction of t.o.'s complexities and irregularities. At this level, such grading can be achieved imperceptibly and informally without artifically stilted language. The *Early-to-Read* series uses a different method. This involves a kind of phasing out process in the actual spelling of words, so that some words have mixed i.t.a. and t.o. spellings, e.g., the word 'know' passes from i.t.a.'s nœ, through the mixed spelling 'now,' before coming finally 'know.'

Timing of transition, too, seem to be different in the two series. In the *Downing Readers* the time for transfer from i.t.a. to t.o. is flexible and is determined by individual differences in the children, although, on average, one can generalize in stating that it usually takes place at about the end of two years. Ohanian's review of the *Early-to-Read* series states that these materials are designed to introduce transition 'usually about April and May' in the first year. Her use of the word 'usually' suggests that some flexibility may be intended with this series also.

Thus in the matter of the methods and timing of the transition stage, too, the teacher must use her professional knowledge of learning theories and her personal knowledge of her own pupils in making her choice between the quite different i.t.a. programs being offered by publishers.

WHAT DOES RESEARCH SAY ABOUT i.t.a.?

Two books published in 1967 contain between them the full story of the seven years of i.t.a. research work in Britain:

1. *The i.t.a. Symposium,* published by the National Foundation for Educational Research in England and Wales, contains a report of the methods and results of the first British i.t.a. experiment. In addition it includes independent reviews of the research report from 11 experts on reading research in Britain, Australia, Canada, and the United States. The book concludes with an overall summing up by Dr. Wall, the Director of the National Foundation for Educational Research.

2. *Evaluating the Initial Teaching Alphabet,* published by Cassell of London in November 1967, is a much fuller account of the whole i.t.a. research project. It reports the second British i.t.a. experiment as well as the first. It provides a history of previous experiments with simplified alphabets, and it relates the i.t.a. approach to theories of the psychology of the reading process. The results of the two i.t.a. experiments are discussed fully and this leads to a number of important conclusions and recommendations.

Briefly, the conclusions reached are that:

(a) The traditional orthography of English is a serious cause of difficulty in the early stages of learning to read and write. In the research, the data showed conclusively that t.o. cuts reading vocabulary at the end of first year to less than half of what it can be with i.t.a.

(b) Transition is not quite as automatic as some people have suggested. While it is not traumatic, nevertheless tests in mid second year show that i.t.a. pupils read t.o. significantly less well than they read i.t.a.–though not less well than t.o. pupils.

(c) However, by the end of the third year, the i.t.a. pupils are about six months ahead in t.o. reading as compared with children who have used only t.o. from the beginning.

Research on the writing of children in the British i.t.a. experiments shows that i.t.a. pupils are superior also in written composition, and that after the transition stage, their t.o. spelling attainments become superior to those of t.o.–only pupils by mid fourth year.

These findings represent the outcomes of the research I conducted. There have been some controversies regarding the methods I used in the research, and teachers who are specially interested in this aspect will find particularly useful two articles I have written in collaboration with some of my colleagues at the Reading Research Unit in London:

1. John Downing, 'Commentary: Methodological Problems in Research on Simplified Alphabets and Regularized Writing-Systems,' *Journal of Typographic Research,* Vol. 1, Pages 191-197, April 1967.

2. John Downing, Daphne Cartwright, Barbara Jones, and William Latham, 'Methodological Problems in the British i.t.a. Research,' *Reading Research Quarterly,* Fall issue, 1967.

WHAT WILL BE i.t.a.'s FUTURE?

The use of i.t.a. for beginning reading and writing seem to be growing steadily. In Britain the number of i.t.a. schools has increased from 20 in 1961 to 2500 in 1967. In America there has been a considerable increase in the number of schools using i.t.a. since its original introduction at the Anita Metzger School in New Jersey. In Canada, there seems to be a growing interest in i.t.a., and its use seems to be growing also, especially in British Columbia. i.t.a. has been taken up by schools in Australia, Bermuda and other parts of the English-speaking world.

Thus the picture of i.t.a.'s progress is promising for such an unusual change in the curriculum, and, now that the research reports described in the previous section of this article have been published, it may be anticiapted that i.t.a.'s use will increase even more rapidly, for the evidence of the damaging effects of t.o. is incontrovertible. It is inconceivable that we can continue to use beginning reading materials printed in t.o. now that it is known that t.o. is responsible for so much waste of effort by teachers and children. Therefore, a wider use of i.t.a. in the schools may be confidently expected as the appropriate next step in this avenue of progress toward improving standards of reading and writing through simplifying and regularizing the conventional English orthography.

However, this prediction must not be interpreted as signifying that the i.t.a. research is completed. This is far from the truth. The present version of i.t.a. is likely to be superseded by further modifications in the years ahead. We know that i.t.a. is much superior to to.o., but i.t.a. users must not become prematurely self-satisfied and create a new orthodoxy. The psycho-linguistic principles underlying i.t.a. should be pursued and developed to the full through further scientific research, and we must be ready for such further improvements as are likely to result.

The results of the seven years of the i.t.a. research project clearly justify the adoption of i.t.a. in its present form by the majority of schools, even though further research is likely to produce, at some time in the future, more improvements in the i.t.a. writing-system itself and in the methods by which it is taught.

48. Self-Discovery, Self-Expression, and the Self-Image in the i.t.a. Classroom*

JOHN A. DOWNING

IN a democracy there is a delicate balance between our concern for the welfare of the individual self and the general well being of the group of society, because the full potential for good in both is necessarily closely interwoven. Sometimes the balance is upset. I believe that in our schools to-day the balance is being biased too much towards society at the expense of the individual and *paradoxically, this over-emphasis on conformity to apparent social demands at the present day is detrimental to society's needs too.* The tremendous acceleration in the technological development of our civilization requires society's members to be more individualistic. We need individuals who can and will discover knowledge and who are able to express themselves and will do so creatively. Also we need people who have healthy self-images which allow them to develop their potential for self-discovery and self-expression with that self-confidence and self-assurance which derives from a successful commerce with their enviornment. On the contrary, the full education development of the individual in these areas is a basis for valid self-evaluation in society. Education's most important aim is to expand the individuals's universe of reality and thus to destroy the inequalities of arrogant privilege whose roots feed on ignorance and unthinking, unquestioning, and uncritical obedience of given rules.

For these reasons, we may unashamedly adopt William Shakespeare's advice as our theme in this discussion of i. t. a. 's significance in the education of girls and boys in the English-speaking nations;

> *This above all—to thine own self be true, And it must follow, as the night the day, Thou canst not then be false to any man.*

CONTROVERSIAL ISSUES IN i.t.a.

I have written about a wide variety of issues in and aspects of i.t.a. in

*Reprinted from the Claremont Reading Conference, February 9-10, 1968, by permission of Malcolm P. Douglass and John A. Downing.

various articles and books. The research project using i.t.a. in Britain took 7 years to complete, and its findings were published in my new book, *Evaluating the Initial Teaching Alphabet,* (1)[1] in December 1967. An international panel of educational and research experts published its opinions of the British i.t.a. research in another book (2) last year, also. In my book I have reported negative as well as positive research findings on i.t.a., and I have. made recommendations for the improvement of the i.t.a. writing-system (3). There are a number of other controversial educational and research issues in i.t.a., and I have reviewed the complete range of topics regarding i.t.a. in another recent article (4). This latter article should help any educator wishing to explore these other aspects of i.t.a. which I do not have time to discuss to-day.

To-day's discussion focuses on the value of i.t.a. in facilitating self-discovery, self-expression, and the development of a healthy self-image. I should warn you right now, before we begin, that many people using i.t.a. neither recognize nor desire these effects of i.t.a., and that, unless teachers consciously seek and plan children's experiences with i.t.a. to achieve these aims, they may not get these effects. *How* i.t.a. is presented in i.t.a. books and in other i.t.a. classroom activities is of vital significance if its use is to benefit our girls and boys.

SELF-DISCOVERY IN i.t.a.

i.t.a.'s most important educational value is the way in which it facilitates the discovery approach. More and more laymen as well as professional educators are recognizing that our present-day and furture society can only survive if we make it our central aim in education to preserve and foster children's natural curiosity and drive for discovery. Man's store of knowledge already has become too vast for any single individual to carry even the knowledge of one specialized discipline "in his head." Therefore, cramming students with facts is a hopelessly outmoded approach. Our aim instead has to be to help children to develop the skills of learning, studying, discovering and structuring which will make them effective in finding and using knowledge stored in libraries, computers, and other such devices.

The most important skills of this type cut right across all the content areas, and there are ways of ensuring that they do this more efficiently and rapidly. Specifically, we must plan children's learning experiences so that they are not narrowly limited to the present task. As Jerome Bruner (5) says:

Learning should not only take us somewhere; it should allow us later to go further more easily.

[1] Numbers in parentheses refer to references at the end of the article.

This applies not only to learning and study skills, but also to the development of *attitudes*. Our educational methods should always be designed deliberately to encourage positive attitudes towards new learning and new discovery.

i.t.a. can play an important role in the application of these principles of "learning how to learn" (as Bruner calls it), and the discovery approach in education. For example, Bruner stresses the importance of

"learning initially not a skill but a general idea, which can then be used as a basis for recognizing subsequent problems as special cases of the idea originally mastered. This type of transfer is at the heart of the educational process."

One such "general idea" is the linguistic structure of English. A grasp of the ground plan of English can be enormous value in learning tasks in all areas of the language arts. Unfortunately, teachers who have strived to give children such a frame of reference have been frustrated by the way in which English is conventionally written or printed, i.e. our traditional orthography (T.O.).

In contrast, the structual relations of written English and spoken English are clarified by the use of i.t.a. What is more, the discovery approach is greatly facilitated by this clarification of the structure of English. For example, compare the i.t.a. and T.O. versions of the sentence "I like my pie." The sound of "eye" occurs in each of these four words. In T.O. this structural feature is concealed because the common phoneme is written differently each time. In i.t.a. it is always written the same so that it looks as well as sounds the same. No artificial and abnormal vocabulary or sentence structure is needed in i.t.a. to bring out this regularity of grapheme-phoneme relations. Meaningful everyday sentences can be used and discovery of these relations will still occur.

This is but one of the ways in which i.t.a. clarifies the structure of English. Two other ways should be mentioned:

(a) The number of phonemes in a word is generally indicated by the number of i.t.a. characters. E.g. the word "thought" has 3 phonemes. In T.O. it has 7 letters, and there is no visual clue to indicate the number of phonemes. In i.t.a. it has 3 i.t.a. characters for the 3 phonemes, thus indicating the structure clearly and correctly.

(b) i.t.a. does not generally use its characters ambiguously. For example, letters in T.O. often represent several different phonemes, e.g. letter *o* in *no, on, one, onion*, etc. T.O's ambiguity gives false clues to structure. This is abolished by i.t.a. But these opportunities in i.t.a. will be to a large extent wasted and frittered away if the materials and teaching methods are not designed to take advantage of i.t.a.'s clarification of structure and consequent facilitation of the discovery approach. For example, the dull formal abstract drills of stereotyped work books seem likely to cancel out these important benefits.

SELF-EXPRESSION IN i.t.a.

Another very important feature of the i.t.a. program which I developed in British Infants schools is the application of i.t.a. in encouraging children's creative writing. This involves the use of *the language experience approach to reading* along side a suitable series of i.t.a. basal readers. But that is not sufficient. Much sooner than is usual in most T.O. language experience classes, the i.t.a. pupil should be encouraged to make his own creative contributions in writing. Indeed, the i.t.a. benefit most valued by British Infants School teachers is the way in which i.t.a. helps children to "speak and think with their pencils."

Again, this important opportunity in i.t.a. is likely to be lost if the i.t.a. program is too stereotyped and textbook centered. Work books may destroy this spontaneous love of creative writing. It may also be severely damaged if too much emphasis is placed on spelling, letter-formation, or writing between guide lines on the paper. Ideally, everything which distracts the attention of the child from the aim of creativity should be removed. Malmquist's (6) research in Sweden has shown clearly the futility and waste that occurs if teachers are pre-occupied with such formal aspects of writing in the first 2 years of school. Creativity is so valuable (and a scarce commodity among adults) that we ought to foster it by showing children how highly we value it. This means de-emphasizing spelling and letter-formation. This is an essential element in the original i.t.a. education program which I developed in Britain.

i.t.a. AND THE SELF-IMAGE

I indicated earlier that attitudes are as important as skills in learning. Bruner's comment on this is highly significant for us.

> Mastery of the fundamental ideas of a field involves not only the grasping of general principles, but also the development of an attitude toward learning and inquiry; toward guessing and hunches, toward the possibility of solving problems on one's own.

Furthermore, he indicates that to develop such attitudes:

> An important ingredient is a sense of excitement about discovery of regularities of previously unrecognized relations and similarities, with a resulting sense of self-confidence in one's abilities.

T.O. does much harm to children's self-respect. They frequently fail *because their reasoning is correct, but English spelling is unreasonable.* Through this they are led to believe that they are "wrong," and, their reasonable hunches are undervalued. In contrast, i.t.a.'s regularity helps more children to be successful in their reasonable hunches, and consequently they are encouraged to further efforts and application of reasoning to problem-solving.

For instance, Wilkinson (7) in her report of the i.t.a. research of Bolton, Lancashire states:

> All of these [teachers] agree that children bring to their task, greater confidence and acquire more quickly the assurance that comes with the belief that they will succeed.

In developing self-confidence, too, it must again be emphasized that i.t.a.'s potential may be wasted if properly designed i.t.a. materials and teaching methods are not used. It is essential to individualize teaching if the self-image benefits of i.t.a. are to be fully realized. In particular, I may mention the way in which this benefit is sometimes lost through too early transition from i.t.a. to T.O. The average child in the original British i.t.a. program which I developed uses i.t.a. for the first two years, although many faster learners transfer to T.O. in the second year and some transfer to T.O. in the first year. Slower learners must be allowed even longer than 2 years to complete the i.t.a. program.

RESPONSIBILITY FOR CREATIVITY-DISCOVERY APPROACH TO i.t.a.

It is only fair that I warn you that the i.t.a. program I have outlined (which we might call the "Creativity-Discovery i.t.a. Approach") is only one of several different methods of applying i.t.a. in beginning reading. For example, Sir James Pitman (8), chief-designer of the i.t.a. symbols and spelling, made it clear, when he first put the i.t.a. alphabet before the public in 1960, that he did not believe that i.t.a. should be associated automatically with any particular educational method. He said:

> It is important to note that 'teaching method' is not involved. The teacher is free to teach any subject, including reading by i.t.a. (9) in whatever way he thinks best.

The methods I have outlined are the ones I have developed in my application of i.t.a. in the schools. As a result of my research I have incorporated these methods in my own published i.t.a. reading program, the *Downing Readers* (10). Other professional colleagues believe that i.t.a. should be taught differently, and I have compared all these different methods in another recent article (11). For example, in my i.t.a. program as I have outlined it to you today, I have stressed (a) the guided discovery approach, (b) creativity in writing rather than formal drills in letter-formation, etc. (c) fostering self-confidence by individualizing the teaching and postponing the transition to T.O. as long as necessary but typically encouraging transfer in the second grade.

To be fair to you and my professional colleagues who hold different views about the best way to maximize i.t.a.'s educational potential, I feel bound to urge you to consider other possible ways of teaching i.t.a. For instance, note the very different approach to i.t.a. stated by Olmaian (12) which she says she discerned in the i.t.a. *Early-to-Read* series by Mazurkiewicz and Tanyzer (13). She stated that in i.t.a. as typiflied by this series: (a) "the mode of teaching and learning is largely through telling and being told respectively and much less through guided discovery." (6) "Children are taught to write each symbol-sound after it is introduced," and "the order of (teaching) the symbol-sounds was determined from two studies." (c) Transition from i.t.a. to T.O. is "encouraged" usually about Arpil and May in first grade.

From Ohanian's review, it seems obvious that these are some very important differences between the Mazurkiewicz and Tanyzer i.t.a. approach and the Downing i.t.a. approach. Perhaps they need separate labels to help educators to discriminate between them. I have suggested the "Creativity—Discovery i.t.a. approach" as the name for mine. It must also be obvious that i.t.a. cannot be regarded as one single method. On the contrary the whole spectrum of methods of teaching reading can be applied in i.t.a. as well as in T.O. You have to choose not only between i.t.a. and T.O., but *within i.t.a. there is a very important choice between widely differing educational approaches.*

Your choice must be free. If you are an i.t.a. teacher or planning to introduce i.t.a. into your school, you should be aware of these differences (and others in other available i.t.a. series) and study them to determine *which educational approach to i.t.a. you think will best suit your pupils.*

Obviously, I believe that the i.t.a. approach which I have developed and described to-day is the superior method, but it is only fair to you also that I confess that the education philosophy and values underlying my i.t.a. approach would be just the same if I were using T.O. In summary, the educational aims and values which I have tried to achieve in my particular approach to i.t.a. are the more fundamental thing for me. I use i.t.a. in my series merely because it is a much better alphabet for securing those aims and values, whereas, T.O. is a very poor tool for this purpose. However, when a new and improved i.t.a. or some other simplified alphabet comes along to do the job even better than the present i.t.a., I will gladly change the alphabet again—but not the fundamental educational aim of providing children with opportunities for self-discovery, self-expression and self-confidence in their first experiences with written and printed English.

References

(1) Downing, John, *Evaluating the Initial Teaching Alphabet.* London: Cassell, 1967.

(2) Downing, John, *et al*, *The i.t.a. Symposium*. Slough, Bucks., England: National Foundation for Educational Research in England and Wales, 1967.

(3) Downing, John, "Can i.t.a. be Improved?" *Elementary English*, 44 (December 1967), 849-855.

(4) Downing, John, "Recent Developments in i.t.a." *California English Journal*, 3 (Fall 1967), 64-74.

(5) Bruner, Jerome S., *The Process of Education*. New York: Vintage Books, 1960.

(6) Malmquist, E., *Overgang fran textning till van lig skrivstil*. Stockholm: Kungl. Skolorerstyrelsen, 1964. (This books has a summary in English. The experiment is also reviewed in the book mentioned as reference number 1 above).

(7) Wilkinson, C. M., "The Initial Teaching Aphabet", in Downing, John, and Brown, Amy L. (Eds.), *Second International Reading Symposium*. London: Cassell, 1967.

(8) Pitman, I. J., "Learning to Read: An Experiment," *Journal of Royal Society of Arts*, 109 (1961), 149-180.

(9) In his original paper Pitman used the abbreviation "A. R." for the "Augmented Roman Alphabet" which only later acquired the name "Initial Teaching Alphabet" and "i.t.a."

(10) Downing, John, *The Downing Readers* (i.t.a. Basal series) London: Initial Teaching Publishing Co., 1964. (Also available from i.t.a. Publications, Inc., New York and Toronto).

(11) Downing Joh, "Progress Report on the Initial Teaching Alphabet," *The B. C. Teacher*, 47 (December 1967), 100-105.

(12) Ohanian, Vera, "Control Populations in i.t.a. Experiments", Elementary English, 43 (April 1966), 373-380.

(13) Mazurkiewicz, A. J. and Tanyzer, J. J., *Early-to-Read* (i.t.a. Basal series). New York: i.t.a. Publications Inc.

49. i.t.a. After Two Years*

REBECCA STEWART, ED.D.

Assistant to the Superintendent
for Elementary Education,
Bethlehem Area School District, Pa.

WHERE does one begin in evaluating the results of the introduction of a new medium of teaching reading to beginners? With teachers, with children, with statistics? With personal reactions? Objective evidence is indeed critical in evaluation, but cold statistics do not reveal the heart-warming changes in children's behavior and learning patterns. Education is necessarily people-changing, an interpersonal experience, and much that the teacher sees happening as the school year marches on toward June, cannot be measured, it can only be described. Therefore, with a common understanding that both objective and subjective evaluations are important, I would like to have us look at the experience in using the initial teaching alphabet in fifteen first grades in 1963-1964 and thirty one first grades in 1964-1965 in the Bethlehem Area Schools. What happened to that first population as they moved into second grade is also crucial.

Let's look objectively at the first-grade population and see what happened to them. All children in first grade during 1963-1964 were considered part of the project population. Approximately two-thirds of this population (referred to as t/o for traditional orthography) continued to receive instruction in a language arts-centered co-basal reading program. One-third of the students in fifteen classrooms located in twelve schools from differing socio-economic sections of the school system used the forty-four sound symbols of the i/t/a as the learning medium. Over forty percent of the i/t/a population was in schools from areas of low socio-economic status. These children tended to fit the current definition of the culturally different, deficient in both verbal and experiential backgrounds, often from homes or localities where Spanish is the language of social interchange. The proportion of 270 children from upper and middle areas to 181 from low socio-economic areas is not representative of the distribution of the total population of the school district and therefore would seem to place the first year's experiment under an initial disadvantage. On the other hand, it could

*From *Elementary English,* **42** (October, 1965) 660-665. Reprinted "with the permission of the National Council of Teachers of English and Rebecca W. Stewart."

and did demonstrate one crucial advantage of the i/t/a—providing a better learning situation for those children who enter first grade with a handicap.

At the beginning of the school year 1963-1964, results of the administration of the California Test of Mental Maturity, Lower Primary, demonstrated that the difference between the populations using different alphabets was small and not significant.

In late May, 1964 Form W and in early September, 1964 Form X of the Lower Primary Level of the California Reading Test were administered to *all* first graders. Not all the i/t/a population had made formal transition to traditionally printed materials, but all took these tests in traditional print—another handicap for the i/t/a population.

One hundred fourteen pairs from the spring administration, reduced to ninety-three pairs in the fall administration from the two populations were identified as matched in sex, chronological age, and socio-economic status, and in I.Q. within two points. To insure a fair test of the i/t/a-taught child's ability to deal with traditional orthography, the 114 children from the i/t/a population had to be in formal transition activities at least one week. An examination of the scores of the matched pairs can answer some significant questions about forgetting. It is recognized that the loss of achievement through the summer hiatus is most apparent to the teacher of second grade. A look at the data in Table I will therefore tell us something about the loss of reading skill for both populations.

TABLE I A Comparison of Total Reading Grade Equivalent Scores Obtained by the Matched Pairs on the California Reading Test (Lower Primary), Form W, May 1964 and Form X, September, 1964

Total Reading Grade Equivalent Scores	i/t/a		t/o	
	Form W May 1964 Percentage	Form X Sept. 1964 Percentage	Form W May 1964 Percentage	Form X Sept. 1964 Percentage
4.0+	1.57	1.07	–	–
3.5–3.9	4.07	10.75	2.37	5.37
3.0–3.4	24.07	21.50	8.57	12.90
2.5–2.9	37.07	35.48	28.67	20.43
2.0–2.4	24.07	22.58	27.07	29.03
1.5–1.9	9.07	8.60	21.07	21.50
1.0–1.4	–	–	11.67	10.75

May   1964 – N = 114 matched pairs
September   1964 – N = 93 matched pairs

The data in Table I seems to indicate that neither population suffered from forgetting, but that the i/t/a population improved in reading skill over the summer as an increase of six percent appears at the 3.5-3.9 interval. Three percent of the t/o population moved to the 3.5-3.9 interval and four percent to the 3.0-3.4 interval.

One of the fears expressed by visitors is that reading comprehension will suffer as a result of the use of a simpler code in the initial task of learning to read and the later transfer to the complex code of the traditional alphabet. The comprehension scores obtained in September do not support this assumption as an examination of the data in Table II will reveal.

TABLE II A Comparison of Comprehension Grade Equivalent Scores Obtained by the Matched Pairs on the California Reading Test (Lower Primary), Form W, May, 1964 and Form X, September, 1964

Reading Grade Equivalent Comprehension	i/t/a Percentage		t/o Percentage	
	Form W May 1964	Form X Sept. 1964	Form W May 1964	Form X Sept. 1964
4.0+	.88	16.13	–	6.45
3.5–3.9	1.75	1.07	2.63	1.07
3.0–3.4	19.29	16.13	6.14	10.75
2.5–2.9	38.59	24.81	27.19	18.28
2.0–2.4	24.56	20.43	31.57	22.58
1.5–1.9	13.16	21.50	22.80	25.81
1.0–1.4	1.75	–	9.65	12.90
.5– .9	–	–	–	2.15
N (Sept. 1964) = 93 matched pairs				

What happened as these children began their second year of formal education? Approximately 15% began developmental reading instruction in a 3^1 reader with the emphasis on thinking and comprehension skills. Approximately 20% were still using the i/t/a program reading in books 5, 6, 7, with the majority in formal transition at the end of book 6 or in book 7 which is printed almost exclusively in traditional print. The remaining 65% were placed in a developmental reading program at the 2^2 level. Wide reading and use of library books for fun and for enrichment in other curriculum areas was encouraged. The students could distinguish long and short vowels and consonants in the beginning, medial, and final positions. These skills are not mastered by the average student in a t/o program until the third grade.

We must confess to being somewhat conservative in assignment of instructional reading levels. Indeed some parents questioned the assignments because children were reading more difficult books for recreation at home. But there is a difference between reading for fun and reading for information and for the development of critical reading skills. We acted on the assumption that the students would pace themselves and that teachers would give them freedom to move ahead as they demonstrated developing skills.

In May the results of the administration of the California Reading Test, Upper Primary, to the total population indicated that there was no significant difference in the comprehension subtest, with a slight but not significant difference in word recognition skills. Again, I remind you of the imbalance in this original population.

TABLE III Means and Standard Deviations of the Reading Achievement Scores of i/t/a and t/o Population

	/t/a N=353		t/o N=868		
	M	SD	M	SD	t ratio
California Reading Test, Upper Primary— April,1965					
Word Recognition	36.4	7.50	34.8	7.95	.670
Comprehension	33.2	10.28	34.2	9.47	.374
Total Reading	69.7	17.10	69.0	16.50	.146

An examination of the results obtained from 196 pairs drawn from the two populations reveals a difference significant at the 1% level of confidence in word recognition and a slight difference not statistically significant in comprehension.

In April, 1965 the teachers reported the instructional level of the basal text used with groups in their classrooms. Teachers who received t/o first graders had been urged to move through the developmental readers as rapidly as children demonstrated competency. The data in Table V speaks for itself.

Spelling instruction was provided both as a group and an individual activity. As a group the classes investigated the spelling patterns—for instance, the many ways the long *i* sound is spelled. Individually, children learned the traditional spellings for words they used in writing activities. The children discovered traditional spelling by using an i/t/a—t/o dictionary and their knowledge of the i/t/a code. In one classroom where it was necessary to combine the i/t/a and t/o students, the t/o children used this dictionary as enthusiastically as the i/t/a children. They also used the pictionary and a junior-edition dictionary, formerly introduced at third grade.

TABLE IV Means and Standard Deviations of the Matched Population of Second Graders on Reading Achievement Scores in April and May, 1965

	i/t/a N=196		t/o N=196				
	M	SD	M	SD	s.e	z	Interpretation
California Reading Test Upper Primary, April, 1965							
Word Recognition	37.19	6.78	35.04	7.92	.651	3.30	Significant 1% level
Comprehension	34.01	19.52	33.98	9.85	.743	.04	Not Significant

TABLE V Second Grade Instructional Levels of the i/t/a and t/o Population as of April 15, 1965

t/o Reader level	i/t/a N=353 Percentage	t/o N=868 Percentage
4−1	7.65	—
3−2	18.70	—
3−1	24.93	25.34
2−2	31.73	38.48
2−1	10.48	29.72
1st	—	6.22
Primer	—	.23
	93.49%	Total 100.00%
i/t/a Reader level		
3-1	1.13	
2-2	4.24	
2-1	.57	
1st	.57	
	6.51%	
	100.00%	

What is most gratifying is the interest in spelling—it's strangely wonderful to the youngsters that English is spelled as it is. And every new spelling pattern is an amazing discovery. Structural and phonetic analysis are taught as helps in spelling correctly, not as part of the instructional reading curriculum.

One visitor, observing a developmental spelling lesson in a second-grade classroom, said "I'm concerned about the spelling list the students are developing. Some of them are not second-grade words." After all, what is a second-grade word? Any word that a second-grader needs to know how to spell in order to express himself?

The spelling section of the Stanford Achievement Test was administered to both populations in May, 1964 and May, 1965. The results in first grade indicated that there was no difference between the two populations in the ability to spell. This relieved our consciences somewhat for it indicated that what parents had feared about the detrimental effect of i/t/a on spelling was unfounded.

The results of the May, 1965 administration of the spelling section of the Stanford Achievement Tests supported the "hunch" which the staff had, that these i/t/a-taught children might be better spellers.

TABLE VI Means and Standard Deviations of the Matched Populations on Spelling Achievement Scores in May, 1964 and April, 1965

	i/t/a		t/o				
	M	SD	M	SD	s.e	z	
May, 1964 N = 114	13.82	4.3	13.81	5.58	.686	.01	Not Significant
May, 1965 N = 196	17.85	7.41	13.85	8.04	.688	5.81	Significant at 1% level

For the first time our second-year classrooms the science curriculum moved beyond the experience-demonstration level. There is a multi-text reference library available with basal texts at first, second and third-grade readability levels, augumented by the resources of the central library. The students checked the results of observation and demonstrations in the texts and discovered that even the books do not always agree.

For the first time a second-grade social studies textbook was provided, but the children rejected it as too easy and babyish. Exposure to third-grade level readers had introduced them to time-and-space concepts which required maps and a globe. The third-grade social studies book was tried in these classrooms and provided the needed challenge to learning.

In some classrooms children learned to use the card catalog and encyclopedias to discover needed information for social studies and science projects.

An unexpected dividend has been the effect on speech problems. Children had to pay attention to speech sounds, their own and others, and this had a beneficial effect in eliminating childish speech patterns. The most dramatic case was the improvement in the speech of one child whose parents had recognized the problem early and had provided pre-school therapy. There was no improvement until the boy discovered that his compositions were unintelligible to his classmates because he was reproducing his speech patterns, for instance, *wun* for *run*. Suddenly he "heard" himself in contrast to others. The parents admitted that i/t/a was the magic ingredient.

Learning with the initial teaching alphabet provides a total language arts approach. Reinforcement of learning is the result of using sound symbols in writing and reading while hearing the phonemes and blending them into morphemes. I believe that using the initial teaching alphabet provides a medium in which the structure of the English language becomes apparent to the learner.

When one examines the compositions the first graders produced in i/t/a last year and as second graders in t/o this year, several fascinating developments are apparent. First, the exposition is almost always in complete sentences. Second, punctuation appears naturally and correctly. Final punctuation, periods and question marks, were discussed as part of teaching, but commas and quotation marks appeared spontaneously. Whether this is the result of observing the teacher's writing of experience charts or awareness of punctuation in reading, nobody really knows. All sentence patterns are present and the range of vocabulary is tremendous.

Evaluation by the teachers of second grade in May, 1965 indicated that though children preferred t/o spelling, this had not affected either the quality or the quantity of their compositions. They reported that punctuation and capitalization were learned easily. Students correctly placed commas in headings, in direct address, and in words in series.

The teachers recommended that more attention be given to accent and syllabification in next year's second grade and that the language program develop an understanding of paragraphing. Structurally, the children's composition moved from opening sentence to conclusion, but they had difficulty in becoming aware of logical subtopics which should be separated into paragraphs.

The population of second-graders was not our only concern in 1964-1965, for two-thirds of our first graders (thirty-one classes) were receiving their introduction to reading through i/t/a. Teaching was less traumatic for the new population of i/t/a teachers, for now there were fifteen experts to consult and materials were available. As a result, the children could move as quickly through the program as achievement levels permitted.

The first year experience of the development of enthusiasm for and independence in learning was duplicated. And though the sixteen inexperienced teachers had in a sense been dragooned into teaching i/t/a, they soon were expressing delight in the differences in motivation and classroom environment, reported initially by the original volunteer teachers.

In April, 1965 teachers of first grade were asked to report the level of the texts used for reading instruction. The results are included in Table VII.

TABLE VII Instructional Level Achievement of the 1964-1965 First-Grade Population in April, 1965

Reader Level	Proportion of i/t/a N = 926	Proportion of t/o N = 453
3–1 t/o	32.18	–
3–1 (i/t/a Book 6)	15.44	–
2–2 (i/t/a Book 5)	17.17	.66
2–1 (i/t/a Book 4)	21.38	26.05
1 (i/t/a Book 3)	4.32	53.42
P (i/t/a Book 2)	5.94	14.57
PP and below	3.56	5.30

A side benefit was the extent to which children revealed their problems and concerns, their joys and sorrows. Teachers said they gained a greater understanding of the child's world and environment, the family relationships and home conditions. With these understandings they could be more accepting of the child's behavior patterns. It was certainly easier to accept the listless and inattentive child when one knew that he got his early sleep in the back seat of a car parked in front of the bowling alley.

One of the music-helping teachers stopped me to report that her first-grade daughter in another school system brought home her preprimer. After reading aloud the usual preprimer story, she looked at her parents and said, "Isn't it stupid!" And then her teacher-mother went on to say "It's too bad she doesn't have i/t/a. You know there was a difference in the classes by mid-year. I could do so much more with i/t/a classes. They were more alert, more interested."

The art supervisor also saw differences in the development of the children. Their representations of figures were more mature and their drawings indicated that they were more observant.

Some children were not promoted in the spring of 1964 and 1965, for no reading program in one year can eliminate the effect of cultural and verbal deprivation or provide a panecea for low mental ability or emotional blocks. But all the children retained in 1964 were reading and writing. In September they returned to first grade but were not typical first-grade repeaters because they had retained what had been taught previously.

In 1963-1964 i/t/a was used in three primary special education classes and was expanded in 1964-1965 to all primary special education classes. The teachers last year had reported, and the behavior of the children in the classroom supported their reports, that these slow learners were experiencing a renewed interest in learning to read and in writing. They no longer were discouraged and disinterested . They chose to go to the library table for books or to use paper and pencils to write stories in their spare time.

Using i/t/a as the initial teaching medium for teaching reading provided a learning environment which made observable differences

> in reading achievement
> in independent learning
> in motivation
> in perseverance
> in the ability to observe
> in the ability to write.

The challenge to the teaching staff is to change the curriculum to provide for developing skills without stifling the creativity and excitement of learning. There is the danger of over-stimulation; there is the danger of superficiality.

The first two years of teaching with i/t/a have not been problem-free—the flood of visitors, the interest of the mass media, and the hundreds of letters continue—and yet we know these externals are unimportant in relation to the opportunities i/t/a have opened for the children and for the teachers. For the children it has meant an early and easier introduction to the joys of reading, the status symbol of the educated man. For the teacher it has been a revelation of the ability of students to persevere, to learn independently, to enjoy a learning task. Most of all there is the satisfaction of seeing all children learn—not all at the same rate or with the same proficiency—but all learning and revelling in the task.

The introduction of reading has traditionally been relegated to the first grade in our public school system. This finds it basis in the study by Morphett and Washburne (1931) in which they found a mental age of six and a half to be optimum for beginning reading. While the results of this study are still being relied upon in most public schools, recent research has caused many reading specialists to question whether there is this relationship between mental age and reading that is implied.

The Denver study (1962), in its first project, revealed that children who had the pre-reading program in kindergarten, demonstrated significantly greater reading skill in first grade, thus providing justification for beginning reading at age five. The second project demonstrated that children above four years benefited greatly from a pre-reading program presented by parents in the home; brighter, younger children also benefited from this same program.

Durkin (1962-1963) in her comparison of early readers to non early readers found that the reading achievement of early readers at the end of third grade ranged from 4.4 to 6.0 with a median of 5.0 The control group which began to read in the first grade, ranged from 2.0 to 6.0 with a median of 4.3 at the end of third grade. She also found that, for all the children who were early readers, actual scores in reading were greater than would have been predicted on the basis of their intelligence as measured by the *Revised Stanford Binet Scale.* Thus, early readers were shown to have profited from their early start giving further supportive evidence to an earlier age than first grade for beginning reading.

Hillerich's study (1963) also revealed that children who had a prereading program in kindergarten demonstrated significantly greater reading achievement the end of first grade as compared to children who had no pre-reading program in kindergarten. Although the mean score in aptitude for the experimental group was slightly lower than that of the control group, the experimental group still scored considerably higher in reading achievement at the end of first grade. Both differences were significant at the .01 level. This study also supports the value of an earlier age than first grade for formal instruction in skills related to reading.

Wise (1965), who conducted a study similar to Hillerich's using a different set of aptitude and achievement tests, confirmed the results of Hillerich's study. Lynn (1963) has found evidence which suggests that accurate perception and learning of whole words can be achieved at a mental age of two and one half to three and one half and earlier.

Eames (1962) found that children five years of age have more accommodative power than at any subsequent age. He also found that the poorest near visual acuity found among five year old pupils was quite sufficient for reading the usual texts. Both of these studies obviate the claim that a six and a half year old mental age is necessary for beginning reading from the standpoint visual maturity.

50. Montessori's Reading Principles Sensitive Period Method Compai Reading Principles of Contempo Reading Specialists

LI

THERE is a current revival of Montessori schools as a poss educating the individual so that he may realize full, personal hum Since Montessori education is proposed as a means to this end, ea must be carefully scrutinized for efficiency toward attainment of

Montessori, having met with rejection in 1917, will meet v her program is not brought into the mainstream of public school the area of reading enjoys exclusive prominence in the primary g schools, it is a possible avenue whereby this integration of met accomplished. The author has, therefore, endeavored to delineate s contrasts between Montessori reading principles and those of reading specialists in order that public school educators may appraise this system.

SENSITIVE PERIODS

Montessori theorized sensitive periods for several areas of among them reading. The sensitive period for reading is the peri child is most amenable to the acquisition of this skill. Because period will occur at varying ages in different children, Montessori in this context and in general terms. She states, "In any case, alm children treated with our method begin to write at four years, and how to read and write, at least as well as children who have finis elementary" (1964-1965, p. 302). She emphatically declares that thi is never obligatory and some children who do not spontaneo themselves for these lessons are left in peace, and do not know ho write. Thus, the sensitive period can be said to occur for most child the ages of four and five.

*From *The Reading Teacher,* **21**, 2 (November, 1967), 163-168. R permission of Lee Elliott and the International Reading Association.

Downing (1962) claims to have had unusual success in teaching reading to children from age two on, via his "Initial Teaching Medium" and also a typewriter which bears the characters of the "Initial Teaching Alphabet." Moore (Caudle, 1965) also claims to have had great success in teaching reading to children from age two on, with his 'talking typewriter.'

To date, no research has been forthcoming to substantially repudiate the research findings of McKee, Durkin, Hillerich, Wise, Eames, Lynn, Moore, and Downing. The positions cited against early reading are based on opinion and the outdated research of Morphett and Washburne. Current research as substantiated the value of an earlier start in reading, placing it between the age of four and five, which is the age of the sensitive period as theorized by Montessori. Thus, Montessori reading principles involving the sensitive period are similar and consistent with current research findings of contemporary reading specialists.

WRITING AND READING

The Montessori method of teaching reading is unique from current reading programs being used in United States public schools in its thorough integration of writing and reading. A program being used in the parochial schools in Hawaii (Spalding, 1957) incorporates writing with a pure phonetic approach to the teaching of reading. This program, bearing elements of similarity to the Montessori method, is the only one of its kind this author was able to locate. While contemporary reading specialists have expressed opinions concerning writing, it is incorporated to little or no extent in their programs.

The three periods into which Montessori divides reading instruction are as follows (1964-1965, p. 271-185):

> *First Period*: Exercise tending to develop the muscular mechanism necessary in holding and using the instrument in writing.
> *Second Period*: Exercise to establish visual-muscular image of the alphabet and muscular memory of the movements necessary to writing.
> *Third Period*: Exercises for the composition of words.

The writing that Montessori refers to in the early stages of instruction does not necessarily involve a communication of ideas but more probably, merely the reproduction of symbols. It utilizes the sensory modalities of visual and auditory, kinesthetic and tactile to facilitate learning of the symbol, whereas contemporary methods utilize the modalities of visual and auditory.

The Montessori method is essentially a pure phonetic approach in that it does teach the child a sound for each letter of the alphabet, and then employs the technique of sounding out, from the spoken word to the letters it consists of and from the letters it consists of to the written word. For purposes of comparison, the author will refer to the McKee *Getting Ready to Read* series (1962) in which word recognition is accomplished chiefly through initial sound and the context in which the word is found. This method also capitalizes on knowledge of the spoken language, which the child already has, by helping him associate the printed form with the spoken form of words that he already knows.

The Montessori method (1964-1965, p. 271-285), as its author describes it, of necessity employs the use of phonics in isolation (b stands for "buh" etc.), though this is not necessarily done in Montessori schools in the United States. Phonics in isolation results in distortion of sounds, few of which can be accurately pronounced in isolation and contemporary reading specialists do not advocate this. The child will, as Montessori observed, come up with a severe distortion of the word intended. The McKee method accomplishes association of letter form to the sound it stands for using a key word which begins with the consonant being taught. Thus, when the child sees a specific letter form, it will immediately trigger the beginning sound of a key word. No consonant sound is ever isolated. A sound is always referred to in connection with a complete word.

This particular phase of the Montessori method may have lent itself with more facility to the Italian language in which it was originated by its author. That a pure phonics approach does not lend itself to the English language is demonstrated by Spache:

> The English language is complex and irregular in its phonetic aspects. A teacher cannot generalize completely about a basic vocabulary, since, for example, the thirteen vowel sounds of language may be represented in one hundred and four ways. Furthermore, the same groups of letters may have very different sounds (1939, pp. 137-150, pp. 191-198).

Clymer (1963) illustrated phonetic irregularity in the English language when he found, out of the forty-four phonic generalizations, only twenty-one possess at least 75 percent utility. The percentage of utility in the remaining twenty-three renders them insignificant. It was further demonstrated that the items of low utility are items having to do with vowels.

Gates (1928) found that pupils who used the phonics method were superior in attention to smaller details of words, but inferior in comprehension and in study of total words, syllables and the longer phonograms. Tate (1937) warned against unbalanced development of the abilities to comprehend words, sentences, and paragraphs through the use of a pure phonics method. McDowell (1953) found that children with a heavy phonics program excelled in alphabetizing and spelling, but were below other pupils in speed and in understanding words and paragraphs.

The Montessori method does not emphasize "understanding of what is read" from the very beginning of instruction. McKee insists that instruction from the beginning be of such a nature that the child learns that meaning lies behind printed symbols and he has not read unless he understands what the words mean. Montessori observed this typical weakness in her own program when she stated, "It was evident that the children, who seemed to read these books with such pleasure, did not take pleasure in the sense, but enjoyed the mechanical ability they had acquired, which consisted in translating the graphic signs into the sounds of a word they recognized" (1964-1965, p. 303). She further states, "Between knowing how to read the words, and how to read the sense of a book, there lies the same distance that exists between knowing how to pronounce a word and how to make a speech" (1964-1965, p. 304).

Montessori's integration of writing and reading could well be a valuable contribution to education. Influenced as this may have been by Seguin, she none the less rejected the method of Seguin on the basis of two fundamental errors: writing in printed capitals and preparation for writing through a study of rational geometry (1964-1965, p. 252). She revised a system of her own which is substantially different.

Hildreth (1963) extolls the virtues of early writing as an aid to reading. Whe feel that writing is an active, motor, muscular response which aids memory of the letter forms and words. Among the numerous advantages are: acquaints beginners with the letters of the alphabet, aids discrimination between similar appearing words, provides a means of reinforcing the recognition of phonetically irregular words, aids in retention of phonic elements, provides self-constructed reading material, teaches left to right direction.

She emphasizes that writing be made a functional skill serving purposes of communication from the beginning. Reading will soon out-distance writing because of the nature of the process and difficulties with English spelling, but rapid gains in reading will be due in part to early writing activities. The present tendency to keep reading and writing apart in beginning reading instruction is unfortunate because of the mutual relation between the two processes.

Fernald (1943) recognizes that handwriting contributes powerfully to learning because of the kinesthetic force involved. She conducted an experiment whereby non readers were taught to read by tracing words and then writing them. She feels that all of us learn, in varying degrees, as we write by hand.

Both Moore (Caudle, 1965) and Downing (1962) have established some relationship between the act of typewriting and reading. Both, however, seem to consider the manipulation of the pencil too difficult and not as meritorious as the typewriter. Thus, research is meagre in the field of writing but logic and some evidence do suggest a strong relationship between writing and reading.

OPEN FOR CONSIDERATION

Montessori's contention, now over sixty years old, that the sensitive period for reading does, in fact, occur most generally in the preschool child, is well substantiated by current research. According to Montessori the sensitive period is one in which the child is most amendable to the acquisition of a given task. It is transient and when artifically induced at a later stage, the values reaped will not be nearly so great.

It is true that a pure phonetic approach does not lend itself with facility to the English language. Yet this is only one phase of the program. It can and has been easily adjusted by the Montessori teachers the author has known and observed.

Montessori's incorporation of writing with reading is unique and ingenious. Montessori teachers have for long years testified to their success with it. There is the possibility that it does greatly facilitate the acquisition of reading skills and where that possibility exists, a close examination by public school educators is warranted.

References

Caudle, F. Pre reading skills through the talking typewriter. *Instructor,* 1965, **75**, 39.

Clymer, T. The utility of phonic generalizations in the primary grades. *The Reading Teacher,* 1963, **16**, 252-258.

Denver Public Schools. Reading instruction in the kindergarten. Denver: Denver Public Schools, 1962. (*mimeo.*)

Downing, J. *The initial teaching alphabet.* New York: McMillan, 1962.

Durkin, Dolores. An earlier start in reading. *Elementary School Journal,* 1962, **63**, 147-151.

Durkin, Dolores. Children who read before grade I. *Elementary School Journal,* 1963, **64**, 143-148.

Eames, T. Physical factors in reading. *The Reading Teacher,* 1962, **15**, 432.

Fernald, Grace. *Remedial techniques in basic school subjects.* New York: McGraw-Hill, 1943.

Gates, A. I. *New methods in primary reading.* New York: Teachers College, Columbia University, 1928.

Hildreth, Gertrude. Early writing as an aid to reading. *Elementary English,* 1963, **40**, 15-20.

Hillerich, R. L. Dare we evaluate paradise. New directions in kindergarten programs. *Proceedings of 1963 New England Kindergarten Conference,* 1963.

McDowell, J. B. A report on the phonetic method of teaching children to read. *Catholic Educational Review,* 1953, **51**, 506-519.

McKee, J., and Harrison, Lucille. *Getting ready to read,* of Reading for meaning series. Boston: Houghton Mifflin, 1962.

Montessori, Maria. *The Montessori method.* Cambridge: Rober Bentley, 1964-65.

Morphett, Mabel, and Washburne, C. When should children begin to read? *Elementary School Journal,* 1931, **31**, 496-503.

Sanderson, A. E., Lynn, R., and Downing, J. A. Reading and mental age, start them young. *Times Education Supplement.* London, England: November 15, 1963, **714**.

Spache, G. Phonics manual for primary and remedial teachers. *Elementary English Review.* 1939. **16**, 147-150, 191-198.

Spalding, Ramona Bishop, and Spalding, W. T. *The writing road to reading.* New York: Whiteside and William Morrow, 1957.

Tate, H. L. The influence of phonics on silent reading in grade I. *Elementary School Journal,* 1937, **37**, 752-763.

Wise, J. The effects of two kindergarten programs upon reading achievement in grade one. Unpublished doctoral dissertation. University of Nebraska, 1965.

51. The Index to Reading Material (Devices and Films for Improving Rate of Reading)*

ANTHONY P. WITHAM

Assistant Supt. of Schools
Monroe, Michigan

GADGETRY in the reading program has long been the source of heated controversy among reading experts. Lack of explicit data from carefully controlled research in this areas has failed to clarify the relative value of instrumentation over traditional and less expensive methods of improving perception, speed and comprehension of reading.

Conclusions drawn from limited research have generally indicated no significant advantages of mechanical aids over ordinary teacher-motivated practices. Additional confusion appears to have emerged from a general lack of sufficient understanding of the goals, methods, and rationale specifically developed for each type of instrumentation.

Teachers employing some form of instrumentation as one facet of the reading program generally report high motivation for self-improvement and short-range gains in rate and comprehension. Statistically valid studies measuring the perserverance of rates and eye movement efficiency achieved by means of mechanical aids are non-existent. This writer is presently conducting a research project which has as one of its objectives the measurement of long range retention of skills developed by a selected instrument.

There are presently available over twenty forms of instrumentation and training films for the reading teacher. Approximately one half of these are designed to improve perceptual skills through some form of *tachistoscopic* training. This type of visual exercise has a variety of goals: accurate form perception and increased visual discrimination; rapid ·visual perception (the ocular and mental intake of visual material); organized retention for a stronger visual memory, better directional attack and an awareness of components as

*From *Elementary English,* 39 (May, 1962) 511-516. Reprinted with the permission of the National Council of teachers of English and Dr. Anthony P. Whitman.

parts of the whole; and finally such by products as increasing attention, concentration, eye-hand coordination and so on.

Tachistoscopic training is frequently employed as a preliminary phase to rapid reading exercises. These devices, which deal with the instantaneous recognition (from 1 to 1/100 of a second) of digits, letters, words, phrases, and so forth, are often used in conjunction with some type of reading pacer of tracing film.

Current investigations are indicating that eye movements are neither the cause nor effect of poor reading but rather a reflection of the skills and habits formed by the reader. Likewise, direct tachistoscopic training has thus far proved to have little lasting effect on reading performance. Recent studies in this area have indicated little correlation between speed of perceiving isolated phrases and speed of reading. More conclusive research is needed before the teacher can decide on the most effective use of tachistoscopes in the reading program.

The remaining devices and films appear to have one major objective—improving *rate* and *comprehension* of narrative reading materials. Most of these techniques attempt to exert varying degrees of eye and/or rate control over the reader. A portion of these pacers are designed for individual use at a typical reading distance (near-point). The student has the advantage of selecting the reading material and determining the rate at his convenience on these portable and comparatively inexpensive accelerators.

The remaining mechanical techniques and training films are designed for group activities and employ various forms of eye movement control at a projected distance (far-point). Rates and content of material are predetermined by the instructor. A range of from 40 to 1000 words-per-minute can be exerted on the group (or individual), depending on the instrument or film selected. Each of these projected programs offer different narrative content, optical projectors, and images on the screen in their efforts to jog the reader from a sluggish and inflexible rate of reading. No opportunity for regression is provided as the constant and controlled rate attempts to encourage the student to economize on the number of eye fixations per line of print. Immediate comprehension tests follow the projected reading. Students are then encouraged to transfer these rates to nearpoint reading materials.

Until more extensive research findings point the way to the most effective use of instrumentation in reading, teachers should (if the budget permits) utilize devices as additional sources of motivation and directed activities in the balanced reading program—and not as the cure-all to reading problems.

Overuse of such aids and their prolonged hibernation in the nearest closet are two abuses which can develop if the principal or supervisor fails to orientate the faculty to the most effective use of the selected instrument in the developmental reading program.

Prices quoted in the Index are *list* prices, subject to the usual school discount.

INSTRUMENTATION FOR READING AND PERCEPTUAL TRAINING

Tachistoscopic Devices

For Individual Use—

EDL *Flash-X*. (K-12). Through timed exposures (1/25 of a second) of pictures, numbers, letters, words and other material, the student is challenged to concentrate, increase speed of recognition, etc. This circular metal disc is designed for individual use with blank cards available for special materials. Flash cards accompanying device: X-1 (readiness pictures); X-2 (primary recognition); X-3 (basic accuracy-numbers); X-4 (letters); X-5 (sight vocabulary-grade 1); X-6 (grade 2); X-7 and X-8 (basic arithmetic); X-9 (advanced set for upper grades and adults); X-12-19 (spelling for grades 2-9). Educational Developmental Laboratories. Flash-X—$7.20. Individual sets of cards—$3.60. Teacher's guide—$.30.

Eye-Span Trainer. (4-12). This device is made of plastic and uses a hand operated shutter for training in flash recognition of numbers, phrases etc. It is available with 29 slides including 264 numbers from 2 to 9 digits in span, 8 slides of phrases, and 4 slides of additional training items. Audi-Visual Research. Complete kit is priced at $7.95.

Keystone Tachette. (K-12). Designed to relate far-point perceptual training to nearpoint. Flash exposure is a constant 1/100 of a second speed. Units of tachistoslides (see *Keystone Tachistoscope)* can be adapted for use with the *Tachette.* Keystone View Company. Individual price—$25.00.

Phrase-O-Scope. (4-12). This miniature tachistoscope is included in the *Rapid Reading Kit,* a self-directive program for increasing rate and comprehension of reading. Junior and adult level materials are available separately. *Reading Skills,* a workbook of some 24 articles stressing rate, is used in conjunction with the *Phrase-O-Scope.* Better Reading Program, Inc. Complete Kits—$12.95.

For Group Use—

EDL *Tach-X Tachistoscope.* (K-12). The *Tach-X* is a 35 mm. filmstrip projector equipped with a timing mechanism that provides exposure speeds of from 1/100 of a second to 1½ second. The accompanying filmstrips include: Set 4c (readiness-color); set 10 (perceptual readiness); set 20 (primary numbers); set 21 (primary letters); set 22 (primary supplementary); set I (words-phrases for grades 1-3); set 30 (intermediate numbers); set 31 (intermediate supplementary); set J (words and phrases for grades 4-6); set 40 (advanced accuracy; set K (words and phrases, grades 7-12); set V (words and phrases, college). Spelling sets available for grades 2-9. Education Developmental Laboratories. Tach-X—$185.00. Prices for individual albums of slides range from $15.00 to $75.00. Activity sheets, technique manual and guide available.

Flash-Tachment. (K-12). This device converts any 2 x 2 slide or filmstrip projector into a classroom tachistoscope. Control of visual after-image is achieved by minimizing screen illumination contrasts. Speeds from 1/25 to 1/100 of a second. You-make-them slides are available for individual preparation in flash-recognition and eye-span training. Audio-Visual Research. *Flash-Tachment* –$5.95. Set of 50 2 x 2 slides, pencil and manual–$3.95.

Keystone Tachistoscope. (K-12). This instrument combines an overhead slide projector with a special *Flashmeter* providing from 1 to 1/100 of a second exposure. The timing device is properly mounted and enclosed for use only on the *Keystone Overhead Projector.* The lever opens the timing device regardless of the setting of speed control, to provide for easy viewing of the image at all times. *Tachistoslides* include: perceptual-span development; Dolch basic sight vocabulary and nouns; phrase and sentence reading; jumping digits; familiar forms; geometric and basic forms; Minnesota efficient reading slides etc. Keystone View Company. Complete program for elementary schools–$445.00; intermediate schools–$468.00; secondary school–$494.00.

Lafayette Tachistoscopes. (4-12). A variety of devices in flash-recognition are available through this producer. Included are: *Constant Illumination Tachistoscope,* designed to eliminate the flash appearance through the use of two projectors operating simultaneously with shutter speeds from 1/100 of a second to 1 second, $328.00; automatic *Projection Tachistoscope,* in which the presentation of both slide and shutter triggering can be set automatically between the limits of 5 seconds and 60 seconds, $275.00; *Tachistoscope,* a 300-watt combination slide and strip film with 5″ lens, $149.00; *Tachitron,* a near-point training instrument, $79.50; all purpose attachment usuable with any make or projector, $92.00. Included with each instrument are 400 training targets in a slide file. Lafayette Instrument Company.

Speeding Your Reading. (9-12). This single film (16 mm.) illustrates the fundamental principles involved in correct reading habits. Emphasizes the development of speed, the meaning of span and how it may be enlarged. Illustrates correct eye movements and shows how to develop more efficient ones. Teaching Aids Exchange. Rental–$2.00; Purchase Price–$50.00.

Tachist-O-Flasher. (1-12). Kit includes the *Flasher* (for use with any filmstrip projector) and accompanying *Tachist-O-Filmstrip* library, including phonics practice, instant words, instant word phrases, reading mastery, prefix and suffix mastery, phrase mastery, seeing skills, number recognition, etc. Science Research Associates. Individual elementary, junior high, and senior high kits priced at $300.00 each. Tachist-O-Flasher–$10.00; 150-watt projector–$39.95 (kits include *Flasher* only).

Tachistoscopic Training Filmstrips. (1-12). This series is divided into seven areas: basic vocabulary group; commonest nouns; word groups; sentences and phrases; familiar objects; number recognition-digits; graded word phrases. The *Speed-I-O-Scope,* an attachment for the regular slide projector, is available to work with the filmstrips. Society for Visual Education. Complete series of graded word phrases (57 strips)–$102.60; digits (7 strips)–$15.75; basic vocabulary et al. (16 strips)–$35.90. Special attachment priced at $89.50.

DEVICES AND FILMS FOR IMPROVING RATE OF READING

For Individual Use–

EDL Skimmer. (7-12). This device produces a bead of light which travels down the fold of the book or material at a constant *skimming* rate (800-100 wpm), resetting automatically at the bottom of each page. A dial calibrated in seconds provides completion timing for *scanning* tasks. Educational Developmental Laboratories. $30.00.

Keystone Reading Pacer. (4-12). Employs a pointer which moves at speeds from 50 to 1000 wpm. The reader can make regressions if necessary. The *Pacer* turns off automatically when the pointer reaches the bottom of the page and starts automatically when moved to the top of the next page. Keystone View Company. $115.00.

Reading Rateometer. (4-12). This portable device can be used with any materials the student may wish to select. By adjusting T-bar to desired rate, the bar paces the reader by moving at a constant rate down the page. *Model A* has a standard range of 70-2500 wpm, *Model B* (for remedial cases) 20-500 wpm range; *Model C* (college-adult) 140-5000 wmpm range. Audio-Visual Research. $39.95.

Shadowscope Reading Pacer. (4-12). A beam of light is presented to the reader which gently sets a compelling pace. Any printed material can be used with the *Shadowscope.* A two-speed range, plus capacity to accept any material, permits use of this device with any group from primary to adult levels. Psychotechnics, Inc. $94.00.

SRA Reading Accelerator. (4-12). This accelerator employs a mechanically-controlled shutter which can be set at any desired speed within a complete range of reading rates by the individual student. When the shutter is released, it moves smoothly down the page, covering one line at a time, obscuring several preceding lines to discourage re-reading. Entirely mechanical, no electrical outlet or batteries are required. Adjusts for any speed between 30 and 3000 wpm. Science Research Associates. Model IIb ($89.50) is designed for schools, reading clinics and home study; Model III ($47.50) is a book size model for portability and economy.

For Group Use–

C-B Developmental Reading Series. (4-12). This program of twenty-four 16 mm. films are divided into three main areas: *Phrase Reading* (16 films); *Keys to Reading* (3 films); and *Pathways to Reading* (5 films). The latter two areas are adjuncts to the *Phrase Reading Series* sub-divided into: beginning, intermediate and advanced levels. The phrase series is arranged to permit review of familiar material at different speeds and with a variety of questions differing in kind and difficulty. In the 175-page manual, the teacher is given the complete text of each of the films while the student workbook offers additional reading selections integrated with the texts of the films. C-B Educational Films, Inc. Complete Phrase Reading Set—$325.00; Keys to Reading—$225.00; Pathways to Reading—$350.00. Films are available separately. Student workbooks—$2.50.

Craig Reader (7-12). A training program utilizing the exapanded line and tachistoscopic techniques in improving rate and comprehension. Device resembles a portable television and can be used individually or with small groups. An automatic film feed for an entire reading cycle is provided in the twenty-one hour lessons which progress from short lines of about 3 words to long lines of over 7 words—always maintaining the one fixation per line reading pattern. Student is encouraged to economize on fixations as one line is exposed at a time. Craig Research, Inc. 20-lesson program including manuals, tests, student workbook, and 55 *Craig-Slides* is priced at $39.50. The Craig Reader—$149.50.

EDL Controlled Reader. (K-12). This device is a factory-modified 500-watt, filmstrip projector. It projects specially prepared, quarter-frame filmstrip reading selection (1-12) at rates varying from 60-1000 wpm. Exposure of the material on the screen is presented in a moving slot which allows the reader to perceive approximately a phrase at a time (or a complete sentence). The slot continues steadily in a left-to-right fashion, uncovering one line of print at specific intervals of time. A library of over 240 reading selections is available. Set 4c-readiness (25 strips-color); set 4d-pre-primer (25 strips); set 4c-first grade (50 stories); set 4f-second grade (50 stories); set 4g-third grade (25 stories); set 3a-intermediate (45 stories); set 2b-junior high (50 stories); set 1b-high school (45 stories). Story and question books are available for each grade level. Teacher's guide accompanies each program. Educational Developmental Laboratories. Filmstrip sets range from $35.00 to $93.00. Controlled Reader—$255.00. *A Controlled Reader, Jr.* (300-watt) is now available for individual and small group training. Filmstrip stories (above) are adaptable to this instrument. $150.00.

Harvard University Reading Films. (9-12). A revised set of 17 films adaptable to any standard 16 mm. silent projector. The empasis is placed upon a central reading habit, the ability to deal successfully with larger and more meaningful units of thoughts. The reading rate increases from 170 to 450 wpm. To obtain the increase in eye span, a method of phrasing control is employed as well as simple pacing. Comprehension checks consist of ten questions on main ideas, inferences etc. on each film and arranged for self-scoring. Test A, B, and C are used in conjunction with the selections for equated forms of measuring reading rate and comprehension. Content is primarily social studies. Teacher's manual contains directions. Harvard University Press. 17 reading films—$275.00. (Rental possible)

Iowa Reading Films. (9-12). Two series of films are available, one at the high school level, the other at the college-adult level. Each series consists of 15 films designed to improve reading rate through controlled reading activities. Films are adapted for standard 16 mm. projector at standard sound speed of 24 frames per second. Within each series, the rate is graduated, the first film being presented at the slowest rate, the last film at the fastest rate. A manual of instructions accompanies each series. Supplementary selections containing twenty articles are available. State University of Iowa. High School series may be rented or purchased at $150.00. Supplementary booklets—$.50 each.

PerceptoScope. (7-12). This is a multi-function projector which can serve as a controller, accelerator, motion picture projector, strip film projector, tachistoscope and timer. A "two-film" feature of the *PerceptoScope* permits simultaneous projection of two films with the rear film superimposing control patterns on subject matter on the front film and automatically regulating its advance. A series of 10 films containing 26 reading articles combined with tachistoscopic material are used for controlled reading training. Forty-one different speeds from 120-4320 wpm are possible. Practice reading and vocabulary books are available. Perceptual Development Laboratories. A total program for 20 students (not including device) is priced at $587.00. The *PerceptoScope Mark II* $1275.00.

Purdue Reading Films. (7-College). This series of 16 mm. training films is designed to be used in the English classroom or within an intensive reading course. They are a group teaching device emphasizing increased speed of perception, regularity in eye movements, widening eye span, and eliminating involuntary regressions. Selections deal with narration, biography, science, history, and personal essay. Three levels and sets are available: *Junior High Series,* (available Spring, 1962) consisting of 12 selections with a range of 90-200 wpm (silent speed) and 135-300 wpm (sound speed)—$87.50; *High School Series,* including 16 selections with a range of 158-470 (silent) and 237-705 (sound) words-per-minute—$115.00; and the *College Series* (revised-1962) offering 16 selections at a 188-511 silent speed and a 282-766 sound speed.—$200.00. In all sets, stops per line begin with 3 and move to 2 fixations. Instructor's guide and 30 comprehension booklets accompany each series. Not available for rental. Prices quoted are not subject to discount. Purdue University.

Addresses of Producers

Audio-Visual Research—523 S. Plymouth Court, Chicago 5, Ill.
Better Reading Program, Inc.—230 East Ohio Street, Chicago 11, Ill.
C-B Educational Film, Inc.—690 Market Street, San Francisco 4, Cal.

Craig Research, Inc.—3410 S. La Cienega Blvd., Los Angeles 16, Cal.
Educational Developmental Labs.—75 Prospect Street, Huntington, N. Y.
Harvard University Press—Cambridge 38, Massachusetts
Keystone View Company—Meadville, Pennsylvania
Lafayette Instrument Company—North 26th Street, Lafayette, Indiana
Perceptual Development Laboratories—6767 Southwest Avenue, St. Louis 17, Mo.
Purdue University, Audio-Visual Center-Lafayette, Indiana
Psychotechnics, Inc.—105 W. Adams Street, Chicago 3, Ill.
Science Research Associates, Inc.—259 East Erie Street, Chicago 11, Ill.
Society for Visual Education—1345 Diversey Parkway, Chicago 14, Ill.
State University of Iowa—Bureau of Audio-Visual Instruction, Iowa City, Iowa
Teaching Aids Exchange—P.O. Box 3527, Long Beach, 3, California

52. Computer at School Helps Teach Students How to Read*

FIRST grade students started classes at Brentwood school (E. Palo Alto, Calif,) here this fall and moved into the computer age.

Brentwood school, in the Ravenswood City School District, is located in a low-income, racially-mixed neighborhood where many of the children have not had much preschool exposure to alphabets and numbers. This system will permit a high degree of attention to the individual pupil, letting him progress according to his ability. Some students will complete their computer-assisted lessons very rapidly, while others who need additional drill can move at their own pace. Conceivably, each student in a class could be working on an entirely different lesson.

Four first grade classes with a total enrollment of 108 are participating in the program. Two classes work with the computer for 30 minutes each morning in reading, and two classes in the afternoon use the facilities to study mathematics. The computer feeds pupils new material as they can handle it, keeps track of answers and scores, and analyzes results on a day-to-day basis so teachers will know how each student is progressing.

U.S.O.E. CHIPS IN ON COSTS

The system grew from joint research and experiments over the past five years by Stanford University's Institute for Mathematical Studies in the Social Sciences, headed by Professor Patrick Suppes, director, and Professor Richard C. Atkinson. The program at Brentwood is supported by a $1 million grant from the U.S. Office of Education.

A 3,200 square-foot building was constructed on the Brentwood school grounds, housing a new IBM 1500 computer system, 16 terminals at which students practice, offices and workrooms. There is also a remote-control teletype circuit to the Stanford Computation Center.

*From *Nation's Schools*, **78**, 4 (October, 1966), 81-84. Copyright 1966, McGraw-Hill, Inc., Chicago. All rights reserved. Reprinted by permission.

Each student sits at a terminal or learning center where he can communicate with the computer by touching a light-pen to a television type screen, by typewriter keyboard, or by speaking into a microphone to reply to a tape-recorded voice from the computer.

The system has the enthusiastic support of Brentwood Principal William Rybensky, District Superintendent Roderic Moore, and Associate Superintendent Philip Smith.

Rybensky emphasized that "computer-assisted instruction," or C.A.I., properly describes the system. The teacher remains the important factor, but the machine assists and supplements.

The teacher carries on her programs in reading or mathematics, scheduled within the usual one-hour blocks of time. She works with one group in her classroom while 16 students go to the computer building for 25 or 30 minutes. Stanford teachers act as proctors during the computer sessions. When pupils finish their lesson, they return to their classroom for additional instruction.

Two innovations at Brentwood this year tie in with the computer program. One is the introduction of a system of levels to replace grading. The faculty believed that fixed grade standards were not flexible enough to reflect the needs of the students. Pupils now work on any of four or five levels or even between levels. Brentwood also adopted a staggered reading program for the primary grades. Half the pupils in each classroom come to school at the regular time and the others an hour later. This divides the class load and give the teacher more time to devote to each pupil.

C.A.I. centers on the computer which pulls from the disc storage the commands for an instructional sequence or problem and tells the terminal devices to display certain numbers, letters and pictures and to play a specific recording. A ready light turns on to tell the pupil that it is time to answer and stays on until the response is completed. The computer evaluates the answer in terms of the response and the child's past performance and decides what question or problem to present next. Each response is recorded so that it identifies the child, what problems he is working on, his response, and his reaction time. This complete history is available to teachers to help determine how to proceed in teaching each particular child.

In addition to the central computer, the system includes disc storage units, tape storage units, card reader and punch, line printer, two proctor stations, and an interphase to 16 student terminals.

At each learning stations there is a cathode ray tube (CRT) which is a television type screen; light-pen to be used with the CRT; modified typewriter keyboard, and audio system which records and plays prerecorded messages. The student is equipped with earphones and a microphone.

The CRT is used to show alphabetic or numerical symbols, including subscript and superscript, on a 7 inch screen with 60 lines and 40 spaces per line.

It also can display line drawings. An indicator can be positioned anywhere along the screen as a pointer, or can move along with words as a "bouncing ball" in a sing-along.

The projector is a random-access 16 mm. film device which shows a still image in black and white or color on a 7 by 9 inch screen. Images are stored in a cartridge with a capacity of 1,024 pictures.

Audio messages lasting one second to 15 minutes come from a random-access control device. Messages are stored in tape cartridges containing three hours of audio material.

STUDENTS USE LIGHT-PENS

When a problem is presented to the child, he can respond by touching a light-pen to the proper answer on the CRT screen. At other times, response is made by keyboard; and the characters struck may or may not be displayed on the CRT. A third method of response is the microphone. The answer is recorded on tape and can be played back as part of the instructional program or used for a later analysis by the teacher.

In the reading program, letter discrimination, word meanings, and sentences can be studied.

Suppose a picture illustrating a running rat were projected on the screen. On the CRT appear the words, "The rat ran." The audio tells the child, "Touch and say the word that answers the question. Who ran?" When the child touches the word "rat" with his light-pen, the audio says, "Yes. Rat." If he makes a mistake, an arrow points to "rat" and he is told, "No. Now touch and say 'rat.' " If no response is made within 30 seconds, he is told the correct answer, the arrow points to it, and he is asked to touch the word. When a correct response is made he is told to go to the next problem.

Rybensky feels there will be problems with certain words involving measurements or dimensions. "Ball," for example, may be difficult to teach by word and one dimension picture. He said the classes were to start a the same level; but as the school year goes along, certain students will need more work on consonants, vowels, and so forth while others will know the material and will be able to bypass it.

Instruction program were prepared at Stanford with the cooperation of the the staff of Brentwood school.

"Our teachers were requested to explain the nature of our children and their needs. They also were asked for their reactions to the proposed programs." Rybensky said. "During the year the programs will be revised somewhat as we go along, and our teachers will contribute to this by feeding back information from their classes."

Daily lessons are prepared by the Stanford staff, which includes teachers trained for elementary school instruction.

To dispel any apprehension that teachers might have had about their role in the program, special inservice training was provided by the Stanford C.A.I. staff in cooperation with the Brentwood school administration. A special course on the system also was offered by San Jose State College Extension to all interested school personnel in the district.

Besides keeping a daily record of a child's achievement, C.A.I. may make a significant contribution to education in the areas of curriculum research and evaluation. It will provide a loboratory for controlled experiments where instructional materials are specified precisely and where a detailed record of each child's performance is available.

JENNESS KEENE, *McGraw-Hill World News.*

53. The O.K. Moore Typewriter Procedure*

DOROTHY K. JOHNSON

I SHALL construct some word pictures for you to provide the background of our research with the automated typewriter.

My first picture is to introduce Dr. Omar Khayyam Moore, who developed his concept of a responsive environment. In order to obtain a complete picture of a person, we need to know more about him than his physical appearance. We are concerned with his philosophy and activities.

DR. OMAR KHAYYAM MOORE

Dr. Moore is a highly creative individual, who was a former professor at Yale but is now affiliated with Rutgers. He is a Sociologist, so his project was initiated as a sociology professor seeking research on culture, on learning theory, and on human higher-order problem solving behavior. Dr. Moore's aim was to determine how humans could learn through a responsive environment. He believes that children between the ages of two and six have a tremendous untapped capacity for learning—and, if placed in a responsive environment can make amazing progress—and this he has proven!

The idea of teaching the very young through their own activity is not a recent innovation, although not very much has been done about it.

Aristotle—the celebrated Greek philosopher, who was a pupil of Plato in the 4th Century B.C. (384-322) recommended it.

Montaigne—the French philosopher in the 16th Century (1533-1592) agreed with Aristotle's views.

Rousseau—the French philosopher in the 18th Century (1712-1778) believed in teaching the very young with real things.

Maria Montessori, who started as a physician in Rome, was a pioneer in early education and child development during the first half of our century,

*From *Journal of the Reading Specialist*, (March, 1966) 87-91. Reprinted with the permission of *Journal of the Reading Specialist*, March 1966, and Dorothy K. Johnson.

believed in work—not for the sake of achievement, but work for the sake of self-development.

John Locke, the English philosopher of the 17th Century (1632-1704) wrote "when a child can talk, 'tis time he should begin to read."

Dr. Moore called his place of work a responsive environments laboratory. There are some specifications necessary for a laboratory to have a real responsive environment.

According to Dr. Moore the environment is responsive if:

1. It allows children to explore within bounds of safety controls. Of course, none of us want children to get hurt.
2. It informs children immediately about the consequences of their action in a constructive way. There are many ways to inform children about their learning. For instance, if a child touches a hot stove, he learns—but not in a constructive way.
3. It permits children to make intensive use of their capabilities for discovering relations—a real learning situation.
4. It is so arranged that it is conducive to the development of problem solving—that is the key to which Dr. Moore worked,—how children can solve problems from their own initative while being safely guarded.

As a result of this theory, Dr. Moore's children can read, write, type and take dictation, as well as compose their own stories before they enter first grade.

I was a first grade teacher for many years, and when this program was suggested to me, I was a real doubting Thomas, but I felt if there was any way to teach children to read, or to help them to learn, I was for finding out! It has been most challenging.

Dr. Moore and his teachers have worked with over on hundred children from the private day school to which the lab is adjacent. Children from two to five years came from the nursery school, kindergarten, and first grade to work at the lab.

The children could stay for thirty minutes or could depart upon request. This activity was voluntary on the part of the children.

Three years ago, five retarded boys and girls, because of their low IQ's (59-72) and behavior problems were rejected by public kindergartens. They worked with Dr. Moore's faculty, and after seven weeks their attitudes and actions improved sufficiently for their schools to agree to accept them.

DR. MOORE'S PLAN IN FREEPORT

Under Dr. Moore's direction and guidance, I established a center to determine whether his technique was applicable to kindergarten children in the public schools.

Through the cooperation of the superintendent, Dr. John Henry Martin, and the generosity of one of the elementary principals, Mr. Christopher Warrell, our center was located at the Atkinson School because of the nearness to the Reading Center. The projection booth of the audio-visual room became our unadorned laboratory.

Since the only automated typewriter at that time (1962) was located at Dr. Moore's lab in Hamden, our only typewriter was an electric one with primary size type.

We did have the benefit of a voice writer for creative work and a viewer from which E. D. L. material was projected.

The attitude of the instructor while working in the booth with the child had to be (a la Dr. Moore) as impersonal as possible, as though the instructor was the automation. Have you ever attempted to be as impersonal as a machine? It isn't easy! When a child starts to tell you with glowing eyes about his birthday party, it takes the ability of a great actor to either ignore or quickly pass over the enthusiasm and repeat the letter to be typed. The theory of keeping the child's mind on the task at hand is essential and could well be applied to many classroom situations. Let's have a time to visit with our children other than in the midst of a teaching situation, unless we can apply the contribution to some phase of learning.

Following Dr. Moore's theory, no praise was given (if we could help it) and no blame was uttered. We presented an opportunity to learn and attempted to aid without pressure or comment.

February, 1962, I started working with two kindergarten children. They came to me before school started in the morning. They proved to be excellent students.

In September, 1962, the program was extended to accommodate seven children. By that time I was fortunate enough to corral one of our corrective reading teachers for part of her time. Miss Ruth Wagner. Then I involved my secretary, Mrs. Jean Hubbard, who was very versatile in working with children as well as coordinating the many facets of the reading department.

RESEARCH AND TEST CENTER

Now to give you a picture of the Research and Test Center as it functioned last year with the aid of two Edison Responsive Environment Machines.

Last January eighteen children were selected from the kindergarten classes in one building to participate in the Edison Responsive Environment experiment. Four children from an elementary special class were also chosen to take part in the project. A matching control group was simultaneously identified in order to weigh the results when we were finished.

Our psychologist used the Binet Intelligence Test as well as reading tests for each child, and matched the children over a range of criteria covering age, sex, race, left or right handedness, language maturity and socioeconomic status as measured by parental job classification. The health department also assisted by administering physical examinations, and tests for hearing, vision and speech.

The children's ages varied from 5.0 to 5.11 years for the kindergarteners and 7.11 to 9.7 years for the special class. We had an equal number of boys and girls.

The IQ distribution of both the experimental and control group ranged from the 140's of the superior group to the 50's of the retarded group.

There was one special exception—a senior in high school who came to us with a reading vocabulary of less than thirty words. The boy was not included in the research, but was with us to see if the machines could help him.

The visual aids room was pressed into service. Three very plain looking booths, approximately eight feet square, dominated the room. Two of the booths housed Edison Reponsive Environment Machines and the third booth contained the original electric typewriter and the viewer.

The booths were insulated so noise would not penetrate, and were air conditioned so the children were comfortable.

There was nothing inside the booth but the machine and a high-chair, which presented rather an incongruous picture.

The booths were monitored through one-way vision glass and an intercom system.

The machines, conceived by Dr. Moore, invented by Richard Kobler and developed at the Edison Research Laboratory, McGraw Edison Company, are marketed by the Responsive Environments Corporation.

The E.R.E. instrument is a computerized typewriter that reporduces several of the sensory responses of a human being. That is—it talks, it listens, it accepts, it responds, it presents pictorial material, it comments or explains, it presents information and responds to being touched. As Mr. Kreisman, general manager of Responsive Environments Corporation, has said, "—the machine becomes an extension of the teacher's personality. She selects the material and can program it."

In perfecting this unusual typewriter, the engineers took all precautions to make the instrument a safe one for young children to use. The typewriter is enclosed in plexiglass so tiny fingers cannot become entangled with the moving parts. Then, too, the machine is jam-proof, making it impossible for a child to depress two keys at once.

The keys of the typewriter are colored, so the student may match his painted nails to the keys, in order to develop correct fingering for typing.

The typewriter has a standard keyboard as far as the alphabet is concerned, but produces primary size type.

Above the typewriter is an exhibitor on which printed material can be displayed. A red pointer band helps the child to keep his place. The pointer band may be adjusted so the child can observe one letter or many words according to his progress. If a child is just beginning, it is possible to select a pointer ban which displays only one letter at a time. As he advances, it is possible for him to see all four lines at a time.

A speaker is built into the machine to project the audio, and a small projector is there to aid the fisual. This is essential to developing concepts. The projector takes regulation size slides.

There are several stages in which the typewriter may be used:

Phase I

It is possible to use the typewriter as you would any typewriter, without a voice—but what a waste this would be!

Phase II

The second phase is the basic step for the children as we introduce them to the program. We present the machine to the children as something in which they would be interested—definitely a play technique.

In this phase, when the child depresses a key there are two results. The voice of the machine will pronounce the name of the key-symbol as the typewriter instantaneously types the symbol in extra large type. This seems to intrigue the child to investigate again and the process is repeated as often as the child desires. Often, the novice will depress the same key many times.

Some children try to locate the voice or ask—"Who is that? Does he stay there all night? Do I know him?"

Phase III

After the child has become acquainted with the keyboard and some of the alphabet, the next phase is offered. A card on which letters of the alphabet have been printed is inserted into the machine so one letter at a time is visible on the exhibitor. As the letter is revealed to the child the machine's voice pronounces the name of the letter, so at this stage the machine is dictating to the child. If the child cannot find the letter the voice automatically repeats. Success is guaranteed because all keys except the correct one are locked. When the child depresses the correct key, the next letter is revealed. The machine informs the child immediately of his action.

The joy in discovery is sadly lacking in most methods of childhood education, according to Dr. Moore. "By the time a child is three years old he has achieved what is probably the most difficult task of his lifetime—he has learned to speak. Nobody instructed him in this skill; he had to develop it unaided. There is plenty of information-processing ability in a mind that can do that."

In our program words soon replaced letters, and the voice spells and pronounces the word so that the child knows what he has typed. A picture is projected on the miniature screen to help the child associate the word with the picture. So there is the audio and the visual to contribute to the child's understanding—for without comprehension there is no reading, just word calling.

For those who believe in a pure phonic system, the machine can be programmed to give the sound of a letter instead of the name.

There is another interesting phase to the E.R.E. machine, when the instrument records the child's voice. This is a great aid in correcting pronunciation or in teaching a foreign language. The machine voice will pronounce a word and the child will repeat it. Then the machine repeats the instructor's voice and the child's contribution, so the child can compare his response to that of the instructor.

Short stores of the look-say type, as well as nursery rhymes were used.

As children progressed the voice naming the letters was ommitted, but the words were pronounced.

At a more advanced stage, the machine dictated the words to be written without any visual aid. This furnished proof of the pupil's accomplishments.

Children were allowed to participate for a maximum of thirty minutes. We worked for a brief five months, with some children working a maximum of thirty-six hours, some working a minimum of twenty-two hours.

OBSERVATIONS

The staff of the Reading and Research Center, with the aid of a statistician, made several observations. The children participating in the E.R.E. program, regardless of intelligence, sex or race, were advanced in comparison with the control group. It was a thrilling experience to watch the children explore and find success in early reading through the typewriter procedures.

Indexes

AUTHOR INDEX

517

SUBJECT INDEX